Essentials of
Contemporary Management

Seventh Edition

Gareth R. Jones

Jennifer M. George
Rice University

Mc
Graw
Hill
Education

ESSENTIALS OF CONTEMPORARY MANAGEMENT, SEVENTH EDITION

Published by McGraw-Hill Education, 2 Penn Plaza, New York, NY 10121. Copyright © 2017 by McGraw-Hill Education. All rights reserved. Printed in the United States of America. Previous editions © 2015, 2013, and 2011. No part of this publication may be reproduced or distributed in any form or by any means, or stored in a database or retrieval system, without the prior written consent of McGraw-Hill Education, including, but not limited to, in any network or other electronic storage or transmission, or broadcast for distance learning.

Some ancillaries, including electronic and print components, may not be available to customers outside the United States.

This book is printed on acid-free paper.

2 3 4 5 6 7 8 9 DOW 21 20 19 18 17 16

ISBN 978-1-259-54547-4
MHID 1-259-54547-4

Senior Vice President, Products & Markets: *Kurt L. Strand*
Vice President, General Manager, Products & Markets: *Michael Ryan*
Vice President, Content Design & Delivery: *Kimberly Meriwether David*
Managing Director: *Susan Gouijnstook*
Director: *Michael Ablassmeir*
Director, Product Development: *Meghan Campbell*
Product Developer: *Gabriela G. Velasco*
Marketing Director: *Robin Lucas*
Marketing Manager: *Casey Keske*
Marketing Specialist: *Sam Deffenbaugh*
Director, Content Design & Delivery: *Terri Schiesl*
Program Manager: *Faye M. Herrig*
Content Project Managers: *Heather Ervolino; Keri Johnson; Karen Jozefowicz*
Buyer: *Laura M. Fuller*
Design: *Tara McDermott/Emily Duehr*
Cover Images/Design Icons (Management Insight, Topics For Discussion, Building Management Skills, Be the Manager, Small Group Breakout): © *VICTOR (Digital Vision Vectors)/Getty RF*
Content Licensing Specialists: *Carrie Burger (Image); DeAnna Dausener (Text)*
Compositor: *SPi Global*
Printer: *R. R. Donnelley*

All credits appearing on page or at the end of the book are considered to be an extension of the copyright page.

Library of Congress Cataloging-in-Publication Data

Jones, Gareth R.
    Essentials of contemporary management / Gareth R. Jones, Jennifer M. George, Rice University.—
Seventh Edition.
        pages cm
    Revised edition of the authors' Essentials of contemporary management, 2015.
    ISBN 978-1-259-54547-4 (alk. paper)
    1. Management. I. George, Jennifer M. II. Title.
HD31.J5974 2017
658—dc23

                                            2015033667

The Internet addresses listed in the text were accurate at the time of publication. The inclusion of a website does not indicate an endorsement by the authors or McGraw-Hill Education, and McGraw-Hill Education does not guarantee the accuracy of the information presented at these sites.

mheducation.com/highered

Brief Contents

Authors

Gareth Jones currently offers pro bono advice on solving management problems to nonprofit organizations in Houston, Texas. He received his BA in Economics Psychology and his PhD in Management from the University of Lancaster, U.K. He was formerly Professor of Management in the Graduate School of Business at Texas A&M University and earlier held teaching and research appointments at Michigan State University, the University of Illinois at Urbana–Champaign, and the University of Warwick, U.K.

He continues to pursue his research interests in strategic management and organizational theory and his well-known research that applies transaction cost analysis to explain many forms of strategic and organizational behavior. He also studies the complex and changing relationships between competitive advantage and information technology in the 2010s.

He has published many articles in leading journals of the field and his research has appeared in the *Academy of Management Review,* the *Journal of International Business Studies,* and *Human Relations.* He published an article about the role of information technology in many aspects of organizational functioning in the *Journal of Management.* One of his articles won the *Academy of Management Journal'*s Best Paper Award, and he is one of the most cited authors in the *Academy of Management Review.* He is, or has served, on the editorial boards of the *Academy of Management Review,* the *Journal of Management,* and *Management Inquiry.*

Gareth Jones has used his academic knowledge to craft leading textbooks in management and three other major areas in the management discipline: organizational behavior, organizational theory, and strategic management. His books are widely recognized for their innovative, contemporary content and for the clarity with which they communicate complex, real-world issues to students.

Jennifer George is the Mary Gibbs Jones Professor of Management and Professor of Psychology in the Jesse H. Jones Graduate School of Business at Rice University. She received her BA in Psychology/Sociology from Wesleyan University, her MBA in Finance from New York University, and her PhD in Management and Organizational Behavior from New York University. Prior to joining the faculty at Rice University, she was a professor in the Department of Management at Texas A&M University.

Professor George specializes in organizational behavior and is well known for her research on mood and emotion in the workplace, their determinants, and their effects on various individual and group-level work outcomes. She is the author of many articles in leading peer-reviewed journals such as the *Academy of Management Journal,* the *Academy of Management Review,* the *Journal of Applied Psychology, Organizational Behavior and Human Decision Processes, Journal of Personality and Social Psychology,* and *Psychological Bulletin.* One of her papers won the Academy of Management's Organizational Behavior Division Outstanding Competitive Paper Award, and another paper won the *Human Relations* Best Paper Award. She is, or has been, on the editorial review boards of the *Journal of Applied Psychology, Academy of Management Journal, Academy of Management Review, Administrative Science Quarterly, Journal of Management, Organizational Behavior and Human Decision Processes, Organization Science, International Journal of Selection and Assessment,* and *Journal of Managerial Issues;* was a consulting editor for the *Journal of Organizational Behavior;* was a member of the SIOP *Organizational Frontiers Series* editorial board; and was an associate editor of the *Journal of Applied Psychology.* She is a fellow in the Academy of Management, the American Psychological Association, the Association for Psychological Science, and the Society for Industrial and Organizational Psychology and a member of the Society for Organizational Behavior. She also has coauthored a textbook titled *Understanding and Managing Organizational Behavior.*

Preface

In this seventh edition of *Essentials of Contemporary Management,* we continue to focus on providing the most up-to-date account of the changes taking place in the world of management and management practices while maintaining our emphasis on making our text relevant and interesting to students. And we know from feedback from instructors and students that the text does engage them. Our increased focus on the challenges and opportunities facing businesses large and small and integrated timely examples bring management issues to life for students.

The number and complexity of the strategic, organizational, and human resource challenges facing managers and all employees have continued to increase throughout the 2000s and into the 2010s. In most companies, managers at all levels continue to play catch-up as they work toward meeting these challenges by implementing new and improved management techniques and practices. Today, relatively small differences in performance between companies, such as in the speed at which they bring new products or services to market or in the ways they motivate their employees to find ways to reduce costs or improve performance, can combine to give a company a significant competitive advantage. Managers and companies that utilize proven management techniques and practices in their decision making and actions increase their effectiveness over time. Companies and managers that are slower to implement new management techniques and practices find themselves at a growing competitive disadvantage that makes it even more difficult to catch up. Thus, in many industries, there is a widening gap between the most successful companies whose performance reaches new heights and their weaker competitors, because their managers have made better decisions about how to use company resources in the most efficient and effective ways.

The challenges facing managers continue to mount as changes in the global environment, such as increasing global outsourcing and rising commodity prices, impact organizations large and small. Moreover, the revolution in information technology (IT) has transformed how managers make decisions across all levels of a company's hierarchy and across all its functions and global divisions. This seventh edition addresses these emerging challenges. For example, we extend our treatment of global outsourcing, examine its pros and cons, and examine the new management problems that emerge when millions of functional jobs in IT, customer service, and manufacturing are performed in countries overseas. Similarly, increasing globalization means that managers must respond to major differences in the legal rules and regulations and ethical values and norms that prevail in countries around the globe.

Other major challenges we continue to expand on in this edition include the impact of the steadily increasing diversity of the workforce on companies and how this increasing diversity makes it imperative for managers to understand how and why people differ so that they can effectively manage and reap the performance benefits of diversity. Similarly, across all functions and levels, managers and employees must continually seek ways to "work smarter" and increase performance. Using new IT to improve all aspects of an organization's operations to enhance efficiency and customer responsiveness is a vital part of this process. So too is the continuing need to innovate and improve the quality of goods and services, and the ways they are produced, to allow an organization to compete effectively. We significantly revised this edition of *Essentials of Contemporary Management* to address these challenges to managers and their organizations.

Major Content Changes

Once again, encouraged by the increasing number of instructors and students who use each new edition of our book, and based on the reactions and suggestions of both users and reviewers, we revised and updated our book in many ways. However, the organization and sequence of chapters remain the same in this new edition. Instructors tell us that they like the way the chapters flow, and the way they build up a picture of management part by part, to provide an excellent learning experience and a comprehensive coverage of management. The way we link and integrate topics, such as our inclusion of entrepreneurship in Chapter 5, "Decision Making, Learning, Creativity, and Entrepreneurship," allows students to make connections among these important topics. As examples of the many changes we made, this new edition expands the coverage of ways to encourage high motivation, creativity, and innovation in organizations and the importance of managers' and organizations' taking steps to protect the natural environment and promote sustainability. Our three-chapter sequence on strategy, structure, and control systems to improve competitive advantage is also updated in many ways. And, in this new edition, throughout the chapters we offer increased coverage of new approaches to leadership and the design of reward systems, new uses of advanced IT at all levels in the organization and across all functions to improve job design and employee motivation, and expanded coverage of the pros and cons associated with global outsourcing.

CHAPTER-BY-CHAPTER CHANGES We made the following specific changes to this edition.

Chapter 1

- New "Management Snapshot" on Scott Parish of Alcon Entertainment.
- New "Manager as a Person" feature on Dennis Corsi, president of Armstrong Consultants, an airport engineering firm.
- New "Managing Globally" feature about GE bringing manufacturing jobs back to the United States.
- New "Ethics in Action" feature on Apple demanding quality from its global suppliers.
- New 2015 "*The Wall Street Journal* Case in the News."

Chapter 2

- New "Management Snapshot" on how "Determination and Broad Interests Lead Jess Lee to the Top at Polyvore."
- New in-text discussion of how some successful entrepreneurs are high on openness to experience and conscientiousness.

- New "Manager as a Person" on "Kevin Plank's Openness to Experience and Conscientiousness Pay Off at Under Armour."
- New "Ethics in Action" on "Telling the Truth at Gentle Giant Moving."
- New in-text discussion of levels of job satisfaction/dissatisfaction in the United States in 2012.
- New 2015 "*Bloomberg Businessweek* Case in the News."

Chapter 3

- Updated "Management Snapshot" on "Ethics and Social Responsibility at Whole Foods Market."
- New "Ethics in Action" on "Safety in the Garment Industry."
- New "Focus on Diversity" on "Effectively Managing Diversity at Sodexo and Principal Financial Group."
- Updated in-text statistics on age of U.S. workforce.
- Updated in-text statistics on men and women in the workforce, gender pay gap, and women in top positions and on boards.
- Updated in-text statistics on median weekly earnings of black and white women and men.
- Updated in-text statistics on number of Hispanics in the U.S. population.
- Updated in-text statistics on poverty in the United States.
- Updated in-text statistics on states prohibiting sexual orientation discrimination.
- New in-text discussion of Merrill Lynch racial discrimination lawsuit settled in 2013 for $160,000,000.
- New in-text discussion of Merrill Lynch/Bank of America gender discrimination lawsuit settled in 2013.
- New 2015 "*The Wall Street Journal* Case in the News."

Chapter 4

- New "Management Snapshot" on the importance of effective global websites.
- New "Managing Globally" feature on reducing water shortages around the world.

- New "Managing Globally" feature on translating athletic success into business leadership.
- New "Management Insight" feature on the cultural challenges faced by expatriates in global business.
- New 2015 *"The Wall Street Journal* Case in the News."

Chapter 5

- New "Management Snapshot" on "Decision Making and Learning Are the Keys to Entrepreneurial Success."
- New "Focus on Diversity" on "Programmed Decision Making at UPS."
- New "Management Insight" on "Decision Making and Learning from Feedback at GarageTek."
- New 2015 *"The Wall Street Journal* Case in the News."

Chapter 6

- New "Management Snapshot" on the turnaround plan for Toys "R" Us.
- New "Manager as a Person" feature on General Motors CEO Mary Barra.
- New "Management Insight" feature on Crocs and the shoe retailer's revised business strategy.
- New "Management Insight" feature on PepsiCo's determination to keep the company intact.
- New 2015 *"Bloomberg Business* Case in the News."

Chapter 7

- New chapter learning objective added to reflect how IT helps managers build strategic alliances and network structures as a way of increasing efficiency and effectiveness.
- New "Management Snapshot" on how Disney lets its studios set unique organizational structures that influence employee creativity.
- New "Management Insight" feature on how one of Wendy's top franchisees focuses on job enlargement for its employees.
- New "Managing Globally" feature on a company reorganization at an international engineering firm that focuses on the needs of local clients.

- New "Management Insight" feature on how an NFL team restored its "team-first" culture.
- New 2015 *"Business Insider* Case in the News."

Chapter 8

- New "Management Snapshot" on Vynamic, a Philadelphia-based health care consulting firm, and its "Zmail" policy.
- New "Management Insight" feature on the military's use of the control process in Afghanistan.
- New "Management Insight" feature on the need for companies to hire employees with strong data analysis skills in this era of "big data."
- New "Management Insight" feature on how Netflix lacks bureaucratic control—on purpose.
- New "Management Insight" feature on "Philanthrofits"—mobile fitness apps that donate money to charity based on the behavior of their users.
- New 2015 *"The Wall Street Journal* Case in the News."

Chapter 9

- New "Management Snapshot" on "High Motivation at the SAS Institute."
- New "Management Insight" on "Motivating and Retaining Employees at The Container Store."
- New "Management Insight" on "Employees Are Motivated at Enterprise Rent-A-Car."
- New section on "Equity and Justice in Organizations."
- Four new key terms: distributive justice, procedural justice, interpersonal justice, and informational justice.
- New 2015 *"The Wall Street Journal* Case in the News."

Chapter 10

- New "Management Snapshot" on "Jim Whitehurst Leads Red Hat."
- New "Management Insight" on "Consideration at Costco."
- Updated in-text statistics on percentages of women in top leadership positions in the United States.

- New "Focus on Diversity" on "Admitting a Mistake Helps Small Business Leader."
- New 2015 *The Wall Street Journal* Case in the News."

Chapter 11

- New "Management Snapshot" on "Using Teams to Innovate at W. L. Gore."
- New "Ethics in Action" on "Leadership in Teams at ICU Medical."
- New "Management Insight" on "Teams Benefit from Deviance and Conformity at IDEO."
- New 2015 *The Wall Street Journal* Case in the News."

Chapter 12

- New "Management Snapshot" on "Effectively Managing Human Resources at the Four Seasons."
- New "Management Insight" on "Recruitment and Selection and Training at Zappos."
- New in-text discussion of online degree programs.
- New in-text examples of companies with formal and mandatory mentoring programs.
- New in-text discussion of companies that provide incentives for employees to improve their health.
- New "Managing Globally" on "Managing Human Resources at Semco."
- Updated in-text statistics on union membership in the United States.
- New 2015 *The Wall Street Journal* Case in the News."

Chapter 13

- New "Management Snapshot" on how wearable technology tracks employee performance.
- New "Management Insight" feature on how companies are using "big data" to find the right talent.
- New "Managing Globally" feature on GE Healthcare's effective global communications.
- New "Ethics in Action" feature on monitoring employees' email and Internet use.
- New 2015 *Fast Company* Case in the News."

Chapter 14

- New "Management Snapshot" on how airlines try many methods to expedite the boarding process.
- New "Management Insight" feature on Panera's new use of technology to speed up service for customers.
- New "Management Insight" feature on how the TJX Companies, a leading discount retailer, makes customer satisfaction its top priority.
- New "Management Insight" feature on Steelcase, a leading office furniture manufacturer, and how the company took its own advice when it came to office layout.
- New 2015 *The Wall Street Journal* Case in the News."

UPDATED RESEARCH CONCEPTS Just as we included pertinent new research concepts in each chapter, so we were careful to eliminate outdated or marginal management concepts. As usual, our goal is to streamline our presentation and keep the focus on recent changes that have the most impact on managers and organizations. In today's world of video downloading, streaming media, and text messaging and tweeting, less is often more—especially when students are often burdened by time pressures stemming from the need to work long hours at paying jobs. New chapter opening "Management Snapshot" cases, the many boxed illustrations inside each chapter, and new "Case in the News" closing cases reinforce updated content critically but succinctly.

We feel confident that the changes to the seventh edition of *Essentials of Contemporary Management* will stimulate and challenge students to think about their future in the world of organizations.

Emphasis on Applied Management

We went to great lengths to bring the manager back into the subject matter of management. That is, we wrote our chapters from the perspective of current or future managers to illustrate, in a hands-on way, the problems and opportunities they face and how they can effectively meet them. For example, in Chapter 3, we provide an integrated treatment of ethics and diversity that clearly explains their significance to practicing managers. In Chapter 6, we provide an integrated treatment of planning, strategy, and competitive advantage, highlighting the crucial choices managers face as they go about performing the planning role. Throughout the text, we emphasize important issues managers face and how management theory, research, and practice can help them and their organizations be effective.

The last two chapters cover the topics of managing information systems, technology, and operations management, topics that tend to be difficult to teach to new management students in an interesting and novel way. Our chapters provide a student-friendly, behavioral approach to understanding the management processes entailed in information systems and operations management. As our reviewers noted, while most books' treatment of these issues is dry and quantitative, ours comes alive with its focus on how managers can manage the people and processes necessary to give an organization a competitive advantage.

Flexible Organization

We designed the grouping of chapters to allow instructors to teach the chapter material in the order that best suits their needs. Instructors are not tied to the planning, organizing, leading, and controlling framework, even though our presentation remains consistent with this approach.

Guided Tour

RICH AND RELEVANT EXAMPLES

An important feature of our book is the way we use real-world examples and stories about managers and companies to drive home the applied lessons to students. Our reviewers were unanimous in their praise of the sheer range and depth of the rich, interesting examples we use to illustrate the chapter material and make it come alive. Moreover, unlike boxed material in other books, our boxes are seamlessly integrated into the text; they are an integral part of the learning experience, and not tacked on to or isolated from the text itself. This is central to our pedagogical approach.

A Management Snapshot opens each chapter, posing a chapter-related challenge and then discussing how managers in one or more organizations responded to that challenge. These vignettes help demonstrate the uncertainty and excitement surrounding the management process.

Toys "R" Us President Hank Mullany (left) and CEO Antonio Urcelay (right) have implemented a business strategy designed to help the company play to its strengths and address its weaknesses. © Bloomberg via Getty Images

MANAGEMENT SNAPSHOT

Toy Retailer Implements Turnaround Plan

How Can Identifying Corporate Strengths and Weaknesses Lead to Better Planning and Strategy?

Toys "R" Us, Inc., with its mascot Geoffrey the Giraffe, is a well-known brand. The toy retailer was founded in 1948 as Children's Supermart and later rebranded as Toys "R" Us after adding toys to its baby furniture business. By 2014, the company had grown to 872 stores in the United States and more than 700 stores outside the United States.

Despite its growth, 2013 was not a good year for Toys "R" Us. Net sales were down, and the company's net loss was $1 billion. Chairman and CEO Antonio Urcelay and President Hank Mullany announced a "TRU Transformation" plan for the company.

"Our 'TRU Transformation' strategy is grounded in consumer research and customer insights and is anchored by three guiding principles—Easy, Expert, Fair," Mullany said. "Among our highest priorities will be to deepen our focus on the customer, build meaningful relationships through loyalty and targeted marketing programs, and improve the shopping experience both in store and online."[1]

Urcelay and Mullany recognize that external factors affect sales at Toys "R" Us. The factors they identified are opportunities and threats, over which the company has no control. They include falling birthrates, changes in the play patterns of children, and the growth of online shopping. While it might be easy for Urcelay and Mullany to blame falling sales on these factors, the two company leaders also looked at internal factors that hurt the business—factors the company does control. "We are encouraged that all of these . . . issues are firmly within our own control to fix," Urcelay said. "And our strategy will address these to improve the business over the short term and put the company on track for the future."

Urcelay and Mullany described four categories of weaknesses at Toys "R" Us and discussed how they could be turned into strengths. First, the retailer said it has provided a weak customer experience both in stores and online. Customers complain that the checkout process in stores is slow and that stores are cluttered and disorganized. The apps for the online store are out of date and frustrating to customers. When customers do buy a product online, they often encounter shipping problems. Toys "R" Us would like to turn this weakness into a strength by making its stores easy, uncluttered places at which to shop, with sales associates who have been trained and who will be perceived as experts on the company's products.

Second, there is a perception that prices at Toys "R" Us are higher than at other retailers. Toys "R" Us

193

MANAGEMENT INSIGHT

Would You Like Some Fritos with That Diet Pepsi?

The story of PepsiCo is a bit fizzy. The company's history tells a tale of related and unrelated diversification. Best known for the soda from which it gets its name, it was founded as the Pepsi-Cola Company in 1902. It merged with Frito-Lay, Inc., in 1965 to become PepsiCo. Along the way, it has diversified into many products related and unrelated to its beverage and packaged snack-food businesses. For example, in unrelated diversification, the company once owned several restaurant chains such as Pizza Hut, Taco Bell, and KFC. The company divested itself of its fast-food division in 1997. Two examples of related diversification include the 1998 purchase of Tropicana and the 2001 purchase of Quaker Oats. The purchase of Tropicana diversified PepsiCo's beverage portfolio to include juices. The purchase of the Quaker Oats Company was mainly to obtain the sports drink Gatorade, which Quaker owned. This purchase further diversified PepsiCo's beverage portfolio to include sports drinks. Also, the acquisition of Quaker's breakfast cereal, pasta, and rice business was not completely unrelated to the Frito-Lay snack-food division.[44]

Not everyone believes the products in PepsiCo's current portfolio are closely related, however. Activist investor Nelson Peltz would like to see PepsiCo split its beverage and food units apart. He argues that the two units would be stronger apart than they are together. "A stand-alone snacks business would offer investors strong growth in sales, margins and free cash flow generation," he said. "And a

ETHICS IN ACTION

Leadership in Teams at ICU Medical

Dr. George Lopez, an internal medicine physician, founded ICU Medical in San Clemente, California, in 1984, after a patient of his accidentally died when an intravenous (IV) line became inadvertently disconnected.[44] Lopez thought there must be a better way to design components of IV lines so that these kinds of tragic accidents don't happen. He developed a product called the Click Lock, which has both a locking mechanism for IV systems and also a protected needle so that health care workers are protected from accidental needle pricks.[45] Today, ICU Medical has more than 2,260 employees and revenues more than $313 million.[46] Lopez is a member of the board of directors, and ICU Medical made *Forbes* magazine's list of "The 200 Best Small Companies."[47] ICU Medical continues to focus on the development and manufacture of products that improve the functioning of IV lines and systems while protecting health care workers from accidental needle pricks.[48] For example, the CLAVE NeedleFree Connector for IV lines is one of ICU Medical's top-selling products.[49]

In the early 1990s, Lopez experienced something not uncommon to successful entrepreneurs as their businesses grow. As the entrepreneur–CEO, he continued to make the maj

MANAGING GLOBALLY

Reorganization Focuses on Local Clients

The Michael Baker Corporation has worked on some high-profile engineering projects around the world. The company had a role in building the 789-mile Trans-Alaska Pipeline in North America, the 135-mile KHMR-American Friendship Highway in Cambodia, the New River Gorge Bridge in West Virginia, the Midfield Terminal Complex at the Pittsburgh International Airport, and a 2,600-mile fiber optic telecommunications network in Mexico. More recently, the company was selected to rehabilitate the Pulaski Skyway, the bridge that connects Newark and Jersey City in New Jersey.[34]

As the need for engineering, construction management, and other services expands nationally and internationally, the company launched a national and global expansion program. In 2013, the company merged with Integrated Mission Solutions to create Michael Baker International.

The company's vision statement includes the words, "Be the go-to company for clients and employees." Its services include architectural, environmental, construc- company has worked with U.S. and al customers.

FOCUS ON DIVERSITY

Programmed Decision Making at UPS

UPS is unrivaled in its use of programmed decision making. Practically all the motions, behaviors, and actions that its drivers perform each day have been carefully honed to maximize efficiency and minimize strain and injuries while delivering high-quality customer service. For example, a 12-step process prescribes how drivers should park their trucks, locate the package they are about to deliver, and step off the truck in 15.5 seconds (a process called "selection" at UPS).[22] Rules and routines such as these are carefully detailed in UPS's "340 Methods" manual (UPS actually has far more than 340 methods). Programmed decision making dictates where drivers should stop to get gas, how they should hold their keys in their hands, and how to lift and lower package

When programmed employees learn tried-a new employees with a 2000s, however, mana methods to suit their re people born after 1980) eration Y trainees seem (90–180 days compared drivers had increased."

MANAGER AS A PERSON

GM's Barra Confronts Challenges

When Mary Barra took over as chief executive officer of General Motors in 2014, it was a challenging time for the automaker. The company had declared bankruptcy in 2009 and was still on the mend. Its net profit for 2013 was low due to several one-time costs, including company restructuring in Europe. But even more important was that within weeks of taking the CEO job, Barra began the recall of more than 2.5 million General Motors cars made between 2003 and 2007. The initial cars recalled were the Cobalt, the HHR, the G5, the Solstice, the Ion, and the Sky.

The cars had faulty ignition switches that would turn off the car while it was being driven, causing accidents and preventing the air bags from deploying. The company said the faulty switches caused at least 31 accidents and at least 12 deaths. More accidents and deaths could come to light as the investigation of the problem continues.

As part of the investigation, it was revealed that problems with the ignition switch emerged as early as 2001 during pre-production tests on the Ion. GM documents indicate that the problem was fixed at the time. However, in 2003, a General Motors service technician observed the problem in an Ion. At the time, the technician suggested that having several other keys on the key ring had worn out the ignition switch. In 2004, a test of the Cobalt that used the same ignition switch, an engineer bumped the key and the car turned off. Despite these indicators, the switch was used for several more years and installed in several more car models.

Our box features are not traditional boxes; that is, they are not disembodied from the chapter narrative. These thematic applications are fully integrated into the reading. Students will no longer be forced to decide whether to read boxed material. These features are interesting and engaging for students while bringing the chapter contents to life.

In-depth examples appear in boxes throughout each chapter. Management Insight boxes illustrate the topics of the chapter, while the Ethics in Action, Managing Globally, and Focus on Diversity boxes examine the chapter topics from each of these perspectives.

Further emphasizing the unique content covered in Chapter 2, "Values, Attitudes, Emotions, and Culture: The Manager as a Person," the Manager as a Person boxes focus on how real managers brought about change within their organizations. These examples allow us to reflect on how individual managers dealt with real-life, on-the-job challenges related to various chapter concepts.

***New!* Expanded Use of Small Business Examples**   To ensure that students see the clear connections between the concepts taught in their Principles of Management course and the application in their future jobs in a medium or small business, Jones and George have expanded the number of examples of the opportunities and challenges facing founders, managers, and employees in small businesses.

EXPERIENTIAL LEARNING FEATURES

We have given considerable time and effort to developing state-of-the-art experiential end-of-chapter learning exercises that drive home the meaning of management to students. These exercises are grouped together at the end of each chapter in a section called "Management in Action." The following activities are included at the end of every chapter:

Topics for Discussion and Action are a set of chapter-related questions and points for reflection. Some ask students to research actual management issues and learn firsthand from practicing managers.

Building Management Skills is a self-developed exercise that asks students to apply what they have learned from their own experience in organizations and from managers or from the experiences of others.

Managing Ethically is an exercise that presents students with an ethical scenario or dilemma and asks them to think about the issue from an ethical perspective to better understand the issues facing practicing managers.

Small Group Breakout Exercise is designed to allow instructors in large classes to utilize interactive experiential exercises.

Be the Manager presents a realistic scenario where a manager or organization faces some kind of challenge, problem, or opportunity. These exercises provide students with a hands-on way of solving "real" problems by applying what they've just learned in the chapter.

Management *in Action*

TOPICS FOR DISCUSSION AND ACTION

Discussion

1. Describe the three steps of planning. Explain how they are related. [LO 6-1]
2. What is the relationship among corporate-, business-, and functional-level strategies, and how do they create value for an organization? [LO 6-2, 6-3]
3. Pick an industry and identify four companies in the industry that pursue one of the four main business-level strategies (low-cost, focused low-cost, etc.). [LO 6-1, 6-2]
4. What is the difference between vertical integration and related diversification? [LO 6-3]

Action

5. Ask a manager about the kinds of planning exercises he or she regularly uses. What are the purposes of these exercises, and what are their advantages or disadvantages? [LO 6-1]
6. Ask a manager to identify the corporate- and business-level strategies used by his or her organization. [LO 6-2, 6-3]

BUILDING MANAGEMENT SKILLS
How to Analyze a Company's Strategy [LO 6-2, 6-3]

Pick a well-known business organization that has received recent media coverage and that provides its annual reports on its website. From the information in the media and annual reports, answer the following questions:

1. What is (are) the main industry(ies) in which the company competes?
2. What business-level strategy does the company seem to be pursuing in this industry? Why?
3. What corporate-level strategies is the company pursuing? Why?
4. Have there been any major changes in its strategy recently? Why?

MANAGING ETHICALLY [LO 6-1, 6-4]

A few years ago, IBM announced that it had fired the three top managers of its Argentine division because of their involvement in a scheme to secure a $250 million contract for IBM to provide and service the computers of one of Argentina's largest state-owned banks. The three executives paid $14 million of the contract money to a third company, CCR, which paid nearly $6 million to phantom companies. This $6 million was then used to bribe the bank executives who agreed to give IBM the contract.

These bribes are not necessarily illegal under Argentine law. Moreover, the three managers argued that all companies have to pay bribes to get new business contracts and they were not doing anything that managers in other companies were not.

Questions

1. Either by yourself or in a group, decide if the business practice of paying bribes is ethical or unethical.
2. Should IBM allow its foreign divisions to pay bribes if all other companies are doing so?
3. If bribery is common in a particular country, what effect would this likely have on the nation's economy and culture?

SMALL GROUP BREAKOUT EXERCISE [LO 6-1, 6-2]
Low Cost or Differentiation?

Form groups of three or four people, and appoint one member as the spokesperson who will communicate your findings to the class when called on by the instructor. Then discuss the following scenario.

You are a team of managers of a major national clothing chain, and you have been charged with finding a way to restore your organization's competitive advantage. Recently, your organization has been experiencing increasing competition from two sources. First, discount stores such as Walmart and Target have been undercutting your prices because they buy their clothes from low-cost foreign manufacturers while you buy most of yours from high-quality domestic suppliers. Discount stores have been attracting your customers who buy at the low end of the price range. Second, small boutiques opening in malls provide high-price designer clothing and are attracting your customers at the high end of the market. Your company has become stuck in the middle, and you have to decide what to do: Should you start to buy abroad so that you can lower your prices and begin to pursue a low-cost strategy? Should you focus on the high end of the market and become more of a differentiator? Or should you try to pursue both a low-cost strategy and a differentiation strategy?

1. Using SWOT analysis, analyze the pros and cons of each alternative.
2. Think about the various clothing retailers in your local malls and city, and analyze the choices they have made about how to compete with one another along the low-cost and differentiation dimensions.

BE THE MANAGER [LO 6-1, 6-2]

A group of investors in your city is considering opening a new upscale supermarket to compete with the major supermarket chains that are currently dominating the city's marketplace. They have called you in to help them determine what kind of upscale supermarket they should open. In other words, how can they best develop a competitive advantage against existing supermarket chains?

Questions

1. List the supermarket chains in your city, and identify their strengths and weaknesses.
2. What business-level strategies are these supermarkets currently pursuing?
3. What kind of supermarket would do best against the competition? What kind of business-level strategy should it pursue?

223

Case in the News Each chapter has one Case in the News that is an actual or shortened version of a current article. The concluding questions encourage students to think about how real managers deal with problems in the business world.

TEACHING RESOURCES

Great care was used in the creation of the supplementary material to accompany *Essentials of Contemporary Management.* Whether you are a seasoned faculty member or a newly minted instructor, you'll find our support materials to be the most thorough and thoughtful ever created.

Instructor's Manual (IM)
The IM supporting this text has been completely updated in order to save instructors' time and support them in delivering the most effective course to their students. For each chapter, this manual provides a chapter overview and lecture outline with integrated PowerPoint® slides, lecture enhancers, notes for end-of-chapter materials, video cases and teaching notes, and more.

PowerPoint® Presentation
Forty slides per chapter feature reproductions of key tables and figures from the text as well as original content. Lecture-enhancing additions such as quick polling questions and examples from outside the text can be used to generate discussion and illustrate management concepts.

Test Bank
The test bank has been thoroughly reviewed, revised, and improved. There are approximately 100 questions per chapter, including true/false, multiple-choice, and essay. Each question is tagged with learning objective, level of difficulty (corresponding to Bloom's taxonomy of educational objectives), and AACSB standards. The AACSB tags allow instructors to sort questions by the various standards and create reports to help give assurance that they are including recommended learning experiences in their curricula.

McGraw-Hill Connect®
Learn Without Limits

Connect is a teaching and learning platform that is proven to deliver better results for students and instructors.

Connect empowers students by continually adapting to deliver precisely what they need, when they need it, and how they need it, so your class time is more engaging and effective.

Course outcomes improve with Connect.

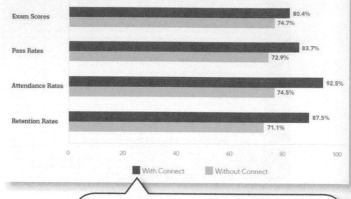

	With Connect	Without Connect
Exam Scores	80.4%	74.7%
Pass Rates	83.7%	72.9%
Attendance Rates	92.5%	74.5%
Retention Rates	87.5%	71.1%

88% of instructors who use **Connect** require it; instructor satisfaction **increases** by 38% when **Connect** is required.

Using **Connect** improves passing rates by **10.8%** and retention by **16.4%**.

Analytics

Connect helps students achieve better grades

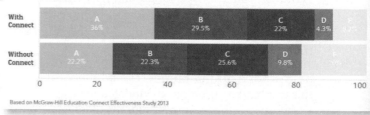

	A	B	C	D	F
With Connect	36%	29.5%	22%	4.3%	
Without Connect	22.2%	22.3%	25.6%	9.8%	

Based on McGraw-Hill Education Connect Effectiveness Study 2013

Connect Insight®

Connect Insight is Connect's new one-of-a-kind visual analytics dashboard—now available for both instructors and students—that provides at-a-glance information regarding student performance, which is immediately actionable. By presenting assignment, assessment, and topical performance results together with a time metric that is easily visible for aggregate or individual results, Connect Insight gives the user the ability to take a just-in-time approach to teaching and learning, which was never before available. Connect Insight presents data that empowers students and helps instructors improve class performance in a way that is efficient and effective.

Students can view their results for any **Connect** course.

Mobile

Connect's new, intuitive mobile interface gives students and instructors flexible and convenient, anytime–anywhere access to all components of the Connect platform.

Adaptive

THE FIRST AND ONLY **ADAPTIVE READING EXPERIENCE** DESIGNED TO TRANSFORM THE WAY STUDENTS READ

More students earn **A's** and **B's** when they use McGraw-Hill Education **Adaptive** products.

SmartBook®

Proven to help students improve grades and study more efficiently, SmartBook contains the same content within the print book, but actively tailors that content to the needs of the individual. SmartBook's adaptive technology provides precise, personalized instruction on what the student should do next, guiding the student to master and remember key concepts, targeting gaps in knowledge and offering customized feedback, and driving the student toward comprehension and retention of the subject matter. Available on smartphones and tablets, SmartBook puts learning at the student's fingertips—anywhere, anytime.

Over **4 billion questions** have been answered, making McGraw-Hill Education products more intelligent, reliable, and precise.

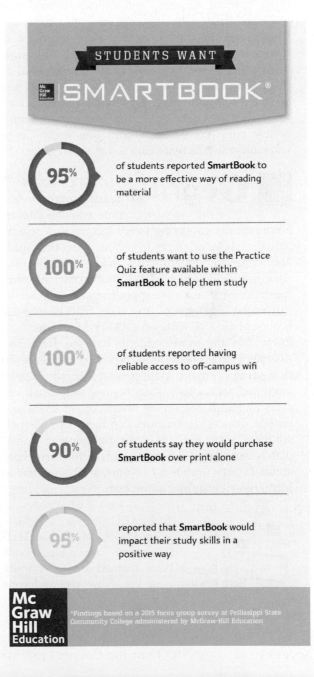

STUDENTS WANT

SMARTBOOK®

95% of students reported **SmartBook** to be a more effective way of reading material

100% of students want to use the Practice Quiz feature available within **SmartBook** to help them study

100% of students reported having reliable access to off-campus wifi

90% of students say they would purchase **SmartBook** over print alone

95% reported that **SmartBook** would impact their study skills in a positive way

McGraw Hill Education

*Findings based on a 2015 focus group survey at Pellissippi State Community College administered by McGraw-Hill Education

 **CREATE** Instructors can now tailor their teaching resources to match the way they teach! With McGraw-Hill Create, **www.mcgrawhillcreate.com,** instructors can easily rearrange chapters, combine material from other content sources, and quickly upload and integrate their own content, such as course syllabi or teaching notes. Find the right content in Create by searching through thousands of leading McGraw-Hill textbooks. Arrange the material to fit your teaching style. Order a Create book and receive a complimentary print review copy in three to five business days or a complimentary electronic review copy via e-mail within one hour. Go to **www.mcgrawhillcreate.com** today and register.

 **TEGRITY CAMPUS** Tegrity makes class time available 24/7 by automatically capturing every lecture in a searchable format for students to review when they study and complete assignments. With a simple one-click start-and-stop process, you capture all computer screens and corresponding audio. Students can replay any part of any class with easy-to-use browser-based viewing on a PC or Mac. Educators know that the more students can see, hear, and experience class resources, the better they learn. In fact, studies prove it. With patented Tegrity "search anything" technology, students instantly recall key class moments for replay online or on iPods and mobile devices. Instructors can help turn all their students' study time into learning moments immediately supported by their lecture. To learn more about Tegrity, watch a two-minute Flash demo at **http://tegritycampus.mhhe.com.**

 **BLACKBOARD® PARTNERSHIP** McGraw-Hill Education and Blackboard have teamed up to simplify your life. Now you and your students can access *Connect* and Create right from within your Blackboard course—all with one single sign-on. The grade books are seamless, so when a student completes an integrated *Connect* assignment, the grade for that assignment automatically (and instantly) feeds your Blackboard grade center. Learn more at **www.omorenow.com.**

MCGRAW-HILL CAMPUS™ McGraw-Hill Campus is a new one-stop teaching and learning experience available to users of any learning management system. This institutional service allows faculty and students to enjoy single sign-on (SSO) access to all McGraw-Hill Higher Education materials, including the award-winning McGraw-Hill *Connect* platform, from directly within the institution's website. With McGraw-Hill Campus, faculty receive instant access to teaching materials (e.g., eTextbooks, test banks, PowerPoint slides, animations, learning objectives, etc.), allowing them to browse, search, and use any instructor ancillary content in our vast library at no additional cost to instructor or students. In addition, students enjoy SSO access to a variety of free content (e.g., quizzes, flash cards, narrated presentations, etc.) and subscription-based products (e.g., McGraw-Hill *Connect*). With McGraw-Hill Campus enabled, faculty and students will never need to create another account to access McGraw-Hill products and services. Learn more at **www.mhcampus.com.**

ASSURANCE OF LEARNING READY Many educational institutions today focus on the notion of *assurance of learning,* an important element of some accreditation standards. *Essentials of Contemporary Management* is designed specifically to support instructors' assurance of learning initiatives with a simple yet powerful solution. Each test bank question for *Essentials of Contemporary Management* maps to a specific chapter learning objective listed in the text.

AACSB TAGGING McGraw-Hill Education is a proud corporate member of AACSB International. Understanding the importance and value of AACSB accreditation, *Essentials of Contemporary Management* recognizes the curricula guidelines detailed in the AACSB standards for business accreditation by connecting selected questions in the text and the test bank to the eight general knowledge and skill guidelines in the AACSB standards. The statements contained in *Essentials of Contemporary Management* are provided only as a guide for the users of this product. The AACSB leaves content coverage and assessment within the purview of individual schools, the mission of the school, and the faculty. While the *Essentials of Contemporary Management* teaching package makes no claim of any specific AACSB qualification or evaluation, we have within *Essentials of Contemporary Management* labeled selected questions according to the eight general knowledge and skills areas.

MCGRAW-HILL CUSTOMER EXPERIENCE GROUP CONTACT INFORMATION At McGraw-Hill Education, we understand that getting the most from new technology can be challenging. That's why our services don't stop after you purchase our products. You can e-mail our Product Specialists 24 hours a day to get product training online. Or you can search our knowledge bank of Frequently Asked Questions on our support website. For Customer Support, call **800-331-5094** or visit **www.mhhe .com/support.** One of our Technical Support Analysts will be able to assist you in a timely fashion.

Acknowledgments

Finding a way to integrate and present the rapidly growing literature on contemporary management and make it interesting and meaningful for students is not an easy task. In writing and revising the several editions of *Essentials of Contemporary Management*, we have been fortunate to have had the assistance of several people who have contributed greatly to the book's final form. First, we are grateful to Michael Ablassmeir, our executive brand manager, for his support and commitment to our project, and for always finding ways to provide the resources that we needed to continually improve and refine our book. Second, we are grateful to Gabriela G. Velasco, our product developer, for so ably coordinating the book's progress, and to her and Casey Keske, our marketing manager, for providing us with concise and timely feedback and information from professors and reviewers that have allowed us to shape the book to the needs of its intended market. We also thank Tara McDermott for executing an awe-inspiring design and Heather Ervolino for coordinating the production process. We are also grateful to the many colleagues and reviewers who provided us with useful and detailed feedback, perceptive comments, and valuable suggestions for improving the manuscript.

Producing any competitive work is a challenge. Producing a truly market-driven textbook requires tremendous effort beyond simply obtaining reviews on a draft manuscript. Our goal behind the development of *Essentials of Contemporary Management* has been clear-cut: to be the most customer-driven essentials of management text and supplement package ever published! The favorable reception that our book has received from its users suggests that our thorough product development plan did lead to a book that has met the expectations of both faculty and students. For the new edition, we have continued to add new reviewers to the over 200 faculty who originally took part in developmental activities ranging from regional focus groups to manuscript reviews and surveys. Consequently, we're confident that the changes we have made to our book and its excellent support package will even more closely meet your expectations and needs.

Our thanks to these faculty who have contributed greatly to *Essentials of Contemporary Management:*

Garry Adams, *Auburn University*
M. Ruhul Amin, *Bloomsburg University of Pennsylvania*
Fred Anderson, *Indiana University of Pennsylvania*
Jacquelyn Appeldorn, *Dutchess Community College*
Barry Armandi, *SUNY–Old Westbury*
Dave Arnott, *Dallas Baptist University*
Debra Arvanites, *Villanova University*
Douglas E. Ashby, *Lewis & Clark Community College*
Joe Atallah, *Devry University*
Kenneth E. Aupperle, *The University of Akron*
Barry S. Axe, *Florida Atlantic University*
Andrea D. Bailey, *Moraine Valley Community College*
Jeff Bailey, *University of Idaho*
Robert M. Ballinger, *Siena College*
Moshe Banai, *Bernard M. Baruch College*
Frank Barber, *Cuyahoga Community College*
Reuel Barksdale, *Columbus State Community College*
Sandy Jeanquart Barone, *Murray State University*
Lorraine P. Bassette, *Prince George's Community College*
Gene Baten, *Central Connecticut State University*
Myra Jo Bates, *Bellevue University*
Josephine Bazan, *Holyoke Community College*
Hrach Bedrosian, *New York University*
Omar Belkhodja, *Virginia State University*
James Bell, *Texas State University–San Marcos*
Ellen A. Benowitz, *Mercer County Community College*
Stephen Betts, *William Paterson University*
Jack C. Blanton, *University of Kentucky*
David E. Blevins, *University of Arkansas at Little Rock*
Mary Jo Boehms, *Jackson State Community College*
Karen Boroff, *Seton Hall University*

Jennifer Bowers, *Florida State University*
Barbara Boyington, *Brookdale Community College*
Dan Bragg, *Bowling Green State University*
Charles Braun, *Marshall University*
Dennis Brode, *Sinclair Community College*
Gil Brookins, *Siena College*
Murray Brunton, *Central Ohio Technical College*
Patricia M. Buhler, *Goldey-Beacom College*
Judith G. Bulin, *Monroe Community College*
David Cadden, *Quinnipiac College*
Thomas Campbell, *University of Texas–Austin*
Thomas Carey, *Western Michigan University*
Barbara Carlin, *University of Houston*
Daniel P. Chamberlin, *Regents University–CRB*
Larry Chasteen, *Stephen F. Austin State University*
Raul Chavez, *Eastern Mennonite University*
Nicolette De Ville Christensen, *Guilford College*
Anthony A. Cioffi, *Lorain County Community College*
Sharon F. Clark, *Lebanon Valley College*
Sharon Clinebell, *University of Northern Colorado*
Dianne Coleman, *Wichita State University*
Elizabeth Cooper, *University of Rhode Island*
Anne Cowden, *California State University–Sacramento*
Thomas D. Craven, *York College of Pennsylvania*
Kent Curran, *University of North Carolina*
Arthur L. Darrow, *Bowling Green State University*
Tom Deckelman, *Walsh College*
D. Anthony DeStadio, *Pittsburgh Technical Institute*
Ron DiBattista, *Bryant College*
Thomas Duening, *University of Houston*
Charles P. Duffy, *Iona College*
Steve Dunphy, *The University of Akron*
Subhash Durlabhji, *Northwestern State University*
Robert A. Eberle, *Iona College*
Karen Eboch, *Bowling Green State University*
Robert R. Edwards, *Arkansas Tech University*
Susan Eisner, *Ramapo College of New Jersey*
William Eldridge, *Kean College*
Pat Ellsberg, *Lower Columbia College*
Stan Elsea, *Kansas State University*
Scott Elston, *Iowa State University*
Judson Faurer, *Metro State College of Denver*
Dale Finn, *University of New Haven*
Charles Flaherty, *University of Minnesota*
Alisa Fleming, *University of Phoenix*
Lucinda Fleming, *Orange County Community College*

Robert Flemming, *Delta State University*
Jeanie M. Forray, *Eastern Connecticut State University*
Marilyn L. Fox, *Minnesota State University*
Mankato Ellen Frank, *Southern Connecticut State University*
Joseph A. Gemma, *Providence College*
Neal Gersony, *University of New Haven*
Donna H. Giertz, *Parkland College*
Leo Giglio, *Dowling College*
David Glew, *Texas A&M University*
Carol R. Graham, *Western Kentucky University*
Matthew Gross, *Moraine Valley Community College*
John Hall, *University of Florida*
Eric L. Hansen, *California State University–Long Beach*
Justin U. Harris, *Strayer College*
Allison Harrison, *Mississippi State University*
Sandra Hartman, *University of New Orleans*
Brad D. Hays, *North Central State College*
Gary Hensel, *McHenry Community College*
Robert A. Herring III, *Winston-Salem State University*
Eileen Bartels Hewitt, *University of Scranton*
Stephen R. Hiatt, *Catawba College*
Tammy Bunn Hiller, *Bucknell University*
Adrienne Hinds, *Northern Virginia Community College*
Anne Kelly Hoel, *University of Wisconsin–Stout*
Eileen Hogan, *Kutztown University*
Jerry Horgesheiner, *Southern Utah State*
Gordon K. Huddleston, *South Carolina State University*
John Hughes, *Texas Tech University*
Larry W. Hughes, *University of Nebraska at Kearney*
Tammy Hunt, *University of North Carolina–Wilmington*
Gary S. Insch, *West Virginia University*
Charleen Jaeb, *Cuyahoga Community College*
Velma Jesser, *Lane Community College*
Richard E. Johe, *Salem College*
Gwendolyn Jones, *The University of Akron*
Kathy Jones, *University of North Dakota*
Marybeth Kardatzke, *North Harris Montgomery Community College District*
Jim Katzenstein, *California State University–Dominguez Hills*

Jehan G. Kavoosi, *Clarion University of Pennsylvania*

Robert J. Keating, *University of North Carolina at Wilmington*

Frank Khoury, *Berkeley College*

Peggi Koenecke, *California State University–Sacramento*

Donald Kopka, *Towson University*

Dennis Lee Kovach, *Community College of Allegheny County–North Campus*

Mark Kunze, *Virginia State University*

Ken Lehmenn, *Forsyth Technical Community College*

Lianlian Lin, *California State Polytechnic University*

Grand Lindstrom, *University of Wyoming*

John Lipinski, *Robert Morris University*

Mary Lou Lockerby, *College of DuPage*

Esther Long, *University of Florida*

E. Geoffrey Love, *University of Illinois*

George S. Lowry, *Randolph–Macon College*

George E. Macdonald Jr., *Laredo Community College*

Bryan Malcolm, *University of Wisconsin*

Z. A. Malik, *Governors State University*

Mary J. Mallott, *George Washington University*

Christine Marchese, *Nassau Community College*

Jennifer Martin, *York College of Pennsylvania*

Lisa McCormick, *Community College of Allegheny County*

Reuben McDaniel, *University of Texas*

Robert L. McKeage, *The University of Scranton*

John A. Miller, *Bucknell University*

Richard R. J. Morin, *James Madison University*

Don Moseley, *University of South Alabama–Mobile*

Behnam Nakhai, *Millersville University of Pennsylvania*

Robert D. Nale, *Coastal Carolina University*

Daniel F. Nehring, *Morehead State University*

Thomas C. Neil, *Clark Atlanta University*

Brian Niehoff, *Kansas State University*

Judy Nixon, *University of Tennessee*

Cliff Olson, *Southern Adventists University*

Karen Overton, *HCC–Northeast College*

Ralph W. Parrish, *University of Central Oklahoma*

Dane Partridge, *University of Southern Indiana*

Sheila J. Pechinski, *University of Maine*

Marc Pendel, *Ball State University*

Fred Pierce, *Northwood University*

Mary Pisnar, *Baldwin Wallace College*

Laynie Pizzolatto, *Nicholls State University*

Eleanor Polster, *Florida International University*

Paul Preston, *University of Texas–San Antonio*

Samuel Rabinowitz, *Rutgers University–Camden*

Gerald Ramsey, *Indiana University Southeast*

Charles Rarick, *Transylvania University*

Deana K. Ray, *Forsyth Technical Community College*

Robert A. Reber, *Western Kentucky University*

Bob Redick, *Lincoln Land Community College*

Douglas Richardon, *Eastfield College*

Tina L. Robbins, *Clemson University*

Deborah Britt Roebuck, *Kennesaw State University*

Harvey Rothenberg, *Regis University*

Catherine Ruggieri, *St. John's University*

George Ruggiero, *Community College of Rhode Island*

Kathleen Rust, *Elmhurst College*

Robert Rustic, *University of Findlay*

Cyndy Ruszkowski, *Illinois State University*

Nestor St. Charles, *Dutchess Community College*

Lynda St. Clair, *Bryant College*

Michael Santoro, *Rutgers University*

John L. Schmidt Jr., *George Mason University*

Gerald Schoenfeld Jr., *James Madison University*

Don Schreiber, *Baylor University*

Robert Schwartz, *University of Toledo*

Amit Shah, *Frostburg State University*

Michael Shapiro, *Dowling College*

Raymond Shea, *Monroe Community College*

Richard Ray Shreve, *Indiana University Northwest*

Sidney Siegel, *Drexel University*

Thomas D. Sigerstad, *Frostburg State University*

Roy L. Simerly, *East Carolina University*

Randi L. Sims, *Nova Southeastern University*

Sharon Sloan, *Northwood University*

Erika E. Small, *Coastal Carolina University*

Brien Smith, *Ball State University*

Marjorie Smith, *Mountain State University*

Raymond D. Smith, *Towson State University*

William A. Sodeman, *University of Southern Indiana*

Carl J. Sonntag, *Pikes Peak Community College*

Robert W. Sosna, *Menlo College*

William Soukup, *University of San Diego*

Rieann Spence-Gale, *Northern Virginia Community College–Alexandria Campus*

H. T. Stanton Jr., *Barton College*

Jerry Stevens, *Texas Tech University*

William A. Stoever, *Seton Hall University*

Charles I. Stubbart, *Southern Illinois University at Carbondale*

James K. Swenson, *Moorhead State University*

Karen Ann Tarnoff, *East Tennessee State University*

Jerry L. Thomas, *Arapahoe Community College*

Joe Thomas, *Middle Tennessee State University*

Kenneth Thompson, *DePaul University*

John Todd, *University of Arkansas*

Thomas Turk, *Chapman University*

Isaiah Ugboro, *North Carolina A & T University*

Linn Van Dyne, *Michigan State University*

Jaen Vanhoegaerden, *Ashridge Management College*

Barry L. Van Hook, *Arizona State University*

Gloria Walker, *Florida Community College*

Stuart H. Warnock, *University of Southern Colorado*

Toomy Lee Waterson, *Northwood University*

Philip A. Weatherford, *Embry-Riddle Aeronautical University*

Ben Weeks, *St. Xavier University*

Emilia S. Westney, *Texas Tech University*

Donita Whitney-Bammerlin, *Kansas State University*

Robert Williams, *University of North Alabama*

W. J. Williams, *Chicago State University*

Shirley A. Wilson, *Bryant College*

Robert H. Woodhouse, *University of St. Thomas*

Michael A. Yahr, *Robert Morris College*

D. Kent Zimmerman, *James Madison University*

Finally, we are grateful to two incredibly wonderful children, Nicholas and Julia, for being all that they are and for the joy they bring to all who know them.

Gareth R. Jones

Jennifer M. George
Jesse H. Jones Graduate School of Business
Rice University

Contents

Part Two The Environment of Management

CHAPTER THREE
Managing Ethics and Diversity   78

CHAPTER FOUR
Managing in the Global Environment   124

Part Three Planning, Decision Making, and Competitive Advantage

CHAPTER FIVE

Decision Making, Learning, Creativity, and Entrepreneurship 160

CHAPTER SIX

Planning, Strategy, and Competitive Advantage 192

Management Snapshot

Management Snapshot

Part Four   Organizing and Change

CHAPTER SEVEN
Designing Organizational Structure   228

Management Snapshot

Disney Lets Studios Set Structure and Culture   229

Overview

CHAPTER EIGHT
Control, Change, and Entrepreneurship   262

Management Snapshot

Zmail Policy Helps Employee Productivity   263

Overview

Part Five Leading Individuals and Groups

CHAPTER NINE

Motivation   300

Management Snapshot
High Motivation at the SAS Institute   301

Overview

CHAPTER TEN

Leaders and Leadership   336

Management Snapshot
Whitehurst Leads Red Hat   337

Overview

CHAPTER ELEVEN
Effective Team Management 368

Management Snapshot
Teams Innovate at W.L. Gore 369

Overview

CHAPTER TWELVE
Building and Managing Human Resources 400

Management Snapshot
Treating Employees Well Leads to Satisfied Customers and Low Turnover at the Four Seasons 401

Overview

Part Six Controlling Essential Activities and Processes

CHAPTER THIRTEEN

Communication and Information Technology Management 438

Management Snapshot
Wearable Technology Tracks Employee Performance 439

Overview

Content Photo Credits: 1: © Image Source/Getty Images RF; 2: © Sam Edwards/age fotostock RF; 3: © Rubberball/Mark Andersen/Getty Images RF; 4: © Neustockimages/E+/Getty Images RF; 5: © Robert Nicholas/age fotostock RF; 6: © Neustockimages/E+/Getty Images RF; 7: © Image Source/Getty Images RF; 8: © claudia veja/Moment/Getty Images RF; 9: © Yuri Arcurs/Cutcaster RF; 10: © Joshua Hodge Photography/Getty Images RF; 11: © Digital Vision/Getty Images RF; 12: © David Lees/Getty Images RF; 13: © Image Source/Getty Images RF; 14: © claudia veja/Moment/Getty Images RF.

1 The Management Process Today

Learning Objectives

After studying this chapter, you should be able to:

LO 1-1 Describe what management is, why management is important, what managers do, and how managers use organizational resources efficiently and effectively to achieve organizational goals.

LO 1-2 Distinguish among planning, organizing, leading, and controlling (the four principal managerial tasks), and explain how managers' ability to handle each one affects organizational performance.

LO 1-3 Differentiate among three levels of management, and understand the tasks and responsibilities of managers at different levels in the organizational hierarchy.

LO 1-4 Distinguish among three kinds of managerial skill, and explain why managers are divided into different departments to perform their tasks more efficiently and effectively.

LO 1-5 Discuss some major changes in management practices today that have occurred as a result of globalization and the use of advanced information technology (IT).

LO 1-6 Discuss the principal challenges managers face in today's increasingly competitive global environment.

© Image Source/Getty Images RF

Broderick Johnson (*left*) and Andrew Kosove (*right*) started Alcon Entertainment, a successful film, TV, and music company, and continue as the company's co-CEOs. Despite turbulent times in the entertainment industry, they have managed to maintain and even expand their business by hiring experienced managers across the organization. © Chris Pizzello/AP Images

MANAGEMENT SNAPSHOT

Alcon Entertainment Hits the Mark

How Does Management Adapt to Changing Technologies?

Scott Parish is the chief financial officer and chief operating officer of Alcon Entertainment, a Los Angeles–based entertainment production company. Alcon was started in 1997 by film producers (and former business students) Broderick Johnson and Andrew Kosove, who remain Alcon's chief executive officers (CEOs). Since its humble beginnings in a rented apartment, the company has grown into a respected and profitable enterprise, making hit movies such as *The Blind Side; P.S., I Love You;* and *What to Expect When You're Expecting.*

Parish left a successful career in logistics and transportation to pursue his dream of working in the motion picture industry. Relocating from Mississippi to California, he took an hourly administrative job at a film production company to learn about the craft. By taking the initiative to develop his understanding of the entertainment business from the ground up, Parish was able to rise in management over the years. Now as a member of Alcon's top team, he is credited with helping grow Alcon from a boutique film company into a respected creator of not just films but television shows and music as well.

However, maintaining Alcon's growth is a significant challenge in a turbulent and changing entertainment business. Managers like Scott Parish must economically produce valuable content that earns profits. Film creation is a complex process. It can take years to shepherd a film from inception to distribution before audiences. As a result, significant planning is invested into production long before the cameras roll. Parish and Alcon's leadership team are constantly on the lookout for innovative ideas that give them an edge at the box office and must identify and produce ideas, which have a strong potential to connect with the intended audience.

Once viable ideas are obtained and screened, Parish must obtain funding for projects that can cost $40 to $80 million each. Financing films often means coordinating with outside investors, so Parish and his team must be able to explain complex film production processes to those unacquainted with the film business. These outside investors represent important stakeholders in the film production process.

After representing Alcon to investors and obtaining needed financing, Parish must build the right team to produce and market new hit films. This means negotiating with and retaining the services of directors and a cast who can help turn concepts into reality. Missteps at this stage of a film's development can be highly detrimental to its eventual success, and Parish and his team must also balance the needs of Hollywood superstars against the creative demands of directors to create products audiences will pay to see and enjoy. Hollywood talent is notoriously difficult to manage, so Parish must negotiate and align the interests of the company with the talent it retains to help make films.

In addition to the challenges of managing film production in a competitive environment, Parish is helping lead Alcon in an entertainment industry being transformed by technological and economic change. Consumers increasingly prefer to watch content digitally, so Alcon has evolved to broaden the ways it distributes content. Previously, film production companies like Alcon worked with movie theaters and brick-and-mortar retailers to sell content. Although these distribution channels are still being used, Alcon's content can now be found digitally on streaming subscription services such as Netflix, for download on Amazon Prime, and on other services.[1] Alcon also retains the rights to its films, meaning it earns residual income from its catalog of film projects. With changing consumer tastes and a recession that has limited consumers' disposable income, managers like Parish are challenged to find new ways of ensuring profitable content creation and distribution.

In a larger sense, the ease of transferring digital content has made digital piracy more prevalent, posing a significant threat to the entertainment industry. Piracy occurs when third parties distribute copyrighted materials that they do not own to others without permission from the copyright holder, typically for commercial gain. However, entertainment production companies only receive revenues when their content is purchased by retailers or consumers, which means piracy has the potential to undermine the production of new movies, music, and television. Indeed, Alcon now adjusts its revenue projections to reflect the threats of piracy. However, the company is not responding passively to this new managerial challenge but is taking action to mitigate the distribution and use of pirated content.

For example, in conjunction with other major studios and entertainment production companies, Alcon has responded to this new economic and technological reality by mobilizing support for CreativeFuture, an industry coalition designed to mitigate digital piracy on the web by informing and educating policymakers and consumers about the long-term effects of digital piracy on the sustainability of the entertainment industry.[2]

Running an entertainment company is difficult work. Managers like Scott Parish must help their companies stay creative and create profitable content in an industry rapidly evolving amid changing consumer tastes and technological change. This requires managers to represent the interests of the organization to the public and an increasingly complex array of external stakeholders.

Overview

The story of Scott Parish's rise to the top of Alcon Entertainment illustrates many of the challenges facing people who become managers. Managing a company is a complex activity, and effective managers must possess many kinds of skills, knowledge, and abilities. Management is an unpredictable process. Making the right decision is difficult, and even effective managers often make mistakes. But the most effective managers, like Scott Parish, learn from their mistakes and continually try to find ways to improve their companies' performance.

In this chapter we look at what managers do and what skills and abilities they must develop to manage their organizations successfully. We also identify the different kinds of managers that organizations need and the skills and abilities they must develop to succeed. Finally, we identify some challenges managers must address if their organizations are to grow and prosper.

What Is Management?

When you think of a manager, what kind of person comes to mind? Do you think of an executive like Scott Parish, who helps direct his company? Or do you see a manager at a fast-food restaurant, who deals directly with employees

organizations
Collections of people who work together and coordinate their actions to achieve a wide variety of goals or desired future outcomes.

management
The planning, organizing, leading, and controlling of human and other resources to achieve organizational goals efficiently and effectively.

LO1-1 Describe what management is, why management is important, what managers do, and how managers utilize organizational resources efficiently and effectively to achieve organizational goals.

organizational performance
A measure of how efficiently and effectively a manager uses resources to satisfy customers and achieve organizational goals.

efficiency
A measure of how well or how productively resources are used to achieve a goal.

effectiveness
A measure of the appropriateness of the goals an organization is pursuing and the degree to which the organization achieves those goals.

and customers, or the person you answer to if you have a part-time job? What do all these people have in common? First, they all work in organizations. **Organizations** are collections of people who work together and coordinate their actions to achieve a wide variety of goals or desired future outcomes.[3] Second, as managers, they are the people responsible for supervising and making the most of an organization's human and other resources to achieve its goals.

Management, then, is the planning, organizing, leading, and controlling of human and other resources to achieve organizational goals efficiently and effectively. An organization's *resources* include assets such as people and their skills, know-how, and experience; machinery; raw materials; computers and information technology; and patents, financial capital, and loyal customers and employees.

Achieving High Performance: A Manager's Goal

One of the most important goals that organizations and their members try to achieve is to provide some kind of good or service that customers value or desire. The principal goal of Scott Parish is to manage Alcon so that it creates a continuous stream of new and improved entertainment content—enjoyable films, television shows, and music—that customers are willing to buy. Like other entertainment companies, Alcon also seeks projects that have the potential to grow into film or television franchises, encouraging repeat business. Likewise, the principal goal of fast-food managers is to produce tasty and convenient food that customers enjoy and come back to buy again and again.

Organizational performance is a measure of how efficiently and effectively managers use available resources to satisfy customers and achieve organizational goals. Organizational performance increases in direct proportion to increases in efficiency and effectiveness (see Figure 1.1). What are efficiency and effectiveness?

Efficiency is a measure of how productively resources are used to achieve a goal.[4] Organizations are efficient when managers minimize the amount of input resources (such as labor, raw materials, and component parts) or the amount of time needed to produce a given output of goods or services. For example, McDonald's develops ever more efficient fat fryers that not only reduce the amount of oil used in cooking, but also speed up the cooking of french fries. UPS develops new work routines to reduce delivery time, such as instructing drivers to leave their truck doors open when going short distances.

To encourage efficiency, Scott Parish has changed the way Alcon compensates many of its actors. Previously, film production companies paid actors using guaranteed compensation without consideration of a movie's success. They would recoup the cost of making a movie only if the film had adequate success at the box office. Unfortunately, that meant film producers like Alcon held all of the risk.

As an alternative, Parish has linked actor compensation to a film's success.[5] This new compensation method means the company risks fewer dollars if a film flops. However, for actors, the new compensation model means they can earn far more than a flat sum of guaranteed compensation. Thus, when a film succeeds, both Alcon and its actors realize the gains. This new compensation model encourages both parties to work efficiently. Alcon also strives to build good relationships and trust with its actors, which in turn brings goodwill to the organization.

Effectiveness is a measure of the *appropriateness* of the goals that managers have selected for the organization to pursue and the degree to which the organization achieves those goals. Organizations are effective when managers choose appropriate

Figure 1.1

Efficiency,
Effectiveness, and
Performance in an
Organization

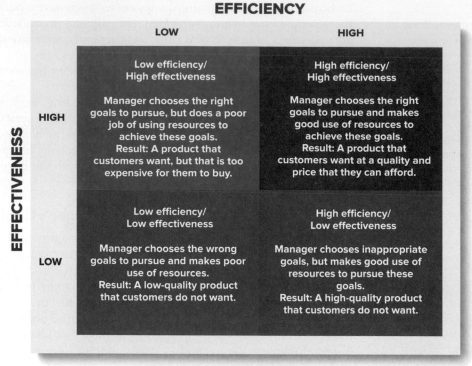

High-performing organizations are efficient *and* effective.

goals and then achieve them. Some years ago, for example, managers at McDonald's decided on the goal of providing breakfast service to attract more customers. The choice of this goal has proved smart: Sales of breakfast food account for more than 30% of McDonald's revenues and are still increasing. Parish's goal is to create a continuous flow of innovative entertainment products at Alcon that resonate with audiences. High-performing organizations, such as Apple, McDonald's, Walmart, Intel, Home Depot, Accenture, and Habitat for Humanity are simultaneously efficient and effective. Effective managers are those who choose the right organizational goals to pursue and have the skills to utilize resources efficiently.

Why Study Management?

The dynamic and complex nature of modern work means that managerial skills are in demand. Organizations need individuals like you who can understand this complexity, respond to environmental contingencies, and make decisions that are ethical and effective. Studying management helps equip individuals to accomplish each of these tasks.

In a broader sense, individuals generally learn through personal experience (think the "school of hard knocks") or through the experiences of others. By studying management in school, you are exposing yourself to the lessons others have learned. The advantage of such social learning is that you are not bound to repeat the mistakes others have made in the past. Furthermore, by studying and practicing the behaviors of good managers and high-performing companies, you will equip yourself to help your future employer succeed.

The economic benefits of becoming a good manager are also impressive. In the United States, general managers earn a median wage of $96,430, with a projected growth rate in job openings of 8% to 14% between now and 2022.[6]

Essential Managerial Tasks

The job of management is to help an organization make the best use of its resources to achieve its goals. How do managers accomplish this objective? They do so by performing four essential managerial tasks: *planning, organizing, leading,* and *controlling.* The arrows linking these tasks in Figure 1.2 suggest the sequence in which managers typically perform them. French manager Henri Fayol first outlined the nature of these managerial activities around the turn of the 20th century in *General and Industrial Management,* a book that remains the classic statement of what managers must do to create a high-performing organization.[7]

Managers at all levels and in all departments—whether in small or large companies, for-profit or not-for-profit organizations, or organizations that operate in one country or throughout the world—are responsible for performing these four tasks, which we look at next. How well managers perform these tasks determines how efficient and effective their organizations are.

LO 1-2 Distinguish among planning, organizing, leading, and controlling (the four principal managerial tasks), and explain how managers' ability to handle each one affects organizational performance.

planning Identifying and selecting appropriate goals; one of the four principal tasks of management.

Planning

To perform the **planning** task, managers identify and select appropriate organizational goals and courses of action; they develop *strategies* for how to achieve high performance. The three steps involved in planning are (1) deciding which goals the organization will pursue, (2) deciding what strategies to adopt to attain those goals, and (3) deciding how to allocate organizational resources to

Figure 1.2
Four Tasks of Management

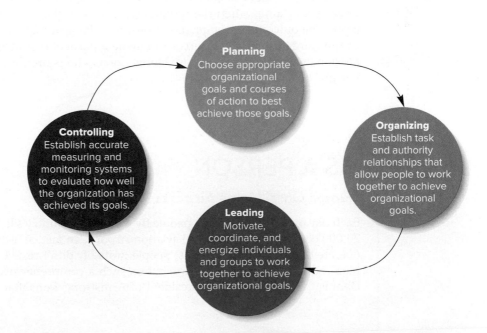

pursue the strategies that attain those goals. How well managers plan and develop strategies determines how effective and efficient the organization is—its performance level.[8]

As an example of planning in action, consider Alcon Entertainment's recent venture into television. Co-CEOs Broderick Johnson and Andrew Kosove are taking Alcon's expertise in film production and applying it to television audiences by producing and distributing quality original programming. Movie and television production have many features in common but operate on different economic models. Films are produced and distributed with partners to reach theater audiences, whereas television shows are produced and offered for channels to distribute to cable, satellite, and streaming audiences.

To help navigate these new challenges, Alcon hired Sharon Hall, formerly of Sony Pictures Television. One of Hall's top priorities is finding ways to create television content that supports and reinforces Alcon's film business.

Alcon is entering a highly competitive market. There are more television stations and shows today than ever before, and competition is fierce to build and maintain audience interest. Thus, the company will need to shape its planning into an effective business **strategy**, which is a cluster of decisions concerning what organizational goals to pursue, what actions to take, and how to use resources to achieve these goals. Alcon recently announced a partnership with the Syfy Channel to produce *The Expanse,* an original sci-fi series.[9]

Alcon originally produced one film at a time, with an emphasis on reducing costs and maximizing efficiency in filmmaking. This constituted a low-cost strategy—a way of obtaining customers by making decisions that allow an organization to produce goods or services more cheaply than its competitors so it can charge lower prices than they do. This low-cost strategy allowed Alcon to weather some disappointing box office results. Alcon's low-cost strategy contrasts with a *differentiation* strategy, in which organizations seek to create highly innovative products that appeal to different types of consumers.[10]

strategy A cluster of decisions about what goals to pursue, what actions to take, and how to use resources to achieve goals.

Planning strategy is complex and difficult, especially because planning is done under uncertainty when the result is unknown so that either success or failure is a possible outcome of the planning process. Managers take major risks when they commit organizational resources to pursue a particular strategy. Another manager passionate about his industry is Dennis Corsi, who is profiled in the "Manager as a Person" box.

MANAGER AS A PERSON

Dennis Corsi Helps Airports Take Off

Each day more than 2 million people fly within the country's large network of nearly 20,000 commercial and general aviation airports. In fact, an estimated 87,000 flights operate daily in U.S. skies. Most people probably don't realize the amount of work required to plan, develop, and maintain such a comprehensive airport system, but Dennis Corsi does. Corsi is president of Armstrong Consultants, a Colorado-based airport engineering firm. He is a pilot and former member of the U.S. Air Force. The knowledge and experience Corsi has acquired over the years, coupled with his managerial talent, have helped Armstrong become a leader in the region.[11]

Headquartered in Grand Junction in western Colorado, Armstrong Consultants helps general and commercial aviation airports plan, engineer, and construct facilities that meet the needs of their customers. Airports receive revenues primarily when aircraft land and refuel at their facilities. However, as aircraft have different landing, takeoff, and taxiing requirements, Armstrong must offer the right mix of facilities to accommodate pilots' needs. For example, some propeller aircraft can use grass airport runways as short as 600 feet, while other business jets require paved runways exceeding one mile in length and more than 100 feet wide. Managers at engineering companies like Armstrong help airports understand and accommodate these different needs. This is where Corsi's more than 23 years of experience in aviation and time spent managing more than 250 airport projects come in handy.[12]

Like other forms of transportation, airports are highly regulated. They must comply with a complicated mix of regulations that specify how they can operate. Managers like Corsi help clients coordinate with local, state, and federal agencies to comply with highly complex regulations. Armstrong has completed more than 1,200 airport improvement projects, which amounts to 30 or more projects each year that must comply with different kinds of regulatory issues.[13] Aviation is also marked by significant technological change and changing consumer needs. Managers like Corsi work hard to stay ahead of the curve, refining their expertise to provide valued insight to clients. Companies like Armstrong also benefit from building and maintaining strong relationships with regulatory agencies, such as the Federal Aviation Administration, which help guide the activities of client airports.

The process of airport planning and engineering is challenging—something Corsi understands well. For example, before facilities are constructed or modified, airports must obtain adequate funding, typically through a combination of local and federal grants that are financed by aviation fuel taxes. Airports then develop forecasts that help identify the types of traffic they expect, as well as the impact on the local economy. These forecasts act as inputs for facility engineering plans, which are developed to guide the use and development of airfield facilities. However, before amending facilities, airports must also obtain adequate state and federal environmental clearances to ensure their activities do not damage the local environment. This includes surveying the area around an airport, estimating light and sound emissions, testing air and water, and forecasting potential impacts to the region. Only then can construction begin at an airport, which presents its own set of challenges.

To help airports with this daunting process, Armstrong retains a staff of engineers, planners, environmental specialists, and construction managers. At the employee-owned company, Corsi and staff must be able to understand the complexities of each of these functional areas and coordinate their activities for multiple clients at once.

Armstrong Consultants and its president, Dennis Corsi, use their aviation knowledge and managerial expertise to help airport clients succeed in a complex business. © Joe Drivas/ Photographer's Choice/Getty Images

Organizing

organizing
Structuring working relationships in a way that allows organizational members to work together to achieve organizational goals; one of the four principal tasks of management.

Organizing is structuring working relationships so organizational members interact and cooperate to achieve organizational goals. Organizing people into departments according to the kinds of job-specific tasks they perform lays out the lines of authority and responsibility between different individuals and groups. Managers must decide how best to organize resources, particularly human resources.

organizational structure A formal system of task and reporting relationships that coordinates and motivates organizational members so they work together to achieve organizational goals.

The outcome of organizing is the creation of an **organizational structure**, a formal system of task and reporting relationships that coordinates and motivates members so they work together to achieve organizational goals. Organizational structure determines how an organization's resources can be best used to create goods and services. As Alcon Entertainment has grown in size and scope, executives face the issue of how to structure the company and maintain its core values. The company that once made one movie per year now produces content in film, television, and music. This requires coordinating the activities of a larger staff working on multiple projects in different markets. Managers like Scott Parish also have the difficult task of maintaining the "filmmaking friendly" culture that helped Alcon grow and thrive. Finally, Parish must work to ensure Alcon's new businesses are working together toward a common objective and doing so in a cost-effective manner. We examine the organizing process in detail in Chapter 9.

Leading

leading Articulating a clear vision and energizing and enabling organizational members so they understand the part they play in achieving organizational goals; one of the four principal tasks of management.

An organization's *vision* is a short, succinct, and inspiring statement of what the organization intends to become and the goals it is seeking to achieve—its desired future state. In **leading**, managers articulate a clear organizational vision for the organization's members to accomplish, and they energize and enable employees so everyone understands the part he or she plays in achieving organizational goals. Leadership involves managers using their power, personality, influence, persuasion, and communication skills to coordinate people and groups so their activities and efforts are in harmony. Leadership revolves around encouraging all employees to perform at a high level to help the organization achieve its vision and goals. Another outcome of leadership is a highly motivated and committed workforce. Alcon Entertainment's employees appreciate the core values and stability of their leadership, which has contributed to their success as a workforce. Likewise, because he worked his way up from an administrative role to a leadership position, Scott Parish is better able to relate to his employees. We discuss the issues involved in managing and leading individuals and groups in Chapters 9 through 12.

Controlling

controlling
Evaluating how well an organization is achieving its goals and taking action to maintain or improve performance; one of the four principal tasks of management.

In **controlling**, the task of managers is to evaluate how well an organization has achieved its goals and to take any corrective actions needed to maintain or improve performance. For example, managers monitor the performance of individuals, departments, and the organization as a whole to see whether they are meeting desired performance standards. Alcon's Scott Parish learned early in his career how important this is; if standards are not being met, managers seek ways to improve performance.

The outcome of the control process is the ability to measure performance accurately and regulate organizational efficiency and effectiveness. To exercise control, managers must decide which goals to measure—perhaps goals pertaining to productivity, quality, or responsiveness to customers—and then they must design control systems that will provide the information necessary to assess performance—that is, determine to what degree the goals have been met. The controlling task also helps managers evaluate how well they themselves are performing the other three tasks of management—planning, organizing, and leading—and take corrective action.

Controlling costs is a delicate practice in Hollywood due to contingencies that affect the production of film, television, and music. Artists' personal and schedule demands, changes in creative direction, and even the weather can affect production costs, posing a challenge to Alcon Entertainment's management team. However, innovative compensation schemes, core values, and stable and respected leadership help give Alcon an advantage over its competitors.

The four managerial tasks—planning, organizing, leading, and controlling—are essential parts of a manager's job. At all levels in the managerial hierarchy, and across all jobs and departments in an organization, effective management means performing these four activities successfully—in ways that increase efficiency and effectiveness.

Levels and Skills of Managers

To perform the four managerial tasks efficiently and effectively, organizations group or differentiate their managers in two main ways—by level in hierarchy and by type of skill. First, they differentiate managers according to their level or rank in the organization's hierarchy of authority. The three levels of managers are first-line managers, middle managers, and top managers—arranged in a hierarchy. Typically first-line managers report to middle managers, and middle managers report to top managers.

department A group of people who work together and possess similar skills or use the same knowledge, tools, or techniques to perform their jobs.

Second, organizations group managers into different departments (or functions) according to their specific job-related skills, expertise, and experiences, such as a manager's engineering skills, marketing expertise, or sales experience. A **department**, such as the manufacturing, accounting, engineering, or sales department, is a group of managers and employees who work together because they possess similar skills and experience or use the same kind of knowledge, tools, or techniques to perform their jobs. Within each department are all three levels of management. Next we examine why organizations use a hierarchy of managers and group them, by the jobs they perform, into departments.

LO 1-3 Differentiate among three levels of management, and understand the tasks and responsibilities of managers at different levels in the organizational hierarchy.

Levels of Management

Organizations normally have three levels of management: first-line managers, middle managers, and top managers (see Figure 1.3). Managers at each level have different but related responsibilities for using organizational resources to increase efficiency and effectiveness.

first-line manager A manager who is responsible for the daily supervision of nonmanagerial employees.

At the base of the managerial hierarchy are **first-line managers**, often called *supervisors*. They are responsible for daily supervision of the nonmanagerial employees who perform the specific activities necessary to produce goods and services. First-line managers work in all departments or functions of an organization.

Examples of first-line managers include the supervisor of a work team in the manufacturing department of a car plant, the head nurse in the obstetrics department of a hospital, and the chief mechanic overseeing a crew of mechanics in the service function of a new car dealership. At Alcon Entertainment, first-line managers are

Figure 1.3
Levels of Managers

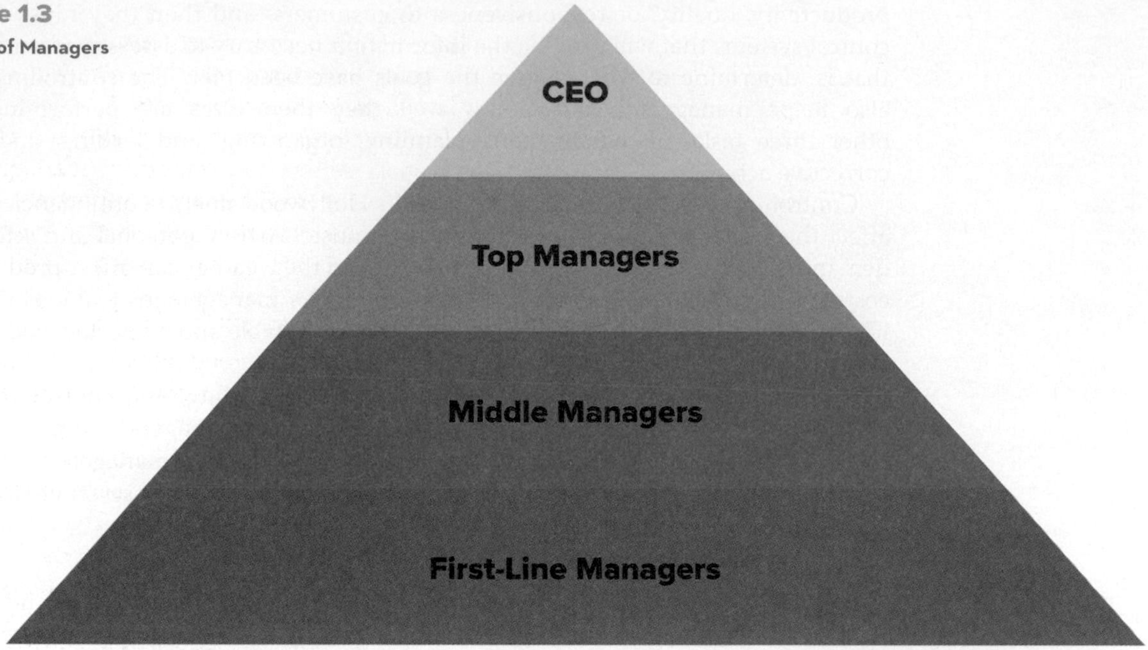

```
                    CEO

                 Top Managers

              Middle Managers

           First-Line Managers
```

often directors who work creatively with talent to produce quality entertainment content. One key to management here is building trust between Alcon's top management and the directors it relies on to create new content.

middle manager
A manager who supervises first-line managers and is responsible for finding the best way to use resources to achieve organizational goals.

Supervising the first-line managers are **middle managers,** responsible for finding the best way to organize human and other resources to achieve organizational goals. To increase efficiency, middle managers find ways to help first-line managers and nonmanagerial employees better use resources to reduce manufacturing costs or improve customer service. To increase effectiveness, middle managers evaluate whether the organization's goals are appropriate and suggest to top managers how goals should be changed. Often the suggestions that middle managers make to top managers can dramatically increase organizational performance. A major part of the middle manager's job is developing and fine-tuning skills and know-how, such as manufacturing or marketing expertise, that allow the organization to be efficient and effective. Middle managers make thousands of specific decisions about the production of goods and services: Which first-line supervisors should be chosen for this particular project? Where can we find the highest-quality resources? How should employees be organized to allow them to make the best use of resources?

Behind a first-class sales force, look for the middle managers responsible for training, motivating, and rewarding the salespeople. Behind a committed staff of high school teachers, look for the principal who energizes them to find ways to obtain the resources they need to do outstanding and innovative jobs in the classroom.

top manager
A manager who establishes organizational goals, decides how departments should interact, and monitors the performance of middle managers.

In contrast to middle managers, **top managers** are responsible for the performance of *all* departments.[14] They have *cross-departmental responsibility*. Top managers establish organizational goals, such as which goods and services the company should produce; they decide how the different departments should interact; and they monitor how well middle managers in each department use resources to achieve goals.[15] Top managers are ultimately responsible for the success or failure of an organization, and their performance (like that of Alcon Television's president,

Ken Chenault, pictured here, is the chairman and CEO of American Express Company. Promoted in 1997, he climbed the ranks from its Travel Related Services Company thanks to his even temper and unrelenting drive. Respected by colleagues for his personality, most will say they can't remember him losing his temper or raising his voice. His open-door policy for subordinates allows him to mentor managers and encourages all to enter and speak their minds.
© Mark Peterson/Redux

top management team A group composed of the CEO, the COO, and the vice presidents of the most important departments of a company.

Sharon Hall) is continually scrutinized by people inside and outside the organization, such as other employees and investors.[16]

The *chief executive officer (CEO)* is a company's most senior and important manager, the one all other top managers report to. Today the term *chief operating officer (COO)* refers to the company's top manager, such as Tim Cook, who was groomed by Steve Jobs to take over as CEO. Together the CEO and COO are responsible for developing good working relationships among the top managers of various departments (manufacturing and marketing, for example); usually these top managers have the title "vice president." A central concern of the CEO is the creation of a smoothly functioning **top management team**, a group composed of the CEO, the COO, and the vice presidents most responsible for achieving organizational goals.[17] Alcon's co-CEOs, Andrew Kosove and Broderick Johnson, are working to build such a team.

The relative importance of planning, organizing, leading, and controlling—the four principal managerial tasks—to any particular manager depends on the manager's position in the managerial hierarchy.[18] The amount of time managers spend planning and organizing resources to maintain and improve organizational performance increases as they ascend the hierarchy (see Figure 1.4).[19] Top managers devote most of their time to planning and organizing, the tasks so crucial to determining an organization's long-term performance. The lower that managers' positions are in the hierarchy, the more time the managers spend leading and controlling first-line managers or nonmanagerial employees.

LO 1-4 Distinguish among three kinds of managerial skill, and explain why managers are divided into different departments to perform their tasks more efficiently and effectively.

conceptual skills The ability to analyze and diagnose a situation and to distinguish between cause and effect.

Managerial Skills

Both education and experience enable managers to recognize and develop the personal skills they need to put organizational resources to their best use. Alcon Entertainment's co-CEOs Andrew Kosove and Broderick Johnson realized from the start that they lacked the experience and expertise in marketing, operations, and planning to guide the company alone. So they recruited experienced managers from other companies, such as Sony Television and New Regency, to help build the company. Research has shown that education and experience help managers acquire and develop three types of skills: *conceptual, human,* and *technical.*[20]

Conceptual skills are demonstrated in the general ability to analyze and diagnose a situation and to distinguish between cause and effect. Top managers require the best conceptual skills because their primary responsibilities are planning and organizing.[21] Managers like Scott Parish must constantly identify new opportunities and mobilize managers and other resources to take advantage of those opportunities.

Formal education and training are important in helping managers develop conceptual skills. Business training at the undergraduate and graduate (MBA) levels provides many of the conceptual tools (theories and techniques in marketing,

Figure 1.4

Relative Amount of
Time That Managers
Spend on the Four
Managerial Tasks

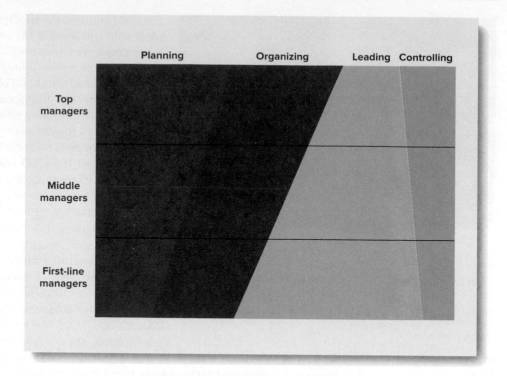

finance, and other areas) that managers need to perform their roles effectively. The study of management helps develop the skills that allow managers to understand the big picture confronting an organization. The ability to focus on the big picture lets managers see beyond the situation immediately at hand and consider choices while keeping in mind the organization's long-term goals.

Today continuing management education and training, including training in advanced IT, are an integral step in building managerial skills because theories and techniques are constantly being developed to improve organizational effectiveness, such as total quality management, benchmarking, and web-based organization and business-to-business (B2B) networks. A quick scan through a magazine such as *Bloomberg Businessweek* or *Fortune* reveals a host of seminars on topics such as advanced marketing, finance, leadership, and human resource management that are offered to managers at many levels in the organization, from the most senior corporate executives to middle managers. Microsoft, IBM, and many other organizations designate a portion of each manager's personal budget to be used at the manager's discretion to attend management development programs.

In addition, organizations may wish to develop a particular manager's abilities in a specific skill area—perhaps to learn an advanced component of departmental skills, such as international bond trading, or to learn the skills necessary to implement total quality management. The organization thus pays for managers to attend specialized programs to develop these skills. Indeed, one signal that a manager is performing well is an organization's willingness to invest in that manager's skill development. Similarly, many nonmanagerial employees who are performing at a high level (because they have studied management) are often sent to intensive management training programs to develop their management skills and to prepare them for promotion to first-level management positions.

human skills
The ability to understand, alter, lead, and control the behavior of other individuals and groups.

Human skills include the general ability to understand, alter, lead, and control the behavior of other individuals and groups. The ability to communicate, to coordinate, and to motivate people, and to mold individuals into a cohesive team distinguishes effective from ineffective managers. Managers like Alcon's Scott Parish require a high level of human skills to motivate and reward their people.

Like conceptual skills, human skills can be learned through education and training, as well as be developed through experience.[22] Organizations increasingly utilize advanced programs in leadership skills and team leadership as they seek to capitalize on the advantages of self-managed teams.[23] To manage personal interactions effectively, each person in an organization needs to learn how to empathize with other people—to understand their viewpoints and the problems they face. One way to help managers understand their personal strengths and weaknesses is to have their superiors, peers, and subordinates provide feedback about their job performance. Thorough and direct feedback allows managers to develop their human skills.

technical skills
The job-specific knowledge and techniques required to perform an organizational role.

Technical skills are the *job-specific* skills required to perform a particular type of work or occupation at a high level. Examples include a manager's specific manufacturing, accounting, marketing, and increasingly, IT skills. Managers need a range of technical skills to be effective. The array of technical skills managers need depends on their position in their organization. The manager of a restaurant, for example, may need cooking skills to fill in for an absent cook, accounting and bookkeeping skills to keep track of receipts and costs and to administer the payroll, and aesthetic skills to keep the restaurant looking attractive for customers.

As noted earlier, managers and employees who possess the same kinds of technical skills typically become members of a specific department and are known as, for example, marketing managers or manufacturing managers.[24] Managers are grouped into different departments because a major part of a manager's responsibility is to monitor, train, and supervise employees so their job-specific skills and expertise increase. Obviously this is easier to do when employees with similar skills are grouped into the same department because they can learn from one another and become more skilled and productive at their particular job.

Figure 1.5 shows how an organization groups managers into departments on the basis of their job-specific skills. It also shows that inside each department, a managerial hierarchy of first-line, middle, and top managers emerges. At Dell, for example, Michael Dell hired experienced top managers to take charge of the marketing, sales, and manufacturing departments and to develop work procedures to help middle and first-line managers control the company's explosive sales growth. When the head of manufacturing found he had no time to supervise computer assembly, he recruited experienced manufacturing middle managers from other companies to assume this responsibility.

core competency
The specific set of departmental skills, knowledge, and experience that allows one organization to outperform another.

Today the term **core competency** is often used to refer to the specific set of departmental skills, knowledge, and experience that allows one organization to outperform its competitors. In other words, departmental skills that create a core competency give an organization a *competitive advantage.* Dell, for example, was the first PC maker to develop a core competency in materials management that allowed it to produce PCs at a much lower cost than its competitors—a major source of competitive advantage. Google is well known for its core competency in research and development (R&D) that allows it to innovate new products at a faster rate than its competitors. From computerized glasses to self-driving cars, Google continues to pioneer the development of technology for the masses.

Figure 1.5
Types and Levels
of Managers

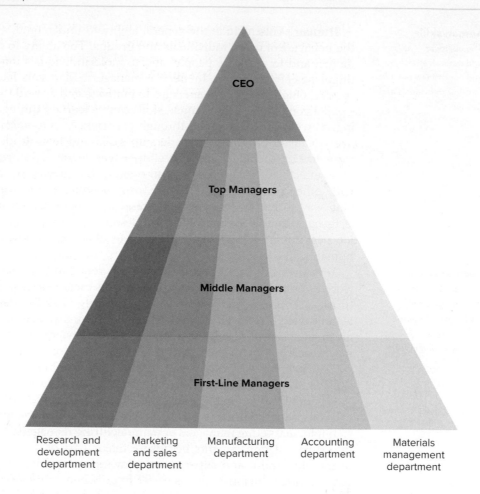

Effective managers need all three kinds of skills—conceptual, human, and technical—to help their organizations perform more efficiently and effectively. The absence of even one type of managerial skill can lead to failure. One of the biggest problems that people who start small businesses confront, for example, is their lack of appropriate conceptual and human skills. Someone who has the technical skills to start a new business does not necessarily know how to manage the venture successfully. Similarly, one of the biggest problems that scientists or engineers who switch careers from research to management confront is their lack of effective human skills. Ambitious managers or prospective managers are constantly in search of the latest educational contributions to help them develop the conceptual, human, and technical skills they need to perform at a high level in today's changing and increasingly competitive global environment.

Developing new and improved skills through education and training has become a priority for both aspiring managers and the organizations they work for. As we discussed earlier, many people are enrolling in advanced management courses; but many companies, such as Microsoft, GE, and IBM, have established their own colleges to train and develop their employees and managers at all levels. Every year these companies put thousands of their employees through management programs designed to identify the employees who the company believes have the competencies that can be developed to become its future top managers. Most organizations closely link promotion to a manager's ability to acquire the competencies that a particular company believes are important.[25] At Apple and 3M, for example, the ability to successfully lead a new product development team is viewed as a vital requirement for promotion; at Accenture and IBM, the ability to attract and retain clients is viewed as a skill their IT consultants must possess. We discuss the various kinds of skills managers need to develop in most of the chapters of this book.

Recent Changes in Management Practices

The tasks and responsibilities of managers have been changing dramatically in recent years. Two major factors that have led to these changes are global competition and advances in information technology. Stiff competition for resources from organizations both at home and abroad has put increased pressure on all managers to improve efficiency and effectiveness. Increasingly, top managers are encouraging lower-level managers to look beyond the goals of their own departments and take a cross-departmental view to find new opportunities to improve organizational performance. Modern IT gives managers at all levels and in all areas access to more and better information and improves their ability to plan, organize, lead, and control. IT also gives employees more job-related information and allows them to become more skilled, specialized, and productive.[26]

Restructuring and Outsourcing

To utilize IT to increase efficiency and effectiveness, CEOs and top management teams have been restructuring organizations and outsourcing specific organizational activities to reduce the number of employees on the payroll and make more productive use of the remaining workforce.

restructuring
Downsizing an organization by eliminating the jobs of large numbers of top, middle, and first-line managers and nonmanagerial employees.

Restructuring involves simplifying, shrinking, or downsizing an organization's operations to lower operating costs, as both Dell and Xerox have been forced to do. The recession that started in 2009 forced most companies—large and small, and profit and nonprofit—to find ways to reduce costs because their customers were spending less money, so their sales and revenues decreased. Restructuring can be done by eliminating product teams, shrinking departments, and reducing levels in the hierarchy, all of which result in the loss of large numbers of jobs of top, middle, or first-line managers, as well as nonmanagerial employees. Modern IT's ability to improve efficiency has increased the amount of downsizing in recent years because IT makes it possible for fewer employees to perform a particular work task. IT increases each person's ability to process information and make decisions more quickly and accurately, for example. U.S. companies are spending over $100 billion a year to purchase advanced IT that can improve efficiency and effectiveness. We discuss the many dramatic effects of IT on management in Chapter 13 and throughout this book.

Restructuring, however, can produce some powerful negative outcomes. It can reduce the morale of remaining employees, who worry about their own job security. And top managers of many downsized organizations realize that they downsized too far when their employees complain they are overworked and when increasing numbers of customers complain about poor service.[27]

outsourcing
Contracting with another company, usually abroad, to have it perform an activity the organization previously performed itself.

Outsourcing involves contracting with another company, usually in a low-cost country abroad, to have it perform a work activity the organization previously performed itself, such as manufacturing, marketing, or customer service. Outsourcing increases efficiency because it lowers operating costs, freeing up money and resources that can be used in more effective ways—for example, to develop new products.

Low-cost global competition dramatically increased outsourcing at the beginning of 2000. In 2013, more than 2.7 million U.S. jobs were outsourced to other countries. India, Indonesia, and China were rated as the best outsourcing countries. Companies primarily reported offshore outsourcing to control costs and gain access to unavailable resources while freeing up internal ones.[28] Tens of thousands of high-paying IT jobs have also moved abroad to countries like India and Russia, where programmers work for one-third the salary of those in the United States.

Large for-profit organizations today typically employ 10% to 20% fewer people than they did 10 years ago because of restructuring and outsourcing. Ford, IBM, AT&T, HP, Dell, and DuPont are among the thousands of organizations that have streamlined their operations to increase efficiency and effectiveness. The argument is that the managers and employees who have lost their jobs will find employment in new and growing U.S. companies where their skills and experience will be better utilized. For example, the millions of manufacturing jobs that have been lost overseas will be replaced by higher-paying U.S. jobs in the service sector that are made possible because of the growth in global trade. At the same time, many companies have experienced growing problems with outsourcing in the 2010s, and the move to insource jobs (that is, to bring them back to the United States) has been increasing as discussed in the following "Managing Globally."

MANAGING GLOBALLY

GE Brings Manufacturing Jobs Back Home

Making headlines by calling outsourcing an "outdated business model," General Electric CEO Jeff Immelt is betting on the benefits of insourcing. After trying to sell its barely breathing, iconic appliance manufacturing operation in Louisville, Kentucky, a few years ago, the CEO changed course and invested $1 billion to revive it. The story of his about-face illustrates a recent trend in U.S. manufacturing: bringing jobs back from overseas.[29]

Built in the 1950s, GE's famed Appliance Park is a massive manufacturing compound that boasts six factory buildings, a power plant, a dedicated fire department, and its own zip code. In its heyday in the early 1970s, Appliance Park employed 23,000 workers and churned out more than 60,000 appliances a week. In many ways, it stood alongside Detroit as an American pillar of manufacturing.

But as with many businesses, and for reasons inside and outside its control, Appliance Park couldn't sustain the growth. It became more beneficial for the company to produce many of its appliances overseas to take advantage of lower wage rates and liberal trade policies. The hustle and bustle at the facility

In an effort to leverage innovation in technology here at home, GE is bringing back manufacturing jobs from overseas, a process known as insourcing. © Kevork Djansezian/AP Images

started to decline in the 1980s through 2000s, to the point where barely more than 1,850 employees produced a limited number of products in 2011. It seemed that GE's appliance division had outsourced itself almost to oblivion, as did the majority of American manufacturing firms during the same period.[30]

Over the past several years, however, several factors have brought jobs back to U.S. shores, creating what has become known as America's "manufacturing renaissance." First, high energy prices abroad made shipping products produced overseas expensive. Second, increasing wage rates and stronger currencies in nations like China made labor less competitive compared with U.S. wage rates. Third, many states have enacted regulations that are more "business friendly," further reducing costs. Finally, the U.S. workforce has continued to increase its productivity, meaning average workers produce more at an increasingly competitive wage rate. These factors have increased demand for U.S. workers, bringing many jobs back to the United States from abroad.

In GE's case, the reason to keep jobs on American soil is more about innovation than anything else. Whereas a product's life cycle—refrigerators, microwaves, stoves, for example—might previously have lasted seven years on average, innovations in technology today have shorten an appliance's life cycle to two or three years. Smarter versions with neater tricks and gadgets are both on the rise and in demand. It no longer makes sense to set up operations overseas when products have shorter life cycles—the savings just aren't there.

A notable example of new product technology is the GE GeoSpring water heater. This innovative product uses ambient air to heat water with about 40% of the electricity of a traditional water heater. It can also be controlled using a smartphone. The GeoSpring's technological differentiation is one reason GE decided to manufacture it in the United States. GE was concerned the water heater could be copied by Chinese competitors, reducing the competitive advantage GE hoped to gain through this innovation.

GE has revived a few of its other manufacturing lines—dishwashers and refrigerators, for instance—and has started making some of the component parts for those lines as well. It is also producing frontloading washers and dryers, which it has never made in the United States. GE and many other companies are finding that the benefits of keeping everything in house—design, manufacturing, sales, marketing—under one roof rather than in different locations far away from each other, ensures the highest-quality product and the conditions to foster innovation.[31]

Empowerment and Self-Managed Teams

LO 1-5 Discuss some major changes in management practices today that have occurred as a result of globalization and the use of advanced information technology (IT).

empowerment The expansion of employees' knowledge, tasks, and decision-making responsibilities.

The second principal way managers have sought to increase efficiency and effectiveness is by empowering lower-level employees and moving to self-managed teams. **Empowerment** is a management technique that involves giving employees more authority and responsibility over how they perform their work activities. The way in which John Deere, the well-known tractor manufacturer, empowered its employees illustrates how this technique can help raise performance. The employees who assemble Deere's vehicles possess detailed knowledge about how Deere products work. Deere's managers realized these employees could become persuasive salespeople if they were given training. So groups of these employees were given intensive sales training and sent to visit Deere's customers and explain to them how to operate and service the company's new products. While speaking with customers, these newly empowered "salespeople" also collect information that helps Deere

Some employees who assemble John Deere tractors are also given intensive sales training so they can visit customers and explain how to operate and service John Deere products.
© Scott Olson/Getty Images

develop new products that better meet customers' needs. The new sales jobs are temporary; employees go on assignment but then return to the production line, where they use their new knowledge to find ways to improve efficiency and quality.

Often companies find that empowering employees can lead to so many kinds of performance gains that they use their reward systems to promote empowerment. For example, Deere's moves to empower employees were so successful that the company negotiated a new labor agreement with its employees to promote empowerment. The agreement specifies that pay increases will be based on employees' learning new skills and completing college courses in areas such as computer programming that will help the company increase efficiency and quality. Deere has continued to make greater use of teams throughout the 2010s, and its profits have soared because its competitors cannot match its user-friendly machines that are the result of its drive to respond to its customers' needs.

IT is being increasingly used to empower employees because it expands employees' job knowledge and increases the scope of their job responsibilities. Frequently IT allows one employee to perform a task that was previously performed by many employees. As a result, the employee has more autonomy and responsibility. IT also facilitates the use of a **self-managed team**, a group of employees who assume collective responsibility for organizing, controlling, and supervising their own work activities.[32] Using IT designed to give team members real-time information about each member's performance, a self-managed team can often find ways to accomplish a task more quickly and efficiently. Moreover, self-managed teams assume many tasks and responsibilities previously performed by first-line managers, so a company can better utilize its workforce.[33] First-line managers act as coaches or mentors whose job is not to tell employees what to do but to provide advice and guidance and help teams find new ways to perform their tasks more efficiently.[34] Using the same IT, middle managers can easily monitor what is happening in these teams and make better resource allocation decisions as a result. We discuss self-managed teams in more detail in Chapter 11.

self-managed team A group of employees who assume responsibility for organizing, controlling, and supervising their own activities and monitoring the quality of the goods and services they provide.

Challenges for Management in a Global Environment

global organizations Organizations that operate and compete in more than one country.

Because the world has been changing more rapidly than ever before, managers and other employees throughout an organization must perform at higher and higher levels.[35] In the last 20 years, rivalry between organizations competing domestically (in the same country) and globally (in countries abroad) has increased dramatically. The rise of **global organizations**, organizations that operate and compete in more than one country, has pressured many organizations to identify better ways to use their resources and improve their performance. The successes of the German chemical companies Schering and Hoechst, Italian furniture manufacturer Natuzzi, Korean electronics companies Samsung and LG, Brazilian plane maker Embraer, and Europe's Airbus Industries are putting pressure on companies in other countries to raise their level of performance to compete successfully against these global organizations.

Even in the not-for-profit sector, global competition is spurring change. Schools, universities, police forces, and government agencies are reexamining their operations because looking at how activities are performed in other countries often reveals better ways to do them. For example, many curriculum and teaching changes in the United States have resulted from the study of methods that Japanese and European school systems use. Similarly, European and Asian hospital systems have learned much from the U.S. system—which may be the most effective, though not the most efficient, in the world.

Today managers who make no attempt to learn from and adapt to changes in the global environment find themselves reacting rather than innovating, and their organizations often become uncompetitive and fail. Five major challenges stand out for managers in today's world: building a competitive advantage, maintaining ethical standards, managing a diverse workforce, utilizing new information systems and technologies, and practicing global crisis management.

Building Competitive Advantage

What are the most important lessons for managers and organizations to learn if they are to reach and remain at the top of the competitive environment of business? The answer relates to the use of organizational resources to build a competitive advantage. **Competitive advantage** is the ability of one organization to outperform other organizations because it produces desired goods or services more efficiently and effectively than its competitors. The four building blocks of competitive advantage are superior *efficiency, quality, innovation,* and *responsiveness to customers* (see Figure 1.6).

Organizations increase their efficiency when they reduce the quantity of resources (such as people and raw materials) they use to produce goods or services. In today's competitive environment, organizations continually search for new ways to use their resources to improve efficiency. Many organizations are training their workforces in the new skills and techniques needed to operate heavily computerized assembly plants. Similarly, cross-training gives employees the range of skills they need to perform many different tasks; and organizing employees in new ways, such

competitive advantage The ability of one organization to outperform other organizations because it produces desired goods or services more efficiently and effectively than they do.

Figure 1.6
Building Blocks of Competitive Advantage

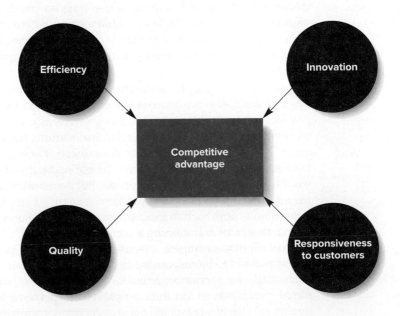

as in self-managed teams, lets them make good use of their skills. These are important steps in the effort to improve productivity. Japanese and German companies invest far more in training employees than do American or Italian companies.

Managers must improve efficiency if their organizations are to compete successfully with companies operating in Mexico, China, Malaysia, and other countries where employees are paid comparatively low wages. New methods must be devised either to increase efficiency or to gain some other competitive advantage—higher-quality goods, for example—if outsourcing and the loss of jobs to low-cost countries are to be prevented.

The challenge from global organizations such as Korean electronics manufacturers, Mexican agricultural producers, and European design and financial companies also has increased pressure on companies to develop the skills and abilities of their workforces in order to improve the quality of their goods and services. One major thrust to improving quality has been to introduce the quality-enhancing techniques known as *total quality management (TQM)*. Employees involved in TQM are often organized into quality control teams and are responsible for finding new and better ways to perform their jobs; they also must monitor and evaluate the quality of the goods they produce. We discuss ways of managing TQM successfully in Chapter 14.

Today companies can win or lose the competitive race depending on their *speed*—how fast they can bring new products to market—or their *flexibility*—how easily they can change or alter the way they perform their activities to respond to actions of their competitors. Companies that have speed and flexibility are agile competitors: Their managers have superior planning and organizing abilities; they can think ahead, decide what to do, and then speedily mobilize their resources to respond to a changing environment. We examine how managers can build speed and flexibility in their organizations in later chapters. Agile companies are adept at responding to changes in their environments. For example, entertainment companies like Alcon are seeking ways to economically produce their content amid tightening profit margins and smaller audiences. One way Alcon has responded to this pressure is by expanding into music production that will support its film and television endeavors.

innovation

The process of creating new or improved goods and services or developing better ways to produce or provide them.

Innovation, the process of creating new or improved goods and services that customers want or developing better ways to produce or provide goods and services, poses a special challenge. Managers must create an organizational setting in which people are encouraged to be innovative. Typically innovation takes place in small groups or teams; management decentralizes control of work activities to team members and creates an organizational culture that rewards risk taking. Innovation doesn't happen by itself; companies have to devote resources that enable innovation. These investments are a balancing act. Consider Google. In 2004, the company was praised for its 80/20 work allocation, where 20% of an employee's time was spent working on individual "pet projects." Innovations such as Gmail came from this program. But the company recently announced it was suspending the 80/20 program because of productivity concerns. Google had banked on the idea that "down" time would enable individuals to innovate, but economic realities and productivity needs meant a change in how the company structured employee work. Instead of a more autonomous approach to innovation, Google is now relying on its Google X lab as a formal means of maintaining a competitive edge.[36]

Organizations compete for customers with their products and services, so training employees to be responsive to customers' needs is vital for all organizations, but particularly for service organizations. Retail stores, banks, and hospitals, for example, depend entirely on their employees to perform behaviors that result in high-quality service at a reasonable cost.[37] As many countries (the United States, Canada, and Switzerland are just a few) move toward a more service-based economy (in part because of the loss of manufacturing jobs to China, Malaysia, and other countries with low labor costs), managing behavior in service organizations is becoming increasingly important. Many organizations are empowering their customer service employees and giving them the authority to take the lead in providing high-quality customer service. As noted previously, empowering nonmanagerial employees and creating self-managed teams change the role of first-line managers and lead to more efficient use of organizational resources.

turnaround management

The creation of a new vision for a struggling company based on a new approach to planning and organizing to make better use of a company's resources and allow it to survive and prosper.

Sometimes the best efforts of managers to revitalize their organization's fortunes fail; and faced with bankruptcy, the directors of these companies are forced to appoint a new CEO who has a history of success in rebuilding a company. **Turnaround management** is the creation of a new vision for a struggling company using a new approach to planning and organizing to make better use of a company's resources and allow it to survive and eventually prosper—something Apple's Steve Jobs excelled at. It involves developing radical new strategies such as how to reduce the number of products sold or change how they are made and distributed, or close corporate and manufacturing operations to reduce costs. Organizations that appoint turnaround CEOs are generally experiencing a crisis because they have become inefficient or ineffective; sometimes this is because of poor management over a continuing period, and sometimes it occurs because a competitor introduces a new product or technology that makes their own products unattractive to customers. For example, Japanese technology firm Sony once dominated the market with a high-visibility brand. In fact, Sony was at the forefront of e-reader technology more than a decade ago with Librie, the first e-book reader with an electronic ink display. Unfortunately, Sony was unable to commercialize this technological breakthrough, and rival Amazon now commands the e-reader market with its Kindle devices and apps. Although it has had a distinctive competency in technological innovation, Sony will need strong leadership to help develop the ability to commercialize its innovations in a fiercely competitive technology sector.[38]

Achieving a competitive advantage requires that managers use all their skills and expertise, as well as their companies' other resources, to find new and improved ways to improve efficiency, quality, innovation, and responsiveness to customers. We revisit this theme often as we examine the ways managers plan strategies, organize resources and activities, and lead and control people and groups to increase efficiency and effectiveness.

Maintaining Ethical and Socially Responsible Standards

Managers at all levels, especially after the recent economic crisis, are under considerable pressure to make the best use of resources to increase the level at which their organizations perform.[39] For example, top managers feel pressure from shareholders to increase the performance of the entire organization to boost its stock price, improve profits, or raise dividends. In turn, top managers may pressure middle managers to find new ways to use organizational resources to increase efficiency or quality and thus attract new customers and earn more revenues—and then middle managers hit on their department's supervisors.

Pressure to increase performance can be healthy for an organization because it leads managers to question how the organization is working, and it encourages them to find new and better ways to plan, organize, lead, and control. However, too much pressure to perform can be harmful.[40] It may induce managers to behave unethically, and even illegally, when dealing with people and groups inside and outside the organization.[41]

A purchasing manager for a nationwide retail chain, for example, might buy inferior clothing as a cost-cutting measure or ignore the working conditions under which products are made to obtain low-priced products. These issues faced the managers of companies that make footwear and clothing in the 1990s, when customers learned about the sweatshop conditions in which garment and shoe workers around the world labored. Today companies such as Nike, Walmart, and Apple are trying to stop sweatshop practices and prevent managers abroad from adopting work practices that harm their workers. They now employ hundreds of inspectors who police the factories overseas that make the products they sell and who can terminate contracts with suppliers when they behave in an unethical or illegal way. Nevertheless, in a 2010 report Apple revealed that its investigations showed that sweatshop conditions still existed in some of the factories it used abroad. Apple said that at least 55 of the 102 factories were ignoring Apple's rule that staff cannot work more than 60 hours a week, for example. Apple is continuing its efforts to reduce these abuses.[42]

Similarly, to secure a large foreign contract, a sales manager in a large company, such as in the defense or electronics industry, might offer bribes to foreign officials to obtain lucrative contracts—even though this is against the law. For example, cosmetics giant Avon recently announced that it will pay $135 million to settle a U.S. bribery probe into its development of new markets. Avon is the world's largest direct sales cosmetics manufacturer, and it is not alone. Companies such as Siemens, KBR/Halliburton, and BAE Systems have all settled bribery probes for amounts exceeding $400 million each.[43]

The issue of social responsibility, discussed in Chapter 3, centers on deciding what obligations a company has toward the people and groups affected by its activities—such as employees, customers, or the cities in which it operates. Some companies have strong views about social responsibility; their managers believe they should protect the interests of others. But some managers may decide to act in an unethical way and put their own interests first, hurting others in the process. A recent example showing why managers must always keep the need to act in an ethical and socially responsible way at the forefront of their decision making is profiled in the following "Ethics in Action" box.

ETHICS IN ACTION

Apple Demands Quality from Its Suppliers

As a worldwide producer of technology, Apple has to coordinate with suppliers around the globe. Many of these suppliers have standards of work that differ significantly from Western expectations, including the use of child labor, work weeks exceeding 60 hours, and work environments that are physically and psychologically crippling.

Apple got into some hot water recently over complaints of excessive work hours, sex discrimination, and other serious abuses at some of its Chinese facilities.[44] The company also came under fire for not carefully monitoring work conditions at supplier factories in other parts of the world, specifically those that mine what are known as "conflict minerals." Such minerals—tantalum, gold, tungsten, and tin, for example—are considered "conflict minerals" because they are found in politically unstable countries such as the Democratic Republic of Congo and other African nations. Tantalum, in particular, is a much-needed component in cell phone production. The issue of mining in conflict zones has become important enough that

Apple suppliers at work in Foxconn Technology Group's Shenzen plant in China. Because of complaints of excessive work hours, sex discrimination, and other abuses at Chinese facilities, Apple has changed how it monitors its suppliers to ensure health and safety guidelines are followed. © Imaginechina/AP Images

in 2012 the Dodd-Frank Act required U.S. companies to disclose whether their production materials come from such countries and to file a report with the Securities and Exchange Commission.[45]

Apple responded to these events by stepping up its supplier compliance and monitoring efforts. Each year, the company publishes an annual Report of Supplier Responsibility that is available to the public. In the 2014 report, Apple listed the extensive measures it is taking to ensure that workers throughout its supply chain are treated fairly and safely. It is conducting routine and surprise audits (451 in 2013) of suppliers, interviewing workers, reviewing financial statements, and monitoring production practices. Apple is also monitoring environmental conditions to ensure that companies support good health and wellness for their employees. Suppliers who fail to meet Apple's standards risk the loss of its business.

The 2014 report showed significant improvement in many areas. Specifically, the company reported that 95% of supplier factories adhere to a less than 60-hour workweek and none of its suppliers mined for minerals in war-zone countries. In addition, Apple started its own Clean Water Program that reuses and recycles water at 13 supplier locations to keep use of this precious resource to a minimum.[46]

A company touted for its meticulous attention to detail and quality has to ensure that it extends that attention throughout its global supply chain.

Managing a Diverse Workforce

A major challenge for managers everywhere is to recognize the ethical need and legal requirement to treat human resources fairly and equitably. Today the age, gender, race, ethnicity, religion, sexual preference, and socioeconomic composition of the workforce presents new challenges for managers. To create a highly trained and motivated workforce, as well as to avoid lawsuits, managers must establish human resource management (HRM) procedures and practices that are legal and fair and do not discriminate against any organizational members.[47] Today most organizations understand that to motivate effectively and take advantage of the talents of a diverse workforce, they must make promotion opportunities available to each and every employee.[48] Managers must recognize the performance-enhancing possibilities of a diverse workforce, such as the ability to take advantage of the skills and experiences of different kinds of people.[49] Accenture provides a good example of a company that has utilized the potential of its diverse employees.

Accenture is a global management consulting company that serves the IT needs of thousands of client companies located in more than 120 countries around the world. A major driving force behind

Global consulting firm Accenture employs a diverse workforce whose talents, values, and experiences match those of the clients they serve around the world. © India Today Group/Getty Images

Accenture's core organizational vision is to manage and promote diversity in order to improve employee performance and client satisfaction. At Accenture, managers at all levels realize consultants bring distinct experiences, talents, and values to their work, and a major management initiative is to take advantage of that diversity to encourage collaboration between consultants to improve the service Accenture provides to each of its clients. Because Accenture's clients are also diverse by country, religion, ethnicity, and so forth, it tries to match its teams of consultants to the attributes of its diverse clients.

Accenture provides hundreds of diversity management training programs to its consultants each year using its 13 teams of global human capital and diversity experts, who collaborate to create its programs. Accenture also encourages each of its consultants to pursue opportunities to "work across different geographies, workforces, and generations to create agile global leaders." Thirty-six percent of its global workforce is composed of women, including 17% of its Global Management Committees and 27% of the external members of its board of directors. Accenture also works to accommodate individuals with disabilities and military veterans, as well as promoting an inclusionary environment for lesbian, gay, bisexual, and transgender employees.[50] The firm also provides diversity training programs to its suppliers and prospective suppliers around the world to show them how diversity can increase their efficiency and effectiveness. In all these ways, Accenture uses its expertise in managing diversity to promote individual and organizational performance—one reason it has become the most successful and fast-growing consultancy company in the world.

Managers who value their diverse employees not only invest in developing these employees' skills and capabilities but also succeed best in promoting performance over the long run. Today more organizations are realizing that people are their most important resource and that developing and protecting human resources is the most important challenge for managers in a competitive global environment. Kevin Rollins, a former CEO of Dell, commented, "I've seen firsthand the power of a diverse workforce. Leveraging the similarities and differences of all team members enables Dell to develop the best products, provide a superior customer experience, and contribute in meaningful ways to the communities where we do business."[51] And as Takahiro Moriguchi of Union Bank of California said when accepting a national diversity award for his company when he was its CEO, "By searching for talent from among the disabled, both genders, veterans, gay, all ethnic groups and all nationalities, we gain access to a pool of ideas, energy, and creativity as wide and varied as the human race itself."[52] We discuss the many issues surrounding the management of a diverse workforce in Chapter 3.

Utilizing IT and E-Commerce

As we have discussed, another important challenge for managers is to continually utilize efficient and effective new IT that can link and enable managers and employees to better perform their jobs—whatever their level in the organization. One example of how IT has changed the jobs of people at all organizational levels comes from UPS, where the average UPS driver makes 120 deliveries a day and figuring out the quickest way to navigate all of these stops is a challenge with economic implications for the global shipping company. UPS estimates that a driver with 25 packages could choose from 15 *trillion* different routes! To help navigate these difficult roads, UPS relies on ORION—its On-Road Integrated Optimization and Navigation system.

Using ORION and other types of technology, UPS drivers plan the most efficient delivery route each day, which saves the company time, money, and fuel. © David Goldman/AP Images

ORION is designed to blend GPS navigation and learning to help drivers optimize driving along their routes. Of course, UPS drivers must also balance promised delivery times, traffic, and other factors into their driving decisions, meaning ORION is a critical technological competency helping the company work effectively and efficiently. To date, UPS estimates that it has saved 85 million miles, 100 million minutes, and 1.5 million gallons of fuel due to ORION and other technologies.[53]

Increasingly, new kinds of IT enable not just individual employees but also self-managed teams by giving them important information and allowing virtual interactions around the globe using the Internet. Increased global coordination helps improve quality and increase the pace of innovation. Microsoft, Hitachi, IBM, and most companies now search for new IT that can help them build a competitive advantage. The importance of IT is discussed in detail in Chapter 13, and throughout the text you will find icons that alert you to examples of how IT is changing the way companies operate.

Summary and Review

WHAT IS MANAGEMENT? A manager is a person responsible for supervising the use of an organization's resources to meet its goals. An organization is a collection of people who work together and coordinate their actions to achieve a wide variety of goals. Management is the process of using organizational resources to achieve organizational goals effectively and efficiently through planning, organizing, leading, and controlling. An efficient organization makes the most productive use of its resources. An effective organization pursues appropriate goals and achieves these goals by using its resources to create goods or services that customers want. [LO 1-1]

MANAGERIAL TASKS The four principal managerial tasks are planning, organizing, leading, and controlling. Managers at all levels of the organization and in all departments perform these tasks. Effective management means managing these activities successfully. [LO 1-2]

LEVELS AND SKILLS OF MANAGERS Organizations typically have three levels of management. First-line managers are responsible for the day-to-day supervision of nonmanagerial employees. Middle managers are responsible for developing and utilizing organizational resources efficiently and effectively. Top managers have cross-departmental responsibility. Three main kinds of managerial skills are conceptual, human, and technical. The need to develop and build technical skills leads organizations to divide managers into departments according to their job-specific responsibilities. Top managers must establish appropriate goals for the entire organization and verify that department managers are using resources to achieve those goals. [LO 1-3, 1-4]

RECENT CHANGES IN MANAGEMENT PRACTICES To increase efficiency and effectiveness, many organizations have altered how they operate. Managers have restructured and downsized operations and outsourced activities to reduce costs. Companies are also empowering their workforces and using self-managed teams to increase efficiency and effectiveness. Managers are increasingly using IT to achieve these objectives. [LO 1-5]

CHALLENGES FOR MANAGEMENT IN A GLOBAL ENVIRONMENT Today's competitive global environment presents many interesting challenges to managers. One of the main challenges is building a competitive advantage by increasing efficiency; quality; speed, flexibility, and innovation; and customer responsiveness. Other challenges are behaving in an ethical and socially responsible way toward people inside and outside the organization, managing a diverse workforce, and utilizing new IT. [LO 1-6]

Management *in Action*

 TOPICS FOR DISCUSSION AND ACTION

Discussion

1. Describe the difference between efficiency and effectiveness, and identify real organizations that you think are, or are not, efficient and effective. [LO 1-1]

2. In what ways can managers at each of the three levels of management contribute to organizational efficiency and effectiveness? [LO 1-3]

3. Identify an organization that you believe is high-performing and one that you believe is low-performing. Give five reasons why you think the performance levels of the two organizations differ so much. [LO 1-2, 1-4]

4. What are the building blocks of competitive advantage?

Why is obtaining a competitive advantage important to managers? [LO 1-5]

5. In what ways do you think managers' jobs have changed the most over the last 10 years? Why have these changes occurred? [LO 1-6]

Action

6. Choose an organization such as a school or a bank; visit it; then list the different organizational resources it uses. How do managers use these resources to maintain and improve its performance? [LO 1-2, 1-4]

7. Visit an organization, and talk to first-line, middle, and top managers about their respective management

roles in the organization and what they do to help the organization be efficient and effective. [LO 1-3, 1-4]

8. Ask a middle or top manager, perhaps someone you already know, to give examples of how he or she performs the managerial tasks of planning, organizing, leading, and controlling. How much time does he or she spend in performing each task? [LO 1-3]

9. Try to find a cooperative manager who will allow you to follow him or her around for a day. List the roles the manager plays, and indicate how much time he or she spends performing them. [LO 1-3, 1-4]

BUILDING MANAGEMENT SKILLS
Thinking about Managers and Management [LO 1-2, 1-3, 1-4]

Think of an organization that has provided you with work experience and the manager to whom you reported (or talk to someone who has had extensive work experience); then answer these questions:

1. Think about your direct supervisor. Of what department is he or she a member, and at what level of management is this person?

2. How do you characterize your supervisor's approach to management? For example, which particular management tasks and roles does this person perform most often? What kinds of management skills does this manager have?

3. Do you think the tasks, roles, and skills of your supervisor are appropriate for the particular job he or she performs? How could this manager improve his or her task performance? How can IT affect this?

4. How did your supervisor's approach to management affect your attitudes and behavior? For example, how well did you perform as a subordinate, and how motivated were you?

5. Think about the organization and its resources. Do its managers use organizational resources effectively? Which resources contribute most to the organization's performance?

6. Describe how the organization treats its human resources. How does this treatment affect the attitudes and behaviors of the workforce?

7. If you could give your manager one piece of advice or change one management practice in the organization, what would it be?

8. How attuned are the managers in the organization to the need to increase efficiency, quality, innovation, or responsiveness to customers? How well do you think the organization performs its prime goals of providing the goods or services that customers want or need the most?

MANAGING ETHICALLY [LO 1-1, 1-3]

Think about an example of unethical behavior that you observed in the past. The incident could be something you experienced as an employee or a customer or something you observed informally.

Questions

1. Either by yourself or in a group, give three reasons why you think the behavior was unethical. For example, what rules or norms were broken? Who benefited or was harmed by what took place? What was the outcome for the people involved?

2. What steps might you take to prevent such unethical behavior and encourage people to behave in an ethical way?

SMALL GROUP BREAKOUT EXERCISE [LO 1-2, 1-3, 1-4]
Opening a New Restaurant

Form groups of three or four people, and appoint one group member as the spokesperson who will communicate your findings to the entire class when called on by the instructor. Then discuss the following scenario:

You and your partners have decided to open a large, full-service restaurant in your local community; it will be open from 7 a.m. to 10 p.m. to serve breakfast, lunch, and dinner. Each of you is investing $50,000 in the venture, and together you have secured a bank loan for $300,000 to begin operations. You and your partners have little experience in managing a restaurant beyond serving meals or eating in restaurants, and you now face the task of deciding how you will manage the restaurant and what your respective roles will be.

1. Decide what each partner's managerial role in the restaurant will be. For example, who will be responsible for the necessary departments and specific activities? Describe your managerial hierarchy.

2. Which building blocks of competitive advantage do you need to establish to help your restaurant succeed? What criteria will you use to evaluate how successfully you are managing the restaurant?

3. Discuss the most important decisions that must be made about (a) planning, (b) organizing, (c) leading, and (d) controlling to allow you and your partners to use organizational resources effectively and build a competitive advantage.

4. For each managerial task, list the issues to solve, and decide which roles will contribute the most to your restaurant's success.

BE THE MANAGER [LO 1-2, 1-5]

Problems at Achieva

You have just been called in to help managers at Achieva, a fast-growing Internet software company that specializes in business-to-business (B2B) network software. Your job is to help Achieva solve some management problems that have arisen because of its rapid growth.

Customer demand to license Achieva's software has boomed so much in just two years that more than 50 new software programmers have been added to help develop a new range of software products. Achieva's growth has been so

swift that the company still operates informally, its organizational structure is loose and flexible, and programmers are encouraged to find solutions to problems as they go along. Although this structure worked well in the past, you have been told that problems are arising.

There have been increasing complaints from employees that good performance is not being recognized in the organization and that they do not feel equitably treated. Moreover, there have been complaints about getting managers to listen to their new ideas and

to act on them. A bad atmosphere is developing in the company, and recently several talented employees left. Your job is to help Achieva's managers solve these problems quickly and keep the company on the fast track.

Questions

1. What kinds of organizing and controlling problems is Achieva suffering from?

2. What kinds of management changes need to be made to solve them?

THE WALL STREET JOURNAL CASE IN THE NEWS [LO 1-1, 1-5, 1-6]

Volkswagen CEO Resigns as Car Maker Races to Stem Emissions Scandal

BERLIN—Volkswagen AG raced Wednesday to contain the widening scandal threatening Germany's most important company, ousting its chief executive and pledging to prosecute those involved in a scheme to cheat U.S. auto-pollution tests.

CEO Martin Winterkorn's resignation follows a calamitous few days after Friday's disclosure by the U.S. Environmental Protection Agency that Europe's biggest auto

maker employed software on some VW and Audi diesel-powered cars to manipulate the results of routine emissions tests.

The crisis threatens to spill beyond the auto maker to the broader German economy. Wolfsburg-based Volkswagen is as much institution as corporation at home, with nearly 300,000 employees, 29 plants across the country and deep ties to the government—Lower Saxony owns 20% of VW.

The company's next CEO faces a daunting task of cleaning up the scandal—the scope of which remains unclear—and keeping its sales expansion on track. Volkswagen hasn't yet said it knows who was responsible or how many employees were involved.

On Tuesday, Volkswagen disclosed that as many as 11 million cars contained software alleged to have duped emissions tests and were possibly subject to a global recall.

The company issued a profit warning and disclosed a €6.5 billion ($7.27 billion) charge to earnings to cover the costs of addressing the matter.

In a statement following Wednesday's meeting of the company's top shareholders and labor representatives, Mr. Winterkorn said he would "accept responsibility" for the "irregularities that have been found in diesel engines" and tendered his resignation to the supervisory board.

"I am shocked by the events of the past few days," he said. "Above all, I am stunned that misconduct on such a scale was possible in the Volkswagen Group."

The executive committee of the supervisory board thanked Mr. Winterkorn for his contributions to the company and said the CEO had "no knowledge of manipulation of the emissions data."

The committee said it would seek prosecution of any Volkswagen employees involved in the affair, and it would establish a special investigative committee to uncover what had happened and who was responsible.

The board subcommittee said it would present by Friday's scheduled supervisory board meeting names of candidates to succeed Mr. Winterkorn, but didn't disclose any.

Two prominent Volkswagen executives on many lists are Herbert Diess and Matthias Müller.

Mr. Diess is a former BMW AG executive who joined Volkswagen in July after being passed over at BMW for the CEO's job. He runs its namesake brand, the company's biggest business. Choosing Mr. Diess would send a signal that Volkswagen shareholders are opting for a fresh start, bringing in an outsider with a strong record in cost-cutting.

Some analysts, however, say Volkswagen has never done well with outside executives. The company's culture is famously clubby and success depends on being well-connected in Wolfsburg and striking a balance between boosting profit margins and maintaining strong ties to labor.

Others think that insular culture makes Mr. Müller, CEO of sports car brand Porsche, a more likely candidate. Mr. Müller gets along well with the Porsche and Piech families who control the company, said people familiar with the matter, and he has deep roots in Volkswagen. He is also well respected in financial circles. "We believe shareholders would welcome such a move," said Arndt Ellinghorst, automotive analyst at Evercore ISI.

Whoever becomes the next CEO, the job of boosting profit margins likely will take a back seat to steering the company through what could be years of rebuilding a brand badly wounded over the past few days. The company's market value is off 29% since Friday.

Volkswagen could face more than $18 billion in fines from the EPA, though analysts say it is unlikely that Volkswagen will have to pay that much. The U.S. Department of Justice has launched a criminal investigation that could result in indictments against Volkswagen executives, analysts said.

The crisis is spreading as regulators and justice officials in Europe and Asia launch investigations, and angry investors and customers file lawsuits seeking damages.

The urgency to repair Volkswagen's reputation goes beyond the benefits to shareholders or even the company's 600,000 employees world-wide. Volkswagen is Germany's largest corporation, generating revenue of almost €203 billion ($227 billion) last year in a country where every seventh job is linked to the nation's export-oriented auto industry.

Damage to Volkswagen could prove a major blow to the broader German economy. Some German politicians, though angry at the company for violating U.S. law, say Volkswagen is being singled out by U.S. authorities.

"It's no coincidence that this discussion comes up now," said Oliver Wittke, a conservative German lawmaker. "Economic interests in the U.S. are also playing a role here."

Under Germany's two-tier corporate governance, the supervisory board oversees the executive management board, but doesn't run the company day-to-day. A five-person subcommittee of the supervisory board, including Wolfgang Porsche, whose grandfather was Beetle inventor Ferdinand Porsche, gathered in Wolfsburg for a crisis meeting. The Porsche-Piech families control about 51% of Volkswagen's voting stock. The second-largest shareholder is the state of Lower Saxony, which holds 20% of the voting rights and has special privileges. State Premier Stephan Weil was present at the meeting. Also in attendance were three representatives of the company's workforce and IG Metall trade union, including Bernd Osterloh, the powerful head of its works council.

It is still unclear who at Volkswagen was responsible for the scheme to trick the EPA. The company hasn't offered a rationale, though outside experts speculate it was to ensure strong engine performance and boost fuel economy amid tough U.S. emissions standards.

The members of the executive committee meeting in Wolfsburg said they were convinced that Mr. Winterkorn knew nothing about it. VW is launching an investigation of its own and will tap external experts. It also asked prosecutors in Braunschweig, the county where VW is located, to investigate.

"I'm pleased that Volkswagen is taking such an aggressive stance on admitting the problem and attacking it," Gina McCarthy, EPA administrator, told The Wall Street Journal on Tuesday.

Mr. Winterkorn's resignation is a bitter end to a long career at Europe's biggest car maker. He was hired by its luxury car brand, Audi, in 1981 as assistant to the director of quality control. A stickler for detail, he became known for his obsession with the quality of its vehicles. He became CEO of the company in 2007 and oversaw a period of unparalleled expansion. He aimed to make Volkswagen the biggest, most profitable and best-run car company in the world. It could overtake current market leader Toyota Motor Corp. in annual sales. In the first half of this year, Volkswagen sold more cars than its rival. But profits are falling as higher costs hit margins, and sales in markets such as China and the U.S. decline. Now, he said, it is time to step down. "Volkswagen needs a fresh start," he said. "I have always been driven by my desire to serve this company, especially our customers and employees. Volkswagen has been, is and will always be my life."

Questions

1. Was the CEO's resignation the right thing to do? Why or why not?

2. In addition to the economic fallout, what other impact could the emissions scandal have on the company's managers? On its employees?

3. How can the company retain current customers?

Source: William Boston, "Volkswagen CEO Resigns as Car Maker Races to Stem Emissions Scandal," *The Wall Street Journal,* www.wsj.com, September 23, 2015.

Endnotes

1. Corporate website, www.alconent.com, accessed February 9, 2015; R. Abrams, "VOD 'Definitely' Not Offsetting Decline on DVD,'" *Variety,* accessed February 4, 2015, http://variety.com.

2. Organization website, http://creativefuture.org, accessed February 4, 2015.

3. G. R. Jones, *Organizational Theory, Design, and Change* (Upper Saddle River, NJ: Pearson, 2011).

4. J. P. Campbell, "On the Nature of Organizational Effectiveness," in P. S. Goodman, J. M. Pennings, et al., *New Perspectives on Organizational Effectiveness* (San Francisco: Jossey-Bass, 1977).

5. Abrams, "VOD 'Definitely' Not Offsetting Decline on DVD."

6. "Summary Report for: 11-1021.00—General and Operations Managers," www.onetonline.org, accessed January 15, 2015.

7. H. Fayol, *General and Industrial Management* (New York: IEEE Press, 1984). Fayol actually identified five different managerial tasks, but most scholars today believe these four capture the essence of Fayol's ideas.

8. P. F. Drucker, *Management Tasks, Responsibilities, and Practices* (New York: Harper & Row, 1974).

9. A. Kondolojy, "Syfy Gives Straight-to-Series Greenlight to 'The Expanse,'" *TV by the Numbers,* accessed January 15, 2015, http://tvbythenumbers.zap2it.com.

10. "Alcon Entertainment [us]," www.imdb.com, accessed February 9, 2015.

11. Corporate website, "About," http://armstrongconsultants.com, accessed January 15, 2015.

12. Grand Junction Economic Partnership, "Feature Local Business: Armstrong Consultants, Inc.," http://gjep.org, accessed January 15, 2015.

13. Ibid.

14. C. P. Hales, "What Do Managers Do? A Critical Review of the Evidence," *Journal of Management Studies,* January 1986, 88–115; A. I. Kraul, P. R. Pedigo, D. D. McKenna, and M. D. Dunnette, "The Role of the Manager: What's Really Important in Different Management Jobs," *Academy of Management Executive,* November 1989, 286–93.

15. A. K. Gupta, "Contingency Perspectives on Strategic Leadership," in D. C. Hambrick, ed., *The Executive Effect: Concepts and Methods for Studying Top Managers* (Greenwich, CT: JAI Press, 1988), 147–78.

16. D. G. Ancona, "Top Management Teams: Preparing for the Revolution," in J. S. Carroll, ed., *Applied Social Psychology and Organizational Settings* (Hillsdale, NJ: Erlbaum, 1990); D. C. Hambrick and P. A. Mason, "Upper Echelons: The Organization as a Reflection of Its Top Managers," *Academy of Management Journal* 9 (1984), 193–206.

17. T. A. Mahony, T. H. Jerdee, and S. J. Carroll, "The Jobs of Management," *Industrial Relations* 4 (1965), 97–110; L. Gomez-Mejia, J. McCann, and R. C. Page, "The Structure of Managerial Behaviors and Rewards," *Industrial Relations* 24 (1985), 147–54.

18. W. R. Nord and M. J. Waller, "The Human Organization of Time: Temporal Realities and Experiences," *Academy of Management Review* 29 (January 2004), 137–40.

19. R. L. Katz, "Skills of an Effective Administrator," *Harvard Business Review,* September–October 1974, 90–102.

20. Ibid.

21. P. Tharenou, "Going Up? Do Traits and Informal Social Processes Predict Advancing in Management," *Academy of Management Journal* 44 (October 2001), 1005–18.

22. C. J. Collins and K. D. Clark, "Strategic Human Resource Practices, Top Management Team Social Networks, and Firm Performance: The Role of Human Resource Practices in Creating Organizational Competitive Advantage," *Academy of Management Journal* 46 (December 2003), 740–52.

23. R. Stewart, "Middle Managers: Their Jobs and Behaviors," in J. W. Lorsch, ed., *Handbook of Organizational Behavior* (Englewood Cliffs, NJ: Prentice-Hall, 1987), 385–91.

24. S. C. de Janasz, S. E. Sullivan, and V. Whiting, "Mentor Networks and Career Success: Lessons for Turbulent Times," *Academy of Management Executive* 17 (November 2003), 78–92.

25. K. Labich, "Making Over Middle Managers," *Fortune,* May 8, 1989, 58–64.

26. B. Wysocki, "Some Companies Cut Costs Too Far, Suffer from Corporate Anorexia," *The Wall Street Journal,* July 5, 1995, A1.

27. Brad Tuttle, "Efficiency Backlash: Businesses Find Too Much Downsizing Can Hurt the Bottom Line," *Time,* accessed February 9, 2015, http://business.time.com.

28. "Job Outsourcing Statistics," *Statistic Brain,* accessed February 9, 2015, www.statisticbrain.com.

29. "More Jobs Coming Back to US from Overseas," *Salary.com,* accessed February 9, 2015, http://business.salary.com; S. Mallaby, "American Industry Is on the Move," *Financial Times,* January 9, 2013.

30. C. Fishman, "The Insourcing Boom," *The Atlantic,* November 28, 2012, www.theatlantic.com/magazine/archive/2012/12/the-insourcing-boom/309166/.

31. D. A. Mann, "GE Puts $100 Million into New Washer Line," *Louisville Business,* August 18, 2015, www.bizjournals.com; "Close to 10,000 Expected at GE Appliance Parks' 60th Birthday Celebration," press release, pressroom.geappliances.com.

32. S. R. Parker, T. D. Wall, and P. R. Jackson, "That's Not My Job: Developing Flexible Work Orientations," *Academy of Management Journal* 40 (1997), 899–929.

33. B. Dumaine, "The New Non-Manager," *Fortune,* February 22, 1993, 80–84.

34. H. G. Baum, A. C. Joel, and E. A. Mannix, "Management Challenges in a New Time," *Academy of Management Journal* 45 (October 2002), 916–31.

35. A. Shama, "Management under Fire: The Transformation of Management in the Soviet Union and Eastern Europe," *Academy of Management Executive* 10 (1993), 22–35.

36. J. Kasperkevic, "Google Secretly Phases Out '20% Time,' " *Inc.,* accessed February 9, 2015, www.inc.com.

37. K. Seiders and L. L. Berry, "Service Fairness: What It Is and Why It Matters," *Academy of Management Executive* 12 (1998), 8–20.

38. R. Adner, "How the Kindle Stomped Sony, or, Why Good Solutions Beat Great Products," *Fast Company,* accessed February 9, 2015, www.fastcodesign.com.

39. T. Donaldson, "Editor's Comments: Taking Ethics Seriously—A Mission Now More Possible," *Academy of Management Review* 28 (July 2003), 363–67.

40. C. Anderson, "Values-Based Management," *Academy of Management Executive* 11 (1997), 25–46.

41. W. H. Shaw and V. Barry, *Moral Issues in Business,* 6th ed. (Belmont, CA: Wadsworth, 1995); T. Donaldson, *Corporations and Morality* (Englewood Cliffs, NJ: Prentice-Hall, 1982).

42. "Supplier Responsibility," www.apple.com, accessed February 9, 2015; press releases 2010, 2012.

43. P. Wahba, "Avon Settles Justice Department Charges of China Bribery for $135 Million," *Fortune,* accessed February 9, 2015, http://fortune.com/2014/12/17/avon-bribery-probe-settlement/.

44. B. Chen, "Apple Says Supplies Don't Come from War Zones," *Economic Times,* February 14, 2014, articles.economictimes.indiatimes.com/2014-02-14/news/47336504_conflict_1_conflict-minerals-foxconn-suppliers.

45. "Apple to Track Suppliers' Sourcing of Conflict Materials," *CBCNews,* February 13, 2014, www.cbc.ca/news/business/apple-to-track-suppliers-sourcing-of-conflict-minerals-1.2535784.

46. "Supplier Responsibility," www.apple.com, accessed February 9, 2015.

47. S. Jackson et al., *Diversity in the Workplace: Human Resource Initiatives* (New York: Guilford Press, 1992).

48. G. Robinson and C. S. Daus, "Building a Case for Diversity," *Academy of Management Executive* 3 (1997), 21–31; S. J. Bunderson and K. M. Sutcliffe, "Comparing Alternative Conceptualizations of Functional Diversity in Management Teams: Process and Performance Effects," *Academy of Management Journal* 45 (October 2002), 875–94.

49. D. Jamieson and J. O'Mara, *Managing Workforce 2000: Gaining a Diversity Advantage* (San Francisco: Jossey-Bass, 1991).

50. "An Inclusive, Diverse Environment: 2012–2013 Corporate Citizenship Report," www.accenture.com, accessed February 9, 2015.

51. Press release, "Dell CEO Kevin Rollins Cites Workforce Diversity as Key to Gaining Competitive Advantages in Business," www.dell.com, March 6, 2006.

52. "Union Bank of California Honored by U.S. Labor Department for Employment Practices," press release, September 11, 2000.

53. Katherine Noyes, "The Shortest Distance Between Two Points? At UPS, It's Complicated," *Fortune,* accessed February 9, 2015, www.fortune.com; M. Wohlsen, "The Astronomical Math Behind UPS's New Tool to Deliver Packages Faster," *Wired,* June 13, 2013, www.wired.com.

History of
Management Thought

The systematic study of management began in the closing decades of the 19th century, after the Industrial Revolution had swept through Europe and America. In the new economic climate, managers of all types of organizations—political, educational, and economic—were increasingly turning their focus toward finding better ways to satisfy customers' needs. Many major economic, technical, and cultural changes were taking place at this time. With the introduction of steam power and the development of sophisticated machinery and equipment, the Industrial Revolution changed the way goods were produced, particularly in the weaving and clothing industries. Small workshops run by skilled workers who produced hand-manufactured products (a system called *crafts production*) were being replaced by large factories in which sophisticated machines controlled by hundreds or even thousands of unskilled or semiskilled workers made products. For example, raw cotton and wool that in the past families or whole villages working together had spun into yarn were now shipped to factories where workers operated machines that spun and wove large quantities of yarn into cloth.

Owners and managers of the new factories found themselves unprepared for the challenges accompanying the change from small-scale crafts production to large-scale mechanized manufacturing. Moreover, many of the managers and supervisors in these workshops and factories were engineers who had only a technical orientation. They were unprepared for the social problems that occur when people work together in large groups (as in a factory or shop system). Managers began to search for new techniques to manage their organizations' resources, and soon they began to focus on ways to increase the efficiency of the worker–task mix. They found help from Frederick W. Taylor.

scientific management
The systematic study of relationships between people and tasks to increase efficiency.

F. W. Taylor and Scientific Management

Frederick W. Taylor (1856–1915) is best known for defining the techniques of **scientific management**, the systematic study of relationships between people and tasks for the purpose of redesigning the work process to increase efficiency. Taylor was a manufacturing manager who eventually became a consultant and taught other managers how to apply his scientific management techniques. Taylor believed that if the amount of time and effort that each worker expends to produce a unit of output (a finished good or service) can be reduced by increasing specialization and the division of labor, the production process will become more efficient. Taylor believed the way to create the most efficient

Frederick W. Taylor, founder of scientific management, and one of the first people to study the behavior and performance of people in the workplace © Bettmann/Corbis

division of labor could best be determined by using scientific management techniques, rather than intuitive or informal rule-of-thumb knowledge. Based on his experiments and observations as a manufacturing manager in a variety of settings, he developed four principles to increase efficiency in the workplace[1]:

- Principle 1: *Study the way workers perform their tasks, gather all the informal job knowledge that workers possess, and experiment with ways of improving the way tasks are performed.*

  To discover the most efficient method of performing specific tasks, Taylor studied in great detail and measured the ways different workers went about performing their tasks. One of the main tools he used was a time and motion study, which involves the careful timing and recording of the actions taken to perform a particular task. Once Taylor understood the existing method of performing a task, he then experimented to increase specialization; he tried different methods of dividing up and coordinating the various tasks necessary to produce a finished product. Usually this meant simplifying jobs and having each worker perform fewer, more routine tasks. Taylor also sought to find ways to improve each worker's ability to perform a particular task—for example, by reducing the number of motions workers made to complete the task, by changing the layout of the work area or the type of tool workers used, or by experimenting with tools of different sizes.

- Principle 2: *Codify the new methods of performing tasks into written rules and standard operating procedures.*

  Once the best method of performing a particular task was determined, Taylor specified that it should be recorded so that the procedures could be taught to all workers performing the same task. These rules could be used to further standardize and simplify jobs—essentially, to make jobs even more routine. In this way efficiency could be increased throughout an organization.

- Principle 3: *Carefully select workers so that they possess skills and abilities that match the needs of the task, and train them to perform the task according to the established rules and procedures.*

  To increase specialization, Taylor believed workers had to understand the tasks that were required and be thoroughly trained in order to perform a task at the required level. Workers who could not be trained to this level were to be transferred to a job where they were able to reach the minimum required level of proficiency.[2]

- Principle 4: *Establish a fair or acceptable level of performance for a task, and then develop a pay system that provides a reward for performance above the acceptable level.*

  To encourage workers to perform at a high level of efficiency, and to provide them with an incentive to reveal the most efficient techniques for performing a task, Taylor advocated that workers benefit from any gains in performance. They should be paid a bonus and receive some percentage of the performance gains achieved through the more efficient work process.

By 1910, Taylor's system of scientific management had become nationally known and in many instances faithfully and fully practiced.[3] However, managers in many organizations chose to implement the new principles of scientific management selectively. This decision ultimately resulted in problems. For example, some managers using scientific management obtained increases in performance, but rather than sharing performance gains with workers through bonuses as Taylor had advocated, they simply increased the amount of work that each worker was expected to do. Many workers experiencing the reorganized work system found that as their performance increased, managers required them to do more work for the same pay. Workers also learned that increases in performance often meant fewer jobs and a greater threat of layoffs because fewer workers were needed. In addition, the specialized, simplified jobs were often monotonous and repetitive, and many workers became dissatisfied with their jobs.

From a performance perspective, the combination of the two management practices—(1) achieving the right mix of worker–task specialization and (2) linking people and tasks by the speed of the production line—resulted in huge savings in cost and huge increases in output that occur in large, organized work settings. For example, in 1908, managers at the Franklin Motor Company using scientific management principles redesigned the work process, and the output of cars increased from 100 cars a month to 45 cars a day; workers' wages, however, increased by only 90%.[4]

Taylor's work has had an enduring effect on the management of production systems. Managers in every organization, whether it produces goods or services, now carefully analyze the basic tasks that workers must perform and try to create a work environment that will allow their organizations to operate most efficiently. We discuss this important issue in Chapter 7.

Weber's Bureaucratic Theory

Side by side with scientific managers studying the person–task mix to increase efficiency, other researchers were focusing on how to increase the efficiency with which organizations were managed. Max Weber, a German professor of sociology, outlined his famous principles of bureaucracy—a formal system of organization and administration designed to ensure efficiency and effectiveness—and created bureaucratic theory. A bureaucratic system of administration is based on five principles:

bureaucracy
A formal system of organization and administration designed to ensure efficiency and effectiveness.

authority
The power to hold people accountable for their actions and to allocate organizational resources.

- Principle 1: *In a bureaucracy, a manager's formal authority derives from the position he or she holds in the organization.*

    Authority is the power to hold people accountable for their actions and to make decisions concerning the use of organizational resources. Authority gives managers the right to direct and control their subordinates' behavior to achieve organizational goals. In a bureaucratic system of administration, obedience is owed to a manager, not because of any personal qualities—such as personality, wealth, or social status—but because the manager occupies a position that is associated with a certain level of authority and responsibility.[5]

- Principle 2: *In a bureaucracy, people should occupy positions because of their performance, not because of their social standing or personal contacts.*

    This principle was not always followed in Weber's time and is often ignored today. Some organizations and industries are still affected by social networks in which personal contacts and relations, not job-related skills, influence hiring and promotion decisions.

- Principle 3: *The extent of each position's formal authority and their responsibilities, and their relationship to other positions in an organization, should be clearly specified.*

Max Weber developed the principles of bureaucracy during Germany's burgeoning industrial revolution to help organizations increase their efficiency and effectiveness.
© akg-images/The Image Works

rules Formal written instructions that specify actions to be taken under different circumstances to achieve specific goals.

standard operating procedures (SOPs) Specific sets of written instructions about how to perform a particular task.

norms Unwritten informal codes of conduct that prescribe how people should act in particular situations and are considered important by most members of a group or organization.

When the tasks and authority associated with various positions in the organization are clearly specified, managers and workers know what is expected of them and what to expect from each other. Moreover, an organization can hold all its employees strictly accountable for their actions when they know their exact responsibilities.

- Principle 4: *Authority can be exercised effectively in an organization when positions are arranged hierarchically, so employees know whom to report to and who reports to them.*[6]

Managers must create an organizational hierarchy of authority that makes it clear who reports to whom and to whom managers and workers should go if conflicts or problems arise. This principle is especially important in the armed forces, FBI, CIA, and other organizations that deal with sensitive issues involving possible major repercussions. It is vital that managers at high levels of the hierarchy be able to hold subordinates accountable for their actions.

- Principle 5: *Managers must create a well-defined system of rules, standard operating procedures, and norms so that they can effectively control behavior within an organization.*

Rules are formal written instructions that specify actions to be taken under different circumstances to achieve specific goals (for example, if A happens, do B). **Standard operating procedures (SOPs)** are specific sets of written instructions about how to perform a certain aspect of a task. A rule might state that at the end of the workday employees are to leave their machines in good order, and a set of SOPs specifies exactly how they should do so, itemizing which machine parts must be oiled or replaced. **Norms** are unwritten, informal codes of conduct that prescribe how people should act in particular situations. For example, an organizational norm in a restaurant might be that waiters should help each other if time permits.

Rules, SOPs, and norms provide behavioral guidelines that increase the performance of a bureaucratic system because they specify the best ways to accomplish organizational tasks. Companies such as McDonald's and Walmart have developed extensive rules and procedures to specify the behaviors required of their employees, such as "Always greet the customer with a smile."

Weber believed that organizations that implement all five principles establish a bureaucratic system that improves organizational performance. The specification of positions and the use of rules and SOPs to regulate how tasks are performed make it easier for managers to organize and control the work of subordinates. Similarly, fair and equitable selection and promotion systems improve managers' feelings of security, reduce stress, and encourage organizational members to act ethically and further promote the interests of the organization.[7]

If bureaucracies are not managed well, many problems can result. Sometimes managers allow rules and SOPs, "bureaucratic red tape," to become so cumbersome that decision making becomes slow and inefficient and organizations are unable to change. When managers rely too much on rules to solve problems and not enough on their own skills and judgment, their behavior becomes inflexible. A key challenge for managers is to use bureaucratic principles to benefit, rather than harm, an organization.

The Work of Mary Parker Follett

If F. W. Taylor is considered the father of management thought, Mary Parker Follett (1868–1933) serves as its mother.[8] Much of her writing about management and the way managers should behave toward workers was a response to her concern that Taylor was ignoring the human side of the organization. She pointed out that management often overlooks the multitude of ways in which employees can contribute to the organization when managers allow them to participate and exercise initiative in their everyday work lives.[9] Taylor, for example, never proposed that managers involve workers in analyzing their jobs to identify better ways to perform tasks, or even ask workers how they felt about their jobs. Instead, he used time and motion experts to analyze workers' jobs for them. Follett, in contrast, argued that because workers know the most about their jobs, they should be involved in job analysis and managers should allow them to participate in the work development process.

Follett proposed, "Authority should go with knowledge . . . whether it is up the line or down." In other words, if workers have the relevant knowledge, then workers, rather than managers, should be in control of the work process itself, and managers should behave as coaches and facilitators—not as monitors and supervisors. In making this statement, Follett anticipated the current interest in self-managed teams and empowerment. She also recognized the importance of having managers in different departments communicate directly with each other to speed decision making. She advocated what she called "cross-functioning": members of different departments working together in cross-departmental teams to accomplish projects—an approach that is increasingly utilized today.[10] She proposed that knowledge and expertise, not managers' formal authority deriving from their position in the hierarchy, should decide who would lead at any particular moment. She believed, as do many management theorists today, that power is fluid and should flow to the person who can best help the organization achieve its goals. Follett took a horizontal view of power and authority, rather than viewing the vertical chain of command as being most essential to effective management. Thus, Follett's approach was very radical for its time.

Mary Parker Follett, an early management thinker who advocated, "Authority should go with knowledge . . . whether it is up the line or down." Photo courtesy of Regina A. Greenwood, from the Ronald G. Greenwood Collection

The Hawthorne Studies and Human Relations

Probably because of its radical nature, Follett's work went unappreciated by managers and researchers until quite recently. Most continued to follow in the footsteps of Taylor, and to increase efficiency, they studied ways to improve various characteristics of the work setting, such as job specialization or the kinds of tools workers used. One series of studies was conducted from 1924 to 1932 at the Hawthorne Works of the Western Electric Company.[11] This research, now known as the Hawthorne studies, was initiated as an attempt to investigate how characteristics of the work setting—specifically the level of lighting or illumination—affect worker fatigue and performance. The researchers conducted an experiment in which they systematically measured worker productivity at various levels of illumination.

The experiment produced some unexpected results. The researchers found that regardless of whether they raised or lowered the level of illumination, productivity

Workers in a telephone manufacturing plant, in 1931. Around this time, researchers at the Hawthorne Works of the Western Electric Company began to study the effects of work setting characteristics—such as lighting and rest periods—on productivity. To their surprise, they discovered that workers' productivity was affected more by the attention they received from researchers than by the characteristics of the work setting—a phenomenon that became known as the Hawthorne effect. © Fox Photos/Hulton Archive/Getty Images

increased. In fact, productivity began to fall only when the level of illumination dropped to the level of moonlight, a level at which presumably workers could no longer see well enough to do their work efficiently.

As you can imagine, the researchers found these results very puzzling. They invited a noted Harvard psychologist, Elton Mayo, to help them. Mayo proposed another series of experiments to solve the mystery. These experiments, known as the relay assembly test experiments, were designed to investigate the effects of other aspects of the work context on job performance, such as the effect of the number and length of rest periods and hours of work on fatigue and monotony.[12] The goal was to raise productivity.

During a two-year study of a small group of female workers, the researchers again observed that productivity increased over time, but the increases could not be solely attributed to the effects of changes in the work setting. Gradually, the researchers discovered that, to some degree, the results they were obtaining were influenced by the fact that the researchers themselves had become part of the experiment. In other words, the presence of the researchers was affecting the results because the workers enjoyed receiving attention and being the subject of study and were willing to cooperate with the researchers to produce the results they believed the researchers desired.

Subsequently, it was found that many other factors also influence worker behavior, and it was not clear what was actually influencing the Hawthorne workers' behavior. However, this particular effect—which became known as the **Hawthorne effect**—seemed to suggest that the attitudes of workers toward their managers affect the level of workers' performance. In particular, the significant finding was that a manager's behavior or leadership approach can affect performance. This finding led many researchers to turn their attention to managerial behavior and leadership. If supervisors could be trained to behave in ways that would elicit cooperative behavior from their subordinates, then productivity could be increased. From this view emerged the **human relations movement**, which advocates that supervisors be behaviorally trained to manage subordinates in ways that elicit their cooperation and increase their productivity.

The importance of behavioral or human relations training became even clearer to its supporters after another series of experiments—the bank wiring room experiments. In a study of workers making telephone-switching equipment, researchers Elton Mayo and F. J. Roethlisberger discovered that the workers, as a group, had deliberately adopted a norm of output restriction to protect their jobs. Other group members subjected workers who violated this informal production norm to sanctions. Those who violated group performance norms and performed above the norm were called "ratebusters"; those who performed below the norm were called "chiselers."

The experimenters concluded that both types of workers threatened the group as a whole. Ratebusters threaten group members because they reveal to managers how fast the work can be done. Chiselers are looked down on because they are not doing

Hawthorne effect
Workers' productivity is affected more by observation or attention received than by physical work setting.

human relations movement
Advocates behavior and leadership training of supervisors to elicit worker cooperation and improve productivity.

their share of the work. Work-group members discipline both ratebusters and chiselers in order to create a pace of work that the workers (not the managers) think is fair. Thus, the work group's influence over output can be as great as the supervisors' influence. Since the work group can influence the behavior of its members, some management theorists argue that supervisors should be trained to behave in ways that gain the goodwill and cooperation of workers so that supervisors, not workers, control the level of work-group performance.

One of the main implications of the Hawthorne studies was that the behavior of managers and workers in the work setting is as important in explaining the level of performance as the technical aspects of the task. Managers must understand the workings of the **informal organization**, the system of behavioral rules and norms that emerge in a group, when they try to manage or change behavior in organizations. Many studies have found that, as time passes, groups often develop elaborate procedures and norms that bond members together, allowing unified action either to cooperate with management in order to raise performance or to restrict output and thwart the attainment of organizational goals.[13] The Hawthorne studies demonstrated the importance of understanding how the feelings, thoughts, and behavior of work-group members and managers affect performance. It was becoming increasingly clear to researchers that understanding behavior in organizations is a complex process that is critical to increasing performance.[14] Indeed, the increasing interest in the area of management known as **organizational behavior**, the study of the factors that have an impact on how individuals and groups respond to and act in organizations, dates from these early studies.

informal organization The system of behavioral rules and norms that emerge in work groups.

organizational behavior The study of factors that impact how workers respond to and act in an organization.

Theory X and Theory Y

Several studies after the Second World War revealed how assumptions about workers' attitudes and behavior affect managers' behavior. Douglas McGregor developed the most influential approach. He proposed that two different sets of assumptions about work attitudes and behaviors dominate the way managers think and affect how they behave in organizations. McGregor named these two contrasting sets of assumptions *Theory X* and *Theory Y*.[15]

According to the assumptions of **Theory X**, the average worker is lazy, dislikes work, and will try to do as little as possible. Moreover, workers have little ambition and wish to avoid responsibility. Thus, the manager's task is to counteract workers' natural tendencies to avoid work. To keep workers' performance at a high level, the manager must supervise them closely and control their behavior by means of "the carrot and stick"—rewards and punishments.

Managers who accept the assumptions of Theory X design and shape the work setting to maximize their control over workers' behaviors and minimize workers' control over the pace of work. These managers believe that workers must be made to do what is necessary for the success of the organization, and they focus on developing rules, SOPs, and a well-defined system of rewards and punishments to control behavior. They see little point in giving workers autonomy to solve their own problems because they think that the workforce neither expects nor desires cooperation. Theory X managers see their role as to closely monitor workers to ensure that they contribute to the production process and do not threaten product quality. Henry Ford, who closely supervised and managed his workforce, fits McGregor's description of a manager who holds Theory X assumptions.

Theory X The assumption that workers will try to do as little as possible and avoid further responsibility unless rewarded or punished for doing otherwise.

Theory Y
The assumption that workers will do what is best for an organization if given the proper work setting, opportunity and encouragement.

In contrast, Theory Y assumes that workers are not inherently lazy, do not naturally dislike work, and, if given the opportunity, will do what is good for the organization. According to Theory Y, the characteristics of the work setting determine whether workers consider work to be a source of satisfaction or punishment; and managers do not need to closely control workers' behavior in order to make them perform at a high level, because workers will exercise self-control when they are committed to organizational goals. The implication of Theory Y, according to McGregor, is that "the limits of collaboration in the organizational setting are not limits of human nature but of management's ingenuity in discovering how to realize the potential represented by its human resources."[16] It is the manager's task to create a work setting that encourages commitment to organizational goals and provides opportunities for workers to be imaginative and to exercise initiative and self-direction.

When managers design the organizational setting to reflect the assumptions about attitudes and behavior suggested by Theory Y, the characteristics of the organization are quite different from those of an organizational setting based on Theory X. Managers who believe that workers are motivated to help the organization reach its goals can decentralize authority and give more control over the job to workers, both as individuals and in groups. In this setting, individuals and groups are still accountable for their activities, but the manager's role is not to control employees but to provide support and advice, to make sure workers have the resources they need to perform their jobs, and to evaluate them on their ability to help the organization meet its goals.

These same kinds of debates are raging today as managers seek to increase both the efficiency and effectiveness of their organizations.

Endnotes

1. F. W. Taylor, *Shop Management* (New York: Harper, 1903); F. W. Taylor, *The Principles of Scientific Management* (New York: Harper, 1911).

2. L. W. Fry, "The Maligned F. W. Taylor: A Reply to His Many Critics," *Academy of Management Review* 1 (1976), 124–29.

3. J. A. Litterer, *The Emergence of Systematic Management as Shown by the Literature from 1870–1900* (New York: Garland, 1986).

4. D. Wren, *The Evolution of Management Thought* (New York: Wiley, 1994), 134.

5. C. Perrow, *Complex Organizations*, 2nd ed. (Glenview, IL: Scott, Foresman, 1979).

6. M. Weber, *From Max Weber: Essays in Sociology*, ed. H. H. Gerth and C. W. Mills (New York: Oxford University Press, 1946), 331.

7. See Perrow, *Complex Organizations*, Ch. 1, for a detailed discussion of these issues.

8. L. D. Parker, "Control in Organizational Life: The Contribution of Mary Parker Follett," *Academy of Management Review* 9 (1984), 736–45.

9. P. Graham, *M. P. Follett—Prophet of Management: A Celebration of Writings from the 1920s* (Boston: Harvard Business School Press, 1995).

10. M. P. Follett, *Creative Experience* (London: Longmans, 1924).

11. E. Mayo, *The Human Problems of Industrial Civilization* (New York: Macmillan, 1933); F. J. Roethlisberger and W. J. Dickson, *Management and the Worker* (Cambridge, MA: Harvard University Press, 1947).

12. D. W. Organ, "Review of *Management and the Worker*, by F. J. Roethlisberger and W. J. Dickson," *Academy of Management Review* 13 (1986), 460–64.

13. D. Roy, "Banana Time: Job Satisfaction and Informal Interaction," *Human Organization* 18 (1960), 158–61.

14. For an analysis of the problems in distinguishing cause from effect in the Hawthorne studies and in social settings in general, see A. Carey, "The Hawthorne Studies: A Radical Criticism," *American Sociological Review* 33 (1967), 403–16.

15. D. McGregor, *The Human Side of Enterprise* (New York: McGraw-Hill, 1960).

16. Ibid., 48.

2

Values, Attitudes, Emotions, and Culture: The Manager as a Person

Learning Objectives

After studying this chapter, you should be able to:

LO 2-1 Describe the various personality traits that affect how managers think, feel, and behave.

LO 2-2 Explain what values and attitudes are, and describe their impact on managerial action.

LO 2-3 Appreciate how moods and emotions influence all members of an organization.

LO 2-4 Describe the nature of emotional intelligence and its role in management.

LO 2-5 Define organizational culture, and explain how managers both create and are influenced by organizational culture.

© Sam Edwards/age fotostock RF

Jess Lee of Polyvore, a fashion and style social commerce website and company. Her ambition, hard work, and persistence, combined with dedication to users and employees, have helped make Polyvore one of the five best websites for one-stop online shopping.
© Bryan Bedder/Getty Images for Lucky Magazine

MANAGEMENT SNAPSHOT

Jess Lee's Determination and Broad Interests Lead to the Top at Polyvore

What Does It Take to Land a Top Position in Silicon Valley?

In her thirties, Jess Lee's rise to the top at Polyvore, a fashion and style social commerce site and company, is a testament to her determination, hard work, persistence, broad interests, originality, and willingness to take risks. When she was growing up in Hong Kong, Lee loved to draw. Her parents had other ideas, and as an entrepreneur who operated a translation organization from their house, her mother instilled in her a sense of the value of being in charge of what you do.[1]

Lee attended Stanford University, where she received a degree in computer science. She had planned on becoming an engineer and had a job lined up when she received a phone call from a Google recruiter inviting her to interview for their associate product manager program. Always up for a challenge, Lee decided to join Google and has not looked back since.[2]

As a product manager working on Google Maps, Lee realized that it was important for the engineers she worked with to hold her in high regard.[3] While her computer science background certainly helped, so did her hard work, determination, and persistence. While she was working at Google, one of her friends introduced her to the Polyvore website. With her love of

art and fashion, Lee became hooked on the site, which enables users to build sets or collages of products from more than 42 million images that typically combine clothing, fashion, and household goods into artistic compilations.[4] Spending an hour or two on the site each evening, Lee decided to let Polyvore's founders know that she liked the site but also give them suggestions for improvements and complaints and problems she had with the site. Her understanding, attention to detail, and close connection to Polyvore and its users made an impression on the founders, who suggested that perhaps she would like to correct all the problems she had uncovered as a Polyvore employee.[5] After a meeting for coffee, the deal was sealed and Lee became a product manager at Polyvore.[6]

Always open to new experiences, Lee engaged in all manner of tasks to help Polyvore create a great user experience, ranging from coding and management to sales. She also undertook a lot of responsibilities at Polyvore that she had never done before, providing challenges and opportunities for learning. In recognition of her dedication and contributions to Polyvore, the founders first decided to make Lee a cofounder and then decided to appoint her CEO.[7] Under her leadership, Polyvore became profitable. Although she is somewhat introverted, Lee has found her own leadership style that works well at Polyvore.[8]

Over 20 million people visit the Polyvore site each month, and the average purchase from a visit to the site is $220.[9] Polyvore earns revenue through affiliate advertising: All products on the site have links to pages where the products can be purchased, and when these links lead to sales, Polyvore receives affiliate fees.[10] Polyvore also earns revenues from native advertising.[11]

Three values are key to Polyvore's culture. One of these values, "delight the user," focuses on the user experience.[12] As a fan and dedicated user of Polyvore before she joined the firm, Lee knows how important the user experience is and seeks to provide users with outstanding products and make sure that they enjoy their time on the site. Another value, "do a few things well," speaks to Polyvore's approach of keeping everything simple.[13] By focusing on what is really important and doing it well while removing tangential activities, Polyvore focuses on high quality and attention to detail.[14] A third value in Polyvore's culture, "make an impact," describes the sense of accomplishment that has always been important to Lee and that she encourages all employees to experience.[15]

An art lover herself, Lee prides herself on providing users with the technology and the site to express their own creativity through the sets they create. Using an analogy from painting, she suggests that Polyvore provides users with a blank canvas on which they can express their creativity.[16]

Time.com named Polyvore one of the five best sites for online shopping on a single site (in other words, one-stop shopping). More specifically, Polyvore was named "Best for Virtual Window Shopping" because users can see collections of products in sets created by other users as well as look through Polyvore's collection of products.[17]

Always open to new experiences and challenges, Lee sees Polyvore expanding beyond fashion, being available on more kinds of devices, and also expanding internationally. Her ambition, hard work, determination, and persistence, combined with her dedication to Polyvore's users and employees, show that Polyvore is in good hands as it seeks to expand.[18]

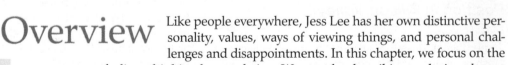

Overview

Like people everywhere, Jess Lee has her own distinctive personality, values, ways of viewing things, and personal challenges and disappointments. In this chapter, we focus on the manager as a feeling, thinking human being. We start by describing enduring characteristics that influence how managers work and how they view other people, their organizations, and the world around them. We also discuss how managers' values, attitudes, and moods play out in organizations, shaping organizational culture. By the end of this chapter, you will appreciate how the personal characteristics of managers influence the process of management in general—and organizational culture in particular.

LO2-1 Describe the various personality traits that affect how managers think, feel, and behave.

Enduring Characteristics: Personality Traits

All people, including managers, have certain enduring characteristics that influence how they think, feel, and behave both on and off the job. These characteristics are **personality traits**: particular tendencies to feel, think, and act in certain ways that can be used to describe the personality of every individual. It is important to understand the personalities of managers because their personalities influence their behavior and their approach to managing people and resources.

personality traits
Enduring tendencies to feel, think, and act in certain ways.

Some managers are demanding, difficult to get along with, and highly critical of other people. Other managers may be as concerned about effectiveness and efficiency as highly critical managers but are easier to get along with, are likable, and frequently praise the people around them. Both management styles may produce excellent results, but their effects on employees are quite different. Do managers deliberately decide to adopt one or the other of these approaches to management? Although they may do so part of the time, in all likelihood, their personalities account for their different approaches. Indeed, research suggests that the way people react to different conditions depends, in part, on their personalities.[19]

The Big Five Personality Traits

We can think of an individual's personality as being composed of five general traits or characteristics: extraversion, negative affectivity, agreeableness, conscientiousness, and openness to experience.[20] Researchers often consider these the Big Five personality traits.[21] Each of them can be viewed as a continuum along which every individual or, more specifically, every manager falls (see Figure 2.1).

Some managers may be at the high end of one trait continuum, others at the low end, and still others somewhere in between. An easy way to understand how these traits can affect a person's approach to management is to describe what people are like at the high and low ends of each trait continuum. As will become evident as you read about each trait, no single trait is right or wrong for being an effective manager. Rather, effectiveness is determined by a complex interaction between the characteristics of managers (including personality traits) and the nature of the job and organization in which they are working. Moreover, personality traits that enhance managerial effectiveness in one situation may impair it in another.

extraversion
The tendency to experience positive emotions and moods and to feel good about oneself and the rest of the world.

EXTRAVERSION Extraversion is the tendency to experience positive emotions and moods and feel good about oneself and the rest of the world. Managers who are high on extraversion (often called *extraverts*) tend to be sociable, affectionate, outgoing, and friendly. Managers who are low on extraversion (often called *introverts*) tend to

Figure 2.1

The Big Five Personality Traits

Managers' personalities can be described by determining which point on each of the following dimensions best characterizes the manager in question:

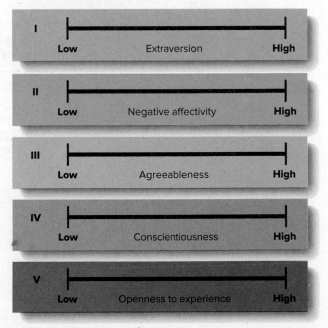

I — Low · Extraversion · High

II — Low · Negative affectivity · High

III — Low · Agreeableness · High

IV — Low · Conscientiousness · High

V — Low · Openness to experience · High

be less inclined toward social interactions and to have a less positive outlook. Being high on extraversion may be an asset for managers whose jobs entail especially high levels of social interaction. Managers who are low on extraversion may nevertheless be highly effective and efficient, especially when their jobs do not require much social interaction. Their quieter approach may enable them to accomplish quite a bit of work in limited time. See Figure 2.2 for an example of a scale that can be used to measure a person's level of extraversion.

Figure 2.2

Measures of Extraversion, Agreeableness, Conscientiousness, and Openness to Experience

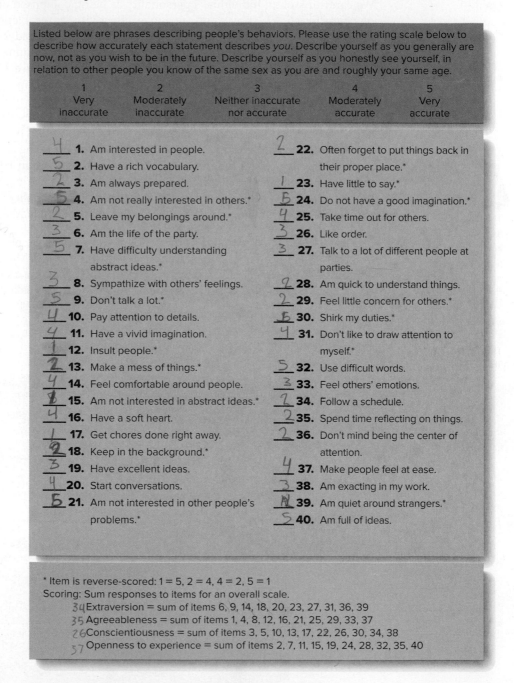

Listed below are phrases describing people's behaviors. Please use the rating scale below to describe how accurately each statement describes *you*. Describe yourself as you generally are now, not as you wish to be in the future. Describe yourself as you honestly see yourself, in relation to other people you know of the same sex as you are and roughly your same age.

1	2	3	4	5
Very inaccurate	Moderately inaccurate	Neither inaccurate nor accurate	Moderately accurate	Very accurate

4 **1.** Am interested in people.
5 **2.** Have a rich vocabulary.
2 **3.** Am always prepared.
5 **4.** Am not really interested in others.*
2 **5.** Leave my belongings around.*
3 **6.** Am the life of the party.
5 **7.** Have difficulty understanding abstract ideas.*
3 **8.** Sympathize with others' feelings.
5 **9.** Don't talk a lot.*
4 **10.** Pay attention to details.
4 **11.** Have a vivid imagination.
1 **12.** Insult people.*
2 **13.** Make a mess of things.*
4 **14.** Feel comfortable around people.
1 **15.** Am not interested in abstract ideas.*
4 **16.** Have a soft heart.
1 **17.** Get chores done right away.
2 **18.** Keep in the background.*
3 **19.** Have excellent ideas.
4 **20.** Start conversations.
5 **21.** Am not interested in other people's problems.*

2 **22.** Often forget to put things back in their proper place.*
1 **23.** Have little to say.*
5 **24.** Do not have a good imagination.*
4 **25.** Take time out for others.
3 **26.** Like order.
3 **27.** Talk to a lot of different people at parties.
2 **28.** Am quick to understand things.
2 **29.** Feel little concern for others.*
5 **30.** Shirk my duties.*
4 **31.** Don't like to draw attention to myself.*
5 **32.** Use difficult words.
3 **33.** Feel others' emotions.
2 **34.** Follow a schedule.
2 **35.** Spend time reflecting on things.
2 **36.** Don't mind being the center of attention.
4 **37.** Make people feel at ease.
3 **38.** Am exacting in my work.
N **39.** Am quiet around strangers.*
5 **40.** Am full of ideas.

* Item is reverse-scored: 1 = 5, 2 = 4, 4 = 2, 5 = 1
Scoring: Sum responses to items for an overall scale.
34 Extraversion = sum of items 6, 9, 14, 18, 20, 23, 27, 31, 36, 39
35 Agreeableness = sum of items 1, 4, 8, 12, 16, 21, 25, 29, 33, 37
26 Conscientiousness = sum of items 3, 5, 10, 13, 17, 22, 26, 30, 34, 38
57 Openness to experience = sum of items 2, 7, 11, 15, 19, 24, 28, 32, 35, 40

Source: L. R. Goldberg, Oregon Research Institute, http://ipip.ori.org/ipip/.

negative affectivity

The tendency to experience negative emotions and moods, to feel distressed, and to be critical of oneself and others.

NEGATIVE AFFECTIVITY Negative affectivity is the tendency to experience negative emotions and moods, feel distressed, and be critical of oneself and others. Managers high on this trait may often feel angry and dissatisfied and complain about their own and others' lack of progress. Managers who are low on negative affectivity do not tend to experience many negative emotions and moods and are less pessimistic and critical of themselves and others. On the plus side, the critical approach of a manager high on negative affectivity may sometimes spur both the manager and others to improve their performance. Nevertheless, it is probably more pleasant to work with a manager who is low on negative affectivity; the better working relationships that such a manager is likely to cultivate also can be an important asset.

agreeableness

The tendency to get along well with other people.

AGREEABLENESS Agreeableness is the tendency to get along well with others. Managers who are high on the agreeableness continuum are likable, tend to be affectionate, and care about other people. Managers who are low on agreeableness may be somewhat distrustful of others, unsympathetic, uncooperative, and even at times antagonistic. Being high on agreeableness may be especially important for managers whose responsibilities require that they develop good, close relationships with others. Nevertheless, a low level of agreeableness may be an asset in managerial jobs that actually require that managers be antagonistic, such as drill sergeants and some other kinds of military managers. See Figure 2.2 for an example of a scale that measures a person's level of agreeableness.

conscientiousness

The tendency to be careful, scrupulous, and persevering.

CONSCIENTIOUSNESS Conscientiousness is the tendency to be careful, scrupulous, and persevering.[22] Managers who are high on the conscientiousness continuum are organized and self-disciplined; those who are low on this trait might sometimes appear to lack direction and self-discipline. Conscientiousness has been found to be a good predictor of performance in many kinds of jobs, including managerial jobs in a variety of organizations.[23] Entrepreneurs who found their own companies, like Jess Lee (a cofounder of Polyvore profiled in "A Manager's Challenge"), often are high on conscientiousness, and their persistence and determination help them to overcome obstacles and turn their ideas into successful new ventures. Figure 2.2 provides an example of a scale that measures conscientiousness.

openness to experience

The tendency to be original, have broad interests, be open to a wide range of stimuli, be daring, and take risks.

OPENNESS TO EXPERIENCE Openness to experience is the tendency to be original, have broad interests, be open to a wide range of stimuli, be daring, and take risks.[24] Managers who are high on this trait continuum may be especially likely to take risks and be innovative in their planning and decision making. Jess Lee, discussed in this chapter's "Management Snapshot" has always been open to new challenges, learning opportunities, and things she hasn't done before—a testament to her high level of openness to experience. Managers who are low on openness to experience may be less prone to take risks and more conservative in their planning and decision making. In certain organizations and positions, this tendency might be an asset. The manager of the fiscal office in a public university, for example, must ensure that all university departments and units follow the university's rules and regulations pertaining to budgets, spending accounts, and reimbursements of expenses. Figure 2.2 provides an example of a measure of openness to experience.

Some successful entrepreneurs who start their own businesses are high on openness to experience and conscientiousness, which has contributed to their accomplishments as entrepreneurs and managers, as is true of Kevin Plank, founder, CEO, and chairman of the board of Under Armour.[25]

MANAGER AS A PERSON

Kevin Plank's Openness to Experience and Conscientiousness Pay Off at Under Armour

When Kevin Plank was a walk-on fullback football player at the University of Maryland in the 1990s, he often became annoyed that his T-shirt was soaked and weighted down with sweat. Always an original thinker, he wondered why athletic apparel couldn't be made out of some kind of polyester blend that would help athletes' and sports aficionados' muscles stay cool while wicking away, and not holding, moisture from sweat.[26] As he was finishing his undergraduate studies at Maryland, he started experimenting with different fabrics, testing their durability, comfort, and water resistance with the help of a local tailor. A prototype of Under Armour's first product—the 0039 compression shirt—was developed.[27]

Upon graduation from the University of Maryland, Plank was offered a position at Prudential Life Insurance. An entrepreneur at heart willing to risk everything to pursue his bold ideas, Plank realized that accepting a secure position with an insurance company would have driven him nuts. So he turned down the Prudential offer and mustered his determination to sell his innovative T-shirt.[28] With little business training or experience, and a lot of perseverance and discipline, Plank pursued the makings of what would become a major competitor of Nike 17 years later with net revenues over $3 billion in 2014.[29] Entering and succeeding in the competitive sports apparel industry dominated by huge players like Nike with vast resources and a widely recognized brand would seem like an impossible feat even for a seasoned businessperson with access to capital. With around $20,000 in the bank and the resolve to turn his idea into a viable venture, Plank succeeded against all odds.[30]

Kevin Plank began by selling his innovative T-shirts from the trunk of his car. Under Armour is now a global company, producing and selling sports and fitness apparel, shoes, and accessories. His success demonstrates how taking risks, while also being determined and disciplined, can lead to success against tough odds. © J. Meric/Getty Images Sport/Getty Images

Very outgoing and confident, Plank used his network of athletic contacts from playing on teams in high school, military school, and the University of Maryland to get the word out about the shirt.[31] From the various teams he had played on, he was familiar enough with around 40 NFL players to contact them and tell them about the shirt. Living out of his car with his trunk full of shirts, Plank drove around to training camps and schools to show athletes and managers his new product. Teaming up with two partners, Plank began running his business from the basement of his grandmother's house in the Georgetown area of Washington, DC, with the help of a $250,000 small business loan. As business and orders picked up, Under Armour outgrew the basement and set up shop on Sharp Street in Baltimore.[32] The rest has literally been history.

Under Armour currently produces and sells apparel, shoes, and accessories for women, men, and youth for athletics, sports, outdoor activities, and fitness.[33] Under Armour is a global company with over 6,000 employees, operating in North

America, Europe, the Middle East, Africa, Asia, and Latin America though most employees work in the United States.[34]

Under Armour is currently headquartered in what used to be the 400,000-square-foot Tide Point complex where Procter & Gamble used to manufacture detergent in Baltimore.[35] Some of the original names of the facilities like Joy and Cheer remain and seem aptly fit for a company like Under Armour.[36] Under Armour has made major contributions to help Baltimore's depressed economy, including employing over 2,000 people in the Baltimore area. Clearly Plank demonstrates that being original, daring, and taking risks while at the same time being highly determined, disciplined, and persevering can help managers and entrepreneurs succeed against tough odds. As Plank puts it, "There's an entrepreneur right now, scared to death . . . Get out of your garage and go take a chance, and start your business."[37]

Successful managers occupy a variety of positions on the Big Five personality trait continua. One highly effective manager may be high on extraversion and negative affectivity; another equally effective manager may be low on both these traits; and still another may be somewhere in between. Members of an organization must understand these differences among managers because they can shed light on how managers behave and on their approach to planning, leading, organizing, or controlling. If subordinates realize, for example, that their manager is low on extraversion, they will not feel slighted when their manager seems to be aloof because they will realize that by nature he or she is simply not outgoing.

Managers themselves also need to be aware of their own personality traits and the traits of others, including their subordinates and fellow managers. A manager who knows that he has a tendency to be highly critical of other people might try to tone down his negative approach. Similarly, a manager who realizes that her chronically complaining subordinate tends to be so negative because of his personality may take all his complaints with a grain of salt and realize that things probably are not as bad as this subordinate says they are.

In order for all members of an organization to work well together and with people outside the organization, such as customers and suppliers, they must understand each other. Such understanding comes, in part, from an appreciation of some fundamental ways in which people differ from one another—that is, an appreciation of personality traits.

Other Personality Traits That Affect Managerial Behavior

Many other specific traits in addition to the Big Five describe people's personalities. Here we look at traits that are particularly important for understanding managerial effectiveness: locus of control; self-esteem; and the needs for achievement, affiliation, and power.

LOCUS OF CONTROL People differ in their views about how much control they have over what happens to and around them. The locus of control trait captures these beliefs.[38] People with an **internal locus of control** believe that they themselves are responsible for their own fate; they see their own actions and behaviors as being major and decisive determinants of important outcomes such as attaining levels of job performance, being promoted, or being turned down for a choice job assignment. Some managers with an internal locus of control see the success of a whole organization resting on their shoulders. One example is Jess Lee in the "Management

internal locus of control The tendency to locate responsibility for one's fate within oneself.

external locus of control The tendency to locate responsibility for one's fate in outside forces and to believe one's own behavior has little impact on outcomes.

self-esteem The degree to which individuals feel good about themselves and their capabilities.

need for achievement The extent to which an individual has a strong desire to perform challenging tasks well and to meet personal standards for excellence.

need for affiliation The extent to which an individual is concerned about establishing and maintaining good interpersonal relations, being liked, and having other people get along.

need for power The extent to which an individual desires to control or influence others.

 LO2-2 Explain what values and attitudes are and describe their impact on managerial action.

Snapshot." An internal locus of control also helps to ensure ethical behavior and decision making in an organization because people feel accountable and responsible for their own actions.

People with an **external locus of control** believe that outside forces are responsible for what happens to and around them; they do not think their own actions make much of a difference. As such, they tend not to intervene to try to change a situation or solve a problem, leaving it to someone else.

Managers need an internal locus of control because they *are* responsible for what happens in organizations; they need to believe that they can and do make a difference, as does Jess Lee at Polyvore. Moreover, managers are responsible for ensuring that organizations and their members behave in an ethical fashion, and for this as well they need an internal locus of control—they need to know and feel they can make a difference.

SELF-ESTEEM Self-esteem is the degree to which individuals feel good about themselves and their capabilities. People with high self-esteem believe that they are competent, deserving, and capable of handling most situations, as does Jess Lee. People with low self-esteem have poor opinions of themselves, are unsure about their capabilities, and question their ability to succeed at different endeavors.[39] Research suggests that people tend to choose activities and goals consistent with their levels of self-esteem. High self-esteem is desirable for managers because it facilitates their setting and keeping high standards for themselves, pushes them ahead on difficult projects, and gives them the confidence they need to make and carry out important decisions.

NEEDS FOR ACHIEVEMENT, AFFILIATION, AND POWER Psychologist David McClelland has extensively researched the needs for achievement, affiliation, and power.[40] The **need for achievement** is the extent to which an individual has a strong desire to perform challenging tasks well and to meet personal standards for excellence. People with a high need for achievement often set clear goals for themselves and like to receive performance feedback. The **need for affiliation** is the extent to which an individual is concerned about establishing and maintaining good interpersonal relations, being liked, and having the people around him or her get along with one another. The **need for power** is the extent to which an individual desires to control or influence others.[41]

Research suggests that high needs for achievement and for power are assets for first-line and middle managers and that a high need for power is especially important for upper-level managers.[42] One study found that U.S. presidents with a relatively high need for power tended to be especially effective during their terms of office.[43] A high need for affiliation may not always be desirable in managers because it might lead them to try too hard to be liked by others (including subordinates) rather than doing all they can to ensure that performance is as high as it can and should be. Although most research on these needs has been done in the United States, some studies suggest that these findings may also apply to people in other countries such as India and New Zealand.[44]

Taken together, these desirable personality traits for managers—an internal locus of control, high self-esteem, and high needs for achievement and power—suggest that managers need to be take-charge people who not only believe their own actions are decisive in determining their own and their organizations' fates but also believe in their own capabilities. Such managers have a personal desire for accomplishment and influence over others.

Values, Attitudes, and Moods and Emotions

What are managers striving to achieve? How do they think they should behave? What do they think about their jobs and organizations? And how do they actually feel at work? We can find some answers to these questions by exploring managers' values, attitudes, and moods.

Values, attitudes, and moods and emotions capture how managers experience their jobs as individuals. *Values* describe what managers are trying to achieve through work and how they think they should behave. *Attitudes* capture their thoughts and feelings about their specific jobs and organizations. *Moods and emotions* encompass how managers actually feel when they are managing. Although these three aspects of managers' work experience are highly personal, they also have important implications for understanding how managers behave, how they treat and respond to others, and how, through their efforts, they help contribute to organizational effectiveness through planning, leading, organizing, and controlling.

Values: Terminal and Instrumental

terminal value
A lifelong goal or objective that an individual seeks to achieve.

instrumental value
A mode of conduct that an individual seeks to follow.

norms Unwritten, informal codes of conduct that prescribe how people should act in particular situations and are considered important by most members of a group or organization.

value system
The terminal and instrumental values that are guiding principles in an individual's life.

The two kinds of personal values are *terminal* and *instrumental*. A **terminal value** is a personal conviction about lifelong goals or objectives; an **instrumental value** is a personal conviction about desired modes of conduct or ways of behaving.[45] Terminal values often lead to the formation of **norms**, which are unwritten, informal codes of conduct, such as behaving honestly or courteously, that prescribe how people should act in particular situations and are considered important by most members of a group or organization.

Milton Rokeach, a leading researcher in the area of human values, identified 18 terminal values and 18 instrumental values that describe each person's value system.[46] By rank ordering, the terminal values from "1 (most important as a guiding principle in one's life)" to "18 (least important as a guiding principle in one's life)" and then rank ordering the instrumental values from 1 to 18, people can give good pictures of their **value systems**—what they are striving to achieve in life and how they want to behave.[47]

Several of Rokeach's terminal values seem to be especially important for managers such as *"a sense of accomplishment (a lasting contribution)"*, *"equality (brotherhood, equal opportunity for all)"*, and *"self-respect (self-esteem)."*[48] A manager who thinks a sense of accomplishment is of paramount importance might focus on making a lasting contribution to an organization by developing a new product that can save or prolong lives, as is true of managers at Medtronic (a company that makes medical devices such as cardiac pacemakers), or by opening a new foreign subsidiary. A manager who places equality at the top of his or her list of terminal values may be at the forefront of an organization's efforts to support, provide equal opportunities to, and capitalize on the many talents of an increasingly diverse workforce.

Other terminal values are likely to be considered important by many managers, such as *"a comfortable life (a prosperous life)"*, *"an exciting life (a stimulating, active life)"*, *"freedom (independence, free choice)"*, and *"social recognition (respect, admiration)."*[49] The relative importance that managers place on each terminal value helps explain what they are striving to achieve in their organizations and what they will focus their efforts on.

Several of Rokeach's instrumental values seem to be important modes of conduct for managers, such as being *"ambitious (hardworking, aspiring)," "broad-minded (open-minded)," "capable (competent, effective)," "responsible (dependable, reliable),"* and *"self-controlled (restrained, self-disciplined)."*[50] Moreover, the relative importance a manager places on these and other instrumental values may be a significant determinant of actual behaviors on the job. A manager who considers being *"imaginative (daring, creative)"*[51] to be highly important, for example, is more likely to be innovative and take risks than is a manager who considers this to be less important (all else being equal). A manager who considers being *"honest (sincere, truthful)"*[52] to be of paramount importance may be a driving force for taking steps to ensure that all members of a unit or organization behave ethically, as indicated in the following "Ethics in Action" box.

ETHICS IN ACTION

Telling the Truth at Gentle Giant Moving

Gentle Giant Moving Company, based in Somerville, Massachusetts, was founded by Larry O'Toole in 1980 and now has over $28 million in revenues and offices in multiple states.[53] Gentle Giant opened its newest office, Chicago Movers–Gentle Giant Moving & Storage, in 2013 in Chicago, Illinois.[54] Although moving is undoubtedly hard work and many people would never think about having a career in this industry, Gentle Giant's unique culture and approach to managing people have not only contributed to the company's success but also give its employees satisfying careers. For example, when Ryan Libby was in college, he worked for Gentle Giant during one of his summer vacations to make some extra money. After graduating from college, he was the assistant manager for the Providence, Rhode Island, Gentle Giant Office. Now Libby is branch manager for Providence.[55] As he puts it, "First it was just a paycheck, and it kind of turned into a long-term career."[56]

At Gentle Giant Moving Company, employees are given leadership training, access to company outings, and the opportunity to advance to management positions. Courtesy of Gentle Giant Moving Company

Libby is just the kind of employee O'Toole seeks to hire—employees who start out driving moving trucks and eventually move into management positions running offices. Whereas some moving companies hire a lot of temporary help in the summer to meet seasonal demand, 60 percent of Gentle Giant employees are employed full-time.[57] Because the demand for moving services is lower in the winter, Gentle Giant uses this time to train and develop employees. Of course new employees receive training in the basics of moving: packing, lifting, and carrying household goods safely. However, employees looking to advance in the company receive training in a host of other areas ranging from project management, communication, problem solving, and customer relations to leadership. An overarching goal of Gentle Giant's training efforts is inculcating in employees the importance of honesty. According to O'Toole, "We really emphasize that what matters most to us is telling the truth."[58]

Training benefits Gentle Giant's employees, customers, and the company as a whole. About one-third of the company's office and management employees started out driving moving trucks. Customers are satisfied because employees are capable, honest, and professional. And the company has continued to grow, prosper, and receive recognition in the business press as well as awards. For example, Gentle Giant was named one of the 15 Top Small Workplaces by *The Wall Street Journal* in collaboration with Winning Workplaces (a nonprofit organization that focuses on helping small and medium-sized companies improve their work environments).[59]

Having fun and getting to know each other as people are also important at Gentle Giant.[60] The company holds parties and arranges outings for employees to sporting events, amusement parks, and other local attractions. Most workdays, O'Toole takes an employee out to lunch. Some college athletes are attracted to work for Gentle Giant because they see moving as a way to keep fit while at the same time having the opportunity to grow and develop on the job and move into a managerial position if they desire.[61]

All in all, managers' value systems signify what managers as individuals are trying to accomplish and become in their personal lives and at work. Thus managers' value systems are fundamental guides to their behavior and efforts at planning, leading, organizing, and controlling.

Attitudes

attitude A collection of feelings and beliefs.

An **attitude** is a collection of feelings and beliefs. Like everyone else, managers have attitudes about their jobs and organizations, and these attitudes affect how they approach their jobs. Two of the most important attitudes in this context are job satisfaction and organizational commitment.

job satisfaction The collection of feelings and beliefs that managers have about their current jobs.

JOB SATISFACTION Job satisfaction is the collection of feelings and beliefs that managers have about their current jobs.[62] Managers who have high levels of job satisfaction generally like their jobs, feel they are fairly treated, and believe that their jobs have many desirable features or characteristics (such as interesting work, good pay and job security, autonomy, or nice coworkers). Figure 2.3 shows sample items from two scales that managers can use to measure job satisfaction. Levels of job satisfaction tend to increase as one moves up the hierarchy in an organization. Upper managers, in general, tend to be more satisfied with their jobs than entry-level employees. Managers' levels of job satisfaction can range from very low to very high.

One might think that in tough economic times, when unemployment is high and layoffs are prevalent, people who have jobs might be relatively satisfied with them. However, this is not necessarily the case. For example, in December 2009, the U.S. unemployment rate was 10 percent, 85,000 jobs were lost from the economy, and the underemployment rate (which includes people who have given up looking for jobs and those who are working part-time because they can't find a full-time position) was 17.3 percent.[63] During these recessionary conditions, job satisfaction levels in the United States fell to record lows.[64]

The Conference Board has been tracking levels of U.S. job satisfaction since 1987, when 61.1 percent of workers surveyed indicated that they were satisfied with their jobs.[65] In 2009 only 45 percent of workers surveyed indicated that they were satisfied with their jobs, an all-time low for the survey.[66] Some sources of job dissatisfaction include uninteresting work, lack of job security, incomes that have not

Figure 2.3

Sample Items from
Two Measures of Job
Satisfaction

Sample items from the Minnesota Satisfaction Questionnaire:

People respond to each of the items in the scale by checking whether they are:

[ ] Very dissatisfied

[ ] Dissatisfied

[ ] Can't decide whether satisfied or not

[ ] Satisfied

[ ] Very satisfied

On my present job, this is how I feel about . . .

_____ **1.** Being able to do things that don't go against my conscience.

_____ **2.** The way my job provides for steady employment.

_____ **3.** The chance to do things for other people.

_____ **4.** The chance to do something that makes use of my abilities.

_____ **5.** The way company policies are put into practice.

_____ **6.** My pay and the amount of work I do.

_____ **7.** The chances for advancement on this job.

_____ **8.** The freedom to use my own judgment.

_____ **9.** The working conditions.

_____ **10.** The way my coworkers get along with each other.

_____ **11.** The praise I get for doing a good job.

_____ **12.** The feeling of accomplishment I get from the job.

The Faces Scale

Workers select the face which best expresses how they feel about their job in general.

11   10   9   8   7   6   5   4   3   2   1

Source: D.J. Weiss et al., *Manual for the Minnesota Satisfaction Questionnaire.* Copyrighted by the Vocational Psychology Research, University of Minnesota; copyright © 1975 by the American Psychological Association.

kept pace with inflation, and having to spend more money on health insurance. For example, three times as many workers in 2009 had to contribute to paying for their health insurance and had rising levels of contributions compared to 1980. Only 43 percent of workers thought their jobs were secure in 2009 compared to 59 percent in 1987. In the 2000s, average household incomes adjusted for inflation declined.[67]

Of all age groups, workers under 25 were the most dissatisfied with their jobs in 2009. More specifically, approximately 64 percent of workers in this age group were dissatisfied with their jobs, perhaps due to declining opportunities and relatively low earnings. Around 22 percent of all respondents didn't think they would still have the same job in a year.[68]

In 2012, 47.3 percent of U.S. workers indicated that they were satisfied with their jobs on the Conference Board survey.[69] This was the seventh year in a row in which less than one-half of Americans were satisfied with their jobs.[70] Factors contributing to levels of satisfaction/dissatisfaction in 2012 included potential for growth on the job, interesting work, communication, recognition, workload, and work–life balance.[71]

In general, it is desirable for managers to be satisfied with their jobs, for at least two reasons. First, satisfied managers may be more likely to go the extra mile for their organization or perform **organizational citizenship behaviors (OCBs)**—behaviors that are not required of organizational members but that contribute to and are necessary for organizational efficiency, effectiveness, and competitive advantage.[72] Managers who are satisfied with their jobs are more likely to perform these "above and beyond the call of duty" behaviors, which can range from putting in long hours when needed to coming up with truly creative ideas and overcoming obstacles to implement them (even when doing so is not part of the manager's job), or to going out of one's way to help a coworker, subordinate, or superior (even when doing so entails considerable personal sacrifice).[73]

organizational citizenship behaviors (OCBs) Behaviors that are not required of organizational members but that contribute to and are necessary for organizational efficiency, effectiveness, and competitive advantage.

A second reason why it is desirable for managers to be satisfied with their jobs is that satisfied managers may be less likely to quit.[74] A manager who is highly satisfied may never even think about looking for another position; a dissatisfied manager may always be on the lookout for new opportunities. Turnover can hurt an organization because it causes the loss of the experience and knowledge that managers have gained about the company, industry, and business environment.

A growing source of dissatisfaction for many lower-level and middle managers, as well as for nonmanagerial employees, is the threat of unemployment and increased workloads from organizational downsizings and layoffs. Organizations that try to improve their efficiency through restructuring and layoffs often eliminate a sizable number of first-line and middle management positions. This decision obviously hurts the managers who are laid off, and it also can reduce the job satisfaction levels of managers who remain. They might fear being the next to be let go. In addition, the workloads of remaining employees often increase dramatically as a result of restructuring, and this can contribute to dissatisfaction.

How managers and organizations handle layoffs is of paramount importance, not only for the layoff victims but also for employees who survive the layoff and keep their jobs.[75] Showing compassion and empathy for layoff victims, giving them as much advance notice as possible about the layoff, providing clear information about severance benefits, and helping layoff victims in their job search efforts are a few of the ways in which managers can humanely manage a layoff.[76] For example, when Ron Thomas, vice president of organizational development for Martha Stewart Living Omnimedia, had to lay off employees as a result of closing the organization's catalog business, he personally called all the catalog businesses he knew to find out about potential positions for laid-off employees.[77] Efforts such as Thomas's to help layoff victims find new jobs can contribute to the job satisfaction of those who survive the layoff. As Thomas puts it, "If you handle a restructuring well, the word gets out that you're a good place to work . . . if we post a job opening today, we'll get 1,500 résumés tomorrow."[78]

Unfortunately, when the unemployment rate is high, laid-off employees sometimes find it difficult to find new jobs and can remain jobless for months.[79] For small businesses, the decision to lay off employees and communicating that decision can be especially painful because managers often have developed close personal relationships with the people they have to let go, know their families, and fear what will happen to them with the loss of a steady income.[80] Shelly Polum, vice president for administration at Ram Tool, a small family-owned manufacturing company in Grafton, Wisconsin, broke down in tears in her office after she had to let employees know they were being laid off.[81] When Charlie Thomas, vice president of Shuqualak Lumber in Shuqualak, Mississippi, had to announce layoffs of close to a quarter of his employees, he wrote a speech that he could not get through without stopping and retreating to his office to pull himself together. As he put it, "I couldn't get it out . . . It just killed my soul."[82] As these managers realize, being laid off can be devastating for employees and their families.

organizational commitment
The collection of feelings and beliefs that managers have about their organization as a whole.

ORGANIZATIONAL COMMITMENT **Organizational commitment** is the collection of feelings and beliefs that managers have about their organization as a whole.[83] Managers who are committed to their organizations believe in what their organizations are doing, are proud of what these organizations stand for, and feel a high degree of loyalty toward their organizations. Committed managers are more likely to go above and beyond the call of duty to help their company and are less likely to quit.[84] Organizational commitment can be especially strong when employees and managers truly believe in organizational values; it also leads to a strong organizational culture.

Organizational commitment is likely to help managers perform some of their figurehead and spokesperson roles (see Chapter 1). It is much easier for a manager to persuade others both inside and outside the organization of the merits of what the organization has done and is seeking to accomplish if the manager truly believes in and is committed to the organization.

Do managers in different countries have similar or different attitudes? Differences in the levels of job satisfaction and organizational commitment among managers in different countries are likely because these managers have different kinds of opportunities and rewards and because they face different economic, political, and sociocultural forces in their organizations' general environments. Levels of organizational commitment from one country to another may depend on the extent to which countries have legislation affecting firings and layoffs and the extent to which citizens of a country are geographically mobile.

LO2-3 Appreciate how moods and emotions influence all members of an organization.

Moods and Emotions

mood A feeling or state of mind.

Just as you sometimes are in a bad mood and at other times are in a good mood, so too are managers. A **mood** is a feeling or state of mind. When people are in a positive mood, they feel excited, enthusiastic, active, or elated.[85] When people are in a negative mood, they feel distressed, fearful, scornful, hostile, jittery, or nervous.[86] People who are high on negative affectivity are especially likely to experience negative moods. People's situations or circumstances also determine their moods; however, receiving a raise is likely to put most people in a good mood regardless of their personality traits. People who are high on negative affectivity are not always in a bad mood and people who are low on extraversion still experience positive moods.[87]

emotions Intense, relatively short-lived feelings.

Emotions are more intense feelings than moods, are often directly linked to whatever caused the emotion, and are more short-lived.[88] However, once whatever has triggered the emotion has been dealt with, the feelings may linger in the form of a less intense mood.[89] For example, a manager who gets very angry when a subordinate has engaged in an unethical behavior may find his anger decreasing in intensity once he has decided how to address the problem. Yet he continues to be in a bad mood the rest of the day, even though he is not directly thinking about the unfortunate incident.[90]

Research has found that moods and emotions affect the behavior of managers and all members of an organization. For example, research suggests that the subordinates of managers who experience positive moods at work may perform at somewhat higher levels and be less likely to resign and leave the organization than the subordinates of managers who do not tend to be in a positive mood at work.[91] Other research suggests that under certain conditions creativity might be enhanced by positive moods, whereas under other conditions negative moods might push people to work harder to come up with truly creative ideas.[92] Recognizing that both mood states have the potential to contribute to creativity in different ways, recent research suggests that employees may be especially likely to be creative to the extent that they experience both mood states (at different times) on the job and to the extent that the work environment is supportive of creativity.[93]

Other research suggests that moods and emotions may play an important role in ethical decision making. For example, researchers at Princeton University found that when people are trying to solve difficult personal moral dilemmas, the parts of their brains that are responsible for emotions and moods are especially active.[94]

More generally, emotions and moods give managers and all employees important information and signals about what is going on in the workplace.[95] Positive emotions and moods signal that things are going well and thus can lead to more expansive, and even playful, thinking. Negative emotions and moods signal that there are problems in need of attention and areas for improvement. So when people are in negative moods, they tend to be more detail-oriented and focused on the facts at hand.[96] Some studies suggest that critical thinking and devil's advocacy may be promoted by a negative mood, and sometimes especially accurate judgments may be made by managers in negative moods.[97]

Managers and other members of an organization need to realize that how they feel affects how they treat others and how others respond to them, including their subordinates. For example, a subordinate may be more likely to approach a manager with a somewhat unusual but potentially useful idea if the subordinate thinks the manager is in a good mood. Likewise, when managers are in very bad moods, their subordinates might try to avoid them at all costs. Figure 2.4 is an example of a scale that can measure the extent to which a person experiences positive and negative moods at work.

Emotional Intelligence

In understanding the effects of managers' and all employees' moods and emotions, it is important to take into account their levels of emotional intelligence. **Emotional intelligence** is the ability to understand and manage one's own moods and emotions and the moods and emotions of other people.[98] Managers with a high level of emotional intelligence are more likely to understand how they are feeling and why, and they are more able to effectively manage their feelings. When managers are experiencing stressful feelings and emotions such as fear or anxiety, emotional intelligence lets them understand why and manage these feelings so they do not get in the way of effective decision making.[99]

Emotional intelligence also can help managers perform their important roles such as their interpersonal roles (figurehead, leader, and liaison).[100] Understanding how your subordinates feel, why they feel that way, and how to manage these feelings is central to developing strong interpersonal bonds with them.[101] More generally, emotional intelligence has the potential to contribute to effective leadership in multiple ways.[102]

For example, emotional intelligence helps managers understand and relate well to other people.[103] It also helps managers maintain their enthusiasm and confidence

emotional intelligence
The ability to understand and manage one's own moods and emotions and the moods and emotions of other people.

LO2-4 Describe the nature of emotional intelligence and its role in management.

Figure 2.4

A Measure of Positive and Negative Mood at Work

People respond to each item by indicating the extent to which the item describes how they felt at work during the past week on the following scale.

1 = Very slightly or not at all   4 = Quite a bit
2 = A little   5 = Very much
3 = Moderately

_____ **1.** Active	_____ **7.** Enthusiastic
_____ **2.** Distressed	_____ **8.** Fearful
_____ **3.** Strong	_____ **9.** Peppy
_____ **4.** Excited	_____ **10.** Nervous
_____ **5.** Scornful	_____ **11.** Elated
_____ **6.** Hostile	_____ **12.** Jittery

Scoring: Responses to items 1, 3, 4, 7, 9, and 11 are summed for a positive mood score; the higher the score, the more positive mood is experienced at work. Responses to items 2, 5, 6, 8, 10, and 12 are summed for a negative mood score; the higher the score, the more negative mood is experienced at work.

Source: A.P. Brief, M.J. Burke, J.M. George, B. Robinson, and J. Webster, "Should Negative Affectivity Remain an Unmeasured Variable in the Study of Job Stress?" *Journal of Applied Psychology* 72 (1988), 193–98; M.J. Burke, A.P. Brief, J.M. George, L. Roberson, and J. Webster, "Measuring Affect at Work: Confirmatory Analyses of Competing Mood Structures with Conceptual Linkage in Cortical Regulatory Systems," *Journal of Personality and Social Psychology* 57 (1989), 1091–102.

organizational culture

The shared set of beliefs, expectations, values, norms, and work routines that influence how individuals, groups, and teams interact with one another and cooperate to achieve organizational goals.

and energize subordinates to help the organization attain its goals.[104] Recent theorizing and research suggest that emotional intelligence may be especially important in awakening employee creativity.[105] Managers themselves are increasingly recognizing the importance of emotional intelligence.

Organizational Culture

LO2-5 Define organizational culture and explain how managers both create and are influenced by organizational culture.

Personality is a way of understanding why all managers and employees, as individuals, characteristically think and behave in different ways. However, when people belong to the same organization, they tend to share certain beliefs and values that lead them to act in similar ways.[106] **Organizational culture** comprises the shared set of beliefs, expectations, values, norms, and work routines that influence how members of an organization relate to one another and work together to achieve organizational goals. In essence, organizational culture reflects the distinctive ways in which organizational members perform their jobs and relate to others inside and outside the organization. It may, for example, be how customers in a particular hotel chain are treated from the time they are greeted at check-in until they leave; or it may be the shared work routines that research teams use to guide new product development. When organizational members share an intense commitment to cultural values, beliefs, and routines and use them to achieve their goals, a *strong* organizational culture exists.[107] When organizational members are not strongly committed to a shared system of values, beliefs, and routines, organizational culture is weak.

The stronger the culture of an organization, the more one can think about it as being the "personality" of an organization because it influences the way its members behave.[108] Organizations that possess strong cultures may differ on a wide variety of dimensions that determine how their members behave toward one another and perform their jobs. For example, organizations differ in how members relate to each other (formally or informally), how important decisions are made (top-down or bottom-up), willingness to change (flexible or unyielding), innovation (creative or predictable), and playfulness (serious or serendipitous). In an innovative design firm like IDEO Product Development in Silicon Valley, employees are encouraged to adopt a playful attitude toward their work, look outside the organization to find inspiration, and adopt a flexible approach toward product design that uses multiple perspectives.[109] IDEO's culture is vastly different from that of companies such as Citibank and ExxonMobil, in which employees treat each other in a more formal or deferential way, employees are expected to adopt a serious approach to their work, and decision making is constrained by the hierarchy of authority.

Managers and Organizational Culture

While all members of an organization can contribute to developing and maintaining organizational culture, managers play a particularly important part in influencing organizational culture[110] because of their multiple and important roles (see Chapter 1). How managers create culture is most vividly evident in start-ups of new companies. Entrepreneurs who start their own companies are typically also the start-ups' top managers until the companies grow and become profitable. Often referred to as the firms' founders, these managers literally create their organizations' cultures.

attraction–selection-attrition (ASA) framework
A model that explains how personality may influence organizational culture.

The founders' personal characteristics play an important role in the creation of organizational culture. Benjamin Schneider, a well-known management researcher, developed a model that helps to explain the role that founders' personal characteristics play in determining organizational culture.[111] His model, called the **attraction–selection–attrition (ASA) framework,** posits that when founders hire employees for their new ventures, they tend to be attracted to and choose employees whose personalities are similar to their own.[112] These similar employees are more likely to stay with the organization. Although employees who are dissimilar in personality might be hired, they are more likely to leave the organization over time.[113] As a result of these attraction, selection, and attrition processes, people in the organization tend to have similar personalities, and the typical or dominant personality profile of organizational members determines and shapes organizational culture.[114]

For example, when David Kelley became interested in engineering and product design challenges in the late 1970s, he realized that who he was as a person meant he would not be happy working in a typical corporate environment. Kelley is high on openness to experience, driven to go where his interests take him, and not content to follow others' directives. Kelley recognized that he needed to start his own business, and with the help of other Stanford-schooled engineers and design experts, IDEO was born.[115]

From the start, IDEO's culture has embodied Kelley's spirited, freewheeling approach to work and design—from colorful and informal workspaces to an emphasis on networking and communicating with as many people as possible to understand a design problem. No project or problem is too big or too small for IDEO; the company designed the Apple Lisa computer and mouse (the precursor of the Mac) and the Palm as well as the Crest Neat Squeeze toothpaste dispenser and the Racer's Edge water bottle.[116] Kelley hates rules, job titles, big corner offices, and all the other trappings of large traditional organizations that stifle creativity. Employees who are attracted to, are selected by, and remain with IDEO value creativity and innovation and embrace onc of IDEO's mottos: "Fail often to succeed sooner."[117]

Although ASA processes are most evident in small firms such as IDEO, they also can operate in large companies.[118] According to the ASA model, this is a naturally occurring phenomenon to the extent that managers and new hires are free to make the kinds of choices the model specifies. However, while people tend to get along well with others who are similar to themselves, too much similarity in an organization can impair organizational effectiveness. That is, similar people tend to view conditions and events in similar ways and thus can be resistant to change. Moreover, organizations benefit from a diversity of perspectives rather than similarity in perspectives (see Chapter 3). At IDEO Kelley recognized early on how important it is to take advantage of the diverse talents and perspectives that people with different personalities, backgrounds, experiences, and education can bring to a design team. Hence, IDEO's design teams include not only engineers but also others who might have a unique insight into a problem, such as anthropologists, communications experts, doctors, and users of a product. When new employees are hired at IDEO, they meet many employees who have different backgrounds and characteristics; the focus is not on hiring someone who will fit in but, rather, on hiring someone who has something to offer and can "wow" different kinds of people with his or her insights.[119]

In addition to personality, other personal characteristics of managers shape organizational culture; these include managers' values, attitudes, moods and emotions, and emotional intelligence.[120] For example, both terminal and instrumental values of managers play a role in determining organizational culture. Managers who highly value freedom and equality, for example, might be likely to stress the importance of autonomy and empowerment in their organizations, as well as fair treatment for all. As another example, managers who highly value being helpful and forgiving

IDEO employees brainstorming—informal communication, casual attire, and flexibility are all hallmarks of this organization. Image courtesy of IDEO

might not only tolerate mistakes but also emphasize the importance of organizational members' being kind and helpful to one another.

Managers who are satisfied with their jobs are committed to their organizations, and experience positive moods and emotions might also encourage these attitudes and feelings in others. The result would be an organizational culture emphasizing positive attitudes and feelings. Research suggests that attitudes like job satisfaction and organizational commitment can be affected by the influence of others. Managers are in a particularly strong position to engage in social influence given their multiple roles. Moreover, research suggests that moods and emotions can be contagious and that spending time with people who are excited and enthusiastic can increase one's own levels of excitement and enthusiasm.

The Role of Values and Norms in Organizational Culture

Shared terminal and instrumental values play a particularly important role in organizational culture. *Terminal values* signify what an organization and its employees are trying to accomplish, and *instrumental values* guide how the organization and its members achieve organizational goals. In addition to values, shared norms also are a key aspect of organizational culture. Recall that norms are unwritten, informal rules or guidelines that prescribe appropriate behavior in particular situations. For example, norms at IDEO include not being critical of others' ideas, coming up with multiple ideas before settling on one, and developing prototypes of new products.[121]

Managers determine and shape organizational culture through the kinds of values and norms they promote in an organization. Some managers, like David Kelley of IDEO, cultivate values and norms that encourage risk taking, creative responses to problems and opportunities, experimentation, tolerance of failure in order to succeed, and autonomy.[122] Top managers at organizations such as Microsoft and Google encourage employees to adopt such values to support their commitment to innovation as a source of competitive advantage.

Other managers, however, might cultivate values and norms that tell employees they should be conservative and cautious in their dealings with others and should consult their superiors before making important decisions or any changes to the status quo. Accountability for actions and decisions is stressed, and detailed records are kept to ensure that policies and procedures are followed. In settings where caution is needed—nuclear power stations, oil refineries, chemical plants, financial institutions, insurance companies—a conservative, cautious approach to making decisions might be appropriate.[123] In a nuclear power plant, for example, the catastrophic consequences of a mistake make a high level of supervision vital. Similarly, in a bank or mutual fund company, the risk of losing investors' money makes a cautious approach to investing appropriate.

Managers of different kinds of organizations deliberately cultivate and develop the organizational values and norms that are best suited to their task and general environments, strategy, or technology. Organizational culture is maintained and transmitted to organizational members through the values of the founder, the process of socialization, ceremonies and rites, and stories and language (see Figure 2.5).

VALUES OF THE FOUNDER From the ASA model just discussed, it is clear that founders of an organization can have profound and long-lasting effects on organizational culture. Founders' values inspire the founders to start their own companies and, in turn, drive the nature of these new companies and their defining characteristics. Thus an organization's founder and his or her terminal and

instrumental values have a substantial influence on the values, norms, and standards of behavior that develop over time within the organization.[124] Founders set the scene for the way cultural values and norms develop because their own values guide the building of the company, and they hire other managers and employees who they believe will share these values and help the organization to attain them. Moreover, new managers quickly learn from the founder what values and norms are appropriate in the organization and thus what is desired of them. Subordinates imitate the style of the founder and, in turn, transmit their values and norms to their subordinates. Gradually, over time, the founder's values and norms permeate the organization.[125]

A founder who requires a great display of respect from subordinates and insists on proprieties, such as formal job titles and formal dress, encourages subordinates to act in this way toward their subordinates. Often, a founder's personal values affect an organization's competitive advantage. For example, McDonald's founder Ray Kroc insisted from the beginning on high standards of customer service and cleanliness at McDonald's restaurants; these became core sources of McDonald's competitive advantage. Similarly, Bill Gates, the founder of Microsoft, pioneered certain cultural values in Microsoft. Employees are expected to be creative and to work hard, but they are encouraged to dress informally and to personalize their offices. Gates also established a host of company events such as cookouts, picnics, and sports events to emphasize to employees the importance of being both an individual and a team player.

SOCIALIZATION Over time, organizational members learn from each other which values are important in an organization and the norms that specify appropriate and inappropriate behaviors. Eventually organizational members behave in accordance with the organization's values and norms—often without realizing they are doing so.

Organizational socialization is the process by which newcomers learn an organization's values and norms and acquire the work behaviors necessary to perform jobs effectively.[126] As a result of their socialization experiences, organizational members internalize an organization's values and norms and behave in accordance with them not only because they think they have to but also because they think these values and norms describe the right and proper way to behave.[127]

At Texas A&M University, for example, all new students are encouraged to go to "Fish Camp" to learn how to be an "Aggie" (the traditional nickname of students at the university). They learn about the ceremonies that have developed over time to commemorate significant events or people in A&M's history. In addition, they learn

organizational socialization The process by which newcomers learn an organization's values and norms and acquire the work behaviors necessary to perform jobs effectively.

how to behave at football games and in class and what it means to be an Aggie. As a result of this highly organized socialization program, by the time new students arrive on campus and start their first semester, they have been socialized into what a Texas A&M student is supposed to do, and they have relatively few problems adjusting to the college environment.

Most organizations have some kind of socialization program to help new employees learn the ropes—the values, norms, and culture of the organization. The military, for example, is well known for the rigorous socialization process it uses to turn raw recruits into trained soldiers. Organizations such as the Walt Disney Company also put new recruits through a rigorous training program to teach them to perform well in their jobs and play their parts in helping Disneyland visitors have fun in a wholesome theme park. New recruits at Disney are called "cast members" and attend Disney University to learn the Disney culture and their parts in it. Disney's culture emphasizes the values of safety, courtesy, entertainment, and efficiency, and these values are brought to life for newcomers at Disney University. Newcomers also learn about the attraction area they will be joining (such as Adventureland or Fantasyland) at Disney University and then receive on-the-job socialization in the area itself from experienced cast members.[128] Through organizational socialization, founders and managers of an organization transmit to employees the cultural values and norms that shape the behavior of organizational members. Thus, the values and norms of founder Walt Disney live on today at Disneyland as newcomers are socialized into the Disney way.

CEREMONIES AND RITES Another way in which managers can create or influence organizational culture is by developing organizational ceremonies and rites—formal events that recognize incidents of importance to the organization as a whole and to specific employees.[129] The most common rites that organizations use to transmit cultural norms and values to their members are rites of passage, of integration, and of enhancement (see Table 2.1).[130]

Rites of passage determine how individuals enter, advance within, and leave the organization. The socialization programs developed by military organizations (such as the U.S. Army) or by large accountancy and law firms are rites of passage. Likewise, the ways in which an organization prepares people for promotion or retirement are rites of passage.

Rites of integration, such as shared announcements of organizational successes, office parties, and company cookouts, build and reinforce common bonds among organizational members. IDEO uses many rites of integration to make its employees feel connected to one another and special. In addition to having wild "end-of-year" celebratory bashes, groups of IDEO employees periodically take time off to go to a sporting event, movie, or meal, or sometimes go on a long bike ride or for a sail. These kinds of shared activities not only reinforce IDEO's culture but also can be a

Table 2.1

Organizational Rites

Type of Rite	Example of Rite	Purpose of Rite
Rite of passage	Induction and basic training	Learn and internalize norms and values
Rite of integration	Office Christmas party	Build common norms and values
Rite of enhancement	Presentation of annual award	Motivate commitment to norms and values

source of inspiration on the job (for example, IDEO has been involved in making movies such as *The Abyss* and *Free Willy*). One 35-member design studio at IDEO led by Dennis Boyle has bimonthly lunch fests with no set agenda—anything goes. While enjoying great food, jokes, and camaraderie, studio members often end up sharing ideas for their latest great products, and the freely flowing conversation that results often leads to creative insights.[131]

A company's annual meeting also may be used as a ritual of integration, offering an opportunity to communicate organizational values to managers, other employees, and shareholders.[132] Walmart, for example, makes its annual stockholders' meeting an extravagant ceremony that celebrates the company's success. The company often flies thousands of its highest-performing employees to its annual meeting at its Bentonville, Arkansas, headquarters for a huge weekend entertainment festival complete with star musical performances. Walmart believes that rewarding its supporters with entertainment reinforces the company's high-performance values and culture. The proceedings are shown live over closed-circuit television in all Walmart stores so all employees can join in the rites celebrating the company's achievements.[133]

Rites of enhancement, such as awards dinners, newspaper releases, and employee promotions, let organizations publicly recognize and reward employees' contributions and thus strengthen their commitment to organizational values. By bonding members within the organization, rites of enhancement reinforce an organization's values and norms.

Stories and language also communicate organizational culture. Stories (whether fact or fiction) about organizational heroes and villains and their actions provide important clues about values and norms. Such stories can reveal the kinds of behaviors that are valued by the organization and the kinds of practices that are frowned on.[134] At the heart of McDonald's rich culture are hundreds of stories that organizational members tell about founder Ray Kroc. Most of these stories focus on how Kroc established the strict operating values and norms that are at the heart of McDonald's culture. Kroc was dedicated to achieving perfection in McDonald's quality, service, cleanliness, and value for money (QSC&V), and these four central values permeate McDonald's culture. For example, an often retold story describes what happened when Kroc and a group of managers from the Houston region were touring various restaurants. One of the restaurants was having a bad day operationally. Kroc was incensed about the long lines of customers, and he was furious when he realized that the products customers were receiving that day were not up to his high standards. To address the problem, he jumped up and stood on the front counter to get the attention of all customers and operating crew personnel. He introduced himself, apologized for the long wait and cold food, and told the customers they could have freshly cooked food or their money back—whichever they wanted. As a result, the customers left happy; and when Kroc checked on the restaurant later, he found that his message had gotten through to its managers and crew—performance had improved. Other stories describe Kroc scrubbing dirty toilets and picking up litter inside or outside a restaurant. These and similar stories are spread around the organization by McDonald's employees. They are the stories that have helped establish Kroc as McDonald's "hero."

Because spoken language is a principal medium of communication in organizations, the characteristic slang or jargon—that is, organization-specific words or phrases—that people use to frame and describe events provides important clues about norms and values. "McLanguage," for example, is prevalent at all levels of McDonald's. A McDonald's employee described as having "ketchup in his or her blood" is someone who is truly dedicated to the McDonald's way—someone who has been completely socialized to its culture. McDonald's has an extensive training program that teaches new employees "McDonald's speak," and new employees are welcomed into the family with a formal orientation that illustrates Kroc's dedication to QSC&V.

The concept of organizational language encompasses not only spoken language but also how people dress, the offices they occupy, the cars they drive, and the degree of formality they use when they address one another. For example, casual dress reflects and reinforces Microsoft's entrepreneurial culture and values. Formal business attire supports the conservative culture found in many banks, which emphasizes the importance of conforming to organizational norms such as respect for authority and staying within one's prescribed role. When employees speak and understand the language of their organization's culture, they know how to behave in the organization and what is expected of them.

At IDEO, language, dress, the physical work environment, and extreme informality all underscore a culture that is adventuresome, playful, risk taking, egalitarian, and innovative. For example, at IDEO, employees refer to taking the consumers' perspective when designing products as "being left-handed." Employees dress in T-shirts and jeans, the physical work environment continually evolves and changes depending on how employees wish to personalize their workspace, no one "owns" a fancy office with a window, and rules are almost nonexistent.[135]

Culture and Managerial Action

While founders and managers play a critical role in developing, maintaining, and communicating organizational culture, this same culture shapes and controls the behavior of all employees, including managers themselves. For example, culture influences how managers perform their four main functions: planning, organizing, leading, and controlling. As we consider these functions, we continue to distinguish between top managers who create organizational values and norms that encourage creative, innovative behavior and top managers who encourage a conservative, cautious approach by their subordinates. We noted earlier that both kinds of values and norms can be appropriate depending on the situation and type of organization.

PLANNING Top managers in an organization with an innovative culture are likely to encourage lower-level managers to participate in the planning process and develop a flexible approach to planning. They are likely to be willing to listen to new ideas and to take risks involving the development of new products. In contrast, top managers in an organization with conservative values are likely to emphasize formal top-down planning. Suggestions from lower-level managers are likely to be subjected to a formal review process, which can significantly slow decision making. Although this deliberate approach may improve the quality of decision making in a nuclear power plant, it can have unintended consequences. In the past, at conservative IBM, the planning process became so formalized that managers spent most of their time assembling complex slide shows and overheads to defend their current positions rather than thinking about what they should do to keep IBM abreast of the changes taking place in the computer industry. When former CEO Lou Gerstner took over, he used every means at his disposal to abolish this culture, even building a brand-new campus-style headquarters to change managers' mind-sets. IBM's culture underwent further changes initiated by its next CEO, Samuel Palmisano, who is now chairman of the board.[136]

ORGANIZING What kinds of organizing will managers in innovative and in conservative cultures encourage? Valuing creativity, managers in innovative cultures are likely to try to create an organic structure—one that is flat, with few levels in the hierarchy, and one in which authority is decentralized so employees are encouraged to work together to solve ongoing problems. A product team structure may be suitable for an organization with an innovative culture. In contrast, managers in a conservative culture are likely to create a well-defined hierarchy of authority and establish clear reporting relationships so employees know exactly whom to report to and how to react to any problems that arise.

LEADING In an innovative culture, managers are likely to lead by example, encouraging employees to take risks and experiment. They are supportive regardless of whether employees succeed or fail. In contrast, managers in a conservative culture are likely to use management by objectives and to constantly monitor subordinates' progress toward goals, overseeing their every move. We examine leadership in detail in Chapter 10 when we consider the leadership styles that managers can adopt to influence and shape employee behavior.

CONTROLLING The ways in which managers evaluate, and take actions to improve, performance differ depending on whether the organizational culture emphasizes formality and caution or innovation and change. Managers who want to encourage risk taking, creativity, and innovation recognize that there are multiple potential paths to success and that failure must be accepted for creativity to thrive. Thus, they are less concerned about employees' performing their jobs in a specific, predetermined manner and in strict adherence to preset goals and more concerned about employees' being flexible and taking the initiative to come up with ideas for improving performance. Managers in innovative cultures are also more concerned about long-term performance than short-term targets because they recognize that real innovation entails much uncertainty that necessitates flexibility. In contrast, managers in cultures that emphasize caution and maintenance of the status quo often set specific, difficult goals for employees, frequently monitor progress toward these goals, and develop a clear set of rules that employees are expected to adhere to.

The values and norms of an organization's culture strongly affect the way managers perform their management functions. The extent to which managers buy into the values and norms of their organization shapes their view of the world and their actions and decisions in particular circumstances. In turn, the actions that managers take can have an impact on the performance of the organization. Thus, organizational culture, managerial action, and organizational performance are all linked together.

While our earlier example of IDEO illustrates how organizational culture can give rise to managerial actions that ultimately benefit the organization, this is not always the case. The cultures of some organizations become dysfunctional, encouraging managerial actions that harm the organization and discouraging actions that might improve performance.[137] Corporate scandals at large companies like Enron, Tyco, and WorldCom show how damaging a dysfunctional culture can be to an organization and its members. For example, Enron's arrogant, "success at all costs" culture led to fraudulent behavior on the part of its top managers.[138] Unfortunately, hundreds of Enron employees paid a heavy price for the unethical behavior of these top managers and the dysfunctional organizational culture. Not only did these employees lose their jobs, but many also lost their life savings in Enron stock and pension funds, which became worth just a fraction of their value before the wrongdoing at Enron came to light. We discuss ethics in depth in the next chapter.

Summary and Review

ENDURING CHARACTERISTICS: PERSONALITY TRAITS Personality traits are enduring tendencies to feel, think, and act in certain ways. The Big Five general traits are extraversion, negative affectivity, agreeableness, conscientiousness, and openness to experience. Other personality traits that affect managerial behavior are locus of control, self-esteem, and the needs for achievement, affiliation, and power. [LO 2-1]

VALUES, ATTITUDES, AND MOODS AND EMOTIONS A terminal value is a personal conviction about lifelong goals or objectives; an instrumental value is a personal conviction about modes of conduct. Terminal and instrumental values have an impact on what managers try to achieve in their organizations and the kinds of behaviors they engage in. An attitude is a collection of feelings and beliefs. Two attitudes important for understanding managerial behaviors include job satisfaction (the collection of feelings and beliefs that managers have about their jobs) and organizational commitment (the collection of feelings and beliefs that managers have about their organizations). A mood is a feeling or state of mind; emotions are intense feelings that are short-lived and directly linked to their causes. Managers' moods and emotions, or how they feel at work on a day-to-day basis, have the potential to impact not only their own behavior and effectiveness but also those of their subordinates. Emotional intelligence is the ability to understand and manage one's own and other people's moods and emotions. [LO 2-2, 2-3, 2-4]

ORGANIZATIONAL CULTURE Organizational culture is the shared set of beliefs, expectations, values, norms, and work routines that influence how members of an organization relate to one another and work together to achieve organizational goals. Founders of new organizations and managers play an important role in creating and maintaining organizational culture. Organizational socialization is the process by which newcomers learn an organization's values and norms and acquire the work behaviors necessary to perform jobs effectively. [LO 2-5]

Management *in Action*

 TOPICS FOR DISCUSSION AND ACTION

Discussion

1. Discuss why managers who have different types of personalities can be equally effective and successful. [LO 2-1]

2. Can managers be too satisfied with their jobs? Can they be too committed to their organizations? Why or why not? [LO 2-2]

3. Assume that you are a manager of a restaurant. Describe what it is like to work for you when you are in a negative mood. [LO 2-3]

4. Why might managers be disadvantaged by low levels of emotional intelligence? [LO 2-4]

Action

5. Interview a manager in a local organization. Ask the manager to describe situations in which

he or she is especially likely to act in accordance with his or her values. Ask the manager to describe situations in which he or she is less likely to act in accordance with his or her values. [LO 2-2]

6. Watch a popular television show, and as you watch it, try to determine the emotional intelligence levels of the characters the actors in the show portray. Rank the characters from highest to lowest in terms of emotional intelligence. As you watched the show, what factors influenced your assessments of emotional intelligence levels? [LO 2-4]

7. Go to an upscale clothing store in your neighborhood, and go to a clothing store that is definitely not upscale. Observe the behavior of employees in each store as well as the store's environment. In what ways are the organizational cultures in each store similar? In what ways are they different? [LO 2-5]

BUILDING MANAGEMENT SKILLS
Diagnosing Culture [LO 2-5]

Think about the culture of the last organization you worked for, your current university, or another organization or club to which you belong. Then answer the following questions:

1. What values are emphasized in this culture?

2. What norms do members of this organization follow?

3. Who seems to have played an important role in creating the culture?

4. In what ways is the organizational culture communicated to organizational members?

MANAGING ETHICALLY [LO 2-1, 2-2]

Some organizations rely on personality and interest inventories to screen potential employees. Other organizations attempt to screen employees by using paper-and-pencil honvesty tests.

Questions

1. Either individually or in a group, think about the ethical implications of using personality and interest inventories to screen potential employees. How might this practice be unfair to potential applicants? How might organizational members who are in charge of hiring misuse it?

2. Because of measurement error and validity problems, some relatively trustworthy people may "fail" an honesty test given by an employer. What are the ethical implications of trustworthy people "failing" honesty tests, and what obligations do you think employers should have when relying on honesty tests for screening?

SMALL GROUP BREAKOUT EXERCISE [LO 2-2, 2-3, 2-4, 2-5]
Making Difficult Decisions in Hard Times

Form groups of three or four people, and appoint one member as the spokesperson who will communicate your findings to the whole class when called on by the instructor. Then discuss the following scenario:

You are on the top management team of a medium-sized company that manufactures cardboard boxes, containers, and other cardboard packaging materials. Your company is facing increasing levels of competition for major corporate customer accounts, and profits have declined significantly. You have tried everything you can to cut costs and remain competitive, with the exception of laying off employees. Your company has had a no-layoff policy for the past 20 years, and you believe that it is an important part of the organization's culture. However, you are experiencing mounting pressure to increase your firm's performance, and your no-layoff policy has been questioned by shareholders. Even though you haven't decided whether to lay off employees and thus break with a 20-year tradition for your company, rumors are rampant in your organization that something is afoot, and employees are worried. You are meeting today to address this problem.

1. Develop a list of options and potential courses of action to address the heightened competition and decline in profitability that your company has been experiencing.

2. Choose your preferred course of action, and justify why you will take this route.

3. Describe how you will communicate your decision to employees.

4. If your preferred option involves a layoff, justify why. If it doesn't involve a layoff, explain why.

BE THE MANAGER [LO 2-1, 2-2, 2-3, 2-4, 2-5]

You have recently been hired as the vice president for human resources in an advertising agency. One problem that has been brought to your attention is the fact that the creative departments at the agency have dysfunctionally high levels of conflict. You have spoken with members of each of these departments, and in each one it seems that a few members of the department are creating all the problems. All these individuals are valued contributors who have many creative ad campaigns to their credit. The high levels of conflict are creating problems in the departments, and negative moods and emotions are much more prevalent than positive feelings. What are you going to do to both retain valued employees and alleviate the excessive conflict and negative feelings in these departments?

BLOOMBERG BUSINESSWEEK CASE IN THE NEWS [LO2-1, 2-2, 2-5]

Wipe Off That Smile: An Amazon Veteran Is Launching a Shopping Site That Is Part Costco, Part Mall, and All Anti-Amazon

The historic downtown commercial district of Montclair, N.J., is known for its restaurants, antique shops, and art-house movie theater. It's not usually home to lavishly funded attacks on the entrenched giants of global e-commerce. Yet on the second floor of a three-story red-brick building on Bloom-field Avenue, across a parking lot from a fancy pizza joint and up an unmarked stairwell, are the offices of one of the biggest bets in the history of online retail: a 100-employee startup called jet.com.

Jet is the brainchild of Marc Lore, the founder and former chief executive officer of Quidsi, a company best known for its most popular website, Diapers.com. He spent years competing with Amazon.com before getting clobbered in a price war and then, in 2010, selling out to the company for $550 million. Lore stayed on at Amazon for more than two years; now he's preparing to assault it.

"We're basically not making a dime on any of the transac we're passing it all back to the consumer"

He wants to reinvent the wholesale shopping club. Jet plans to open for business on a "friends-and-family" basis in January and will start limited sign-ups on February 20. Customers will find just about everything, from clothes, books, and electronics to baby goods and athletic gear. After a 90-day free trial period, Jet customers will be asked to pay $49.99 a year for access to what Lore claims will be prices that are 10 percent to 15 percent lower than anywhere else online.

Like Costco, Jet plans to make money on membership fees. Every other savings will be passed along to the buyer. And like EBay and the dominant Chinese e-commerce player, Alibaba.com, it will function primarily as a marketplace, allowing other merchants to compete to offer their wares to customers. But there's a twist: Shoppers can squeeze out more savings if they can control the urge for instant gratification and let Jet figure out how to deliver the goods as economically as possible. For example, prices can drop when a shopper combines multiple orders into a single shipment or is willing to wait for a seller offering a more economical shipping option.

"The bottom line is, we're basically not making a dime on any of the transactions. We're passing it all back to the consumer," Lore says from a conference room in his Montclair headquarters. "We want to build a different type of relationship with the consumer. When we show you a product, it's not because we are making money on it and not because we are closing out a line. It's because we think it's a good deal."

Lore reassembled members of his old Quidsi band and has raised one of the largest seed funding rounds of all time. Before completing a single sale, he's collected $80 million from venture capital firms NEA, Bain Capital Ventures, Western Technology Investment, and Accel Partners, the firm that backed Facebook, and plans to raise hundreds of millions more. It may be the riskiest bet on an unproven e-commerce business model since Amazon itself raised billions in debt in the late '90s, when it was still highly unprofitable.

"This idea is massive," says Patrick Lee, a partner at Western Technology Investment. "If Marc is right on this one, it will be multiple times bigger than Quidsi ever was."

Lore founded Quidsi in 2005 with his childhood friend Vinit Bharara and built it while Amazon focused on media categories and hard goods like TVs and kitchenware. Lore and Bharara built a reputation for excellent service, adding a personal touch that resonated with customers. Diapers and other necessities, packed in blue, red, and green boxes—often with a handwritten note inside—arrived promptly at the doorsteps of grateful new parents. By 2010, Quidsi was pulling in about $300 million in annual sales.

Then Amazon took notice of Quidsi's rise and, in the fall of that year, cut diaper prices by a third. Lore calculated at one point that Amazon was on track to lose $100 million over three months on diapers alone. Quidsi's profitability sank, and Lore was forced to sell out to Amazon during the Great Recession, when additional capital to fund the fight was impossible to obtain.

Lore and Bharara spent a little less than two and a half years inside Amazon. (Bharara is an investor in Jet but has founded his own startup, online magazine Cafe.com.) Lore, whose default mode is tactful and earnest, tries to steer away from criticizing Amazon but frequently can't help himself. "I felt like I did everything I could do there," he says. "Little by little, they started wanting more and more control."

A few weeks after Lore left, Amazon cut out the distinctive colored delivery boxes. It was a move to reduce costs, but to Lore it symbolized an operating philosophy he doesn't share. "It was a superlogical decision, and I'm sure the numbers worked out fine," he says. "But you can't put a number on what it means to create a personal connection to the consumer."

Lore watched these moves from afar, as he was trying and failing at an early retirement. He has two teenage daughters and, after he left Amazon, spent a few months with his family living in California wine country. He also invested in Lot18, a wine delivery company, though he sold his stake back to the company when he realized he had ideas about the business but as a passive investor couldn't actually see them through.

It was there in Northern California, amid the rolling vineyards, that Lore had what he considers his e-commerce epiphany. Big players like Amazon, walmart.com, and Google are all scrambling to offer the fastest possible service, catering to today's typical wealthier-than-average online shoppers who care more about convenience than value. Although shipping can appear to be free, it's often baked in as higher prices. "There's this huge middle class of people that are going to be spending more and more dollars online, and for them it's going to be all about price," Lore says.

He took inspiration from Costco, which invented a new category of discount retail, the members-only warehouse. It saved money by locating its cavernous, no-frills stores in out-of-the-way places and stocking them with a limited variety of supersize products—and it passed those savings on to shoppers in the form of lower prices. Costco, Sam's Club, and other chains now have more than 100 million paying members in the United States.

A few weeks after he left Amazon, Lore had lunch in New York with Sameer Gandhi at Accel and said he wanted to bring the membership-based shopping club model online. It was just a germ of an idea, but Gandhi wrote him a check for $1 million anyway because Lore had a record of making and then delivering on big promises. "When you are ready to do it, here is your seed money," Gandhi told him.

Lore's first task was finding new ways to squeeze costs out of e-commerce transactions. He started with packaging and shipping. With Jet.com, customers will be able to make multiple online purchases from a range of sellers and combine the merchandise in one box, which is then cheaper to ship. Jet turns these savings over to the customer. When Jet.com members add more items to their shopping cart, they'll see the price for each product fall.

The trick will be to persuade shoppers to load up their carts instead of buying individual items impulsively. "We need to open people's eyes a little bit," says Mike Hanrahan, a former executive at Quidsi and now Jet's chief technology officer. "If we can educate them that, 'Look, instead of buying one thing every week, come back every two weeks and buy two things and you will save a few percent,' it's actually a lot of money."

Buyers will also save by being offered items from sellers located near them. In a perfectly efficient online transaction, customers would buy only after filling their digital carts from nearby stores. Jet is more likely to emphasize merchandise that is physically close to the buyer and, again, pass the savings along.

The Jet model wouldn't have worked a few years ago, but now that nearly every merchant is online and looking for new ways to compete with the likes of Amazon, it might. So far, Jet has signed up Sony Store, electronics retailer TigerDirect.com, Sears Hometown & Outlet Stores, and hundreds of smaller retailers. BabyAge, a Jet.com seller based in Jenkins Township, Pa., spends $5 to ship to the East Coast, on average, and $15 to California. Usually the site sets prices that cover the highest possible shipping costs. But using a set of online pricing tools that Jet is making available to its sellers, it can reward the most efficient transactions. For example, a Graco stroller that might cost $119 on Amazon will cost $108 for anyone on Jet buying from BabyAge in the Northeast. "This is going to produce regional specialty in e-commerce, because now I'll be able to sell for less than Amazon," says Jack Kiefer, the company's CEO.

Jet customers will get to choose whether to use a debit card instead of a credit card, and if they do, once again they'll watch the prices for individual products fall by roughly 1.5 percent. Similarly they'll have the choice to opt for delivery times of a week or more and to tap the savings that come from shipping via ground instead of air. Jet itself will sell some high-volume items such as diapers, dog food, and paper towels from fulfillment centers in Reno, Nev., and Swedesboro, N.J.

Because software can be used to track every possible decision they make on the site, customers will be able to watch their savings add up and judge whether it's worth the annual fee. "It's going to be a no-brainer," Lore claims. "Every household in America should have a Jet membership. Why not spend $50 bucks to save $200?"

Lore, 43, is that rarest of tech entrepreneurs, a very Jersey guy who's as much a student of Bruce Springsteen as Steve Jobs. He spent his early years on Staten Island, before his family moved to Lincroft, N.J., while he was in middle school. His father owned a computer consulting firm, and his mother raised the kids—Lore has two younger siblings. His parents fought frequently, to which he attributes his visceral distaste for conflict.

"If someone is unhappy here and doesn't see an opportunity for growth, OK, good luck, go to Wal-Mart"

Lore was showing an entrepreneurial bent by age 6, when he charged family members 5¢ each to watch Casper the Friendly Ghost on a slide projector; he came up with a story for each frame. By 14 he was trading stocks using his parents' money and buying and selling baseball cards at trade shows.

Bharara, his childhood friend, calls Lore "a human calculator" who's almost eerily talented with numbers. Lore didn't apply himself in high school, however, frequently opting to sneak down to the casinos in Atlantic City and count cards in blackjack. His track coach, fearing that Lore might flunk out of high school during his junior year, refused to let him train until he improved his grades. Something clicked, and Lore raised his grade point average to 3.9 and got a near-perfect score on his math SAT. He got into Bucknell University and became the first member of his family to attend college.

After graduation, Lore spent a few years working in risk management for Bankers Trust and Credit Suisse First Boston in New York and then for Japan's Sanwa Bank in London, raising red flags on chancy trades and generally getting ignored by the hotshot traders who were making a killing with credit-default swaps and other newfangled derivatives. One morning when he was 27 years old, Lore fell to the floor in his office, feeling an electric jolt in his chest. It was stress and the result of overwork, not a heart attack, but Lore got the message, left finance, and started following his entrepreneurial passions.

His first company, The Pit, let sports fans value and trade sports collectibles like shares of stock. He sold the business to the Topps trading card company in 2001 for a modest $5.7 million, less than 12 months after starting it. Lore moved to seattle to run a division of Topps, which is why, a few years later, he found himself at a picnic for his daughter's private school, hobnobbing with another school parent: Jeff Bezos.

Lore had just started Quidsi, then called 1800Diapers, and at the barbecue he joked to Bezos, "I hope to give you a run for your money." Bezos didn't seem to remember that encounter years later, when they met again after Amazon acquired Quidsi.

Lore says he has "no bad feelings toward Jeff and Amazon." But in many ways he has conceived of Jet.com's culture as the antithesis of Amazon's, which is known for its confrontational style, internal secrecy, and deliberate avoidance of friendly consensus. It also requires employees to sign noncompete agreements and, in fact, locked Lore into one that expires early this year.

At Jet, there will be no annual performance reviews, because Lore thinks feedback should be immediate and civil. Board presentations are posted online for the entire company to see. And Lore isn't making any of his employees sign noncompetes; he says that "what goes around comes around," and that without such stipulations "there's more loyalty and trust that is built."

"If someone is unhappy here and doesn't see an opportunity for growth, OK, good luck, go to Wal-Mart," he says. "I want to prove to myself that a different kind of culture can work and that you don't have to be like that to be successful."

The implicit criticism of Amazon, the company that nearly drove Quidsi out of business but eventually made Lore wealthy, isn't lost on some outside observers. "There's definitely a history of folks being acquired by Amazon, living inside it, learning from it, and coming out with a bit of a chip on their shoulder," says Scot Wingo, who's CEO of ChannelAdvisor, a company that helps other retailers sell online and has been briefed on Jet. "They go inside, and it creates a bit of animosity when they come out."

Jet is building new offices in Hoboken, on the Hudson River overlooking the Manhattan skyline, which should be ready shortly after the site goes nationwide in March. The floor plan will be completely open. Lore himself won't have a desk; he says he'll roam between meetings.

The startup's success is hardly assured. Sellers won't come to the service until it's got customers, and to get those it has to persuade many online shoppers, who are quite satisfied hunting for bargains at Wal-Mart, EBay, and Amazon, to try something new and pony up $50 for the privilege. (Jet.com plans to use much of its seed money on a massive branding campaign that will feature television, radio, and outdoor advertising.) "It's extremely hard to change people's behavior, though they proved with Diapers.com that they could get millions of people to buy diapers from them," says Wingo.

There's also the possibility that Lore's powerful competitors will see Jet's price cuts and respond by going even lower. Amazon did that before and drove Diapers.com into the red. Lore is betting in part that, this time, Amazon simply has its hands full. Bezos's company is spending billions to expand in India and China while continuing expensive forays into cloud computing and hardware such as its Kindle Fire phones. Bezos could cut prices, but that would exacerbate Amazon's losses at a time when investors are already showing impatience: Amazon stock fell 22 percent in 2014.

Either way, Lore will probably need a lot more capital. He's talking to Google Ventures and other investors about raising a second round of funding. He may also find interest abroad—China's Alibaba and Japan's Rakuten are both looking for ways to enter the U.S. market. "He has the ability to raise capital like no one I've ever seen," says Bharara of his friend. "I mean that in the best way. He sells using math together with a big vision and the ability to execute it. It's a very powerful combination."

Lore's investors, many of whom hit it big on Quidsi, seem almost giddy about the size and risks of the bet. "All of us in the investment syndicate realized that if this was going to succeed, it needed to have significant resources," says Accel's Gandhi. "It's the kind of thing we all like to do: very ambitious and full of things that can go wrong."

Questions

1. How would you describe Marc Lore's personality in terms of the Big Five personality traits?

2. How would you describe Marc Lore's personality in terms of the other personality traits that affect managerial behavior?

3. Which terminal and instrumental values do you think might be especially important to him?

4. In what ways do you think that Lore will influence the culture at jet.com?

Source: Brad Stone, "Wipe Off That Smile: An Amazon Veteran Is Launching a Shopping Site That's Part Costco, Part Mall, and All Anti-Amazon," *Bloomberg Businessweek,* January 12–18, 2015, pp. 42–47.

Endnotes

1. A. Bryant, "In a Corporate Culture, It's a Gift to Be Simple," *The New York Times,* November 22, 2013, B2; L. Dishman, "What's In Store: How Polyvore's Stylish Social Commerce Is Cracking Retail 3.0," *Forbes,* www.forbes.com/sites/lydiadishman/2012/12/21/whats-in-store-how-polyvores-stylish-social-commerce-is-cracking-retail-3-0/, February 21, 2014.; About—Polyvore, www.polyvore.com/cgi/about, February 21, 2014.; L. Orsini,"The Art of Technology and Vice Versa: Polyvore's Jess Lee," *ReadWrite,* www.readwrite.com/2013/09/16/polyvore-jess-lee-art-technology-fashion-design-builders#feed=/series/builders&awesm=~ozruSxdDwrOX2T, February 21, 2014.

2. Bryant, "In a Corporate Culture, It's a Gift to Be Simple."

3. Ibid.; L. Dishman, "Polyvore's Jess Lee Turns Fashion Lovers into Style Trendsetters," *Fast Company,* www.fastcompany.com/1793703/polyvores-jess-lee-turns-fashion-lovers-style-trendsetters, February 21, 2014.

4. Orsini, "The Art of Technology and Vice Versa: Polyvore's Jess Lee"; Dishman, "Polyvore's Jess Lee Turns Fashion Lovers into Style Trendsetters"; A. Preiser, "Polyvore Takes on the Home," *ELLE Decor,* www.elledecor.com/shopping/shop-talk/polyvore-home-decor, February 21, 2014.

5. Orsini, "The Art of Technology and Vice Versa: Polyvore's Jess Lee."

6. Bryant, "In a Corporate Culture, It's a Gift to Be Simple."

7. Ibid.; "Jess Lee Co-Founder and CEO," www.polyvore.com/cgi/about.team, February 18, 2015.

8. V.A. Kansara, "Founder Stories: Jess Lee's Journey from Polyvore Superuser to CEO," *Business of Fashion,* www.businessoffashion.com/2013/08/founder-stories-jess-lees-journey-from-polyvore-superuser-to-ceo-marissa-mayer-google.html, February 21, 2014.

9. L. Dishman, "What's in Store: How Polyvore's Stylish Social Commerce Is Cracking Retail 3.0," *Forbes,* www.forbes.com/sites/lydiadishman/2012/12/21/whats-in-store-how-polyvores-stylish-social-commerce-is-cracking-retail-3-0/, February 21, 2014.; J. Graham, "Polyvore Releases iPad App," *USA Today,* www.usatoday.com/story/tech/columnist/talkingtech/2013/10/31/polyvore-releases-ipad-app/3296915/, February 21, 2014.

10. J. Xavier, "Hackers' Way Meets Runway: Silicon Valley Startups Take Aim at Fashion Industry," *Silicon Valley Business Journals,* www.bizjournals.com/sanjose/print-edition/2014/02/21/hackers-way-meets-runway-fashion.html, February 21, 2014.

11. K. Liyakasa, "Polyvore: Connecting Commerce to the Sphere of Social Data," *AdExchanger,* www.adexchanger.com/ecommerce-2/polyvore-connecting-commerce-to-the-sphere-of-social-data/, February 21, 2014.

12. About—Polyvore, www.polyvore.com/cgi/about, February 21, 2014.; C. Gregoire, "This CEO's Secret to a Happy, Productive Workplace—and Game-Changing Innovation," *Huffington Post,* www.huffingtonpost.com/2013/08/14/the-simple-trick-that-mad_n_3742942.html, February 21, 2014.

13. About—Polyvore, www.polyvore.com/cgi/about, February 21, 2014.

14. A. Bryant, "In a Corporate Culture, It's a Gift to Be Simple," *The New York Times,* November 22, 2013, B2.

15. About—Polyvore.

16. Orsini,"The Art of Technology and Vice Versa: Polyvore's Jess Lee."

17. Techlicious / E. Harper, "The 5 Best Sites for One-Stop Online Shopping," *Time,* www.techland.time.com/2013/12/03/the-5-best-sites-for-one-stop-online-shopping/, March 11, 2014.

18. Bryant, "In a Corporate Culture, It's a Gift to Be Simple."

19. S. Carpenter, "Different Dispositions, Different Brains," *Monitor on Psychology,* February 2001, 66–68.

20. J.M. Digman, "Personality Structure: Emergence of the Five-Factor Model," *Annual Review of Psychology* 41 (1990), 417–40; R.R. McCrae and P.T. Costa, "Validation of the Five-Factor Model of Personality across Instruments and Observers," *Journal of Personality and Social Psychology* 52 (1987), 81–90; R.R. McCrae and P.T. Costa, "Discriminant Validity of NEO-PIR Facet Scales," *Educational and Psychological Measurement* 52 (1992), 229–37.

21. Digman, "Personality Structure"; McCrae and Costa, "Validation of the Five-Factor Model"; McCrae and Costa, "Discriminant Validity"; R.P. Tett and D.D. Burnett, "A Personality Trait-Based Interactionist Model of Job Performance," *Journal of Applied Psychology* 88, no. 3 (2003), 500–17; J.M. George, "Personality, Five-Factor Model," in S. Clegg and J.R. Bailey, eds., *International Encyclopedia of Organization Studies* (Thousand Oaks, CA: Sage, 2007).

22. L.A. Witt and G.R. Ferris, "Social Skills as Moderator of Conscientiousness–Performance Relationship: Convergent Results across Four Studies," *Journal of Applied Psychology* 88, no. 5 (2003), 809–20; M.J. Simmering, J.A. Colquitte, R.A. Noe, and C.O.L.H. Porter, "Conscientiousness, Autonomy Fit, and Development: A Longitudinal Study," *Journal of Applied Psychology* 88, no. 5 (2003), 954–63.

23. M.R. Barrick and M.K. Mount, "The Big Five Personality Dimensions and Job Performance: A Meta-Analysis," *Personnel Psychology* 44 (1991), 1–26; S. Komar, D.J. Brown, J.A. Komar, and C. Robie, "Faking and the Validity of Conscientiousness: A Monte Carlo Investigation," *Journal of Applied Psychology* 93 (2008), 140–54.

24. Digman, "Personality Structure"; McCrae and Costa, "Validation of the Five-Factor Model"; McCrae and Costa, "Discriminant Validity."

25. Under Armour, Inc.—Executive Team, www.investor.underarmour.com/management.cfm, March 12, 2014; "Under Armour Reports Full Year New Revenues Growth of 32%; Announces Creation of World's Largest Digital Health and Fitness

Community," www.vabiz.com/releasedetail.cfm?ReleaseID=894686, February 18, 2015.

26. D. Roberts, "Under Armour Gets Serious," *Fortune,* November 7, 2011, 152–62; K. Plank, as told to Mark Hyman, "How I Did It: Kevin Plank: For the Founder of Apparel-Maker Under Armour, Entrepreneurship Is 99% Perspiration and 1% Polyester," *Inc.,* www.inc.com/magazine/20031201/howididit_Printer_Friendly.html, March 26, 2012.

27. Roberts, "Under Armour Gets Serious"; Plank, as told to Mark Hyman, "How I Did It"; "Under Armour's Kevin Plank: Creating the Biggest, Baddest Brand on the Planet," *Knowledge@Wharton,* January 5, 2011, www.knowledge.wharton.upenn.edu/printer_friendly.cfm?articleid=2665, March 26, 2012; "2011 Under Armour Annual Report," Under Armour, Inc.—Annual Report & Proxy, www.investor.underarmour.com/annuals.cfm?sh_print=yes&, March 30, 2012.

28. Roberts, "Under Armour Gets Serious."

29. "Under Armour Reports Fourth Quarter Net Revenues Growth of 35% and Full Year Net Revenues Growth of 27%; Raises Full Year 2014 Outlook," www.investor.underarmour.com/releasedetail.cfm?ReleaseID=821996, March 12, 2014; "Under Armour Reports Full Year Revenues Growth of 32%."

30. Roberts, "Under Armour Gets Serious"; "Creating the Biggest, Baddest Brand on the Planet."

31. Roberts, "Under Armour Gets Serious."

32. Roberts, "Under Armour Gets Serious."

33. "2011 Under Armour Annual Report."

34. "2011 Under Armour Annual Report."

35. Roberts, "Under Armour Gets Serious."; M. Urger, "Shining Armour," baltimoremagazine.net, August 2013, 173–77, 244, 245.

36. Roberts, "Under Armour Gets Serious"; "Creating the Biggest, Baddest Brand on the Planet."

37. Roberts, "Under Armour Gets Serious."

38. J.B. Rotter, "Generalized Expectancies for Internal versus External Control of Reinforcement," *Psychological Monographs* 80 (1966), 1–28; P. Spector, "Behaviors in Organizations as a Function of Employees' Locus of Control," *Psychological Bulletin* 91 (1982), 482–97.

39. J. Brockner, *Self-Esteem at Work* (Lexington, MA: Lexington Books, 1988).

40. D.C. McClelland, *Human Motivation* (Glenview, IL: Scott, Foresman, 1985); D.C. McClelland, "How Motives, Skills, and Values Determine What People Do," *American Psychologist* 40 (1985), 812–25; D.C. McClelland, "Managing Motivation to Expand Human Freedom," *American Psychologist* 33 (1978), 201–10.

41. D.G. Winter, *The Power Motive* (New York: Free Press 1973).

42. M.J. Stahl, "Achievement, Power, and Managerial Motivation: Selecting Managerial Talent with the Job Choice Exercise," *Personnel Psychology* 36 (1983), 775–89; D.C. McClelland and D.H. Burnham, "Power Is the Great Motivator," *Harvard Business Review* 54 (1976), 100–110.

43. R.J. House, W.D. Spangler, and J. Woycke, "Personality and Charisma in the U.S. Presidency: A Psychological Theory of Leader Effectiveness," *Administrative Science Quarterly* 36 (1991), 364–96.

44. G.H. Hines, "Achievement, Motivation, Occupations and Labor Turnover in New Zealand," *Journal of Applied Psychology* 58 (1973), 313–17; P.S. Hundal, "A Study of Entrepreneurial Motivation: Comparison of Fast- and Slow-Progressing Small Scale Industrial Entrepreneurs in Punjab, India," *Journal of Applied Psychology* 55 (1971), 317–23.

45. M. Rokeach, *The Nature of Human Values* (New York: Free Press 1973).

46. Ibid.

47. Ibid.

48. M. Rokeach, *The Nature of Human Values* (New York: Free Press, 1973).

49. Ibid.

50. Ibid.

51. Ibid.

52. Ibid.

53. K.K. Spors, "Top Small Workplaces 2007: Gentle Giant Moving," *The Wall Street Journal,* October 1, 2007, R4–R5; "Gentle Giant Sees Revenue Boost, *Boston Business Journal,* January 15, 2008, www.gentlegiant.com/news-011508-1.htm, February 5, 2008; Company History: Gentle Giant Moving Company, "Company History," www.gentlegiant.com/history.php, February 3, 2010; "Massachusetts Moving Company Gentle Giant Moving Company Celebrates 30 Years in Operation," January 25, 2010, www.gentlegiant.com/press/press20100125.php, February 3, 2010.

54. Spors, "Top Small Workplaces 2007"; Full Service Moving Company—Gentle Giant History, www.gentlegiant.com/moving-companies/full-service-moving.aspx, March 13, 2014.; Chicago Movers—Gentle Giant Moving Company, www.gentlegiant.com/Locations/Illinois.aspx, March 13, 2014; "History of Gentle Giant," www.gentlegiant.com/moving-companies/full-service-moving.aspx, February 18, 2015.

55. Full Service Moving Company—Gentle Giant History, www.gentlegiant.com/moving-companies/full-service-moving.aspx, March 30, 2012; R. Libby, branch manager, Providence, RI, www.gentlegiant.com/moving-companies/furniture-movers/ryan-libby.aspx, March 13, 2014.

56. Libby, "Moving Services and Moving Tips from Gentle Giant Moving Company."

57. Spors, "Top Small Workplaces 2007."

58. Ibid.

59. Spors, "Top Small Workplaces 2007"; "Gentle Giant Receives Top Small Workplace Award," www.gentlegiant.com/topsmallworkplace.htm, January 5, 2008; "Corporate Overview," www.gentlegiant.com/company.php, February 3, 2010.

60. Spors, "Top Small Workplaces 2007."

61. Ibid.

62. A.P. Brief, *Attitudes In and Around Organizations* (Thousand Oaks, CA: Sage, 1998).

63. P.S. Goodman, "U.S. Job Losses in December Dim Hopes for Quick

Upswing," *The New York Times,* www.nytimes.com/2010/01/09/business/economy/09jobs.html?pagewanted=print, February 3, 2010; U.S. Bureau of Labor Statistics, "Economic News Release Employment Situations Summary," www.data.bls.gov/cgi-bin/print.pl/news.release/empsit.nr0.htm, February 3, 2010; B. Steverman, "Layoffs: Short-Term Profits, Long-Term Problems," *BusinessWeek,* www.businessweek.com/print/investor/content/jan2010/pi20100113_133780.htm, February 3, 2010.

64. J. Aversa, "Americans' Job Satisfaction Falls to Record Low," www.news.yahoo.com/s/ap/20100105/ap_on_bi_ge/us_unhappy_workers/print, February 3, 2010.

65. The Conference Board, press release/news, "U.S. Job Satisfaction at Lowest Level in Two Decades," January 5, 2010, www.conference-board.org/utilities/pressPrinterFriendly.cfm?press_ID=3820, February 3, 2010.

66. Aversa, "Americans' Job Satisfaction"; Conference Board, press release/news, "U.S. Job Satisfaction."

67. Ibid.

68. Ibid.

69. G. Levanon, "The Determinants of Job Satisfaction," www.hcexchange.conference-board.org/blog/post.cfm?post=1927, March 13, 2014.

70. Job Satisfaction: 2013 Edition—The Conference Board, www.conference-board.org/publications/publicationdetail.cfm?publicationid=2522, March 13, 2014.

71. Levanon, "The Determinants of Job Satisfaction."

72. D.W. Organ, *Organizational Citizenship Behavior: The Good Soldier Syndrome* (Lexington, MA: Lexington Books, 1988).

73. J.M. George and A.P. Brief, "Feeling Good—Doing Good: A Conceptual Analysis of the Mood at Work—Organizational Spontaneity Relationship," *Psychological Bulletin* 112 (1992), 310–29.

74. W.H. Mobley, "Intermediate Linkages in the Relationship between Job Satisfaction and Employee Turnover," *Journal of Applied Psychology* 62 (1977), 237–40.

75. C. Hymowitz, "Though Now Routine, Bosses Still Stumble during Layoff Process," *The Wall Street Journal,* June 25, 2007, B1; J. Brockner, "The Effects of Work Layoffs on Survivors: Research, Theory and Practice," in B.M. Staw and L.L. Cummings, eds., *Research in Organizational Behavior,* vol. 10 (Greenwich, CT: JAI Press, 1988), 213–55.

76. Hymowitz, "Though Now Routine."

77. Ibid.

78. Ibid.

79. Goodman, "U.S. Job Losses in December Dim Hopes for Quick Upswing."

80. M. Luo, "For Small Employers, Rounds of Shedding Workers and Tears," *The New York Times,* May 7, 2009, A1, A3.

81. Luo, "Rounds of Shedding Workers and Tears."

82. Ibid.

83. N. Solinger, W. van Olffen, and R.A. Roe, "Beyond the Three-Component Model of Organizational Commitment," *Journal of Applied Psychology* 93 (2008), 70–83.

84. J.E. Mathieu and D.M. Zajac, "A Review and Meta-Analysis of the Antecedents, Correlates, and Consequences of Organizational Commitment," *Psychological Bulletin* 108 (1990), 171–94.

85. D. Watson and A. Tellegen, "Toward a Consensual Structure of Mood," *Psychological Bulletin* 98 (1985), 219–35.

86. Watson and Tellegen, "Toward a Consensual Structure of Mood."

87. J.M. George, "The Role of Personality in Organizational Life: Issues and Evidence," *Journal of Management* 18 (1992), 185–213.

88. H.A. Elfenbein, "Emotion in Organizations: A Review and Theoretical Integration," in J.P. Walsh and A.P. Brief, eds., *The Academy of Management Annals,* vol. 1 (New York: Lawrence Erlbaum Associates, 2008), 315–86.

89. J.P. Forgas, "Affect in Social Judgments and Decisions: A Multi-Process Model," in M. Zanna, ed., *Advances in Experimental and Social Psychology,* vol. 25 (San Diego, CA: Academic Press, 1992), 227–75; J.P. Forgas and J.M. George, "Affective Influences on Judgments and Behavior in Organizations: An Information Processing Perspective," *Organizational Behavior and Human Decision Processes* 86 (2001), 3–34; J.M. George, "Emotions and Leadership: The Role of Emotional Intelligence," *Human Relations* 53 (2000), 1027–55; W.N. Morris, *Mood: The Frame of Mind* (New York: Springer-Verlag, 1989).

90. George, "Emotions and Leadership."

91. J.M. George and K. Bettenhausen, "Understanding Prosocial Behavior, Sales Performance, and Turnover: A Group Level Analysis in a Service Context," *Journal of Applied Psychology* 75 (1990), 698–709.

92. George and Brief, "Feeling Good—Doing Good"; J.M. George and J. Zhou, "Understanding When Bad Moods Foster Creativity and Good Ones Don't: The Role of Context and Clarity of Feelings," paper presented at the Academy of Management Annual Meeting, 2001; A.M. Isen and R.A. Baron, "Positive Affect as a Factor in Organizational Behavior," in B.M. Staw and L.L. Cummings, eds., *Research in Organizational Behavior,* vol. 13 (Greenwich, CT: JAI Press, 1991), 1–53.

93. J.M. George and J. Zhou, "Dual Tuning in a Supportive Context: Joint Contributions of Positive Mood, Negative Mood, and Supervisory Behaviors to Employee Creativity," *Academy of Management Journal* 50 (2007), 605–22; J.M. George, "Creativity in Organizations," in J.P. Walsh and A.P. Brief, eds., *The Academy of Management Annals,* vol. 1 (New York: Lawrence Erlbaum Associates, 2008), 439–77.

94. J.D. Greene, R.B. Sommerville, L.E. Nystrom, J.M. Darley, and J.D. Cohen, "An FMRI Investigation of Emotional Engagement in Moral Judgment," *Science,* September 14, 2001, 2105–08; L. Neergaard, "Brain Scans Show Emotions Key to Resolving Ethical Dilemmas," *Houston Chronicle,* September 14, 2001, 13A.

95. George and Zhou, "Dual Tuning in a Supportive Context."

96. George and Zhou, "Dual Tuning in a Supportive Context;" J.M. George, "Dual Tuning: A Minimum Condition for Understanding Affect in Organizations?" *Organizational Psychology Review,* no. 2 (2011), 147–64.

97. R.C. Sinclair, "Mood, Categorization Breadth, and Performance Appraisal: The Effects of Order of Information Acquisition and Affective State on Halo, Accuracy, Informational Retrieval, and Evaluations," *Organizational Behavior and Human Decision Processes* 42 (1988), 22–46.

98. D. Goleman, *Emotional Intelligence* (New York: Bantam Books, 1994); J.D. Mayer and P. Salovey, "The Intelligence of Emotional Intelligence," *Intelligence* 17 (1993), 433–42; J.D. Mayer and P. Salovey, "What Is Emotional Intelligence?" in P. Salovey and D. Sluyter, eds., *Emotional Development and Emotional Intelligence: Implications for Education* (New York: Basic Books, 1997); P. Salovey and J.D. Mayer, "Emotional Intelligence," *Imagination, Cognition, and Personality* 9 (1989–1990), 185–211.

99. S. Epstein, *Constructive Thinking* (Westport, CT: Praeger, 1998).

100. "Leading by Feel," *Inside the Mind of the Leader,* January 2004, 27–37.

101. P.C. Early and R.S. Peterson, "The Elusive Cultural Chameleon: Cultural Intelligence as a New Approach to Intercultural Training for the Global Manager," *Academy of Management Learning and Education* 3, no. 1 (2004), 100–15.

102. George, "Emotions and Leadership"; S. Begley, "The Boss Feels Your Pain," *Newsweek,* October 12, 1998, 74; D. Goleman, *Working with Emotional Intelligence* (New York: Bantam Books, 1998).

103. "Leading by Feel," *Inside the Mind of the Leader,* January 2004, 27–37.

104. George, "Emotions and Leadership."

105. J. Zhou and J.M. George, "Awakening Employee Creativity: The Role of Leader Emotional Intelligence," *Leadership Quarterly* 14 (2003), 545–68.

106. H.M. Trice and J.M. Beyer, *The Cultures of Work Organizations* (Englewood Cliffs, NJ: Prentice-Hall, 1993).

107. J.B. Sørensen, "The Strength of Corporate Culture and the Reliability of Firm Performance," *Administrative Science Quarterly* 47 (2002), 70–91.

108. "Personality and Organizational Culture," in B. Schneider and D.B. Smith, eds., *Personality and Organizations* (Mahway, NJ: Lawrence Erlbaum, 2004), 347–69; J.E. Slaughter, M.J. Zickar, S. Highhouse, and D.C. Mohr, "Personality Trait Inferences about Organizations: Development of a Measure and Assessment of Construct Validity," *Journal of Applied Psychology* 89, no. 1 (2004), 85–103.

109. T. Kelley, *The Art of Innovation: Lessons in Creativity from IDEO, America's Leading Design Firm* (New York: Random House, 2001).

110. "Personality and Organizational Culture."

111. B. Schneider, "The People Make the Place," *Personnel Psychology* 40 (1987), 437–53.

112. "Personality and Organizational Culture."

113. Ibid.

114. B. Schneider, H.B. Goldstein, and D.B. Smith, "The ASA Framework: An Update," *Personnel Psychology* 48 (1995), 747–73; J. Schaubroeck, D.C. Ganster, and J.R. Jones, "Organizational and Occupational Influences in the Attraction–Selection–Attrition Process," *Journal of Applied Psychology* 83 (1998), 869–91.

115. Kelley, *The Art of Innovation.*

116. www.ideo.com, February 5, 2008.

117. Kelley, *The Art of Innovation.*

118. "Personality and Organizational Culture."

119. Kelley, *The Art of Innovation.*

120. George, "Emotions and Leadership."

121. Kelley, *The Art of Innovation.*

122. Ibid.

123. D.C. Feldman, "The Development and Enforcement of Group Norms," *Academy of Management Review* 9 (1984), 47–53.

124. G.R. Jones, *Organizational Theory, Design, and Change* (Upper Saddle River, NJ: Prentice-Hall, 2003).

125. H. Schein, "The Role of the Founder in Creating Organizational Culture," *Organizational Dynamics* 12 (1983), 13–28.

126. J.M. George, "Personality, Affect, and Behavior in Groups," *Journal of Applied Psychology* 75 (1990), 107–16.

127. J. Van Maanen, "Police Socialization: A Longitudinal Examination of Job Attitudes in an Urban Police Department," *Administrative Science Quarterly* 20 (1975), 207–28.

128. www.intercotwest.com/Disney; M.N. Martinez, "Disney Training Works Magic," *HRMagazine,* May 1992, 53–57.

129. P.L. Berger and T. Luckman, *The Social Construction of Reality* (Garden City, NY: Anchor Books, 1967).

130. H.M. Trice and J.M. Beyer, "Studying Organizational Culture through Rites and Ceremonials," *Academy of Management Review* 9 (1984), 653–69.

131. Kelley, *The Art of Innovation.*

132. H.M. Trice and J.M. Beyer, *The Cultures of Work Organizations* (Englewood Cliffs, NJ: Prentice-Hall, 1993).

133. B. Ortega, "Walmart's Meeting Is a Reason to Party," *The Wall Street Journal,* June 3, 1994, A1.

134. H.M. Trice and J.M. Beyer, "Studying Organizational Culture through Rites and Ceremonies," *Academy of Management Review* 9 (1984), 653–69.

135. Kelley, *The Art of Innovation.*

136. www.ibm.com; IBM Investor Relations—Corporate Governance, Executive Officers, "Executive Officers," www.ibm.com/investor/governance/executive-officers.wss, February 5, 2010; "Board of Directors," IBM Annual Report 2011—Board of Directors and Senior Leadership, www.ibm.com/annualreport/2011/board-of-directors.html, April 4, 2012.

137. K.E. Weick, *The Social Psychology of Organization* (Reading, MA: Addison Wesley, 1979).

138. B. McLean and P. Elkind, *The Smartest Guys in the Room: The Amazing Rise and Scandalous Fall of Enron* (New York: Penguin Books, 2003); R. Smith and J.R. Emshwiller, *24 Days: How Two Wall Street Journal Reporters Uncovered the Lies That Destroyed Faith in Corporate America* (New York: HarperCollins, 2003); M. Swartz and S. Watkins, *Power Failure: The Inside Story of the Collapse of ENRON* (New York: Doubleday, 2003).

PART 2

3 Managing Ethics and Diversity

Learning Objectives

After studying this chapter, you should be able to:

LO 3-1 Illustrate how ethics help managers determine the right way to behave when dealing with different stakeholder groups.

LO 3-2 Explain why managers should behave ethically and strive to create ethical organizational cultures.

LO 3-3 Appreciate the increasing diversity of the workforce and of the organizational environment.

LO 3-4 Grasp the central role that managers play in the effective management of diversity.

LO 3-5 Understand why the effective management of diversity is both an ethical and a business imperative.

LO 3-6 Understand the two major forms of sexual harassment and how they can be eliminated.

© Rubberball/Mark Andersen/Getty Images RF

Where do your grocery dollars go? Whole Foods Market's goal is to make shopping fun and socially responsible. Customers' money supports an organization that monitors its suppliers, rewards its employees, and seeks to reduce its impact on the environment.
© AP Images

MANAGEMENT SNAPSHOT

Ethics and Social Responsibility at Whole Foods Market

How Can Managers Ethically Satisfy the Needs of Multiple Stakeholders?

The first Whole Foods Market opened in Austin, Texas, in 1980 as a supermarket for natural foods and had 19 employees.[1] Today it is the world's leading retailer of natural and organic foods, with 409 stores in North America and the United Kingdom.[2] Whole Foods specializes in selling chemical- and drug-free meat, poultry, and produce; its products are the "purest" possible, meaning it selects the ones least adulterated by artificial additives, sweeteners, colorings, and preservatives.[3] Despite the high prices it charges for its pure produce, sales per store are growing, and its total sales had grown to over $14 billion by 2014.[4] Sales for the first quarter of 2015 were $4.7 billion.[5] Why has Whole Foods been so successful? Co-founder and CO-CEO John Mackey says it is because of the principles he established to manage his company since its beginning—principles founded on the need to behave in an ethical and socially responsible way toward everybody affected by its business.

Mackey says he started his business for three reasons—to have fun, to make money, and to contribute to the well-being of other people.[6] The company's mission is based on its members' collective responsibility to the well-being of the people and groups it affects, its *stakeholders;* at Whole Foods these are customers, team members, investors, suppliers, the community, and the natural environment. Mackey measures his company's success by how well it satisfies the needs of these stakeholders. His ethical stance toward customers is that they are guaranteed that Whole Foods products are 100% organic, hormone-free, or as represented. To help achieve this promise, Whole Foods insists that its suppliers also behave in an ethical way, so it knows, for example, that the beef it sells comes from cows pastured on grass, not corn-fed in feed lots, and the chicken it sells is from free-range hens and not from hens that have been confined in tiny cages that prevent movement.

Mackey's management approach toward "team members," as Whole Foods employees are called, is also based on a well-defined ethical position. He says, "We put great emphasis at Whole Foods on the 'Whole People' part of the company mission. We believe in helping support our team members to grow as individuals—to become 'Whole People.' We allow tremendous individual initiative at Whole Foods, and that's why our company is so innovative and creative."[7] Mackey claims that each supermarket in the chain is unique because in each one team members are constantly experimenting with new and better ways to serve customers and improve their well-being. As team members learn, they become "self-actualized" or self-fulfilled, and this increase in their well-being translates into a desire to increase the well-being of other stakeholders. Evidence of Whole Foods Market's commitment to team members is the fact that Whole Foods Market has been included in *Fortune* magazine's "100 Best Companies to Work For" for 18 years running. Whole Foods also has been recognized by *Fortune* for being a "Most Diverse" Company.[8]

Mackey's strong views on ethics and social responsibility also serve shareholders. Mackey does not believe that the object of being in business is to primarily maximize profits for shareholders; he puts customers first.

He believes, however, that companies that behave ethically and strive to satisfy the needs of customers and employees simultaneously satisfy the needs of investors because high profits are the result of loyal customers and committed employees. Indeed, since Whole Foods issued shares to the public in 1992, the value of those shares has increased substantially. Giving back to local communities and protecting the natural environment are also key priorities at Whole Foods.[9] Clearly, taking a strong position on ethics and social responsibility has worked so far at Whole Foods.

Overview

While a strong code of ethics can influence the way employees behave, what causes people to behave unethically in the first place? Moreover, how do managers and employees determine what is ethical or unethical? In this chapter, we examine the nature of the obligations and responsibilities of managers and the companies they work for toward the people and society that are affected by their actions. First, we examine the nature of ethics and the sources of ethical problems. Second, we discuss the major groups of people, called *stakeholders,* who are affected by the way companies operate. Third, we look at four rules or guidelines that managers can use to decide whether a specific business decision is ethical or unethical and why it is important for people and companies to behave in an ethical way.

We then turn to the issue of the effective management of diversity. This first requires that organizations, their managers, and all employees behave ethically and follow legal rules and regulations in the ways diverse employees are hired, promoted, and treated. Second, effectively managing diversity means learning to appreciate and respond appropriately to the needs, attitudes, beliefs, and values that diverse employees bring to an organization and finding ways to use their skills and talents to benefit them and the company they work for. Finally, we discuss steps managers can take to eradicate sexual harassment in organizations. By the end of this chapter, you will understand the central role that the effective management of ethics and diversity plays in shaping the practice of business and the life of a people, society, and nation.

LO 3-1 Illustrate how ethics help managers determine the right way to behave when dealing with different stakeholder groups.

The Nature of Ethics

Suppose you see a person being mugged. Will you act in some way to help even though you risk being hurt? Will you walk away? Perhaps you might not intervene, but will you call the police? Does how you act depend on whether the person being mugged is a fit male, an elderly person, or a homeless person? Does it depend on whether other people are around so you can tell yourself, "Oh well, someone else will help or call the police. I don't need to"?

Ethical Dilemmas

ethical dilemma
The quandary people find themselves in when they have to decide if they should act in a way that might help another person or group even though doing so might go against their own self-interest.

The situation just described is an example of an **ethical dilemma**, the quandary people find themselves in when they have to decide if they should act in a way that might help another person or group and is the right thing to do, even though doing so might go against their own self-interest.[10] A dilemma may also arise when a person has to choose between two different courses of action, knowing that whichever course he or she selects will harm one person or group even while it may benefit another. The ethical dilemma here is to decide which course of action is the lesser of two evils.

People often know they are confronting an ethical dilemma when their moral scruples come into play and cause them to hesitate, debate, and reflect upon the rightness or goodness of a course of action. Moral scruples are thoughts and feelings that tell a person what is right or wrong; they are a part of a person's ethics. **Ethics** are the inner guiding moral principles, values, and beliefs that people use to analyze or interpret a situation and then decide what is the right or appropriate way to behave. Ethics also indicate what is inappropriate behavior and how a person should behave to avoid harming another person.

ethics The inner guiding moral principles, values, and beliefs that people use to analyze or interpret a situation and then decide what is the right or appropriate way to behave.

The essential problem in dealing with ethical issues, and thus solving moral dilemmas, is that no absolute or indisputable rules or principles can be developed to decide whether an action is ethical or unethical. Put simply, different people or groups may dispute which actions are ethical or unethical depending on their personal self-interest and specific attitudes, beliefs, and values—concepts we discussed in Chapter 3. How are we and companies and their managers and employees to decide what is ethical and so act appropriately toward other people and groups?

Ethics and the Law

The first answer to this question is that society as a whole, using the political and legal process, can lobby for and pass laws that specify what people can and cannot do. Many different kinds of laws govern business—for example, laws against fraud and deception and laws governing how companies can treat their employees and customers. Laws also specify what sanctions or punishments will follow if those laws are broken. Different groups in society lobby for which laws should be passed based on their own personal interests and beliefs about right and wrong. The group that can summon the most support can pass laws that align with its interests and beliefs. Once a law is passed, a decision about what the appropriate behavior is with regard to a person or situation is taken from the personally determined ethical realm to the societally determined legal realm. If you do not conform to the law, you can be prosecuted; and if you are found guilty of breaking the law, you can be punished. You have little say in the matter; your fate is in the hands of the court and its lawyers.

In studying the relationship between ethics and law, it is important to understand that *neither laws nor ethics are fixed principles* that do not change over time. Ethical beliefs change as time passes; and as they do so, laws change to reflect the changing ethical beliefs of a society. It was seen as ethical, and it was legal, for example, to acquire and possess slaves in ancient Rome and Greece and in the United States until the late 19th century. Ethical views regarding whether slavery was morally right or appropriate changed, however. Slavery was made illegal in the United States when those in power decided that slavery degraded the meaning of being human. Slavery makes a statement about the value or worth of human beings and about their right to life, liberty, and the pursuit of happiness. And if we deny these rights to other people, how can we claim to have any natural rights to these things?

Moreover, what is to stop any person or group, that becomes powerful enough to take control of the political and legal process, from enslaving us and denying us the right to be free and to own property? In denying freedom to others, one risks losing it oneself, just as stealing from others opens the door for them to steal from us in return. "Do unto others as you would have them do unto you" is a common ethical or moral rule that people apply in such situations to decide what is the right thing to do.

Changes in Ethics over Time

There are many types of behavior—such as murder, theft, slavery, rape, and driving while intoxicated—that most people currently believe are unacceptable and unethical and should therefore be illegal. However, the ethics of many other actions and behaviors are open to dispute. Some people might believe a particular behavior—for example, smoking tobacco or possessing guns—is unethical and so should be made illegal. Others might argue that it is up to the individual or group to decide if such behaviors are ethical and thus whether a particular behavior should remain legal.

As ethical beliefs change over time, some people may begin to question whether existing laws that make specific behaviors illegal are still appropriate. They might argue that although a specific behavior is deemed illegal, this does not make it unethical and thus the law should be changed. In 46 states, for example, it is illegal to possess or use marijuana (cannabis). To justify this law, it is commonly argued that smoking marijuana leads people to try more dangerous drugs. Once the habit of taking drugs has been acquired, people can get hooked on them. More powerful drugs such as heroin and other narcotics are addictive, and most people cannot stop using them without help. Thus, the use of marijuana, because it might lead to further harm, might be considered an unethical practice.

It has been documented medically, however, that marijuana use can help people with certain illnesses. For example, for cancer sufferers who are undergoing chemotherapy and for those with AIDS who are on potent medications, marijuana offers relief from many treatment side effects, such as nausea and lack of appetite. Yet, in the United States, it is illegal in many states for doctors to prescribe marijuana for these patients, so their suffering continues. Since 1996, however, 23 states have made it legal to prescribe marijuana for medical purposes; nevertheless, the federal government has sought to stop such state legislation. The U.S. Supreme Court ruled in 2005 that only Congress or the states could decide whether medical marijuana use should be made legal, and people in many states are currently lobbying for a relaxation of state laws against its use for medical purposes.[11] In Canada, there has been a widespread movement to decriminalize marijuana. While not making the drug legal, decriminalization removes the threat of prosecution even for uses that are not medically related and allows the drug to be taxed. Initiatives are under way in several states to decriminalize the possession of small amounts of marijuana for personal use as well as to make it more widely available to people legally for medical purposes. A major ethical debate is currently raging over this issue in many states and countries.

The important point to note is that while ethical beliefs lead to the development of laws and regulations to prevent certain behaviors or encourage others, laws themselves change or even disappear as ethical beliefs change. In Britain, in 1830, a person could be executed for more than 350 different crimes, including sheep stealing.

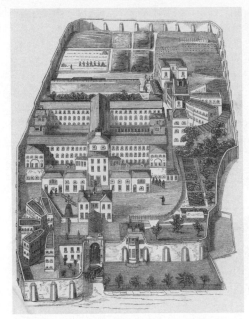

Coldbath Fields Prison in London, circa 1810. The British criminal justice system in the 1800s was severe. A person could be executed for more than 350 different crimes, including sheep stealing. As ethical beliefs change over time, so do laws. © Hulton Archive/Getty Images

Today the death penalty is no longer legal in Britain. Thus, both ethical and legal rules are *relative:* No absolute or unvarying standards exist to determine how we should behave, and people are caught up in moral dilemmas all the time. Because of this we have to make ethical choices.

The previous discussion highlights an important issue in understanding the relationship between ethics, law, and business. Throughout the 2010s, many scandals plagued major companies such as J.P. Morgan Chase, HSBC, Standard Chartered Bank, ING, Barclays, and Capital One. Managers at some of these companies engaged in risky trades, interest rate manipulation, illegal trade facilitation, drug money laundering, and deception of customers.

In other cases no laws were broken, yet outrage was expressed over perceptions of unethical actions. One example of this is the Occupy Wall Street movement, a protest that began on September 17, 2011, in a park close to New York City's Wall Street financial district. The movement was prompted in part by the perceived unethical influence of the financial services sector on the government. On its web page (occupywall-street.org), the organization says it is "fighting back against the corrosive power of major banks and multinational corporations over the democratic process, and the role of Wall Street in creating an economic collapse that has caused the greatest recession in generations." It also raised issues of social and economic inequality.

Some of the goals of this protest were to reduce the influence of corporations on government and allow a more balanced distribution of income. While the protesters did not allege that what financial institutions were doing was illegal, they asserted that the actions of financial institutions were not congruent with ethical business practices.

In 2011, President Barack Obama commented on Occupy Wall Street's concerns about the way policies are influenced by the financial sector: "It expresses the frustrations that the American people feel that we had the biggest financial crisis since the Great Depression, huge collateral damage all throughout the country, all across Main Street. And yet you're still seeing some of the same folks who acted irresponsibly trying to fight efforts to crack down on abusive practices that got us into this problem in the first place."[12]

Stakeholders and Ethics

Just as people have to work out the right and wrong ways to act, so do companies. When the law does not specify how companies should behave, their managers must decide the right or ethical way to behave toward the people and groups affected by their actions. Who are the people or groups that are affected by a company's business decisions? If a company behaves in an ethical way, how does this benefit people and society? Conversely, how are people harmed by a company's unethical actions?

The people and groups affected by how a company and its managers behave are called its stakeholders. **Stakeholders** supply a company with its productive resources; as a result, they have a claim on and a stake in the company.[13] Because stakeholders

stakeholders

The people and groups that supply a company with its productive resources and so have a claim on and a stake in the company.

Figure 3.1

Types of Company
Stakeholders

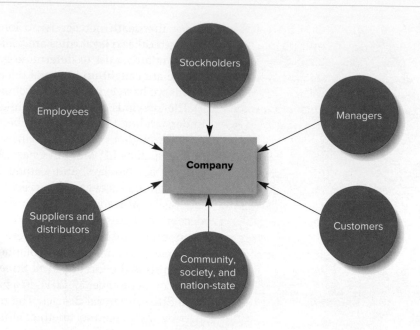

can directly benefit or be harmed by its actions, the ethics of a company and its managers are important to them. Who are a company's major stakeholders? What do they contribute to a company, and what do they claim in return? Here we examine the claims of these stakeholders—stockholders; managers; employees; suppliers and distributors; customers; and community, society, and nation-state as Figure 3.1 depicts.

Stockholders

Stockholders have a claim on a company because when they buy its stock or shares they become its owners. When the founder of a company decides to publicly incorporate the business to raise capital, shares of the stock of that company are issued. This stock grants its buyers ownership of a certain percentage of the company and the right to receive any future stock dividends. For example, in 2005, Microsoft decided to pay the owners of its 5 billion shares a special dividend payout of $32 billion. Bill Gates received $3.3 billion in dividends based on his stockholding, and he donated this money to the Bill and Melinda Gates Foundation, to which he has reportedly donated more than $28 billion to date, with the promise of much more to come; and Warren Buffet committed to donate at least $30 billion to the Gates Foundation over the next decade. The two richest people in the world have decided to give away a large part of their wealth to serve global ethical causes—in particular to address global health concerns such as malnutrition, malaria, tuberculosis, and AIDS. Gates is also donating about $1.8 billion to the Gates Foundation to help eradicate polio as part of the Polio Eradication & Endgame Strategic Plan 2013–2018.[14]

Stockholders are interested in how a company operates because they want to maximize the return on their investment. Thus, they watch the company and its managers closely to ensure that management is working diligently to increase the company's profitability.[15] Stockholders also want to ensure that managers are behaving ethically and not risking investors' capital by engaging in actions that could hurt the company's reputation. No company wants the reputation described by the

Occupy Wall Street protesters, who alleged that business organizations value money over people and work in the self-interest of a privileged few. However, experts warn businesses not to ignore the movement. Harvard bloggers say the persistence of Occupy Wall Street is "a signal that there is authentic, deep-seated unhappiness with the failings of the U.S. economic system. It's an indicator that economic inequality is perceived as an important issue—one requiring businesses' immediate attention."[16]

Managers

Managers are a vital stakeholder group because they are responsible for using a company's financial, capital, and human resources to increase its performance and thus its stock price.[17] Managers have a claim on an organization because they bring to it their skills, expertise, and experience. They have the right to expect a good return or reward by investing their human capital to improve a company's performance. Such rewards include good salaries and benefits, the prospect of promotion and a career, and stock options and bonuses tied to company performance.

Rajat Kumar Gupta, former Goldman Sachs board member, exits federal court in New York after being convicted of insider trading and sentenced to two years in prison. © Craig Ruttle/AP Images

Managers are the stakeholder group that bears the responsibility to decide which goals an organization should pursue to most benefit stakeholders and how to make the most efficient use of resources to achieve those goals. In making such decisions, managers frequently must juggle the interests of different stakeholders, including themselves.[18] These sometimes difficult decisions challenge managers to uphold ethical values because some decisions that benefit certain stakeholder groups (managers and stockholders) harm other groups (individual workers and local communities). For example, in economic downturns or when a company experiences performance shortfalls, layoffs may help cut costs (thus benefiting shareholders) at the expense of the employees laid off. Many U.S. managers have recently faced this difficult decision. Until the 2009 financial crisis sent unemployment soaring over 10 percent, on average about 1.6 million U.S. employees out of a total labor force of 140 million were affected by mass layoffs each year; and more than 3 million jobs from the United States, Europe, and Japan have been outsourced to Asia since 2005. Layoff decisions are always difficult: They not only take a heavy toll on workers, their families, and local communities but also mean the loss of the contributions of valued employees to an organization. In 2014 Michelin North America (Canada) announced it would slash 500 jobs from its Granton tire plant over the next 18 months. The company was Nova Scotia's largest private manufacturer.[19]

As we discussed in Chapter 1, managers must be motivated and given incentives to work hard in the interests of stockholders. Their behavior must also be scrutinized to ensure that they do not behave illegally or unethically, pursuing goals that threaten stockholders and the company's interests.[20] Unfortunately, we have seen in the 2010s how easy it is for top managers to find ways to ruthlessly pursue their self-interest at the expense of stockholders and employees because laws and regulations are not strong enough to force them to behave ethically.

In a nutshell, the problem has been that in many companies corrupt managers focus not on building the company's capital and stockholders' wealth but on maximizing their own personal capital and wealth. In an effort to prevent future scandals, the Securities and Exchange Commission (SEC), the government's top business watchdog, has begun to rework the rules governing a company's relationship with its auditor, as well as regulations concerning stock options, and to increase the power of outside directors to scrutinize a CEO. The SEC's goal is to outlaw many actions that were previously classified as merely unethical. For example, companies are now forced to reveal to stockholders the value of the stock options they give their top executives and directors and when they give them these options; this shows how much such payments reduce company profits. Managers and directors can now be prosecuted if they disguise or try to hide these payments. In the 2010s, the SEC announced many new rules requiring that companies disclose myriad details of executive compensation packages to investors; already the boards of directors of many companies have stopped giving CEOs perks such as free personal jet travel, membership in exclusive country clubs, and luxury accommodations on "business trips." Also, in 2010 Congress passed new laws preventing the many unethical and illegal actions of managers of banks and other financial institutions that led to the 2009 financial crisis. One of these regulations, the "Volcker Rule," seeks to reduce the chances that banks will put depositors' money at risk.[21]

Indeed, many experts argue that the rewards given to top managers, particularly the CEO and COO, grew out of control in the 2000s. Top managers are today's "aristocrats," and through their ability to influence the board of directors and raise their own pay, they have amassed personal fortunes worth hundreds of millions of dollars. For example, according to a study by the Federal Reserve, U.S. CEOs now get paid about 600 times what the average worker earns, compared to about 40 times in 1980—a staggering increase. In 2014, the median CEO pay was $8.64 million.[22] We noted in Chapter 1 that besides their salaries, top managers often receive tens of millions in stock bonuses and options—even when their companies perform poorly.

Is it ethical for top managers to receive such vast amounts of money from their companies? Do they earn it? Remember, this money could have gone to shareholders in the form of dividends. It could also have reduced the huge salary gap between those at the top and those at the bottom of the hierarchy. Many people argue that the growing disparity between the rewards given to CEOs and other employees is unethical and should be regulated. CEO pay has skyrocketed because CEOs are the people who set and control one another's salaries and bonuses; they can do this because they sit on the boards of other companies as outside directors. Others argue that because top managers play an important role in building a company's capital and wealth, they deserve a significant share of its profits. Some recent research has suggested that the companies whose CEO compensation includes a large percentage of stock options tend to experience big share losses more often than big gains, and that on average, company performance improves as stock option use declines.[23] The debate over how much money CEOs and other top managers should be paid is still raging, particularly because the financial crisis beginning in 2009 showed how much money the CEOs of troubled financial companies earned even as their companies' performance and stock prices collapsed. For example, Countrywide Mortgage, which pioneered the subprime business, suffered losses of more than $1.7 billion in 2007, and its stock fell 80 percent; yet its CEO Angelo Mozilo still received $20 million in stock awards and sold stock options worth $121 million before the company's price collapsed.

Employees

A company's employees are the hundreds of thousands of people who work in its various departments and functions, such as research, sales, and manufacturing. Employees expect to receive rewards consistent with their performance. One principal way that a company can act ethically toward employees and meet their expectations is by creating an occupational structure that fairly and equitably rewards employees for their contributions. Companies, for example, need to develop recruitment, training, performance appraisal, and reward systems that do not discriminate against employees and that employees believe are fair.

Suppliers and Distributors

No company operates alone. Every company is in a network of relationships with other companies that supply it with the inputs (such as raw materials, components, contract labor, and clients) that it needs to operate. It also depends on intermediaries such as wholesalers and retailers to distribute its products to the final customers. Suppliers expect to be paid fairly and promptly for their inputs; distributors expect to receive quality products at agreed-upon prices. Once again, many ethical issues arise in how companies contract and interact with their suppliers and distributors. Important issues concerning safety specifications are governed by the contracts a company signs with its suppliers and distributors, for example; however, lax oversight can have tragic consequences, as the accompanying "Ethics in Action" feature shows.

ETHICS IN ACTION

Safety in the Garment Industry

Why did more than 150 international brands and retailers, including Abercrombie & Fitch, American Eagle Outfitters, Fruit of the Loom, and PVH, sign the Accord on Fire and Building Safety in Bangladesh in 2013? The accord is a five-year agreement stating that the signing companies and organizations commit to meet the minimum safety standards for the textile industry in Bangladesh.

Could it be that the buying power of consumers in their mid-twenties—consumers very concerned about the plight of the global worker—encouraged brands and retailers to sign the agreement? Sébastien Breteau, founder and chief executive officer of AsiaInspection,[24] a quality control service provider of supplier audits, product inspections, and lab testing for consumer goods and food importers, believes that young people have raised awareness of social accountability in global supply chain management. "This generation cares a lot about transparency," he said. "They want to know that what they are buying doesn't kill the planet."[25] This means that organizations who do not monitor their suppliers carefully risk paying a steep price with young consumers.

Several industrial accidents in 2013 catalyzed social accountability in global supply chain management, according to Breteau's firm. Probably the most tragic of the tipping points was the collapse of the Rana Plaza in Dhaka, Bangladesh. The collapse of the eight-story commercial building killed 1,132 workers and injured more than 2,500 on April 24, 2013. The day before the collapse, building inspectors had found cracks in the structure and warned business owners to evacuate. A few shops and a bank heeded the warning, but owners of garment factories in the building ordered employees to come to work. The collapse was the deadliest disaster in the history of the garment industry worldwide.

There are parallels between the collapse of Rana Plaza and a tragedy in the history of American garment factories. In 1911, a fire destroyed the Triangle Shirtwaist Factory and killed 146 garment workers. The factory was on the top floors of a building in Greenwich Village, New York City. When the fire broke out, workers found the exit doors locked from the outside, a common practice at the time to stop theft and unauthorized breaks. Many workers died by jumping out the windows to escape the flames. The outrage that followed the Triangle fire was a catalyst for change in factory conditions, much like the outrage that followed the Rana Plaza collapse. In the aftermath of the fire, the Factory Investigating Commission was formed and, much like the Accord on Fire and Building Safety in Bangladesh, began factory inspections. Many factories in New York City were found to have the same conditions that caused the Triangle fire, such as flammable materials, locked exit doors, and inadequate fire alarms and fire suppression systems. Between 1911 and 1913, 60 new laws were passed to improve factory conditions.

In March 2014 engineering teams organized through the Accord issued inspection reports on 10 Bangladesh factories. The reports indicated many factories did not have adequate fire alarm and sprinkler systems and that some fire exits were locked.[26] Also, many factories had dangerously high weight loads on floors, which is believed to be a cause of the Rana Plaza collapse.

Following the Rana Plaza collapse, clients of the Breteau's inspection firm have become less reluctant to commit to the creation and enforcement of programs to audit factory working conditions. "Suddenly, we saw a switch in our clients' attitude to social accountability," according to Breteau. "They became very serious about running audit programs through their supply chains."[27] The company's audit programs include quality management standards according to the ISO 9001 or U.S. C-TPAT standards, social compliance according to SA 8000 standards, and ethical trading according to Sedex Ethical Trade Audits.

Will this change in attitudes toward social accountability in global supply chains have a lasting impact? *Forbes* blogger Robert Bowman, managing editor of SupplyChainBrain, a website and magazine covering global supply chains, names several reasons why retailers have failed to take aggressive action to stop unsafe working conditions in the past. From the retailers' point of view, it can be difficult to keep track of complex supply chains. Multiple layers of suppliers and subcontractors in some supply chains make it complicated to know exactly how and where goods are being produced, Bowman says. From the consumer's point of view, shocking revelations of poor labor practices cause temporary indignation. After headlines and media stories about sweatshops and safety violations, shoppers quickly return to being indifferent about how clothing is produced, Bowman says. However, the shocking collapse of Rana Plaza and the resulting signatures on the Accord on Fire and Building Safety in Bangladesh bode well for real change in global supply chain ethics.

Many other issues depend on business ethics. For example, numerous products sold in U.S. stores have been outsourced to countries that do not have U.S.-style regulations and laws to protect the workers who make these products. All companies must take an ethical position on the way they obtain and make the products they sell. Commonly this stance is published on a company's website.

Customers

Customers are often regarded as the most critical stakeholder group because if a company cannot attract them to buy its products, it cannot stay in business. Thus, managers and employees must work to increase efficiency and effectiveness in order to create loyal customers and attract new ones. They do so by selling customers quality products at a fair price and providing good after-sales service. They can also strive to improve their products over time and provide guarantees to customers about the integrity of their products like the Soap Dispensary.

Community, Society, and Nation

The effects of the decisions made by companies and their managers permeate all aspects of the communities, societies, and nations in which they operate. *Community* refers to physical locations like towns or cities or to social milieus like ethnic neighborhoods in which companies are located. A community provides a company with the physical and social infrastructure that allows it to operate; its utilities and labor force; the homes in which its managers and employees live; the schools, colleges, and hospitals that serve their needs; and so on.

Through the salaries, wages, and taxes it pays, a company contributes to the economy of its town or region and often determines whether the community prospers or declines. Similarly, a company affects the prosperity of a society and a nation and, to the degree that a company is involved in global trade, all the countries it operates in and thus the prosperity of the global economy. We have already discussed the many issues surrounding global outsourcing and the loss of jobs in the United States, for example.

Although the individual effects of the way each McDonald's restaurant operates might be small, for instance, the combined effects of how all McDonald's and other fast-food companies do business are enormous. In the United States alone, more than 500,000 people work in the fast-food industry, and many thousands of suppliers like farmers, paper cup manufacturers, builders, and so on depend on it for their livelihood. Small wonder then that the ethics of the fast-food business are scrutinized closely. This industry was the major lobbyer against attempts to raise the national minimum wage (which was raised to $7.25 an hour in 2009, where it remains in 2014 up from $5.15—a figure that had not changed since 1997), for example, because a higher minimum wage would substantially increase its operating costs. However, responding to protests about chickens raised in cages where they cannot move, McDonald's—the largest egg buyer in the United States—issued new ethical guidelines concerning cage size and related matters that its egg suppliers must abide by if they are to retain its business. What ethical rules does McDonald's use to decide its stance toward minimum pay or minimum cage size?

Business ethics are also important because the failure of a company can have catastrophic effects on a community; a general decline in business activity affects a whole nation. The decision of a large company to pull out of a community, for example, can threaten the community's future. Some companies may attempt to improve their profits by engaging in actions that, although not illegal, can hurt communities and nations. One of these actions is pollution. For example, many U.S. companies reduce costs by trucking their waste to Mexico, where it is legal to dump waste in the Rio Grande. The dumping pollutes the river from the Mexican side, but the U.S. side of the river is increasingly experiencing pollution's negative effects.

Rules for Ethical Decision Making

When a stakeholder perspective is taken, questions on company ethics abound.[28] What is the appropriate way to manage the claims of all stakeholders? Company decisions that favor one group of stakeholders, for example, are likely to harm the interests of others.[29] High prices charged to customers may bring high returns to shareholders and high salaries to managers in the short run. If in the long run customers turn to companies that offer lower-cost products, however, the result may be declining sales, laid-off employees, and the decline of the communities that support the high-priced company's business activity.

When companies act ethically, their stakeholders support them. For example, banks are willing to supply them with new capital, they attract highly qualified job applicants, and new customers are drawn to their products. Thus, ethical companies grow and expand over time, and all their stakeholders benefit. The results of unethical behavior are loss of reputation and resources, shareholders selling their shares, skilled managers and employees leaving the company, and customers turning to the products of more reputable companies.

When making business decisions, managers must consider the claims of all stakeholders.[30] To help themselves and employees make ethical decisions and behave in ways that benefit their stakeholders, managers can use four ethical rules or principles to analyze the effects of their business decisions on stakeholders: the *utilitarian, moral rights, justice,* and *practical* rules (Figure 3.2).[31] These rules are useful guidelines that help managers decide on the appropriate way to behave in situations where it is necessary to balance a company's self-interest and the interests of its stakeholders. Remember, the right choices will lead resources to be used where they can create

Figure 3.2
Four Ethical Rules

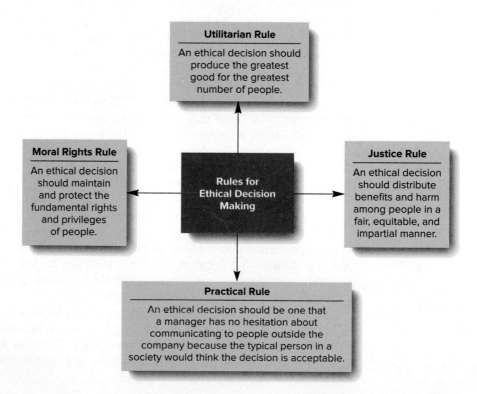

Utilitarian Rule

An ethical decision should produce the greatest good for the greatest number of people.

Moral Rights Rule

An ethical decision should maintain and protect the fundamental rights and privileges of people.

Rules for Ethical Decision Making

Justice Rule

An ethical decision should distribute benefits and harm among people in a fair, equitable, and impartial manner.

Practical Rule

An ethical decision should be one that a manager has no hesitation about communicating to people outside the company because the typical person in a society would think the decision is acceptable.

the most value. If all companies make the right choices, all stakeholders will benefit in the long run.[32]

utilitarian rule An ethical decision is a decision that produces the greatest good for the greatest number of people.

UTILITARIAN RULE The **utilitarian rule** is that an ethical decision is a decision that produces the greatest good for the greatest number of people. To decide which is the most ethical course of business action, managers should first consider how different possible courses of business action would benefit or harm different stakeholders. They should then choose the course of action that provides the most benefits, or, conversely, the one that does the least harm, to stakeholders.[33]

The ethical dilemma for managers is this: How do you measure the benefit and harm that will be done to each stakeholder group? Moreover, how do you evaluate the rights of different stakeholder groups, and the relative importance of each group, in coming to a decision? Because stockholders own the company, shouldn't their claims be held above those of employees? For example, managers might face a choice of using global outsourcing to reduce costs and lower prices or continuing with high-cost production at home. A decision to use global outsourcing benefits shareholders and customers but will result in major layoffs that will harm employees and the communities in which they live. Typically, in a capitalist society such as the United States, the interests of shareholders are put above those of employees, so production will move abroad. This is commonly regarded as being an ethical choice because in the long run the alternative, home production, might cause the business to collapse and go bankrupt, in which case greater harm will be done to all stakeholders.

moral rights rule An ethical decision is one that best maintains and protects the fundamental or inalienable rights and privileges of the people affected by it.

MORAL RIGHTS RULE Under the **moral rights rule**, an ethical decision is one that best maintains and protects the fundamental or inalienable rights and privileges of the people affected by it. For example, ethical decisions protect people's rights to freedom, life and safety, property, privacy, free speech, and freedom of conscience. The adage "Do unto others as you would have them do unto you" is a moral rights principle that managers should use to decide which rights to uphold. Customers must also consider the rights of the companies and people who create the products they wish to consume.

From a moral rights perspective, managers should compare and contrast different courses of business action on the basis of how each course will affect the rights of the company's different stakeholders. Managers should then choose the course of action that best protects and upholds the rights of *all* stakeholders. For example, decisions that might significantly harm the safety or health of employees or customers would clearly be unethical choices.

The ethical dilemma for managers is that decisions that will protect the rights of some stakeholders often will hurt the rights of others. How should they choose which group to protect? For example, in deciding whether it is ethical to snoop on employees, or search them when they leave work to prevent theft, does an employee's right to privacy outweigh an organization's right to protect its property? Suppose a coworker is having personal problems and is coming in late and leaving early, forcing you to pick up the person's workload. Do you tell your boss even though you know this will probably get that person fired?

justice rule An ethical decision distributes benefits and harms among people and groups in a fair, equitable, or impartial way.

JUSTICE RULE The **justice rule** is that an ethical decision distributes benefits and harms among people and groups in a fair, equitable, or impartial way. Managers should compare and contrast alternative courses of action based on the degree to which they will fairly or equitably distribute outcomes to stakeholders. For example, employees who are similar in their level of skill, performance, or responsibility should receive similar pay; allocation of outcomes should not be based on differences such as gender, race, or religion.

The ethical dilemma for managers is to determine the fair rules and procedures for distributing outcomes to stakeholders. Managers must not give people they like bigger raises than they give to people they do not like, for example, or bend the rules to help their favorites. On the other hand, if employees want managers to act fairly toward them, then employees need to act fairly toward their companies by working hard and being loyal. Similarly, customers need to act fairly toward a company if they expect it to be fair to them—something people who illegally copy digital media should consider.

PRACTICAL RULE   Each of these rules offers a different and complementary way of determining whether a decision or behavior is ethical, and all three rules should be used to sort out the ethics of a particular course of action. Ethical issues, as we just discussed, are seldom clear-cut, however, because the rights, interests, goals, and incentives of different stakeholders often conflict. For this reason, many experts on ethics add a fourth rule to determine whether a business decision is ethical: The **practical rule** is that an ethical decision is one that a manager has no hesitation or reluctance about communicating to people outside the company because the typical person in a society would think it is acceptable. A business decision is probably acceptable on ethical grounds if a manager can answer yes to each of these questions:

1. Does my decision fall within the accepted values or standards that typically apply in business activity today?

2. Am I willing to see the decision communicated to all people and groups affected by it—for example, by having it reported in newspapers or on television?

3. Would the people with whom I have a significant personal relationship, such as family members, friends, or even managers in other organizations, approve of the decision?

Applying the practical rule to analyze a business decision ensures that managers are taking into account the interests of all stakeholders.[34]

Why Should Managers Behave Ethically?

Why is it so important that managers, and people in general, should act ethically and temper their pursuit of self-interest by considering the effects of their actions on others? The answer is that the relentless pursuit of self-interest can lead to a collective disaster when one or more people start to profit from being unethical because this encourages other people to act in the same way.[35] More and more people jump onto the bandwagon, and soon everybody is trying to manipulate the situation to serve their personal ends with no regard for the effects of their action on others. This is called the "tragedy of the commons."

Suppose that in an agricultural community there is common land that everybody has an equal right to use. Pursuing self-interest, each farmer acts to make the maximum use of the free resource by grazing his or her own cattle and sheep. Collectively all the farmers overgraze the land, which quickly becomes worn out. Then a strong wind blows away the exposed topsoil, so the common land is destroyed. The pursuit of individual self-interest with no consideration of societal interests leads to disaster for each individual and for the whole society because scarce resources are destroyed.[36] Consider digital piracy: The tragedy that would result if all people were

practical rule
An ethical decision is one that a manager has no reluctance about communicating to people outside the company because the typical person in a society would think it is acceptable.

LO 3-2 Explain why managers should behave ethically and strive to create ethical organizational cultures.

to steal digital media would be the disappearance of music, movie, and book companies as creative people decided there was no point in working hard to produce original songs, stories, and so on.

We can look at the effects of unethical behavior on business activity in another way. Suppose companies and their managers operate in an unethical society, meaning one in which stakeholders routinely try to cheat and defraud one another. If stakeholders expect each other to cheat, how long will it take them to negotiate the purchase and shipment of products? When they do not trust each other, stakeholders will probably spend hours bargaining over fair prices, and this is a largely unproductive activity that reduces efficiency and effectiveness.[37] The time and effort that could be spent improving product quality or customer service are lost to negotiating and bargaining. Thus, unethical behavior ruins business commerce, and society has a lower standard of living because fewer goods and services are produced, as Figure 3.3 illustrates.

On the other hand, suppose companies and their managers operate in an ethical society, meaning stakeholders believe that they are dealing with others who are basically moral and honest. In this society, stakeholders have a greater reason to trust others. **Trust** is the willingness of one person or group to have faith or confidence

trust The willingness of one person or group to have faith or confidence in the goodwill of another person, even though this puts them at risk.

Figure 3.3
Some Effects of Ethical and Unethical Behavior

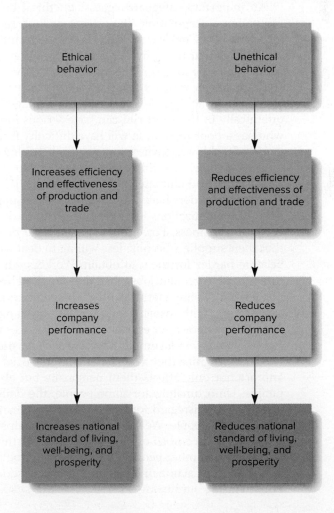

in the goodwill of another person, even though this puts them at risk (because the other might act in a deceitful way). When trust exists, stakeholders are likely to signal their good intentions by cooperating and providing information that makes it easier to exchange and price goods and services. When one person acts in a trustworthy way, this encourages others to act in the same way. Over time, as greater trust between stakeholders develops, they can work together more efficiently and effectively, which raises company performance (see Figure 3.3). As people see the positive results of acting in an honest way, ethical behavior becomes a valued social norm, and society in general becomes increasingly ethical.

As noted in Chapter 1, a major responsibility of managers is to protect and nurture the resources under their control. Any organizational stakeholders—managers, workers, stockholders, and suppliers—who advance their own interests by behaving unethically toward other stakeholders, either by taking resources or by denying resources to others, waste collective resources. If other individuals or groups copy the behavior of the unethical stakeholder, the rate at which collective resources are misused increases, and eventually few resources are available to produce goods and services. Unethical behavior that goes unpunished creates incentives for people to put their unbridled self-interests above the rights of others.[38] When this happens, the benefits that people reap from joining together in organizations disappear quickly.

An important safeguard against unethical behavior is the potential for loss of reputation.[39] **Reputation**, the esteem or high repute that people or organizations gain when they behave ethically, is an important asset. Stakeholders have valuable reputations that they must protect because their ability to earn a living and obtain resources in the long run depends on how they behave.

reputation The esteem or high repute that individuals or organizations gain when they behave ethically.

If a manager misuses resources and other parties regard that behavior as being at odds with acceptable standards, the manager's reputation will suffer. Behaving unethically in the short run can have serious long-term consequences. A manager who has a poor reputation will have difficulty finding employment with other companies. Stockholders who see managers behaving unethically may refuse to invest in their companies, and this will decrease the stock price, undermine the companies' reputations, and ultimately put the managers' jobs at risk.[40]

All stakeholders have reputations to lose. Suppliers who provide shoddy inputs find that organizations learn over time not to deal with them, and eventually they go out of business. Powerful customers who demand ridiculously low prices find that their suppliers become less willing to deal with them, and resources ultimately become harder for them to obtain. Workers who shirk responsibilities on the job find it hard to get new jobs when they are fired. In general, if a manager or company is known for being unethical, other stakeholders are likely to view that individual or organization with suspicion and hostility, creating a poor reputation. But a manager or company known for ethical business practices will develop a good reputation.[41]

In summary, in a complex, diverse society, stakeholders, and people in general, need to recognize they are part of a larger social group. How they make decisions and act not only affects them personally but also affects the lives of many other people. Unfortunately, for some people, the daily struggle to survive and succeed or their total disregard for others' rights can lead them to lose that bigger connection to other people. We can see our relationships to our families and friends, to our school, church, and so on. But we must go further and keep in mind the effects of our actions on other people—people who will be judging our actions and whom we might harm by acting unethically. Our moral scruples are like those "other people" but are inside our heads.

Sources of an Organization's Code of Ethics

Codes of ethics are formal standards and rules, based on beliefs about right or wrong, that managers can use to help themselves make appropriate decisions with regard to the interests of their stakeholders.[42] Ethical standards embody views about abstractions such as justice, freedom, equity, and equality. An organization's code of ethics derives from three principal sources in the organizational environment: *societal* ethics, *professional* ethics, and the *individual* ethics of the organization's managers and employees (see Figure 3.4).

societal ethics Standards that govern how members of a society are to deal with each other on issues such as fairness, justice, poverty, and the rights of the individual.

SOCIETAL ETHICS Societal ethics are standards that govern how members of a society deal with each other in matters involving issues such as fairness, justice, poverty, and the rights of the individual. Societal ethics emanate from a society's laws, customs, and practices and from the unwritten attitudes, values, and norms that influence how people interact with each other. People in a particular country may automatically behave ethically because they have internalized values and norms that specify how they should behave in certain situations. Not all values and norms are internalized, however. The typical ways of doing business in a society and laws governing the use of bribery and corruption are the result of decisions made and enforced by people with the power to determine what is appropriate.

Societal ethics vary among societies. For example, ethical standards accepted in the United States are not accepted in all other countries. In many economically poor countries, bribery is standard practice to get things done, such as getting a telephone installed or a contract awarded. In the United States and many other Western countries, bribery is considered unethical and often illegal.

Societal ethics control self-interested behavior by individuals and organizations—behavior threatening to society's collective interests. Laws spelling out what is good

Figure 3.4

Sources of an Organization's Code of Ethics

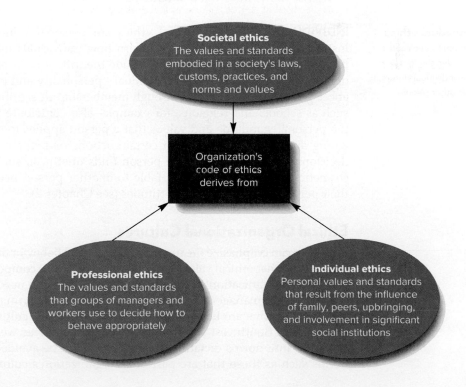

or appropriate business practice provide benefits to everybody. Free and fair competition among organizations is possible only when laws and rules level the playing field and define what behavior is acceptable or unacceptable in certain situations. For example, it is ethical for a manager to compete with managers in other companies by producing a higher-quality or lower-priced product, but it is not ethical (or legal) to do so by spreading false claims about competitors' products, bribing stores to exclude competitors' products, or blowing up competitors' factories.

professional ethics Standards that govern how members of a profession are to make decisions when the way they should behave is not clear-cut.

PROFESSIONAL ETHICS Professional ethics are standards that govern how members of a profession, managers or workers, make decisions when the way in which they should behave is not clear-cut.[43] Medical ethics govern the way doctors and nurses are to treat patients. Doctors are expected to perform only necessary medical procedures and to act in the patient's interest and not in their own. The ethics of scientific research require scientists to conduct their experiments and present their findings in ways that ensure the validity of their conclusions. Like society at large, most professional groups can impose punishments for violations of ethical standards. Doctors and lawyers can be prevented from practicing their professions if they disregard professional ethics and put their own interests first.

Within an organization, professional rules and norms often govern how employees such as lawyers, researchers, and accountants make decisions and act in certain situations, and these rules and norms may become part of the organization's code of ethics. When they do, workers internalize the rules and norms of their profession (just as they do those of society) and often follow them automatically when deciding how to behave.[44] Because most people follow established rules of behavior, people often take ethics for granted. However, when professional ethics are violated, such as when scientists fabricate data to disguise the harmful effects of products, ethical issues rise to the forefront of attention.

individual ethics Personal values and attitudes that govern how individuals interact with other people.

INDIVIDUAL ETHICS Individual ethics are personal values (both terminal and instrumental) and attitudes that govern how individuals interact with other people.[45] Sources of individual ethics include the influence of one's family, peers, and upbringing in general, and an individual's personality and experience. The experiences gained over a lifetime—through membership in significant social institutions such as schools and religions, for example—also contribute to the development of the personal standards and values that a person applies to decide what is right or wrong and whether to perform certain actions or make certain decisions. Many decisions or behaviors that one person finds unethical, such as using animals for cosmetics testing, may be acceptable to another person because of differences in their personalities, values, and attitudes (see Chapter 2).

Ethical Organizational Cultures

Managers can emphasize the importance of ethical behavior and social responsibility by ensuring that ethical values and norms are a central component of organizational culture. An organization's code of ethics guides decision making when ethical questions arise, but managers can go one step farther by ensuring that important ethical values and norms are key features of an organization's culture. For example, Herb Kelleher and Southwest Airlines' culture value employee well-being; this emphasis translates into norms dictating that layoffs should be avoided.[46] Ethical values and norms such as these that are part of an organization's culture help organizational members resist self-interested action and recognize that they are part of something bigger than themselves.[47]

Managers' role in developing ethical values and standards in other employees is very important. Employees naturally look to those in authority to provide leadership, and managers become ethical role models whose behavior is scrutinized by their subordinates. If top managers are not ethical, their subordinates are not likely to behave in an ethical manner. Employees may think that if it's all right for a top manager to engage in dubious behavior, it's all right for them, too. The actions of top managers such as CEOs and the president of the United States are scrutinized so closely for ethical improprieties because these actions represent the values of their organizations and, in the case of the president, the values of the nation.

Managers can also provide a visible means of support to develop an ethical culture. Increasingly, organizations are creating the role of ethics officer, or **ethics ombudsman**, to monitor their ethical practices and procedures. The ethics ombudsman is responsible for communicating ethical standards to all employees, for designing systems to monitor employees' conformity to those standards, and for teaching managers and nonmanagerial employees at all levels of the organization how to respond to ethical dilemmas appropriately.[48] Because the ethics ombudsman has organizationwide authority, organizational members in any department can communicate instances of unethical behavior by their managers or coworkers without fear of retribution. This arrangement makes it easier for everyone to behave ethically. In addition, ethics ombudsmen can provide guidance when organizational members are uncertain about whether an action is ethical. Some organizations have an organizationwide ethics committee to provide guidance on ethical issues and help write and update the company code of ethics.

ethics ombudsman An ethics officer who monitors an organization's practices and procedures to be sure they are ethical.

The Increasing Diversity of the Workforce and the Environment

One of the most important management issues to emerge over the last 40 years has been the increasing diversity of the workforce. **Diversity** is dissimilarities—differences—among people due to age, gender, race, ethnicity, religion, sexual orientation, socioeconomic background, education, experience, physical appearance, capabilities/disabilities, and any other characteristic that is used to distinguish between people (see Figure 3.5).

Diversity raises important ethical issues and social responsibility issues. It is also a critical issue for organizations—one that if not handled well can bring an organization to its knees, especially in our increasingly global environment. There are several reasons why diversity is such a pressing concern and an issue both in the popular press and for managers and organizations:

LO 3-3 Appreciate the increasing diversity of the workforce and of the organizational environment.

- There is a strong ethical imperative in many societies that diverse people must receive equal opportunities and be treated fairly and justly. Unfair treatment is also illegal.

- Effectively managing diversity can improve organizational effectiveness.[49] When managers effectively manage diversity, they not only encourage other managers to treat diverse members of an organization fairly and justly but also realize that diversity is an important organizational resource that can help an organization gain a competitive advantage.

- There is substantial evidence that diverse individuals continue to experience unfair treatment in the workplace as a result of biases, stereotypes, and overt

Figure 3.5

Sources of Diversity in
the Workplace

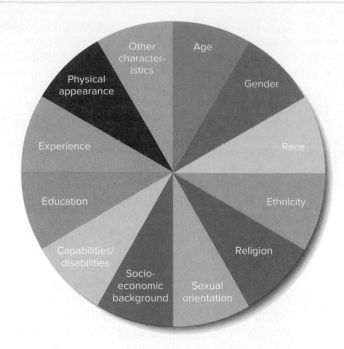

discrimination.[50] In one study, résumés of equally qualified men and women were sent to high-priced Philadelphia restaurants (where potential earnings are high). Though equally qualified, men were more than twice as likely as women to be called for a job interview and more than five times as likely to receive a job offer.[51] Findings from another study suggest that both women and men tend to believe that women will accept lower pay than men; this is a possible explanation for the continuing gap in pay between men and women.[52]

Other kinds of diverse employees may face even greater barriers. For example, the federal Glass Ceiling Commission Report indicated that African Americans have the hardest time being promoted and climbing the corporate ladder, that Asians are often stereotyped into technical jobs, and that Hispanics are assumed to be less well educated than other minority groups.[53] (The term **glass ceiling** alludes to the invisible barriers that prevent minorities and women from being promoted to top corporate positions.)[54]

Before we can discuss the multitude of issues surrounding the effective management of diversity, we must document just how diverse the U.S. workforce is becoming.

glass ceiling

A metaphor alluding to the invisible barriers that prevent minorities and women from being promoted to top corporate positions.

Age

According to data from the U.S. Census Bureau and the CIA's World Fact Book, the median age of a person in the United States is the highest it has ever been, 37.6 years.[55] Moreover, by 2030, it is projected that close to 20 percent of the U.S. population will be 65 or over.[56] The Age Discrimination in Employment Act of 1967 prohibits age discrimination.[57] Major equal employment opportunity legislation that prohibits discrimination among diverse groups is summarized in Table 3.1.

The aging of the population suggests that managers need to be vigilant to ensure that employees are not discriminated against because of age. Moreover, managers need

Table 3.1

Major Equal Employment Opportunity Laws Affecting Human Resources Management

Year	Law	Description
1963	Equal Pay Act	Requires that men and women be paid equally if they are performing equal work.
1964	Title VII of the Civil Rights Act	Prohibits discrimination in employment decisions on the basis of race, religion, sex, color, or national origin; covers a wide range of employment decisions, including hiring, firing, pay, promotion, and working conditions.
1967	Age Discrimination in Employment Act	Prohibits discrimination against workers over the age of 40 and restricts mandatory retirement.
1978	Pregnancy Discrimination Act	Prohibits discrimination against women in employment decisions on the basis of pregnancy, childbirth, and related medical decisions.
1990	Americans with Disabilities Act	Prohibits discrimination against disabled individuals in employment decisions and requires that employers make accommodations for disabled workers to enable them to perform their jobs.
1991	Civil Rights Act	Prohibits discrimination (as does Title VII) and allows for the awarding of punitive and compensatory damages, in addition to back pay, in cases of intentional discrimination.
1993	Family and Medical Leave Act	Requires that employers provide 12 weeks of unpaid leave for medical and family reasons, including paternity and illness of a family member.

to ensure that the policies and procedures they have in place treat all workers fairly, regardless of their ages. Additionally, effectively managing diversity means employees of diverse ages are able to learn from each other, work well together, and take advantage of the different perspectives each has to offer.

Gender

Women and men both have substantial participation rates in the U.S. workforce (approximately 55.6 percent of the U.S. workforce is male and 44.4 percent female),[58] yet women's median weekly earnings are estimated to be $706 compared to $860 for men.[59] Thus, the gender pay gap appears to be as unfortunately real as the glass ceiling. According to the nonprofit organization Catalyst, which studies women in business, while women compose about 51.5 percent of the employees in managerial and professional positions,[60] only around 14.6 percent of executive officers in the 500 largest U.S. companies (that is, the *Fortune* 500) are women, and only 8.1 percent of the top earner executive officers are women.[61] These women, such as Virginia Rometty, CEO of IBM, and Indra Nooyi, CEO of PepsiCo, stand out among their male peers and often receive a disparate amount of attention in the media. Women are also very underrepresented on boards of directors—they currently hold 16.9 percent of the board seats of *Fortune* 500 companies.[62] However, as Sheila Wellington, former president of Catalyst, indicates, "Women either control or influence nearly all consumer purchases, so it's important to have their perspective represented on boards."[63]

Additionally, research conducted by consulting firms suggests that female executives outperform their male colleagues in skills such as motivating others,

A female executive enjoying the company plane is not as rare a sight today as it used to be; nevertheless, the glass ceiling remains a real barrier to women in the business workforce. © ColorBlind Images/ Blend Images LLC RF

promoting good communication, turning out high-quality work, and being good listeners.[64] For example, the Hagberg Group performed in-depth evaluations of 425 top executives in a variety of industries, with each executive rated by approximately 25 people. Of the 52 skills assessed, women received higher ratings than men on 42 skills, although at times the differences were small.[65] Results of a study conducted by Catalyst found that organizations with higher proportions of women in top management positions had significantly better financial performance than organizations with lower proportions of female top managers.[66] Another study conducted by Catalyst found that companies with three or more women on their boards of directors performed better in terms of returns on equity, sales, and invested capital than companies with fewer or no women on their boards.[67] Studies such as these make one wonder why the glass ceiling continues to hamper the progress of women in business.

Race and Ethnicity

The U.S. Census Bureau distinguished between the following races in the 2010 census: American Indian or Alaska Native; Asian Indian; black, African American, or Negro; Chinese; Filipino; Japanese; Korean; Vietnamese; other Asian; Native Hawaiian; Guamanian or Chamorro; Samoan; Other Pacific Islander; white; and other races.[68] Although *ethnicity* refers to a grouping of people based on some shared characteristic such as national origin, language, or culture, the U.S. Census Bureau treats ethnicity in terms of whether a person is Hispanic, Latino, or of Spanish origin or not.[69] Hispanics, also referred to as Latinos, are people whose origins are in Spanish cultures such as those of Cuba, Mexico, Puerto Rico, and South and Central America. Hispanics can be of different races.[70] According to a recent poll, most Hispanics prefer to be identified by their country of origin (such as Mexican, Cuban, or Salvadoran) rather than by the overarching term *Hispanic.*[71]

The racial and ethnic diversity of the U.S. population is increasing quickly, as is the diversity of the workforce.[72] According to the U.S. Census Bureau, approximately one of every three U.S. residents belongs to a minority group (is not a non-Hispanic white).[73] More specifically, 16.3 percent of the population is Hispanic or Latino, 83.7 percent of the population is not Hispanic or Latino, and 63.7 percent of the population is white alone (that is, white and not Hispanic or Latino).[74] For those individuals self-identifying one race in the 2010 U.S. census, approximately 72.4 percent of the population is white, 12.6 percent is black or African American, 0.9 percent is American Indian or Alaska Native, 4.8 percent is Asian, 0.2 percent is Native Hawaiian and other Pacific Islander, and 6.2 percent is another race; 2.9 percent of the population self-identified two or more races.[75] According to projections released by the U.S. Census Bureau, the composition of the U.S. population in 2050 will be quite different from its composition today; in 2050, the U.S. population is projected to be 54 percent minority.[76]

The increasing racial and ethnic diversity of the workforce and the population as a whole underscores the importance of effectively managing diversity. Statistics compiled by the Bureau of Labor Statistics suggest that much needs to be done in terms of ensuring that diverse employees have equal opportunities. For example, median weekly earnings for black men are approximately 75.1 percent of median earnings for white men; median weekly earnings for black women are approximately 83.9 percent of median earnings for white women.[77] In the remainder of this chapter, we focus on the fair treatment of diverse employees and explore why this is such an important challenge and what managers can do to meet it. We begin by taking a broader perspective and considering how increasing racial and ethnic diversity in an organization's environment (such as customers and suppliers) affects decision making and organizational effectiveness.

At a general level, managers and organizations are increasingly being reminded that stakeholders in the environment are diverse and expect organizational decisions and actions to reflect this diversity. For example, the NAACP (National Association for the Advancement of Colored People) and Children Now (an advocacy group) have lobbied the entertainment industry to increase the diversity in television programming, writing, and producing.[78] The need for such increased diversity is more than apparent. For example, while Hispanics make up 17 percent of the U.S. population (or 53 million potential TV viewers), less than 5 percent of the characters in prime-time TV shows are Hispanics, according to a study conducted by Children Now.[79] Moreover, less than 5 percent of the evening network TV news stories are reported by Hispanic correspondents, according to the Center for Media and Public Affairs.[80]

Pressure is mounting on networks to increase diversity for a variety of reasons revolving around the diversity of the population as a whole, TV viewers, and consumers. For example, home and automobile buyers are increasingly diverse, reflecting the increasing diversity of the population as a whole.[81] Moreover, managers have to be especially sensitive to avoid stereotyping different groups when they communicate with potential customers. For example, Toyota Motor Sales USA made a public apology to the Reverend Jesse Jackson and his Rainbow Coalition for using a print advertisement depicting an African-American man with a Toyota RAV4 sport utility image embossed on his gold front tooth.[82]

Religion

Title VII of the Civil Rights Act prohibits discrimination based on religion (as well as based on race/ethnicity, country of origin, and sex; see Table 3.1). In addition to enacting Title VII, in 1997, the federal government issued "The White House Guidelines on Religious Exercise and Expression in the Federal Workplace."[83] These guidelines, while technically applicable only in federal offices, also are frequently relied on by large corporations. The guidelines require that employers make reasonable accommodations for religious practices, such as observances of holidays, as long as doing so does not entail major costs or hardships.[84]

A key issue for managers in religious diversity is recognizing and being aware of different religions and their beliefs, with particular attention being paid to when religious holidays fall. For example, critical meetings should not be scheduled during a holy day for members of a certain faith, and managers should be flexible in allowing people to have time off for religious observances. According to Lobna Ismail, director of a diversity training company in Silver Spring, Maryland, when managers acknowledge, respect, and make even small accommodations for religious diversity, employee loyalty is often enhanced. For example, allowing employees to leave work early on certain days instead of taking a lunch break or posting holidays for different religions on the company calendar can go a long way toward making individuals of diverse religions feel respected and valued as well as enabling them to practice their faith.[85] According to research conducted by the Tanenbaum Center for Inter-religious Understanding in New York, while only about 23 percent of employees who feel they are victims of religious discrimination actually file complaints, about 45 percent of these employees start looking for other jobs.[86]

Capabilities/Disabilities

The Americans with Disabilities Act (ADA) of 1990 prohibits discrimination against persons with disabilities and also requires that employers make reasonable accommodations to enable these people to effectively perform their jobs. On the surface, few would argue with the intent of this legislation. However, as managers attempt to implement policies and procedures to comply with the ADA, they face a number of interpretation and fairness challenges.

On one hand, some people with real disabilities warranting workplace accommodations are hesitant to reveal their disabilities to their employers and claim the accommodations they deserve.[87] On the other hand, some employees abuse the ADA by seeking unnecessary accommodations for disabilities that may or may not exist.[88] Thus, it is perhaps not surprising that the passage of the ADA does not appear to have increased employment rates significantly for those with disabilities.[89] A key challenge for managers is to promote an environment in which employees needing accommodations feel comfortable disclosing their need and, at the same time, to ensure that the accommodations not only enable those with disabilities to effectively perform their jobs but also are perceived to be fair by those not disabled.[90]

In addressing this challenge, often managers must educate both themselves and their employees about the disabilities, as well as the real capabilities, of those who are disabled. For example, during a Disability Awareness Week, administrators at the University of Notre Dame sought to increase the public's knowledge of disabilities while also heightening awareness of the abilities of persons who are disabled.[91] The University of Houston conducted a similar program called "Think Ability."[92] According to Cheryl Amoruso, director of the University of Houston's Center for Students with Disabilities, many people are unaware of the prevalence of disabilities as well as misinformed about their consequences.[93] She suggests, for example, that although students may not be able to see, they can still excel in their coursework and have successful careers.[94] Accommodations enabling such students to perform up to their capabilities are covered under the ADA.

The ADA also protects employees with acquired immune deficiency syndrome (AIDS) from being discriminated against in the workplace. AIDS is caused by the human immunodeficiency virus (HIV) and is transmitted through sexual contact, infected needles, and contaminated blood products. HIV is not spread through casual nonsexual contact. Yet out of ignorance, fear, or prejudice, some people wish to avoid all contact with anyone infected with HIV. Infected individuals may not necessarily develop AIDS, and some individuals with HIV are able to remain effective performers of their jobs while not putting others at risk.[95]

AIDS awareness training can help people overcome their fears and also give managers a tool to prevent illegal discrimination against HIV-infected employees.

Such training focuses on educating employees about HIV and AIDS, dispelling myths, communicating relevant organizational policies, and emphasizing the rights of HIV-positive employees to privacy and an environment that allows them to be productive.[96] The need for AIDS awareness training is underscored by some of the problems HIV-positive employees experience once others in their workplace become aware of their condition.[97] Moreover, organizations are required to make reasonable accommodations to enable people with AIDS to effectively perform their jobs.

Thus, managers have an obligation to educate employees about HIV and AIDS, dispel myths and the stigma of AIDS, and ensure that HIV-related discrimination is not occurring in the workplace. For example, Home Depot has provided HIV training and education to its store managers; such training was sorely needed given that over half of the managers indicated that it was the first time they had the opportunity to talk about AIDS.[98] Moreover, advances in medication and treatment mean that more infected individuals are able to continue working or are able to return to work after their condition improves. Thus, managers need to ensure that these employees are fairly treated by all members of their organizations.[99] And managers and organizations that do not treat HIV-positive employees in a fair manner, as well as provide reasonable accommodations (such as allowing time off for doctor visits or to take medicine), risk costly lawsuits.

Socioeconomic Background

The term *socioeconomic background* typically refers to a combination of social class and income-related factors. From a management perspective, socioeconomic diversity (and in particular diversity in income levels) requires that managers be sensitive and responsive to the needs and concerns of individuals who might not be as well off as others. U.S. welfare reform in the middle to late 1990s emphasized the need for single mothers and others receiving public assistance to join or return to the workforce. In conjunction with a strong economy, this led to record declines in the number of families, households, and children living below the poverty level, according to the 2000 U.S. census.[100] However, the economic downturns in the early and late 2000s suggest that some past gains that lifted families out of poverty have been reversed. In a strong economy, it is much easier for poor people with few skills to find jobs; in a weak economy, when companies lay off employees in hard times, people who need their incomes the most are unfortunately often the first to lose their jobs.[101] And in recessionary times, it is difficult for laid-off employees to find new positions. For example, in December 2009, there were an average of 6.1 unemployed workers for every open position.[102]

According to statistics released by the US Census Bureau, the official poverty rate in the United States in 2012 was 15.0 percent or 46.5 million people; in 2009 the poverty rate was 14.3 percent or 43.6 million people.[103] The Census Bureau relies on predetermined threshold income figures, based on family size and composition, adjusted annually for inflation, to determine the poverty level. Families whose income falls below the threshold level are considered poor.[104] For example, in 2012, a family of four was considered poor if their annual income fell below $23,492.[105] When workers earn less than $15 per hour, it is often difficult, if not impossible, for them to meet their families' needs.[106] Moreover, increasing numbers of families are facing the challenge of finding suitable child care arrangements that enable the adults to work long hours and/or through the night to maintain an adequate income level. New information technology has led to more businesses operating 24 hours a day, creating real challenges for workers on the night shift, especially those with children.[107]

Hundreds of thousands of parents across the country are scrambling to find someone to care for their children while they are working the night shift, commuting several hours a day, working weekends and holidays, or putting in long hours on one or more jobs. This has led to the opening of day-care facilities that operate around the clock as well as to managers seeking ways to provide such care for children of their employees. For example, the Children's Choice Learning Center in Las Vegas, Nevada, operates around the clock to accommodate employees working nights in neighboring casinos, hospitals, and call centers. Randy Donahue, a security guard who works until midnight, picks his children up from the center when he gets off work; his wife is a nurse on the night shift.[108]

Judy Harden, who focuses on families and child care issues for the United Workers Union, indicates that the demands families are facing necessitate around-the-clock and odd-hour child care options. Many parents simply do not have the choice of working at hours that allow them to take care of their children at night and/or on weekends, never mind when the children are sick.[109] Some parents and psychologists feel uneasy having children separated from their families for so much time and particularly at night. Most agree that, unfortunately for many families, this is not a choice but a necessity.[110]

Socioeconomic diversity suggests that managers need to be sensitive and responsive to the needs and concerns of workers who may be less fortunate than themselves in terms of income and financial resources, child care and elder care options, housing opportunities, and existence of sources of social and family support. Moreover—and equally important—managers should try to give such individuals opportunities to learn, advance, and make meaningful contributions to their organizations while improving their economic well-being.

Sexual Orientation

According to research conducted by Gary Gates of the Williams Institute at the UCLA School of Law, approximately 3.5 percent of adults in the United States, or 9 million U.S. residents, self-identify as lesbian, gay, bisexual, or transgender (LGBT).[111] Although no federal law prohibits discrimination based on sexual orientation, 21 states and the District of Columbia have such laws, and a 1998 executive order prohibits sexual orientation discrimination in civilian federal offices.[112] Moreover, an increasing number of organizations recognize the minority status of LGBT employees, affirm their rights to fair and equal treatment, and provide benefits to same-sex partners of gay and lesbian employees.[113] For example, a vast majority of *Fortune* 500 companies prohibit discrimination based on sexual orientation, and a majority of the *Fortune* 500 provide domestic partner benefits.[114] More generally, managers can take many steps to ensure that sexual orientation is not used to unfairly discriminate among employees.

Other Kinds of Diversity

Other kinds of diversity are important in organizations, are critical for managers to deal with effectively, and also are potential sources of unfair treatment. For example, organizations and teams need members with diverse backgrounds and experiences. This is clearly illustrated by the prevalence of cross-functional teams in organizations whose members might come from various departments such as marketing, production, finance, and sales (teams are covered in depth in Chapter 11). A team responsible for developing and introducing a new product, for example, often needs the expertise of employees not only from research and design and engineering but also from marketing, sales, production, and finance.

Other types of diversity can affect how employees are treated in the workplace. For example, employees differ from each other in how attractive they are (based on the standards of the cultures in which an organization operates) and in body weight. Whether individuals are attractive, unattractive, thin, or overweight in most cases has no bearing on their job performance unless they have jobs in which physical appearance plays a role, such as modeling. Yet sometimes these physical sources of diversity affect advancement rates and salaries. A study published in the *American Journal of Public Health* found that highly educated obese women earned approximately 30 percent less per year than women who were not obese and men (regardless of whether or not the men were obese).[115] Clearly managers need to ensure that all employees are treated fairly, regardless of their physical appearance.

Managers and the Effective Management of Diversity

The increasing diversity of the environment—which, in turn, increases the diversity of an organization's workforce—increases the challenges managers face in effectively managing diversity. Each of the kinds of diversity just discussed presents a particular set of issues managers need to appreciate before they can respond to them effectively. Understanding these issues is not always a simple matter, as many informed managers have discovered. Research on how different groups are currently treated and the unconscious biases that might adversely affect them is vital because it helps managers become aware of the many subtle and unobtrusive ways in which diverse employee groups can come to be treated unfairly over time. Managers can take many more steps to become sensitive to the ongoing effects of diversity in their organizations, take advantage of all the contributions diverse employees can make, and prevent employees from being unfairly treated.

LO 3-4 Grasp the central role that managers play in the effective management of diversity.

Critical Managerial Roles

In each of their managerial roles (see Chapter 1), managers can either promote the effective management of diversity or derail such efforts; thus, they are critical to this process. For example, in their interpersonal roles, managers can convey that the effective management of diversity is a valued goal and objective (figurehead role), can serve as a role model and institute policies and procedures to ensure that all organizational members are treated fairly (leader role), and can enable diverse individuals and groups to coordinate their efforts and cooperate with each other both inside the organization and at the organization's boundaries (liaison role). Table 3.2 summarizes ways in which managers can ensure that diversity is effectively managed as they perform their different roles.

Given the formal authority that managers have in organizations, they typically have more influence than rank-and-file employees. When managers commit to supporting diversity, their authority and positions of power and status influence other members of an organization to make a similar commitment.[116] Research on social influence supports such a link: People are likely to be influenced and persuaded by others who have high status.[117]

Table 3.2

Managerial Roles and the Effective Management of Diversity

Type of Role	Specific Role	Example
Interpersonal	Figurehead	Conveys that the effective management of diversity is a valued goal and objective.
	Leader	Serves as a role model and institutes policies and procedures to ensure that diverse members are treated fairly.
	Liaison	Enables diverse individuals to coordinate their efforts and cooperate with one another.
Informational	Monitor	Evaluates the extent to which all employees are treated fairly.
	Disseminator	Informs employees about diversity policies and initiatives and the intolerance of discrimination.
	Spokesperson	Supports diversity initiatives in the wider community and speaks to diverse groups to interest them in career opportunities.
Decisional	Entrepreneur	Commits resources to develop new ways to effectively manage diversity and eliminate biases and discrimination.
	Disturbance handler	Takes quick action to correct inequalities and curtail discriminatory behavior.
	Resource allocator	Allocates resources to support and encourage the effective management of diversity.
	Negotiator	Works with organizations (e.g., suppliers) and groups (e.g., labor unions) to support and encourage the effective management of diversity.

Consider the steps that managers at Sodexo and Principal Financial Group have taken to effectively manage diversity as profiled in the accompanying "Focus on Diversity" feature.

FOCUS ON DIVERSITY

Effectively Managing Diversity at Sodexo and Principal Financial Group

Managers at Sodexo, Inc., a major food and facilities management company serving over 15 million consumers per day in businesses, health care facilities, schools and universities, and government agencies, take many steps to ensure that diversity is effectively managed.[118] Sodexo encourages managers to interact with diverse groups to gain a better appreciation and understanding of their experiences. When Ron Bond attended a meeting of the Women's Food Service Forum with some of his female coworkers, he stood out as one of the few men in attendance among 1,500 women. Thinking back on his own experiences when, for example, he started out his career and women were rare in the management ranks, Bond gained a deeper appreciation of what it means to be different in a group or organization. As he suggested, "That's a profound experience . . . I can begin to feel what it must have felt like to be different."[119]

Magic Johnson and Sodexo president and CEO George Chavel present Northwestern University student Sarah Suh with the Stephen J. Brady STOP Hunger scholarship at Sodexo's Diversity Business Leadership Summit in Chicago in 2013. Courtesy of Sodexo

Sodexo provides employees and managers with extensive diversity training, encourages managers to mentor and coach employees who are different from themselves, and bases 25 percent of top managers' bonuses on their performance on diversity initiatives, including hiring and training diverse employees.[120] Managers are encouraged to sponsor affinity groups for employees that differ from themselves. For example, Bond sponsored the women's affinity group, which provided a forum for female employees to connect with each other and address their mutual concerns (such as a lactation room so new mothers can pump breast milk). Sponsoring such groups helps managers become aware of and address concerns of some employee groups they might never have thought of otherwise. Bond realized that having a lactation room was "just one of those things I'd never thought about."[121]

Lorna Donatone managed a unit of Sodexo that provides food services for cruise companies. Of Swedish and German ancestry and raised in Nebraska, she sponsored Sodexo's Latino affinity group and discovered a better way to serve her unit's customers. Donatone learned to rely more on more bilingual materials to promote the services she provided to cruise companies and their customers. As senior vice president and global chief diversity officer for Sodexo Dr. Rohini Anand indicated, "To really engage people, you have to create a series of epiphanies and take leaders through those epiphanies."[122]

Sodexo's effective management of diversity has not gone unnoticed in the business community, and the company and its diverse employees have received numerous awards and recognition for their diversity initiatives.[123] Frequently ranked as a best place to work for diverse employees by magazines such as *DiversityInc., Working Mother,* and *Latina Style,* Sodexo was ranked second in *DiversityInc.*'s listing of "The Top 50 Companies for Diversity" in 2014.[124]

Principal Financial Group, headquartered in Des Moines, Iowa, operates in a vastly different industry: financial products, services, and insurance.[125] Yet Principal Financial also has been recognized for its effective management of diversity.[126] To ensure that opportunities are open for diverse employees, Principal has offered its employees flexible work schedules since 1974—decades before many other companies provided this option. And employees who take advantage of this and other benefits, such as having 12 weeks off work after the birth of a child, do not find their career progress hampered as is sometimes the case at other companies.[127]

When Valarie Vest was a regional client service director at Principal and on her second maternity leave, her supervisors called to offer her a promotion to a position that included more responsibility, more travel, and relocation to a different city. They thought she was the best candidate for the position and let her decide if she wanted to take it. She was delighted to accept the position, which included managing 10 employees.[128]

Principal seeks to hire diverse employees and then gives them the resources and opportunities to help them reach their potential while helping Principal achieve its goals. These resources and opportunities include, but are not limited to, mentoring programs, multicultural celebrations, on-site child care, development programs, and domestic partner benefits.[129] Additionally, there are a variety of employee resource groups that all employees can join to network, engage in career development activities, and become involved in the community.[130]

Sodexo and Principal Financial Group are among the growing numbers of companies that are reaping the benefits of an increasingly diverse workforce.

LO 3-5
Understand why the effective management of diversity is both an ethical and a business imperative.

When managers commit to diversity, their commitment legitimizes the diversity management efforts of others.[131] In addition, resources are devoted to such efforts, and all members of an organization believe that their diversity-related efforts are supported and valued. Consistent with this reasoning, top management commitment and rewards for the support of diversity are often cited as critical ingredients in the success of diversity management initiatives.[132] Additionally, seeing managers express confidence in the abilities and talents of diverse employees causes other organizational members to be similarly confident and helps reduce any prejudice they may have as a result of ignorance or stereotypes.[133]

Two other important factors emphasize why managers are so central to the effective management of diversity. The first factor is that women, African Americans, Hispanics, and other minorities often start out at a slight disadvantage due to how they are perceived by others in organizations, particularly in work settings where they are a numerical minority. As Virginia Valian, a psychologist at Hunter College who studies gender, indicates, "In most organizations women begin at a slight disadvantage. A woman does not walk into the room with the same status as an equivalent man, because she is less likely than a man to be viewed as a serious professional."[134]

The second factor is that research suggests that slight differences in treatment can accumulate and result in major disparities over time. Even small differences—such as a small favorable bias toward men for promotions—can lead to major differences in the number of male and female managers over time.[135] Thus, while women and other minorities are sometimes advised not to make "a mountain out of a molehill" when they perceive they have been unfairly treated, research conducted by Valian and others suggests that molehills (slight differences in treatment based on irrelevant distinctions such as race, gender, or ethnicity) can turn into mountains over time (major disparities in important outcomes such as promotions) if they are ignored.[136] Once again, managers have the obligation, from both an ethical and a business perspective, to prevent any disparities in treatment and outcomes due to irrelevant distinctions such as race or ethnicity.

Effectively Managing Diversity Makes Good Business Sense

Diverse organizational members can be a source of competitive advantage, helping an organization provide customers with better goods and services.[137] The variety of points of view and approaches to problems and opportunities that diverse employees provide can improve managerial decision making. Suppose that the Budget Gourmet frozen food company is trying to come up with creative ideas for new frozen meals that will appeal to health-conscious, time-conscious customers tired of the same old frozen fare. Which group do you think is likely to come up with the most creative ideas: a group of white women with marketing degrees from Yale University who grew up in upper-middle-class families in the Northeast or a racially mixed group of men and women who grew up in families with varying income levels in different parts of the country and attended a variety of geographically dispersed business schools? Most people would agree that the diverse group is likely to have a wider range of creative ideas. Although this example is simplistic, it underscores one way in which diversity can lead to a competitive advantage.

Just as the workforce is becoming increasingly diverse, so too are the customers who buy an organization's goods or services. In an attempt to suit local customers' needs and tastes, organizations like Target often vary the selection of products available in stores in different cities and regions.[138]

Diverse members of an organization are likely to be attuned to what goods and services diverse segments of the market want and do not want. Automakers, for example, are increasingly assigning women to their design teams to ensure that the needs and desires of female customers are taken into account in new car design.

For Darden Restaurants, the business case for diversity rests on market share and growth. Darden seeks to satisfy the needs and tastes of diverse customers by providing menus in Spanish in communities with large Hispanic populations.[139] Similarly, market share and growth and the identification of niche markets led Tracey Campbell to cater to travelers with disabilities.[140] She heads InnSeekers, a telephone and online listing resource for bed and breakfasts. Nikki Daruwala works for the Calvert Group in Bethesda, Maryland, a mutual fund that emphasizes social responsibility and diversity. She indicates that profit alone is more than enough of an incentive to effectively manage diversity. As she puts it, "You can look at an automaker. There are more women making decisions about car buying or home buying . . . $3.72 trillion per year are spent by women."[141]

Another way that effective management of diversity can improve profitability is by increasing retention of valued employees, which decreases the costs of hiring replacements for those who quit as well as ensures that all employees are highly motivated. In terms of retention, given the current legal environment, more and more organizations are attuned to the need to emphasize the importance of diversity in hiring. Once hired, if diverse employees think they are being unfairly treated, however, they will be likely to seek opportunities elsewhere. Thus, recruiting diverse employees has to be followed with ongoing effective management of diversity to retain valued organizational members.

If diversity is not effectively managed and turnover rates are higher for members of groups who are not treated fairly, profitability will suffer on several counts. Not only are the future contributions of diverse employees lost when they quit, but the organization also has to bear the costs of hiring replacement workers. According to the Employment Management Association, on average it costs more than $10,000 to hire a new employee; other estimates are significantly higher. For example, Ernst & Young estimates it costs about $1,200,000 to replace 10 professionals, and the diversity consulting firm Hubbard & Hubbard estimates replacement costs average one-and-a-half times an employee's annual salary.[142] Moreover, additional costs from failing to effectively manage diversity stem from time lost due to the barriers diverse members of an organization perceive as thwarting their progress and advancement.[143]

Effectively managing diversity makes good business sense for another reason. More and more, managers and organizations concerned about diversity are insisting that their suppliers also support diversity.[144]

Finally, from both business and ethical perspectives, effective management of diversity is necessary to avoid costly lawsuits such as those settled by Advantica (owner of the Denny's chain) and the Coca-Cola Company. In 2000, Coca-Cola settled a class action suit brought by African-American employees at a cost of $192 million. The damage such lawsuits cause goes beyond the monetary awards to the injured parties; it can tarnish a company's image. One positive outcome of Coca-Cola's 2000 settlement is the company's recognition of the need to commit additional resources to diversity management initiatives. Coca-Cola is increasing its use of minority suppliers, instituting a formal mentoring program, and instituting days to celebrate diversity with its workforce.[145] These efforts have paid off, and Coca-Cola has appeared on *DiversityInc.*'s list of the "Top 50 Companies for Diversity."

In 2013 Merrill Lynch agreed to settle a racial discrimination lawsuit, brought by 700 black brokers, which spent around eight years in the U.S. federal court system; the settlement cost was $160,000,000.[146] After the suit was initially filed, Merrill Lynch was bought by Bank of America. As part of the settlement, Merrill Lynch agreed to change its policies, take proactive steps to ensure that discrimination does not take place, and ensure that black brokers have fair opportunities to be successful. This three-year initiative is being overseen by a committee composed of black brokers.[147] Also in 2013, Bank of America agreed to settle a discrimination lawsuit brought by female employees of Merrill Lynch for $39 million; from around 1998 to 2013, Merrill Lynch paid close to $500,000,000 to settle discrimination claims.[148] As part of the settlement, Merrill Lynch consented to alter its policies to help ensure that women have fair opportunities to be successful.[149] Initiatives undertaken as result of both of these lawsuits should help ensure that Merrill Lynch effectively manages diversity. By now it should be clear that effectively managing diversity is a necessity on both ethical and business grounds.

Sexual Harassment

Sexual harassment seriously damages both the people who are harassed and the reputation of the organization in which it occurs. It also can cost organizations large amounts of money. In 1995, for example, Chevron Corporation agreed to pay $2.2 million to settle a sexual harassment lawsuit filed by four women who worked at the Chevron Information Technology Company in San Ramon, California. One woman involved in the suit said she had received violent pornographic material through the company mail. Another, an electrical engineer, said she had been asked to bring pornographic videos to Chevron workers at an Alaska drill site.[150] More recently, in 2001, TWA spent $2.6 million to settle a lawsuit that alleged female employees were sexually harassed at JFK International Airport in New York. According to the EEOC, not only was sexual harassment tolerated at TWA, but also company officials did little to curtail it when it was brought to their attention.[151]

Unfortunately, the events at Chevron and TWA are not isolated incidents.[152] In 2011, two lawsuits were filed against American Apparel and its founder and CEO, Dov Charney, alleging sexual harassment.[153] Of the 607 women surveyed by the National Association for Female Executives, 60 percent indicated that they had experienced some form of sexual harassment.[154] In a survey conducted by the Society for Human Resource Management of 460 companies, 36 percent of the companies indicated that, within the last 24 months, one or more employees claimed that they had been sexually harassed.[155] Sexual harassment victims can be women or men, and their harassers do not necessarily have to be of the opposite sex.[156] However, women are the most frequent victims of sexual harassment, particularly those in male-dominated occupations or those who occupy positions stereotypically associated with certain gender relationships, such as a female secretary reporting to a male boss. Though it occurs less frequently, men can also be victims of sexual harassment.

LO 3-6
Understand the two major forms of sexual harassment and how they can be eliminated.

For instance, several male employees at Jenny Craig filed a lawsuit claiming they were subject to lewd and inappropriate comments from female coworkers and managers.[157] Sexual harassment is not only unethical; it is also illegal. Managers have an ethical obligation to ensure that they, their coworkers, and their subordinates never engage in sexual harassment, even unintentionally.

Forms of Sexual Harassment

quid pro quo sexual harassment Asking for or forcing an employee to perform sexual favors in exchange for receiving some reward or avoiding negative consequences.

There are two basic forms of sexual harassment: quid pro quo sexual harassment and hostile work environment sexual harassment. **Quid pro quo sexual harassment** occurs when a harasser asks or forces an employee to perform sexual favors to keep a job, receive a promotion, receive a raise, obtain some other work-related opportunity, or avoid receiving negative consequences such as demotion or dismissal.[158] This "Sleep with me, honey, or you're fired" form of harassment is the more extreme type and leaves no doubt in anyone's mind that sexual harassment has taken place.[159]

hostile work environment sexual harassment Telling lewd jokes, displaying pornography, making sexually oriented remarks about someone's personal appearance, and other sex-related actions that make the work environment unpleasant.

Hostile work environment sexual harassment is more subtle. It occurs when organizational members face an intimidating, hostile, or offensive work environment because of their sex.[160] Lewd jokes, sexually oriented comments or innuendos, vulgar language, displays of pornography, displays or distribution of sexually oriented objects, and sexually oriented remarks about one's physical appearance are examples of hostile work environment sexual harassment.[161] A hostile work environment interferes with organizational members' ability to perform their jobs effectively and has been deemed illegal by the courts. Managers who engage in hostile work environment harassment or allow others to do so risk costly lawsuits for their organizations. For example, in February 2004, a federal jury awarded Marion Schwab $3.24 million after deliberating on her sexual harassment case against FedEx.[162] Schwab was the only female tractor-trailer driver at the FedEx facility serving the Harrisburg International Airport vicinity in Middletown, Pennsylvania, from 1997 to 2000. During that period, she was the target of sexual innuendos, was given inferior work assignments, and was the brunt of derogatory comments about her appearance and the role of women in society. On five occasions the brakes on her truck were tampered with. The federal EEOC sued FedEx, and Schwab was part of the suit.[163]

The courts have recently recognized other forms of hostile work environment harassment, in addition to sexual harassment. For example, in June 2006, a California jury awarded $61 million in punitive and compensatory damages to two FedEx Ground drivers. The drivers, who are of Lebanese descent, indicated that they faced a hostile work environment and high levels of stress because a manager harassed them with racial slurs for two years.[164]

Steps Managers Can Take to Eradicate Sexual Harassment

Managers have an ethical obligation to eradicate sexual harassment in their organizations. There are many ways to accomplish this objective. Here are four initial steps managers can take to deal with the problem:[165]

- *Develop and clearly communicate a sexual harassment policy endorsed by top management.* This policy should include prohibitions against both quid pro quo and hostile work environment sexual harassment. It should contain (1) examples of types of behavior that are unacceptable, (2) a procedure for employees to use to report instances of harassment, (3) a discussion of the disciplinary actions that will be taken when harassment has taken place, and (4) a commitment to educate and train organizational members about sexual harassment.

- *Use a fair complaint procedure to investigate charges of sexual harassment.* Such a procedure should (1) be managed by a neutral third party, (2) ensure that complaints are dealt with promptly and thoroughly, (3) protect and fairly treat victims, and (4) ensure that alleged harassers are fairly treated.

- *When it has been determined that sexual harassment has taken place, take corrective actions as soon as possible.* These actions can vary depending on the severity of the harassment. When harassment is extensive, prolonged, of a quid pro quo nature, or severely objectionable in some other manner, corrective action may include firing the harasser.

- *Provide sexual harassment education and training to all organizational members, including managers.* The majority of *Fortune* 500 firms currently provide this education and training for their employees. Managers at DuPont, for example, developed DuPont's "A Matter of Respect" program to help educate employees about sexual harassment and eliminate its occurrence. The program includes a four-hour workshop in which participants are given information that defines sexual harassment, sets forth the company's policy against it, and explains how to report complaints and access a 24-hour hotline. Participants watch video clips showing actual instances of harassment. One clip shows a saleswoman having dinner with a male client who, after much negotiating, seems about to give her company his business when he suddenly suggests that they continue their conversation in his hotel room. The saleswoman is confused about what to do. Will she be reprimanded if she says no and the deal is lost? After watching a video, participants discuss what they have seen, why the behavior is inappropriate, and what organizations can do to alleviate the problem.[166] Throughout the program, managers stress to employees that they do not have to tolerate sexual harassment or get involved in situations in which harassment is likely to occur.

Barry S. Roberts and Richard A. Mann, experts on business law and authors of several books on the topic, suggest a number of additional factors that managers and all members of an organization need to keep in mind about sexual harassment:[167]

- Every sexual harassment charge should be taken seriously.

- Employees who go along with unwanted sexual attention in the workplace can be sexual harassment victims.

- Employees sometimes wait before they file complaints of sexual harassment.

- An organization's sexual harassment policy should be communicated to each new employee and reviewed with current employees periodically.

- Suppliers and customers need to be familiar with an organization's sexual harassment policy.

- Managers should give employees alternative ways to report incidents of sexual harassment.

- Employees who report sexual harassment must have their rights protected; this includes being protected from any potential retaliation.

- Allegations of sexual harassment should be kept confidential; those accused of harassment should have their rights protected.

- Investigations of harassment charges and any resultant disciplinary actions need to proceed in a timely manner.

- Managers must protect employees from sexual harassment from third parties they may interact with while performing their jobs, such as suppliers or customers.[168]

Summary and Review

ETHICS AND STAKEHOLDERS Ethics are moral principles or beliefs about what is right or wrong. These beliefs guide people in their dealings with other individuals and groups (stakeholders) and provide a basis for deciding whether behavior is right and proper. Many organizations have a formal code of ethics derived primarily from societal ethics, professional ethics, and the individual ethics of the organization's top managers. Managers can apply ethical standards to help themselves decide on the proper way to behave toward organizational stakeholders. Ethical organizational cultures are those in which ethical values and norms are emphasized. Ethical organizational cultures can help organizations and their members behave in a socially responsible manner. [LO 3-1, 3-2]

INCREASING DIVERSITY OF WORKFORCE AND ENVIRONMENT Diversity is differences among people due to age, gender, race, ethnicity, religion, sexual orientation, socioeconomic background, and capabilities/disabilities. The workforce and the organizational environment have become increasingly diverse. Effectively managing diversity is an ethical imperative and can improve organizational effectiveness. [LO 3-3, 3-5]

MANAGING DIVERSITY The effective management of diversity is not only an essential responsibility of managers but an ethical and a business imperative. In each of their managerial roles, managers can encourage organizationwide acceptance and valuing of diversity. [LO 3-4, 3-5]

SEXUAL HARASSMENT Two forms of sexual harassment are quid pro quo sexual harassment and hostile work environment sexual harassment. Steps that managers can take to eradicate sexual harassment include development, communication, and enforcement of a sexual harassment policy, use of fair complaint procedures, prompt corrective action when harassment occurs, and sexual harassment training and education. [LO 3-6]

Management *in Action*

TOPICS FOR DISCUSSION AND ACTION

Discussion

1. When are ethics and ethical standards especially important in organizations? [LO 3-1]

2. Why might managers do things that conflict with their own ethical values? [LO 3-1]

3. How can managers ensure that they create ethical organizational cultures? [LO 3-2]

4. Why are gay and lesbian workers and workers who test positive for HIV sometimes discriminated against? [LO 3-3]

5. Why might some employees resent workplace accommodations that are dictated by the Americans with Disabilities Act? [LO 3-3]

Action

6. Choose a *Fortune* 500 company not mentioned in the chapter. Conduct research to determine what steps this organization has taken to effectively manage diversity and eliminate sexual harassment. [LO 3-4, 3-5, 3-6]

BUILDING MANAGEMENT SKILLS [LO 3-3, 3-4, 3-5, 3-6]
Solving Diversity-Related Problems

Think about the last time that you (1) were treated unfairly because you differed from a decision maker on a particular dimension of diversity or (2) observed someone else being treated unfairly because that person differed from a decision maker on a particular dimension of diversity. Then answer these questions:

1. Why do you think the decision maker acted unfairly in this situation?

2. In what ways, if any, were biases, stereotypes, or overt discrimination involved in this situation?

3. Was the decision maker aware that he or she was acting unfairly?

4. What could you or the person who was treated unfairly have done to improve matters and rectify the injustice on the spot?

5. Was any sexual harassment involved in this situation? If so, what kind was it?

6. If you had authority over the decision maker (e.g., if you were his or her manager or supervisor), what steps would you take to ensure that the decision maker no longer treated diverse individuals unfairly?

MANAGING ETHICALLY [LO 3-1]

Some companies require that their employees work very long hours and travel extensively. Employees with young children, employees taking care of elderly relatives, and employees who have interests outside the workplace sometimes find that their careers are jeopardized if they try to work more reasonable hours or limit their work-related travel. Some of these employees feel that it is unethical for their manager to expect so much of them in the workplace and not understand their needs as parents and caregivers.

Questions

1. Either individually or in a group, think about the ethical implications of requiring long hours and extensive amounts of travel for some jobs.

2. What obligations do you think managers and companies have to enable employees to have a balanced life and meet nonwork needs and demands?

SMALL GROUP BREAKOUT EXERCISE [LO 3-3, 3-4, 3-5]
Determining If a Problem Exists

Form groups of three or four people, and appoint one member as the spokesperson who will communicate your findings to the whole class when called on by the instructor. Then discuss the following scenario:

You and your partners own and manage a local chain of restaurants, with moderate to expensive prices, that are open for lunch and dinner during the week and for dinner on weekends. Your staff is diverse, and you believe that you are effectively managing diversity. Yet on visits to the different restaurants you have noticed that your African American employees tend to congregate together and communicate mainly with each other. The same is true for your Hispanic employees and your white employees. You are meeting with your partners today to discuss this observation.

1. Discuss why the patterns of communication that you

observed might be occurring in your restaurants.

2. Discuss whether your observation reflects an underlying problem. If so, why? If not, why not?

3. Discuss whether you should address this issue with your staff and in your restaurants. If so, how and why? If not, why not?

BE THE MANAGER [LO 3-3, 3-4, 3-5, 3-6]

You are Maria Herrera and have been recently promoted to the position of director of financial analysis for a medium-sized consumer goods firm. During your first few weeks on the job, you took the time to have lunch with each of your subordinates to try to get to know them better. You have 12 direct reports who are junior and senior financial analysts who support different product lines. Susan Epstein, one of the female financial analysts you had lunch with, made the following statement: "I'm so glad we finally have a woman in charge. Now, hopefully things will get better around here." You pressed Epstein to elaborate, but she clammed up. She indicated that she didn't want to unnecessarily bias you and that the problems were pretty self-evident. In fact, Epstein was surprised that you didn't know what she was talking about and jokingly mentioned that perhaps you should spend some time undercover, observing her group and their interactions with others.

You spoke with your supervisor and the former director who had been promoted and had volunteered to be on call if you had any questions. Neither man knew of any diversity-related issues in your group. In fact, your supervisor's response was, "We've got a lot of problems, but fortunately that's not one of them."

Question

1. What are you going to do to address this issue?

THE WALL STREET JOURNAL CASE IN THE NEWS [LO 3-3, 3-4, 3-5, 3-6]

Men Enlist in Fight for Gender Equality

The head of the women's networking group at **Cardinal Health** Inc. is a powerful executive who rose through the management ranks while balancing family and career. He's also a guy.

Finance chief Mike Kaufmann's unusual role highlights a significant shift for U.S. corporate diversity efforts: More big businesses are enlisting men in their push to attain gender equality and diversity at the top.

Companies long viewed women's advancement as the women's problem. But despite years of women-only corporate events, women have progressed slowly into the executive suite or stalled altogether, diversity experts say.

Cardinal shifted gears after women said, "When men are involved with us, it turbocharges the system," recalls George Barrett, chief executive of the health-care services concern.

About 60 male bosses from Cardinal, Dell Inc. and three other major employers recently completed a six-month program organized by Catalyst, a non-profit group that tracks and advocates women's advancement. Participants learned to improve women's prospects partly by building alliances with men. "Guys listen to guys," notes Catalyst President Deborah Gillis.

The leadership consultancy that helped Catalyst put together its program, a firm called White Men

As Full Diversity Partners LLC, says it advised 17 Fortune 500 companies last year to increase men's involvement in advancing women.

"Corporate leaders have come to recognize that men must work alongside women to create meaningful gender-equity improvements," says Bill Proudman, a co-founder. The firm coaches men to examine their mind-sets and shift behaviors so they can foster a more inclusive work culture, he adds.

The National Association for Female Executives also included executive men for the first time at its December meeting. Attendees pledged to urge male colleagues to become champions of women. Many men took immediate action, such as creating mentorship programs, association president Betty Spence says.

These moves reflect research that suggests men carry considerable clout but fear being called out for helping women to move ahead. "Having a guy lead our women's initiative seemed strange to some men I work with," Mr. Kaufmann says.

In addition, several female staffers opposed his 2010 appointment. They said, "We don't need men saving women,'" recollects Carole Watkins, chief human resources officer.

Mr. Kaufmann contends that men must be highly involved to change the balance of power in senior management. Among other things, he has urged men to participate in the women's networking group, and male members now exceed 125. Half of Cardinal's six operating presidents are now female, compared with a third five years ago.

In 2013, women held 14.6% of executive officer positions at Fortune 500 firms, virtually unchanged since 2010, Catalyst reports. But American businesses don't see a financial payoff from gender diversity "until women constitute at least 22% of a senior executive team," concluded a 2014 study by McKinsey & Co.

Catalyst's initiative, launched last May, teaches middle managers and senior executives to understand hurdles facing women, men's privileged status and "unconscious bias"—everyone's implicit preference for certain groups. Unconscious bias often influences important workplace decisions.

Cardinal sales manager Jason Hamilton initially resisted joining the program because of his busy schedule. In hindsight, he says, "I found myself very moved" by the experience. Speaking at a Cardinal national sales convention in July, he described a "new man's man" who

stands up for gender equality. He expressed hope "that [model] will equate to more sales."

Mr. Hamilton says he now actively recruits internal female candidates for vacancies. Previously, he adds, "I didn't pay as much attention."

Doug Hillary, a Dell vice president, says the Catalyst program made him realize he might unconsciously favor male staffers who log long hours at the office. So he asked a female lieutenant with two youngsters whether he adequately accommodated her family needs. He learned that he unwittingly scheduled many staff conference calls when she was dropping kids off at school.

Since then, Mr. Hillary has tried to limit those calls, a move he believes benefits all working parents. He also joined Dell's networking group for women and has encouraged his male colleagues to do the same.

Rockwell Automation Inc. has sought to accelerate the advancement and retention of women and minorities by sending 800 mostly male leaders to multiday sessions conducted by White Men As Full Diversity Partners. One result: the emergence of "change inclusion teams," which are nearly all run by white men. Some have devised tactics to curb gender barriers at the industrial-equipment maker.

For instance, the inclusion team for U.S. field salespeople discouraged the "old boys' network" type of socializing at the bar after company conferences. Instead, it arranged chili cookoffs and other alternate events, recalls regional sales manager John Ahlborn, its first leader. Certain male team members confronted customers over uninvited sexual advances toward their female coworkers.

Between 2010 and 2014, the proportion of U.S. executive roles held by women climbed to 23% from 13%, Rockwell says.

American Express Co. uses other tactics, such as mandatory one-time training for the top brass of the credit-card company about how men's and women's brains work differently.

A well-developed area of women's brains regulates decision-making, for example. They frequently don't pursue larger roles because they weigh various outcomes before acting. By contrast, men's brain structure leads them to focus on "getting the job done," says Valerie Grillo, AmEx's chief diversity officer.

Such insights helped Neal J. Sample, a division head, persuade vice president Rathi Murthy to consider a rapid promotion. "Am I ready?" Ms. Murthy remembers wondering.

She won Mr. Sample's promise of continued full support in the position. "He knew that as a woman, I needed that small nudge," Ms. Murthy says. She succeeded him as the division's chief information officer in January.

Questions

1. Why is Mike Kaufmann leading the women's networking group at Cardinal Health?

2. What have some male managers learned from participating in Catalyst's initiative for middle and top managers to understand the challenges faced by women in the workplace?

3. What are some of the potential advantages of having white men participate in and/or lead corporate diversity efforts?

4. What are some of the potential disadvantages of having white men participate in and/or lead corporate diversity efforts?

Source: Joann S. Lublin, "Men Enlist in Fight for Gender Equality," *The Wall Street Journal*, March 11, 2015, p. B7.

Endnotes

1. "Whole Foods Market History," www.wholefoodsmarket.com/company-info/whole-foods-market-history, March 13, 2013.

2. www.wholefoodsmarket.com, 2012.; www.media.wholefoodsmarket.com, February 18, 2015.

3. "The Green Machine," *Newsweek*, March 21, 2005, E8–E10.

4. www.wholefoodsmarket.com, 2012.; "Whole Foods Market Reports Fourth Quarter Results," www.assets.wholefoodsmarket.com.s3.amazonaws.com/www/company-info/investor-relations/financial-press-releases/2014/Q414-Financial.pdf, February 18, 2015.

5. "Whole Foods Market Reports First Quarter Results," www.wholefoodsmarket.com/sites/default/files/media/global/company%20info/pdf, March 13, 2013.; "Whole Foods Market Delivers Record Q1 Sales and EPS," www.assets.wholefoodsmarket.com.s3.amazonaws.com/www/company-info/investor-relations/financial-press-releases/2015/1Q15-Financial.pdf, February 18, 2015.

6. "John Mackey's Blog: 20 Questions with Sunni's Salon," www.wholefoodsmarket.com, 2006.

7. Ibid.

8. "Fortune 100 Rankings/whole Foods Market," www.wholefoodsmarket.com/career/fortune-100-rankings, March 13, 2013.; "Fast Facts," www.media.wholefoodsmarket.com/fast-facts, February 18, 2105; "Top Companies—Most Diverse," www.archive.fortune.com/magazines/fortune/best-companies/2012/minorities, February 18, 2015; M. Moskowitz and R. Levering, "The 100 Best Companies to Work For," *Fortune*, March 15, 2015, pp. 140–154.

9. "Declaration of Interdependence/whole Foods Market," www.wholefoodsmarket.com/mission-values/core-values/declaration-interdependence, March 13, 2013.

10. www.apple.com, press release, 2012.

11. D. Kravets, "Supreme Court to Hear Case on Medical Pot," www.yahoo.com, June 29, 2004; C. Lane, "A Defeat for Users of Medical Marijuana," www.washington-post.com, June 7, 2005.

12. M. Bruce, "Obama Says Wall St. Protests Voice Widespread Frustrations," October 6, 2011, abcnews.go.com/blogs/politics/2011/10/obama-says-wall-st-protests-voice-widespread-frustrations/.

13. R.E. Freeman, *Strategic Management: A Stakeholder Approach* (Marshfield, MA: Pitman, 1984).

14. S. Bianchi, "Bill Gates Seeks $1.5 Billion More to Eradicate Polio by 2018," *Bloomberg*, April 25, 2013, www.bloomberg.com/news/2013-04-25/bill-gates-seeks-1-5-billion-more-to-eradicate-polio-by-2018.html.

15. J.A. Pearce, "The Company Mission as a Strategic Tool," *Sloan Management Review*, Spring 1982, 15–24.

16. H. Bapuji and S. Riaz, "Occupy Wall Street: What Businesses Need to Know," *Harvard Business Review*, October 14, 2011, blogs.hbr.org/2011/10/occupy-wall-street-what-business/.

17. C.I. Barnard, *The Functions of the Executive* (Cambridge, MA: Harvard University Press, 1948).

18. Freeman, *Strategic Management*.

19. "Michelin Job Cuts at Granton Plant 'Devastating': Company Says Market for Small Car and Truck Tires Is Diminishing," March 3, 2014, www.cbc.ca/news/canada/nova-scotia/michelin-job-cuts-at-granton-plant-devastating-1.2557903.

20. P.S. Adler, "Corporate Scandals: It's Time for Reflection in Business Schools," *Academy of Management Executive* 16 (August 2002), 148–50.

21. C. Main, "Volcker Rule, EU Bank Deadlock, Deutsche Bank Risk: Compliance," *Bloomberg*, December 10, 2013, www.bloomberg.com/news/2013-12-10/volcker-rule-eu-bank-deadlock-deutsche-bank-risk-compliance.html.

22. R. Kerber, "Growth in Compensation for U.S. CEOs May Have Slowed," *Reuters*, March 17, 2014, www.reuters.com/article/2014/03/17/us-compensation-ceos-2013-insight-idUSBREA2G05520140317.

23. W.G. Sanders and D.C. Hambrick, "Swinging for the Fences: The Effects of CEO Stock Options on Company Risk Taking and Performance," *Academy of Management Journal* 53, no. 5 (2007), 1055–78.

24. www.asiainspection.com/who-we-are, February 20, 2105.

25. R. Bowman, "Is This the Year When Supply Chains Become Socially Responsible?" *Forbes*, March 11, 2014, www.forbes.com/sites/robertbowman/2014/03/11/is-this-the-year-when-supply-chains-become-socially-responsible/.

26. S. Greenhouse, "Bangladesh Inspections Find Gaps in Safety," *The New York Times*, March 11, 2014, www.nytimes.com/2014/03/12/business/safety-flaws-found-in-new-inspections-of-factories-in-bangladesh.html?hpw8rref=business.

27. Ibid.

28. T.L. Beauchamp and N.E. Bowie, eds., *Ethical Theory and Business* (Englewood Cliffs, NJ: Prentice-Hall, 1929); A. MacIntyre, *After Virtue* (South Bend, IN: University of Notre Dame Press, 1981).

29. R.E. Goodin, "How to Determine Who Should Get What," *Ethics*, July 1975, 310–21.

30. E.P. Kelly, "A Better Way to Think about Business" (book review), *Academy of Management Executive* 14 (May 2000), 127–29.

31. T.M. Jones, "Ethical Decision Making by Individuals in Organization: An Issue Contingent Model," *Academy of Management Journal* 16 (1991), 366–95; G.F. Cavanaugh, D.J. Moberg, and M. Velasquez, "The Ethics of Organizational Politics," *Academy of Management Review* 6 (1981), 363–74.

32. L.K. Trevino, "Ethical Decision Making in Organizations: A Person–Situation Interactionist Model," *Academy of Management Review* 11 (1986), 601–17; W.H. Shaw and V. Barry, *Moral Issues in Business*, 6th ed. (Belmont, CA: Wadsworth, 1995).

33. T.M. Jones, "Instrumental Stakeholder Theory: A Synthesis of Ethics and Economics," *Academy of Management Review* 20(195), 404–37.

34. B. Victor and J.B. Cullen, "The Organizational Bases of Ethical Work Climates," *Administrative Science Quarterly* 33 (1988), 101–25.

35. D. Collins, "Organizational Harm, Legal Consequences and Stakeholder Retaliation," *Journal of Business Ethics* 8 (1988), 1–13.

36. R.C. Solomon, *Ethics and Excellence* (New York: Oxford University Press, 1992).

37. T.E. Becker, "Integrity in Organizations: Beyond Honesty and Conscientiousness," *Academy of Management Review* 23 (January 1998), 154–62.

38. S.W. Gellerman, "Why Good Managers Make Bad Decisions," in K.R. Andrews, ed, *Ethics in Practice: Managing the Moral Corporation* (Boston: Harvard Business School Press, 1989).

39. J. Dobson, "Corporate Reputation: A Free Market Solution to Unethical Behavior," *Business and Society* 28 (1989), 1–5.

40. M.S. Baucus and J.P. Near, "Can Illegal Corporate Behavior Be Predicted? An Event History Analysis," *Academy of Management Journal* 34 (1991), 9–36.

41. Trevino, "Ethical Decision Making."

42. A. S. Waterman, "On the Uses of Psychological Theory and Research in the Process of Ethical Inquiry," *Psychological Bulletin* 103, no. 3 (1988): 283–98.

43. M. S. Frankel, "Professional Codes: Why, How, and with What Impact?" *Ethics* 8 (1989): 109–15.

44. J. Van Maanen and S. R. Barley, "Occupational Communities: Culture and Control in Organizations," in B. Staw and L. Cummings, eds., *Research in Organizational Behavior*, vol. 6 (Greenwich, CT: JAI Press, 1984), 287–365.

45. Jones, "Ethical Decision Making by Individuals in Organizations."

46. M. Conlin, "Where Layoffs Are a Last Resort," *BusinessWeek*, October 8, 2001, *BusinessWeek* Archives; *Southwest Airlines Fact Sheet*, June 19, 2001, www.swabiz.com.

47. G. R. Jones, *Organizational Theory: Text and Cases* (Reading, MA: Addison-Wesley, 1997).

48. P. E. Murphy, "Creating Ethical Corporate Structure," *Sloan Management Review* (Winter 1989), 81–87.

49. W.B. Swann, Jr., J.T. Polzer, D.C. Seyle, and S.J. Ko, "Finding Value in Diversity: Verification of Personal and Social Self-Views in Diverse Groups," *Academy of Management Review* 29, no. 1 (2004), 9–27.

50. "Usual Weekly Earnings Summary," *News: Bureau of Labor Statistics*, April 16, 2004 (www.bls.gov/news .release/whyeng.nr0.htm); "Facts on Affirmative Action in Employment and Contracting," *Americans for a Fair Chance*, January 28, 2004 (fairchance.civilrights.org/ research_center/details. cfm?id=18076); "Household Data Annual Averages," www.bls.gov, April 28, 2004.

51. "Prejudice: Still on the Menu," *BusinessWeek*, April 3, 1995, 42.

52. "She's a Woman, Offer Her Less," *BusinessWeek*, May 7, 2001, 34.

53. "Glass Ceiling Is a Heavy Barrier for Minorities, Blocking Them from Top Jobs," *The Wall Street Journal*, March 14, 1995, A1.

54. "Catalyst Report Outlines Unique Challenges Faced by African-American Women in Business," *Catalyst* news release, February 18, 2004.

55. C. Gibson, "Nation's Median Age Highest Ever, but 65-and-Over Population's Growth Lags, Census 2000 Shows," *U.S. Census Bureau News*, May 30, 2001 (www.census .gov); "U.S. Census Press Releases: Nation's Population One-Third Minority," *U.S. Census Bureau News*, May 10, 2006 (www.census .gov/Press-Release/www/releases/ archives/population/006808.html); "The World Factbook," *Central Intelligence Agency*, www.cia.gov/ library/publications/the-world-factbook/fields/2177.html, April 5, 2012; "The World Factbook," Central Intelligence Agency, www.cia.gov/ library/publications/the-world-factbook/fields/2177.html, April 1, 2014.

56. "Table 2: United States Population Projections by Age and Sex: 2000–2050," *U.S. Census Board, International Data Base, 94*, April 28, 2004 (www.census.gov/ipc/www. idbprint.html); "An Older and More Diverse Nation by Midcentury," August 14, 2008, Newsroom: Population, www.census.gov/ newsroom/releases/archives/ population/cb08-123.html, April 5, 2012.

57. U.S. Equal Employment Opportunity Commission, "Federal Laws Prohibiting Job Discrimination—Questions and Answers," www.eeoc .gov, June 20, 2001.

58. "Sex by Industry by Class of Worker for the Employed Civilian Population 16 Years and Over," *American FactFinder*, October 15, 2001 (factfinder.census.gov); "2002 Catalyst Census of Women Corporate Officers and Top Earners in the *Fortune* 500," www. catalystwomen.org, August 17, 2004; "WB—Statistics & Data," www.dol.gov/wb/stats/main .htm?PrinterFriendly=true&, February 9, 2010; "Statistical Overview of Women in the Workplace," *Catalyst*, December 2011, www.catalyst.org/ publication/219/statistical-overview-of-women-in-the-workplace, April 4, 2012; "Usual Weekly Earnings of Wage and Salary Workers Fourth Quarter 2013," Bureau of Labor Statistics U.S. Department of Labor, January 22, 2014, www.bls.gov/ news.release/pdf/wkyemg.pdf, April 1, 2014.

59. "Profile of Selected Economic Characteristics: 2000," *American FactFinder*, October 15, 2001 (factfinder.census.gov); "Usual Weekly Earnings Summary," www.bls.gov/news.release, August 17, 2004; "WB—Statistics & Data"; "Usual Weekly Earnings of Wage and Salary Workers Fourth Quarter 2011," January 24, 2012, *Bureau of Labor Statistics, U.S. Department of Labor (BLS)*, www.bls.gov/news. release/pdf/wkyeng.pdf, April 5, 2012.; "Usual Weekly Earnings of Wage and Salary Workers Fourth Quarter 2013."

60. "Women in Management in the United States, 1960–Present," July 2011, *Catalyst*, www.catalyst. org/publication/207/women-in-management-in-the-united-states-1960-p, April 5, 2012.; "Statistical Overview of Women in the Workplace," Knowledge Center — Catalyst.org, March 3, 2014, www. catalyst.org/knowledge/statistical-overview-women-workplace, April 1, 2014.

61. "2000 Catalyst Census of Women Corporate Officers and Top Earners of the *Fortune* 500," www.catalystwomen.org, October 21, 2001; S. Wellington, M. Brumit Kropf, and P.R. Gerkovich, "What's Holding Women Back?" *Harvard Business Review,* June 2003, 18–19; D. Jones, "The Gender Factor," *USA Today.com,* December 30, 2003; "2002 Catalyst Census of Women Corporate Officers and Top Earners in the *Fortune* 500"; "2007 Catalyst Census of Women Corporate Officers and Top Earners of the *Fortune* 500"; www.catalyst.org/knowledge/titles/title.php?page=cen_COTE_07, February 8, 2008; "No News Is Bad News: Women's Leadership Still Stalled in Corporate America," December 14, 2011, *Catalyst,* www.catalyst.org/press-release/199/no-news-is-bad-news-womens-leadership-still-sta . . . , April 5, 2012; "Statistical Overview of Women in the Workplace"; "Fortune 500 Executive Officer Top Earner Positions Held by Women," Knowledge Center—Catalyst.org, www.catalyst.org/knowledge/women-executive-officer-top-earners-fortune-500-0, April 1, 2014.

62. T. Gutner, "Wanted: More Diverse Directors," *BusinessWeek,* April 30, 2001, 134; "2003 Catalyst Census of Women Board Directors," www.catalystwomen.org, August 17, 2004; "2007 Catalyst Census of Women Board Directors of the *Fortune* 500,"; "Statistical Overview of Women in the Workplace"; "Statistical Overview of Women in the Workplace."

63. Gutner, "Wanted: More Diverse Directors"; "2003 Catalyst Census of Women Board Directors."

64. R. Sharpe, "As Leaders, Women Rule," *BusinessWeek,* November 20, 2000, 75–84.

65. Ibid.

66. "New Catalyst Study Reveals Financial Performance Is Higher for Companies with More Women at the Top," *Catalyst* news release, January 26, 2004.

67. P. Sellers, "Women on Boards (NOT!)," *Fortune,* October 15, 2007, 105.

68. U.S. Census 2010, U.S. Department of Commerce, U.S. Census Bureau;

K.R. Hums, N.A. Jones, and R.R. Ramirez, "Overview of Race and Hispanic Original: 2010," *2010 Census Briefs,* March 2011, *United States Census Bureau,* www.census.gov/prod/cen2010/briefs/c2010br-02.pdf, April 5, 2012.

69. U.S. Census 2010.

70. B. Guzman, "The Hispanic Population," U.S. Census Bureau, May 2001; U.S. Census Bureau, "Profiles of General Demographic Characteristics," May 2001; U.S. Census Bureau, "Revisions to the Standards for the Classification of Federal Data on Race and Ethnicity," November 2, 2000, 1–19.

71. L. Chavez, "Just Another Ethnic Group," *The Wall Street Journal,* May 14, 2001, A22.

72. Bureau of Labor Statistics, "Civilian Labor Force 16 and Older by Sex, Age, Race, and Hispanic Origin, 1978, 1988, 1998, and Projected 2008," stats.bls.gov/emp, October 16, 2001.

73. "An Older and More Diverse Nation by Midcentury," August 14, 2008, www.census.gov/newsroom/releases/archives/population/cb08-123.html, April 5, 2012; Humes, Jones, and Ramirez, "Overview of Race and Hispanic Original: 2010."

74. Humes, Jones, and Ramirez, "Overview of Race and Hispanic Original: 2010."

75. "U.S. Census Bureau, Profile of General Demographic Characteristics: 2000," *Census 2000,* www.census.gov; "U.S. Census Press Releases: Nation's Population One-Third Minority," *U.S. Census Bureau News,* May 10, 2006 (www.census.gov/Press-Release/www/releases/archives/population/006808.html); Humes, Jones, and Ramirez, "Overview of Race and Hispanic Original: 2010."

76. "An Older and More Diverse Nation by Midcentury."

77. "Usual Weekly Earnings of Wage and Salary Workers Fourth Quarter 2011," January 24, 2012, Bureau of Labor Statistics U.S. Department of Labor (BLS), www.bls.gov/news.release/pdf/wkyeng.pdf, April 5, 2012.; "Usual Weekly Earnings of Wage and Salary Workers Fourth Quarter 2013," Bureau of Labor Statistics U.S. Department of Labor, January 22, 2014, www.bls.gov/

news.release/pdf/wkyemg.pdf, April 1, 2014.

78. J. Flint, "NBC to Hire More Minorities on TV Shows," *The Wall Street Journal,* January 6, 2000, B13.

79. J. Poniewozik, "What's Wrong with This Picture?" *Time,* June 1, 2001 (www.Time.com); "Hispanic Heritage Month 2013: Sept. 15 – Oct. 15," U.S. Census Bureau News, www.census.gov/newsroom/releases/pdf/cb13ff-19-hispancheritage.pdf.

80. Poniewozik, "What's Wrong with This Picture?"

81. National Association of Realtors, "Real Estate Industry Adapting to Increasing Cultural Diversity," *PR Newswire,* May 16, 2001.

82. "Toyota Apologizes to African Americans over Controversial Ad," *Kyodo News Service,* Japan, May 23, 2001.

83. J.H. Coplan, "Putting a Little Faith in Diversity," *BusinessWeek Online,* December 21, 2000.

84. Ibid.

85. Ibid.

86. K. Holland, "When Religious Needs Test Company," *The New York Times,* February 25, 2007, BU17.

87. J.N. Cleveland, J. Barnes-Farrell, and J.M. Ratz, "Accommodation in the Workplace," *Human Resource Management Review* 7 (1997), 77–108; A. Colella, "Coworker Distributive Fairness Judgments of the Workplace Accommodations of Employees with Disabilities," *Academy of Management Review* 26 (2001), 100–16.

88. Colella, "Coworker Distributive Fairness"; D. Stamps, "Just How Scary Is the ADA," *Training* 32 (1995), 93–101; M.S. West and R.L. Cardy, "Accommodating Claims of Disability: The Potential Impact of Abuses," *Human Resource Management Review* 7 (1997), 233–46.

89. G. Koretz, "How to Enable the Disabled," *BusinessWeek,* November 6, 2000 (*BusinessWeek* Archives).

90. Colella, "Coworker Distributive Fairness."

91. "Notre Dame Disability Awareness Week 2004 Events," www.nd.edu/~bbuddies/daw.html, April 30, 2004.

92. P. Hewitt, "UH Highlights Abilities, Issues of the Disabled," *Houston Chronicle*, October 22, 2001, 24A.

93. Center for Students with DisAbilities (CSD)—University of Houston, www.uh.edu/csd/about_us/staff .html, April 1, 2014.

94. "Notre Dame Disability Awareness"; Hewitt, "UH Highlights Abilities, Issues of the Disabled."

95. J.M. George, "AIDS/AIDS-Related Complex," in L.H. Peters, C.R. Greer, and S.A. Youngblood, eds., *The Blackwell Encyclopedic Dictionary of Human Resource Management* (Oxford, UK: Blackwell, 1997), 6–7.

96. J.M. George, "AIDS Awareness Training," 6.

97. S. Armour, "Firms Juggle Stigma, Needs of More Workers with HIV," *USA Today*, September 7, 2000, B1.

98. Ibid.

99. Ibid.; S. Vaughn, "Career Challenge; Companies' Work Not Over in HIV and AIDS Education," *Los Angeles Times*, July 8, 2001.

100. R. Brownstein, "Honoring Work Is Key to Ending Poverty," *Detroit News*, October 2, 2001, 9; G. Koretz, "How Welfare to Work Worked," *BusinessWeek*, September 24, 2001 (*BusinessWeek* Archives).

101. "As Ex-Welfare Recipients Lose Jobs, Offer Safety Net," *The Atlanta Constitution*, October 10, 2001, A18.

102. C.S. Rugaber, "Job Openings in a Squeeze," *Houston Chronicle*, February 10, 2010, D1.

103. Press releases, U.S. Census Bureau, "Income, Poverty and Health Insurance Coverage in the United States: 2008," www.census.gov/ Press-Release/www/releases/ archives/income_wealth/014227 .html, February 8, 2010; "The 2009 HHS Poverty Guidelines," www. aspe.hhs.gov/poverty/09poverty .shtml, February 8, 2010; "Income, Poverty and Health Insurance Coverage in the United States: 2010," September 13, 2011, www. census.gov/newsroom/releases/ archives/income_wealth/cb11-157.html, April 5, 2012.; "About Poverty—Highlights—U.S. Census Bureau," www.census.gov/hhes/ www/poverty/about/overview/ index.html, April 1, 2014.

104. U.S. Census Bureau, "Poverty—How the Census Bureau Measures Poverty," *Census 2000*, September 25, 2001; "How the Census Bureau Measures Poverty," www.census .gov/hhes/www/poverty/about/ overview/measure.html, April 1, 2014.

105. Press releases, U.S. Census Bureau, "Income, Poverty and Health Insurance Coverage in the United States: 2008," www.census.gov/ Press-Release/www/releases/ archives/income_wealth/014227 .html, February 8, 2010; "The 2009 HHS Poverty Guidelines," www. aspe.hhs.gov/poverty/09poverty .html, February 8, 2010; "Income, Poverty and Health Insurance Coverage in the United States: 2010," September 13, 2011, www.census .gov/newsroom/releases/archives/ income_wealth/cb11-157.html, April 5, 2012.; "Income, Poverty and Health Insurance Coverage in the United States: 2012," www.census .gov/newsroom/releases/archives/ income_wealth/cb13-165.html, April 1, 2014.

106. I. Lelchuk, "Families Fear Hard Times Getting Worse/$30,000 in the Bay Area Won't Buy Necessities, Survey Says," *San Francisco Chronicle*, September 26, 2001, A13; S.R. Wheeler, "Activists: Welfare-to-Work Changes Needed," *Denver Post*, October 10, 2001, B6.

107. B. Carton, "Bedtime Stories: In 24-Hour Workplace, Day Care Is Moving to the Night Shift," *The Wall Street Journal*, July 6, 2001, A1, A4.

108. Ibid.; "Mission, Core Values, and Philosophy," *Children's Choice Features*, www.childrenschoice.com/ AboutUs/MissionCoreValuesand Philosophy/tabid/59/Default.aspx, February 9, 2010.

109. Carton, "Bedtime Stories."

110. Ibid.

111. G.J. Gates, "How Many People Are Lesbian, Gay, Bisexual, and Transgender?" April 2011, *The William Institute*, www. williamsinstitute.law.ucla.edu/ wp-content/uploads/Gates-How-Many-People-LGBT-Apr-2011.pdf, April 5, 2012.

112. S.E. Needleman, "More Programs Move to Halt Bias against Gays," *The Wall Street Journal*, November 26, 2007, B3; "How the Census Bureau Measures Poverty," www. census.gov/hhes/www/poverty/ about/overview/measure.html, April 1, 2014.

113. K. Fahim, "United Parcel Service Agrees to Benefits in Civil Unions," *The New York Times*, July 31, 2007, A19.

114. J. Hempel, "Coming Out in Corporate America," *BusinessWeek*, December 15, 2003, 64–72; "LGBT Equality at the Fortune 500," *Human Rights Campaign*, www.hrc.org/ resources/entry/lgbt-equality-at-the-fortune-500, April 5, 2012.

115. "For Women, Weight May Affect Pay," *Houston Chronicle*, March 4, 2004, 12A.

116. V. Valian, *Why So Slow? The Advancement of Women* (Cambridge, MA: MIT Press, 2000).

117. S.T. Fiske and S.E. Taylor, *Social Cognition*, 2nd ed. (New York: McGraw-Hill, 1991); Valian, *Why So Slow?*

118. P. Dvorak, "Firms Push New Methods to Promote Diversity," *The Wall Street Journal*, December 18, 2006, B3; www. sodexousa.com/, February 7, 2008, "About Us," www.sodexousa.com/ usen/aboutus/aboutus.asp; February 8, 2010; "Catalyst Honors Initiatives at Sodexo and Commonwealth Bank of Australia with the 2012 Catalyst Award," January 24, 2012, www.sodexousa. com/usen/newsroom/press/press12/ sodexo_catalyst_award.asp, April 5, 2012.; "Sodexo in USA," www. sodexousa.com/usen/about-us/ About_us/sodexo-in-USA.aspx, March 28, 2014.

119. Dvorak, "Firms Push New Methods."

120. Ibid.

121. Ibid.

122. Ibid.; "Sodexo Executive Dr. Rohini Anand Honored with Mosaic Woman Leadership Award," November 17, 2011, www.sodexousa. com/usen/newsroom/press/press11/ rohinianandmosaicaward.asp, April 5, 2012.

123. "Sodexho Named Large Employer of the Year by Pike Area (Alabama) Committee," www.sodexousa .com/press-releases/pr110907_2

.asp, February 6, 2008; "No. 6 Sodexo—DiversityInc.com," www.diversityinc.com/content/1757/article/5454/?No_6_Sodexo, February 9, 2010; "Sodexo Tops 2009 HACR List of Most Inclusive Companies for Hispanics," www.sodexousa.com/usen/newsroom/press/press10/hacrcorporateinclusion.asp, February 8, 2010.

124. "Corporate Diversity," www.sodexousa.com/press-factsheets/press_fact_corporate.asp, February 6, 2008; "Sodexho Named to Atlanta Tribune's Top Companies for Minorities," www.sodexousa.com/-press-releases/pr111207_1.asp, February 6, 2008; "Sodexho Recognized as Leader in Corporate Social Responsibility by Montgomery County Chamber of Commerce," www.sodexousa.com/press-releases/pr111507.asp, February 6, 2008; "Catalyst Honors Initiatives at Sodexo and Commonwealth Bank of Australia with the 2012 Catalyst Award," January 24, 2012, www.sodexousa.com/usen/newsroom/press/press12/sodexo_catalyst_award.asp, April 5, 2012.; "The DiversityInc Top 50," DiversityInc, June 2013, 29–76.; "The 2014 Diversity Inc. Top 50 Companies for Diversity," www.diversity.com/the-diversityinc-top-50-companies-for-diversity-2014/, February 23, 2015.

125. "Principal.com—About the Principal," www.principal.com/about/index.htm?print, February 8, 2010; "Principal Financial Group Company Overview—Principal.com," www.principal.com/about/corporate.htm?print, March 28, 2014.; www.principal.com/index.shtm, February 20, 2105.

126. "100 Best Companies to Work for 2008: Principal Financial Group snapshot/FORTUNE," www.money.cnn.com/magazines/fortune/bestcompanies/2008/snapshots/21.html, February 8, 2010; "100 Best Companies to Work For 2009: Principal Financial Group—PFG—from Fortune," www.money.cnn.com/magazines/fortune/bestcompanies/2009/snapshots/17.html, February 8, 2010; J. Hempel, "In the Land of

Women," Fortune, February 4, 2008, 68–69; "Diversity: The Principal Financial Group Earns High Marks in 2010 Corporate Equality . . . ," www.echelonmagazine.com/index.php?id=1123, February 8, 2010; "Human Rights Campaign Foundation, Corporate Equality Index, 2010"; "HRC/Corporate Equality Index," www.hrc.org/issues/workplace/cei.htm, February 22, 2010.

127. Hempel, "In the Land of Women."

128. Ibid.

129. "Principal.com—Careers: Diversity," www.principal.com/careers/workinghere/diversity.htm?print, February 8, 2010; "Principal.com—Careers at The Principal." www.principal.com/careers/workinghere/benefits_main.htm?print, February 8, 2010.

130. Ibid

131. Valian, Why So Slow?

132. S. Rynes and B. Rosen, "A Field Survey of Factors Affecting the Adoption and Perceived Success of Diversity Training," Personnel Psychology 48 (1995), 247–70; Valian, Why So Slow?

133. V. Brown and F.L. Geis, "Turning Lead into Gold: Leadership by Men and Women and the Alchemy of Social Consensus," Journal of Personality and Social Psychology 46 (1984), 811–24; Valian, Why So Slow?

134. Valian, Why So Slow?

135. J. Cole and B. Singer, "A Theory of Limited Differences: Explaining the Productivity Puzzle in Science," in H. Zuckerman, J.R. Cole, and J.T. Bruer, eds., The Outer Circle: Women in the Scientific Community (New York: Norton, 1991), 277–310; M.F. Fox, "Sex, Salary, and Achievement: Reward Dualism in Academia," Sociology of Education 54 (1981), 71–84; J.S. Long, "The Origins of Sex Differences in Science," Social Forces 68 (1990), 1297–1315; R.F. Martell, D.M. Lane, and C. Emrich, "Male–Female Differences: A Computer Simulation," American Psychologist 51 (1996), 157–58; Valian, Why So Slow?

136. Cole and Singer, "A Theory of Limited Differences"; Fox, "Sex, Salary, and Achievement"; Long, "The Origins of Sex Differences";

Martell, Lane, and Emrich, "Male–Female Differences: A Computer Simulation"; Valian, Why So Slow?

137. G. Robinson and K. Dechant, "Building a Case for Business Diversity," Academy of Management Executive 3 (1997), 32–47.

138. A. Patterson, "Target 'Micromarkets' Its Way to Success; No 2 Stores Are Alike," The Wall Street Journal, May 31, 1995, A1, A9.

139. "The Business Case for Diversity: Experts Tell What Counts, What Works," DiversityInc.com, October 23, 2001.

140. B. Hetzer, "Find a Niche—and Start Scratching," BusinessWeek, September 14, 1998 (BusinessWeek Archives). B. Hetzer, "Find a Niche—and Start Scratching," BusinessWeek, September 14, 1998 (BusinessWeek Archives).

141. K. Aaron, "Woman Laments Lack of Diversity on Boards of Major Companies," The Times Union, May 16, 2001 (www.timesunion.com).

142. "The Business Case for Diversity."

143. B. Frankel, "Measuring Diversity Is One Sure Way of Convincing CEOs of Its Value," DiversityInc.com, October 5, 2001.

144. A. Stevens, "Lawyers and Clients," The Wall Street Journal, June 19, 1995, B7.

145. J. Kahn, "Diversity Trumps the Downturn," Fortune, July 9, 2001, 114–16.

146. K. Weise, "The Mann Who Took on Merrill," Bloomberg Businessweek, November 28, 2013, 56–61.

147. Ibid.; P. McGeehan, "Merrill Lynch In Big Payout for Bias Case," The New York Times, August 28, 2013.

148. P. McGeehan, "Bank of America to Pay $39 Million in Gender Bias Case," The New York Times, September 6, 2013.

149. Ibid.

150. "Chevron Settles Claims of 4 Women at Unit as Part of Sex Bias Suit," The Wall Street Journal, January 22, 1995, B12.

151. D.K. Berman, "TWA Settles Harassment Claims at JFK Airport for $2.6 Million," The Wall Street Journal, June 25, 2001, B6.

152. A. Lambert, "Insurers Help Clients Take Steps to Reduce Sexual Harassment," Houston Business

Journal, March 19, 2004 (Houston
.bizjournals.com/Houston/
stories/2004/03/22/focus4.html).

153. L.M. Holson, "Chief of American
Apparel Faces Second Harassment
Suit," *The New York Times*, March 24,
2011: B2.

154. T. Segal, "Getting Serious about
Sexual Harassment," *BusinessWeek*,
November 9, 1992, 78–82.

155. J. Green, "The Silencing of
Sexual Harassment," *Bloomberg
BusinessWeek*, November 21–27,
2011, 27–28.

156. U.S. Equal Employment Opportunity
Commission, "Facts about Sexual
Harassment," www.eeoc.gov/facts/
fs-sex.html, May 1, 2004.

157. B. Carton, "Muscled Out? At Jenny
Craig, Men Are Ones Who Claim
Sex Discrimination," *The Wall Street
Journal*, November 29, 1994, A1, A7.

158. R.L. Paetzold and A.M.
O'Leary-Kelly, "Organizational
Communication and the Legal
Dimensions of Hostile Work
Environment Sexual Harassment,"
in G.L. Kreps, ed., *Sexual
Harassment: Communication
Implications* (Cresskill, NJ: Hampton
Press, 1993).

159. M. Galen, J. Weber, and A.Z. Cuneo,
"Sexual Harassment: Out of the
Shadows," *Fortune*, October 28, 1991,
30–31.

160. A.M. O'Leary-Kelly, R.L. Paetzold,
and R.W. Griffin, "Sexual
Harassment as Aggressive
Action: A Framework for
Understanding Sexual
Harassment," paper presented at
the annual meeting of the Academy
of Management, Vancouver,
August 1995.

161. B.S. Roberts and R.A. Mann,
"Sexual Harassment in the
Workplace: A Primer," www3.
uakron.edu/lawrev/robert1.html,
May 1, 2004.

162. "Former FedEx Driver Wins EEOC
Lawsuit," *Houston Chronicle*,
February 26, 2004, 9B.

163. "Former FedEx Driver Wins EEOC
Lawsuit."

164. J. Robertson, "California Jury
Awards $61M for Harassment,"
www.news.Yahoo.com, June 4, 2006.

165. S.J. Bresler and R. Thacker, "Four-
Point Plan Helps Solve Harassment
Problems," *HR Magazine*, May 1993,
117–24.

166. "Du Pont's Solution," *Training*,
March 1992, 29.

167. Ibid.

168. Ibid.

4

Managing in the Global Environment

Learning Objectives

After studying this chapter, you should be able to:

LO 4-1 Explain why the ability to perceive, interpret, and respond appropriately to the global environment is crucial for managerial success.

LO 4-2 Differentiate between the global task and global general environments.

LO 4-3 Identify the main forces in the global task and general environments, and describe the challenges that each force presents to managers.

LO 4-4 Explain why the global environment is becoming more open and competitive, and identify the forces behind the process of globalization that increase the opportunities, complexities, challenges, and threats managers face.

LO 4-5 Discuss why national cultures differ and why it is important that managers be sensitive to the effects of falling trade barriers and regional trade associations on the political and social systems of nations around the world.

© Neustockimages/E+/Getty Images RF (left)
© Plush Studios/DH Kong/Getty Images RF (right)

MANAGEMENT SNAPSHOT

Going Global Requires Effective Websites

How Should Managers Think About Globalization on the Internet?

Being a global organization is one thing; having a global presence on the Internet is another. Many organizations do not have a truly global website. For organizations selling goods on the Internet, the checkout process alone is full of challenges. Users who want to buy something will typically be directed to an online checkout form to fill out with shipping and billing information. These forms alone present challenges. For example, when asking customers for information, a U.S. company's website form might ask for the person's "last name." In other cultures, the last name is called the "family name" or "surname." Also, in many cultures, last names are much longer than many Western names and require more spaces in the website's forms.

Then there's the name of the checkout area on the website. What do you call the place where a customer can store the names of goods until they are purchased? In the United States, Amazon uses the term "shopping cart" in its checkout process. In the United Kingdom, it uses the phrase, "shopping basket."

There are other concerns to be addressed in the checkout process, including having users select their country or region versus using geolocation, offering support via phone, providing billing and shipping information that is country or region specific, and specifying acceptable payment platforms such as Paypal or Visa Checkout.

The 2015 Web Globalization Report Card from Global by Design provides input into the challenges of globalizing a website. The report describes the best and worst practices in website globalization and ranks the best and worst sites. It praises companies at the top of the list, including Google, Facebook, and Booking.com, for their efforts at localization. These efforts include using local images instead of stock photos, having culture-specific content, and using language that is not only translated but also culturally nuanced. The 25 companies whose websites ranked at the top of the list supported an average of 50 languages. Use of a global design template also helped company web pages score near the top of the list. While localization is important, the report stresses the importance of a consistent look across countries.

At the other end of the list are those who received poor scores, including big names like Walmart. Their shortcomings, according to the report card, were often the opposite of what the best companies did right. Not every website with a low score did all of these things wrong, but they did some combination of poor practices that put them toward the bottom of the list. Many fell short on localization, especially on language translation. Many did not have or had inconsistent "global gateways" to local websites. Another big problem was the lack of a global design template.

"Lack of global consistency is an issue with many websites," according to John Yunker, author of the Web Globalization Report Card, "That is, each country web team appears to have gone off on its own and created a website from scratch instead of working across company to share common design templates and resources."[1]

Overview

Top managers of a global company like Amazon operate in an environment where they compete with other companies for scarce and valuable resources. Managers of companies large and small have found that to survive and prosper in the 21st century, most companies must become **global organizations**, which operate and compete not only domestically, at home, but also globally, in countries around the world. Operating in the global environment is uncertain and unpredictable because it is complex and changes constantly.

global organization
An organization that operates and competes in more than one country.

LO 4-1 Explain why the ability to perceive, interpret, and respond appropriately to the global environment is crucial for managerial success.

If organizations are to adapt successfully to this changing environment, their managers must learn to understand the forces that operate in it and how these forces give rise to opportunities and threats. In this chapter we examine why the environment, both domestically and globally, has become more open, vibrant, and competitive. We examine how forces in the task and general environments affect global organizations and their managers. By the end of this chapter, you will appreciate the changes that are taking place in the environment and understand why it is important for managers to develop a global perspective as they strive to increase organizational efficiency and effectiveness.

What Is the Global Environment?

The **global environment** is a set of forces and conditions in the world outside an organization's boundary that affect how it operates and shape its behavior.[2] These forces change over time and thus present managers with *opportunities* and *threats*. Some changes in the global environment, such as the development of efficient new production technology, the availability of lower-cost components, or the opening of new global markets, create opportunities for managers to make and sell more products, obtain more resources and capital, and thereby strengthen their organization. In contrast, the rise of new global competitors, a global economic recession, or an oil shortage poses threats that can devastate an organization if managers are unable to sell its products. The quality of managers' understanding of forces in the global environment and their ability to respond appropriately to those forces are critical factors affecting organizational performance.

global environment
The set of global forces and conditions that operate beyond an organization's boundaries but affect a manager's ability to acquire and utilize resources.

In this chapter we explore the nature of these forces and consider how managers can respond to them. To identify opportunities and threats caused by forces in the global environment, it is helpful for managers to distinguish between the *task environment* and the more encompassing *general environment* (see Figure 4.1).

The **task environment** is the set of forces and conditions that originate with global suppliers, distributors, customers, and competitors; these forces and conditions

Figure 4.1
Forces in the Global Environment

task environment
The set of forces and conditions that originate with suppliers, distributors, customers, and competitors and affect an organization's ability to obtain inputs and dispose of its outputs because they influence managers daily.

general environment
The wide-ranging global, economic, technological, sociocultural, demographic, political, and legal forces that affect an organization and its task environment.

affect an organization's ability to obtain inputs and dispose of its outputs. The task environment contains the forces that have the most *immediate* and *direct* effect on managers because they pressure and influence managers daily. When managers turn on the radio or television, arrive at their offices in the morning, open their mail, or look at their computers or mobile devices, they are likely to learn about problems facing them because of changing conditions in their organization's task environment.

The **general environment** includes the wide-ranging global, economic, technological, sociocultural, demographic, political, and legal forces that affect the organization and its task environment. For the individual manager, opportunities and threats resulting from changes in the general environment are often more difficult to identify and respond to than are events in the task environment. However, changes in these forces can have major impacts on managers and their organizations.

The Task Environment

Forces in the task environment result from the actions of suppliers, distributors, customers, and competitors both at home and abroad (see Figure 4.1). These four groups affect a manager's ability to obtain resources and dispose of outputs daily, weekly, and monthly and thus have a significant impact on short-term decision making.

Suppliers

Suppliers are the individuals and organizations that provide an organization with the input resources (such as raw materials, component parts, or employees) it needs to produce goods and services. In return, the suppliers receive payment for those goods and services. An important aspect of a manager's job is to ensure a reliable supply of input resources.

Consider Dell as an example. Dell has many suppliers of component parts such as microprocessors (Intel and AMD) and disk drives (Quantum and Seagate Technologies). It also has suppliers of preinstalled software, including the operating system and specific applications software (Microsoft and Adobe). Dell's providers of capital, such as banks and financial institutions, are also important suppliers. Cisco Systems and Oracle are important providers of hardware and software for technology companies.

Dell has several suppliers of labor. One source is the educational institutions that train future Dell employees and therefore provide the company with skilled workers. Another is trade unions, organizations that represent employee interests and can control the supply of labor by exercising the right of unionized workers to strike. Unions also can influence the terms and conditions under which labor is employed. Dell's workers are not unionized; when layoffs became necessary because of the financial crisis and recession that began in 2009, the company had few problems laying off workers to reduce costs. In organizations and industries where unions are strong, however, such as the transportation industry, an important part of a manager's job is negotiating and administering agreements with unions and their representatives.

Changes in the nature, number, or type of suppliers produce opportunities and threats to which managers must respond if their organizations are to prosper. For example, a major supplier-related threat that confronts managers arises when suppliers' bargaining position is so strong that they can raise the prices of the inputs they supply to the organization. A supplier's bargaining position is especially strong when (1) the supplier is the sole source of an input and (2) the input is vital to the organization.[3] For example, for 17 years G. D. Searle was the sole supplier of NutraSweet, the artificial sweetener used in most diet soft drinks. Not only was NutraSweet an important ingredient in diet soft drinks, but it also was one for which there was no acceptable substitute (saccharin and other artificial sweeteners raised health concerns). Searle earned its privileged position because it invented and held the patent for NutraSweet, and patents prohibit other organizations from introducing competing products for 17 years. As a result Searle was able to demand a high price for NutraSweet, charging twice the price of an equivalent amount of sugar; and paying that price raised the costs of soft drink manufacturers such as Coca-Cola and PepsiCo. When Searle's patent expired many other companies introduced products similar to NutraSweet, and prices fell.[4] In the 2000s Splenda, which was made by McNeil Nutritionals, owned by Tate & Lyle, a British company, replaced NutraSweet as the artificial sweetener of choice, and NutraSweet's price fell further; Splenda began to command a high price from soft drink companies.[5] However, a new sweetener introduced in 2008 has gained market share from Splenda. The noncaloric, natural sweetener Truvia, which is manufactured by Cargill, moved to the number 2 position in 2014.[6]

In contrast, when an organization has many suppliers for a particular input, it is in a relatively strong bargaining position with those suppliers and can demand low-cost, high-quality inputs from them. Often an organization can use its power with suppliers to force them to reduce their prices, as Dell frequently does. Dell, for example, is constantly searching for low-cost suppliers abroad to keep its PC prices competitive. At a global level, organizations can buy products from suppliers overseas or become their own suppliers by manufacturing their products abroad.

It is important that managers recognize the opportunities and threats associated with managing the global supply chain. On one hand, gaining access to low-cost products made abroad represents an opportunity for U.S. companies to lower their input costs. On the other hand, managers who fail to use low-cost overseas suppliers create a threat and put their organizations at a competitive disadvantage.[7] Levi Strauss, for example, was slow to realize that it could not compete with the low-priced jeans sold by Walmart and other retailers, but it was eventually forced to close all its U.S. jean factories and outsource manufacturing to low-cost overseas suppliers to cut the price of its jeans to a competitive level. Now it sells its low-priced jeans in Walmart. The downside to global outsourcing is, of course, the loss of millions of U.S. jobs, an issue we have discussed in previous chapters.

A common problem facing managers of large global companies such as Ford, Sony, and Dell is managing the development of a global supplier network that will allow their companies to keep costs down and quality high. For example, Boeing's 777 jet was originally built using many components from more than 500 global suppliers; eight made parts for the 777 fuselage, doors, and wings.[8] Boeing chose these suppliers because they were the best in the world at performing their particular activities, and Boeing's goal was to produce a high-quality final product.[9] Pleased with the outcome, Boeing decided to outsource a greater percentage of components to global suppliers when it designed the new 787 Dreamliner; however, many serious problems delayed the introduction of the aircraft for several years.[10]

The purchasing activities of global companies have become increasingly complicated as a result of the development of a whole range of skills and competencies in different countries around the world. It is clearly in companies' interests to search out the lowest-cost, best-quality suppliers. Advances in technology and the global reach of the Internet continue to make it easier for companies to coordinate complicated, long-distance exchanges involving the purchasing of inputs and the disposal of outputs—something Sony has taken advantage of as it trims the number of its suppliers to reduce costs.

global outsourcing
The purchase or production of inputs or final products from overseas suppliers to lower costs and improve product quality or design.

Global outsourcing occurs when a company contracts with suppliers in other countries to make the various inputs or components that go into its products or to assemble the final products to reduce costs. For example, Apple contracts with companies in Taiwan and China to make inputs such as the chips, batteries, and LCD displays that power its digital devices; then it contracts with outsourcers such as Foxconn to assemble its final products—such as iPods, iPhones, and iPads. Apple also outsources the distribution of its products around the world by contracting with companies such as FedEx or DHL.

Global outsourcing has grown enormously to take advantage of national differences in the cost and quality of resources such as labor or raw materials that can significantly reduce manufacturing costs or increase product quality or reliability. Today such global exchanges are becoming so complex that some companies specialize in managing other companies' global supply chains. Global companies use the services of overseas intermediaries or brokers, which are located close to potential suppliers, to find the suppliers that can best meet the needs of a particular company. They can design the most efficient supply chain for a company to outsource the component and assembly operations required to produce its final products. Because

The purchasing activities of global companies have become increasingly complicated in recent years. Hundreds of suppliers around the world produce parts for Boeing's 787 Dreamliner.
© John Van Hasselt/Corbis

these suppliers are located in thousands of cities in many countries, finding them is difficult. Li & Fung, based in Hong Kong, is one broker that has helped hundreds of major U.S. companies to outsource their component or assembly operations to suitable overseas suppliers, especially suppliers in mainland China.[11]

Although outsourcing to take advantage of low labor costs has helped many companies perform better, in the 2010s its risks have also become apparent, especially when issues such as reliability, quality, and speed are important. Several years ago, General Electric moved the production of its hybrid water heater from China to Kentucky due to rising wages in China and increasing transportation costs. Moving production back to the United States also gave the company more control over product quality. When all the savings were taken into account, the Kentucky plant was able to produce a better product at a lower cost than the plant in China.[12] Apple also brought the manufacturing of its Mac Pro from overseas to Austin, Texas.[13]

On the other hand, some companies do not outsource manufacturing; they prefer to establish their own assembly operations and factories around the world to protect their proprietary technology. For example, most global automakers own their production operations in China to retain control over global decision making and to keep their operations secret. An interesting example of how organizations have tried to control what happens in their supply chains is discussed in the "Managing Globally" feature.

MANAGING GLOBALLY

Stopping Global Water Shortages

How much water did it take to manufacture the outfit you are wearing right now? The textile industry has a huge water footprint. First, it takes water to grow cotton, the material that accounts for 90% of the textile industry's use of natural fibers.[14] One estimate suggests that nearly 400 gallons of water are needed to produce each cotton T-shirt.[15] The farming of cotton accounts for 2.6% of annual global water usage and is the largest water consumption factor in the supply chain of the textile industry.[16] And it's not just quantity. Cotton production has a direct impact on water quality through the use of pesticides, herbicides, and fertilizers.

Second, problems continue beyond the growing of raw materials. The textile industry uses and pollutes water while dyeing fabrics. It can take more than 6 gallons of water to dye one T-shirt. The polyester apparel industry alone uses 2.4 trillion gallons of water a year.[17] The process of treating, rinsing, and dyeing fabric accounts for about 20% of the world's industrial water pollution.[18] Dye houses in China and India have been accused of overusing local water supplies as well as dumping toxic wastewater into local waterways.[19] In response to concerns about the use and pollution of water to make fabric and garments, several manufacturers

In an effort to reduce the water footprint of its global supply chain, Nike now uses an innovative process that dyes polyester without using water or chemicals. The company began selling products manufactured using this process in 2014 under the label Nike ColorDry. © Elliot Fine/Moment Mobile/Getty Images

have sought no-water and reduced-water ways of working in their supply chains.

In 2014 Levi Strauss & Co. made more than 100,000 pairs of jeans using 100% recycled water in China. This batch alone saved about 3 million gallons of water in addition to the 203 million gallons the company's Water<Less jeans brand had already saved.[20] The company also plans to retrofit facilities in Nicaragua and South Asia to recycle water in the production process.

Nike and Adidas also are cutting back on water use in their supply chains by using an innovative process that dyes polyester without using water or chemicals. The process, developed by DyeCoo Textile Systems in the Netherlands, dyes fabric by turning carbon dioxide into a liquid by putting it under extreme pressure. As the carbon dioxide cools, it turns back into a gas that can be recycled and used again.[21] The first garment produced by Nike using the process was the running singlet worn by Kenyan marathoner Abel Kirui in the 2012 Olympics. The company began selling products manufactured using the process in 2014 under the name Nike ColorDry.[22] Adidas also started waterless dyeing in 2012, producing a limited collection of 50,000 T-shirts with the Yeh Group, which owns a textile mill in Thailand. A full line of "DryDye" apparel is now available around the world.[23]

Nike COO Eric Sprunk said, "NIKE, Inc., innovates not only in the design of our products but also in how they are made. We see sustainability and business growth as complementary, and our strategy is to prioritize relationships with factory groups that demonstrate a desire to invest in sustainable practices and technologies. Our collaboration with Far Eastern and DyeCoo, to develop and scale the ColorDry process, is an important milestone on our path toward manufacturing innovation."[24]

Distributors

Distributors are organizations that help other organizations sell their goods or services to customers. The decisions managers make about how to distribute products to customers can have important effects on organizational performance. For example, package delivery companies such as Federal Express, UPS, and the U.S. Postal Service have become vital distributors for the millions of items bought online and shipped to customers by dot-com companies both at home and abroad.

The changing nature of distributors and distribution methods can bring opportunities and threats for managers. If distributors become so large and powerful that they can control customers' access to a particular organization's goods and services, they can threaten the organization by demanding that it reduce the prices of its goods and services.[25] For example, the huge retail distributor Walmart controls its suppliers' access to millions of customers and thus can demand that its suppliers reduce their prices to keep its business. If an organization such as Procter & Gamble refuses to reduce its prices, Walmart might respond by buying products only from Procter & Gamble's competitors—companies such as Unilever and Colgate. To reduce costs, Walmart also has used its power as a distributor to demand that suppliers adopt a wireless radio frequency scanning technology to reduce the cost of shipping and stocking products in its stores.[26]

In 2014, the Bridgestone Corporation joined more than two dozen Japanese automotive suppliers who had already pleaded guilty to conspiring to fix the prices of parts sold to automakers. The Tokyo-based company was accused of conspiring to allocate sales, prearrange bids, and fix prices of parts sold. It paid a $425 million fine, higher than the fines given to other suppliers because of a previous price-fixing conviction.[27]

Customers

customers

Individuals and groups that buy the goods and services an organization produces.

Customers are the individuals and groups that buy the goods and services an organization produces. For example, Dell's customers can be segmented into several distinct groups: (1) individuals who purchase PCs for home and mobile use, (2) small companies, (3) large companies, and (4) government agencies and educational institutions. Changes in the number and types of customers or in customers' tastes and needs create opportunities and threats. An organization's success depends on its responsiveness to customers—whether it can satisfy their needs. In the PC industry, customers are demanding smaller computers with faster speeds, increased mobility, new apps, and lower prices—and PC makers must respond to the changing types and needs of customers, such as by introducing tablets and other mobile devices. A school, too, must adapt to the changing needs of its customers. For example, if more Spanish-speaking students enroll, additional classes in English as a second language may need to be scheduled. A manager's ability to identify an organization's main customer groups, and make the products that best satisfy their particular needs, is a crucial factor affecting organizational and managerial success.

The most obvious opportunity associated with expanding into the global environment is the prospect of selling goods and services to millions or billions of new customers, as Amazon.com's CEO Jeff Bezos discovered when he expanded his company's operations in many countries. Similarly, Accenture and Cap Gemini, two large consulting companies, established regional operating centers around the globe, and they recruit and train thousands of overseas consultants to serve the needs of customers in their respective world regions.

Today many products have gained global customer acceptance. This consolidation is occurring both for consumer goods and for business products and has created enormous opportunities for managers. The worldwide acceptance of Coca-Cola, Apple iPads, McDonald's hamburgers, and Samsung smartphones is a sign that the tastes and preferences of customers in different countries may not be so different after all. Likewise, large global markets exist for business products such as telecommunications equipment, electronic components, and computer and financial services. Thus Cisco and Siemens sell their telecommunications equipment; Intel, its microprocessors; and Oracle and SAP, their business systems management software, to customers all over the world.

Competitors

competitors

Organizations that produce goods and services that are similar to a particular organization's goods and services.

One of the most important forces an organization confronts in its task environment is competitors. **Competitors** are organizations that produce goods and services that are similar and comparable to a particular organization's goods and services.

In other words, competitors are organizations trying to attract the same customers. Dell's competitors include other domestic PC makers (such as Apple and HP) as well as overseas competitors (such as Sony and Toshiba in Japan; Lenovo, the Chinese company that bought IBM's PC division; and Acer, the Taiwanese company that bought Gateway). Similarly, online stockbroker E*Trade has other competitors such as TD Ameritrade, Scottrade, and Charles Schwab.

Rivalry between competitors is potentially the most threatening force managers must deal with. A high level of rivalry typically results in price competition, and falling prices reduce customer revenues and profits. In the early 2000s competition in the PC industry became intense because Dell was aggressively cutting costs and prices to increase its global market share. IBM had to exit the PC business after it lost billions in its battle against low-cost rivals, and Gateway and HP also suffered losses while Dell's profits soared. By 2006, however, HP's fortunes had recovered because it had found ways to lower its costs and offer stylish new PCs, and Apple was growing rapidly, so Dell's profit margins shrunk. In 2009, HP overtook Dell to become the largest global PC maker, and by 2010 Apple's and Acer's sales were also expanding rapidly. Dell's managers had failed to appreciate how fast its global competitors were catching up and had not developed the right strategies to keep the company at the top. By the end of 2014, after a long and harsh battle with investors over the future of the company, Michael Dell took the company private and is focusing on new products and a stake in the corporate cloud computing sector.[28]

Although extensive rivalry between existing competitors is a major threat to profitability, so is the potential for new competitors to enter the task environment. **Potential competitors** are organizations that are not presently in a task environment but have the resources to enter if they so choose. In 2010, Amazon.com, for example, was not in the furniture or large appliance business, but it could enter these businesses if its managers decided it could profitably sell such products online—and in 2015 it does sell furniture and large appliances. When new competitors enter an industry, competition increases and prices and profits decrease—as furniture and electronic stores such as Best Buy have discovered as they battle Amazon.com.

potential competitors
Organizations that presently are not in a task environment but could enter if they so choose.

BARRIERS TO ENTRY In general, the potential for new competitors to enter a task environment (and thus increase competition) is a function of barriers to entry. **Barriers to entry** are factors that make it difficult and costly for a company to enter a particular task environment or industry.[29] In other words, the more difficult and costly it is to enter the task environment, the higher are the barriers to entry. The higher the barriers to entry, the fewer the competitors in an organization's task environment and thus the lower the threat of competition. With fewer competitors, it is easier to obtain customers and keep prices high.

barriers to entry
Factors that make it difficult and costly for an organization to enter a particular task environment or industry.

Barriers to entry result from three main sources: economies of scale, brand loyalty, and government regulations that impede entry (see Figure 4.2). **Economies of scale** are the cost advantages associated with large operations. Economies of scale result from factors such as manufacturing products in very large quantities, buying inputs in bulk, or making more effective use of organizational resources than do competitors by fully utilizing employees' skills and knowledge. If organizations already in the task environment are large and enjoy significant economies of scale, their costs are lower than the costs that potential entrants will face, and newcomers will find it expensive to enter the industry. Amazon.com, for example, enjoys significant economies of scale relative to most other online companies because of its highly efficient distribution system.[30]

economies of scale
Cost advantages associated with large operations.

Figure 4.2

Barriers to Entry and Competition

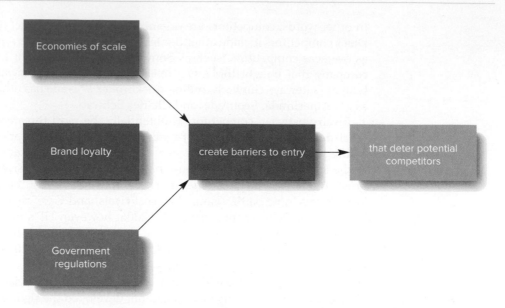

brand loyalty
Customers' preference for the products of organizations currently existing in the task environment.

Brand loyalty is customers' preference for the products of organizations currently in the task environment. If established organizations enjoy significant brand loyalty, a new entrant will find it difficult and costly to obtain a share of the market. Newcomers must bear huge advertising costs to build customer awareness of the goods or services they intend to provide. Today Google, Amazon.com, and Apple enjoy a high level of brand loyalty and have some of the highest website hit rates, which allows them to increase their marketing revenues.

In some cases, *government regulations* function as a barrier to entry at both the industry and the country levels. Many industries that were deregulated, such as air transport, trucking, utilities, and telecommunications, experienced a high level of new entry after deregulation; this forced existing companies in those industries to operate more efficiently or risk being put out of business. At the national and global levels, administrative barriers are government policies that create barriers to entry and limit imports of goods by overseas companies. Japan is well known for the many ways in which it attempts to restrict the entry of overseas competitors or lessen their impact on Japanese firms. Japan has come under intense pressure to relax and abolish regulations such as those governing the import of rice, for example.

The Japanese rice market, like many other Japanese markets, was closed to overseas competitors until 1993 to protect Japan's thousands of high-cost, low-output rice farmers. Rice cultivation is expensive in Japan because of the country's mountainous terrain, and Japanese consumers have always paid high prices for rice. Under overseas pressure, the Japanese government opened the market; but overseas competitors are allowed to export to Japan only 8% of its annual rice consumption to protect its farmers.

An O-bento lunch. Now that Japan imports rice from the United States, Japanese rice farmers, who cannot compete against lower-priced imports, have been forced to leave fields idle or grow less profitable crops. Philip Game/Lonely Planet Images/Getty Images

In the 2000s, however, an alliance between organic rice grower Lundberg Family Farms of California and the Nippon Restaurant Enterprise Co. found a new way to break into the Japanese rice market. Because there is no tariff on rice used in processed foods, Nippon converts the U.S. organic rice into "O-bento," an organic hot boxed lunch packed with rice, vegetables, chicken, beef, and salmon, all imported from the United States. The lunches, which cost about $4 compared to a Japanese rice bento that costs about $9, are sold at railway stations and other outlets throughout Japan and have become very popular. A storm of protest from Japanese rice farmers arose because the entry of U.S. rice growers forced them to leave their rice fields idle or grow less profitable crops. Other overseas companies are increasingly forming alliances with Japanese companies to find new ways to break into the high-priced Japanese market, and little by little, Japan's restrictive trade practices are being whittled away.

In summary, intense rivalry among competitors creates a task environment that is highly threatening and makes it increasingly difficult for managers to gain access to the resources an organization needs to make goods and services. Conversely, low rivalry results in a task environment where competitive pressures are more moderate and managers have greater opportunities to acquire the resources they need to make their organizations effective.

The General Environment

Economic, technological, sociocultural, demographic, political, and legal forces in the general environment often have important effects on forces in the task environment that determine an organization's ability to obtain resources—effects that managers may not be aware of. For example, the sudden, dramatic upheavals in the mortgage and banking industry that started in 2007 were brought about by a combination of the development of complex new financial lending instruments called derivatives; a speculative boom in commodities and housing prices; and lax government regulation that allowed unethical bankers and financial managers to exploit the derivatives to make immense short-term profits. These events triggered the economic crisis beginning in 2008 that caused stock markets around the world to plummet, devastating the retirement savings of hundreds of millions of ordinary people, and caused layoffs of millions of employees as companies slashed their workforces because customers reduced their spending. Fortunately, by 2013 sound economic policies resulted in a major recovery.

The implication is clear: Managers must continuously analyze forces in the general environment because these forces affect ongoing decision making and planning. How well managers can perform this task determines how quickly an organization can respond to the changes taking place. Next we discuss the major forces in the general environment and examine their impact on an organization's task environment.

economic forces

Interest rates, inflation, unemployment, economic growth, and other factors that affect the general health and well-being of a nation or the regional economy of an organization.

Economic Forces

Economic forces affect the general health and well-being of a country or world region. They include interest rates, inflation, unemployment, and economic growth. Economic forces produce many opportunities and threats for managers. Low levels of unemployment and falling interest rates give people more money to spend, and as a result organizations can sell more goods and services. Good economic times affect the supply of resources that become easier or more inexpensive to acquire, and organizations have an opportunity to flourish. High-tech companies enjoyed this throughout the 1990s when computer and electronics companies like Sony made record profits as the global economy boomed because of advances in IT and growing global trade.

In contrast, worsening macroeconomic conditions, like those in the 2010s, pose a major threat because they reduce managers' ability to gain access to the resources their organizations need to survive and prosper. Profit-seeking organizations such as hotels and retail stores have fewer customers during economic downturns; hotel rates dropped by 14% in 2009 compared to 2008, for example, just as retail sales plunged. Nonprofits such as charities and colleges also saw donations decline by more than 20% because of the economic downturn.

Poor economic conditions make the environment more complex and managers' jobs more difficult and demanding. Companies often need to reduce the number of their managers and employees, streamline their operations, and identify ways to acquire and use resources more efficiently and effectively. Successful managers realize the important effects that economic forces have on their organizations, and they pay close attention to what is occurring in the economy at the national and regional levels to respond appropriately.

Technological Forces

technology The combination of skills and equipment that managers use in designing, producing, and distributing goods and services.

Technology is the combination of tools, machines, computers, skills, information, and knowledge that managers use to design, produce, and distribute goods and services; **technological forces** are outcomes of changes in that technology. The overall pace of technological change has accelerated greatly in the last decades because technological advances in microprocessors and computer hardware and software have spurred technological advances in most businesses and industries. The effects of changing technological forces are still increasing in magnitude.

technological forces Outcomes of changes in the technology managers use to design, produce, or distribute goods and services.

Technological forces can have profound implications for managers and organizations. Technological change can make established products obsolete—for example, cathode-ray tube (CRT) computer monitors and televisions (such as Sony's Trinitron), bound sets of encyclopedias, and newspapers and magazines—forcing managers to find new ways to satisfy customer needs. Although technological change can threaten an organization, it also can create a host of new opportunities for designing, making, or distributing new and better kinds of goods and services. AMD recently launched processors with powerful graphics capabilities for games and high-performance apps. The chips use heterogeneous systems architecture, commonly known as HSA, to speed up computers. Innovations like this drive the technology revolution, which spurs demand for all kinds of new digital computing devices and services.[31]

Changes in IT are altering the nature of work itself within organizations, including that of the manager's job. Today telecommuting, videoconferencing, and text messaging are everyday activities that let managers supervise and coordinate geographically dispersed employees. Salespeople in many companies work from home offices and commute electronically to work. They communicate with other employees through companywide electronic communication networks using tablet PCs and smartphones to orchestrate "face-to-face" meetings with coworkers across the country or globe.

Sociocultural Forces

sociocultural forces Pressures emanating from the social structure of a country or society or from the national culture.

Sociocultural forces are pressures emanating from the social structure of a country or society or from the national culture, such as the concern for diversity, discussed in the previous chapter. Pressures from both sources can either constrain or

social structure The traditional system of relationships established between people and groups in a society.

facilitate the way organizations operate and managers behave. **Social structure** is the traditional system of relationships established between people and groups in a society. Societies differ substantially in social structure. In societies that have a high degree of social stratification, there are many distinctions among individuals and groups. Caste systems in India and Tibet and the recognition of numerous social classes in Great Britain and France produce a multilayered social structure in each of those countries. In contrast, social stratification is lower in relatively egalitarian New Zealand and in the United States, where the social structure reveals few distinctions among people. Most top managers in France come from the upper classes of French society, but top managers in the United States come from all strata of American society.

Societies also differ in the extent to which they emphasize the individual over the group. Such differences may dictate how managers need to motivate and lead employees.

national culture The set of values that a society considers important and the norms of behavior that are approved or sanctioned in that society.

National culture is the set of values that a society considers important and the norms of behavior that are approved or sanctioned in that society. Societies differ substantially in the values and norms they emphasize. For example, in the United States individualism is highly valued, but in Korea and Japan individuals are expected to conform to group expectations.[32] National culture, discussed at length later in this chapter, also affects how managers motivate and coordinate employees and how organizations do business. Ethics, an important aspect of national culture, were discussed in detail in Chapter 3.

Pick your poison. The American trend toward fitness has prompted traditional soft drink manufacturers to expand their offerings into a staggering array of energy drinks. © Photo by John Nordell/The Christian Science Monitor via Getty Images

Social structure and national culture not only differ across societies but also change within societies over time. In the United States, attitudes toward the roles of women, sex, marriage, and gays and lesbians changed in each past decade. Many people in Asian countries such as Hong Kong, Singapore, Korea, and even China think the younger generation is far more individualistic and "American-like" than previous generations. Currently, throughout much of eastern Europe, new values that emphasize individualism and entrepreneurship are replacing communist values based on collectivism and obedience to the state. The pace of change is accelerating.

Individual managers and organizations must be responsive to changes in, and differences among, the social structures and national cultures of all the countries in which they operate. In today's increasingly integrated global economy, managers are likely to interact with people from several countries, and many managers live and work abroad. Effective managers are sensitive to differences between societies and adjust their behavior accordingly.

Managers and organizations also must respond to social changes within a society. In the last decades, for example, Americans have become increasingly interested in their personal health and fitness. Managers who recognized this trend early and took advantage of the opportunities that resulted from it were able to reap significant gains for their organizations, such as chains of health clubs. PepsiCo used the opportunity presented by the fitness trend and took market share from archrival Coca-Cola by being the first to introduce diet colas and fruit-based soft drinks. Then Quaker Oats made Gatorade the most popular energy drink, and now others like Red Bull, Monster, and Rockstar are increasing in popularity. The health trend, however, did not offer opportunities to all companies; to some it posed a threat. Tobacco companies came under intense pressure due to consumers' greater awareness of negative health impacts from smoking. The rage for "low-carb" foods in the 2000s increased demand for meat and protein, and bread and doughnut companies such as Kraft and Krispy Kreme suffered—until the recent recession boosted the sale of inexpensive products such as macaroni and cheese.

Demographic Forces

demographic forces Outcomes of changes in, or changing attitudes toward, the characteristics of a population, such as age, gender, ethnic origin, race, sexual orientation, and social class.

Demographic forces are outcomes of changes in, or changing attitudes toward, the characteristics of a population, such as age, gender, ethnic origin, race, sexual orientation, and social class. Like the other forces in the general environment, demographic forces present managers with opportunities and threats and can have major implications for organizations. We examine the nature of these challenges throughout this book.

Today most industrialized nations are experiencing the aging of their populations as a consequence of falling birth and death rates and the aging of the baby boom generation. Consequently, the absolute number of older people has increased substantially, which has generated opportunities for organizations that cater to older people, such as the home health care, recreation, and medical industries, which have seen an upswing in demand for their services. The aging of the population also has several implications for the workplace. Most significant are a relative decline in the number of young people joining the workforce and an increase in the number of active employees who are postponing retirement beyond the traditional age of 65. Indeed, the continuing financial crisis in the 2010s has made it impossible for millions of older people to retire because their savings have been decimated. These changes suggest that organizations need to find ways to motivate older employees and use their skills and knowledge—an issue that many Western societies have yet to tackle.

Political and Legal Forces

political and legal forces Outcomes of changes in laws and regulations, such as deregulation of industries, privatization of organizations, and increased emphasis on environmental protection.

Political and legal forces are outcomes of changes in laws and regulations. They result from political and legal developments that take place within a nation, within a world region, or across the world, and significantly affect managers and organizations everywhere. Political processes shape a nation's laws and the international laws that govern the relationships between nations. Laws constrain the operations of organizations and managers and thus create both opportunities and threats.[33] For example, throughout much of the industrialized world there has been a strong trend toward deregulation of industries previously controlled by the state and privatization of organizations once owned by the state such as airlines, railways, and utility companies.

Another important political and legal force affecting managers and organizations is the political integration of countries that has been taking place during the last several decades. Increasingly, nations are forming political unions that allow free exchange of resources and capital. The growth of the European Union (EU) is one example: Common laws govern trade and commerce between EU member countries, and the European Court has the right to examine the business of any global organization and to approve any proposed mergers between overseas companies that operate inside the EU. For example, Microsoft's anticompetitive business practices came under scrutiny, and it was fined hundreds of millions for its uncompetitive practice of bundling its Internet Explorer web browser with its software. As part of its agreement with the European Court, Microsoft agreed that, beginning in 2010, it would ship its Windows 7 software with a choice of 10 web browsers (such as Chrome, Safari, and Firefox). Also, in 2012, after months of delay, the court allowed the merger between Motorola and Google to proceed although the court was also investigating Google for possible anticompetitive online advertising practices. In 2015, there are ongoing negotiations between the United States and the European Union regarding the Transatlantic Trade and Investment Partnership (T-TIP). The agreement would lower trade barriers to make it easier for organizations in the United States and the EU to buy and sell each other's goods and services.[34]

Indeed, international agreements to abolish laws and regulations that restrict and reduce trade between countries have been having profound effects on global organizations. The falling legal trade barriers create enormous opportunities for companies to sell goods and services internationally. But by allowing overseas companies to compete in a nation's domestic market for customers, falling trade barriers also pose a serious threat because they increase competition in the task environment. For example, the Obama administration has been negotiating for the United States to join the Trans-Pacific Partnership (TPP), a trade agreement whose possible members include 11 other countries (Australia, Brunei, Canada, Chile, Japan, Malaysia, Mexico, New Zealand, Peru, Singapore, and Vietnam). The partnership may allow the United States to break into the Japanese rice market. Australia and New Zealand hope the trade agreement will open up markets for their dairy products. However, U.S. car companies, sugar producers, and textile makers have expressed concern about increased foreign competition if the United States joins the pact. Public Citizen, a nonprofit consumer advocacy group, believes TPP will provide organizations with incentives to offshore their facilities, which would harm manufacturing industries in the United States.[35]

LO 4-4 Explain why the global environment is becoming more open and competitive, and identify the forces behind the process of globalization that increase the opportunities, complexities, challenges, and threats that managers face.

Deregulation, privatization, and the removal of legal barriers to trade are just a few of the many ways in which changing political and legal forces can challenge organizations and managers. Others include increased emphasis on environmental protection and the preservation of endangered species, increased emphasis on workplace safety, and legal constraints against discrimination on the basis of race, gender, or age. Managers face major challenges when they seek to take advantage of the opportunities created by changing political, legal, and economic forces.

The Changing Global Environment

The 21st century has banished the idea that the world is composed of distinct national countries and markets that are separated physically, economically, and culturally. Managers need to recognize that companies compete in a truly global marketplace, which is the source of the opportunities and threats they must respond to. Managers continually confront the challenges of global competition such as establishing operations in a country abroad, obtaining inputs from suppliers abroad, or managing in a different national culture.[36] (See Figure 4.3.)

In essence, as a result of falling trade barriers, managers view the global environment as open—that is, as an environment in which companies are free to buy goods and services from, and sell goods and services to, whichever companies and countries they choose. They also are free to compete against each other to attract customers around the world. All large companies must establish an international network of operations and subsidiaries to build global competitive advantage. Coca-Cola and

Figure 4.3

The Peters Projection World Map shows the accurate area of landmasses. Africa appears much larger here than in many conventional maps. In today's open global environment, this large continent is starting to take on an increasingly important role.

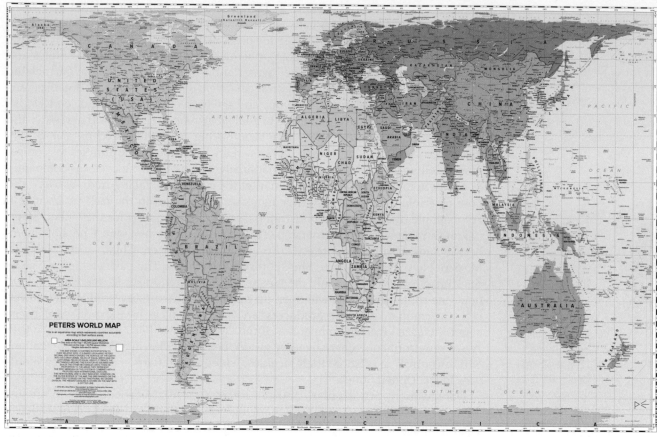

PepsiCo, for example, have competed aggressively for decades to develop the strongest global soft drink empire, just as Toyota and Honda have built hundreds of car plants around the world to provide the vehicles that global customers like.

In this section we first explain how this open global environment is the result of globalization and the flow of capital around the world. Next we examine how specific economic, political, and legal changes, such as the lowering of barriers to trade and investment, have increased globalization and led to greater interaction and exchanges between organizations and countries. Then we discuss how declining barriers of distance and culture have also increased the pace of globalization, and we consider the specific implications of these changes for managers and organizations. Finally we note that nations still differ widely from each other because they have distinct cultural values and norms and that managers must appreciate these differences to compete successfully across countries.

The Process of Globalization

Perhaps the most important reason why the global environment has become more open and competitive is the increase in globalization. **Globalization** is the set of specific and general forces that work together to integrate and connect economic,

globalization The set of specific and general forces that work together to integrate and connect economic, political, and social systems across countries, cultures, or geographical regions so that nations become increasingly interdependent and similar.

political, and social systems *across* countries, cultures, or geographic regions. The result of globalization is that nations and peoples become increasingly *interdependent* because the same forces affect them in similar ways. The fates of peoples in different countries become interlinked as the world's markets and businesses become increasingly interconnected. And as nations become more interdependent, they become more similar to one another in the sense that people develop a similar liking for products as diverse as mobile phones, iPads, jeans, soft drinks, sports teams, Japanese cars, foods such as curry, green tea, and Colombian coffee. One outcome of globalization is that more women are joining the ranks of leadership. To help women transition to leadership positions, Ernst & Young, a global organization, has begun a special program across the world, as the accompanying "Managing Globally" feature describes.

MANAGING GLOBALLY

Translating Athletic Success into Business Leadership

The 2012 London Olympics were a watershed moment for female athletes. For the first time ever, every country sending athletes to the games had women on the team, and women were able to participate in all sports.

Beth Brooke-Marciniak, global vice chair of public policy at EY, leads a drive to recruit female athletes because their confidence, high standards, discipline, and team experience may make them excellent business leaders. © Buda Mendes/Getty Images For Laureus

"Coming out of London there was so much momentum around women. . . . It reinforced to us that women are an emerging market. The leadership potential that exists in these elite athletes is so consistent with our beliefs in somehow trying to unlock the potential to foster more women's economic empowerment and leadership," said Beth Brooke-Marciniak, global vice chair, public policy, at EY (formerly Ernst & Young).[37]

Between the 2012 London Olympics and the 2016 Rio Olympics, EY is working to create a network of retired elite female athletes, former Olympians, and top female leaders to encourage female athletes to pursue powerful careers after retiring from sports. EY is an official supporter of the Rio games.[38]

The background of this global network involved a study by EY in May 2013 that confirmed a connection between sports and leadership. The study included a survey of 821 female senior managers and executives at companies around the world with annual revenues in excess of $250 million. Results found that almost all female leaders played sports at some point in their lives. More specifically, 96% of the women surveyed with board-level jobs played sports at the primary, secondary, postsecondary, or college level. The women in the study agreed that experience in playing sports leads to positive behaviors in the workplace, especially teamwork. Of the study respondents, 72% said there seemed to be a correlation between playing sports and teamwork. Also, 76% said that behaviors and techniques from sports can be adopted to improve team performance in the workplace. While the study does not conclude that every athlete will become a strong organizational leader, it does conclude that sports can help women develop leadership skills that will serve organizations well.[39]

EY's survey confirms the findings of a 2002 survey of more than 400 senior women executives commissioned by Mass-Mutual Financial Group and Oppenheimer, which found 80% or more of those surveyed had participated in an organized sport growing up and that the majority of those surveyed believed sports helped them to become more disciplined and build their leadership skills. Beyond the results of these two surveys, there's anecdotal evidence. For example, Brazilian President Dilma Rousseff played volleyball. Basketball players who became high-level leaders include Mondelez International CEO Irene Rosenfeld, former U.S. Secretary of State Hillary Clinton, and DuPont CEO Ellen Kullman.[40]

These women found success after their sports careers ended, but that is not always the case. EY contends that many female athletes encounter difficulties in moving their success from the playing field to the corporate office.[41] The EY Women Athletes Business Network has three steps designed to make that transition easier and increase the impact of female leadership[42]:

1. Bringing together former elite athletes, former Olympians, and women in EY's business network to form mentoring relationships and provide opportunities.

2. Using multimedia platforms to tell inspirational stories of women who found participation in sports to be important to their success.

3. Conducting research about the relationship between women's participation in sports and their leadership skills as well as their effect on global education, health, and development.

"Ernst & Young [EY] has seen the power of diversity and inclusion, and we want to build a better working world by expanding opportunities for women leaders. With their inherent confidence, high standards, discipline, and experience in working as a team, female athletes have tremendous value for businesses like ours, governments, and NGOs around the world," said Brooke-Marciniak, a Title IX scholarship recipient herself. "We have a long history of convening networks, helping female entrepreneurs scale their companies, and driving the global dialogue around the advancement of women. The impact of women at the London games was historic, and we want to continue this momentum by helping transform elite female athletes into exceptional leaders."[43]

But what drives or spurs globalization? What makes companies like IKEA, Toyota, or Microsoft want to venture into an uncertain global environment? The answer is that the path of globalization is shaped by the ebb and flow of *capital*—valuable wealth-generating assets or resources that people move through companies, countries, and world regions to seek their greatest returns or profits. Managers, employees, and companies like IKEA and Samsung are motivated to try to profit or benefit by using their skills to make products customers around the world want to buy. The four principal forms of capital that flow between countries are these:

- *Human capital:* the flow of people around the world through immigration, migration, and emigration.
- *Financial capital:* the flow of money capital across world markets through overseas investment, credit, lending, and aid.
- *Resource capital:* the flow of natural resources, parts, and components between companies and countries, such as metals, minerals, lumber, energy, food products, microprocessors, and auto parts.
- *Political capital:* the flow of power and influence around the world using diplomacy, persuasion, aggression, and force of arms to protect the right or access of a country, world region, or political bloc to the other forms of capital.

Most of the economic advances associated with globalization are the result of these four capital flows and the interactions between them, as nations compete on the world stage to protect and increase their standards of living and to further the political goals and social causes that are espoused by their societies' cultures. The next sections look at the factors that have increased the rate at which capital flows between companies and countries. In a positive sense, the faster the flow, the more capital is being utilized where it can create the most value, such as people moving to where their skills earn them more money, or investors switching to the stocks or bonds that give them higher dividends or interest, or companies finding lower-cost sources of inputs. In a negative sense, however, a fast flow of capital also means that individual countries or world regions can find themselves in trouble when companies and investors move their capital to invest it in more productive ways in other countries or world regions—often those with lower labor costs or rapidly expanding markets. When capital leaves a country, the results are higher unemployment, recession, and a lower standard of living for its people.

Declining Barriers to Trade and Investment

One of the main factors that has speeded globalization by freeing the movement of capital has been the decline in barriers to trade and investment, discussed earlier. During the 1920s and 1930s many countries erected formidable barriers to international trade and investment in the belief that this was the best way to promote their economic well-being. Many of these barriers were high tariffs on imports of manufactured goods. A **tariff** is a tax that a government imposes on goods imported into one country from another. The aim of import tariffs is to protect domestic industries and jobs, such as those in the auto or steel industry, from overseas competition by raising the price of these products from abroad. In 2009, for example, the U.S. government increased the tariffs on vehicle tires imported from China to protect U.S. tire makers from unfair competition. The elevated tariffs expired in 2012, and in 2013 the passenger tire imports from China increased by more than 55% to 46 million units, an all-time high. The U.S. Commerce Department recently announced that Chinese-made tires for passenger cars were unfairly subsidized and may be subject again to punitive tariffs in the near future.[44]

The reason for removing tariffs is that, very often, when one country imposes an import tariff, others follow suit and the result is a series of retaliatory moves as countries progressively raise tariff barriers against each other. In the 1920s this behavior

tariff A tax that a government imposes on imported or, occasionally, exported goods.

depressed world demand and helped usher in the Great Depression of the 1930s and massive unemployment. Beginning with the 2009 economic crisis, the governments of most countries have worked hard in the 2010s not to fall into the trap of raising tariffs to protect jobs and industries in the short run because they know the long-term consequences of this would be the loss of even more jobs. Governments of countries that resort to raising tariff barriers ultimately reduce employment and undermine the economic growth of their countries because capital and resources will always move to their most highly valued use—wherever that is in the world.

GATT AND THE RISE OF FREE TRADE After World War II, advanced Western industrial countries, having learned from the Great Depression, committed themselves to the goal of removing barriers to the free flow of resources and capital between countries. This commitment was reinforced by acceptance of the principle that free trade, rather than tariff barriers, was the best way to foster a healthy domestic economy and low unemployment.[45]

free-trade doctrine
The idea that if each country specializes in the production of the goods and services that it can produce most efficiently, this will make the best use of global resources.

The **free-trade doctrine** predicts that if each country agrees to specialize in the production of the goods and services that it can produce most efficiently, this will make the best use of global capital resources and will result in lower prices.[46] For example, if Indian companies are highly efficient in the production of textiles and U.S. companies are highly efficient in the production of computer software, then, under a free-trade agreement, capital would move to India and be invested there to produce textiles, while capital from around the world would flow to the United States and be invested in its innovative computer software companies. Consequently, prices of both textiles and software should fall because each product is being produced where it can be made at the lowest cost, benefiting consumers and making the best use of scarce capital. This doctrine is also responsible for the increase in global outsourcing and the loss of millions of U.S. jobs in textiles and manufacturing as capital has been invested in factories in Asian countries such as China and Malaysia. However, millions of U.S. jobs have also been created because of new capital investments in the high-tech, IT, and service sectors, which in theory should offset manufacturing job losses in the long run.

Historically, countries that accepted this free-trade doctrine set as their goal the removal of barriers to the free flow of goods, services, and capital between countries. They attempted to achieve this through an international treaty known as the General Agreement on Tariffs and Trade (GATT). In the half-century since World War II, there have been eight rounds of GATT negotiations aimed at lowering tariff barriers. The last round, the Uruguay Round, involved 117 countries and succeeded in lowering tariffs by more than 30% from the previous level. It also led to the dissolving of GATT and its replacement by the World Trade Organization (WTO), which continues the struggle to reduce tariffs and has more power to sanction countries that break global agreements. On average, the tariff barriers among the governments of developed countries declined from more than 40% in 1948 to about 3% today, causing a dramatic increase in world trade.[47]

Declining Barriers of Distance and Culture

Historically, barriers of distance and culture also closed the global environment and kept managers focused on their domestic market. The management problems Unilever, the huge British-based soap and detergent maker, experienced at the turn of the 20th century illustrate the effect of these barriers.

Founded in London during the 1880s by William Lever, a Quaker, Unilever had a worldwide reach by the early 1900s and operated subsidiaries in most major countries of the British Empire, including India, Canada, and Australia. Lever had a very hands-on, autocratic management style and found his far-flung business empire difficult to control. The reason for Lever's control problems was that communication over great distances was difficult. It took six weeks to reach India by ship from England, and international telephone and telegraph services were unreliable.

Another problem Unilever encountered was the difficulty of doing business in societies that were separated from Britain by barriers of language and culture. Different countries have different sets of national beliefs, values, and norms, and Lever found that a management approach that worked in Britain did not necessarily work in India or Persia (now Iran). As a result, management practices had to be tailored to suit each unique national culture. After Lever's death in 1925, top management at Unilever lowered or *decentralized* (see Chapter 7) decision-making authority to the managers of the various national subsidiaries so they could develop a management approach that suited the country in which they were operating. One result of this strategy was that the subsidiaries grew distant and remote from one another, which reduced Unilever's performance.[48]

Since the end of World War II, a continuing stream of advances in communications and transportation technology has worked to reduce the barriers of distance and culture that affected Unilever and all global organizations. Over the last decades, global communication has been revolutionized by developments in satellites, digital technology, the Internet and global computer networks, and video teleconferencing that allow transmission of vast amounts of information and make reliable, secure, and instantaneous communication possible between people and companies anywhere in the world. This revolution has made it possible for a global organization—a tiny garment factory in Li & Fung's network or a huge company such as IKEA or Unilever—to do business anywhere, anytime, and to search for customers and suppliers around the world.

One of the most important innovations in transportation technology that has opened the global environment has been the growth of commercial jet travel. New York is now closer in travel time to Tokyo than it was to Philadelphia in the days of the 13 colonies—a fact that makes control of far-flung international businesses much easier today than in William Lever's era. In addition to speeding travel, modern communications and transportation technologies have also helped reduce the cultural distance between countries. The Internet and its millions of websites facilitate the development of global communications networks and media that are helping to create a worldwide culture above and beyond unique national cultures. Moreover, television networks such as CNN, MTV, ESPN, BBC, and HBO can now be transmitted to many countries, and Hollywood films are streamed live via the Internet throughout the world.

Effects of Free Trade on Managers

The lowering of barriers to trade and investment and the decline of distance and culture barriers has created enormous opportunities for companies to expand the market for their goods and services through exports and investments in overseas countries. The shift toward a more open global economy has created not only more opportunities to sell goods and services in markets abroad but also the opportunity to buy more from other countries. For example, apparel maker Ralph Lauren was heavily criticized when it was discovered the uniforms it made for the 2012 U.S. Olympic team were manufactured in China. Americans were not ready for their team uniforms to be made in another country. For the 2014 U.S. Olympic team, the Ralph Lauren uniforms were made in the United States. A manager's job is more challenging in a dynamic global environment because of the increased intensity of competition that goes hand in hand with the lowering of barriers to trade and investment.

REGIONAL TRADE AGREEMENTS The growth of regional trade agreements such as the North American Free Trade Agreement (NAFTA), and more recently the Central American Free Trade Agreement (CAFTA), also presents opportunities and threats for managers and their organizations. In North America, NAFTA, which became effective in 1994, aimed to abolish the tariffs on 99% of the goods traded between Mexico, Canada, and the United States by 2004. Although it did not achieve this lofty goal, NAFTA has removed most barriers on the cross-border flow of resources, giving, for example, financial institutions and retail businesses in Canada and the United States unrestricted access to the Mexican marketplace. After NAFTA was signed, there was a flood of investment into Mexico from the United States, as well as many other countries such as Japan. Walmart, Costco, Ford, and many major U.S. retail chains expanded their operations in Mexico; Walmart, for example, is stocking many more products from Mexico in its U.S. stores, and its Mexican store chain is also expanding rapidly.

The establishment of free-trade areas creates an opportunity for manufacturing organizations because it lets them reduce their costs. They can do this either by shifting production to the lowest-cost location within the free-trade area (for example, U.S. auto and textile companies shifting production to Mexico) or by serving the whole region from one location rather than establishing separate operations in each country. Some managers, however, view regional free-trade agreements as a threat because they expose a company based in one member country to increased competition from companies based in the other member countries. NAFTA has had this effect; today Mexican managers in some industries face the threat of head-to-head competition against efficient U.S. and Canadian companies. But the opposite is true as well: U.S. and Canadian managers are experiencing threats in labor-intensive industries, such as the flooring tile, roofing, and textile industries, where Mexican businesses have a cost advantage.

There are many regional trade agreements around the world. For example, founded in 1999, the African Union's purpose is both political and economic. Its goals include removing any remnants of colonization and apartheid, as well as creating cooperation for development. Complementing the role of the African Union is the Southern African Development Community, a 15-country group whose goals include socioeconomic development and poverty eradication. Another trade agreement is the Cooperation Council for the Arab States of the Gulf, which is made up of several countries, including Qatar, Oman, Bahrain, the United Arab Emirates, Kuwait, and Saudi Arabia. As part of the agreement, countries work on regional cooperation and economic relations.[49]

The Role of National Culture

Despite evidence that countries are becoming more similar because of globalization, and that the world may become "a global village," the cultures of different countries still vary widely because of vital differences in their values, norms, and attitudes. As noted earlier, national culture includes the values, norms, knowledge, beliefs, moral principles, laws, customs, and other practices that unite the citizens of a country. National culture shapes individual behavior by specifying appropriate and inappropriate behavior and interaction with others. People learn national culture in their everyday lives by interacting with those around them. This learning starts at an early age and continues throughout their lives.

Cultural Values and Norms

values Ideas about what a society believes to be good, right, desirable, or beautiful.

The basic building blocks of national culture are values and norms. **Values** are beliefs about what a society considers to be good, right, desirable, or beautiful—or their opposites. They provide the basic underpinnings for notions of individual freedom, democracy, truth, justice, honesty, loyalty, social obligation, collective responsibility, the appropriate roles for men and women, love, sex, marriage, and so on. Values are more than merely abstract concepts; they are invested with considerable emotional significance. People argue, fight, and even die over values such as freedom or dignity.

Although deeply embedded in society, values are not static; they change over time, but change is often the result of a slow and painful process. For example, the value systems of many formerly communist states such as Georgia, Hungary, and Romania have undergone significant changes as those countries move away from values that emphasize state control toward values that emphasizes individual freedom. Social turmoil often results when countries undergo major changes in their values, as is happening today in Asia, South America, and the Middle East.

norms Unwritten, informal codes of conduct that prescribe how people should act in particular situations and are considered important by most members of a group or organization.

Norms are unwritten, informal codes of conduct that prescribe appropriate behavior in particular situations and are considered important by most members of a group or organization. They shape the behavior of people toward one another. Two types of norms play a major role in national culture: mores and folkways. **Mores** are norms that are considered to be of central importance to the functioning of society and to social life. Accordingly, the violation of mores brings serious retribution. Mores include proscriptions against murder, theft, adultery, and incest. In many societies mores have been enacted into law. Thus, all advanced societies have laws against murder and theft. However, there are many differences in mores from one society to another. In the United States, for example, drinking alcohol is widely accepted; but in Saudi Arabia consumption of alcohol is viewed as a serious violation of social mores and is punishable by imprisonment.

mores Norms that are considered to be central to the functioning of society and to social life.

folkways The routine social conventions of everyday life.

Folkways are the routine social conventions of everyday life. They concern customs and practices such as dressing appropriately for particular situations, good social manners, eating with the correct utensils, and neighborly behavior. Although folkways define how people are expected to behave, violation of folkways is not a serious or moral matter. People who violate folkways are often thought to be eccentric or ill-mannered, but they are not usually considered immoral or wicked. In many countries, strangers are usually excused for violating folkways because they are unaccustomed to local behavior; but if they repeat the violation, they are censured because they are expected to learn appropriate behavior. Hence the importance for managers working in countries abroad to gain wide experience.

LO 4-5 Discuss why national cultures differ and why it is important that managers be sensitive to the effects of falling trade barriers and regional trade associations on the political and social systems of nations around the world.

Hofstede's Model of National Culture

Researchers have spent considerable time and effort identifying similarities and differences in the values and norms of different countries. One model of national culture was developed by Geert Hofstede.[50] As a psychologist for IBM, Hofstede

individualism

A worldview that values individual freedom and self-expression and adherence to the principle that people should be judged by their individual achievements rather than by their social background.

collectivism

A worldview that values subordination of the individual to the goals of the group and adherence to the principle that people should be judged by their contribution to the group.

power distance

The degree to which societies accept the idea that inequalities in the power and well-being of their citizens are due to differences in individuals' physical and intellectual capabilities and heritage.

collected data on employee values and norms from more than 100,000 IBM employees in 64 countries. Based on his research, Hofstede developed five dimensions along which national cultures can be placed (see Figure 4.4).[51]

INDIVIDUALISM VERSUS COLLECTIVISM The first dimension, which Hofstede labeled "individualism versus collectivism," has a long history in human thought. **Individualism** is a worldview that values individual freedom and self-expression and adherence to the principle that people should be judged by their individual achievements rather than by their social background. In Western countries, individualism usually includes admiration for personal success, a strong belief in individual rights, and high regard for individual entrepreneurs.[52]

In contrast, **collectivism** is a worldview that values subordination of the individual to the goals of the group and adherence to the principle that people should be judged by their contribution to the group. Collectivism was widespread in communist countries but has become less prevalent since the collapse of communism in most of those countries. Japan is a noncommunist country where collectivism is highly valued.

Collectivism in Japan traces its roots to the fusion of Confucian, Buddhist, and Shinto thought that occurred during the Tokugawa period in Japanese history (1600–1870s). A central value that emerged during this period was strong attachment to the group—whether a village, a work group, or a company. Strong identification with the group is said to create pressures for collective action in Japan, as well as strong pressure for conformity to group norms and a relative lack of individualism.[53]

Managers must realize that organizations and organizational members reflect their national culture's emphasis on individualism or collectivism. Indeed, one of the major reasons why Japanese and American management practices differ is that Japanese culture values collectivism and U.S. culture values individualism.

POWER DISTANCE By **power distance** Hofstede meant the degree to which societies accept the idea that inequalities in the power and well-being of their citizens are due to differences in individuals' physical and intellectual capabilities and heritage. This concept also encompasses the degree to which societies accept the economic

Figure 4.4

Hofstede's Model of National Culture

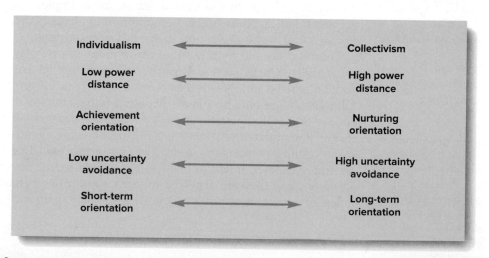

and social differences in wealth, status, and well-being that result from differences in individual capabilities.

Societies in which inequalities are allowed to persist or grow over time have *high power distance.* In high-power-distance societies, workers who are professionally successful amass wealth and pass it on to their children, and, as a result, inequalities may grow over time. In such societies, the gap between rich and poor, with all the attendant political and social consequences, grows very large. In contrast, in societies with *low power distance,* large inequalities between citizens are not allowed to develop. In low-power-distance countries, the government uses taxation and social welfare programs to reduce inequality and improve the welfare of the least fortunate. These societies are more attuned to preventing a large gap between rich and poor and minimizing discord between different classes of citizens.

Advanced Western countries such as the United States, Germany, the Netherlands, and the United Kingdom have relatively low power distance and high individualism. Economically poor Latin American countries such as Guatemala and Panama, and Asian countries such as Malaysia and the Philippines, have high power distance and low individualism.[54] These findings suggest that the cultural values of richer countries emphasize protecting the rights of individuals and, at the same time, provide a fair chance of success to every member of society.

achievement orientation A worldview that values assertiveness, performance, success, and competition.

ACHIEVEMENT VERSUS NURTURING ORIENTATION Societies that have an **achievement orientation** value assertiveness, performance, success, competition, and results. Societies that have a **nurturing orientation** value the quality of life, warm personal relationships, and services and care for the weak. Japan and the United States tend to be achievement-oriented; the Netherlands, Sweden, and Denmark are more nurturing-oriented.

nurturing orientation A worldview that values the quality of life, warm personal friendships, and services and care for the weak.

UNCERTAINTY AVOIDANCE Societies as well as individuals differ in their tolerance for uncertainty and risk. Societies low on **uncertainty avoidance** (such as the United States and Hong Kong) are easygoing, value diversity, and tolerate differences in personal beliefs and actions. Societies high on uncertainty avoidance (such as Japan and France) are more rigid and skeptical about people whose behaviors or beliefs differ from the norm. In these societies, conformity to the values of the social and work groups to which a person belongs is the norm, and structured situations are preferred because they provide a sense of security.

uncertainty avoidance The degree to which societies are willing to tolerate uncertainty and risk.

LONG-TERM VERSUS SHORT-TERM ORIENTATION The last dimension that Hofstede described is orientation toward life and work.[55] A national culture with a **long-term orientation** rests on values such as thrift (saving) and persistence in achieving goals. A national culture with a **short-term orientation** is concerned with maintaining personal stability or happiness and living for the present. Societies with a long-term orientation include Taiwan and Hong Kong, well known for their high rate of per capita savings. The United States and France have a short-term orientation, and their citizens tend to spend more and save less.

long-term orientation A worldview that values thrift and persistence in achieving goals.

short-term orientation A worldview that values personal stability or happiness and living for the present.

National Culture and Global Management

Differences among national cultures have important implications for managers. First, because of cultural differences, management practices that are effective in one country might be troublesome in another. General Electric's managers learned this while trying to manage Tungsram, a Hungarian lighting products company GE acquired for $150 million. GE was attracted to Tungsram, widely regarded as one of

Hungary's best companies, because of Hungary's low wage rates and the possibility of using the company as a base from which to export lighting products to western Europe. GE transferred some of its best managers to Tungsram and hoped it would soon become a leader in Europe. Unfortunately many problems arose.

One problem resulted from major misunderstandings between the American managers and the Hungarian workers. The Americans complained that the Hungarians were lazy; the Hungarians thought the Americans were pushy. The Americans wanted strong sales and marketing functions that would pamper customers. In the prior command economy, sales and marketing activities were unnecessary. In addition, Hungarians expected GE to deliver Western-style wages, but GE came to Hungary to take advantage of the country's low-wage structure. As Tungsram's losses mounted, GE managers had to admit that, because of differences in basic attitudes between countries, they had underestimated the difficulties they would face in turning Tungsram around. Nevertheless, by 2001 these problems had been solved, and the increased efficiency of GE's Hungarian operations has made General Electric a major player in the European lighting market.[56]

Often, management practices must be tailored to suit the cultural contexts within which an organization operates. An approach effective in the United States might not work in Japan, Hungary, or Mexico because of differences in national culture. For example, U.S.-style pay-for-performance systems that emphasize the performance of individuals might not work well in Japan, where individual performance in pursuit of group goals is the value that receives emphasis.

Managers doing business with individuals from another country must be sensitive to the value systems and norms of that country and behave accordingly. For example, Friday is the Islamic Sabbath. Thus it would be impolite and inappropriate for a U.S. manager to schedule a busy day of activities for Saudi Arabian managers on a Friday.

A culturally diverse management team can be a source of strength for an organization participating in the global marketplace. Compared to organizations with culturally homogeneous management teams, organizations that employ managers from a variety of cultures have a better appreciation of how national cultures differ, and they tailor their management systems and behaviors to the differences.[57] Indeed, one advantage that many Western companies have over their Japanese competitors is greater willingness to create global teams composed of employees from different countries around the world who can draw on and share their different cultural experiences and knowledge to provide service that is customized to the needs of companies in different countries. For example, because IT services account for more than half of IBM's $90 billion annual revenues, it has been searching for ways to better use its talented workforce to both lower costs and offer customers unique, specialized kinds of services that its competitors cannot. IBM has developed several kinds of techniques to accomplish this.[58]

In the 2000s, IBM created "competency centers" around the world staffed by employees who share the same specific IT skill. Most of IBM's employees are concentrated in competency centers located in the countries in which IBM has the most clients and

Computer technicians at work in a server room. IBM's competency centers customize teams of workers who can manage their own tasks. © Comstock/Stockbyte/Getty images RF

does the most business. These employees have a wide variety of skills, developed from their previous work experience, and the challenge facing IBM is to use these experts efficiently. To accomplish this, IBM used its own IT expertise to develop sophisticated software that allows it to create self-managed teams composed of IBM experts who have the optimum mix of skills to solve a client's particular problems. First, IBM programmers analyze the skills and experience of its more than 80,000 global employees and enter the results into the software program. Then they analyze and code the nature of a client's specific problem and input that information. IBM's program matches each specific client problem to the skills of IBM's experts and identifies a list of "best fit" employees. One of IBM's senior managers narrows this list and decides on the actual composition of the self-managed team. Once selected, team members, from wherever they happen to be in the world, assemble as quickly as possible and go to work analyzing the client's problem. Together, team members use their authority. This new IT lets IBM create an ever-changing set of global self-managed teams that form to develop the software and service package necessary to solve the problems of IBM's global clients. At the same time, IBM's IT also optimizes the use of its whole talented workforce because each employee is placed in his or her "most highly valued use"—that is, in the team where the employee's skills can best increase efficiency and effectiveness. There are many factors involved in working for a global organization. The accompanying "Management Insight" describes how managers might educate themselves about some of the issues.

MANAGEMENT INSIGHT

Cultural Challenges Faced by Expatriates in Global Business

Where in the world would you like to be an expatriate? The annual Expat Explorer Survey by HSBC Bank International could help you decide. The survey ranks the best places in the world to be an expatriate worker. The results are available on the company's website (http://expatexplorer.hsbc.com) and can help people understand what it would be like to be an expatriate in different countries.

The HSBC site also allows users to submit tips based on their expatriate experiences. For example, an expatriate named Miki provides a list of five tips on how to live in Japan:

1. Say "Konnichiwa" (hello) to get conversations started with your new neighbors.
2. If you want to make new friends, attend a Japanese drinks party, which is part of the culture for many companies.
3. Ask for help at any time because Japanese people are friendly and like to offer support.
4. Enjoy Japanese food.
5. Visit hot springs called "onsen" throughout the country—they are considered great tourist attractions.

Other information on the site is more general. For example, New Zealand, South Africa, and Germany are rated highly for raising children. France, Belgium, Germany, and Taiwan get high marks for health care access and quality. When it comes to earning disposable income, Thailand, Vietnam, Taiwan, China, and Bahrain are at the top of the list.

The HSBC survey ranks countries based on experience, economics, and raising children abroad. The economics factor includes income, disposable income, and host economic satisfaction.

The experience factor includes a long list of issues from entertainment and work–life balance to local culture and making local friends to local weather and learning the local language. The raising children factor also includes a long list of issues from quality and cost of child care to access to better education to children learning a new language.

While the factors in the survey can be chosen to tailor a list of the best countries for an individual expatriate, the survey does rank the countries from best to worst. Among the "best" countries on the three factors are Switzerland, Singapore, China, Germany, and Bahrain. The "worst" countries on the three factors include Italy, Brazil, United Kingdom, and Egypt. The United States ranked 30 out of 34 due to poor scores on experience and raising children abroad.

Another interesting finding of the most recent Expat Explorer report is that economies classified as emerging and growth leading economies, or EAGLEs, are proving to be popular destinations for companies looking to send their employees abroad. These countries include Brazil, Turkey, India, China, Mexico, and Taiwan. Other topics of survey response compilations include tips for getting a car, finding a school for your children, arranging your paperwork, getting through immigration, settling in, and avoiding homesickness.

There are several lists on how to adapt to life in the United States, with tips such as travel around the United States and don't just stay in one city or state, be aware of how important your credit rating is, research schools because there are huge disparities in education for your children, and visit all of the national parks across the country.

The site contains a disclaimer that content on the site is the opinion of users and not verified by HSBC.[59]

Summary and Review

WHAT IS THE GLOBAL ENVIRONMENT? The global environment is the set of forces and conditions that operate beyond an organization's boundaries but affect a manager's ability to acquire and use resources. The global environment has two components: the task environment and the general environment. [LO 4-1]

THE TASK ENVIRONMENT The task environment is the set of forces and conditions that originate with global suppliers, distributors, customers, and competitors and influence managers daily. The opportunities and threats associated with forces in the task environment become more complex as a company expands globally. [LO 4-2, 4-3]

THE GENERAL ENVIRONMENT The general environment comprises wide-ranging global economic, technological, sociocultural, demographic, political, and legal forces that affect an organization and its task environment. [LO 4-2, 4-3]

THE CHANGING GLOBAL ENVIRONMENT In recent years there has been a marked shift toward a more open global environment in which capital flows more freely as people and companies search for new opportunities to create profit and wealth. This has hastened the process of globalization. Globalization is the set of specific and general forces that work together to integrate and connect economic, political, and social systems across countries, cultures, or geographic regions so that nations become increasingly interdependent and similar. The process of globalization has been furthered by declining barriers to international trade and investment and declining barriers of distance and culture. [LO 4-4, 4-5]

Management *in Action*

TOPICS FOR DISCUSSION AND ACTION

Discussion

1. Why is it important for managers to understand the forces in the global environment that are acting on them and their organizations? [LO 4-1]

2. Which organization is likely to face the most complex task environment—a biotechnology company trying to develop a cure for cancer or a large retailer like The Gap or Macy's? Why? [LO 4-2, 4-3]

3. The population is aging because of declining birth rates, declining death rates, and the aging of the baby boom generation. What might some of the implications of this demographic trend be for (a) a pharmaceutical company and (b) the home construction industry? [LO 4-1, 4-2, 4-3]

4. How do political, legal, and economic forces shape national culture? What characteristics of national culture do you think have the most important effect on how successful a country is in doing business abroad? [LO 4-3, 4-5]

5. After the passage of NAFTA, many U.S. companies shifted production operations to Mexico to take advantage of lower labor costs and lower standards for environmental and worker protection. As a result, they cut their costs and were better able to survive in an increasingly competitive global environment. Was their behavior ethical—that is, did the ends justify the means? [LO 4-4]

Action

6. Choose an organization and ask a manager in that organization to list the number and strengths of forces in the organization's task environment. Ask the manager to pay particular attention to identifying opportunities and threats that result from pressures and changes in customers, competitors, and suppliers. [LO 4-1, 4-2, 4-3]

BUILDING MANAGEMENT SKILLS

Analyzing an Organization's Environment [LO 4-1, 4-2, 4-3]

Pick an organization with which you are familiar. It can be an organization in which you have worked or currently work or one that you interact with regularly as a customer (such as the college you are attending). For this organization do the following:

1. Describe the main forces in the global task environment that are affecting the organization.

2. Describe the main forces in the global general environment

that are affecting the organization.

3. Explain how environmental forces affect the job of an individual manager within this organization. How do they

determine the opportunities and threats that its managers must confront?

MANAGING ETHICALLY [LO 4-4, 4-5]

Home Depot misjudged the market in China. The world's largest home improvement chain entered the Chinese market in 2006 and decided to leave it six years later. The company was unable to sell its do-it-yourself brand to Chinese consumers. Cheap labor in China means many people can hire someone else to do home improvement work for them. In addition, apartment-based living in China meant there was not much demand for products such as lumber.[60]

Questions

1. What could Home Depot have done to avoid its mistake in China?

2. In what cultures might Home Depot find better success?

SMALL GROUP BREAKOUT EXERCISE [LO 4-1, 4-2]
How to Enter the Copying Business

Form groups of three to five people, and appoint one group member as the spokesperson who will communicate your findings to the whole class when called on by the instructor. Then discuss the following scenario:

You and your partners have decided to open a small printing and copying business in a college town of 100,000 people. Your business will compete with companies like FedEx Office. You know that over 50% of small businesses fail in their first year, so to increase your chances of success, you have decided to perform a detailed analysis of the task environment of the copying business to discover what opportunities and threats you will encounter.

1. Decide what you must know about (a) your future customers, (b) your future competitors, and (c) other critical forces in the task environment if you are to be successful.

2. Evaluate the main barriers to entry into the copying business.

3. Based on this analysis, list some steps you would take to help your new copying business succeed.

BE THE MANAGER [LO 4-1, 4-2]

The Changing Environment of Retailing

You are the new manager of a major clothing store that is facing a crisis. This clothing store has been the leader in its market for the last 15 years. In the last three years, however, two other major clothing store chains have opened, and they have steadily been attracting customers away from your store—your sales are down 30%. To find out why, your store surveyed former customers and learned that they perceive your store as not keeping up with changing fashion trends and new forms of customer service. In examining how the store operates, you found out that the 10 purchasing managers who buy the clothing and accessories for the store have been buying from the same clothing suppliers and have become reluctant to try new ones. Moreover, salespeople rarely, if ever, make suggestions for changing how the store operates, and they don't respond to customer requests; the culture of the store has become conservative and risk-averse.

Questions

1. Analyze the major forces in the task environment of a retail clothing store.

2. Devise a program that will help other managers and employees to better understand and respond to their store's task environment.

Why Auto Makers Are Building New Factories in Mexico, Not the U.S.

Array of Free-Trade Pacts Favors Mexico over U.S. South as Site for North American Assembly Plants

A barren patch in the rugged hills along the Tennessee River is a sign of how Mexico has accelerated past the U.S. South in the global competition for auto investment.

The tract of cleared woodland lies alongside a factory Volkswagen AG set out to build in 2008. VW took an option on the adjacent 800 acres as a place where its Audi unit might build a North American plant someday.

But four years later, when Audi decided to move global production of its Q5 SUV to North America, the prize went to Mexico. Audi now is finishing a $1.3 billion factory in a gritty south-central Mexico town called San Jose Chiapa. The plant's massive buildings rise like supertankers from dun-colored fields where families scrape by raising corn and beans.

Mexico's low wages and improved logistics were part of the draw. But for Audi, which plans to ship the factory's output all over the world, what tipped the scales was Mexico's unrivaled trade relationships.

"Mexico had more than 40 different free-trade agreements," said Rupert Stadler, Audi's chief executive. The pacts give exporters from Mexico duty-free access to markets that contain 60% of the world's economic output.

The U.S. is negotiating to expand its own array of free-trade agreements, but progress has been slow amid congressional opposition to giving the White House special trade authority known as "fast track." Foes worry that the trade agreements could drive jobs to low-wage countries.

With some luxury-car makers, at least, the reverse may be true. The Audi deal shows that besides its low-cost labor, Mexico's trade pacts give it allure in the global car market, threatening the American South's industrial renewal.

Seven Asian and European auto makers have opened new Mexican assembly plants, or disclosed plans for one, in little more than a year. Other car companies have financed significant expansions in Mexico, among them Nissan Motor Co., General Motors Co., Ford Motor Co. and Fiat Chrysler Automobiles NV.

Last week, VW said it would spend $1 billion expanding a Mexican plant to build a small SUV for the U.S. and some foreign markets. All told, auto makers and parts suppliers have earmarked more than $20 billion of new investments, Mexican officials say.

While the bulk of Mexico's auto exports go to the U.S. and Canada, its partners in the North American Free Trade Agreement, auto makers increasingly are turning to Mexico as a platform for selling world-wide.

The trade-related cost edge can be large. When Audi rival BMW AG ships cars to Europe from BMW's two-decade-old Spartanburg, S.C., plant, it is hit with a 10% duty on each one. For a $50,000 vehicle, that $5,000 is a much bigger factor than differences in labor costs.

In July, BMW said it would build a factory in Mexico's central San Luis Potosi state to produce 150,000 still-unspecified vehicles annually by 2019. Mexico's "large number of international free trade agreements . . . was a decisive factor in

the choice of location," BMW said at the time.

The wave of investment has turned Mexico into the world's seventh-largest producer of cars— it passed Brazil last year—and the fourth-largest exporter after Germany, Japan and South Korea. Mexico has just eclipsed Japan to become the No. 2 supplier of vehicles to the U.S. market after Canada. Industry analysts see Mexico's current annual production of 3.2 million cars and light trucks rising more than 50% to five million by 2018.

That would still be far below U.S. annual production of 11.4 million. Of these, six Southeastern states produce about 3.9 million. Auto makers began flocking to the U.S. South in the 1980s for its largely nonunion labor, good transportation and energy grids, and the region came to be seen as the new Detroit of the North American auto industry. Now, as Mexico gears up, the stakes are high for Dixie.

The South continues to hold economic appeal for car companies. Daimler AG, BMW and others are expanding existing assembly plants in Alabama and South Carolina. Just this month, Daimler disclosed another investment, a planned $500 million expansion of an existing plant near Charleston, S.C.

But it has been more than six years since an auto maker picked the U.S. South for a "greenfield" plant, meaning one where the company didn't already have facilities. Such projects have all gone to Mexico lately.

South Korea's Kia Motors Corp., which six years ago picked Georgia for its first North American factory, passed on several U.S. sites for its second one and chose a location near Monterrey, Mexico. An alliance between Nissan and Daimler said in June it would build a $1.4 billion plant in Mexico's Aguascalientes state to make Infiniti and Mercedes compacts. Nissan, which has three assembly plants in the U.S. South plus North American headquarters in Nashville, also finished a $2 billion plant expansion in Mexico in late 2013.

"We see a number of wins, back to back, in Mexico that might have gone here," said Greg Canfield, Alabama's economic development secretary. "What we're seeing in Alabama and the South is the recognition that we really have a new competitor."

Global Supplier

In Audi's case, the company wanted a North American plant not only to feed the strong U.S. market for a midsize SUV such as the Q5, which it currently makes in Germany, but also to supply the model to Europe and much of the rest of the world.

From the start, Audi preferred to piggyback on parent VW's North American infrastructure such as roads and suppliers. In the site competition, that meant largely a two-horse race between VW's existing North American plants, one at Chattanooga and one in the south-central Mexican state of Puebla.

The place Audi chose, San Jose Chiapa, seems at first glance like the middle of nowhere, a cinder-block town of about 10,000 residents. But the port of Veracruz on the Gulf of Mexico is reachable in less than half a day by rail or truck, and the factories of suppliers to the VW plant are an hour's drive west.

Puebla state officials sweetened San Jose Chiapa's allure by agreeing to finance a training center and

donate 1,200 acres of land. Plans are under way to build a model community with homes, shops, schools and cinemas for families of the 20,000 people expected to work at Audi's assembly plants and parts suppliers.

"It's like a bomb exploded here," said Josue Martinez, a bricklayer who serves as mayor of San Jose Chiapa. "For this town, there is a before and an after the Audi plant."

Producing the Q5 in Mexico isn't without risk. The plant will assemble every Q5 sold world-wide except in China and India, so any factory glitch would interrupt global sales for a popular model.

Audi is taking some unusual steps to control its risk. First, to ensure quality, the company created a consultancy that fanned out to 160 parts suppliers in Mexico, encouraging some to change plant design or improve weak production processes.

Audi also developed a process to evaluate raw materials, a task normally left to suppliers. One goal was to have most of the plant's raw materials priced in dollars, so costs wouldn't be subject to exchange-rate swings, as they would if some materials were imported. "A natural hedge," Audi calls this strategy.

The company created an inventory of local sources for every part and for all raw materials used in the Q5, and has required suppliers to source from its list. "We thought if every supplier does it by himself, it will fail," said Bernd Martens, Audi's procurement chief. "So, we did it at Audi."

Audi now is training 600 people from Puebla state at its headquarters in Ingolstadt, Germany. Visiting on 18-month stints, the Mexicans, mostly supervisory level, study German, train on Audi systems and are indoctrinated with the company's intense focus on quality.

Spanish conversations float through the air at cafes in the Bavarian town on the Danube. Once a week, Audi's Mexican workers and German colleagues crowd into the Havana Bar for salsa dancing.

"When we have a problem in Mexico, we have to know who can help us in Ingolstadt," said Isaul Lopez Gutierrez, who will run a team of system analysts in Puebla. His oldest daughter, a 7-year-old, attends a German school.

Audi figured that siting its Q5 plant in Mexico would enable it to save 50% on labor costs, compared with Tennessee, Mr. Stadler said. It also should save slightly more on parts in Mexico than in the U.S., said Mr. Martens.

A crucial factor was trade. Mexico has 10 free-trade arrangements encompassing 45 countries—counting EU members separately—plus other trade deals in Latin America and the Asian Pacific, according to the government's trade office. In contrast, the U.S. has free-trade agreements with 20 countries, mostly smaller economies such as Chile, Jordan and Panama, said the U.S. trade representative's office.

U.S. officials are negotiating with officials from Japan and 10 other Asian and Latin American countries in hopes of completing in coming months a framework known as the Trans-Pacific Partnership. But the agreement, which officials say would help the countries compete with China, needs the legislation known as fast track to ease its passage in Congress. If introduced and passed this year, fast track could also expedite the passage of a trade agreement with the EU that is in the early stages of negotiation.

Tough for Tennessee

Because of the free-trade agreements Mexico already has, Audi's consideration of Chattanooga for the Q5 plant "never seemed real," said Tennessee Republican Sen. Bob Corker. Mexico's greater array of trade pacts "puts us at a disadvantage. This is something that is very important to our country," he said.

But Obama administration officials have run into determined resistance from some fellow Democrats. "Bitter experience tells us that bad trade deals devastate jobs, devastate wages," said Rep. Rosa DeLauro of Connecticut, who is leading opposition to fast track among Democrats in the House.

After Audi settled on Mexico in 2012, officials of the U.S. Commerce Department visited Chattanooga to meet with business and government leaders. Gathered around a long walnut-colored conference table at Chamber of Commerce offices, the locals said Audi's decision needed to be a wake-up call about Mexico's trade advantage. The discussion "wasn't so much about the Audi project itself—it was about an example that could probably translate into other projects that are going to be looking at Chattanooga," said Charles Wood, an executive with the Chattanooga Chamber of Commerce.

Six Southern states commissioned a study of how to compete with Mexico. The report by the Center for Automotive Research suggested tightening the density of parts suppliers and training workforces for higher-value production jobs.

In Tennessee, the auto industry accounts for three-quarters of manufacturing jobs, according to a Brookings Institution study. The state now offers adult residents free training to learn the advanced skills needed today by auto makers, said Tennessee's economic-development commissioner, Randy Boyd.

Looking out his office window on downtown Nashville, Mr. Boyd came back to Mexico's trade edge. "We'd love to compete on even terms," he said. "This will definitely be an issue if Mexico has that advantage and we don't."

Questions

1. Explain the reasons behind Audi's decision to build its Q5 SUV in Mexico rather than in the United States.

2. Describe how Audi's strategy to train supervisory staff from the Mexican plant in Germany will have a positive impact on the operations at the new facility.

3. Audi took the unusual step of preparing a source list for every part of the Q5 model that local suppliers must use. What is the advantage of this management decision? Is there a disadvantage?

Source: Dudley Althaus and William Boston, "Why Auto Makers Are Building New Factories in Mexico, Not the U.S.," *The Wall Street Journal,* accessed March 17, 2015, www.wsj.com.

Endnotes

1. J. Yunker, "The Top 25 Global Websites from the 2015 Web Globalization Report Card," *Global by Design,* accessed March 17, 2015, www.globalbydesign .com; J. Yunker, "The Global Web Revolution: A Look Back at the Language Growth of eBay, Coke, Amazon, and Others," *Smartling* blog, accessed March 17, 2015, www. smartling.com; D. Berthiaume, "Visa Expanding Online Payment Service Visa Checkout to 16 Global Markets," *Chain Store Age,* accessed March 17, 2015, www.chainstoreage .com; R. Laing, "5 Ways to Win at Website Localization," *Mashable,* accessed March 17, 2015, http:// mashable.com.

2. L. J. Bourgeois, "Strategy and Environment: A Conceptual Integration," *Academy of Management Review* 5 (1985), 25–39.

3. M. E. Porter, *Competitive Strategy* (New York: Free Press, 1980).

4. "Coca-Cola versus Pepsi-Cola and the Soft Drink Industry," Harvard Business School Case 9-391–179.

5. www.splenda.com, 2015.

6. D. Engber, "The Quest for a Natural Sugar Substitute," *The New York Times,* January 1, 2014, www. nytimes.com.

7. A. K. Gupta and V. Govindarajan, "Cultivating a Global Mind-Set," *Academy of Management Executive* 16 (February 2002), 116–27.

8. "Boeing's Worldwide Supplier Network," *Seattle Post-Intelligencer,* April 9, 1994, p. 13.

9. I. Metthee, "Playing a Larger Part," *Seattle Post-Intelligencer,* April 9, 1994, p. 13.

10. S. Denning, "What Went Wrong at Boeing? *Forbes,* January 21, 2013, www.forbes.com.

11. Company website, "What We Do," www.lifung.com, accessed March 10, 2015.

12. S. Denning, "Why Apple and GE Are Bringing Back Manufacturing," *Forbes,* accessed March 10, 2015, www.forbes.com.

13. S. Oliver, "Tim Cook Lauds 'American Manufacturing

Expertise' During Visit to Texas Mac Pro Factory," *Apple Insider,* accessed March 10, 2015, http://appleinsider.com.

14. J. Lee, "The Apparel Industry's Answer to Global Water Shortages," *Triple Pundit,* March 12, 2015, www.triplepundit.com.

15. K. Drennan, "Reduce Your Wardrobe's Water Footprint," *Green Living,* accessed March 12, 2015, www.greenlivingonline.com.

16. "Water Pollution," *Eco360,* accessed March 12, 2015, www.sustainablecommunication.org.

17. D. Ferris, "Nike, Adidas Want to Dye Your Shirt with No Water," *Forbes,* accessed March 12, 2015, www.forbes.com.

18. "Water Pollution."

19. L. Kaye, "Clothing to Dye For: The Textile Sector Must Confront Water Risks," *The Guardian,* accessed March 12, 2015, www.theguardian.com.

20. R. Hosseini, "Recycling Water to Make Your Jeans," (blog) www.levistrauss.com, accessed March 12, 2015.

21. "Nike Moves to Water-Free, Chemical-Free Dyeing," *GreenBiz,* accessed March 12, 2015, www.greenbiz.com.

22. A. Brettman, "6 Questions about Nike's Water-Less Fabric Dyeing Technology," *The Oregonian,* accessed March 12, 2015, www.oregonlive.com.

23. P. Meister, "One Million Yards of Water-Saving DryDye Fabric—and Counting!" *Adidas Group* blog, accessed March 12, 2015, http://blog.adidas-group.com.

24. Company website, "Nike, Inc., Unveils ColorDry Technology and High-Tech Facility to Eliminate Water and Chemicals in Dyeing," http://news.nike.com, accessed March 12, 2015.

25. M. E. Porter, *Competitive Advantage* (New York: Free Press, 1985).

26. M. Malone, "Did Wal-Mart Love RFID to Death?" *ZDNet,* accessed March 12, 2015, http://zdnet.com.

27. A. Grossman, "Bridgestone Agrees to Pay $425 Million Fine in Price-Fixing Probe," *The Wall Street Journal,* accessed March 12, 2015, http://blogs.wsj.com.

28. J. Ellett, "Dell's CMO Reveals Plan for Success As a Private Company," *Forbes,* accessed March 15, 2015, www.forbes.com.

29. For views on barriers to entry from an economics perspective, see Porter, *Competitive Strategy.* For the sociological perspective, see J. Pfeffer and G. R. Salancik, *The External Control of Organization: A Resource Dependence Perspective* (New York: Harper & Row, 1978).

30. S. Banjo, "Wal-Mart's E-Stumble with Amazon," *The Wall Street Journal,* accessed March 12, 2015, www.wsj.com.

31. M. Hachman, "AMD Reveals High-End 'Carrizo' APU, the First Chip to Fully Embrace Audacious HSA Tech," *PCWorld,* accessed March 12, 2015, www.pcworld.com.

32. N. Goodman, *An Introduction to Sociology* (New York: HarperCollins, 1991); C. Nakane, *Japanese Society* (Berkeley: University of California Press, 1970).

33. For a detailed discussion of the importance of the structure of law as a factor explaining economic change and growth, see D. C. North, *Institutions, Institutional Change, and Economic Performance* (Cambridge: Cambridge University Press, 1990).

34. European Commission, "About TTIP," http://ec.europa.eu, accessed March 12, 2015.

35. D. Lee, "The Trans-Pacific Partnership: Who Wins, Who Loses, Why It Matters," *Los Angeles Times,* accessed March 12, 2015, www.latimes.com; organization website, "Trans-Pacific Partnership (TPP): Job Loss, Lower Wages and Higher Drug Prices," www.citizen.org.

36. M. A. Carpenter and J. W. Fredrickson, "Top Management Teams, Global Strategic Posture, and the Moderating Role of Uncertainty," *Academy of Management Journal* 44 (June 2001), 533–46.

37. A. Glass, "Ernst & Young Launches Women Athletes Global Leadership Network," *Forbes,* accessed March 12, 2015, www.forbes.com.

38. Organization website, "EY: Official Supporter of the Rio 2016 Olympic Games," www.rio2016.com.

39. Company website, "Women Athletes Business Network: Perspectives on Sport and Teams," www.ey.com, accessed March 12, 2015.

40. E. Kinlin, "From Athletics to Leadership," *Women Executives,* accessed March 12, 2015, http://kinlin.com.

41. "EY Women Athletes Global Leadership Network," *Leaders,* accessed March 12, 2015, www.leadersmag.com.

42. Glass, "Ernst & Young Launces Women Athletes Global Leadership Network."

43. "Ernst & Young to Launch Leadership Network for Elite Female Athletes to Address Unmet Global Need," *PRWeb,* accessed March 12, 2015, www.prweb.com.

44. William Mauldin, "U.S. Moves to Impose Tariffs on Chinese Tires," *The Wall Street Journal,* accessed March 12, 2015, www.wsj.com; B. Davis, "Chinese Car Tire Imports to U.S. at an All-Time High," www.tirebusiness.com, March 18, 2014.

45. For a summary of these theories, see P. Krugman and M. Obstfeld, *International Economics: Theory and Policy* (New York: HarperCollins, 1991). Also see C. W. L. Hill, *International Business* (New York: McGraw-Hill, 1997), chap. 4.

46. A. M. Rugman, "The Quest for Global Dominance," *Academy of Management Executive* 16 (August 2002), 157–60.

47. www.wto.org.com, 2015.

48. C. A. Bartlett and S. Ghoshal, *Managing across Borders* (Boston: Harvard Business School Press, 1989).

49. Organization website, "AU in a Nutshell," www.au.int, accessed March 12, 2015; organization website, www.sadc.int, accessed March 12, 2015; organization website, "Areas of Cooperation Achievements," www.gcc-sg.org, accessed March 12, 2015.

50. G. Hofstede, B. Neuijen, D. D. Ohayv, and G. Sanders, "Measuring Organizational Cultures: A Qualitative and Quantitative Study across Twenty Cases," *Administrative Science Quarterly* 35 (1990), 286–316.

51. M. H. Hoppe, "Introduction: Geert Hofstede's Culture's Consequences:

International Differences in Work-Related Values," *Academy of Management Executive* 18 (February 2004), 73–75.

52. R. Bellah, *Habits of the Heart: Individualism and Commitment in American Life* (Berkeley: University of California Press, 1985).

53. R. Bellah, *The Tokugawa Religion* (New York: Free Press, 1957); C. Nakane, *Japanese Society* (Berkeley: University of California Press, 1970).

54. G. Hofstede, "The Cultural Relativity of Organizational Practices and Theories," *Journal of International Business Studies,* Fall 1983, 75–89.

55. Hofstede et al., "Measuring Organizational Cultures."

56. J. Perlez, "GE Finds Tough Going in Hungary," *The New York Times,* July 25, 1994, C1, C3; www.ge.com, 2015.

57. J. P. Fernandez and M. Barr, *The Diversity Advantage* (New York: Lexington Books, 1994).

58. www.ibm.com, 2015.

59. Company website, "Expat Explorer Report 2014," http://expatexplorer.hsbc.com, accessed March 17, 2015.

60. L. Burkitt, "Home Depot Learns Chinese Prefer 'Do-It-for-Me,'" *The Wall Street Journal,* accessed March 17, 2015, www.wsj.com.

PART 3

5 Decision Making, Learning, Creativity, and Entrepreneurship

Learning Objectives

After studying this chapter, you should be able to:

LO 5-1 Understand the nature of managerial decision making, differentiate between programmed and nonprogrammed decisions, and explain why nonprogrammed decision making is a complex, uncertain process.

LO 5-2 Describe the six steps managers should take to make the best decisions.

LO 5-3 Identify the advantages and disadvantages of group decision making, and describe techniques that can improve it.

LO 5-4 Explain the role that organizational learning and creativity play in helping managers to improve their decisions.

LO 5-5 Describe how managers can encourage and promote entrepreneurship to create a learning organization, and differentiate between entrepreneurs and intrapreneurs.

© Robert Nicholas/age fotostock RF

Lifelong learning and good decision making have been crucial to the success of 1-800-Flowers.com Inc. James McCann, Chairman and CEO, bartended, worked in the administration of a group home for boys, got a degree in psychology, and then built a small florist shop into a global business. © Bloomberg via Getty Images

MANAGEMENT SNAPSHOT

Decision Making and Learning

Why Is Decision Making and Learning of Utmost Importance for Entrepreneurs and Managers?

All managers must make decisions day in and day out under considerable uncertainty. And sometimes those decisions come back to haunt them if they turn out poorly. Sometimes, even highly effective managers make bad decisions. And factors beyond a manager's control can cause a good decision to result in unexpected negative consequences. Effective managers recognize the critical importance of making decisions on an ongoing basis as well as learning from prior decisions.

Decision making and learning have been key to Jim McCann's success in building a small florist shop into a global business with $756.3 million in 2014 revenues headquartered in Carle Place, New York.[1] In fact, learning and decision making have been mainstays for McCann throughout his life. Growing up in Queens, New York, McCann learned from his father, who had a small painting business. While he was bartending at night and going to college in the day, a friend let him know about an opportunity to work evenings in a group home for teenage boys. McCann decided to seize this opportunity, and while continuing to go to college in the day, he worked and slept (in his own room) in the St. John's Home for Boys in Queens.[2] When he graduated, he continued to work at the home in administration for 14 years.[3]

McCann continued to bartend at night to make some extra money for his family, and one of his customers told him that he was planning on selling a small flower shop.[4] McCann ending up buying the store for $10,000, continued to work at the home for boys, and learned the flower business—and the rest has made history.[5]

When he bought the store, he decided he wanted to turn it into a larger organization.[6] Ten years later he had over 20 flower stores and quit his job at the home for boys to work full time on his flower shop business.[7]

In the late 1980s McCann heard a commercial on the radio for 1-800-Flowers, the first company that enabled customers to call a toll-free number to order flowers.[8] McCann decided to be a distributor for this company, and became the florist for New York. However, over time, McCann stopped getting orders from this source of customers. McCann went to Dallas where the company was based and found out that its owners had ceased operating because of a lack of business.[9]

McCann decided to try to buy the business with his savings from his own business, while saving money by not involving lawyers, accountants, or bankers in the transaction.[10] He offered the owners $2 million for their 800 flower business and they accepted. Soon after, McCann discovered that in buying the business, he had become responsible for the $7 million in debt that the business had accrued and that his decision to buy 1-800-Flowers amounted to a big mistake.[11]

Determined to turn around this mistake, McCann turned his store in Queens into a telemarketing firm for flowers, but business was lackluster.[12] While on a trip to Dallas, he seized an opportunity to expand his business presented to him by Larry Zarin, who was marketing Kellogg's Nutri-Grain.[13] Zarin and McCann agreed that they would put advertisements on boxes of Nutri-Grain indicating that if customers bought the cereal, they could buy a dozen roses from 1-800-Flowers for $14.99. To their amazement, they received 30,000 orders for flowers. A similar promotion worked with Zales jewelry stores, helping make the company known across the country (its network of florists is called BloomNet).[14]

In the early 1990s, McCann and his brother and partner, Chris, decided they wanted to put their business online and they were the first organization to have an online transaction over AOL.[15] The company went public in 1999 and raised funds to create a better technological platform.[16]

Jim and Chris McCann continue to make decisions and learn to this day. 1-800-Flowers.com has become active in the social-mobile-local retail space and sells gifts for all occasions as well as flowers.[17] Clearly, learning and decision making have been crucial ingredients for the entrepreneurial success story behind 1-800-Flowers.com.[18]

Overview

The "Management Snapshot" illustrates how decision making and learning are an ongoing challenge for managers that can profoundly influence organizational effectiveness. McCann's decision to seize an opportunity and buy a small flower shop and his subsequent decisions along the way have had a dramatic effect on his business.[19] The decisions managers make at all levels in companies large and small can change the growth and prosperity of these companies and the well-being of their employees, customers, and other stakeholders. Yet such decisions can be difficult to make because they are fraught with uncertainty.

In this chapter, we examine how managers make decisions, and we explore how individual, group, and organizational factors affect the quality of the decisions they make and ultimately determine organizational performance. We discuss the nature of managerial decision making and examine some models of the decision-making process that help reveal the complexities of successful decision making. Then we outline the main steps of the decision-making process. Next we examine how managers can promote organizational learning and creativity and improve the quality of decision making throughout an organization. Finally, we discuss the important role of entrepreneurship in promoting organizational creativity, and we differentiate between entrepreneurs and intrapreneurs. By the end of this chapter, you will appreciate the critical role of management decision making in creating a high-performing organization.

LO 5-1
Understand the nature of managerial decision making, differentiate between programmed and nonprogrammed decisions, and explain why nonprogrammed decision making is a complex, uncertain process.

The Nature of Managerial Decision Making

Every time managers act to plan, organize, direct, or control organizational activities, they make a stream of decisions. In opening a new restaurant, for example, managers have to decide where to locate it, what kinds of food to provide, which people to employ, and so on. Decision making is a basic part of every task managers perform.

As we discussed in the previous chapter, one of the main tasks facing a manager is to manage the organizational environment. Forces in the external environment give rise to many opportunities and threats for managers and their organizations. In addition, inside an organization managers must address many opportunities and threats that may arise as organizational resources are used. To deal with these opportunities and threats, managers must make decisions—that is, they must select one solution from a set of alternatives. **Decision making** is the process by which managers respond to opportunities and threats by analyzing the options and making determinations, or *decisions,* about specific organizational goals and courses of action. Good decisions result in the selection of appropriate goals and courses of action that increase organizational performance; bad decisions lower performance.

Decision making in response to opportunities occurs when managers search for ways to improve organizational performance to benefit customers, employees, and other stakeholder groups. In the "Management Snapshot," Jim McCann seized the opportunities to buy a flower shop and expand his business in multiple ways including going online. *Decision making in response to threats* occurs when events inside or outside the organization adversely affect organizational performance and managers search for ways to increase performance.[20] Decision making is central to being a manager, and whenever managers engage in planning, organizing, leading, and controlling—their four principal tasks—they are constantly making decisions.

Managers are always searching for ways to make better decisions to improve organizational performance. At the same time, they do their best to avoid costly mistakes that will hurt organizational performance. Examples of spectacularly good decisions include Martin Cooper's decision to develop the first cell phone at Motorola and Apple's decision to develop the iPod.[21] Examples of spectacularly bad decisions include the decision by managers at NASA and Morton Thiokol to launch the *Challenger* space shuttle—a decision that killed six astronauts in 1986—and the decision by NASA to launch the *Columbia* space shuttle in 2003, which killed seven astronauts.

Programmed and Nonprogrammed Decision Making

Regardless of the specific decisions a manager makes, the decision-making process is either programmed or nonprogrammed.[22]

PROGRAMMED DECISION MAKING Programmed decision making is a *routine,* virtually automatic process. Programmed decisions are decisions that have been made so many times in the past that managers have developed rules or guidelines to be applied when certain situations inevitably occur. Programmed decision making takes place when a school principal asks the school board to hire a new teacher whenever student enrollment increases by 40 students; when a manufacturing supervisor hires new workers whenever existing workers' overtime increases by more than 10 percent; and when an office manager orders basic office supplies, such as paper and pens, whenever the inventory of supplies drops below a certain level. Furthermore, in the last example, the office manager probably orders the same amount of supplies each time.

This decision making is called *programmed* because office managers, for example, do not need to repeatedly make new judgments about what should be done. They can rely on long-established decision rules such as these:

- *Rule 1:* When the storage shelves are three-quarters empty, order more copy paper.
- *Rule 2:* When ordering paper, order enough to fill the shelves.

decision making
The process by which managers respond to opportunities and threats by analyzing options and making determinations about specific organizational goals and courses of action.

programmed decision making
Routine, virtually automatic decision making that follows established rules or guidelines.

Managers can develop rules and guidelines to regulate all routine organizational activities. For example, rules can specify how a worker should perform a certain task, and rules can specify the quality standards that raw materials must meet to be acceptable. Most decision making that relates to the day-to-day running of an organization is programmed decision making. Examples include deciding how much inventory to hold, when to pay bills, when to bill customers, and when to order materials and supplies. Programmed decision making occurs when managers have the information they need to create rules that will guide decision making. There is little ambiguity involved in assessing when the stockroom is empty or counting the number of new students in class.

As profiled in the accompanying "Focus on Diversity" feature, effectively training new employees is essential to reap the benefits of programmed decision making.

FOCUS ON DIVERSITY

Programmed Decision Making at UPS

UPS is unrivaled in its use of programmed decision making. Practically all the motions, behaviors, and actions that its drivers perform each day have been carefully honed to maximize efficiency and minimize strain and injuries while delivering high-quality customer service. For example, a 12-step process prescribes how drivers should park their trucks, locate the package they are about to deliver, and step off the truck in 15.5 seconds (a process called "selection" at UPS).[23] Rules and routines such as these are carefully detailed in UPS's "340 Methods" manual (UPS actually has far more than 340 methods). Programmed decision making dictates where drivers should stop to get gas, how they should hold their keys in their hands, and how to lift and lower packages.[24]

When programmed decision making is so heavily relied on, ensuring that new employees learn tried-and-true routines is essential. UPS has traditionally taught new employees with a two-week period of lectures followed by practice.[25] In the 2000s, however, managers began to wonder if they needed to alter their training methods to suit their new Generation Y trainees (Generation Y typically refers to people born after 1980), who were not so keen on memorization and drills.[26] Generation Y trainees seemed to require more training time to become effective drivers (90–180 days compared to a typical average of 30–45 days), and quit rates for new drivers had increased.[27]

Given the fundamental importance of performance programs for UPS operations, managers decided to try to alter the training new hires receive so it would be better received by Generation Y trainees. In the late 2000s, UPS opened an innovative Landover, Maryland, training center called UPS Integrad, which has over 11,000 square feet and cost over $30 million to build and equip. Integrad was developed over a three-year period through a collaborative effort of over 170 people, including UPS top managers (many of whom started their careers with UPS as drivers), teams from Virginia Tech and MIT, animators from the Indian company Brainvisa, and forecasters from the Institute for the Future with the support of a grant from the Department of Labor for $1.8 million.[28] Results thus far suggest that Integrad training results in greater driver proficiency and fewer first-year accidents and injuries.[29]

Training at Integrad emphasizes hands-on learning.[30] For example, at Integrad, a UPS truck with transparent sides is used to teach trainees selection so they can actually see the instructor performing the steps and then practice the steps themselves rather than trying to absorb the material in a lecture. Trainees can try different movements and see, with the help of computer diagrams and simulations, how following UPS routines will help protect them from injury and how debilitating work as a driver can be if they do not follow routines. Video recorders track and document what trainees do correctly and incorrectly so they can see it for themselves rather than relying on feedback from an instructor, which they might question. As Stephen Jones, Director of International Training & Development at UPS,[31] indicates, "Tell them what they did incorrectly, and they'll tell you, 'I didn't do that. You saw wrong.' This way we've got it on tape and they can see it for themselves."[32]

At Integrad, trainees get practice driving in a pseudo town that has been constructed in a parking lot.[33] They also watch animated demonstrations on computer screens, participate in simulations, take electronic quizzes, and receive scores on various components that are retained in a database to track learning and performance. Recognizing that Generation Y trainees have a lot of respect for expertise and reputation, older employees also are brought in to facilitate learning at Integrad. For example, long-time UPS employee Don Petersik, who has since retired from UPS,[34] trained facilitators at Integrad and shared stories with them to reinforce the UPS culture—such as the time he was just starting out as a preloader and, unknown to him, the founder of UPS, Jim Casey, approached him and said, "Hi, I'm Jim. I work for UPS."[35] As Petersik indicated, "What's new about the company now is that our teaching style matches your learning styles."[36] Clearly, when learning programmed decision making is of utmost importance, as it is at UPS, it is essential to take into account diversity in learning styles and approaches.

NONPROGRAMMED DECISION MAKING Suppose, however, managers are not certain that a course of action will lead to a desired outcome. Or in even more ambiguous terms, suppose managers are not even sure what they are trying to achieve. Obviously rules cannot be developed to predict uncertain events.

Nonprogrammed decision making is required for these *nonroutine* decisions. Nonprogrammed decisions are made in response to unusual or novel opportunities and threats. Nonprogrammed decision making occurs when there are no ready-made decision rules that managers can apply to a situation. Rules do not exist because the situation is unexpected or uncertain and managers lack the information they would need to develop rules to cover it. Examples of nonprogrammed decision making include decisions to invest in a new technology, develop a new kind of product, launch a new promotional campaign, enter a new market, expand internationally, or start a new business as did Jim McCann in the "Management Snapshot."

How do managers make decisions in the absence of decision rules? They may rely on their **intuition**—feelings, beliefs, and hunches that come readily to mind, require little effort and information gathering, and result in on-the-spot decisions.[37] Or they may make **reasoned judgments**—decisions that require time and effort and result from careful information gathering, generation of alternatives, and evaluation of alternatives. "Exercising" one's judgment is a more rational process than "going with" one's intuition. For reasons that we examine later in this chapter, both intuition and judgment often are flawed and can result in poor decision making. Thus, the likelihood of error is much greater in nonprogrammed decision making than in programmed

nonprogrammed decision making Nonroutine decision making that occurs in response to unusual, unpredictable opportunities and threats.

intuition Feelings, beliefs, and hunches that come readily to mind, require little effort and information gathering, and result in on-the-spot decisions.

reasoned judgment A decision that requires time and effort and results from careful information gathering, generation of alternatives, and evaluation of alternatives.

Nonprogrammed decision making covers areas with no previous benchmarks or rubrics, such as seen in this photo. © AP Images/RF

decision making.[38] In the remainder of this chapter, when we talk about decision making, we are referring to *nonprogrammed* decision making because it causes the most problems for managers and is inherently challenging.

Sometimes managers have to make rapid decisions and don't have time to carefully consider the issues involved. They must rely on their intuition to quickly respond to a pressing concern. For example, when fire chiefs, captains, and lieutenants manage firefighters battling dangerous, out-of-control fires, they often need to rely on their expert intuition to make on-the-spot decisions that will protect the lives of the firefighters and save the lives of others, contain the fires, and preserve property—decisions made in emergency situations entailing high uncertainty, high risk, and rapidly changing conditions.[39] In other cases, managers do have time to make reasoned judgments, but there are no established rules to guide their decisions, such as when deciding whether to proceed with a proposed merger. Regardless of the circumstances, making nonprogrammed decisions can result in effective or ineffective decision making.

The classical and administrative decision-making models reveal many of the assumptions, complexities, and pitfalls that affect decision making. These models help reveal the factors that managers and other decision makers must be aware of to improve the quality of their decision making. Keep in mind, however, that the classical and administrative models are just guides that can help managers understand the decision-making process. In real life the process is typically not cut-and-dried, but these models can help guide a manager through it.

The Classical Model

classical decision-making model

A prescriptive approach to decision making based on the assumption that the decision maker can identify and evaluate all possible alternatives and their consequences and rationally choose the most appropriate course of action.

One of the earliest models of decision making, the **classical model**, is *prescriptive*, which means it specifies how decisions *should* be made. Managers using the classical model make a series of simplifying assumptions about the nature of the decision-making process (see Figure 5.1). The premise of the classical model is that once managers recognize the need to make a decision, they should be able to generate a complete list of *all* alternatives and consequences and make the best choice. In other words, the classical model assumes that managers have access to *all* the information they need to make the **optimum decision**, which is the most appropriate decision possible in light of what they believe to be the most desirable consequences for the organization. Furthermore, the classical model assumes managers can easily list their own preferences for each alternative and rank them from least to most preferred to make the optimum decision.

optimum decision

The most appropriate decision in light of what managers believe to be the most desirable consequences for the organization.

The Administrative Model

James March and Herbert Simon disagreed with the underlying assumptions of the classical model of decision making. In contrast, they proposed that managers in the real world do *not* have access to all the information they need to make a decision. Moreover, they pointed out that even if all information were readily available,

Figure 5.1

The Classical Model of Decision Making

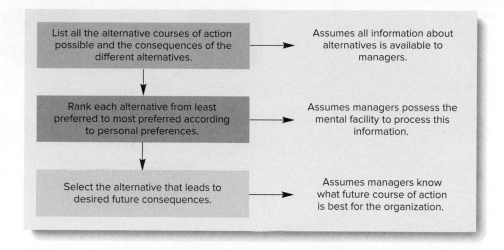

| List all the alternative courses of action possible and the consequences of the different alternatives. | → | Assumes all information about alternatives is available to managers. |

| Rank each alternative from least preferred to most preferred according to personal preferences. | → | Assumes managers possess the mental facility to process this information. |

| Select the alternative that leads to desired future consequences. | → | Assumes managers know what future course of action is best for the organization. |

---

administrative model An approach to decision making that explains why decision making is inherently uncertain and risky and why managers usually make satisfactory rather than optimum decisions.

many managers would lack the mental or psychological ability to absorb and evaluate it correctly. As a result, March and Simon developed the **administrative model** of decision making to explain why decision making is always an inherently uncertain and risky process—and why managers can rarely make decisions in the manner prescribed by the classical model. The administrative model is based on three important concepts: *bounded rationality, incomplete information,* and *satisficing.*

BOUNDED RATIONALITY March and Simon pointed out that human decision-making capabilities are bounded by people's cognitive limitations—that is, limitations in their ability to interpret, process, and act on information.[40] They argued that the limitations of human intelligence constrain the ability of decision makers to determine the optimum decision. March and Simon coined the term **bounded rationality** to describe the situation in which the number of alternatives a manager must identify is so great and the amount of information so vast that it is difficult for the manager to even come close to evaluating it all before making a decision.[41]

bounded rationality Cognitive limitations that constrain one's ability to interpret, process, and act on information.

INCOMPLETE INFORMATION Even if managers had unlimited ability to evaluate information, they still would not be able to arrive at the optimum decision because they would have incomplete information. Information is incomplete because the full range of decision-making alternatives is unknowable in most situations, and the consequences associated with known alternatives are uncertain.[42] In other words, information is incomplete because of risk and uncertainty, ambiguity, and time constraints (see Figure 5.2).

risk The degree of probability that the possible outcomes of a particular course of action will occur.

RISK AND UNCERTAINTY As we saw in Chapter 4, forces in the organizational environment are constantly changing. **Risk** is present when managers know the possible outcomes of a particular course of action and can assign probabilities to them. For example, managers in the biotechnology industry know that new drugs have a 10 percent probability of successfully passing advanced clinical trials and a 90 percent probability of failing. These probabilities reflect the experiences of thousands of drugs that have gone through advanced clinical trials. Thus when managers in the biotechnology industry decide to submit a drug for testing, they know that there is only a 10 percent chance that the drug will succeed, but at least they have some information on which to base their decision.

Figure 5.2
Why Information Is
Incomplete

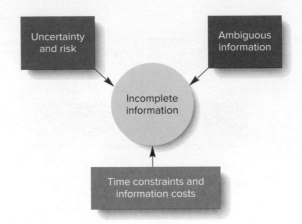

uncertainty
Unpredictability.

When **uncertainty** exists, the probabilities of alternative outcomes *cannot* be determined and future outcomes are *unknown*. Managers are working blind. Because the probability of a given outcome occurring is not known, managers have little information to use in making a decision. For example, in 1993, when Apple Computer introduced the Newton, its personal digital assistant (PDA), managers had no idea what the probability of a successful product launch for a PDA might be. Because Apple was the first to market this totally new product, there was no body of well-known data that Apple's managers could draw on to calculate the probability of a successful launch. Uncertainty plagues most managerial decision making.[43] Although Apple's initial launch of its PDA was a disaster due to technical problems, an improved version was more successful.

**ambiguous
information**
Information that can be
interpreted in multiple
and often conflicting
ways.

AMBIGUOUS INFORMATION A second reason why information is incomplete is that much of the information managers have at their disposal is **ambiguous information**. Its meaning is not clear—it can be interpreted in multiple and often conflicting ways.[44] Take a look at Figure 5.3. Do you see a young woman or an old woman? In a similar fashion, managers often interpret the same piece of information differently and make decisions based on their own interpretations.

TIME CONSTRAINTS AND INFORMATION COSTS The third reason why information is incomplete is that managers have neither the time nor the money to search for all possible alternative solutions and evaluate all the potential consequences of those alternatives. Consider the situation confronting a Ford Motor Company purchasing manager who has one month to choose a supplier for a small engine part. There are 20,000 potential suppliers for this part in the United States alone. Given the time available, the purchasing manager cannot contact all potential suppliers and ask each for its terms (price, delivery schedules, and so on). Moreover, even if the time were available, the costs of obtaining the information, including the manager's own time, would be prohibitive.

satisficing Searching
for and choosing
an acceptable, or
satisfactory, response
to problems and
opportunities, rather
than trying to make the
best decision.

SATISFICING March and Simon argued that managers do not attempt to discover every alternative when faced with bounded rationality, an uncertain future, unquantifiable risks, considerable ambiguity, time constraints, and high information costs. Rather, they use a strategy known as **satisficing**, which is exploring a limited sample of all potential alternatives.[45] When managers satisfice, they search for and choose acceptable, or satisfactory, ways to respond to problems and opportunities rather

Figure 5.3

Ambiguous Information: Young Woman or Old Woman?

than trying to make the optimal decision.[46] In the case of the Ford purchasing manager's search, for example, satisficing may involve asking a limited number of suppliers for their terms, trusting that they are representative of suppliers in general, and making a choice from that set. Although this course of action is reasonable from the perspective of the purchasing manager, it may mean that a potentially superior supplier is overlooked.

March and Simon pointed out that managerial decision making is often more art than science. In the real world, managers must rely on their intuition and judgment to make what seems to them to be the best decision in the face of uncertainty and ambiguity.[47] Moreover, managerial decision making is often fast-paced; managers use their experience and judgment to make crucial decisions under conditions of incomplete information. Although there is nothing wrong with this approach, decision makers should be aware that human judgment is often flawed. As a result, even the best managers sometimes make poor decisions.[48]

Steps in the Decision-Making Process

LO 5-2 Describe the six steps managers should take to make the best decisions.

Using the work of March and Simon as a basis, researchers have developed a step-by-step model of the decision-making process and the issues and problems that managers confront at each step. Perhaps the best way to introduce this model is to examine the real-world nonprogrammed decision making of Scott McNealy at a crucial point in Sun Microsystems' history. McNealy was a founder of Sun Microsystems and was the chairman of the board of directors until Sun was acquired by Oracle in 2010.[49]

In early August 1985, Scott McNealy, then CEO of Sun Microsystems[50] (a hardware and software computer workstation manufacturer focused on network solutions), had to decide whether to go ahead with the launch of the new Carrera workstation computer, scheduled for September 10. Sun's managers had chosen the date nine months earlier when the development plan for the Carrera was first proposed. McNealy knew it would take at least a month to prepare for the September 10 launch, and the decision could not be put off.

Customers were waiting for the new machine, and McNealy wanted to be the first to provide a workstation that took advantage of Motorola's powerful 16-megahertz 68020 microprocessor. Capitalizing on this opportunity would give Sun a significant edge over Apollo, its main competitor in the workstation market. McNealy knew, however, that committing to the September 10 launch date was risky. Motorola was having production problems with the 16-megahertz 68020 microprocessor and could not guarantee Sun a steady supply of these chips. Moreover, the operating system software was not completely free of bugs.

If Sun launched the Carrera on September 10, the company might have to ship some machines with software that was not fully operational, was likely to crash the system, and utilized Motorola's less powerful 12-megahertz 68020 microprocessor instead of the 16-megahertz version.[51] Of course, Sun could later upgrade the microprocessor and operating system software in any machines purchased by early customers, but the company's reputation would suffer. If Sun did not go ahead with the September launch, the company would miss an important opportunity.[52] Rumors were circulating in the industry that Apollo would be launching a new machine of its own in December.

McNealy clearly had a difficult decision to make. He had to decide quickly whether to launch the Carrera, but he did not have all the facts. He did not know, for example, whether the microprocessor or operating system problems could be resolved by September 10; nor did he know whether Apollo was going to launch a competing machine in December. But he could not wait to find these things out—he had to make a decision. We'll see what he decided later in the chapter.

Many managers who must make important decisions with incomplete information face dilemmas similar to McNealy's. Managers should consciously follow six steps to make a good decision (see Figure 5.4).[53] We review these steps in the remainder of this section.

Recognize the Need for a Decision

The first step in the decision-making process is to recognize the need for a decision. Scott McNealy recognized this need, and he realized a decision had to be made quickly.

Figure 5.4

Six Steps in Decision Making

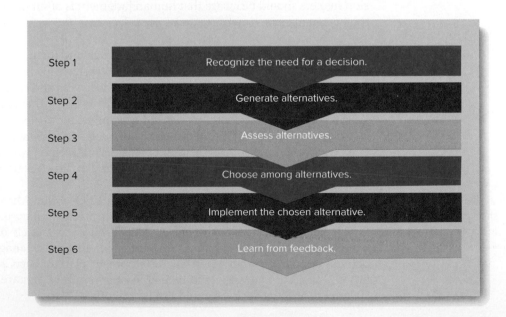

Step 1   Recognize the need for a decision.

Step 2   Generate alternatives.

Step 3   Assess alternatives.

Step 4   Choose among alternatives.

Step 5   Implement the chosen alternative.

Step 6   Learn from feedback.

Some stimuli usually spark the realization that a decision must be made. These stimuli often become apparent because changes in the organizational environment result in new kinds of opportunities and threats. This happened at Sun Microsystems. The September 10 launch date had been set when it seemed that Motorola chips would be readily available. Later, with the supply of chips in doubt and bugs remaining in the system software, Sun was in danger of failing to meet its launch date.

The stimuli that spark decision making are as likely to result from the actions of managers inside an organization as they are from changes in the external environment.[54] An organization possesses a set of skills, competencies, and resources in its employees and in departments such as marketing, manufacturing, and research and development. Managers who actively pursue opportunities to use these competencies create the need to make decisions. Managers thus can be proactive or reactive in recognizing the need to make a decision, but the important issue is that they must recognize this need and respond in a timely and appropriate way.[55]

Generate Alternatives

Having recognized the need to make a decision, a manager must generate a set of feasible alternative courses of action to take in response to the opportunity or threat. Management experts cite failure to properly generate and consider different alternatives as one reason why managers sometimes make bad decisions.[56] In the Sun Microsystems decision, the alternatives seemed clear: go ahead with the September 10 launch or delay the launch until the Carrera was 100 percent ready for market introduction. Often, however, the alternatives are not so obvious or so clearly specified.

One major problem is that managers may find it difficult to come up with creative alternative solutions to specific problems. Perhaps some of them are used to seeing the world from a single perspective—they have a certain "managerial mindset." Many managers find it difficult to view problems from a fresh perspective. According to best-selling management author Peter Senge, we all are trapped within our personal mental models of the world—our ideas about what is important and how the world works.[57] Generating creative alternatives to solve problems and take advantage of opportunities may require that we abandon our existing mind sets and develop new ones—something that usually is difficult to do.

The importance of getting managers to set aside their mental models of the world and generate creative alternatives is reflected in the growth of interest in the work of authors such as Peter Senge and Edward de Bono, who have popularized techniques for stimulating problem solving and creative thinking among managers.[58] Later in this chapter, we discuss the important issues of organizational learning and creativity in detail.

Assess Alternatives

Once managers have generated a set of alternatives, they must evaluate the advantages and disadvantages of each one.[59] The key to a good assessment of the alternatives is to define the opportunity or threat exactly and then specify the criteria that *should* influence the selection of alternatives for responding to the problem or opportunity. One reason for bad decisions is that managers often fail to specify the criteria that are important in reaching a decision.[60] In general, successful managers use four criteria to evaluate the pros and cons of alternative courses of action (see Figure 5.5):

1. *Legality:* Managers must ensure that a possible course of action will not violate any domestic or international laws or government regulations.

2. *Ethicalness:* Managers must ensure that a possible course of action is ethical and will not unnecessarily harm any stakeholder group. Many decisions managers make may help some organizational stakeholders and harm others (see Chapter 3). When examining alternative courses of action, managers need to be clear about the potential effects of their decisions.

3. *Economic feasibility:* Managers must decide whether the alternatives are economically feasible—that is, whether they can be accomplished given the organization's performance goals. Typically managers perform a cost–benefit analysis of the various alternatives to determine which one will have the best net financial payoff.

4. *Practicality:* Managers must decide whether they have the capabilities and resources required to implement the alternative, and they must be sure that the alternative will not threaten the attainment of other organizational goals. At first glance, an alternative might seem economically superior to other alternatives; but if managers realize it is likely to threaten other important projects, they might decide it is not practical after all.

Often, a manager must consider these four criteria simultaneously. Scott McNealy framed the problem at hand at Sun Microsystems quite well. The key question was whether to go ahead with the September 10 launch date. Two main criteria were influencing McNealy's choice: the need to ship a machine that was as "complete" as possible (the *practicality* criterion) and the need to beat Apollo to market with a new workstation (the *economic feasibility* criterion). These two criteria conflicted. The first suggested that the launch should be delayed; the second, that the launch

Figure 5.5

General Criteria for
Evaluating Possible
Courses of Action

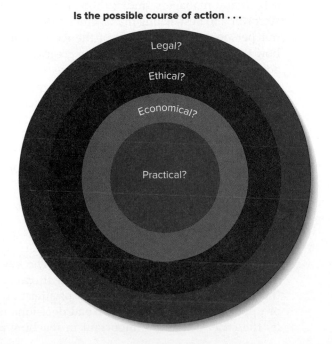

Is the possible course of action . . .

Legal?

Ethical?

Economical?

Practical?

should go ahead. McNealy's actual choice was based on the relative importance that he assigned to these two criteria. In fact, Sun Microsystems went ahead with the September 10 launch, which suggests that McNealy thought the need to beat Apollo to market was the more important criterion.

Some of the worst managerial decisions can be traced to poor assessment of the alternatives, such as the decision to launch the *Challenger* space shuttle, mentioned earlier. In that case, the desire of NASA and Morton Thiokol managers to demonstrate to the public the success of the U.S. space program in order to ensure future funding (*economic feasibility*) conflicted with the need to ensure the safety of the astronauts (*ethicalness*). Managers deemed the economic criterion more important and decided to launch the space shuttle even though there were unanswered questions about safety. Tragically, some of the same decision-making problems that resulted in the *Challenger* tragedy led to the demise of the *Columbia* space shuttle 17 years later, killing all seven astronauts on board.[61] In both the *Challenger* and the *Columbia* disasters, safety questions were raised before the shuttles were launched; safety concerns took second place to budgets, economic feasibility, and schedules; top decision makers seemed to ignore or downplay the inputs of those with relevant technical expertise; and speaking up was discouraged.[62] Rather than making safety a top priority, decision makers seemed overly concerned with keeping on schedule and within budget.[63]

Choose among Alternatives

Once the set of alternative solutions has been carefully evaluated, the next task is to rank the various alternatives (using the criteria discussed in the previous section) and make a decision. When ranking alternatives, managers must be sure *all* the information available is brought to bear on the problem or issue at hand. As the Sun Microsystems case indicates, however, identifying all *relevant* information for a decision does not mean the manager has *complete* information; in most instances, information is incomplete.

Perhaps more serious than the existence of incomplete information is the often-documented tendency of managers to ignore critical information, even when it is available. We discuss this tendency in detail later when we examine the operation of cognitive biases and groupthink.

Implement the Chosen Alternative

Once a decision has been made and an alternative has been selected, it must be implemented, and many subsequent and related decisions must be made. After a course of action has been decided—say, to develop a new line of women's clothing—thousands of subsequent decisions are necessary to implement it. These decisions would involve recruiting dress designers, obtaining fabrics, finding high-quality manufacturers, and signing contracts with clothing stores to sell the new line.

Although the need to make subsequent decisions to implement the chosen course of action may seem obvious, many managers make a decision and then fail to act on it. This is the same as not making a decision at all. To ensure that a decision is implemented, top managers must assign to middle managers the responsibility for making the follow-up decisions necessary to achieve the goal. They must give middle managers sufficient resources to achieve the goal, and they must hold the middle managers accountable for their performance. If the middle managers succeed in implementing the decision, they should be rewarded; if they fail, they should be subject to sanctions.

Learn from Feedback

The final step in the decision-making process is learning from feedback. Effective managers always conduct a retrospective analysis to see what they can learn from past successes or failures. Managers who do not evaluate the results of their decisions do not learn from experience; instead they stagnate and are likely to make the same mistakes again and again.[64] To avoid this problem, managers must establish a formal procedure with which they can learn from the results of past decisions. The procedure should include these steps:

1. Compare what actually happened to what was expected to happen as a result of the decision.
2. Explore why any expectations for the decision were not met.
3. Derive guidelines that will help in future decision making.

Managers who always strive to learn from past mistakes and successes are likely to continuously improve the decisions they make. A significant amount of learning can take place when the outcomes of decisions are evaluated, and this assessment can produce enormous benefits. Learning from feedback is particularly important for entrepreneurs who start their own businesses, as profiled in the accompanying "Management Insight" feature.

MANAGEMENT INSIGHT

Decision Making and Learning from Feedback at GarageTek

Decision making has been an ongoing challenge for Marc Shuman, founder and president of GarageTek, headquartered in Melville, New York.[65] Since founding his company about 15 years ago,[66] he has met this challenge time and time again, recognizing when decisions need to be made and learning from feedback about prior decisions.

Shuman was working with his father in a small business, designing and building interiors of department stores, when he created and installed a series of wall panels with flexible shelving for a store to display its merchandise. When he realized that some of his employees were using the same concept in their own homes to organize the clutter in their basements and garages, he recognized that he had a potential opportunity to start a new business, GarageTek, designing and installing custom garage systems to organize and maximize storage capacities and uses for home garage space.[67] A strong housing market at the time, the popularity of closet organizing systems, and the recognition that many people's lives were getting busier and more complicated led him to believe that home owners would be glad to pay someone to design and install a system that would help them gain control over some of the clutter in their lives.[68]

Schuman decided to franchise his idea because he feared that other entrepreneurs were probably

The interior of a garage showing a GarageTek custom system designed to organize storage capacity and uses for home garage space. The franchise has experienced its ups and downs, but, thanks to good management, business continues to grow. Courtesy GarageTek

having similar thoughts and competition could be around the corner.[69] Within three years GarageTek had 57 franchises in 33 states, contributing revenues to the home office of around $12 million. While this would seem to be an enviable track record of success, Shuman recognized that although many of the franchises were succeeding, some were having serious problems. With the help of a consulting company, Shuman and home office managers set about trying to figure out why some franchises were failing. They gathered detailed information about each franchise: the market served, pricing strategies, costs, managerial talent, and franchisee investment. From this information, Shuman learned that the struggling franchises tended either to have lower levels of capital investment behind them or to be managed by nonowners.[70]

Shuman learned from this experience. He now has improved decision criteria for accepting new franchisees to help ensure that their investments of time and money lead to a successful franchise.[71] Shuman also decided to give new franchisees much more training and support than he had in the past. New franchisees now receive two weeks of training at the home office that culminates in their preparing a one-year marketing and business plan;[72] on-site assistance in sales, marketing, and operations; a multivolume training manual; a sales and marketing kit; and access to databases and GarageTek's intranet. Franchisees learn from each other through monthly conference calls and regional and national meetings.[73]

By 2014, GarageTek had franchises covering 60 markets in the United States and also had expanded overseas into the United Kingdom, Australia, New Zealand, South Africa, and Russia.[74] And Shuman continues to make decisions day in and day out; in his words, "We're not, by any stretch, done."[75]

Group Decision Making

Many (or perhaps most) important organizational decisions are made by groups or teams of managers rather than by individuals. Group decision making is superior to individual decision making in several respects. When managers work as a team to make decisions and solve problems, their choices of alternatives are less likely to fall victim to the biases and errors discussed previously. They are able to draw on the combined skills, competencies, and accumulated knowledge of group members and thereby improve their ability to generate feasible alternatives and make good decisions. Group decision making also allows managers to process more information and to correct one another's errors. And in the implementation phase, all managers affected by the decisions agree to cooperate. When a group of managers makes a decision (as opposed to one top manager making a decision and imposing it on subordinate managers), the probability that the decision will be implemented successfully increases.

Some potential disadvantages are associated with group decision making. Groups often take much longer than individuals to make decisions. Getting two or more managers to agree to the same solution can be difficult because managers' interests and preferences are often different. In addition, just like decision making by individual managers, group decision making can be undermined by biases. A major source of group bias is *groupthink*.

The Perils of Groupthink

Groupthink is a pattern of faulty and biased decision making that occurs in groups whose members strive for agreement among themselves at the expense of accurately

LO 5-3 Identify the advantages and disadvantages of group decision making, and describe techniques that can improve it.

groupthink A pattern of faulty and biased decision making that occurs in groups whose members strive for agreement among themselves at the expense of accurately assessing information relevant to a decision.

assessing information relevant to a decision.[76] When managers are subject to groupthink, they collectively embark on a course of action without developing appropriate criteria to evaluate alternatives. Typically, a group rallies around one central manager, such as the CEO, and the course of action that manager supports. Group members become blindly committed to that course of action without evaluating its merits. Commitment is often based on an emotional, rather than an objective, assessment of the optimal course of action.

The decision President Kennedy and his advisers made to launch the unfortunate Bay of Pigs invasion in Cuba in 1962, the decisions made by President Johnson and his advisers from 1964 to 1967 to escalate the war in Vietnam, the decision made by President Nixon and his advisers in 1972 to cover up the Watergate break-in, and the decision made by NASA and Morton Thiokol in 1986 to launch the ill-fated *Challenger* shuttle—all were likely influenced by groupthink. After the fact, decision makers such as these who may fall victim to groupthink are often surprised that their decision-making process and outcomes were so flawed.

When groupthink occurs, pressures for agreement and harmony within a group have the unintended effect of discouraging individuals from raising issues that run counter to majority opinion. For example, when managers at NASA and Morton Thiokol fell victim to groupthink, they convinced each other that all was well and that there was no need to delay the launch of the *Challenger* space shuttle.

Devil's Advocacy

devil's advocacy
Critical analysis of a preferred alternative, made in response to challenges raised by a group member who, playing the role of devil's advocate, defends unpopular or opposing alternatives for the sake of argument.

The existence of groupthink raises the question of how to improve the quality of group and individual decision making so managers make decisions that are realistic and are based on thorough evaluation of alternatives. One technique known to counteract groupthink is devil's advocacy.[77]

Devil's advocacy is a critical analysis of a preferred alternative to ascertain its strengths and weaknesses before it is implemented.[78] Typically one member of the decision-making group plays the role of devil's advocate. The devil's advocate critiques and challenges the way the group evaluated alternatives and chose one over the others. The purpose of devil's advocacy is to identify all the reasons that might make the preferred alternative unacceptable. In this way, decision makers can be made aware of the possible perils of recommended courses of action.

Diversity among Decision Makers

LO 5-4 Explain the role that organizational learning and creativity play in helping managers to improve their decisions.

Another way to improve group decision making is to promote diversity in decision-making groups (see Chapter 3).[79] Bringing together managers of both genders from various ethnic, national, and functional backgrounds broadens the range of life experiences and opinions that group members can draw on as they generate, assess, and choose among alternatives. Moreover, diverse groups are sometimes less prone to groupthink because group members already differ from each other and thus are less subject to pressures for uniformity.

Organizational Learning and Creativity

The quality of managerial decision making ultimately depends on innovative responses to opportunities and threats. How can managers increase their ability to make nonprogrammed decisions that will allow them to adapt to, modify, and even drastically alter their task environments so they can continually increase organizational performance? The answer is by encouraging organizational learning.[80]

Get off email and lose the desk! Giving yourself and your employees the time and space to know that contributions off the beaten track are valued increases the ability to think outside the box.
© Morgan Lane Photography/Alamy RF

organizational learning The process through which managers seek to improve employees' desire and ability to understand and manage the organization and its task environment.

learning organization An organization in which managers try to maximize the ability of individuals and groups to think and behave creatively and thus maximize the potential for organizational learning to take place.

creativity A decision maker's ability to discover original and novel ideas that lead to feasible alternative courses of action.

Organizational learning is the process through which managers seek to improve employees' desire and ability to understand and manage the organization and its task environment so employees can make decisions that continuously raise organizational effectiveness.[81] A **learning organization** is one in which managers do everything possible to maximize the ability of individuals and groups to think and behave creatively and thus maximize the potential for organizational learning to take place. At the heart of organizational learning is **creativity**, which is the ability of a decision maker to discover original and novel ideas that lead to feasible alternative courses of action. Encouraging creativity among managers is such a pressing organizational concern that many organizations hire outside experts to help them develop programs to train their managers in the art of creative thinking and problem solving.

Creating a Learning Organization

How can managers foster a learning organization? Learning theorist Peter Senge identified five principles for creating a learning organization (see Figure 5.6):[82]

1. For organizational learning to occur, top managers must allow every person in the organization to develop a sense of *personal mastery.* Managers must empower employees and allow them to experiment, create, and explore what they want.

2. As part of attaining personal mastery, organizations need to encourage employees to develop and use *complex mental models*—sophisticated ways of thinking that challenge them to find new or better ways of performing a task—to deepen their understanding of what is involved in a particular activity. Here Senge argued that managers must encourage employees to develop a taste for experimenting and risk taking.[83]

3. Managers must do everything they can to promote group creativity. Senge thought that *team learning* (learning that takes place in a group or team) is more important than individual learning in increasing organizational learning. He pointed out that most important decisions are made in subunits such as groups, functions, and divisions.

4. Managers must emphasize the importance of *building a shared vision*—a common mental model that all organizational members use to frame problems or opportunities.

5. Managers must encourage *systems thinking.* Senge emphasized that to create a learning organization, managers must recognize the effects of one level of learning on another. Thus, for example, there is little point in creating teams to facilitate team learning if managers do not also take steps to give employees the freedom to develop a sense of personal mastery.

Building a learning organization requires that managers change their management assumptions radically. Developing a learning organization is neither a quick nor an easy process. Senge worked with Ford Motor Company to help managers

Figure 5.6

Senge's Principles for
Creating a Learning
Organization

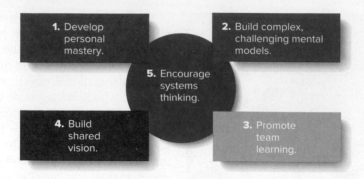

Figure 5.6

Senge's Principles for
Creating a Learning
Organization

make Ford a learning organization. Why would Ford want this? Top management believed that to compete successfully Ford must improve its members' ability to be creative and make the right decisions.

Increasingly, managers are being called on to promote global organizational learning. For example, managers at Walmart have used the lessons derived from its failures and successes in one country to promote global organizational learning across the many countries in which it now operates. When Walmart entered Malaysia, it was convinced customers there would respond to its one-stop shopping format. It found, however, that Malaysians enjoy the social experience of shopping in a lively market or bazaar and thus did not like the impersonal efficiency of the typical Walmart store. As a result, Walmart learned the importance of designing store layouts to appeal specifically to the customers of each country in which it operates.

When purchasing and operating a chain of stores in another country, such as the British ASDA chain, Walmart now strives to retain what customers value in the local market while taking advantage of its own accumulated organizational learning. For example, Walmart improved ASDA's information technology used for inventory and sales tracking in stores and enrolled ASDA in Walmart's global purchasing operations, which has enabled the chain to pay less for certain products, sell them for less, and, overall, significantly increase sales. At the same time Walmart empowered local ASDA managers to run the stores; as the president of ASDA indicates, "This is still essentially a British business in the way it's run day to day."[84] Clearly, global organizational learning is essential for companies such as Walmart that have significant operations in multiple countries.

Promoting Individual Creativity

Research suggests that when certain conditions are met, managers are more likely to be creative. People must be given the opportunity and freedom to generate new ideas.[85] Creativity declines when managers look over the shoulders of talented employees and try to "hurry up" a creative solution. How would you feel if your boss said you had one week to come up with a new product idea to beat the competition? Creativity results when employees have an opportunity to experiment, to take risks, and to make mistakes and learn from them. And employees must not fear that they will be looked down on or penalized for ideas that might at first seem outlandish; sometimes those ideas yield truly innovative products and services.[86] Highly innovative companies such as Google, Apple, and Facebook are well known for the wide degree of freedom they give their managers and employees to experiment and develop innovative goods and services.[87]

Once managers have generated alternatives, creativity can be fostered by giving them constructive feedback so they know how well they are doing. Ideas that seem to be going nowhere can be eliminated and creative energies refocused in other directions. Ideas that seem promising can be promoted, and help from other managers can be obtained.[88]

Top managers must stress the importance of looking for alternative solutions and should visibly reward employees who come up with creative ideas. Being creative can be demanding and stressful. Employees who believe they are working on important, vital issues are motivated to put forth the high levels of effort that creativity demands. Creative people like to receive the acclaim of others, and innovative organizations have many kinds of ceremonies and rewards to recognize creative employees.

Employees on the front line are often in a good position to come up with creative ideas for improvements but may be reluctant to speak up or share their ideas. To encourage frontline employees to come up with creative ideas and share them, some managers have used contests and rewards.[89] Contests and rewards signal the importance of coming up with creative ideas and encourage employees to share them. Examples of companies that have benefited from contests and rewards for creativity include Hammond's Candies in Denver, Colorado; Borrego Solar Systems in San Diego, California; and Infosurv in Atlanta, Georgia.

Promoting Group Creativity

To encourage creativity at the group level, organizations can use group problem-solving techniques that promote creative ideas and innovative solutions. These techniques can also prevent groupthink and help managers uncover biases. Here we look at three group decision-making techniques: *brainstorming*, the *nominal group technique*, and the *Delphi technique*.

BRAINSTORMING *Brainstorming* is a group problem-solving technique in which managers meet face-to-face to generate and debate a wide variety of alternatives from which to make a decision.[90] Generally from 5 to 15 managers meet in a closed-door session and proceed like this:

- One manager describes in broad outline the problem the group is to address.
- Group members share their ideas and generate alternative courses of action.
- As each alternative is described, group members are not allowed to criticize it; everyone withholds judgment until all alternatives have been heard. One member of the group records the alternatives on a flip chart.
- Group members are encouraged to be as innovative and radical as possible. Anything goes; and the greater the number of ideas put forth, the better. Moreover, group members are encouraged to "piggyback" or build on each other's suggestions.
- When all alternatives have been generated, group members debate the pros and cons of each and develop a short list of the best alternatives.

production blocking
A loss of productivity in brainstorming sessions due to the unstructured nature of brainstorming.

Brainstorming is useful in some problem-solving situations—for example, when managers are trying to find a name for a new perfume or car model. But sometimes individuals working alone can generate more alternatives. The main reason for the loss of productivity in brainstorming appears to be **production blocking**, which occurs because group members cannot always simultaneously make sense of all the alternatives being generated, think up additional alternatives, and remember what they were thinking.[91]

nominal group technique A decision-making technique in which group members write down ideas and solutions, read their suggestions to the whole group, and discuss and then rank the alternatives.

NOMINAL GROUP TECHNIQUE To avoid production blocking, the **nominal group technique** is often used. It provides a more structured way of generating alternatives in writing and gives each manager more time and opportunity to come up with potential solutions. The nominal group technique is especially useful when an issue is controversial and when different managers might be expected to champion different courses of action. Generally, a small group of managers meets in a closed-door session and adopts the following procedures:

- One manager outlines the problem to be addressed, and 30 or 40 minutes are allocated for group members, working individually, to write down their ideas and solutions. Group members are encouraged to be innovative.

- Managers take turns reading their suggestions to the group. One manager writes all the alternatives on a flip chart. No criticism or evaluation of alternatives is allowed until all alternatives have been read.

- The alternatives are then discussed, one by one, in the sequence in which they were proposed. Group members can ask for clarifying information and critique each alternative to identify its pros and cons.

- When all alternatives have been discussed, each group member ranks all the alternatives from most preferred to least preferred, and the alternative that receives the highest ranking is chosen.[92]

delphi technique A decision-making technique in which group members do not meet face-to-face but respond in writing to questions posed by the group leader.

DELPHI TECHNIQUE Both the nominal group technique and brainstorming require that managers meet to generate creative ideas and engage in joint problem solving. What happens if managers are in different cities or in different parts of the world and cannot meet face-to-face? Videoconferencing is one way to bring distant managers together to brainstorm. Another way is to use the **Delphi technique**, which is a written approach to creative problem solving.[93] The Delphi technique works like this:

- The group leader writes a statement of the problem and a series of questions to which participating managers are to respond.

- The questionnaire is sent to the managers and departmental experts who are most knowledgeable about the problem. They are asked to generate solutions and mail the questionnaire back to the group leader.

- A team of top managers records and summarizes the responses. The results are then sent back to the participants, with additional questions to be answered before a decision can be made.

- The process is repeated until a consensus is reached and the most suitable course of action is apparent.

LO 5-5 Describe how managers can encourage and promote entrepreneurship to create a learning organization, and differentiate between entrepreneurs and intrapreneurs.

Entrepreneurship and Creativity

Entrepreneurs are individuals who notice opportunities and decide how to mobilize the resources necessary to produce new and improved goods and services. Entrepreneurs make all of the planning, organizing, leading, and controlling decisions necessary to start new business ventures. Thus, entrepreneurs are an important source of creativity in the organizational

entrepreneur An individual who notices opportunities and decides how to mobilize the resources necessary to produce new and improved goods and services.

social entrepreneur An individual who pursues initiatives and opportunities and mobilizes resources to address social problems and needs in order to improve society and well-being through creative solutions.

intrapreneur A manager, scientist, or researcher who works inside an organization and notices opportunities to develop new or improved products and better ways to make them.

world. These people, such as David Filo and Jerry Yang (founders of Yahoo!), make vast fortunes when their businesses succeed. Or they are among the millions of people who start new business ventures only to lose their money when they fail. Despite the fact that many small businesses fail in the first three to five years, many men and women in today's workforce want to start their own companies.[94]

Social entrepreneurs are individuals who pursue initiatives and opportunities to address social problems and needs to improve society and well-being, such as reducing poverty, increasing literacy, protecting the natural environment, or reducing substance abuse.[95] Social entrepreneurs seek to mobilize resources to solve social problems through creative solutions.[96]

Many managers, scientists, and researchers employed by companies engage in entrepreneurial activity, and they are an important source of organizational creativity. They are involved in innovation, developing new and improved products and ways to make them. Such employees notice opportunities for either quantum or incremental product improvements and are responsible for managing the product development process. These individuals are known as **intrapreneurs** to distinguish them from entrepreneurs who start their own businesses. But in general, entrepreneurship involves creative decision making that gives customers new or improved goods and services.

There is an interesting relationship between entrepreneurs and intrapreneurs. Many managers with intrapreneurial talents become dissatisfied if their superiors decide neither to support nor to fund new product ideas and development efforts that the managers think will succeed. What do intrapreneurial managers who feel they are getting nowhere do? Often, they decide to leave their current organizations and start their own companies to take advantage of their new product ideas! In other words, intrapreneurs become entrepreneurs and found companies that often compete with the companies they left. To avoid losing these individuals, top managers must find ways to facilitate the entrepreneurial spirit of their most creative employees. In the remainder of this section, we consider issues involved in promoting successful entrepreneurship in both new and existing organizations.

Entrepreneurship and New Ventures

The fact that a significant number of entrepreneurs were frustrated intrapreneurs provides a clue about the personal characteristics of people who are likely to start a new venture and bear all the uncertainty and risk associated with being an entrepreneur.

CHARACTERISTICS OF ENTREPRENEURS Entrepreneurs are likely to possess a particular set of the personality characteristics we discussed in Chapter 2. First, they are likely to be high on the personality trait of *openness to experience,* meaning they are predisposed to be original, to be open to a wide range of stimuli, to be daring, and to take risks. Entrepreneurs also are likely to have an *internal locus of control,* believing that they are responsible for what happens to them and that their own actions determine important outcomes such as the success or failure of a new business. People with an external locus of control, in contrast, would be unlikely to leave a secure job in an organization and assume the risk associated with a new venture.

Entrepreneurs are likely to have a high level of *self-esteem* and feel competent and capable of handling most situations—including the stress and uncertainty surrounding a plunge into a risky new venture. Entrepreneurs are also likely to have a high *need for achievement* and have a strong desire to perform challenging tasks and meet high personal standards of excellence.

ENTREPRENEURSHIP AND MANAGEMENT Given that entrepreneurs are predisposed to activities that are somewhat adventurous and risky, in what ways can people become involved in entrepreneurial ventures? One way is to start a business from scratch. Taking advantage of modern IT, some people start solo ventures or partnerships.

When people who go it alone succeed, they frequently need to hire other people to help them run the business. Michael Dell, for example, began his computer business as a college student and within weeks had hired several people to help him assemble computers from the components he bought from suppliers. From his solo venture grew Dell Computer.

> **entrepreneurship**
> The mobilization of resources to take advantage of an opportunity to provide customers with new or improved goods and services.

Some entrepreneurs who start a new business have difficulty deciding how to manage the organization as it grows; **entrepreneurship** is *not* the same as management. Management encompasses all the decisions involved in planning, organizing, leading, and controlling resources. Entrepreneurship is noticing an opportunity to satisfy a customer need and then deciding how to find and use resources to make a product that satisfies that need. When an entrepreneur has produced something customers want, entrepreneurship gives way to management because the pressing need becomes providing the product both efficiently and effectively. Frequently a founding entrepreneur lacks the skills, patience, and experience to engage in the difficult and challenging work of management. Some entrepreneurs find it hard to delegate authority because they are afraid to risk their company by letting others manage it. As a result, they become overloaded and the quality of their decision making declines. Other entrepreneurs lack the detailed knowledge necessary to establish state-of-the-art information systems and technology or to create the operations management procedures that are vital to increase the efficiency of their organizations' production systems. Thus, to succeed, it is necessary to do more than create a new product; an entrepreneur must hire managers who can create an operating system that will let a new venture survive and prosper.

Intrapreneurship and Organizational Learning

The intensity of competition today, particularly from agile small companies, has made it increasingly important for large established organizations to promote and encourage intrapreneurship to raise their level of innovation and organizational learning. As we discussed earlier, a learning organization encourages all employees to identify opportunities and solve problems, thus enabling the organization to continuously experiment, improve, and increase its ability to provide customers with new and improved goods and services. The higher the level of intrapreneurship, the higher will be the level of learning and innovation. How can organizations promote organizational learning and intrapreneurship?

> **product champion** A manager who takes "ownership" of a project and provides the leadership and vision that take a product from the idea stage to the final customer.

PRODUCT CHAMPIONS One way to promote intrapreneurship is to encourage individuals to assume the role of **product champion**, a manager who takes "ownership" of a project and provides the leadership and vision that take a product from the idea stage to the final customer. 3M, a company well known for its attempts to promote intrapreneurship, encourages all its managers to become product champions and identify new product ideas. A product champion becomes responsible for developing a business plan for the product. Armed with this business plan, the champion appears before 3M's product development committee, a team of senior 3M managers who probe the strengths and weaknesses of the plan to decide whether it should be funded. If the plan is accepted, the product champion assumes responsibility for product development.

SKUNKWORKS The idea behind the product champion role is that employees who feel ownership for a project are inclined to act like outside entrepreneurs and go to great lengths to make the project succeed. Using skunkworks and new venture divisions can also strengthen this feeling of ownership. A **skunkworks** is a group of intrapreneurs who are deliberately separated from the normal operation of an organization—for example, from the normal chain of command—to encourage them to devote all their attention to developing new products. The idea is that if these people are isolated, they will become so intensely involved in a project that development time will be relatively brief and the quality of the final product will be enhanced. The term *skunkworks* was coined at the Lockheed Corporation, which formed a team of design engineers to develop special aircraft such as the U2 spy plane. The secrecy with which this unit functioned and speculation about its goals led others to refer to it as "the skunkworks."

skunkworks A group of intrapreneurs who are deliberately separated from the normal operation of an organization to encourage them to devote all their attention to developing new products.

REWARDS FOR INNOVATION To encourage managers to bear the uncertainty and risk associated with the hard work of entrepreneurship, it is necessary to link performance to rewards. Increasingly companies are rewarding intrapreneurs on the basis of the outcome of the product development process. Intrapreneurs are paid large bonuses if their projects succeed, or they are granted stock options that can make them millionaires if their products sell well. Both Microsoft and Google, for example, have made hundreds of their employees multimillionaires as a result of the stock options they were granted as part of their reward packages. In addition to receiving money, successful intrapreneurs can expect to receive promotion to the ranks of top management. Most of 3M's top managers, for example, reached the executive suite because they had a track record of successful intrapreneurship. Organizations must reward intrapreneurs equitably if they wish to prevent them from leaving and becoming outside entrepreneurs who might form a competitive new venture. Nevertheless, intrapreneurs frequently do so.

Summary and Review

THE NATURE OF MANAGERIAL DECISION MAKING Programmed decisions are routine decisions made so often that managers have developed decision rules to be followed automatically. Nonprogrammed decisions are made in response to situations that are unusual or novel; they are nonroutine decisions. The classical model of decision making assumes that decision makers have complete information; are able to process that information in an objective, rational manner; and make optimum decisions. March and Simon argued that managers exhibit bounded rationality, rarely have access to all the information they need to make optimum decisions, and consequently satisfice and rely on their intuition and judgment when making decisions. **[LO5-1]**

STEPS IN THE DECISION-MAKING PROCESS When making decisions, managers should take these six steps: recognize the need for a decision, generate alternatives, assess alternatives, choose among alternatives, implement the chosen alternative, and learn from feedback. **[LO5-2]**

GROUP DECISION MAKING Many advantages are associated with group decision making, but there are also several disadvantages. One major source of poor decision making is groupthink. Afflicted decision makers collectively embark on a dubious course of action without questioning the assumptions that underlie their decision. Managers can improve the quality of group decision making by using techniques such as devil's advocacy and dialectical inquiry and by increasing diversity in the decision-making group. **[LO5-3]**

ORGANIZATIONAL LEARNING AND CREATIVITY Organizational learning is the process through which managers seek to improve employees' desire and ability to understand and manage the organization and its task environment so employees can make decisions that continuously raise organizational effectiveness. Managers must take steps to promote organizational learning and creativity at the individual and group levels to improve the quality of decision making. **[LO5-4]**

ENTREPRENEURSHIP Entrepreneurship is the mobilization of resources to take advantage of an opportunity to provide customers with new or improved goods and services. Entrepreneurs start new ventures of their own. Intrapreneurs work inside organizations and manage the product development process. Organizations need to encourage intrapreneurship because it leads to organizational learning and innovation. **[LO5-5]**

Management *in Action*

 TOPICS FOR DISCUSSION AND ACTION

Discussion

1. What are the main differences between programmed decision making and nonprogrammed decision making? **[LO5-1]**

2. In what ways do the classical and administrative models of decision making help managers appreciate the complexities of real-world decision making? **[LO5-1]**

3. Why do capable managers sometimes make bad decisions? What can individual managers do to improve their decision-making skills? **[LO5-1, 5-2]**

4. In what kinds of groups is groupthink most likely to be a problem? When is it least likely to be a problem? What steps can group members take to ward off groupthink? **[LO5-3]**

5. What is organizational learning, and how can managers promote it? **[LO5-4]**

6. What is the difference between entrepreneurship and intrapreneurship? **[LO5-5]**

Action

7. Ask a manager to recall the best and the worst decisions he or she ever made. Try to determine why these decisions were so good or so bad. **[LO5-1, 5-2, 5-3]**

8. Think about an organization in your local community or your university, or an organization that you are familiar with, that is doing poorly. Now think of questions managers in the organization should ask stakeholders to elicit creative ideas for turning around the organization's fortunes. **[LO5-4]**

BUILDING MANAGEMENT SKILLS

How Do You Make Decisions? [LO 5-1, 5-2, 5-4]

Pick a decision you made recently that has had important consequences for you. It may be your decision about which college to attend, which major to select, whether to take a part-time job, or which part-time job to take. Using the material in this chapter, analyze how you made the decision:

1. Identify the criteria you used, either consciously or unconsciously, to guide your decision making.

2. List the alternatives you considered. Were they all possible alternatives? Did you unconsciously (or consciously) ignore some important alternatives?

3. How much information did you have about each alternative?

   Were you making the decision on the basis of complete or incomplete information?

4. Try to remember how you reached the decision. Did you sit down and consciously think through the implications of each alternative, or did you make the decision on the basis of intuition? Did you use any rules of thumb to help you make the decision?

5. In retrospect, do you think your choice of alternative was shaped by any of the cognitive biases discussed in this chapter?

6. Having answered the previous five questions, do you think in retrospect that you made a reasonable decision? What, if anything, might you do to improve your ability to make good decisions in the future?

MANAGING ETHICALLY [LO5-3]

Sometimes groups make extreme decisions—decisions that are either more risky or more conservative than they would have been if individuals acting alone had made them. One explanation for the tendency of groups to make extreme decisions is diffusion of responsibility. In a group, responsibility for the outcomes of a decision is spread among group members, so each person feels less than fully accountable. The group's decision is extreme because no individual has taken full responsibility for it.

Questions

1. Either alone or in a group, think about the ethical implications of extreme decision making by groups.

2. When group decision making takes place, should members of a group each feel fully accountable for outcomes of the decision? Why or why not?

SMALL GROUP BREAKOUT EXERCISE [LO5-3, 5-4]

Brainstorming

Form groups of three or four people, and appoint one member as the spokesperson who will communicate your findings to the class when called on by the instructor. Then discuss the following scenario:

You and your partners are trying to decide which kind of restaurant to open in a centrally located shopping center that has just been built in your city. The problem confronting you is that the city already has many restaurants that provide different kinds of food at all price ranges. You have the resources to open any type of restaurant. Your challenge is to decide which type is most likely to succeed.

Use brainstorming to decide which type of restaurant to open. Follow these steps:

1. As a group, spend 5–10 minutes generating ideas about the alternative restaurants that the

members think will be most likely to succeed. Each group member should be as innovative and creative as possible, and no suggestions should be criticized.

2. Appoint one group member to write down the alternatives as they are identified.

3. Spend the next 10–15 minutes debating the pros and cons of the alternatives. As a group, try to reach a consensus on which alternative is most likely to succeed.

After making your decision, discuss the pros and cons of the brainstorming method, and decide whether any production blocking occurred.

When called on by the instructor, the spokesperson should be prepared to share your group's decision with the class, as well as the reasons for the group's decision.

BE THE MANAGER [LO5-1, 5-2, 5-3, 5-4, 5-5]

You are a top manager who was recently hired by an oil field services company in Oklahoma to help it respond more quickly and proactively to potential opportunities in its market. You report to the chief operating officer (COO), who reports to the CEO, and you have been on the job for eight months. Thus far you have come up with three initiatives you carefully studied, thought were noteworthy, and proposed and justified to the COO. The COO seemed cautiously interested when you presented the proposals, and each time he indicated he would think about them and discuss them with the CEO because considerable resources were involved. Each time you never heard back from the COO, and after a few weeks elapsed, you casually asked the COO if there was any news on the proposal in question. For the first proposal, the COO said, "We think it's a good idea, but the timing is off. Let's shelve it for the time being and reconsider it next year." For the second proposal, the COO said, "Mike [the CEO] reminded me that we tried that two years ago and it wasn't well received in the market. I am surprised I didn't remember it myself when you first described the proposal, but it came right back to me once Mike mentioned it." For the third proposal, the COO simply said, "We're not convinced it will work."

You believe your three proposed initiatives are viable ways to seize opportunities in the marketplace, yet you cannot proceed with any of them. Moreover, for each proposal, you invested considerable time and even worked to bring others on board to support the proposal, only to have it shot down by the CEO. When you interviewed for the position, both the COO and the CEO claimed they wanted "an outsider to help them step out of the box and innovate." Yet your experience to date has been just the opposite. What are you going to do?

THE WALL STREET JOURNAL CASE IN THE NEWS [LO5-1, 5-2]

Aetna Sets Wage Floor: $16 an Hour

Anna Wilde Mathews and Theo Francis

Amid signs of a tightening labor market, **Aetna** Inc. plans to boost the incomes of its lowest-paid workers by as much as a third in a bid to draw top prospects and reduce turnover.

The move by the big health insurer highlights larger debates over the pace of the economic recovery and the compensation of people toward the bottom of the wage scale. Around 12% of Aetna's domestic work force will receive a raise to a floor of $16 an hour. Aetna, which also said it will cut health-care costs for many of the same employees next year, follows **Gap** Inc., **Starbucks** Corp. and others in raising the lower limit on worker wages.

Aetna Chief Executive Mark T. Bertolini said the company's shift reflects changes in the insurance industry, which is increasingly selling coverage to individuals. "We're preparing our company for a future where we're going to have a much more consumer-oriented business," he said, and Aetna wants "a better and more informed work force."

Economists and policy makers have been on the lookout for signs of growth in workers' pay, which has lagged behind other markers of improved economic activity, including rising employment and economic output. While many economists say wage inflation remains a remote concern, some point to scattered signs of pressure as an indicator that the recovery may be accelerating and spreading its benefits to a wider group.

"We are getting closer and closer to the inflection point where we will see broad wage pressure," said Torsten Slok, chief international economist at Deutsche Bank. "We are getting to the stage where companies can no longer find the right workers."

5,700
The number of workers who stand to get raises starting in April.

Aetna's decision also comes amid a broader conversation about the incomes of those toward the bottom of the wage scale. State and local governments around the country have moved to raise minimum wages, often generating pushback from business groups. Some companies—mostly in the heavily low-wage retail and restaurant industries—have come under fire from labor groups over their pay. And the Securities and Exchange Commission is crafting a rule requiring publicly traded companies to disclose how much their CEOs make relative to their average worker.

Aetna said it appeared that none of the approximately 5,700 workers set to benefit, who include part-timers, are currently making the minimum wage in their localities. Starting this April, their hourly wage will be raised to $16, an 11% increase on average but an increase of as much as 33% for some workers.

Job ads from Aetna and its competitors, along with wage reports on job-hunting websites, suggest that low-level health-insurer workers in customer-service, billing claims-processing and similar positions, including both seasoned workers and entry-level employees are often paid $13 to $15 an hour.'

Next year, the company will also let workers with household income below a certain threshold choose health coverage with lower out-of-pocket charges without paying more in monthly premiums, a shift it said could save a worker with a family as much as $4,000 a year. The company said that as many as 7,000 employees may be eligible. Like a growing number of its employer clients, Aetna offers only high-deductible plans to employees

Mr. Bertolini said Aetna expects to offer a benefits program to employer clients that's similar to the one it's rolling out to its own workers.

The total cost to Aetna for both changes will be $14 million in 2015 and approximately $25.5 million next year, the company said. Aetna has projected operating revenue for 2015 of at least $62 billion, with operating profit of at least $2.4 billion. Overseas Aetna employees won't be affected nor will those working for third-party contractors that provide janitorial, security, cafeteria or other services.

Mr. Bertolini said Aetna hopes to reduce its turnover costs of around $120 million a year and improve the quality of job prospects and the engagement of workers who interact with consumers and health-care providers. He said he isn't certain the changes will pay for themselves in purely financial terms, but the cost is small relative to Aetna's size. 'I'm willing to make the investment to see whether or not this happens," he said.

Mr. Bertolini, who said he had recently asked Aetna executives to read economist Thomas Piketty's book on wealth inequality, also framed the move in more idealistic terms: "It's not just about paying people, it's about the whole social compact," Mr. Bertolini said, adding, "Why can't private industry step forward and make the innovative decisions on how to do this?"

Mr. Bertolini said the timing was partly tied to the economic recovery, which, he suggested, will heighten the competition for employees "now that there are more places for them to go."

So far, even as the economy and the labor market have improved, wages have grown slowly. On Friday, the Labor Department said unemployment fell to 5.6% in December from 5.8% in November, and employers added 252,000 jobs, capping the best year of job growth in nearly 15 years. By contrast, average hourly earnings fell slightly-likely reflecting seasonal part-time holiday hiring—bringing 2014's increase to 1.7%.

Economists said Mr. Berto lini's bet could pay off. "There's a very strong relationship between wages and turnover," said Lawrence Katz, a Harvard economist.

Questions

1. Is the decision managers at Aetna made to have a $16 an hour wage floor a programmed or nonprogrammed decision?

2. How did managers recognize the need to make this decision?

3. To what extent do you think satisficing was involved in making this decision?

4. How would you evaluate this decision according to the four criteria that managers use to evaluate the advantages and disadvantages of different courses of action?

Source: "Aetna Sets Wage Floor: $16 an Hour" by A. W. Mathews and T. Francis. *The Wall Street Journal,* January 13, 2015, pp. B1, B6.

Endnotes

1. "Planting the Seeds for 1-800-Flowers.com," *Fortune*, March, 17, 2014, 47–50; "James McCann: Executive Profile & Biography," *Businessweek*, http://investing.businessweek.com/research/stocks/people/person.asp?personId=234954&ticker=FLWS; "1-800-FLOWERS.COM, Inc. Reports Financial Results from Continuing Operations for its Fiscal 2014 Fourth Quarter and Full Year," http://investor.1800flowers.com/releasedetail.cfm? Release ID=870329, February 23, 2015.

2. "Planting the Seeds for 1-800-Flowers.com."

3. Ibid.

4. Ibid.; D. Schawbel, "Jim McCann: How He Turned 1-800-Flowers.com into a Household Name," *Forbes*, www.forbes.com/sites/danschawbel/2014/01/27/jim-mccann-how-he-turned-1-800-flowers-com-into-a-household-name/, April 14, 2014.

5. "Planting the Seeds for 1-800-Flowers.com"; "Jim McCann: From Bartender to 30 Million Clients—Off the Cuff," *Yahoo News*, www.news.yahoo.com/blogs/off-the-cuff/jim-mccann-bartender-30-million-clients-094417515.html.

6. "Planting the Seeds for 1-800-Flowers.com."

7. Ibid.

8. Ibid.

9. Ibid.

10. Ibid.

11. Ibid.

12. Ibid.

13. Ibid.

14. Ibid.

15. Ibid.

16. Ibid.

17. "1-800-Flowers.com, Inc.—Investor Overview," www.investor.1800flowers.com/index.cfm?pg=profile, April 16, 2014.; "SoLoMo—An Interview with Christopher G. McCann," www.files.shareholder.com/downloads/FLWS/3092623901x0x504093/5f089d9d-6e25-4fd2-9600-5dc331cd5292/LEADERS-Christopher-McCann-1-800-FLOWERS.pdf, April 14, 2014.

18. "Planting the Seeds for 1-800-Flowers.com."

19. Ibid.

20. G.P. Huber, *Managerial Decision Making* (Glenview, IL: Scott, Foresman, 1993).

21. "Martin Cooper—History of Cell Phone and Martin Cooper," www.inventors.about.com/cs/inventorsalphabet/a/martin_cooper.htm?p=1, February 16, 2010; "Motorola Demonstrates Portable Telephone to Be Available for Public Use by 1976," April 3, 1973, www.motorola.com, February 17, 2009; "The Cellular Telephone Concept—An Overview," September 10, 1984, www.motorola.com, February 17, 2009;" "iPod," www.apple.com/, February 16, 2010.

22. H.A. Simon, *The New Science of Management* (Englewood Cliffs, NJ: Prentice-Hall, 1977).

23. N.A. Hira, "The Making of a UPS Driver," *Fortune*, November 12, 2007, 118–29.

24. Ibid.; J. Lovell, "Left-Hand Turn Elimination," *The New York Times*, December 9, 2007, www.nytimes.com/2007/12/09/magazine/09left-handturn.html?_r=2&oref=slogin&r, February 20, 2008.

25. Hira, "The Making of a UPS Driver."

26. L. Osburn, "Expecting the World on a Silver Platter," *Houston Chronicle*, September 17, 2007, D1, D6.

27. Hira, "The Making of a UPS Driver"; UPS Integrad—UPS Corporate Responsibility, www.community.ups.com/Safety/Training+For+Safety/UPS+Integrad, April 18, 2012.

28. Hira, "The Making of a UPS Driver"; "Welcome to UPS Careers," www.ups.managehr.com/Home.htm, February 20, 2008; "UPS Integrad—UPS Corporate Responsibility"; "Empowered People," www.community.ups.com/committed-to-more/employees-saftey/, February 24, 2015.

29. "UPS Integrad—UPS Corporate Responsibility."

30. Hira, "The Making of a UPS Driver"; "UPS Integrad—UPS Corporate Responsibility."

31. "Best Webcast Series: Evolving the Leadership Development Culture at UPS," *American Society for Training & Development*, www.webcasts.astd.org/webinar/811, April 17, 2014.

32. Hira, "The Making of a UPS Driver."

33. Ibid.; "UPS Integrad—UPS Corporate Responsibility."

34. D. Petersik, "Oxygen Learning," www.oxygenlearning.com/who-we-are/don-petersik/, April 17, 2014.

35. Hira, "The Making of a UPS Driver."

36. Ibid.

37. D. Kahneman, "Maps of Bounded Rationality: A Perspective on Intuitive Judgment and Choice," *Prize Lecture*, December 8, 2002; E. Jaffe, "What Was I Thinking? Kahneman Explains How Intuition Leads Us Astray," *American Psychological Society* 17, no. 5 (May 2004), 23–26; E. Dane and M. Pratt, "Exploring Intuition and Its Role in Managerial Decision Making," *Academy of Management Review* 32 (2007), 33–54.

38. One should be careful not to generalize too much here, however; for as Peter Senge has shown, programmed decisions rely on the implicit assumption that the environment is in a steady state. If environmental conditions change, sticking to a routine decision rule can produce disastrous results. See P. Senge, *The Fifth Discipline: The Art and Practice of the Learning Organization* (New York: Doubleday, 1990).

39. Kahneman, "Maps of Bounded Rationality"; Jaffe, "What Was I Thinking?"

40. H.A. Simon, *Administrative Behavior* (New York: Macmillan, 1947), 79.

41. H.A. Simon, *Models of Man* (New York: Wiley, 1957).

42. K.J. Arrow, *Aspects of the Theory of Risk Bearing* (Helsinki: Yrjo Johnssonis Saatio, 1965).

43. Arrow, *Aspects of the Theory of Risk Bearing*.

44. R.L. Daft and R.H. Lengel, "Organizational Information Requirements, Media Richness and Structural Design," *Management Science* 32 (1986), 554–71.

45. R. Cyert and J. March, *Behavioral Theory of the Firm* (Englewood Cliffs, NJ: Prentice-Hall, 1963).

46. J.G. March and H.A. Simon, *Organizations* (New York: Wiley, 1958).

47. H.A. Simon, "Making Management Decisions: The Role of Intuition and Emotion," *Academy of Management Executive* 1 (1987), 57–64.

48. M.H. Bazerman, *Judgment in Managerial Decision Making* (New York: Wiley, 1986). Also see Simon, *Administrative Behavior*.

49. "Scott G. McNealy Profile," *Forbes.com,* www.people.forbes.com/profile/scott-g-mcnealy/75347, February 16, 2010; Sun Oracle, "Overview and Frequently Asked Questions," www.oracle.com, February 16, 2010.

50. "Sun Microsystems—Investor Relations: Officers and Directors," www.sun.com/aboutsun/investor/sun_facts/officers_directors.html, June 1, 2004; "How Sun Delivers Value to Customers," *Sun Microsystems—Investor Relations: Support & Training,* June 1, 2004 (www.sun.com/aboutsun/investor/sun_facts/core_strategies.html); "Sun at a Glance," *Sun Microsystems—Investor Relations: Sun Facts,* June 1, 2004 (www.sun.com/aboutsun/investor/sun_facts/index.html); "Plug in the System, and Everything Just Works," *Sun Microsystems— Investor Relations: Product Portfolio,* June 1, 2004 (www.sun.com/aboutsun/investor/sun_facts/portfolio/html).

51. N.J. Langowitz and S.C. Wheelright, "Sun Microsystems, Inc. (A)," Harvard Business School Case 686–133.

52. R.D. Hof, "How to Kick the Mainframe Habit," *BusinessWeek,* June 26, 1995, 102–104.

53. Bazerman, *Judgment in Managerial Decision Making;* Huber, *Managerial Decision Making;* J.E. Russo and P.J. Schoemaker, *Decision Traps* (New York: Simon & Schuster, 1989).

54. M.D. Cohen, J.G. March, and J.P. Olsen, "A Garbage Can Model of Organizational Choice," *Administrative Science Quarterly* 17 (1972), 1–25.

55. Cohen, March, and Olsen, "A Garbage Can Model."

56. Bazerman, *Judgment in Managerial Decision Making.*

57. Senge, *The Fifth Discipline.*

58. E. de Bono, *Lateral Thinking* (London: Penguin, 1968); Senge, *The Fifth Discipline.*

59. Russo and Schoemaker, *Decision Traps.*

60. Bazerman, *Judgment in Managerial Decision Making.*

61. B. Berger, "NASA: One Year after *Columbia*—Bush's New Vision Changes Agency's Course Midstream," *Space News Business Report,* January 26, 2004 (www.space.com/spacenews/businessmonday_040126.html).

62. J. Glanz and J. Schwartz, "Dogged Engineer's Effort to Assess Shuttle Damage," *The New York Times,* September 26, 2003, A1.

63. M.L. Wald and J. Schwartz, "NASA Chief Promises a Shift in Attitude," *The New York Times,* August 28, 2003, A23.

64. Russo and Schoemaker, *Decision Traps.*

65. S. Clifford, "Marc Shuman Was Determined to Expand Fast," *Inc.,* March, 2006, 44–50; D. Kocieniewski, "After $12,000, There's Even Room to Park the Car," *The New York Times,* February 20, 2006; "The World's Cleanest Garage," www.garagetek.com, May 30, 2006 (www.garagetek.com/nav.asp); "What Is Garagetek?" www.garagetek.com, May 30, 2006 (www.garagetek.com/content_CNBC.asp); L. Christie, "7 Franchises: Riding the Housing Boom," CNNMoney.com, March 7, 2006 (www.money.cnn.com/2006/03/07/smbusiness/homefranchises/index.htm); "745 Businesses to Start Now!" *Entrepreneur,* January 2005, 88, 192, 193; "Franchise Opportunities Available," www.garagetek.com/FranchiseOpportunities/ February 16, 2010; "GarageTek Inc.: Private Company Information," *BusinessWeek,* www.investing.businessweek.com/research/stocks/private/snapshot.asp?privcapId=126174 . . . , February 15, 2010; "Garage Makover," *Inc.,* July 2007, 53.; "About GarageTek—Garage Storage & Organizational Systems—Garag Solutions," www.garagetek.com/AboutUs/, April 15, 2014.

66. "About Us," *Garagetek,* www.garagetek.com/AboutUs/, April 17, 2012.

67. Clifford, "Marc Shuman Was Determined to Expand Fast."

68. Ibid.

69. "Franchise Opportunities," *GarageTek,* www.garagetek.com/FranchiseOpportunities/GarageTek-Opportunities.aspx, February 14, 2008.

70. Clifford, "Marc Shuman Was Determined to Expand Fast."

71. Ibid.

72. "Franchise Opportunities Available," *Garagetek,* www.garagetek.com/FranchiseOpportunities/, April 17, 2012.

73. Clifford, "Marc Shuman Was Determined to Expand Fast."

74. "About Us," About GarageTek—Garage Storage & Organizational Systems—Garage Solutions, www.garagetek.com/AboutUs/, April 15, 2014.; "About Garage Tek," www.garagetek.com/AboutUs, February 24, 2015.

75. Clifford, "Marc Shuman Was Determined to Expand Fast."

76. I.L. Janis, *Groupthink: Psychological Studies of Policy Decisions and Disasters,* 2nd ed. (Boston: Houghton Mifflin, 1982).

77. C.R. Schwenk, *The Essence of Strategic Decision Making* (Lexington, MA: Lexington Books, 1988).

78. See R.O. Mason, "A Dialectic Approach to Strategic Planning," *Management Science* 13 (1969) 403–14; R.A. Cosier and J.C. Aplin, "A Critical View of Dialectic Inquiry in Strategic Planning," *Strategic Management Journal* 1 (1980), 343–56; I.I. Mitroff and R.O. Mason, "Structuring III—Structured Policy Issues: Further Explorations in a Methodology for Messy Problems," *Strategic Management Journal* 1 (1980), 331–42.

79. M.C. Gentile, *Differences That Work: Organizational Excellence through Diversity* (Boston: Harvard Business School Press, 1994); F. Rice, "How to Make Diversity Pay," *Fortune,* August 8, 1994, 78–86.

80. B. Hedberg, "How Organizations Learn and Unlearn," in W.H. Starbuck and P.C. Nystrom, eds., *Handbook of Organizational Design,* vol. 1 (New York: Oxford University Press, 1981), 1–27.

81. Senge, *The Fifth Discipline.*

82. Ibid.

83. P.M. Senge, "The Leader's New Work: Building Learning Organizations," *Sloan Management Review,* Fall 1990, 7–23.

84. W. Zellner, K.A. Schmidt, M. Ihlwan, and H. Dawley, "How Well Does Walmart Travel?" *BusinessWeek,* September 3, 2001, 82–84.

85. J.M George, "Creativity in Organizations," in J.P. Walsh and A.P. Brief, eds., *The Academy of Management Annals,* Vol. 1 (New York: Erlbaum, 2008), 439–77.

86. Ibid.

87. C. Saltr, "FAST 50: The World's Most Innovative Companies," *Fast Company,* March 2008, 73–117.

88. R.W. Woodman, J.E. Sawyer, and R.W. Griffin, "Towards a Theory of Organizational Creativity," *Academy of Management Review* 18 (1993), 293–321.

89. T. Evans, "Entrepreneurs Seek to Elicit Workers' Ideas," *The Wall Street Journal,* December 22, 2009, B7; D. Dahl, "Rounding Up Staff Ideas," Inc.com, February 1, 2010, www.inc.com/magazine/20100201/rounding-up-staff-ideas_Printer_Friendly.html,

February 12, 2010; "About Borrego Solar," www.borregosolar.com/solar-energy-company/solar-contractor.php, February 15, 2010.

90. T.J. Bouchard Jr., J. Barsaloux, and G. Drauden, "Brainstorming Procedure, Group Size, and Sex as Determinants of Problem Solving Effectiveness of Individuals and Groups," *Journal of Applied Psychology* 59 (1974), 135–38.

91. M. Diehl and W. Stroebe, "Productivity Loss in Brainstorming Groups: Towards the Solution of a Riddle," *Journal of Personality and Social Psychology* 53 (1987), 497–509.

92. D.H. Gustafson, R.K. Shulka, A. Delbecq, and W.G. Walster, "A Comparative Study of Differences in Subjective Likelihood Estimates Made by Individuals, Interacting Groups, Delphi Groups, and Nominal Groups," *Organizational Behavior and Human Performance* 9 (1973), 280–91.

93. N. Dalkey, *The Delphi Method: An Experimental Study of Group Decision Making* (Santa Monica, CA: Rand Corp., 1989).

94. T. Lonier, "Some Insights and Statistics on Working Solo," www.workingsolo.com.

95. I.N. Katsikis and L.P. Kyrgidou, "The Concept of Sustainable Entrepreneurship: A Conceptual Framework and Empirical Analysis," *Academy of Management Proceedings,* 2007, 1–6, web.ebscohost.com/ehost/delivery?vid=7&hid=102&sid=434afdf5-5ed9-45d4-993b-, January 24, 2008; "What Is a Social Entrepreneur?" www.ashoka.org/social_entrepreneur, February 20, 2008; C. Hsu, "Entrepreneur for Social Change," *U.S.News.com,* October 31, 2005, www.usnews.com/usnews/news/articles/051031/31drayton.htm; D.M. Sullivan, "Stimulating Social Entrepreneurship: Can Support from Cities Make a Difference?" *Academy of Management Perspectives,* February 2007, 78.

96. Katsikis and Kyrgidou, "The Concept of Sustainable Entrepreneurship"; "What Is a Social Entrepreneur?"; Hsu, "Entrepreneur for Social Change"; Sullivan, "Stimulating Social Entrepreneurship."

6

Planning, Strategy, and Competitive Advantage

Learning Objectives

After studying this chapter, you should be able to:

LO 6-1 Identify the three main steps of the planning process, and explain the relationship between planning and strategy.

LO 6-2 Differentiate between the main types of strategies, and explain how they give an organization a competitive advantage that may lead to superior performance.

LO 6-3 Differentiate between the main types of corporate-level strategies, and explain how they are used to strengthen a company's business-level strategy and competitive advantage.

LO 6-4 Describe the vital role managers play in implementing strategies to achieve an organization's mission and goals.

© Mint Images Limited/Alamy RF (Left)
© Neustockimages/E+/Getty Images RF (Right)

Toys "R" Us President Hank Mullany (left) and CEO Antonio Urcelay (right) have implemented a business strategy designed to help the company play to its strengths and address its weaknesses. © Bloomberg via Getty Images

MANAGEMENT SNAPSHOT

Toy Retailer Implements Turnaround Plan

How Can Identifying Corporate Strengths and Weaknesses Lead to Better Planning and Strategy?

Toys "R" Us, Inc., with its mascot Geoffrey the Giraffe, is a well-known brand. The toy retailer was founded in 1948 as Children's Supermart and later rebranded as Toys "R" Us after adding toys to its baby furniture business. By 2014, the company had grown to 872 stores in the United States and more than 700 stores outside the United States.

Despite its growth, 2013 was not a good year for Toys "R" Us. Net sales were down, and the company's net loss was $1 billion. Chairman and CEO Antonio Urcelay and President Hank Mullany announced a "TRU Transformation" plan for the company.

"Our 'TRU Transformation' strategy is grounded in consumer research and customer insights and is anchored by three guiding principles—Easy, Expert, Fair," Mullany said. "Among our highest priorities will be to deepen our focus on the customer, build meaningful relationships through loyalty and targeted marketing programs, and improve the shopping experience both in store and online."[1]

Urcelay and Mullany recognize that external factors affect sales at Toys "R" Us. The factors they identified are opportunities and threats, over which the company has no control. They include falling birthrates, changes in the play patterns of children, and the growth of online shopping. While it might be easy for Urcelay and Mullany to blame falling sales on these factors, the two company leaders also looked at internal factors that hurt the business—factors the company does control. "We are encouraged that all of these . . . issues are firmly within our own control to fix," Urcelay said. "And our strategy will address these to improve the business over the short term and put the company on track for the future."

Urcelay and Mullany described four categories of weaknesses at Toys "R" Us and discussed how they could be turned into strengths. First, the retailer said it has provided a weak customer experience both in stores and online. Customers complain that the checkout process in stores is slow and that stores are cluttered and disorganized. The apps for the online store are out of date and frustrating to customers. When customers do buy a product online, they often encounter shipping problems. Toys "R" Us would like to turn this weakness into a strength by making its stores easy, uncluttered places at which to shop, with sales associates who have been trained and who will be perceived as experts on the company's products.

Second, there is a perception that prices at Toys "R" Us are higher than at other retailers. Toys "R" Us would like to turn this weakness into a strength by making sure its prices are perceived as fair and by reducing the many exclusions to its price-matching policy. The company also plans to use data from its loyalty program to send targeted offers to customers and to communicate more simplified offers to customers.

Third, the retailer has struggled with inventory management. Customers often find that sought-after items are out of stock. Toys "R" Us had already begun to work on this issue before the 2013 financial returns were known. The company has expanded its ability to ship online orders from stores and distribution centers, resulting in a much more flexible inventory system. It also is using a "product life cycle management" system to get the right goods into stores at the right times. In addition, clearance sales events will move merchandise that has been around the store for too long.

Finally, the retailer plans to right size its cost structure. The company is assessing its business structure and operations to increase efficiency and effectiveness. As a part of this assessment, the company found 500 positions to eliminate. "As we look to the future, our strategy will establish a path to sustainable business growth, building upon the company's unique strengths," Urcelay said. "Toys 'R' Us is one of the most recognized brands in the world with a strong international presence and a large and loyal customer base."

One year into the "TRU Transformation" plan, Urcelay and Mullany are pleased with the company's progress. Profit margins, inventory management, and the customer shopping experience have improved, and the global e-commerce business continues to grow. They know there is still much work to do; however, the transformation plan has put the company on a success business path.[2]

Overview

planning Identifying and selecting appropriate goals and courses of action; one of the four principal tasks of management.

LO 6-1 Identify the three main steps of the planning process and explain the relationship between planning and strategy.

As the opening case suggests, in a fast-changing competitive environment such as the global toy industry, managers must continually evaluate how well products are meeting customer needs, and they must engage in thorough, systematic planning to find new strategies to better meet those needs. This chapter explores the manager's role both as planner and as strategist. First, we discuss the nature and importance of planning, the kinds of plans managers develop, and the levels at which planning takes place. Second, we discuss the three major steps in the planning process: (1) determining an organization's mission and major goals, (2) choosing or formulating strategies to realize the mission and goals, and (3) selecting the most effective ways to implement and put these strategies into action. We also examine techniques such as SWOT analysis that can help managers improve the quality of their planning; and we discuss a range of strategies managers can use to give their companies a competitive advantage over their rivals. By the end of this chapter, you will understand the vital role managers carry out when they plan, develop, and implement strategies to create a high-performing organization.

Planning and Strategy

strategy A cluster of decisions about what goals to pursue, what actions to take, and how to use resources to achieve goals.

Planning, as we noted in Chapter 1, is a process managers use to identify and select appropriate goals and courses of action for an organization.[3] The organizational plan that results from the planning process details the goals of the organization and the specific strategies managers will implement to attain those goals. Recall from Chapter 1 that a **strategy** is a cluster of related managerial decisions and actions to help an organization attain one of its goals. Thus planning is both a goal-making and a strategy-making process.

Figure 6.1

Three Steps in Planning

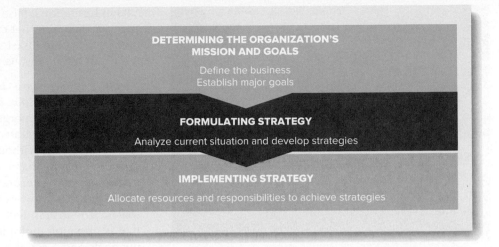

DETERMINING THE ORGANIZATION'S
MISSION AND GOALS

Define the business
Establish major goals

FORMULATING STRATEGY

Analyze current situation and develop strategies

IMPLEMENTING STRATEGY

Allocate resources and responsibilities to achieve strategies

mission statement

A broad declaration
of an organization's
purpose that identifies
the organization's
products and customers
and distinguishes the
organization from its
competitors.

In most organizations, planning is a three-step activity (see Figure 6.1). The first step is determining the organization's mission and goals. A **mission statement** is a broad declaration of an organization's overriding purpose, what it is seeking to achieve from its activities; this statement also identifies what is *unique or important* about its products to its employees and customers; finally it *distinguishes or differentiates* the organization in some ways from its competitors. (Three examples of mission statements, those created by LinkedIn, Twitter, and Facebook, are illustrated later in Figure 6.4.)

The second step is formulating strategy. Managers analyze the organization's current situation and then conceive and develop the strategies necessary to attain the organization's mission and goals. The third step is implementing strategy. Managers decide how to allocate the resources and responsibilities required to implement the strategies among people and groups within the organization.[4] In subsequent sections of this chapter we look in detail at the specifics of these steps. But first we examine the general nature and purpose of planning.

The Nature of the Planning Process

Essentially, to perform the planning task, managers (1) establish and discover where an organization is at the *present time;* (2) determine where it should be in the future, its *desired future state;* and (3) decide how to *move it forward* to reach that future state. When managers plan, they must forecast what may happen in the future to decide what to do in the present. The better their predictions, the more effective will be the strategies they formulate to take advantage of future opportunities and counter emerging competitive threats in the environment. As previous chapters noted, however, the external environment is uncertain and complex, and managers typically must deal with incomplete information and bounded rationality. This is why planning and strategy making are so difficult and risky; and if managers' predictions are wrong and strategies fail, organizational performance falls.

Why Planning Is Important

Almost all managers participate in some kind of planning because they must try to predict future opportunities and threats and develop a plan and strategies that will result in a high-performing organization. Moreover, the absence of a plan often

A group of managers meets to plot their company's strategy. Their ability to assess opportunities and challenges and to forecast the future doesn't just depend on intelligence. Such tools as SWOT analysis can significantly bolster the accuracy of their predictions.
© Ryan McVay/Getty Images/RF

results in hesitations, false steps, and mistaken changes of direction that can hurt an organization or even lead to disaster. Planning is important for four main reasons:

1. *Planning is necessary to give the organization a sense of direction and purpose.*[5] A plan states what goals an organization is trying to achieve and what strategies it intends to use to achieve them. Without the sense of direction and purpose that a formal plan provides, managers may interpret their own specific tasks and jobs in ways that best suit themselves. The result will be an organization that is pursuing multiple and often conflicting goals and a set of managers who do not cooperate and work well together. By stating which organizational goals and strategies are important, a plan keeps managers on track so they use the resources under their control efficiently and effectively.

2. *Planning is a useful way of getting managers to participate in decision making about the appropriate goals and strategies for an organization.* Effective planning gives all managers the opportunity to participate in decision making. At Intel, for example, top managers, as part of their annual planning process, regularly request input from lower-level managers to determine what the organization's goals and strategies should be.

3. *A plan helps coordinate managers of the different functions and divisions of an organization to ensure that they all pull in the same direction and work to achieve its desired future state.* Without a well-thought-out plan, for example, it is possible that the manufacturing function will make more products than the sales function can sell, resulting in a mass of unsold inventory. In fact, this happened in 2015 when the Northeast experienced harsh winter weather, which slowed car sales and left carmakers with unsold inventory. To sell extra cars, many carmakers had to offer deep discounts to sell off their excess stock.

4. *A plan can be used as a device for controlling managers within an organization.* A good plan specifies not only which goals and strategies the organization is committed to but also *who* bears the responsibility for putting the strategies into action to attain the goals. When managers know they will be held accountable for attaining a goal, they are motivated to do their best to make sure the goal is achieved.

Henri Fayol, the originator of the model of management we discussed in Chapter 1, said that effective plans should have four qualities: unity, continuity, accuracy, and flexibility.[6] *Unity* means that at any time only one central, guiding plan is put into operation to achieve an organizational goal; more than one plan to achieve a goal would cause confusion and disorder. *Continuity* means that planning is an ongoing process in which managers build and refine previous plans and continually modify plans at all levels—corporate, business, and functional—so they fit together into one broad framework. *Accuracy* means that managers need to make every attempt to collect and use all available information in the planning process. Of course managers must recognize that uncertainty exists and that information is almost always incomplete (for reasons we discussed in Chapter 5). Despite the need for continuity and accuracy, however, Fayol emphasized that the planning process should be *flexible* enough so plans can be altered and changed if the situation changes; managers must not be bound to a static plan.

Levels of Planning

In large organizations planning usually takes place at three levels of management: corporate, business or division, and department or functional. Consider how General Electric (GE) operates. One of the world's largest global organizations, GE competes in more than 100 different businesses or industries.[7] GE has three main levels of management: corporate level, business or divisional level, and functional level (see Figure 6.2). At the corporate level are CEO and Chairman Jeffrey Immelt, his top management team, and their corporate support staff. Together they are responsible for planning and strategy making for the organization as a whole.

Below the corporate level is the business level. At the business level are the different *divisions* or *business units* of the company that compete in distinct industries; GE has more than 100 divisions, including Aviation, Energy Management, Oil and Gas, Healthcare, and Transportation. In 2015, GE sold off its GE Capital unit for more than $26 billion. Each division or business unit has its own set of *divisional managers* who control planning and strategy for their particular division or unit. So, for example, Transportation's divisional managers plan how to operate globally to reduce costs while meeting the needs of customers in different countries.

Going down one more level, each division has its own set of *functions* or *departments,* such as manufacturing, marketing, human resource management (HRM), and research and development (R&D). For example, Aviation has its own

Figure 6.2

Levels of Planning at General Electric

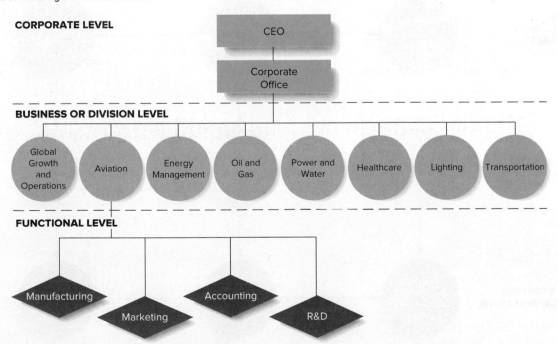

marketing function, as do Healthcare and Transportation. Each division's *functional managers* are responsible for the planning and strategy making necessary to increase the efficiency and effectiveness of their particular function. So, for example, GE Lighting's marketing managers are responsible for increasing the effectiveness of its advertising and sales campaigns in different countries to improve lightbulb sales.

Levels and Types of Planning

As just discussed, planning at GE, as at all other large organizations, takes place at each level. Figure 6.3 shows the link between these three levels and the three steps in the planning and strategy-making process illustrated in Figure 6.1.

The **corporate-level plan** contains top management's decisions concerning the organization's mission and goals, overall (corporate-level) strategy, and structure (see Figure 6.3). **Corporate-level strategy** specifies in which industries and national markets an organization intends to compete and why. One of the goals stated in GE's corporate-level plan is that GE should be first or second in market share in every industry in which it competes. A division that cannot attain this goal may be sold to another company. GE Medical Systems was sold to Thompson of France for this reason. Another GE goal is to acquire other companies that can help a division build its market share to reach its corporate goal of being first or second in an industry. In 2015, GE expected to win European Union approval to purchase the power and grid businesses of French multinational Alstom for more than $13 billion.[8]

corporate-level plan Top management's decisions pertaining to the organization's mission, overall strategy, and structure.

corporate-level strategy A plan that indicates in which industries and national markets an organization intends to compete.

Figure 6.3
Levels and Types of Planning

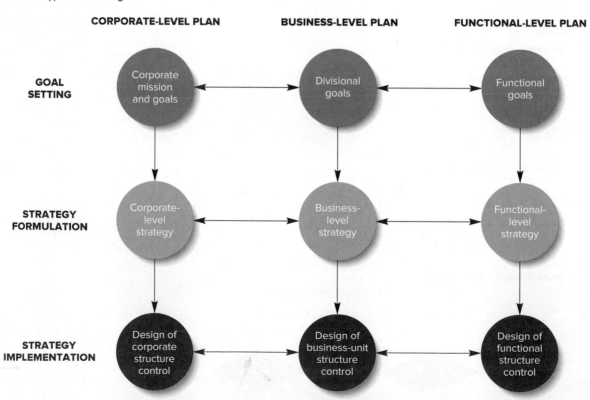

In general, corporate-level planning and strategy are the primary responsibility of top or corporate managers. The corporate-level goal of GE is to be the first or second leading company in every industry in which it competes. Jeffrey Immelt and his top management team decide which industries GE should compete in to achieve this goal. The corporate-level plan provides the framework within which divisional managers create their business-level plans. At the business level, the managers of each division create a **business-level plan** that details (1) the long-term divisional goals that will allow the division to meet corporate goals and (2) the division's business-level strategy and structure necessary to achieve divisional goals. Business-level strategy outlines the specific methods a division, business unit, or organization will use to compete effectively against its rivals in an industry. Managers at GE's Lighting division (currently number two in the global lighting industry, behind the Dutch company Philips NV) develop strategies designed to help their division take over the number one spot and better contribute to GE's corporate goals. The lighting division's specific strategies might focus on ways to reduce costs in all departments to lower prices and so gain market share from Philips. For example, GE has expanded its European lighting operations in Hungary, which is a low-cost location.[9]

At the functional level, the business-level plan provides the framework within which functional managers devise their plans. A **functional-level plan** states the goals that the managers of each function will pursue to help their division attain its business-level goals, which, in turn, will allow the entire company to achieve its corporate goals. **Functional-level strategy** is a plan of action that managers of individual functions (such as manufacturing or marketing) can follow to improve the ability of each function to perform its task-specific activities in ways that add value to an organization's goods and services and thereby increase the value customers receive. Thus, for example, consistent with the lighting division's strategy of driving down costs, its manufacturing function might adopt the goal "To reduce production costs by 20% over the next three years," and functional strategies to achieve this goal might include (1) investing in state-of-the-art European production facilities and (2) developing an electronic global business-to-business network to reduce the costs of inputs and inventory holding.

In the planning process, it is important to ensure that planning across the three different levels is *consistent*—functional goals and strategies should be consistent with divisional goals and strategies, which, in turn, should be consistent with corporate goals and strategies, and vice versa. When consistency is achieved, the whole company operates in harmony; activities at one level reinforce and strengthen those at the other levels, increasing efficiency and effectiveness. To help accomplish this, each function's plan is linked to its division's business-level plan, which, in turn, is linked to the corporate plan. Although few organizations are as large and complex as GE, most plan in the same way as GE and have written plans, which are frequently updated, to guide managerial decision making.

Time Horizons of Plans

Plans differ in their **time horizons,** the periods of time over which they are intended to apply or endure. Managers usually distinguish among *long-term plans,* with a time horizon of five years or more; *intermediate-term plans,* with a horizon between one and five years; and *short-term plans,* with a horizon of one year or less. Typically corporate- and business-level goals and strategies require long- and intermediate-term plans, and functional-level goals and strategies require intermediate- and short-term plans.

---

business-level plan Divisional managers' decisions pertaining to divisions' long-term goals, overall strategy, and structure.

functional-level plan Functional managers' decisions pertaining to the goals that they propose to pursue to help the division attain its business-level goals.

functional-level strategy A plan of action to improve the ability of each of an organization's functions to perform its task-specific activities in ways that add value to an organization's goods and services.

time horizon The intended duration of a plan.

Although most companies operate with planning horizons of five years or more, this does not mean that managers undertake major planning exercises only once every five years and then "lock in" a specific set of goals and strategies for that period. Most organizations have an annual planning cycle that is usually linked to the annual financial budget (although a major planning effort may be undertaken only every few years). So a corporate- or business-level plan that extends over several years is typically treated as a *rolling plan*—a plan that is updated and amended every year to take account of changing conditions in the external environment. Thus the time horizon for an organization's 2016 corporate-level plan might be 2021, for the 2017 plan it might be 2022, and so on. The use of rolling plans is essential because of the high rate of change in the environment and the difficulty of predicting competitive conditions five years in the future. Rolling plans enable managers to make midcourse corrections if environmental changes warrant or to change the thrust of the plan altogether if it no longer seems appropriate. The use of rolling plans allows managers to plan flexibly without losing sight of the need to plan for the long term.

Standing Plans and Single-Use Plans

Another distinction often made between plans is whether they are standing plans or single-use plans. Managers create standing and single-use plans to help achieve an organization's specific goals. *Standing plans* are used in situations in which programmed decision making is appropriate. When the same situations occur repeatedly, managers develop policies, rules, and standard operating procedures (SOPs) to control the way employees perform their tasks. A policy is a general guide to action; a rule is a formal, written guide to action; and a standing operating procedure is a written instruction describing the exact series of actions that should be followed in a specific situation. For example, an organization may have a standing plan about ethical behavior by employees. This plan includes a policy that all employees are expected to behave ethically in their dealings with suppliers and customers; a rule that requires any employee who receives from a supplier or customer a gift worth more than $50 to report the gift; and an SOP that obliges the recipient of the gift to make the disclosure in writing within 30 days.

In contrast, *single-use plans* are developed to handle nonprogrammed decision making in unusual or one-of-a-kind situations. Examples of single-use plans include *programs,* which are integrated sets of plans for achieving certain goals, and *projects,* which are specific action plans created to complete various aspects of a program. For instance, NASA is working on a major program to launch a rover in 2020 to investigate a specific environment on the surface of Mars. One project in this program is to develop the scientific instruments to bring samples back from Mars.[10]

Determining the Organization's Mission and Goals

As we discussed earlier, determining the organization's mission and goals is the first step of the planning process. Once the mission and goals are agreed upon and formally stated in the corporate plan, they guide the next steps by defining which strategies are appropriate.[11] Figure 6.4 presents the mission statements for three Internet-based companies: LinkedIn, Twitter, and Facebook.

Figure 6.4
Mission Statements for Three Internet-Based Companies

COMPANY	MISSION STATEMENT
LinkedIn	Our mission is simple: Connect the world's professionals to make them more productive and successful.
Twitter	Our mission: To give everyone the power to create and share ideas and information instantly, without barriers.
Facebook	Facebook's mission is to give people the power to share and make the world more open and connected.

Sources: Company website, "Mission," www.linkedin.com, accessed March 23, 2015; company website, "About," https://about.twitter.com, accessed March 23, 2015, company website, "Our Mission," www.facebook.com, accessed September 1, 2015.

Defining the Business

To determine an organization's *mission*—the overriding reason it exists to provide customers with goods or services they value—managers must first *define its business* so they can identify what kind of value customers are receiving. To define the business, managers must ask three related questions about a company's products: (1) *Who* are our customers? (2) *What* customer needs are being satisfied? (3) *How* are we satisfying customer needs?[12] Managers ask these questions to identify the customer needs that the organization satisfies and how the organization satisfies those needs. Answering these questions helps managers identify not only the customer needs they are satisfying now but also the needs they should try to satisfy in the future and who their true competitors are. All this information helps managers plan and establish appropriate goals.

Establishing Major Goals

Once the business is defined, managers must establish a set of primary goals to which the organization is committed. Developing these goals gives the organization a sense of direction or purpose. In most organizations, articulating major goals is the job of the CEO, although other managers have input into the process. Thus, at GE, CEO Immelt's primary goal is still to be one of the two best performers in every industry in which the company competes, even though this is highly challenging. However, the best statements of organizational goals are ambitious—that is, they *stretch* the organization and require that each of its members work to improve company performance.[13] The role of **strategic leadership**, the ability of the CEO and top managers to convey a compelling vision of what they want to achieve to their subordinates, is important here. If subordinates buy into the vision and model their behaviors on their leaders, they develop a willingness to undertake the hard, stressful work that is necessary for creative, risk-taking strategy making.[14] Many popular books such as *Built to Last* provide lucid accounts of strategic leaders establishing "big, hairy, audacious goals (BHAGs)" that serve as rallying points to unite their subordinates.[15]

Although goals should be challenging, they should also be realistic. Challenging goals give managers at all levels an incentive to look for ways to improve organizational performance, but a goal that is clearly unrealistic and impossible to attain may prompt managers to give up.[16] GE's Jeff Immelt has to be careful not to set unrealistic sales targets for the company's various divisions that might discourage their top managers, for example.

strategic leadership The ability of the CEO and top managers to convey a compelling vision of what they want the organization to achieve to their subordinates.

Finally, the time period in which a goal is expected to be achieved should be stated. Time constraints are important because they emphasize that a goal must be attained within a reasonable period; they inject a sense of urgency into goal attainment and act as a motivator. For example, Taco Bell's managers committed themselves to reviving its line of fast-food offerings and to increase sales significantly while taking away customers from other fast-food chains. By 2015, Taco Bell rolled out a breakfast menu on a national basis, which has increased overall sales.[17]

Formulating Strategy

strategy formulation The development of a set of corporate, business, and functional strategies that allow an organization to accomplish its mission and achieve its goals.

In **strategy formulation** managers work to develop the set of strategies (corporate, divisional, and functional) that will allow an organization to accomplish its mission and achieve its goals. Strategy formulation begins with managers' systematically analyzing the factors or forces inside an organization and outside in the global environment that affect the organization's ability to meet its goals now and in the future. SWOT analysis and the five forces model are two handy techniques managers can use to analyze these factors.

SWOT Analysis

SWOT analysis A planning exercise in which managers identify organizational strengths (S) and weaknesses (W) and environmental opportunities (O) and threats (T).

SWOT analysis is a planning exercise in which managers identify *internal* organizational strengths (S) and weaknesses (W) and *external* environmental opportunities (O) and threats (T). Based on a SWOT analysis, managers at the different levels of the organization select the corporate, business, and functional strategies to best position the organization to achieve its mission and goals (see Figure 6.5). In Chapter 4 we discussed forces in the task and general environments that have the potential to affect an organization. We noted that changes in these forces can produce opportunities that an organization might take advantage of and threats that may harm its current situation.

The first step in SWOT analysis is to identify an organization's strengths and weaknesses. Table 6.1 lists many important strengths (such as high-quality skills in marketing and in research and development) and weaknesses (such as rising manufacturing costs and outdated technology). The task facing managers is to

Figure 6.5

Planning and Strategy Formulation

Table 6.1

Questions for SWOT Analysis

Potential Strengths	Potential Opportunities	Potential Weaknesses	Potential Threats
Well-developed strategy?	Expand core business(es)?	Poorly developed strategy?	Attacks on core business(es)?
Strong product lines?	Exploit new market segments?	Obsolete, narrow product lines?	Increase in domestic competition?
Broad market coverage?	Widen product range?	Rising manufacturing costs?	Increase in foreign competition?
Manufacturing competence?	Extend cost or differentiation advantage?	Decline in R&D innovations?	Change in consumer tastes?
Good marketing skills?	Diversify into new growth businesses?	Poor marketing plan?	Fall in barriers to entry?
Good materials management systems?	Expand into foreign markets?	Poor materials management systems?	Rise in new or substitute products?
R&D skills and leadership?	Apply R&D skills in new areas?	Loss of customer goodwill?	Increase in industry rivalry?
Human resource competencies?	Enter new related businesses?	Inadequate human resources?	New forms of industry competition?
Brand-name reputation?	Vertically integrate forward?	Loss of brand name?	Potential for takeover?
Cost of differentiation advantage?	Vertically integrate backward?	Growth without direction?	Changes in demographic factors?
Appropriate management style?	Overcome barriers to entry?	Loss of corporate direction?	Changes in economic factors?
Appropriate organizational structure?	Reduce rivalry among competitors?	Infighting among divisions?	Downturn in economy?
Appropriate control systems?	Apply brand-name capital in new areas?	Loss of corporate control?	Rising labor costs?
Ability to manage strategic change?	Seek fast market growth?	Inappropriate organizational structure and control systems?	Slower market growth?
Others?	Others?	High conflict and politics?	Others?
		Others?	

identify the strengths and weaknesses that characterize the present state of their organization.

The second step in SWOT analysis begins when managers embark on a full-scale SWOT planning exercise to identify potential opportunities and threats in the environment that affect the organization now or may affect it in the future. Examples of possible opportunities and threats that must be anticipated (many of which were discussed in Chapter 4) are listed in Table 6.1. Scenario planning is often used to strengthen this analysis.

With the SWOT analysis completed, and strengths, weaknesses, opportunities, and threats identified, managers can continue the planning process and determine specific strategies for achieving the organization's mission and goals. The resulting strategies should enable the organization to attain its goals by taking advantage of opportunities, countering threats, building strengths, and correcting organizational weaknesses. To appreciate how managers use SWOT analysis to formulate strategy, consider the example of General Motors. When Mary Barra became the company's first female CEO in 2014, the company was recovering from bankruptcy and profits were down. Yet those were not the biggest strategic challenges Barra would face in her first few weeks as CEO. For more details, see the discussion in the accompanying "Manager as a Person" feature.

MANAGER AS A PERSON

GM's Barra Confronts Challenges

When Mary Barra took over as chief executive officer of General Motors in 2014, it was a challenging time for the automaker. The company had declared bankruptcy in 2009 and was still on the mend. Its net profit for 2013 was low due to several one-time costs, including company restructuring in Europe. But even more important was that within weeks of taking the CEO job, Barra began the recall of more than 2.5 million General Motors cars made between 2003 and 2007. The initial cars recalled were the Cobalt, the HHR, the G5, the Solstice, the Ion, and the Sky.

The cars had faulty ignition switches that would turn off the car while it was being driven, causing accidents and preventing the air bags from deploying. The company said the faulty switches caused at least 31 accidents and at least 12 deaths. More accidents and deaths could come to light as the investigation of the problem continues.

As part of the investigation, it was revealed that problems with the ignition switch emerged as early as 2001 during pre-production tests on the Ion. GM documents indicate that the problem was fixed at the time. However, in 2003, a General Motors service technician observed the problem in an Ion. At the time, the technician suggested that having several other keys on the key ring had worn out the ignition switch. In 2004, in a test of the Cobalt that used the same ignition switch, an engineer bumped the key and the car turned off. Despite these indicators, the switch was used for several more years and installed in several more car models.

This is the General Motors that Barra inherited: recovering from bankruptcy, experiencing less net profit, and dealing with a significant scandal around why it took more than a decade to recall cars that were causing accidents and deaths. One might expect that Barra would seek to avoid responsibility for the recall, given that the problems occurred before she became CEO. However, she has taken ownership of the recall and the company's failings.[18]

"We are putting the customer first, and that is guiding every decision we make. That is how we want today's GM to be judged. How we handle the recall will be an important test of that commitment," she said. "But it cannot stop there. We need to continue on the path of putting the customer first in everything we do. It's not something that only gets decided by senior leadership. We all have to own it . . . and we're using this opportunity to change much more about our business."[19]

Barra has publicly stated that problems within General Motors allowed the ignition switch to reach the market and vowed to make the development process much faster in the future. She also released a series of videos to answer consumer questions about the recall and whether the cars are safe to drive. She created the position of vice president for global vehicle safety and gave the position a more direct link to company leadership than past

Despite encountering enormous challenges at GM, CEO Mary Barra has decided not to change the company's basic strategy.
© Mark Lennihan/AP Images

safety officers were given. She testified before Congress when hearings were held about the recall.

Despite all the challenges she has faced, Barra does not seem inclined to change the company's strategy. She was quoted in February 2014 as saying, "There's no right turn or left turn in our strategy. We have a sound strategy. We need to accelerate the implementation of it. I want to make sure that employees around the globe understand the plan is the plan. Because I don't want to lose a minute."[20]

Barra's decision not to change the strategy of General Motors does not ignore the company's strengths, weaknesses, opportunities, and threats. In strengths, she perceives that General Motors has a strong lineup of vehicles to bring to the market. However, she notes a weakness in that some of the General Motors brands, specifically Cadillac and Chevrolet.

She sees an opportunity for General Motors to grow in China and to become more global in general. While General Motors is already a leader in China, Barra believes there is still room for growth. In fact, she wants to create a new position of president of international operations to take the company's global strategy to the next level. She also plans to have General Motors pursue trends in the car industry such as fuel efficiency and autonomous driving. Also important, Barra said, will be finding ways to integrate smartphones and other consumer electronic devices into cars in a manner that will allow for their safe use while driving.

In threats, she has noted the costs of materials and competition from other brands in Europe and the ongoing economic woes in Russia. Barra recently announced that General Motors will close its Opel manufacturing plant in Russia and pull the Opel brand completely from the Russian market.[21] The U.S. Department of Justice's ongoing investigation of the ignition switch and the timing of the recall is certainly a threat, but one for which Barra's handling has received much praise. One business writer listed Barra's strong communication skills as strength that will help the company as it deals with the recall and the investigation.[22]

The analysis of General Motors strengths, weaknesses, opportunities, and threats finds the company with much to do: "We clearly have a lot of work ahead to make all of our regions solidly and consistently profitable," Barra said. "It's going to be a multi-year journey that will include brand building, significant reductions in material and logistics cost and overall lower fixed cost."[23]

The Five Forces Model

A well-known model that helps managers focus on the five most important competitive forces, or potential threats, in the external environment is Michael Porter's five forces model. We discussed the first four forces in the following list in Chapter 4. Porter identified these five factors as major threats because they affect how much profit organizations competing within the same industry can expect to make:

- *The level of rivalry among organizations in an industry:* The more that companies compete against one another for customers—for example, by lowering the prices of their products or by increasing advertising—the lower is the level of industry profits (low prices mean less profit).

- *The potential for entry into an industry:* The easier it is for companies to enter an industry—because, for example, barriers to entry, such as brand loyalty, are low— the more likely it is for industry prices and therefore industry profits to be low.

- *The power of large suppliers:* If there are only a few large suppliers of an important input, then suppliers can drive up the price of that input, and expensive inputs result in lower profits for companies in an industry.
- *The power of large customers:* If only a few large customers are available to buy an industry's output, they can bargain to drive down the price of that output. As a result, industry producers make lower profits.
- *The threat of substitute products:* Often the output of one industry is a substitute for the output of another industry (plastic may be a substitute for steel in some applications, for example; similarly, bottled water is a substitute for cola). When a substitute for their product exists, companies cannot demand high prices for it or customers will switch to the substitute, and this constraint keeps their profits low.

Porter argued that when managers analyze opportunities and threats, they should pay particular attention to these five forces because they are the major threats an organization will encounter. It is the job of managers at the corporate, business, and functional levels to formulate strategies to counter these threats so an organization can manage its task and general environments, perform at a high level, and generate high profits. At General Motors, CEO Mary Barra performed such analysis to identify the opportunities and threats the company faces.

hypercompetition
Permanent, ongoing, intense competition brought about in an industry by advancing technology or changing customer tastes.

Today competition is tough in most industries, whether companies make cars, soup, computers, or dolls. The term **hypercompetition** applies to industries that are characterized by permanent, ongoing, intense competition brought about by advancing technology or changing customer tastes and fads and fashions.[24] Clearly, planning and strategy formulation are much more difficult and risky when hypercompetition prevails in an industry.

Formulating Business-Level Strategies

Michael Porter, the researcher who developed the five forces model, also developed a theory of how managers can select a business-level strategy—a plan to gain a competitive advantage in a particular market or industry.[25] Porter argued that business-level strategy creates a competitive advantage because it allows an organization (or a division of a company) to *counter and reduce* the threat of the five industry forces. That is, successful business-level strategy reduces rivalry, prevents new competitors from entering the industry, reduces the power of suppliers or buyers, and lowers the threat of substitutes—and this raises prices and profits.

LO 6-2
Differentiate between the main types of business-level strategies and explain how they give an organization a competitive advantage that may lead to superior performance.

According to Porter, to obtain these higher profits managers must choose between two basic ways of increasing the value of an organization's products: *differentiating the product* to increase its value to customers or *lowering the costs* of making the product. Porter also argues that managers must choose between serving the whole market or serving just one segment or part of a market. Based on those choices, managers choose to pursue one of four business-level strategies: low cost, differentiation, focused low cost, or focused differentiation (see Table 6.2).

Low-Cost Strategy

low-cost strategy
Driving the organization's costs down below the costs of its rivals.

With a **low-cost strategy**, managers try to gain a competitive advantage by focusing the energy of all the organization's departments or functions on driving the company's costs down below the costs of its industry rivals. This strategy, for example, would require that manufacturing managers search for new ways to reduce

Table 6.2

Porter's Business-Level Strategies

	Number of Market Segments Served	
Strategy	**Many**	**Few**
Low cost	✓	
Focused low cost		✓
Differentiation	✓	
Focused differentiation		✓

production costs, R&D managers focus on developing new products that can be manufactured more cheaply, and marketing managers find ways to lower the costs of attracting customers. According to Porter, companies pursuing a low-cost strategy can sell a product for less than their rivals sell it and yet still make a good profit because of their lower costs. Thus such organizations enjoy a competitive advantage based on their low prices. For example, BIC pursues a low-cost strategy: It offers customers razor blades priced lower than Gillette's and ballpoint pens less expensive than those offered by Cross or Waterman. Also, when existing companies have low costs and can charge low prices, it is difficult for new companies to enter the industry because entering is always an expensive process.

Differentiation Strategy

differentiation strategy
Distinguishing an organization's products from the products of competitors on dimensions such as product design, quality, or after-sales service.

With a **differentiation strategy**, managers try to gain a competitive advantage by focusing all the energies of the organization's departments or functions on *distinguishing* the organization's products from those of competitors on one or more important dimensions, such as product design, quality, or after-sales service and support. Often the process of making products unique and different is expensive. This strategy, for example, frequently requires that managers increase spending on product design or R&D to differentiate products, and costs rise as a result. Organizations that successfully pursue a differentiation strategy may be able to charge a *premium price* for their products; the premium price lets organizations pursuing a differentiation strategy recoup their higher costs. Coca-Cola, PepsiCo, and Procter & Gamble are some of the many well-known companies that pursue a strategy of differentiation. They spend enormous amounts of money on advertising to differentiate, and create a unique image for, their products. Also, differentiation makes industry entry difficult because new companies have no brand name to help them compete and customers don't perceive other products to be close substitutes, so this also allows premium pricing and results in high profits.

"Stuck in the Middle"

According to Porter's theory, managers cannot simultaneously pursue both a low-cost strategy and a differentiation strategy. Porter identified a simple correlation: Differentiation raises costs and thus necessitates premium pricing to recoup those high costs. For example, if BIC suddenly began to advertise heavily to try to build a strong global brand image for its products, BIC's costs would rise. BIC then could no longer make a profit simply by pricing its blades or pens lower than Gillette or Cross. According to Porter, managers must choose between a low-cost strategy and a differentiation strategy. He refers to managers and organizations that have not made this choice as being "stuck in the middle."

Organizations stuck in the middle tend to have lower levels of performance than do those that pursue a low-cost or a differentiation strategy. To avoid being stuck in the middle, top managers must instruct departmental managers to take actions that will result in either low cost or differentiation.

However, exceptions to this rule can be found. For example, Southwest Airlines has written its mission statement to say "dedication to the highest quality of customer service delivered with a sense of warmth, friendliness, individual pride, and company spirit."[26] Based on this statement, the company seems to be pursuing a differentiation strategy based on customer service. Yet the average price of a one-way ticket on a Southwest flight continues to be among the lowest, which suggests a cost leadership strategy. Likewise, Apple has a story that mixes cost leadership with differentiation. Apple CEO Tim Cook emphasizes that Apple's strategy is to focus on making great products—a differentiation strategy. He said the company never had the goal of selling a low-cost phone.[27] However, he said, the company did find a way to reach its goal of providing a great experience with a phone while reducing its cost. Cook emphasizes that differentiation was the goal, but low cost also became possible. These examples suggest that although Porter's ideas may be valid in most cases, well-managed companies such as Southwest Airlines and Apple may pursue both low costs and differentiated products.

Focused Low-Cost and Focused Differentiation Strategies

Both the differentiation strategy and the low-cost strategy are aimed at serving many or most segments of a particular market, such as for cars, toys, foods, or computers. Porter identified two other business-level strategies that aim to serve the needs of customers in only one or a few market segments.[28] Managers pursuing a **focused low-cost strategy** serve one or a few segments of the overall market and aim to make their organization the lowest-cost company serving that segment. By contrast, managers pursuing a **focused differentiation strategy** serve just one or a few segments of the market and aim to make their organization the most differentiated company serving that segment.

Companies pursuing either of these strategies have chosen to *specialize* in some way by directing their efforts at a particular kind of customer (such as serving the needs of babies or affluent customers) or even the needs of customers in a specific geographic region (customers on the East or West Coast). BMW, for example, pursues a focused differentiation strategy, producing cars exclusively for higher-income customers. By contrast, Toyota pursues a differentiation strategy and produces cars that appeal to consumers in almost all segments of the car market, from basic transportation (Toyota Corolla) through the middle of the market (Toyota Camry) to the high-income end of the market (Lexus).

Increasingly, smaller companies are finding it easier to pursue a focused strategy and compete successfully against large, powerful, low-cost and differentiated companies because of advances in technology that lower costs and enable them to reach and attract customers. By establishing a storefront on the web, thousands of small, specialized companies have been able to carve out a profitable niche against large bricks-and-mortar competitors. Zara is a flagship brand for Spanish global retailer, Inditex, whose sales have soared in recent years, and that provides an excellent example of the way even a small bricks-and-mortar company can use technology to pursue

focused low-cost strategy Serving only one segment of the overall market and trying to be the lowest-cost organization serving that segment.

focused differentiation strategy Serving only one segment of the overall market and trying to be the most differentiated organization serving that segment.

Zara models an incredibly successful strategy in jumping on trends and turning out new fashion lines in record time, while its smart store layout allows shoppers to quickly find which styles appeal to them.
© Bloomberg via Getty Images

a focused strategy and compete globally.[29] Zara has managed to position itself as the low-price, low-cost leader in the fashion segment of the clothing market, against differentiators such as Gucci, Dior, and Armani, because it has applied technology to its specific needs. Zara manages its design and manufacturing process in a way that minimizes the inventory it has to carry—the major cost borne by a clothing retailer. However, technological advances also give its designers instantaneous feedback on which clothes are selling well and in which countries, and this gives Zara a competitive advantage from differentiation. Specifically, Zara can manufacture more of a particular kind of dress or suit to meet high customer demand, decide which clothing should be sold in its rapidly expanding network of global stores, and constantly change the mix of clothes it offers customers to keep up with fashion—at low cost.

Zara's approach to technology also lets it efficiently manage the interface between its design and manufacturing operations. Zara takes only five weeks to design a new collection and then a week to make it. Fashion houses like Chanel and Armani, by contrast, can take six or more months to design a collection and then three more months to make it available in stores.[30] This short time to market gives Zara great flexibility and allows the company to respond quickly to the rapidly changing fashion market, in which fashions can change several times a year. Because of the quick manufacturing-to-sales cycle and just-in-time fashion, Zara offers its clothes collections at relatively low prices and still makes profits that are the envy of the fashion clothing industry.

Zara has been able to pursue a focused strategy that is simultaneously low-cost and differentiated because it has developed many strengths in functions such as clothing design, marketing, and technology that have given it a competitive advantage. Developing functional-level strategies that strengthen business-level strategy and increase competitive advantage is a vital managerial task. Discussion of this important issue is left until the next chapter. First, we need to go up one planning level and examine how corporate strategy helps an organization achieve its mission and goals.

LO 6-3 Differentiate between the main types of corporate-level strategies and explain how they are used to strengthen a company's business-level strategy and competitive advantage.

Formulating Corporate-Level Strategies

Once managers have formulated the business-level strategies that will best position a company, or a division of a company, to compete in an industry and outperform its rivals, they must look to the future. If their planning has been successful the company will be generating high profits, and their task now is to plan how to invest these profits to increase performance over time.

Recall that *corporate-level strategy* is a plan of action that involves choosing in which industries and countries a company should invest its resources to achieve its mission and goals. In choosing a corporate-level strategy, managers ask, How should the growth and development of our company be managed to increase its ability to create value for customers (and thus increase its performance) over the long run? Managers of effective organizations actively seek new opportunities to use a company's resources to create new and improved goods and services for customers.

Examples of organizations whose product lines are growing rapidly are Google, Intel, Apple, and Toyota, whose managers pursue any feasible opportunity to use their companies' skills to provide customers with new products.

In addition, some managers must help their organizations respond to threats due to changing forces in the task or general environment that have made their business-level strategies less effective and reduced profits. For example, customers may no longer be buying the kinds of goods and services a company is producing (high-salt soup, bulky televisions, or gas-guzzling SUVs), or other organizations may have entered the market and attracted away customers (this happened to Sony in the 2000s after Apple and Samsung began to produce better MP3 players, laptops, and flat-screen televisions). Top managers aim to find corporate strategies that can help the organization strengthen its business-level strategies and thus respond to these changes and improve performance.

The principal corporate-level strategies that managers use to help a company grow and keep it at the top of its industry, or to help it retrench and reorganize to stop its decline, are (1) concentration on a single industry, (2) vertical integration, (3) diversification, and (4) international expansion. An organization will benefit from pursuing any of these strategies only when the strategy helps further increase the value of the organization's goods and services so more customers buy them. Specifically, to increase the value of goods and services, a corporate-level strategy must help a company, or one of its divisions, either (1) lower the costs of developing and making products or (2) increase product differentiation so more customers want to buy the products even at high or premium prices. Both of these outcomes strengthen a company's competitive advantage and increase its performance.

Concentration on a Single Industry

concentration on a single industry
Reinvesting a company's profits to strengthen its competitive position in its current industry.

Most growing companies reinvest their profits to strengthen their competitive position in the industry in which they are currently operating; in doing so, they pursue the corporate-level strategy of **concentration on a single industry**. Most commonly, an organization uses its functional skills to develop new kinds of products, or it expands the number of locations in which it uses those skills. For example, Apple continuously introduces improved mobile wireless digital devices such as the iPhone and iPad, whereas McDonald's, which began as one restaurant in California, focused all its efforts on using its resources to quickly expand across the globe to become the biggest and most profitable U.S. fast-food company. The way Crocs focuses on the shoe business is discussed in the following "Management Insight" box.

MANAGEMENT INSIGHT

Revised Strategy Puts Crocs on Sound Footing

Crocs is one company that has stuck to its product. The company makes shoes—and not just any shoes. The company makes shoes from something called Croslite, a trademarked resin that makes Crocs comfortable, soft, and lightweight. The company was founded in 2002 and hit its popularity peak in 2007, when it sold 50 million pairs.[31] The best-known product of the company is its clog, a chunky and brightly colored shoe. The company expanded its product line to include accessories and apparel, but its main business remains shoes made of its special resin.

Yet by 2009, the company was struggling. Sales were hurt by the recession that began in 2008 and by knockoff shoes that cut into sales of Crocs and helped saturate the market. As if that weren't bad enough, there also was a backlash from consumers. Some people hated the footwear enough to start a social media campaign against Crocs. One blog, called I Hate Crocs, lamented that "blaringly, violently distasteful and while most trends of such an obviously unfashionable nature don't tend to survive for exceptionally long, Crocs have."[32] There also were videos posted to YouTube of people destroying the shoes and a Facebook page with more than 1.3 million likes.

By the end of 2008, the company posted a $200 million loss, paralleling the $200 million profit it made in 2007. To recover, the company expanded its shoe line to include more fashionable—but still comfortable—shoes. Then, in 2013, the company fired its CEO and secured a $200 million investment from the private equity firm Blackstone. To reduce losses in 2014, the company closed stores and laid off employees in an effort to return to profitability.[33] In early 2015, Gregg Ribatt joined the company as CEO, bringing many years of experience in the footwear industry to his new position. With new leadership in place and plans under way to streamline operations, Crocs is planning to stay in the shoe business.[34]

On the other hand, when organizations are performing effectively, they often decide to enter *new industries* in which they can use their growing profits to establish new operating divisions to create and make a wider range of more valuable products. Thus they begin to pursue vertical integration or diversification—such as Coca-Cola, PepsiCo, and General Electric, discussed earlier.

Vertical Integration

vertical integration
Expanding a company's operations either backward into an industry that produces inputs for its products or forward into an industry that uses, distributes, or sells its products.

When an organization is performing well in its industry, managers often see new opportunities to create value either by producing the inputs it uses to make its products or by distributing and selling its products to customers. For example, as Tesla Motors works toward its goal of mass-producing an electric car that will sell for $35,000 by 2017, it recognizes it will need batteries for the vehicle. To meet that need, Tesla will become its own battery supplier by building a large battery factory. Not only does Tesla expect the factory to supply its needs, it also expects the factory to help lower the cost of the batteries.[35] **Vertical integration** is a corporate-level strategy in which a company expands its business operations either backward into a new industry that produces inputs for the company's products (*backward vertical integration*) or forward into a new industry that uses, distributes, or sells the company's products (*forward vertical integration*).[36] A steel company that buys iron ore mines and enters the raw materials industry to supply the ore needed to make steel is engaging in backward vertical integration. A PC maker that decides to enter the retail industry and open a chain of company-owned retail outlets to sell its PCs is engaging in forward integration. For example, Apple entered the retail industry when it set up a chain of Apple stores to sell its computers and other mobile devices.

Figure 6.6 illustrates the four main stages in a typical raw material to customer value chain; value is added to the product at each stage by the activities involved in each industry. For a company based in the assembly stage, backward integration would involve establishing a new division in the intermediate manufacturing or raw material production industries; and forward integration would involve establishing

Figure 6.6

Stages in a Vertical Value Chain

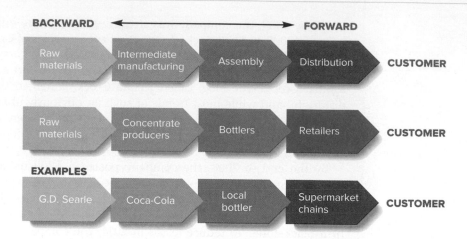

a new division to distribute its products to wholesalers or a retail division to sell directly to customers. A division at one stage or one industry receives the product produced by the division in the previous stage or industry, transforms it in some way—adding value—and then transfers the output at a higher price to the division at the next stage in the chain.

As an example of how this industry value chain works, consider the cola segment of the soft drink industry. In the raw material industry, suppliers include sugar companies and manufacturers of artificial sweeteners such as NutraSweet and Splenda, which are used in diet colas. These companies sell their products to companies in the soft drink industry that make concentrate—such as Coca-Cola and PepsiCo, which mix these inputs with others to produce the cola concentrate. In the process, they add value to these inputs. The concentrate producers then sell the concentrate to companies in the bottling and distribution industry, which add carbonated water to the concentrate and package the resulting drinks—again adding value to the concentrate. Next the bottlers distribute and sell the soft drinks to retailers, including stores such as Costco and Walmart and fast-food chains such as McDonald's. Companies in the retail industry add value by making the product accessible to customers, and they profit from direct sales to customers. Thus value is added by companies at each stage in the raw material to consumer chain.

The reason managers pursue vertical integration is that it allows them either to add value to their products by making them special or unique or to lower the costs of making and selling them. An example of using forward vertical integration to increase differentiation is Apple's decision to open its own stores to make its unique products more accessible to customers who could try them out before they bought them. So too is Coca-Cola and PepsiCo's decision to buy their bottlers so they can better differentiate their products and lower costs in the future.

Although vertical integration can strengthen an organization's competitive advantage and increase its performance, it can also reduce an organization's flexibility to respond to changing environmental conditions and create threats that must be countered by changing the organization's strategy. For example, when Procter & Gamble acquired the Gillette Company in 2005, Duracell batteries, a vertical integration for Gillette, came with it. However, Duracell stood out as an oddball among the other products in P&G's portfolio, and some analysts suggested that P&G sell off Duracell, which it did in 2014 to Warren Buffett's Berkshire Hathaway for $3 billion.[37]

Thus, when considering vertical integration as a strategy to add value, managers must be careful because sometimes it may *reduce* a company's ability to create value when the environment changes. This is why so many companies have divested themselves of units that draw attention and resources away from an organization's primary purpose.

Diversification

diversification

Expanding a company's business operations into a new industry in order to produce new kinds of valuable goods or services.

related diversification

Entering a new business or industry to create a competitive advantage in one or more of an organization's existing divisions or businesses.

synergy Performance gains that result when individuals and departments coordinate their actions.

Diversification is the corporate-level strategy of expanding a company's business operations into a new industry in order to produce new kinds of valuable goods or services.[38] Examples include PepsiCo's diversification into the snack food business with the purchase of Frito Lay, and Cisco's diversification into consumer electronics when it purchased Linksys. There are two main kinds of diversification: related and unrelated.

RELATED DIVERSIFICATION Related diversification is the strategy of entering a new business or industry to create a competitive advantage in one or more of an organization's existing divisions or businesses. Related diversification can add value to an organization's products if managers can find ways for its various divisions or business units to share their valuable skills or resources so that synergy is created.[39] Synergy is obtained when the value created by two divisions cooperating is greater than the value that would be created if the two divisions operated separately and independently. For example, suppose two or more divisions of a diversified company can use the same manufacturing facilities, distribution channels, or advertising campaigns—that is, share functional activities. Each division has to invest fewer resources in a shared functional activity than it would have to invest if it performed the functional activity by itself. Related diversification can be a major source of cost savings when divisions share the costs of performing a functional activity.[40] Similarly, if one division's R&D skills can improve another division's products and increase their differentiated appeal, this synergy can give the second division an important competitive advantage over its industry rivals—so the company as a whole benefits from diversification.

The way Procter & Gamble's disposable diaper and paper towel divisions cooperate is a good example of the successful production of synergies. These divisions share the costs of procuring inputs such as paper and packaging; a joint sales force sells both products to retail outlets; and both products are shipped using the same distribution system. This resource sharing has enabled both divisions to reduce their costs, and as a result, they can charge lower prices than their competitors and so attract more customers.[41] In addition, the divisions can share the research costs of developing new and improved products, such as finding more absorbent material, that increase both products' differentiated appeal. This is something that is also at the heart of 3M's corporate strategy. From the beginning, 3M has pursued related diversification and created new businesses by leveraging its skills in research and development. Today the company has five business groups that share resources such as technology and marketing. The five groups are industrial, consumer, safety and graphics, health care, and electronics and energy. In 2014, the company spent more than 5% of revenue on research and development. By 2017, 3M expects to spend 6% of revenue on research and development and see about 40% of revenue come from products launched over the past five years.[42]

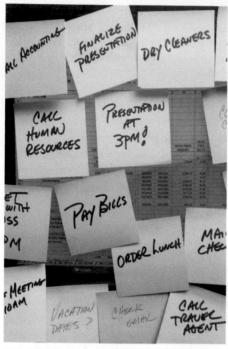

How did we ever survive without Post-it Notes? 3M's intense focus on solving customer problems results in new products that sell well, including countless variations of the original sticky note.
© Bill Varie/Corbis

How does 3M do it? First, the company is a science-based enterprise with a strong tradition of innovation and risk taking. Risk taking is encouraged and failure is not punished but is seen as a natural part of the process of creating new products and business. Second, 3M's management is relentlessly focused on the company's customers and the problems they face. Many of 3M's products have come from helping customers to solve difficult problems. Third, managers set stretch goals that require the company to create new products and businesses at a rapid rate. Fourth, employees are given considerable autonomy to pursue their own ideas; indeed, 15% of employees' time can be spent working on projects of their own choosing without management approval. Many products have resulted from this autonomy, including the ubiquitous Post-it Notes. Fifth, while products belong to business units and business units are responsible for generating profits, the technologies belong to every unit within the company. Anyone at 3M is free to try to develop new applications for a technology developed by its business units. Finally, 3M organizes many companywide meetings where researchers from its different divisions are brought together to share the results of their work.[43] Whether a company such as PepsiCo should keep its businesses together or split is discussed in the accompanying "Management Insight" feature.

MANAGEMENT INSIGHT

Would You Like Some Fritos with That Diet Pepsi?

The story of PepsiCo is a bit fizzy. The company's history tells a tale of related and unrelated diversification. Best known for the soda from which it gets its name, it was founded as the Pepsi-Cola Company in 1902. It merged with Frito-Lay, Inc., in 1965 to become PepsiCo. Along the way, it has diversified into many products related and unrelated to its beverage and packaged snack-food businesses. For example, in unrelated diversification, the company once owned several restaurant chains such as Pizza Hut, Taco Bell, and KFC. The company divested itself of its fast-food division in 1997. Two examples of related diversification include the 1998 purchase of Tropicana and the 2001 purchase of Quaker Oats. The purchase of Tropicana diversified PepsiCo's beverage portfolio to include juices. The purchase of the Quaker Oats Company was mainly to obtain the sports drink Gatorade, which Quaker owned. This purchase further diversified PepsiCo's beverage portfolio to include sports drinks. Also, the acquisition of Quaker's breakfast cereal, pasta, and rice business was not completely unrelated to the Frito-Lay snack-food division.[44]

Not everyone believes the products in PepsiCo's current portfolio are closely related, however. Activist investor Nelson Peltz would like to see PepsiCo split its beverage and food units apart. He argues that the two units would be stronger apart than they are together. "A stand-alone snacks business would offer investors strong growth in sales, margins and free cash flow generation," he said. "And a stand-alone beverage business would provide strong, stable, free cash flow that may be optimized through an effective balance sheet and capital return program."[45] A *Wall Street Journal* survey released in 2014 indicated that the majority of institutional investors support splitting up the company.[46]

At least two powerful voices do not want to see the company split. Warren Buffet, chairman and chief executive officer of Berkshire Hathaway and someone to whom many investors will listen, said: "I think that Frito-Lay is an extremely good business. It's a better business than the soft drink business, but I think the soft drink business is a good business too, and I don't see any reason to split them up."[47]

The second powerful voice belongs to PepsiCo CEO Indra Nooyi, who has led the company since 2006. In her previous roles with the company, Nooyi directed the divestment of the restaurant businesses as well as the acquisition of Tropicana and Quaker Oats. Nooyi insists that beverages and snacks go together, both for consumers and for business logistics. She says that the company's broad portfolio of products and size helps bring shoppers into retailers' stores: "Our portfolio works, we have scale."[48]

For now, PepsiCo is keeping its beverage and food units together. But the arguments about whether these units are related or unrelated will likely continue.[49]

In sum, to pursue related diversification successfully, managers search for new businesses where they can use the existing skills and resources in their departments and divisions to create synergies, add value to new products and businesses, and improve their competitive position and that of the entire company. In addition, managers may try to acquire a company in a new industry because they believe it possesses skills and resources that will improve the performance of one or more of their existing divisions. If successful, such skill transfers can help an organization to lower its costs or better differentiate its products because they create synergies between divisions.

UNRELATED DIVERSIFICATION Managers pursue **unrelated diversification** when they establish divisions or buy companies in new industries that are *not* linked in any way to their current businesses or industries. One main reason for pursuing unrelated diversification is that sometimes managers can buy a poorly performing company, transfer their management skills to that company, turn around its business, and increase its performance—all of which create value.

Another reason for pursuing unrelated diversification is that purchasing businesses in different industries lets managers engage in *portfolio strategy*, which is apportioning financial resources among divisions to increase financial returns or spread risks among different businesses, much as individual investors do with their own portfolios. For example, managers may transfer funds from a rich division (a "cash cow") to a new and promising division (a "star") and, by appropriately allocating money between divisions, create value. Though used as a popular explanation in the 1980s for unrelated diversification, portfolio strategy ran into increasing criticism in the 1990s because it simply does not work.[50] Why? As managers expand the scope of their organization's operations and enter more and more industries, it becomes increasingly difficult for top managers to be knowledgeable about all of the organization's diverse businesses. Managers do not have the time to process all of the information required to adequately assess the strategy and performance of each division, and so the performance of the entire company often falls.

unrelated diversification

Entering a new industry or buying a company in a new industry that is not related in any way to an organization's current businesses or industries.

215

This problem has occurred at GE, as its then CEO Reg Jones commented: "I tried to review each business unit plan in great detail. This effort took untold hours and placed a tremendous burden on the corporate executive office. After a while I began to realize that no matter how hard we would work, we could not achieve the necessary in-depth understanding of the 40-odd business unit plans."[51] Unable to handle so much information, top managers are overwhelmed and eventually make important resource allocation decisions on the basis of only a superficial analysis of the competitive position of each division. This usually results in value being lost rather than created.[52]

Thus, although unrelated diversification can potentially create value for a company, research evidence suggests that *too much* diversification can cause managers to lose control of their organization's core business. As a result, diversification can reduce value rather than create it.[53] Because of this, during the last decade there has been an increasing trend for diversified companies to divest many of their unrelated, and sometimes related, divisions. Managers in companies such as Tyco, Dial, and Textron have sold off many or most of their divisions and focused on increasing the performance of the core division that remained—in other words, they went back to a strategy of concentrating on a single industry.[54] In 2014, Honeywell International announced it would divest its brake pad and braking system components business to better focus its corporate objectives on the company's core technologies. Before the announcement, Honeywell's 2014 outlook was lukewarm at best. After the announcement, the company said it expected earnings growth of between 8% and 12%.[55]

International Expansion

As if planning whether to vertically integrate, diversify, or concentrate on the core business were not a difficult enough task, corporate-level managers also must decide on the appropriate way to compete internationally. A basic question confronts the managers of any organization that needs to sell its products abroad and compete in more than one national market: To what extent should the organization customize features of its products and marketing campaign to different national conditions?

If managers decide that their organization should sell the same standardized product in each national market in which it competes, and use the same basic marketing approach, they adopt a **global strategy**. Such companies undertake little, if any, customization to suit the specific needs of customers in different countries. But if managers decide to customize products and marketing strategies to specific national conditions, they adopt a **multidomestic strategy**. Panasonic has traditionally pursued a global strategy, selling the same basic TVs, camcorders, and DVD and MP3 players in every country in which it does business and often using the same basic marketing approach. Unilever, the European food and household products company, has pursued a multidomestic strategy. Thus, to appeal to German customers, for example, Unilever's German division sells a different range of food products and uses a different marketing approach than its North American division.

Both global and multidomestic strategies have advantages and disadvantages. The major advantage of a global strategy is the significant cost savings associated with not having to customize products and marketing approaches to different national conditions. For example, Rolex watches, Ralph Lauren or Tommy Hilfiger clothing, Chanel or Armani clothing or accessories or perfume, Dell computers, Chinese-made plastic toys and buckets, and U.S.-grown rice and wheat are all products that can be sold using the same marketing across many countries by simply changing

global strategy
Selling the same standardized product and using the same basic marketing approach in each national market.

multidomestic strategy Customizing products and marketing strategies to specific national conditions.

the language. Thus, companies can save a significant amount of money. The major disadvantage of pursuing a global strategy is that by ignoring national differences, managers may leave themselves vulnerable to local competitors that differentiate their products to suit local tastes.

Global food makers Kellogg's and Nestlé learned this when they entered the Indian processed food market, which is worth more than $100 billion a year. These companies did not understand how to customize their products to the tastes of the Indian market and initially suffered large losses. When Kellogg's launched its breakfast cereals in India, for example, it failed to understand that most Indians eat cooked breakfasts because milk is normally not pasteurized. Today, with the growing availability of pasteurized or canned milk, it offers exotic cereals made from basmati rice and flavored with mango to appeal to customers. Similarly, Nestlé's Maggi noodles failed to please Indian customers until it gave them a "marsala" or mixed curry spice flavor; today its noodles have become a staple in Indian school lunches.[56]

The advantages and disadvantages of a multidomestic strategy are the opposite of those of a global strategy. The major advantage of a multidomestic strategy is that by customizing product offerings and marketing approaches to local conditions, managers may be able to gain market share or charge higher prices for their products. The major disadvantage is that customization raises production costs and puts the multidomestic company at a price disadvantage because it often has to charge prices higher than the prices charged by competitors pursuing a global strategy. Obviously the choice between these two strategies calls for trade-offs.

Managers at Gillette, the well-known razor blade maker that is now part of Procter & Gamble (P&G), created a strategy that combined the best features of both international strategies. Like P&G, Gillette has always been a global organization because its managers quickly saw the advantages of selling its core product, razor blades, in as many countries as possible. Gillette's strategy over the years has been pretty constant: Find a new country with a growing market for razor blades, form a strategic alliance with a local razor blade company and take a majority stake in it, invest in a large marketing campaign, and then build a modern factory to make razor blades and other products for the local market. For example, when Gillette entered Russia after the breakup of the Soviet Union, it saw a huge opportunity to increase sales. It formed a joint venture with a local company called Leninets Concern, which made a razor known as the Sputnik, and then with this base began to import its own brands into Russia. When sales grew sharply, Gillette decided to offer more products in the market and built a new plant in St. Petersburg.[57]

In establishing factories in countries where labor and other costs are low and then distributing and marketing its products to countries in that region of the world, Gillette pursued a global strategy. However, all of Gillette's research and development and design activities are located in the United States. As it develops new kinds of razors, it equips its foreign factories to manufacture them when it decides that local customers are ready to trade up to the new product. So, for example, Gillette's latest

The offices of Hindustan Lever Limited in Mumbai, India. Unilever uses a multidomestic strategy to market its products globally.
© Indranil Mukherjee/AFP/Getty Images

razor may be introduced in a country abroad years later than in the United States. Thus Gillette customizes its products to the needs of different countries and so also pursues a multidomestic strategy.

By pursuing this kind of international strategy, Gillette achieves low costs and still differentiates and customizes its product range to suit the needs of each country or world region. P&G pursues a similar international strategy, and the merger between them to create the world's largest consumer products company came about because of the value that could be realized by pursuing related diversification at a global level. For example, P&G's corporate managers realized that substantial global synergies could be obtained by combining their global manufacturing, distribution, and sales operations across countries and world regions. These synergies have saved billions of dollars. At the same time, by pooling their knowledge of the needs of customers in different countries, the combined companies can better differentiate and position products throughout the world. P&G's strategy continues to work. *Fortune* recently named the company to its World's Most Admired Companies list for 2015.[58]

CHOOSING A WAY TO EXPAND INTERNATIONALLY As we have discussed, a more competitive global environment has proved to be both an opportunity and a threat for organizations and managers. The opportunity is that organizations that expand globally can open new markets, reach more customers, and gain access to new sources of raw materials and to low-cost suppliers of inputs. The threat is that organizations that expand globally are likely to encounter new competitors in the foreign countries they enter and must respond to new political, economic, and cultural conditions.

Before setting up foreign operations, managers of companies such as Amazon.com, Lands' End, GE, P&G, and Boeing needed to analyze the forces in the environment of a particular country (such as Korea or Brazil) to choose the right method to expand and respond to those forces in the most appropriate way. In general, four basic ways to operate in the global environment are importing and exporting, licensing and franchising, strategic alliances, and wholly owned foreign subsidiaries, Gillette's preferred approach. We briefly discuss each one, moving from the lowest level of foreign involvement and investment required of a global organization and its managers, and the least amount of risk, to the high end of the spectrum (see Figure 6.7).

Importing and Exporting   The least complex global operations are exporting and importing. A company engaged in **exporting** makes products at home and sells them abroad. An organization might sell its own products abroad or allow a local organization in the foreign country to distribute its products. Few risks are associated with

exporting Making products at home and selling them abroad.

Figure 6.7

Four Ways to Expand Internationally

Level of foreign involvement and investment
and degree of risk

exporting because a company does not have to invest in developing manufacturing facilities abroad. It can further reduce its investment abroad if it allows a local company to distribute its products.

importing Selling products at home that are made abroad.

A company engaged in **importing** sells products at home that are made abroad (products it makes itself or buys from other companies). For example, most of the products that Pier 1 Imports and The Limited sell to their customers are made abroad. In many cases the appeal of a product—Irish crystal, French wine, Italian furniture, or Indian silk—is that it is made abroad. The Internet has made it much easier for companies to tell potential foreign buyers about their products; detailed product specifications and features are available online, and informed buyers can communicate easily with prospective sellers.

licensing Allowing a foreign organization to take charge of manufacturing and distributing a product in its country or world region in return for a negotiated fee.

LICENSING AND FRANCHISING In **licensing**, a company (the licenser) allows a foreign organization (the licensee) to take charge of both manufacturing and distributing one or more of its products in the licensee's country or world region in return for a negotiated fee. Chemical maker DuPont might license a local factory in India to produce nylon or Teflon. The advantage of licensing is that the licenser does not have to bear the development costs associated with opening up in a foreign country; the licensee bears the costs. The risks associated with this strategy are that the company granting the license has to give its foreign partner access to its technological know-how and so risks losing control of its secrets.

franchising Selling to a foreign organization the rights to use a brand name and operating know-how in return for a lump-sum payment and a share of the profits.

Whereas licensing is pursued primarily by manufacturing companies, franchising is pursued primarily by service organizations. In **franchising**, a company (the franchiser) sells to a foreign organization (the franchisee) the rights to use its brand name and operating know-how in return for a lump-sum payment and share of the franchiser's profits. Hilton Hotels might sell a franchise to a local company in Chile to operate hotels under the Hilton name in return for a franchise payment. The advantage of franchising is that the franchiser does not have to bear the development costs of overseas expansion and avoids the many problems associated with setting up foreign operations. The downside is that the organization that grants the franchise may lose control over how the franchisee operates, and product quality may fall. In this way franchisers, such as Hilton, Avis, and McDonald's, risk losing their good names. American customers who buy McDonald's hamburgers in Korea may reasonably expect those burgers to be as good as the ones they get at home. If they are not, McDonald's reputation will suffer over time. Once again, the Internet facilitates communication between partners and allows them to better meet each other's expectations.

strategic alliance An agreement in which managers pool or share their organization's resources and know-how with a foreign company, and the two organizations share the rewards and risks of starting a new venture.

STRATEGIC ALLIANCES One way to overcome the loss-of-control problems associated with exporting, licensing, and franchising is to expand globally by means of a strategic alliance. In a **strategic alliance**, managers pool or share their organization's resources and know-how with those of a foreign company, and the two organizations share the rewards or risks of starting a new venture in a foreign country. Sharing resources allows a U.S. company, for example, to take advantage of the high-quality skills of foreign manufacturers and the specialized knowledge of foreign managers about the needs of local customers and to reduce the risks involved in a venture. At the same time, the terms of the alliance give the U.S. company more control over how the good or service is produced or sold in the foreign country than it would have as a franchiser or licenser.

joint venture
A strategic alliance among two or more companies that agree to jointly establish and share the ownership of a new business.

A strategic alliance can take the form of a written contract between two or more companies to exchange resources, or it can result in the creation of a new organization. A **joint venture** is a strategic alliance among two or more companies that agree to jointly establish and share the ownership of a new business.[59] An organization's level of involvement abroad increases in a joint venture because the alliance normally involves a capital investment in production facilities abroad in order to produce goods or services outside the home country. Risk, however, is reduced. The Internet and global teleconferencing provide the increased communication and coordination necessary for global partners to work together. For example, Coca-Cola and Nestlé formed a joint venture to market Nestea in more than 52 markets worldwide.[60] Recently, Avon and KORRES, a Greek natural skin care company, entered into a long-term strategic alliance in which Avon will manufacture and market KORRES products in Latin America. Although Avon is already established in Latin America, adding KORRES products will allow Avon to pursue the natural and organic beauty market.[61]

wholly owned foreign subsidiary
Production operations established in a foreign country independent of any local direct involvement.

WHOLLY OWNED FOREIGN SUBSIDIARIES When managers decide to establish a **wholly owned foreign subsidiary**, they invest in establishing production operations in a foreign country independent of any local direct involvement. Many Japanese car component companies, for example, have established their own operations in the United States to supply U.S.-based Japanese carmakers such as Toyota and Honda with high-quality car components.

Operating alone, without any direct involvement from foreign companies, an organization receives all of the rewards and bears all of the risks associated with operating abroad.[62] This method of international expansion is much more expensive than the others because it requires a higher level of foreign investment and presents managers with many more threats. However, investment in a foreign subsidiary or division offers significant advantages: It gives an organization high potential returns because the organization does not have to share its profits with a foreign organization, and it reduces the level of risk because the organization's managers have full control over all aspects of their foreign subsidiary's operations. Moreover, this type of investment allows managers to protect their technology and know-how from foreign organizations. Large well-known companies such as DuPont, GM, and P&G, which have plenty of resources, make extensive use of wholly owned subsidiaries.

Obviously, global companies can use many of these different corporate strategies simultaneously to create the most value and strengthen their competitive position. We discussed earlier how P&G pursues related diversification at the global level while it pursues an international strategy that is a mixture of global and multidomestic. P&G also pursues vertical integration: It operates factories that make many of the specialized chemicals used in its products; it operates in the container industry and makes the thousands of different glass and plastic bottles and jars that contain its products; it prints its own product labels; and it distributes its products using its own fleet of trucks. Although P&G is highly diversified, it still puts the focus on its core individual product lines because it is famous for pursuing brand management—it concentrates resources around each brand, which in effect is managed as a "separate company." So P&G is trying to add value in every way it can from its corporate and business strategies.

At the business level P&G aggressively pursues differentiation and charges premium prices for its products. However, it also strives to lower its costs and pursues the corporate-level strategies just discussed to achieve this.

Planning and Implementing Strategy

LO 6-4 Describe the vital role managers play in implementing strategies to achieve an organization's mission and goals.

After identifying appropriate business and corporate strategies to attain an organization's mission and goals, managers confront the challenge of putting those strategies into action. Strategy implementation is a five-step process:

1. Allocating responsibility for implementation to the appropriate individuals or groups.
2. Drafting detailed action plans that specify how a strategy is to be implemented.
3. Establishing a timetable for implementation that includes precise, measurable goals linked to the attainment of the action plan.
4. Allocating appropriate resources to the responsible individuals or groups.
5. Holding specific individuals or groups responsible for the attainment of corporate, divisional, and functional goals.

The planning process goes beyond just identifying effective strategies; it also includes plans to ensure that these strategies are put into action. Normally the plan for implementing a new strategy requires the development of new functional strategies, the redesign of an organization's structure, and the development of new control systems; it might also require a new program to change an organization's culture. These are issues we address in the next three chapters.

Summary and Review

PLANNING Planning is a three-step process: (1) determining an organization's mission and goals; (2) formulating strategy; and (3) implementing strategy. Managers use planning to identify and select appropriate goals and courses of action for an organization and to decide how to allocate the resources they need to attain those goals and carry out those actions. A good plan builds commitment for the organization's goals, gives the organization a sense of direction and purpose, coordinates the different functions and divisions of the organization, and controls managers by making them accountable for specific goals. In large organizations planning takes place at three levels: corporate, business or divisional, and functional or departmental. Long-term plans have a time horizon of five years or more; intermediate-term plans, between one and five years; and short-term plans, one year or less. **[LO 6-1]**

DETERMINING MISSION AND GOALS AND FORMULATING STRATEGY Determining the organization's mission requires that managers define the business of the organization and establish major goals. Strategy formulation requires that managers perform a SWOT analysis and then choose appropriate strategies at the corporate, business, and functional levels. At the business level, managers are responsible for developing a successful low-cost and/or differentiation strategy, either for the whole market or a particular segment of it. At the functional level, departmental managers develop strategies to help the organization either add value to its products by differentiating them or lower the costs of value creation. At the corporate level, organizations use strategies such as concentration on a single industry, vertical integration, related and unrelated diversification, and international expansion to strengthen their competitive advantage by increasing the value of the goods and services provided to customers. **[LO 6-1, 6-2, 6-3]**

IMPLEMENTING STRATEGY Strategy implementation requires that managers allocate responsibilities to appropriate individuals or groups; draft detailed action plans that specify how a strategy is to be implemented; establish a timetable for implementation that includes precise, measurable goals linked to the attainment of the action plan; allocate appropriate resources to the responsible individuals or groups; and hold individuals or groups accountable for the attainment of goals. **[LO 6-4]**

Management *in Action*

TOPICS FOR DISCUSSION AND ACTION

Discussion

1. Describe the three steps of planning. Explain how they are related. **[LO 6-1]**

2. What is the relationship among corporate-, business-, and functional-level strategies, and how do they create value for an organization? **[LO 6-2, 6-3]**

3. Pick an industry and identify four companies in the industry that pursue one of the four main business-level strategies (low-cost, focused low-cost, etc.). **[LO 6-1, 6-2]**

4. What is the difference between vertical integration and related diversification? **[LO 6-3]**

Action

5. Ask a manager about the kinds of planning exercises he or she regularly uses. What are the purposes of these exercises, and what are their advantages or disadvantages? **[LO 6-1]**

6. Ask a manager to identify the corporate- and business-level strategies used by his or her organization. **[LO 6-2, 6-3]**

BUILDING MANAGEMENT SKILLS

How to Analyze a Company's Strategy   [LO 6-2, 6-3]

Pick a well-known business organization that has received recent media coverage and that provides its annual reports on its website. From the information in the media and annual reports, answer the following questions:

1. What is (are) the main industry(ies) in which the company competes?

2. What business-level strategy does the company seem to be pursuing in this industry? Why?

3. What corporate-level strategies is the company pursuing? Why?

4. Have there been any major changes in its strategy recently? Why?

MANAGING ETHICALLY   [LO 6-1, 6-4]

A few years ago, IBM announced that it had fired the three top managers of its Argentine division because of their involvement in a scheme to secure a $250 million contract for IBM to provide and service the computers of one of Argentina's largest state-owned banks. The three executives paid

$14 million of the contract money to a third company, CCR, which paid nearly $6 million to phantom companies. This $6 million was then used to bribe the bank executives who agreed to give IBM the contract.

These bribes are not necessarily illegal under Argentine law. Moreover, the three managers argued that all companies have to pay bribes to get new business contracts and they were not doing anything that managers in other companies were not.

Questions

1. Either by yourself or in a group, decide if the business practice of paying bribes is ethical or unethical.

2. Should IBM allow its foreign divisions to pay bribes if all other companies are doing so?

3. If bribery is common in a particular country, what effect would this likely have on the nation's economy and culture?

SMALL GROUP BREAKOUT EXERCISE [LO 6-1, 6-2]
Low Cost or Differentiation?

Form groups of three or four people, and appoint one member as the spokesperson who will communicate your findings to the class when called on by the instructor. Then discuss the following scenario.

You are a team of managers of a major national clothing chain, and you have been charged with finding a way to restore your organization's competitive advantage. Recently, your organization has been experiencing increasing competition from two sources. First, discount stores such as Walmart and Target have been undercutting your prices because they buy their clothes from low-cost foreign manufacturers while you buy most of yours from high-quality domestic suppliers. Discount stores have been attracting your customers who buy at the low end of the price range. Second, small boutiques opening in malls provide high-price designer clothing and are attracting your customers at the high end of the market. Your company has become stuck in the middle, and you have to decide what to do: Should you start to buy abroad so that you can lower your prices and begin to pursue a low-cost strategy? Should you focus on the high end of the market and become more of a differentiator? Or should you try to pursue both a low-cost strategy and a differentiation strategy?

1. Using SWOT analysis, analyze the pros and cons of each alternative.

2. Think about the various clothing retailers in your local malls and city, and analyze the choices they have made about how to compete with one another along the low-cost and differentiation dimensions.

BE THE MANAGER [LO 6-1, 6-2]

A group of investors in your city is considering opening a new upscale supermarket to compete with the major supermarket chains that are currently dominating the city's marketplace. They have called you in to help them determine what kind of upscale supermarket they should open. In other words, how can they best develop a competitive advantage against existing supermarket chains?

Questions

1. List the supermarket chains in your city, and identify their strengths and weaknesses.

2. What business-level strategies are these supermarkets currently pursuing?

3. What kind of supermarket would do best against the competition? What kind of business-level strategy should it pursue?

"Our industry does not respect tradition. It only respects innovation," Satya Nadella said in February 2014 when he was appointed chief executive officer of Microsoft. After 39 years, the company Bill Gates co-founded had come to be perceived as an out-of-touch behemoth that relied too much on its Windows operating system and failed to move into new markets, like mobile. Key products such as Microsoft Office—the suite of applications that includes Word and Excel—had been designed around Windows, with only parts converted to work on Apple's iOS and Google's Android systems. Nadella's accession would be a chance to reorient the company, getting it to introduce products that looked outside Windows and to develop new business models.

Nadella has aggressively pursued this course. Since December, Microsoft has bought two small companies that focus on mobile productivity apps for iOS and Android phones and tablets. To appeal to younger users, the company last September purchased Mojang, maker of the popular Minecraft video game, for $2.5 billion, and it's adding features to Windows such as 3D holograms that users view through a headset and control with hand gestures. The newest version of Microsoft's Power BI (business intelligence) product—a dashboard for data analysis—was released in January, first for iOS systems. "Microsoft hasn't really shown any sort of vision like this in a long, long time," Michael Silver, an analyst at Gartner and longtime Microsoft watcher, said in January when it unveiled the holograms. "All it took was replacing the senior management."

In Nadella's first year, Microsoft stock rose 14 percent, and sales increased 12 percent. The new CEO, unlike his predecessor Steve Ballmer, is popular with investors, venture capitalists, and startups. Even employees like Nadella, surprising for a chief executive who signed off on the largest layoffs in Microsoft's history—18,000 job cuts were announced last July. Staff say they appreciate Nadella's strategy shifts and attempts to make the company leaner and less bureaucratic.

The big issue Nadella faces is how to generate more revenue with new software and features, such as cloud subscriptions and free apps replacing pricey Windows and Office licenses. Revenue is projected to increase 8.6 percent, to $94.3 billion, this fiscal year, slowing from last year's double-digit growth, according to data compiled by Bloomberg. "He's hit all the low-hanging fruit—that said, these things were not easy to do," says Brad Silverberg, a venture capitalist and former Microsoft executive.

"Where there are execution issues, we will address them," Nadella said on a conference call in January. "Where there are macroeconomic issues, we will weather them." Microsoft declined to make Nadella available for an interview.

Windows, which once dominated computing and ran on more than 90 percent of computing devices, now runs on 11 percent of computers and gadgets, according to a report from Sanford C. Bernstein. Nadella and Windows chief Terry Myerson are looking at ways to update the software.

Nadella uses the Power BI dashboard to track and compile huge amounts of information on product usage and financial performance to see what works and what doesn't, says James Phillips, general manager of the product. Nadella also measures and coordinates executive performance with metrics from the dashboard. "Satya has been leading the charge for everyone in the company to be more data-oriented," says Chief Strategy Officer Mark Penn.

Microsoft's quarterly earnings report in January highlights the hurdles Nadella faces. While cloud software sales to businesses more than doubled in the quarter that ended Dec. 31, sales of traditional Office and Windows software to companies fell short of analysts' estimates. Windows sales to personal computer makers who put the program on their machines dropped 13 percent. In total, profit declined 11 percent from the previous year, to $5.86 billion, while sales rose 8 percent, to $26.5 billion.

Revenue is being hurt by fluctuating currencies, while the Chinese government is investigating Microsoft over alleged anticompetitive practices and seeking to end purchases of its software. The government of Russian President Vladimir Putin says it wants to reduce reliance on Microsoft.

Internally, Nadella and his executives make the point whenever they can that the day could come when new and younger generations of computer and software users might not use its products. At one board meeting last year, Windows chief Myerson showed a slide with pictures of students using Apple Macs and iPads, according to Microsoft spokesman Peter Wootton.

In 2014, Nadella told employees at a town hall that they should skip meetings if they don't really need to be there. And he's advised workers to come to him directly if they feel the bureaucracy is stifling. "The organization knows it's go-time," says Phillips. "There are changes in the market we need to respond to."

Nadella's also changed the way engineering teams are structured, eliminating testers to speed up software releases and adding data scientists and designers to the teams. He's looking at cutting some middle managers to make decisions faster and to eliminate layers of bureaucracy, Wootton says.

Eli Lilly Chief Technology Officer Mike Meadows says Microsoft is more open and listening to what customers need. He was glad to see the company demonstrate its products on iPads at Microsoft's chief information officer conference last fall—Lilly's 20,000 salespeople use Apple tablets, Meadows says. "They're starting to demonstrate more understanding of reality," he says. "They would say, 'We were going in this direction already,' but Satya lit a fire."

The bottom line: Nadella is working to push Microsoft out of its Windows slump and into cloud computing and apps for iOS and Android.

Questions

1. What kind of planning missteps helped cause Microsoft's decline over the past few years?

2. How is Nadella trying to eliminate some of the bureaucracy that has hurt the company's ability to innovate?

3. What business strategies has Nadella implemented that will help revitalize the technology giant?

Source: Dina Bass, "Microsoft CEO Satya Nadella Looks to Future Beyond Windows," *Bloomberg Business*, February 19, 2015, www.bloomberg.com.

Endnotes

1. Company website, "Toys 'R' Us, Inc. Reports Results for Fourth Quarter and Full Year Fiscal 2013," press release, and "Toys 'R' Us, Inc. Outlines 'TRU Transformation' Strategy," press release, www.toysrusinc.com, accessed March 31, 2015.

2. Company website, "Toys 'R' Us, Inc. Provides 'TRU Transformation' Strategic Update," press release, www.toysrusinc.com, accessed March 31, 2015.

3. A. Chandler, *Strategy and Structure: Chapters in the History of the American Enterprise* (Cambridge, MA: MIT Press, 1962).

4. Ibid.

5. H. Fayol, *General and Industrial Management* (1884; New York: IEEE Press, 1984).

6. Ibid., 18.

7. Company website, "2014 GE Annual Report," www.ge.com, accessed March 23, 2015; GE Ventures, "Why Work with Us," www.geventures.com, accessed March 23, 2015.

8. Reuters, "GE Expected to Win EU Approval for $14 Billion Alstom Deal," *Fortune*, accessed September 1, 2015, http://fortune.com.

9. www.ge.com, 2015.

10. Organization website, "NASA Announces Mars 2020 Rover Payload to Explore the Red Planet As Never Before," www.nasa.gov, accessed March 23, 2015.

11. J. A. Pearce, "The Company Mission as a Strategic Tool," *Sloan Management Review*, Spring 1992, 15–24.

12. D. F. Abell, *Defining the Business: The Starting Point of Strategic Planning* (Englewood Cliffs, NJ: Prentice-Hall, 1980).

13. G. Hamel and C. K. Prahalad, "Strategic Intent," *Harvard Business Review*, May–June 1989, 63–73.

14. D. I. Jung and B. J. Avolio, "Opening the Black Box: An Experimental Investigation of the Mediating Effects of Trust and Value Congruence on Transformational and Transactional Leadership," *Journal of Organizational Behavior*, December 2000, 949–64; B. M. Bass and B. J. Avolio, "Transformational and Transactional Leadership: 1992 and Beyond," *Journal of European Industrial Training*, January 1990, 20–35.

15. J. Porras and J. Collins, *Built to Last: Successful Habits of Visionary Companies* (New York: HarperCollins, 1994).

16. E. A. Locke, G. P. Latham, and M. Erez, "The Determinants of Goal Commitment," *Academy of Management Review* 13 (1988), 23–39.

17. M. Watrous, "Breakfast a Bright Spot for Yum!" *Food Business News*, accessed March 24, 2015, www.foodbusinessnews.net.

18. M. Burden, "GM CEO: Behavior Change Will Improve Company," *The Detroit News*, accessed March 24, 2015, www.detroitnews.com; M. Wolff, "GM's Barra Shames Voiceless CEOs," *USA Today*, accessed March 24, 2015, www.usatoday.com.

19. J. Jelter, "GM CEO Mary Barra on Recalls: We Have to Own It," *Market Watch*, accessed March 24, 2014, http://blogs.marketwatch.com.

20. P. Sellers, "Car Talk (and More!) with Mary Barra, GM's New Chief," *Fortune*, accessed March 24, 2015, http://fortune.com.

21. J. Ellingworth, "General Motors Beats a Retreat Out of Russia," *Yahoo Finance*, accessed March 24, 2015, http://finance.yahoo.com.

22. N. Bromey, "GM's Mary Barra Earning High Marks for Response to Ignition-Recall Crisis," *Detroit Free Press*, accessed March 24, 2015, www.freep.com.

23. "General Motors' CEO Discusses Q4 2013 Results—Earnings Call Transcript," *Yahoo Finance,* accessed March 24, 2015, http://finance.yahoo.com.

24. R. D. Aveni, *Hypercompetition* (New York: Free Press, 1994).

25. M. E. Porter, *Competitive Strategy* (New York: Free Press, 1980).

26. Company website, "About Southwest: Mission," www.southwest.com, accessed March 25, 2015.

27. S. Grobart, "Tim Cook: The Complete Interview," *Bloomberg Businessweek,* accessed March 25, 2015, www.bloomberg.com.

28. Porter, *Competitive Strategy.*

29. Company website, "Zara Brand," www.inditex.com, accessed March 25, 2015; G. Petro, "The Future of Fashion Retailing: The Zara Approach (Part 2 of 3)," *Forbes,* accessed March 25, 2015, www.forbes.com.

30. L. Cochrane, "Fashion: How the Global Market Is Changing Seasonal Collections," *The Guardian,* accessed March 25, 2015, www.theguardian.com.

31. Company website, "About Crocs," www.crocs.com, accessed March 25, 2015.

32. V. Ravina, "I Hate Crocs dot com," September 28, 2011, http://ihatecrocsblog.blogspot.com.

33. E. Volkman, "Are Crocs Coming Back in Style? Blackstone Group Thinks So," *Daily Finance,* March 7, 2014, www.dailyfinance.com; S. Kapner, "Crocs to Restructure, Cutting Jobs and Stores," *The Wall Street Journal,* accessed March 25, 2015, www.wsj.com.

34. Ben Geier, "You'll Never Believe How Many Pairs of Crocs Were Sold Last Year," *Fortune,* accessed April 8, 2015, http://fortune.com; "Gregg Ribatt Begins New Role as CEO of Crocs Inc.," *Market Watch,* accessed March 25, 2015, www.marketwatch.com.

35. M. Ramsey, "Will Tesla's $5 Billion Gigafactory Make a Battery Nobody Else Wants?" *The Wall Street Journal,* accessed March 25, 2015, http://blogs.wsj.com.

36. M. K. Perry, "Vertical Integration: Determinants and Effects," in R. Schmalensee and R. D. Willig, *Handbook of Industrial Organization,* vol. 1 (New York: Elsevier Science, 1989).

37. R. Collings, "Procter & Gamble's Duracell Is Sold for $3B," *The Deal Pipeline,* accessed March 26, 2015, www.thedeal.com.

38. E. Penrose, *The Theory of the Growth of the Firm* (Oxford: Oxford University Press, 1959).

39. M. E. Porter, "From Competitive Advantage to Corporate Strategy," *Harvard Business Review* 65 (1987), 43–59.

40. D. J. Teece, "Economies of Scope and the Scope of the Enterprise," *Journal of Economic Behavior and Organization* 3 (1980), 223–47.

41. M. E. Porter, *Competitive Advantage: Creating and Sustaining Superior Performance* (New York: Free Press, 1985).

42. Company website, www.3M.com, accessed March 25, 2015.

43. Company website, "2014 Annual Report," www.3M.com, accessed March 25, 2015.

44. Company website, "Our History," www.pepsico.com, accessed March 29, 2015.

45. M. Rocco, "Nelson Peltz Renews Call to Split PepsiCo," *Fox Business,* accessed March 29, 2015, www.foxbusiness.com.

46. L. Baertlein, "Most Investors in Survey Back Pepsi Split; Buffet Opposes," *Reuters,* accessed March 29, 2015, www.reuters.com.

47. Ibid.

48. P. Wahba, "PepsiCo CEO Says Bigger Is Better in Wooing Wal-Mart, Other Retailers," *Fortune,* accessed March 29, 2015, http://fortune.com.

49. P. Sellers, "Pepsi and Peltz Call a Truce—and Here's Who Wins," *Fortune,* accessed March 29, 2015, http://fortune.com.

50. For a review of the evidence, see C.W.L. Hill and G. R. Jones, *Strategic Management: An Integrated Approach,* 5th ed. (Boston: Houghton Mifflin, 2011), chap. 10.

51. C. R. Christensen et al., *Business Policy Text and Cases* (Homewood, IL: Irwin, 1987), 778.

52. C. W. L. Hill, "Conglomerate Performance over the Economic Cycle," *Journal of Industrial Economics* 32 (1983), 197–213.

53. V. Ramanujam and P. Varadarajan, "Research on Corporate Diversification: A Synthesis," *Strategic Management Journal* 10 (1989), 523–51. Also see A. Shleifer and R. W. Vishny, "Takeovers in the 1960s and 1980s: Evidence and Implications," in R. P. Rumelt, D. E. Schendel, and D. J. Teece, eds., *Fundamental Issues in Strategy* (Boston: Harvard Business School Press, 1994).

54. J. R. Williams, B. L. Paez, and L. Sanders, "Conglomerates Revisited," *Strategic Management Journal* 9 (1988), 403–14.

55. Zacks Equity Research, "Honeywell Q4 Earnings Beat by a Sliver," *Yahoo Finance,* accessed March 29, 2015, http://finance.yahoo.com; Zacks Equity Research, "Honeywell to Divest Friction Material Biz," *Yahoo Finance,* January 8, 2014, http://finance.yahoo.com.

56. "Noodles in India," *Euromonitor International,* accessed March 30, 2015, www.euromonitor.com.

57. "Gillette Co.'s New $40 Million Razor Blade Factory in St. Petersburg, Russia," *Boston Globe,* June 7, 2000, C6.

58. "Fortune Most Admired Companies: 2015," http://fortune.com, accessed March 30, 2015; company website, www.pg.com, accessed March 30, 2015.

59. B. Kogut, "Joint Ventures: Theoretical and Empirical Perspectives," *Strategic Management Journal* 9 (1988), 319–33.

60. Company overview, "BPW," https://www.linkedin.com, accessed March 30, 2015.

61. "Avon and KORRES Enter into Strategic Alliance in Latin America," *PR Newswire,* accessed March 30, 2015, www.prnewswire.com.

62. N. Hood and S. Young, *The Economics of the Multinational Enterprise* (London: Longman, 1979).

PART 4

7 Designing Organizational Structure

Learning Objectives

After studying this chapter, you should be able to:

LO 7-1 Identify the factors that influence managers' choice of an organizational structure.

LO 7-2 Explain how managers group tasks into jobs that are motivating and satisfying for employees.

LO 7-3 Describe the types of organizational structures managers can design, and explain why they choose one structure over another.

LO 7-4 Explain why managers must coordinate jobs, functions, and divisions using the hierarchy of authority and integrating mechanisms.

LO 7-5 Describe how information technology (IT) is helping managers build strategic alliances and network structures to increase efficiency and effectiveness.

© Image Source/Getty Images RF

MANAGEMENT SNAPSHOT

Disney Lets Studios Set Structure and Culture

How Can Organizational Structure Influence Employee Creativity?

What do Snow White, Iron Man, and Buzz Lightyear have in common? The studios that produced these movies are all owned by the Walt Disney Company. Disney owns several organizations, including Walt Disney Animation Studios, Marvel Studios, and Pixar Animation Studios.

While the three studios are all owned by the same company and roughly do the same thing (produce movies), they have different stories and different organizational cultures. Walt Disney Animation Studios is the oldest of the three, established by Walt and Roy Disney under the name Disney Brothers Cartoon Studio in 1923. Its first feature film was *Snow White and the Seven Dwarfs* in 1937. In 2013, it released its 53rd animated film, *Frozen,* which became the number one animated film of all time and the fifth-highest grossing film of all time.[1]

Marvel was founded in 1939 as Timely Publications. In 1941, it introduced the comic book *Captain America* with a cover picture of the hero punching Adolf Hitler. In 1991, Marvel Studios was established as a film production unit. Marvel has more than 8,000 characters, including the Avengers, Green Goblin, Iron Man, Spider-Man, and the X-Men. Most of these characters live in the Marvel universe, in fictional cities similar to New York and Los Angeles. The Walt Disney Company bought Marvel in 2009.[2] In 2002, investor and then-owner of Marvel Ronald Perelman said, "It is a mini-Disney in terms of intellectual property. Disney's got much more highly recognized characters and softer characters, whereas our characters are termed action heroes. But at Marvel we are now in the business of the creation and marketing of characters."[3]

Pixar Animation Studios was founded in 1979 as Graphics Group. It was originally the computer division of Lucasfilm and became its own corporation in 1986 with funding from Apple cofounder Steve Jobs. Its first feature film was *Toy Story* in 1995, which eventually was nominated for awards by the Academy of Motion Pictures Arts and Sciences.[4] The Walt Disney Company bought Pixar in 2006.

Although *Toy Story* was a success, Pixar cofounder Ed Catmull found there were structural issues within the company. Pixar had insisted that communication happen through proper hierarchical channels, which led to hard feelings between the creative and production departments. While working on *A Bug's Life,* the film that followed *Toy Story,* Pixar created a rule that anyone could talk to anyone else, regardless of level. The resulting communication structure helped Pixar foster a more creative culture.[5]

In his recently published book, *Creativity, Inc.: Overcoming the Unseen Forces That Stand in the Way of True Inspiration,* Catmull, now president of Walt Disney Animation Studios and Pixar, discussed the merger of Disney and Pixar. He said that when two organizations merge, there is typically a push to consolidate workflows and to reduce redundancies. However, when Disney and Pixar came together, they did something different.

"We took the exact opposite approach, which was to say to each studio, 'You may look at the tools that the other has, you may use them if you want, but the choice is entirely yours.' They each have a development group that's coming up with different ideas, but because we said, 'You don't have to take ideas from anybody else,' they felt freer to talk with each other."[6]

Yet some lessons from Pixar were applied at Disney, according to Catmull. When Pixar joined Disney in 2006, Disney employees were demoralized by a few lackluster film projects, including *Chicken Little* and *Home on the Range.* Pixar practices, such as creating an environment in which workers can be candid and where innovative ideas can move forward, were applied at Disney. After the ideas took hold, the studio produced several big hits, including *Tangled* and *Frozen.*[7]

"The one thing we were really adamant about was that the two studios not be integrated together. We established an absolute rule, which we still adhere to, that neither studio can do any production work for the other. For me, the local ownership is really important. We put in place mechanisms to keep each studio's culture unique," Catmull said. "It's a model that Bob's using at Marvel. Marvel has a completely different culture than Pixar does, or Disney Animation, and he lets them run it their way. You want to have mechanisms to bridge between them, but you don't interfere with that local culture."[8]

Overview

As the example of Disney Animation, Pixar, and Marvel Studios suggests, organizational culture is a powerful influence on how employees work. The way an organization's structure is designed also affects employee behavior and how well the organization functions. In a quickly changing global environment, managers at all levels of an organization must identify the best way to organize people and resources to increase efficiency and effectiveness.

organizational structure A formal system of task and reporting relationships that coordinates and motivates organizational members so that they work together to achieve organizational goals.

By the end of this chapter, you will be familiar with the main types of organizational structure as well as with the important factors that determine how managers design such structures. Then, in Chapter 8, we examine issues related to the design of an organization's control systems.

Designing Organizational Structure

Organizing is the process by which managers establish the structure of working relationships among employees to allow them to achieve organizational goals efficiently and effectively. **Organizational structure** is the formal system of task and job reporting relationships that determines how employees use resources to achieve organizational goals.[9] **Organizational design** is the process by which managers create a specific type of organizational structure and culture so a company can operate in the most efficient and effective way.[10]

LO7-1 Identify the factors that influence managers' choice of an organizational structure.

According to *contingency theory,* managers design organizational structures to fit the factors or circumstances that are affecting the company the most and causing them the most uncertainty.[11] Thus, there is no one best way to design an organization: Design reflects each organization's specific situation, and researchers have argued that in some situations stable, mechanistic structures may be most

Figure 7.1

Factors Affecting Organizational Structure

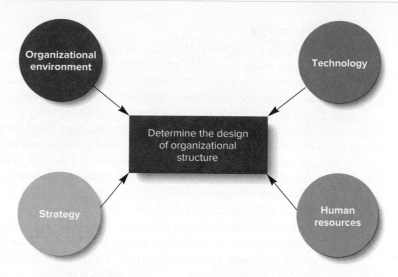

organizational design The process by which managers make specific organizing choices that result in a particular kind of organizational structure.

appropriate while in others flexible, organic structures might be the most effective. Four factors are important determinants of the type of organizational structure or organizing method managers select: the nature of the organizational environment, the type of strategy the organization pursues, the technology (and particularly *information technology*) the organization uses, and the characteristics of the organization's human resources (see Figure 7.1).[12]

The Organizational Environment

In general, the more quickly the external environment is changing and the greater the uncertainty within it, the greater are the problems facing managers in trying to gain access to scarce resources. In this situation, to speed decision making and communication and make it easier to obtain resources, managers typically make organizing choices that result in more flexible structures and entrepreneurial cultures.[13] They are likely to decentralize authority, empower lower-level employees to make important operating decisions, and encourage values and norms that emphasize change and innovation—a more organic form of organizing.

In contrast, if the external environment is stable, resources are readily available, and uncertainty is low, then less coordination and communication among people and functions are needed to obtain resources. Managers can make organizing choices that bring more stability or formality to the organizational structure and can establish values and norms that emphasize obedience and being a team player. Managers in this situation prefer to make decisions within a clearly defined hierarchy of authority and to use detailed rules, standard operating procedures (SOPs), and restrictive norms to guide and govern employees' activities—a more mechanistic form of organizing.

As we discussed in Chapter 4, change is rapid in today's global marketplace, and increasing competition both at home and abroad is putting greater pressure on managers to attract customers and increase efficiency and effectiveness. Consequently, interest in finding ways to structure organizations—such as through empowerment and self-managed teams—to allow people and departments to behave flexibly has been increasing.

Strategy

Chapter 6 suggested that once managers decide on a strategy, they must choose the right means to implement it. Different strategies often call for the use of different organizational structures and cultures. For example, a differentiation strategy aimed at increasing the value customers perceive in an organization's goods and services usually succeeds best in a flexible structure with a culture that values innovation; flexibility facilitates a differentiation strategy because managers can develop new or innovative products quickly—an activity that requires extensive cooperation among functions or departments. In contrast, a low-cost strategy that is aimed at driving down costs in all functions usually fares best in a more formal structure with more conservative norms, which gives managers greater control over the activities of an organization's various departments.[14]

In addition, at the corporate level, when managers decide to expand the scope of organizational activities by vertical integration or diversification, for example, they need to design a flexible structure to provide sufficient coordination among the different business divisions.[15] As discussed in Chapter 6, many companies have been divesting businesses because managers have been unable to create a competitive advantage to keep them up to speed in fast-changing industries. By moving to a more flexible structure, managers gain more control over their different businesses. Finally, expanding internationally and operating in many different countries challenges managers to create organizational structures that allow organizations to be flexible on a global level.[16] As we discuss later, managers can group their departments or divisions in several ways to allow them to effectively pursue an international strategy.

Technology

Recall that technology is the combination of skills, knowledge, machines, and computers that are used to design, make, and distribute goods and services. As a rule, the more complicated the technology that an organization uses, the more difficult it is to regulate or control it because more unexpected events can arise. Thus, the more complicated the technology, the greater is the need for a flexible structure and progressive culture to enhance managers' ability to respond to unexpected situations—and give them the freedom and desire to work out new solutions to the problems they encounter. In contrast, the more routine the technology, the more appropriate is a formal structure, because tasks are simple and the steps needed to produce goods and services have been worked out in advance.

What makes a technology routine or complicated? One researcher who investigated this issue, Charles Perrow, argued that two factors determine how complicated or nonroutine technology is: task variety and task analyzability.[17] *Task variety* is the number of new or unexpected problems or situations that a person or function encounters in performing tasks or jobs. *Task analyzability* is the degree to which programmed solutions are available to people or functions to solve the problems they encounter. Nonroutine or complicated technologies are characterized by high task variety and low task analyzability; this means that many varied problems occur and that solving these problems requires significant nonprogrammed decision making. In contrast, routine technologies are characterized by low task variety and high task analyzability; this means that the problems encountered do not vary much and are easily resolved through programmed decision making.

Examples of nonroutine technology are found in the work of scientists in an R&D laboratory who develop new products or discover new drugs, and they are seen in the planning exercises an organization's top management team uses to chart the organization's future strategy. Examples of routine technology include typical mass-production or assembly operations, where workers perform the same task repeatedly and where managers have already identified the programmed solutions necessary to perform a task efficiently. Similarly, in service organizations such as fast-food restaurants, the tasks that crew members perform in making and serving fast food are routine.

Human Resources

A final important factor affecting an organization's choice of structure and culture is the characteristics of the human resources it employs. In general, the more highly skilled its workforce, and the greater the number of employees who work together in groups or teams, the more likely an organization is to use a flexible, decentralized structure and a professional culture based on values and norms that foster employee autonomy and self-control. Highly skilled employees, or employees who have internalized strong professional values and norms of behavior as part of their training, usually desire greater freedom and autonomy and dislike close supervision.

Flexible structures, characterized by decentralized authority and empowered employees, are well suited to the needs of highly skilled people. Similarly, when people work in teams, they must be allowed to interact freely and develop norms to guide their own work interactions, which also is possible in a flexible organizational structure. Thus, when designing organizational structure and culture, managers must pay close attention to the needs of the workforce and to the complexity and kind of work employees perform.

In summary, an organization's external environment, strategy, technology, and human resources are the factors to be considered by managers in seeking to design the best structure and culture for an organization. The greater the level of uncertainty in the organization's environment, the more complex its strategy and technologies, and the more highly qualified and skilled its workforce, the more likely managers are to design a structure and a culture that are flexible, can change quickly, and allow employees to be innovative in their responses to problems, customer needs, and so on. The more stable the organization's environment, the less complex and more well understood its strategy or technology, and the less skilled its workforce, the more likely managers are to design an organizational structure that is formal and controlling and a culture whose values and norms prescribe how employees should act in particular situations.

Later in the chapter we discuss how managers can create different kinds of organizational cultures. First, however, we discuss how managers can design flexible or formal organizational structures. The way an organization's structure works depends on the organizing choices managers make about three issues:

- How to group tasks into individual jobs.
- How to group jobs into functions and divisions.
- How to allocate authority and coordinate or integrate functions and divisions.

job design

The process by which managers decide how to divide tasks into specific jobs.

Grouping Tasks into Jobs: Job Design

The first step in organizational design is **job design**, the process by which managers decide how to divide into specific jobs the tasks that have to be performed to provide customers with goods and services. Managers at McDonald's, for example, have decided how best to divide the tasks required to provide customers with fast, cheap food

LO7-2 Explain how managers group tasks into jobs that are motivating and satisfying for employees.

in each McDonald's restaurant. After experimenting with different job arrangements, McDonald's managers decided on a basic division of labor among chefs and food servers. Managers allocated all the tasks involved in actually cooking the food (putting oil in the fat fryers, opening packages of frozen french fries, putting beef patties on the grill, making salads, and so on) to the job of chef. They allocated all the tasks involved in giving the food to customers (such as greeting customers, taking orders, putting fries and burgers into bags, adding salt, pepper, and napkins, and taking money) to food servers. In addition, they created other jobs—the job of dealing with drive-through customers, the job of keeping the restaurant clean, and the job of overseeing employees and responding to unexpected events. The result of the job design process is a *division of labor* among employees, one that McDonald's managers have discovered through experience is most efficient.

Establishing an appropriate division of labor among employees is a critical part of the organizing process, one that is vital to increasing efficiency and effectiveness. At McDonald's, the tasks associated with chef and food server were split into different jobs because managers found that, for the kind of food McDonald's serves, this approach was most efficient. It is efficient because when each employee is given fewer tasks to perform (so that each job becomes more specialized), employees become more productive at performing the tasks that constitute each job.

At Subway sandwich shops, however, managers chose a different kind of job design. At Subway, there is no division of labor among the people who make the sandwiches, wrap the sandwiches, give them to customers, and take the money. The roles of chef and food server are combined into one. This different division of tasks and jobs is efficient for Subway and not for McDonald's because Subway serves a limited menu of mostly submarine-style sandwiches that are prepared to order. Subway's production system is far simpler than McDonald's, because McDonald's menu is much more varied and its chefs must cook many different kinds of foods. In 2014, Subway changed its children's menu to promote healthful options and trained its employees to encourage children to choose apples as part of their meals.[18]

At Subway, the roles of chef and server are combined into one, making the job "larger" than the jobs of McDonald's more specialized food servers. The idea behind job enlargement is that increasing the range of tasks performed by employees will reduce boredom.
© Jeffrey Allan Salter/Corbis

Managers of every organization must analyze the range of tasks to be performed and then create jobs that best allow the organization to give customers the goods and services they want. In deciding how to assign tasks to individual jobs, however, managers must be careful not to take **job simplification**, the process of reducing the number of tasks that each worker performs, too far.[19] Too much job simplification may reduce efficiency rather than increase it if workers find their simplified jobs boring and monotonous, become demotivated and unhappy, and, as a result, perform at a low level.

job simplification
The process of reducing the number of tasks that each worker performs.

Job Enlargement and Job Enrichment

In an attempt to create a division of labor and design individual jobs to encourage workers to perform at a higher level and be more satisfied with their work, several researchers have proposed ways other than job simplification to group tasks into jobs: job enlargement and job enrichment.

job enlargement

Increasing the number of different tasks in a given job by changing the division of labor.

Job enlargement is increasing the number of different tasks in a given job by changing the division of labor.[20] For example, because Subway food servers make the food as well as serve it, their jobs are "larger" than the jobs of McDonald's food servers. The idea behind job enlargement is that increasing the range of tasks performed by a worker will reduce boredom and fatigue and may increase motivation to perform at a high level—increasing both the quantity and the quality of goods and services provided. The range of tasks performed by a worker will reduce boredom and fatigue and may increase motivation to perform at a higher level—increasing both the quantity and quality of goods and services provided. The accompanying "Management Insight" feature describes how one Wendy's franchisee tried to improve service by enlarging jobs through employee training.

job enrichment

Increasing the degree of responsibility a worker has over his or her job.

Job enrichment is increasing the degree of responsibility a worker has over a job by, for example, (1) empowering workers to experiment to find new or better ways of doing the job, (2) encouraging workers to develop new skills, (3) allowing workers to decide how to do the work and giving them the responsibility for deciding how to respond to unexpected situations, and (4) allowing workers to monitor and measure their own performance.[21] The idea behind job enrichment is that increasing workers' responsibility increases their involvement in their jobs and thus increases their interest in the quality of the goods they make or the services they provide.

MANAGEMENT INSIGHT

Wendy's Franchisee Focuses on Enlarging Jobs

Wendy's fast-food chain is changing its image. The company has redesigned its corporate logo and selected a new look for its restaurants, which includes new employee uniforms, wireless Internet, and flat-screen televisions. It also added lounge areas with fireplaces and faux leather chairs. What's the idea behind having a living room area at a fast-food restaurant? "The hearth at home is a gathering place," said Tré Musco, who is the chief executive of Tesser, the design firm hired to oversee Wendy's remodeling efforts. "It's warm, it's comfortable, it says stay and relax, as opposed to, this is fast food, get in and get out as quickly as possible." Customers who dine in tend to spend a little more money, so having a welcoming environment can increase sales. Wendy's reported a 25% jump in sales at the remodeled restaurants.[22]

The company plans to remodel more than 600 restaurants in the new design by the end of 2015. The company also has a schedule for when franchise-owned restaurants will be updated. But at least one franchise owner is innovating in a way that has a similar effect, without the remodel.

In addition to Wendy's stores getting a makeover, one of its top franchisees focuses on employee training as way of improving customer service, enlarging jobs, and maintaining quality. © Gene J. Puskar/AP Images

Meritage Hospitality Group, which owns 151 quick service and casual dining operations in six states, is improving customer service through employee training. First, the company committed to bringing on board 10 well-trained workers to each of its 48 stores in Michigan—that's almost 500 new workers. The company held a job fair and looked for friendly, caring people. Then the company provided extensive training for all employees. In fact, they hired the new position of corporate trainer to do one-on-one training with cashiers. Employees are encouraged to look for ways to initiate a conversation with customers and create a personal connection. They also are encouraged to have a regular customer's order ready before the customer orders. Finally, Meritage instituted contests among staff in its restaurants. One contest between the day shift and the night shift was to see who could get the most customer names in a given day.[23]

As a result of the effort, sales increased, customer complaints went down, and customer compliments went up. "Our biggest tip is to invest the time in training," said Al Pruitt, president of Wendy's for Meritage. "If you spend time on your people, you will always get a return on your investment."[24]

In general, managers who make design choices that increase job enrichment and job enlargement are likely to increase the degree to which people behave flexibly rather than rigidly or mechanically. Narrow, specialized jobs are likely to lead people to behave in predictable ways; workers who perform a variety of tasks and who are allowed and encouraged to discover new and better ways to perform their jobs are likely to act flexibly and creatively. Thus, managers who enlarge and enrich jobs create a flexible organizational structure, and those who simplify jobs create a more formal structure. If workers are grouped into self-managed work teams, the organization is likely to be flexible because team members provide support for each other and can learn from one another.

The Job Characteristics Model

J. R. Hackman and G. R. Oldham's job characteristics model is an influential model of job design that explains in detail how managers can make jobs more interesting and motivating.[25] Hackman and Oldham's model also describes the likely personal and organizational outcomes that will result from enriched and enlarged jobs.

According to Hackman and Oldham, every job has five characteristics that determine how motivating the job is. These characteristics determine how employees react to their work and lead to outcomes such as high performance and satisfaction and low absenteeism and turnover:

- *Skill variety:* The extent to which a job requires that an employee use a wide range of different skills, abilities, or knowledge. Example: The skill variety required by the job of a research scientist is higher than that called for by the job of a McDonald's food server.

- *Task identity:* The extent to which a job requires that a worker perform all the tasks necessary to complete the job, from the beginning to the end of the production process. Example: A craftsworker who takes a piece of wood and transforms it into a custom-made desk has higher task identity than does a worker who performs only one of the numerous operations required to assemble a flat-screen TV.

- *Task significance:* The degree to which a worker feels his or her job is meaningful because of its effect on people inside the organization, such as coworkers, or on people outside the organization, such as customers. Example: A teacher who sees the effect of his or her efforts in a well-educated and well-adjusted student enjoys high task significance compared to a dishwasher who monotonously washes dishes as they come to the kitchen.

- *Autonomy:* The degree to which a job gives an employee the freedom and discretion needed to schedule different tasks and decide how to carry them out. Example: Salespeople who have to plan their schedules and decide how to allocate their time among different customers have relatively high autonomy compared to assembly-line workers, whose actions are determined by the speed of the production line.

- *Feedback:* The extent to which actually doing a job provides a worker with clear and direct information about how well he or she has performed the job. Example: An air traffic controller whose mistakes may result in a midair collision receives immediate feedback on job performance; a person who compiles statistics for a business magazine often has little idea of when he or she makes a mistake or does a particularly good job.

Hackman and Oldham argue that these five job characteristics affect an employee's motivation because they affect three critical psychological states. The more employees feel that their work is *meaningful* and that they are *responsible for work outcomes and responsible for knowing how those outcomes affect others,* the more motivating work becomes and the more likely employees are to be satisfied and to perform at a high level. Moreover, employees who have jobs that are highly motivating are called on to use their skills more and to perform more tasks, and they are given more responsibility for doing the job. All of the foregoing are characteristic of jobs and employees in flexible structures where authority is decentralized and where employees commonly work with others and must learn new skills to complete the range of tasks for which their group is responsible.

Grouping Jobs into Functions and Divisions: Designing Organizational Structure

Once managers have decided which tasks to allocate to which jobs, they face the next organizing decision: how to group jobs together to best match the needs of the organization's environment, strategy, technology, and human resources. Typically, managers first decide to group jobs into departments and they design a *functional structure* to use organizational resources effectively. As an organization grows and becomes more difficult to control, managers must choose a more complex organizational design, such as a divisional structure or a matrix or product team structure. The different ways in which managers can design organizational structure are discussed next. Selecting and designing an organizational structure to increase efficiency and effectiveness is a significant challenge. As noted in Chapter 6, managers reap the rewards of a well-thought-out strategy only if they choose the right type of structure to implement the strategy. The ability to make the right kinds of organizing choices is often what differentiates effective from ineffective managers and creates a high-performing organization.

LO7-3 Describe the types of organizational structures managers can design, and explain why they choose one structure over another.

Functional Structure

A *function* is a group of people, working together, who possess similar skills or use the same kind of knowledge, tools, or techniques to perform their jobs.

Figure 7.2 The Functional Structure of Pier 1 Imports

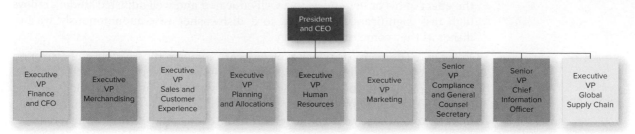

functional structure

An organizational structure composed of all the departments that an organization requires to produce its goods or services.

Manufacturing, sales, and research and development are often organized into functional departments. A **functional structure** is an organizational structure composed of all the departments that an organization requires to produce its goods or services. Figure 7.2 shows the functional structure that Pier 1 Imports, the home furnishings company, uses to supply its customers with a range of goods from around the world to satisfy their desires for new and innovative products.

Pier 1's main functions are finance and administration, merchandising (purchasing the goods), sales and customer experience (managing the retail outlets), marketing, planning and allocation (managing credit and product distribution), and human resources. Each job inside a function exists because it helps the function perform the activities necessary for high organizational performance. Thus, within the marketing function are all the jobs necessary to efficiently advertise Pier 1's products to increase their appeal to customers (for example, promotion, photograph, and visual communication).

There are several advantages to grouping jobs according to function. First, when people who perform similar jobs are grouped together, they can learn from observing one another and thus become more specialized and can perform at a higher level. The tasks associated with one job often are related to the tasks associated with another job, which encourages cooperation within a function. In Pier 1's marketing department, for example, the person designing the photography program for an ad campaign works closely with the person responsible for designing store layouts and with visual communication experts. As a result, Pier 1 can develop a strong, focused marketing campaign to differentiate its products.

Second, when people who perform similar jobs are grouped together, it is easier for managers to monitor and evaluate their performance.[26] Imagine if marketing experts, purchasing experts, and real-estate experts were grouped together in one function and supervised by a manager from merchandising. Obviously, the merchandising manager would not have the expertise to evaluate all these different people appropriately. A functional structure allows workers to evaluate how well coworkers are performing their jobs, and if some workers are performing poorly, more experienced workers can help them develop new skills.

Finally, managers appreciate functional structure because it allows them to create the set of functions they need to scan and monitor the competitive environment and obtain information about the way it is changing.[27] With the right set of functions in place, managers are then in a good position to develop a strategy that allows the organization to respond to its changing situation. Employees in the marketing group can specialize in monitoring new marketing developments that will allow Pier 1 to better target its customers. Employees in merchandising can monitor all potential suppliers of home furnishings both at home and abroad to find the goods most likely to appeal to Pier 1's customers and manage Pier 1's global supply chain.

Pier 1 organizes its operations by function, which means that employees can more easily learn from one another and improve the service they provide to customers.
© Tim Boyle/Getty Images

As an organization grows, and particularly as its task environment and strategy change because it is beginning to produce a wider range of goods and services for different kinds of customers, several problems can make a functional structure less efficient and effective.[28] First, managers in different functions may find it more difficult to communicate and coordinate with one another when they are responsible for several different kinds of products, especially as the organization grows both domestically and internationally. Second, functional managers may become so preoccupied with supervising their own specific departments and achieving their departmental goals that they lose sight of organizational goals. If that happens, organizational effectiveness will suffer because managers will be viewing issues and problems facing the organization only from their own, relatively narrow, departmental perspectives.[29] Both of these problems can reduce efficiency and effectiveness.

Divisional Structures: Product, Geographic, and Market

divisional structure
An organizational structure composed of separate business units within which are the functions that work together to produce a specific product for a specific customer.

As the problems associated with growth and diversification increase over time, managers must search for new ways to organize their activities to overcome the problems associated with a functional structure. Most managers of large organizations choose a **divisional structure** and create a series of business units to produce a specific kind of product for a specific kind of customer. Each *division* is a collection of functions or departments that work together to produce the product. The goal behind the change to a divisional structure is to create smaller, more manageable units within the organization. There are three forms of divisional structure (see Figure 7.3).[30] When managers organize divisions according to the *type of good or service* they provide, they adopt a product structure. When managers organize divisions according to the *area of the country or world* they operate in, they adopt a geographic structure. When managers organize divisions according to *the type of customer* they focus on, they adopt a market structure.

Figure 7.3
Product, Geographic,
and Market Structures

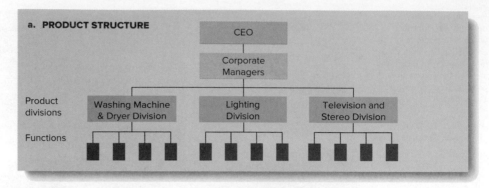

a. PRODUCT STRUCTURE

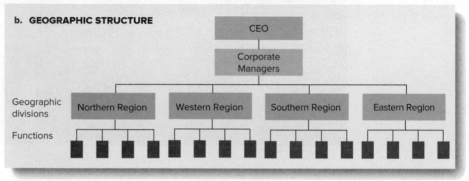

b. GEOGRAPHIC STRUCTURE

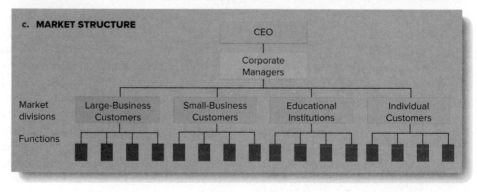

c. MARKET STRUCTURE

PRODUCT STRUCTURE Imagine the problems that managers at Pier 1 would encounter if they decided to diversify into producing and selling cars, fast food, and health insurance—in addition to home furnishings—and tried to use their existing set of functional managers to oversee the production of all four kinds of products. No manager would have the necessary skills or abilities to oversee those four products. No individual marketing manager, for example, could effectively market cars, fast food, health insurance, and home furnishings at the same time. To perform a functional activity successfully, managers must have experience in specific markets or industries. Consequently, if managers decide to diversify into new industries or to expand their range of products, they commonly design a product structure to organize their operations (see Figure 7.3a).

Using a **product structure**, managers place each distinct product line or business in its own self-contained division and give divisional managers the responsibility for devising an appropriate business-level strategy to allow the division to compete

product structure An organizational structure in which each product line or business is handled by a self-contained division.

When Glaxo Wellcome and SmithKline Beecham merged, managers resolved the problem of how to coordinate the activities of thousands of research scientists by organizing them into product divisions focusing on clusters of diseases. © Kim Steele/Photodisc Green/Getty Images RF

effectively in its industry or market.[31] Each division is self-contained because it has a complete set of all the functions—marketing, R&D, finance, and so on—that it needs to produce or provide goods or services efficiently and effectively. Functional managers report to divisional managers, and divisional managers report to top or corporate managers.

Grouping functions into divisions focused on particular products has several advantages for managers at all levels in the organization. First, a product structure allows functional managers to specialize in only one product area, so they are able to build expertise and fine-tune their skills in this particular area. Second, each division's managers can become experts in their industry; this expertise helps them choose and develop a business-level strategy to differentiate their products or lower their costs while meeting the needs of customers. Third, a product structure frees corporate managers from the need to supervise directly each division's day-to-day operations; this latitude allows corporate managers to create the best corporate-level strategy to maximize the organization's future growth and ability to create value. Corporate managers are likely to make fewer mistakes about which businesses to diversify into or how to best expand internationally, for example, because they are able to take an organizationwide view.[32] Corporate managers also are likely to evaluate better how well divisional managers are doing, and they can intervene and take corrective action as needed.

The extra layer of management, the divisional management layer, can improve the use of organizational resources. Moreover, a product structure puts divisional managers close to their customers and lets them respond quickly and appropriately to the changing task environment. One pharmaceutical company that has recently adopted a new product structure to better organize its activities with great success is GlaxoSmithKline. The need to innovate new kinds of prescription drugs in order to boost performance is a continual battle for pharmaceutical companies. Over the past decade, many of these companies have been merging to try to increase their research productivity, and one of them, GlaxoSmithKline, was created from the merger between Glaxo Wellcome and SmithKline Beecham. Prior to the merger, both companies experienced a steep decline in the number of new prescription drugs their scientists were able to invent. The problem facing the new company's top managers was how to best use and combine the talents of the scientists and researchers from both of the former companies to allow them to quickly innovate promising new drugs.

Top managers realized that after the merger there would be enormous problems associated with coordinating the activities of the thousands of research scientists who were working on hundreds of different kinds of drug research programs. Understanding the problems associated with large size, the top managers decided to group the researchers into eight smaller product divisions to allow them to focus on particular clusters of diseases such as heart disease or viral infections. The members of each product division were told that they would be rewarded based on the number of new prescription drugs they were able to invent and the speed with which they could bring these new drugs to the market. GlaxoSmithKline's new product structure has worked well, its research productivity doubled after the reorganization, and a record number of new drugs are moving into clinical trials. However, the need to innovate and stay competitive remains, and GlaxoSmithKline plans more restructuring before 2016.[33]

GEOGRAPHIC STRUCTURE When organizations expand rapidly both at home and abroad, functional structures can create special problems because managers in one central location may find it increasingly difficult to deal with the different problems and issues that may arise in each region of a country or area of the world. In these cases, a **geographic structure**, in which divisions are broken down by geographic location, is often chosen (see Figure 7.3b). To achieve the corporate mission of providing next-day mail service, Fred Smith, CEO of FedEx, chose a geographic structure and divided up operations by creating a division in each region. Large retailers such as Macy's, Neiman Marcus, and Brooks Brothers also use a geographic structure. Since the needs of retail customers differ by region—for example, surfboards in California and down parkas in the Midwest—a geographic structure gives retail regional managers the flexibility they need to choose the range of products that best meets the needs of regional customers.

In adopting a *global geographic structure,* such as shown in Figure 7.4a, managers locate different divisions in each of the world regions where the organization operates. Managers are most likely to do this when they pursue a multidomestic strategy because customer needs vary widely by country or world region. For example, if

geographic structure
An organizational structure in which each region of a country or area of the world is served by a self-contained division.

Figure 7.4
Global Geographic and Global Product Structures

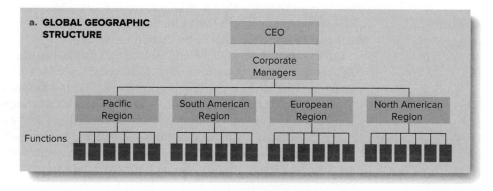

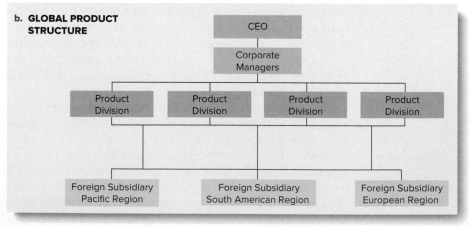

products that appeal to U.S. customers do not sell in Europe, the Pacific Rim, or South America, managers must customize the products to meet the needs of customers in those different world regions; a global geographic structure with global divisions may allow them to do this. The accompanying "Managing Globally" feature describes how one company reorganized itself in an effort to offer more services to customers in each region it serves.

MANAGING GLOBALLY

Reorganization Focuses on Local Clients

The Michael Baker Corporation has worked on some high-profile engineering projects around the world. The company had a role in building the 789-mile Trans-Alaska Pipeline in North America, the 135-mile KHMR-American Friendship Highway in Cambodia, the New River Gorge Bridge in West Virginia, the Midfield Terminal Complex at the Pittsburgh International Airport, and a 2,600-mile fiber optic telecommunications network in Mexico. More recently, the company was selected to rehabilitate the Pulaski Skyway, the bridge that connects Newark and Jersey City in New Jersey.[34]

As the need for engineering, construction management, and other services expands nationally and internationally, the company launched a national and global expansion program. In 2013, the company merged with Integrated Mission Solutions to create Michael Baker International.

The company's vision statement includes the words, "Be the go-to company for clients and employees." Its services include architectural, environmental, construction, planning, and program management. The company has worked with U.S. and foreign allied governments and with commercial customers.

The renovation of the Pulaski Skyway in New Jersey is one of Michael Baker International's projects. The engineering and consulting firm recently reorganized its operations into seven global regions to offer more services and more local project leadership.
© Mel Evans/AP Images

Michael Baker International has more than 5,000 employees in more than 90 national and international offices. In 2014, the company reorganized into an operations-centric structure in seven regions. In announcing the reorganization, the firm suggested that its new structure would allow it to offer more services to customers in each region. The reorganization also would allow more local leadership of projects.[35]

"This reorganization is a result of extensive review, market analysis, client demand, and discussion with personnel at all levels of the company identifying and highlighting opportunities for building a balanced business in each of our regions," stated Kurt Bergman, chief executive officer. "The new organization promotes empowered business leaders at the office and regional levels, supported by national market and practice leads, to build and manage well-balanced portfolios reflective of the complete continuum of services provided by the Michael Baker International enterprise."[36]

In contrast, to the degree that customers abroad are willing to buy the same kind of product or slight variations thereof, managers are more likely to pursue a global strategy. In this case they are more likely to use a global product structure. In a *global product structure,* each product division, not the country and regional managers, takes responsibility for deciding where to manufacture its products and how to market them in countries worldwide (see Figure 7.4b). Product division managers manage their own global value chains and decide where to establish foreign subsidiaries to distribute and sell their products to customers in foreign countries.

MARKET STRUCTURE Sometimes the pressing issue facing managers is to group functions according to the type of customer buying the product in order to tailor the products the organization offers to each customer's unique demands. A PC maker such as Dell, for example, has several kinds of customers, including large businesses (which might demand networks of computers linked to a mainframe computer), small companies (which may need just a few PCs linked together), educational users in schools and universities (which might want thousands of independent PCs for their students), and individual users (who may want a high-quality multimedia PC so they can play the latest video games).

market structure
An organizational structure in which each kind of customer is served by a self-contained division; also called *customer structure.*

To satisfy the needs of diverse customers, a company might adopt a **market structure**, which groups divisions according to the particular kinds of customers they serve (see Figure 7.3c). A market structure lets managers be responsive to the needs of their customers and allows them to act flexibly in making decisions in response to customers' changing needs. To spearhead its turnaround, for example, Dell created four streamlined market divisions that each focus on being responsive to one particular type of customer: individual consumers, small businesses, large companies, and government and state agencies. Organizations need to continually evaluate their structures to ensure that operations are working according to plan. The accompanying "Management Insight" feature provides an example of what can happen in an organization when leaders do not know what is happening.

MANAGEMENT INSIGHT

Restoring a Team-First Culture

In the middle of the 2013 NFL season, Miami Dolphins offensive lineman Jonathan Martin abruptly quit and entered a hospital to be treated for emotional distress. He said he had been bullied by three of his teammates.[37]

The National Football League investigated the team and found Martin had been subjected to daily harassment by Richie Incognito, a guard for the Miami Dolphins, as well as by John Jerry and Mike Pouncey, both offensive linemen who also played for the team. The harassment included racial slurs about Martin being African American, sexual taunts about his mother and sister, and jokes that Martin was gay.

The team's owner, Stephen Ross, said, "When we asked the NFL to conduct this independent review, we felt it was important to take a step back and thoroughly research these serious allegations. As an organization, we are committed to a culture of team-first accountability and respect for one another."[38]

The investigation and subsequent report identified Incognito as the main instigator of the harassment. After the report was released, Jim Turner, who coached the offensive line, was fired for not stopping the harassment and for taking part in some taunting. Kevin O'Neill, who was the team's head athletic trainer at the time, was fired for not cooperating with the investigation. In addition, the investigation concluded that Dolphins head coach, Joe Philbin, did not take part in or know about the harassment that Martin was subjected to.[39]

"After interviewing Coach Philbin at length, we were impressed with his commitment to promoting integrity and accountability throughout the Dolphins organization—a point echoed by many players," the report stated. "We are convinced that had Coach Philbin learned of the underlying misconduct, he would have intervened promptly to ensure that Martin and others were treated with dignity."[40]

Philbin said that the information contained in the report about vulgar language and behavior was disappointing and violated the team's fundamental values. He also indicated that he would be responsible for making sure such events do not happen again. "That ultimately rests on my shoulders," he said. "And I will be accountable moving forward for making sure that we emphasize a team-first culture of respect toward one another."[41]

Matrix and Product Team Designs

Moving to a product, geographic, or market divisional structure allows managers to respond more quickly and flexibly to the particular circumstances they confront. However, when information technology or customer needs are changing rapidly and the environment is uncertain, even a divisional structure may not give managers enough flexibility to respond to the environment quickly. To operate effectively under these conditions, managers must design the most flexible kind of organizational structure available: *a matrix structure* or a *product team structure* (see Figure 7.5).

matrix structure
An organizational structure that simultaneously groups people and resources by function and by product.

MATRIX STRUCTURE In a **matrix structure**, managers group people and resources in two ways simultaneously: by function and by product.[42] Employees are grouped by *functions* to allow them to learn from one another and become more skilled and productive. In addition, employees are grouped into *product teams* in which members of different functions work together to develop a specific product. The result is a complex network of reporting relationships among product teams and functions that makes the matrix structure very flexible (see Figure 7.5a). Each person in a product team reports to two managers: (1) a functional boss, who assigns individuals to a team and evaluates their performance from a functional perspective, and (2) the boss of the product team, who evaluates their performance on the team. Thus team members are known as *two-boss employees.* The functional employees assigned to product teams change over time as the specific skills that the team needs change. At the beginning of the product development process, for example, engineers and R&D specialists are assigned to a product team because their skills are needed to develop new products. When a provisional design has been established, marketing experts are assigned to the team to gauge how customers will respond to the new product. Manufacturing personnel join when it is time to find the most efficient way to produce the product. As their specific jobs are completed, team members leave and are reassigned to new teams. In this way the matrix structure makes the most use of human resources.

To keep the matrix structure flexible, product teams are empowered and team members are responsible for making most of the important decisions involved in product development.[43] The product team manager acts as a facilitator, controlling

Figure 7.5

Matrix and Product
Team Structures

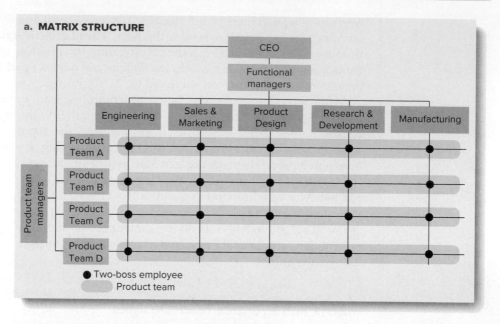

a. **MATRIX STRUCTURE**

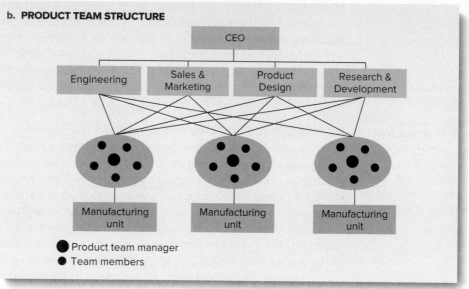

b. **PRODUCT TEAM STRUCTURE**

the financial resources and trying to keep the project on time and within budget. The functional managers try to ensure that the product is the best it can be to maximize its differentiated appeal.

High-tech companies that operate in environments where new product development takes place monthly or yearly have used matrix structures successfully for many years, and the need to innovate quickly is vital to the organization's survival. The flexibility afforded by a matrix structure lets managers keep pace with a changing and increasingly complex environment.[44]

PRODUCT TEAM STRUCTURE The dual reporting relationships that are at the heart of a matrix structure have always been difficult for managers and employees to deal with. Often the functional boss and the product boss make conflicting demands on team members, who do not know which boss to satisfy first. Also, functional and product team bosses may come into conflict over precisely who is in charge of which team members and for how long. To avoid these problems, managers have devised a way of organizing people and resources that still allows an organization to be flexible but makes its structure easier to operate: a product team structure.

product team structure
An organizational structure in which employees are permanently assigned to a cross-functional team and report only to the product team manager or to one of his or her direct subordinates.

cross-functional team A group of managers brought together from different departments to perform organizational tasks.

The **product team structure** differs from a matrix structure in two ways: (1) It does away with dual reporting relationships and two-boss employees, and (2) functional employees are permanently assigned to a cross-functional team that is empowered to bring a new or redesigned product to market. A **cross-functional team** is a group of managers brought together from different departments to perform organizational tasks. When managers are grouped into cross-functional teams, the artificial boundaries between departments disappear, and a narrow focus on departmental goals is replaced with a general interest in working together to achieve organizational goals. For example, when mattress company Sealy saw its sales slipping, it pulled together a cross-functional team that was allowed to work outside the organization's hierarchy and quickly designed a new mattress. With everyone focused on the goal, team members created a mattress that broke previous sales records.[45]

Members of a cross-functional team report only to the product team manager or to one of his or her direct subordinates. The heads of the functions have only an informal, advisory relationship with members of the product teams—the role of functional managers is only to counsel and help team members, share knowledge among teams, and provide new technological developments that can help improve each team's performance (see Figure 7.5b).[46] Increasingly, organizations are making empowered cross-functional teams an essential part of their organizational architecture to help them gain a competitive advantage in fast-changing organizational environments.

Coordinating Functions and Divisions

The more complex the structure a company uses to group its activities, the greater are the problems of *linking and coordinating* its different functions and divisions. Coordination becomes a problem because each function or division develops a different orientation toward the other groups that affects how it interacts with them. Each function or division comes to view the problems facing the company from its own perspective; for example, they may develop different views about the major goals, problems, or issues facing a company.

LO7-4 Explain why managers must coordinate jobs, functions, and divisions using the hierarchy of authority and integrating mechanisms.

At the functional level, the manufacturing function typically has a short-term view; its major goal is to keep costs under control and get the product out the factory door on time. By contrast, the product development function has a long-term viewpoint because developing a new product is a relatively slow process and high product quality is seen as more important than low costs. Such differences in viewpoint may make manufacturing and product development managers reluctant to cooperate and coordinate their activities to meet company goals. At the divisional level, in a company with a product structure, employees may become concerned more with making *their* division's products a success than with the profitability of the entire company. They may refuse, or simply not see, the need to cooperate and share information or knowledge with other divisions.

The problem of linking and coordinating the activities of different functions and divisions becomes more acute as the number of functions and divisions increases.

We look first at how managers design the hierarchy of authority to coordinate functions and divisions so they work together effectively. Then we focus on integration and examine the different integrating mechanisms managers can use to coordinate functions and divisions.

Allocating Authority

As organizations grow and produce a wider range of goods and services, the size and number of their functions and divisions increase. To coordinate the activities of people, functions, and divisions and to allow them to work together effectively, managers must develop a clear hierarchy of authority.[47] **Authority** is the power vested in a manager to make decisions and use resources to achieve organizational goals by virtue of his or her position in an organization. The **hierarchy of authority** is an organization's *chain of command*—the relative authority that each manager has—extending from the CEO at the top, down through the middle managers and first-line managers, to the nonmanagerial employees who actually make goods or provide services. Every manager, at every level of the hierarchy, supervises one or more subordinates. The term **span of control** refers to the number of subordinates who report directly to a manager.

Figure 7.6 shows a simplified picture of the hierarchy of authority at McDonald's as of July 2015. The fast-food giant's new president and CEO, Steve Easterbrook, has taken bold steps to revise the company's organizational structure in an effort to "reset and turnaround the business." Easterbrook, who took over as CEO in March 2015, is the manager who has the ultimate responsibility for the company's overall performance, and he has the authority to decide how to use organizational resources to benefit McDonald's stakeholders. Peter Bensen, formerly the company's CFO, was named to the newly created position of chief administrative officer, responsible for oversight of global departments that support operations, including finance, supply chain and sustainability, restaurant development, franchising, information technology, and restaurant solutions. McDonald's four new divisions focus on combining markets with similar needs, challenges, and opportunities for growth—rather than a geographic approach to company operations. Also in the top management hierarchy is Robert Gibbs, executive vice president and chief communications officer. Unlike other managers, Gibbs is not a **line manager**, someone in the direct line or chain of command who has formal authority over people and resources. Rather, Gibbs is a **staff manager**, responsible for one of McDonald's specialist functions—communications. He reports directly to Easterbrook.[48]

authority The power to hold people accountable for their actions and to make decisions concerning the use of organizational resources.

hierarchy of authority An organization's chain of command, specifying the relative authority of each manager.

span of control The number of subordinates who report directly to a manager.

line manager Someone in the direct line or chain of command who has formal authority over people and resources at lower levels.

staff manager Someone responsible for managing a specialist function, such as finance or marketing.

Figure 7.6   **The Hierarchy of Authority and Span of Control at McDonald's Corporation**

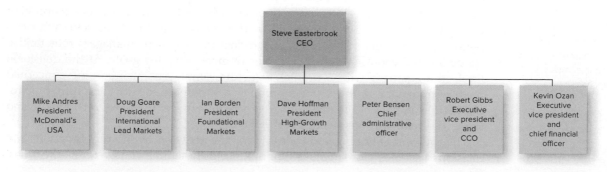

Managers at each level of the hierarchy confer on managers at the next level down the authority to decide how to use organizational resources. Accepting this authority, those lower-level managers are accountable for how well they make those decisions. Managers who make the right decisions are typically promoted, and organizations motivate managers with the prospects of promotion and increased responsibility within the chain of command.

Below Andres are the other main levels in the McDonald's USA chain of command—executive vice presidents of its Northeast, South, Central, and West regions, zone managers, regional managers, and supervisors. A hierarchy is also evident in each company-owned McDonald's restaurant. At the top is the store manager; at lower levels are the first assistant, shift managers, and crew personnel. McDonald's managers have decided that this hierarchy of authority best allows the company to pursue its business-level strategy of providing fast food at reasonable prices.

TALL AND FLAT ORGANIZATIONS As an organization grows in size (normally measured by the number of its managers and employees), its hierarchy of authority normally lengthens, making the organizational structure taller. A *tall* organization has many levels of authority relative to company size; a *flat* organization has fewer levels relative to company size (see Figure 7.7).[49] As a hierarchy becomes taller, problems that make the organization's structure less flexible and slow managers' response to changes in the organizational environment may result.

Communication problems may arise when an organization has many levels in the hierarchy. It can take a long time for the decisions and orders of upper-level managers to reach managers further down in the hierarchy, and it can take a long time for top managers to learn how well their decisions worked. Feeling out of touch, top managers may want to verify that lower-level managers are following orders and may require written confirmation from them. Middle managers, who know they will be held strictly accountable for their actions, start devoting too much time to the process of making decisions to improve their chances of being right. They might even try to avoid responsibility by making top managers decide what actions to take.

Another communication problem that can result is the distortion of commands and messages being transmitted up and down the hierarchy, which causes managers at different levels to interpret what is happening differently. Distortion of orders and messages can be accidental, occurring because different managers interpret messages from their own narrow, functional perspectives. Or distortion can be intentional, occurring because managers low in the hierarchy decide to interpret information in a way that increases their own personal advantage.

Another problem with tall hierarchies is that they usually indicate that an organization is employing many managers, and managers are expensive. Managerial salaries, benefits, offices, and secretaries are a huge expense for organizations. Large companies such as IBM and GM pay their managers millions of dollars a year. During the recent recession, hundreds of thousands of managers were laid off as companies restructured and downsized their workforces to reduce costs. However, in 2015, a gradual recovery is under way.[50]

THE MINIMUM CHAIN OF COMMAND To ward off the problems that result when an organization becomes too tall and employs too many managers, top managers need to ascertain whether they are employing the right number of middle and first-line managers and whether they can redesign their organizational architecture to

Figure 7.7

Flat and Tall
Organizations

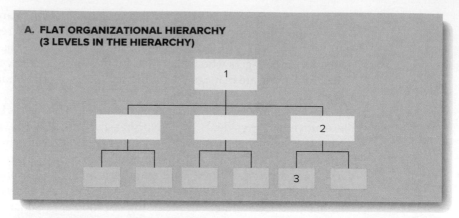

A. **FLAT ORGANIZATIONAL HIERARCHY
(3 LEVELS IN THE HIERARCHY)**

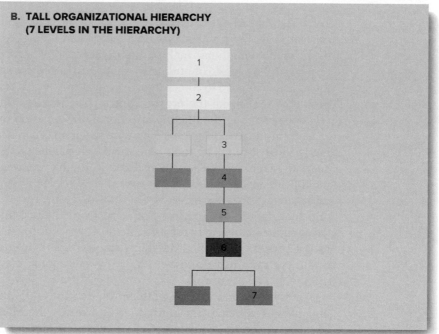

B. **TALL ORGANIZATIONAL HIERARCHY
(7 LEVELS IN THE HIERARCHY)**

reduce the number of managers. Top managers might well follow a basic organizing principle—the principle of the minimum chain of command—which states that top managers should always construct a hierarchy with the fewest levels of authority necessary to efficiently and effectively use organizational resources.

Effective managers constantly scrutinize their hierarchies to see whether the number of levels can be reduced—for example, by eliminating one level and giving the responsibilities of managers at that level to managers above and by empowering employees below. One manager who has worked to empower employees is David Novak, executive chairman (and former CEO) of YUM! Brands. Instead of dictating what the company's Taco Bell, KFC, and Pizza Hut brands should do, Novak turned the corporate headquarters into a support center for worldwide operations. He also wrote a book called *Taking People with You: The Only Way to Make BIG Things Happen,* which outlines the leadership program Novak developed to motivate employees and align them with the organization's goals.[51]

decentralizing authority Giving lower-level managers and nonmanagerial employees the right to make important decisions about how to use organizational resources.

CENTRALIZATION AND DECENTRALIZATION OF AUTHORITY Another way in which managers can keep the organizational hierarchy flat is by **decentralizing authority**—that is, by giving lower-level managers and nonmanagerial employees the right to make important decisions about how to use organizational resources.[52] If managers at higher levels give lower-level employees the responsibility of making important decisions and only *manage by exception,* then the problems of slow and distorted communication noted previously are kept to a minimum. Moreover, fewer managers are needed because their role is not to make decisions but to act as coach and facilitator and to help other employees make the best decisions. In addition, when decision-making authority is low in the organization and near the customer, employees are better able to recognize and respond to customer needs.

Decentralizing authority allows an organization and its employees to behave in a flexible way even as the organization grows and becomes taller. This is why managers are so interested in empowering employees, creating self-managed work teams, establishing cross-functional teams, and even moving to a product team structure. These design innovations help keep the organizational architecture flexible and responsive to complex task and general environments, complex technologies, and complex strategies.

Although more and more organizations are taking steps to decentralize authority, *too much* decentralization has certain disadvantages. If divisions, functions, or teams are given too much decision-making authority, they may begin to pursue their own goals at the expense of organizational goals. Managers in engineering design or R&D, for example, may become so focused on making the best possible product they fail to realize that the best product may be so expensive few people are willing or able to buy it. Also, too much decentralization can cause lack of communication among functions or divisions; this prevents the synergies of cooperation from ever materializing, and organizational performance suffers.

Top managers must seek the balance between centralization and decentralization of authority that best meets the four major contingencies an organization faces (see Figure 7.1). If managers are in a stable environment, are using well-understood technology, and are producing stable kinds of products (such as cereal, canned soup, or books), there is no pressing need to decentralize authority, and managers at the top can maintain control of much of organizational decision making.[53] However, in uncertain, changing environments where high-tech companies are producing state-of-the-art products, top managers must often empower employees and allow teams to make important strategic decisions so the organization can keep up with the changes taking place. No matter what its environment, a company that fails to control the balance between centralization and decentralization will find its performance suffering.

Integrating and Coordinating Mechanisms

Much coordination takes place through the hierarchy of authority. However, several problems are associated with establishing contact among managers in different functions or divisions. As discussed earlier, managers from different functions and divisions may have different views about what must be done to achieve organizational goals. But if the managers have equal authority (as functional managers typically do), the only manager who can tell them what to do is the CEO, who has the ultimate authority to resolve conflicts. The need to solve everyday conflicts, however, wastes top management time and slows strategic decision making; indeed, one sign of a poorly performing structure is the number of problems sent up the hierarchy for top managers to solve.

To increase communication and coordination among functions or between divisions and to prevent these problems from emerging, top managers incorporate various **integrating mechanisms** into their organizational architecture. The greater the complexity of an organization's structure, the greater is the need for coordination among people, functions, and divisions to make the organizational structure work efficiently and effectively. Thus when managers adopt a divisional, matrix, or product team structure, they must use complex integrating mechanisms to achieve organizational goals. Several integrating mechanisms are available to managers to increase communication and coordination.[54] Figure 7.8 lists these mechanisms, as well as examples of the individuals or groups who might use them.

LIAISON ROLES Managers can increase coordination among functions and divisions by establishing liaison roles. When the volume of contacts between two functions increases, one way to improve coordination is to give one manager in each function or division the responsibility for coordinating with the other. These managers may meet daily, weekly, monthly, or as needed. A liaison role is illustrated in Figure 7.8; the small dot represents the person within a function who has responsibility for coordinating with the other function. Coordinating is part of the liaison's full-time job, and usually an informal relationship develops among the people involved, greatly easing strains between functions. Furthermore, liaison roles provide a way of transmitting information across an organization, which is important in large organizations whose employees may know no one outside their immediate function or division.

TASK FORCES When more than two functions or divisions share many common problems, direct contact and liaison roles may not provide sufficient coordination. In these cases, a more complex integrating mechanism, a **task force**, may be

integrating mechanisms
Organizing tools that managers can use to increase communication and coordination among functions and divisions.

task force A committee of managers from various functions or divisions who meet to solve a specific, mutual problem; also called *ad hoc committee*.

Figure 7.8   Types and Examples of Integrating Mechanisms

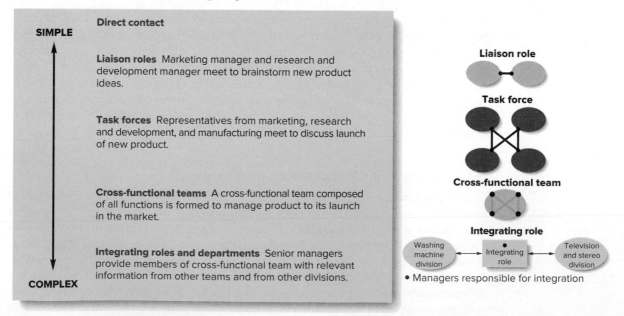

appropriate (see Figure 7.8). One manager from each relevant function or division is assigned to a task force that meets to solve a specific, mutual problem; members are responsible for reporting to their departments on the issues addressed and the solutions recommended. Task forces are often called *ad hoc committees* because they are temporary; they may meet on a regular basis or only a few times. When the problem or issue is solved, the task force is no longer needed; members return to their normal roles in their departments or are assigned to other task forces. Typically task force members also perform many of their normal duties while serving on the task force.

CROSS-FUNCTIONAL TEAMS In many cases the issues addressed by a task force are recurring problems, such as the need to develop new products or find new kinds of customers. To address recurring problems effectively, managers are increasingly using permanent integrating mechanisms such as cross-functional teams. An example of a cross-functional team is a new product development committee that is responsible for the choice, design, manufacturing, and marketing of a new product. Such an activity obviously requires a great deal of integration among functions if new products are to be successfully introduced, and using a complex integrating mechanism such as a cross-functional team accomplishes this. As discussed earlier, in a product team structure people and resources are grouped into permanent cross-functional teams to speed products to market. These teams assume long-term responsibility for all aspects of development and making the product.

INTEGRATING ROLES An integrating role is a role whose only function is to increase coordination and integration among functions or divisions to achieve performance gains from synergies. Usually managers who perform integrating roles are experienced senior managers who can envisage how to use the resources of the functions or divisions to obtain new synergies. At PepsiCo, Amy Chen, now a senior sales manager, coordinated with several company divisions to create a program that would deliver meals during the summer months to children from low-income families. The resulting program, Food for Good, delivers meals to children who would normally receive a lunch at school.[55] The more complex an organization and the greater the number of its divisions, the more important integrating roles are.

In summary, to keep an organization responsive to changes in its task and general environments as it grows and becomes more complex, managers must increase coordination among functions and divisions by using complex integrating mechanisms. Managers must decide on the best way to organize their structures—that is, choose the structure that allows them to make the best use of organizational resources.

strategic alliance
An agreement in which managers pool or share their organization's resources and know-how with another company, and the two organizations share the rewards and risks of starting a new venture.

Strategic Alliances, B2B Network Structures, and IT

Recently, increasing globalization and the use of new information technology (IT) have brought about two innovations in organizational architecture that are sweeping through U.S. and European companies: strategic alliances and business-to-business (B2B) network structures. A **strategic alliance** is a formal agreement that commits two or more companies to exchange or share their resources in order to produce and market a product.[56] Strategic alliances are typically formed because companies share similar interests and believe they can benefit from cooperating with each other. For example, in 2014, The Coca-Cola Company entered a strategic alliance with the InterContinental Hotels Group (IHG). As part of the alliance, IHG will

B2B network structure A series of global strategic alliances that an organization creates with suppliers, manufacturers, and distributors to produce and market a product.

serve select Coke products in its 3,200 hotels. Both companies are well-known brands and are both headquartered in Atlanta, Georgia.[57]

The growing sophistication of IT using global intranets, videoconferencing, and cloud computing makes it much easier to manage strategic alliances and encourage managers to share information and cooperate with each other across the globe. One outcome of this increased use of technology has been the growth of strategic alliances into an IT-based network structure for businesses. A **B2B network structure** is a formal series of global strategic alliances that one or several organizations create with suppliers, manufacturers, and distributors to product and market a product. Network structures allow an organization to manage its global value chain and to find new ways to reduce costs while increasing the quality of products—without incurring the high costs of operating a complex organizational structure (such as the costs of employing many managers). More and more U.S. and European companies rely on global network structures to gain access to low-cost foreign sources of inputs, as discussed in Chapter 6. Athletic apparel giants such as Nike and Adidas have used this approach extensively.

Nike is the largest and most profitable athletic shoe manufacturer in the world. The key to Nike's success is the network structure that Nike founder and CEO Philip Knight created to allow his company to produce and market shoes. As noted in Chapter 6, the most successful companies today are trying to pursue simultaneously a low-cost and a differentiation strategy. Knight decided early that to do this at Nike he needed organizational architecture that would allow his company to focus on some functions, such as design, and leave others, such as manufacturing, to other organizations.

By far the largest function at Nike's Oregon headquarters is the design function, composed of talented designers who pioneered innovations in sports shoe design such as the air pump and Air Jordans that Nike introduced so successfully. Designers use computer-aided design (CAD) to design Nike shoes, and they electronically store all new product information, including manufacturing instructions. When the designers have finished their work, they electronically transmit all the blueprints for the new products to a network of Southeast Asian suppliers and manufacturers with which Nike has formed strategic alliances.[58] Instructions for the design of a new sole may be sent to a supplier in Taiwan; instructions for the leather uppers, to a supplier in Malaysia. The suppliers produce the shoe parts and send them for final assembly to a manufacturer in China with which Nike has established another strategic alliance. From China the shoes are shipped to distributors throughout the world. Ninety-nine percent of the more than 100 million pairs of shoes that Nike sells each year are made in Southeast Asia.

This network structure gives Nike two important advantages. First, Nike is able to respond to changes in athletic shoe fashion very quickly. Using its global IT system, Nike literally can change the instructions it gives each of its suppliers overnight, so that within a few weeks its foreign manufacturers are producing new kinds of shoes.[59] Any alliance partners that fail to perform up to Nike's standards are replaced with new partners through the regular B2B marketplace.

outsource To use outside suppliers and manufacturers to produce goods and services.

Second, Nike's costs are very low because wages in Southeast Asia are a fraction of what they are in the United States, and this difference gives Nike a low-cost advantage. Also, Nike's ability to **outsource** and use foreign manufacturers to produce all its shoes abroad allows Knight to keep the organization's U.S. structure flat and flexible. Nike is able to use a relatively inexpensive functional structure to organize its activities.

The use of network structures is increasing rapidly as companies recognize the many opportunities they offer to reduce costs and increase organizational flexibility. Supply chain spending by U.S. firms is expected to increase by more than 10% over the new few years.[60] The push to reduce costs has led to the development of B2B marketplaces in which most or all of the companies in a specific industry (for example, auto makers) use the same platform link to each other and establish industry specifications and standards. Then these companies jointly list the quantity and specifications of the inputs they require and solicit bids from thousands of potential suppliers from around the world. Suppliers also use the same software platform, so electronic bidding, auctions, and transactions are possible between buyers and sellers on a global basis. The idea is that high-volume, standardized transactions can help drive down costs at the industry level.

The ability of managers to develop a network structure to produce or provide the goods and services customers want, rather than create a complex organizational structure to do so, has led many researchers and consultants to popularize the idea of a **boundaryless organization**. Such an organization is composed of people linked by technology—computers, email, computer-aided design systems, videoconferencing, and cloud-based software—who may rarely, if ever, see one another face-to-face. People are utilized when their services are needed, much as in a matrix structure, but they are not formal members of an organization; they are functional experts who form an alliance with an organization, fulfill their contractual obligations, and then move on to the next project.

Large consulting companies, such as Accenture, IBM, and McKinsey & Co., utilize their global consultants in this way. Consultants are connected by laptops to an organization's **knowledge management system**, its company-specific virtual information system that systematizes the knowledge of its employees and facilitates the sharing and integration of expertise within and between functions and divisions through real-time interconnected technology.

boundaryless organization An organization whose members are linked by computers, email, computer-aided design systems, videoconferencing, and cloud-based software, and who rarely, if ever, see one another face-to-face.

knowledge management system A company-specific virtual information system that systematizes the knowledge of its employees and facilitates the sharing and integration of their expertise.

Summary and Review

DESIGNING ORGANIZATIONAL STRUCTURE The four main determinants of organizational structure are the external environment, strategy, technology, and human resources. In general, the higher the level of uncertainty associated with these factors, the more appropriate is a flexible, adaptable structure as opposed to a formal, rigid one. [LO 7-1]

GROUPING TASKS INTO JOBS Job design is the process by which managers group tasks into jobs. To create more interesting jobs, and to get workers to act flexibly, managers can enlarge and enrich jobs. The job characteristics model provides a tool managers can use to measure how motivating or satisfying a particular job is. [LO 7-2]

GROUPING JOBS INTO FUNCTIONS AND DIVISIONS Managers can choose from many kinds of organizational structures to make the best use of organizational resources. Depending on the specific organizing problems they face, managers can choose from functional, product, geographic, market, matrix, product team, and hybrid structures. [LO 7-3]

COORDINATING FUNCTIONS AND DIVISIONS No matter which structure managers choose, they must decide how to distribute authority in the organization, how many levels to have in the hierarchy of authority, and what balance to strike between centralization and decentralization to keep the number of levels in the hierarchy to a minimum. As organizations grow, managers must increase integration and coordination among functions and divisions. Six integrating mechanisms are available to facilitate this: direct contact, liaison roles, task forces, cross-functional teams, integrating roles, and the matrix structure. [LO 7-3, 7-4]

STRATEGIC ALLIANCES, B2B NETWORK STRUCTURES, AND IT To avoid many of the communication and coordination problems that emerge as organizations grow, managers are using IT to develop new ways of organizing. In a strategic alliance, managers enter into an agreement with another organization to provide inputs or to perform a functional activity. If managers enter into a series of these agreements, they create a network structure. A network structure, most commonly based on some shared form of IT, can be formed around one company, or a number of companies can join together to create an industry B2B network. Increasingly, technology encourages more cross-functional communication among departments and with other organizations. As this continues, the concept of a *boundaryless,* or virtual, organization has become commonplace, in which employees and other members are linked electronically and may not encounter each other in face-to-face work situations. [LO 7-5]

Management *in Action*

 TOPICS FOR DISCUSSION AND ACTION

Discussion

1. Would a flexible or a more formal structure be appropriate for these organizations: (a) a large department store, (b) a Big Four accounting firm, (c) a biotechnology company? Explain your reasoning. [LO 7-1, 7-2]

2. Using the job characteristics model as a guide, discuss how a manager can enrich or enlarge subordinates' jobs. [LO 7-2]

3. How might a salesperson's job or an administrative assistant's job be enlarged or enriched to make it more motivating? [LO 7-2, 7-3]

4. When and under what conditions might managers change from a functional to (a) a product, (b) a geographic, or (c) a market structure? [LO 7-1, 7-3]

5. How do matrix structures and product team structures differ? Why is the product team structure more widely used? [LO 7-1, 7-3, 7-4]

6. As high-powered, low-cost wireless technologies continue to grow, many managers soon may not need to come to an office to do their jobs but may work at home. What are the pros and cons of such an arrangement? [LO 7-5]

Action

7. Find and interview a manager, and identify the kind of organizational structure that his or her organization uses to coordinate its people and resources. Why is the organization using that structure? Do you think a different structure would be more appropriate? If so which one? [LO 7-1, 7-3, 7-4]

8. With the same or another manager, discuss the distribution of authority in the organization. Does the manager think that decentralizing authority and empowering employees are appropriate? [LO 7-1, 7-3]

9. What are the advantages and disadvantages of business-to-business networks? [LO 7-5]

BUILDING MANAGEMENT SKILLS

Understanding Organizing [LO 7-1, 7-2, 7-3]

Think of an organization with which you are familiar, perhaps one you have worked for—such as a store, restaurant, office, church, or school. Then answer the following questions:

1. Which contingencies are most important in explaining how the organization is organized? Do you think it is organized in the best way?

2. Using the job characteristics model, how motivating do you think the job of a typical employee is in this organization?

3. Can you think of any ways in which a typical job could be enlarged or enriched?

4. What kind of organizational structure does the organization use? If it is part of a chain, what kind of structure does the entire organization use? What

other structures discussed in the chapter might allow the organization to operate more effectively? For example, would the move to a product team structure lead to greater efficiency or effectiveness? Why or why not?

5. How many levels are there in the organization's hierarchy? Is authority centralized or decentralized? Describe the span of control of the top manager and of middle or first-line managers.

6. Is the distribution of authority appropriate for the organization

and its activities? Would it be possible to flatten the hierarchy by decentralizing authority and empowering employees?

7. What are the principal integrating mechanisms used in the organization? Do they provide sufficient coordination among individuals and functions? How might they be improved?

8. Now that you have analyzed the way this organization is structured, what advice would you give its managers to help them improve the way it operates?

MANAGING ETHICALLY [LO 7-1, 7-3]

Suppose an organization is downsizing and laying off many of its middle managers. Some top managers charged with deciding whom to terminate might decide to keep the subordinates they like, and who are obedient to them, rather than the ones who are difficult or the best performers. They might also decide to lay off the most highly paid subordinates even if they are high performers. Think of the ethical issues involved

in designing a hierarchy, and discuss the following issues.

Questions

1. What ethical rules (see Chapter 3) should managers use to decide which employees to terminate when redesigning their hierarchy?

2. Some people argue that employees who have worked for an organization for many

years have a claim on the organization at least as strong as that of its shareholders. What do you think of the ethics of this position—can employees claim to "own" their jobs if they have contributed significantly to the organization's past success? How does a socially responsible organization behave in this situation?

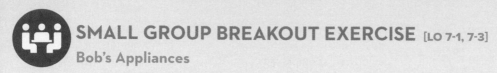
Form groups of three or four people, and appoint one member as the spokesperson who will communicate your findings to the class when called on by the instructor. Then discuss the following scenario:

Bob's Appliances sells and services household appliances such as washing machines, dishwashers, ranges, and refrigerators. Over the years, the company has developed a good reputation for the quality of its customer service, and many local builders patronize the store. Recently, other national retailers, including Best Buy, Lowe's, and Costco, have begun to offer appliances for sale. To attract more customers, however, these stores also carry a complete range of consumer electronics products—televisions, stereos, and computers. Bob Lange, the owner of Bob's Appliances, has decided that if he is to stay in business, he must widen his product range and compete directly with the chains.

Lange decides to build a 20,000-square-foot store and service center, and he is now hiring new employees to sell and service the new line of consumer electronics. Because of his company's increased size, Lange is not sure of the best way to organize the employees. Currently, he uses a functional structure; employees are divided into sales, purchasing and accounting, and repair. Bob is wondering whether selling and servicing consumer electronics is so different from selling and servicing appliances that he should move to a product structure (see the figure) and create separate sets of functions for each of his two lines of business.[61]

Question

1. You are a team of local consultants whom Bob has called in to advise him as he makes this crucial choice. Which structure do you recommend? Why?

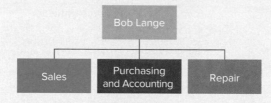

FUNCTIONAL STRUCTURE

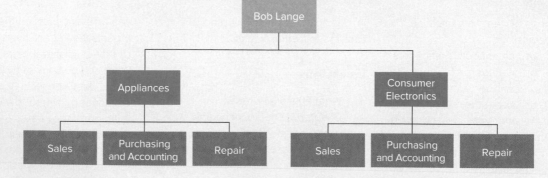

PRODUCT STRUCTURE

BE THE MANAGER [LO 7-1, 7-3, 7-4]

Speeding Up Website Design

You have been hired by a website design, production, and hosting company whose new animated website designs are attracting a lot of attention and a lot of customers. Currently, employees are organized into different functions such as hardware, software design, graphic art, and website hosting, as well as functions such as marketing and human resources. Each function takes its turn to work on a new project from initial customer request to final online website hosting.

The problem the company is experiencing is that it typically takes one year from the initial idea stage to the time that the website is up and running; the company wants to shorten this time by half to protect and expand its market niche. In talking to other managers, you discover that they believe the company's current functional structure is the source of the problem—it is not allowing employees to develop websites fast enough to satisfy customers' demands. They want you to design a better structure.

Questions

1. Discuss ways in which you can improve how the current functional structure operates so that it speeds website development.

2. Discuss the pros and cons of moving to a (a) multidivisional, (b) matrix, or (c) product team structure to reduce website development time.

3. Which of these structures do you think is most appropriate, and why?

BUSINESS INSIDER CASE IN THE NEWS [LO 7-1, 7-2, 7-3, 7-4]

80% of Zappos Employees No Longer Have a Manager

When Zappos announced late last year that it would eliminate titles and traditional managers from its company, some were skeptical about whether the online shoe retailer could pull it off.

But the company tells *Business Insider* that 80% of its 1,500 employees are now working under Holacracy, a relatively new organizational philosophy meant to offer workers more flexibility by replacing traditional job titles with a fluctuating number of roles that each employee is assigned.

Rather than being accountable to a single boss in a traditional hierarchy, each employee reports to the other people in their "circles." Each circle has an organizational goal to achieve, and each role that people

fill within the circle is a task necessary for accomplishing that goal.

Of course Holacracy has not made Zappos a company entirely without hierarchy. The job of assigning roles within in a circle is left to a singular person known as the "lead link," and many circles contain subcircles that they oversee.

For instance, Zappos CEO Tony Hsieh is the lead link on the company's broadest circle, the 10-member internal board, which is tasked with fulfilling the company's overall purpose.

John Bunch, the Zappos employee tasked with running the company's transition to Holacracy, tells *Business Insider* that Hsieh's power is different under Holacracy.

However, Bunch declines to say whether Hsieh's sway has increased or decreased at the company he joined as CEO in 2000 and sold to Amazon 9 years later for $1.2 billion.

Hsieh holds "many, many, many roles" across the company, Bunch says, including being the "department expert" in a circle devoted to teaching other businesses about Zappos' famously quirky corporate culture.

And while employees no longer have titles internally, Bunch says they have what Zappos calls "#titles" to explain what they do all day to people outside the company.

Thus far, Bunch says the company is on pace to meet its goal of having all of its employees operating under Holacracy by the end of the year.

In his mind, one of the biggest challenges posed by the new system has been teaching employees not only what Holacracy is but how to use it, a process he compares to teaching 1,500 people how to speak a new language.

The organizational philosophy, created in 2009 by software developer Brian Robertson, is characterized by a series of governance meetings in which circle members iron out "tensions," the issues that are preventing the circle from running as smoothly as possible.

"I think you hear a spectrum of reactions," Bunch says when asked what his employees are saying about the transition. "Each employee is on their own personal journey in terms of learning what Holacracy is all about, and learning how to use it, and discovering if they think this is the right system."

Still, it's unclear how much the company has functionally changed since it began its transition at the end of last year.

Bunch says that several areas of the company have used Holacracy to make necessary changes to how they approach certain organizational challenges, but he declines to say which changes were made or which areas of the company were behind them.

Additionally, Bunch says a lot of the company's hiring, firing, and salary decisions are made the same way they were a year ago, but that over time, the company will evolve those systems to make them more in line with Holacracy.

"I don't want to paint a rose-colored picture where I say everything is up and running and we've reached our highest potential, but we have seen some bright spots," Bunch says.

Ultimately, he hopes the move to Holacracy will pay off by helping the company better realize its goals of openness and excellent internal communication, and that the looser organizational structure will allow employees to push the company into areas it has not previously ventured into.

"One of the markers of success for Holacracy would be to look back in five years and say, 'Wow I would never have envisioned Zappos taking on that area, and look at them, they're having success with it,'" Bunch says.

Questions

1. How might fluctuating job roles affect employees' productivity?

2. As an employee, what advantages and disadvantages do you see to Holacracy?

3. Search the Internet and outline additional changes that have occurred at Zappos since the new management structure was implemented. Do you think the structure will be a success? Why or why not?

Source: Aaron Taube, "80% of Zappos Employees No Longer Have a Manager," *Business Insider,* November 4, 2014, www.businessinsider.com.

Endnotes

1. D. Price, "Managing Creativity: Lessons from Pixar and Disney Animation," *Harvard Business Review,* accessed April 15, 2015, http://blogs.hbr.org; A. Stewart, "'Frozen' Reaches $1.29 Billion to Become Fifth-Highest Grossing Film Globally," *Variety,* accessed April 15, 2015, http://variety.com.

2. Company website, "Captain America Comics," http://marvel.com, accessed April 15, 2015.

3. Company website, "Excerpt from *Comic Wars,*" www.randomhouse.com, accessed April 15, 2015.

4. Company website, "The Pixar Timeline 1979 to Present," http://pixar.com, accessed April 15, 2015.

5. E. Catmull, "Building a Sense of Purpose at Pixar," *McKinsey & Company Insights,* accessed April 15, 2015, www.mckinsey.com.

6. Price, "Managing Creativity: Lessons from Pixar and Disney Animation."

7. "How Pixar Changed Disney Animation," *CBC News,* accessed April 15, 2015, www.cbc.ca.

8. Price, "Managing Creativity: Lessons from Pixar and Disney Animation."

9. G. R. Jones, *Organizational Theory, Design and Change: Text and Cases* (Upper Saddle River: Prentice Hall, 2011).

10. J. Child, *Organization: A Guide for Managers and Administrators* (New York: Harper & Row, 1977).

11. P. R. Lawrence and J. W. Lorsch, *Organization and Environment* (Boston: Graduate School of Business Administration, Harvard University, 1967).

12. R. Duncan, "What Is the Right Organizational Design?"

Organizational Dynamics, Winter 1979, 59–80.

13. T. Burns and G. R. Stalker, *The Management of Innovation* (London: Tavistock, 1966).

14. D. Miller, "Strategy Making and Structure: Analysis and Implications for Performance," *Academy of Management Journal* 30 (1987), 7–32.

15. A. D. Chandler, *Strategy and Structure* (Cambridge, MA: MIT Press, 1962).

16. J. Stopford and L. Wells, *Managing the Multinational Enterprise* (London: Longman, 1972).

17. C. Perrow, *Organizational Analysis: A Sociological View* (Belmont, CA: Wadsworth, 1970).

18. Government website, "First Lady Michelle Obama Announces Commitment by Subway®

Restaurants to Promote Healthier Choices to Kids," www.whitehouse.gov, accessed April 15, 2015.

19. F. W. Taylor, *The Principles of Scientific Management* (New York: Harper, 1911).

20. R. W. Griffin, *Task Design: An Integrative Approach* (Glenview, IL: Scott, Foresman, 1982).

21. Ibid.

22. V. Wong, "Let's Go to Wendy's and Cuddle by the Fireplace," *Bloomberg Businessweek,* accessed April 15, 2015, ww.bloomberg.com.

23. "Meritage Reports Acquisition of Wendy's Restaurants in Tallahassee, Florida," *Market Wired,* accessed April 15, 2015, www.marketwired.com.

24. J. Daley, "Wendy's Franchise Owner Launches a Big Training Initiative," *Entrepreneur,* accessed April 15, 2015, www.entrepreneur.com.

25. J. R. Hackman and G. R. Oldham, *Work Redesign* (Reading, MA: Addison-Wesley, 1980).

26. J. R. Galbraith and R. K. Kazanjian, *Strategy Implementation: Structure, System, and Process,* 2nd ed. (St. Paul, MN: West, 1986).

27. Lawrence and Lorsch, *Organization and Environment.*

28. Jones, *Organizational Theory.*

29. Lawrence and Lorsch, *Organization and Environment.*

30. R. H. Hall, *Organizations: Structure and Process* (Englewood Cliffs, NJ: Prentice Hall, 1972); R. Miles, *Macro Organizational Behavior* (Santa Monica, CA: Goodyear, 1980).

31. Chandler, *Strategy and Structure.*

32. G. R. Jones and C. W. L. Hill, "Transaction Cost Analysis of Strategy-Structure Choice," *Strategic Management Journal* 9 (1988), 159–72.

33. Company website, "About Us," www.gsk.com, accessed April 10, 2015; Albertina Torsoli and Makiko Kitamura, "Glaxo Plans Changes to Compensation Program for U.S. Sales Team," *Chicago Tribune,* accessed April 10, 2015, www.chicagotribune.com.

34. Company website, "About Us," www.mbakerintl.com, accessed April 16, 2015.

35. Company website, "Vision Statement," www.mbakerintl.com, accessed April 16, 2015.

36. "Michael Baker International Unveils New Organizational Structure for National and International Expansion," *Business Wire,* accessed April 16, 2015, www.businesswire.com.

37. C. Mortensen, "Jonathan Martin Went to Hospital," http://espn.go.com, accessed April 16, 2015.

38. "Incognito, Others Tormented Martin," http://espn.go.com, accessed April 16, 2015.

39. "Heads Roll Following Report on Miami Dolphins Bullying Scandal," *The Blaze,* accessed April 16, 2015, www.theblaze.com.

40. "Incognito, Others Tormented Martin."

41. "Heads Roll Following Report on Miami Dolphins Bullying Scandal."

42. S. M. Davis and P. R. Lawrence, *Matrix* (Reading, MA: Addison-Wesley, 1977); J. R. Galbraith, "Matrix Organization Designs: How to Combine Functional and Project Forms," *Business Horizons* 14 (1971), 29–40.

43. L. R. Burns, "Matrix Management in Hospitals: Testing Theories of Matrix Structure and Development," *Administrative Science Quarterly* 34 (1989), 349–68.

44. C. W. L. Hill, *International Business* (Homewood, IL: Irwin, 2003).

45. Kotter International, "5 Innovation Secrets from Sealy," *Forbes,* accessed April 15, 2015, www.forbes.com.

46. Jones, *Organizational Theory.*

47. P. Blau, "A Formal Theory of Differentiation in Organizations," *American Sociological Review* 35 (1970), 684–95.

48. Company website, "McDonald's Announces Initial Steps in Turnaround Plan Including Worldwide Business Restructuring and Financial Updates," http://news.mcdonalds.com, accessed September 3, 2015; "Executive Team," www.aboutmcdonalds.com, accessed September 3, 2015.

49. Child, *Organization.*

50. D. Schawbel, "10 Workplace Trends for 2015," *Forbes,* accessed April 15, 2015, www.forbes.com; J. Schoen, "Many Feel Like Recession Still Hasn't Ended," *USA Today,* accessed April 15, 2015, www.usatoday.com.

51. Company website, "Board of Directors," and "YUM! Brands Chairman and CEO David Novak Shares Break-Through Leadership Strategies in New Book, *Taking People with You: The Only Way to Make Big Things Happen,*" www.yum.com, accessed April 16, 2015.

52. P. M. Blau and R. A. Schoenherr, *The Structure of Organizations* (New York: Basic Books, 1971).

53. Jones, *Organizational Theory.*

54. J. R. Galbraith, *Designing Complex Organizations* (Reading, MA: Addison-Wesley, 1977), chap. 1; Galbraith and Kazanjian, *Strategy Implementation,* chap. 7.

55. "PepsiCo's Amy Chen: Doing Good for the Bottom Line—and the World," *Knowledge @ Wharton,* accessed April 16, 2015, http://knowledge.wharton.upenn.edu.

56. B. Kogut, "Joint Ventures: Theoretical and Empirical Perspectives," *Strategic Management Journal* 9 (1988), 319–32.

57. "IHG Announces Strategic Alliance with The Coca-Cola Company," *PR Newswire,* accessed April 16, 2015, www.prnewswire.com.

58. G. S. Capowski, "Designing a Corporate Identity," *Management Review,* June 1993, 37–38.

59. J. Marcia, "Just Doing It," *Distribution,* January 1995, 36–40.

60. L. Columbus, "Gartner Predicts CRM Will Be a $36B Market by 2017," *Forbes,* accessed April 16, 2015, www.forbes.com.

61. Copyright © 2006, Gareth R. Jones.

Control, Change, and Entrepreneurship

Learning Objectives

After studying this chapter, you should be able to:

LO 8-1 Define organizational control, and explain how it increases organizational effectiveness.

LO 8-2 Describe the four steps in the control process and the way it operates over time.

LO 8-3 Identify the main output controls, and discuss their advantages and disadvantages as means of coordinating and motivating employees.

LO 8-4 Explain how clan control or organizational culture creates an effective organizational architecture.

LO 8-5 Discuss the relationship between organizational control and change, and explain why managing change is a vital management task.

LO 8-6 Understand the role of entrepreneurship in the control and change process.

© claudia veja/Moment/Getty Images RF

Vynamic, a Philadelphia-based health care consultancy firm, introduced a corporate-wide ban on emails on the weekends and between 10 P.M. and 6 A.M. during the week for both managers and employees, which has helped improved productivity and work–life balance for the company's workforce.
© Glowimages/Getty Images RF

MANAGEMENT SNAPSHOT

Zmail Policy Helps Employee Productivity

How Can Managers Create a New Culture?

In terms of challenges in the modern workplace, email may be at the top of the list. Overuse of this communications method and the problems surrounding it continue to hinder employee effectiveness and efficiency. Recent research suggests that the average worker spends more than 13 hours per week on email—and those hours certainly are not limited to time spent in the office.[1] In this 24/7 world, with people connected to multiple devices simultaneously, how can managers help their employees handle email so that the quality of their work and their work–life balance don't suffer? Philadelphia-based Vynamic may have the answer for both managers and workers: a Zmail policy.

Vynamic is a health care consultancy firm that prides itself on a strong and healthy organizational culture. Several years ago, employees started to complain about the stress of constant email contact at all hours. CEO Dan Calista describes a common scenario that many professionals experience in this digital world. An employee checks email before going to sleep. Next thing the person knows, he or she is now thinking about the email instead of getting a restful stretch of "ZZZs." Thus, the Zmail policy was

born—Vynamic employees (including managers) are requested not to send emails between 10 p.m. and 6 a.m. during the week and all day Saturday and Sunday.

The company recognizes that some employees like to spend a few hours over the weekend reviewing pertinent emails and sending communications to clients and colleagues when no one is distracting them. For some people, there are benefits to this type of work habit. However, Calista recommends saving the email as a draft and sending it off first thing Monday morning. He asks, "Why is it so important to you that the other person join your weekend time?"

Despite the ban on late night and weekend emails, employees are expected to communicate with clients and colleagues as necessary to keep business moving forward. Calista says that unplugging from email and mentally disconnecting from work is not only liberating, it might also help employees become more productive after a good night's sleep. Vynamic employees have embraced the Zmail policy as an important benefit to working for the company: over the past five years, less than 10% of its consultants have left the organization.[2]

Not all companies have the tools or the time to implement organizational controls like the one initiated by Vynamic. However, there are ways that managers and employees alike can get a handle on managing the email challenge. The following tips can be useful to professionals at all levels of an organization:

- Turn off notifications so you are not distracted by each and every message received.

- Don't check email more than three times a day, and select specific times in the workday to check for messages.

- If you need information from a colleague in less than three hours, use a different mode of communication than an email request—how about picking up the phone and asking? This allows coworkers to work on other tasks without dreading one more email notification, and it models behavior that coworkers might adapt, resulting in fewer email messages for everyone.

- Respond to both simple and urgent messages, file those that do not require a reply, and flag any that require more thought and follow-up.

- Use group lists. If you email the same group of people over and over, put them in a group so you do not have to type everyone's email addresses each time you send a message. This also allows you to sort messages to and from the group for easy archiving or deletion.

- If you feel you must hold on to some messages, create folders in which to store them so they are not in your inbox.

- Empty the trash at the end of the day. Sometimes you will need to retrieve an email from the trash, so make this the last thing you do each day.[3]

Overview   As the experience at Vynamic suggests, the ways in which managers decide to control and regulate the behavior of their employees has important effects on their performance. When managers make choices about how to influence and shape employees' behavior and performance, they are using organizational control. And control is the essential ingredient that is needed to bring about and manage organizational change efficiently and effectively.

As discussed in Chapter 7, the first task facing managers is to establish the structure of task and job reporting relationships that allows organizational members to use resources most efficiently and effectively. Structure alone, however, does not provide the incentive or motivation for people to behave in ways that help achieve organizational goals. The purpose of organizational control is to provide managers with a means of directing and motivating subordinates to work toward achieving organizational goals and to provide managers with specific feedback on how well an organization and its members are performing.

Organizational structure provides an organization with a skeleton, and control and culture give it the muscles, sinews, nerves, and sensations that allow managers to regulate and govern its activities. The managerial functions of organizing and controlling are inseparable, and effective managers must learn to make them work together in a harmonious way.

In this chapter, we look in detail at the nature of organizational control and describe the steps in the control process. We discuss three types of control available to managers to control and influence organizational members—output control, behavior control, and clan control (which operates through the values and norms of an organization's culture).[4] Then we discuss the important issue of organizational change, change that is possible only when managers have put in place a control system that allows them to alter the way people and groups behave. Finally, we look at the role of entrepreneurs and entrepreneurship in changing the way a company operates. By the end of this chapter, you will appreciate the rich variety of control systems available to managers and understand why developing an appropriate control system is vital to increasing the performance of an organization and its members.

What Is Organizational Control?

As we noted in Chapter 1, *controlling* is the process whereby managers monitor and regulate how efficiently and effectively an organization and its members are performing the activities necessary to achieve organizational goals. As discussed in previous chapters, when planning and organizing, managers develop the organizational strategy and structure that they hope will allow the organization to use resources most effectively to create value for customers. In controlling, managers monitor and evaluate whether the organization's strategy and structure are working as intended, how they could be improved, and how they might be changed if they are not working.

Control, however, does not mean just reacting to events after they have occurred. It also means keeping an organization on track, anticipating events that might occur, and then changing the organization to respond to whatever opportunities or threats have been identified. Control is concerned with keeping employees motivated, focused on the important problems confronting the organization, and working together to make the changes that will help an organization perform better over time.

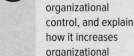

LO 8-1 Define organizational control, and explain how it increases organizational effectiveness.

The Importance of Organizational Control

To understand the importance of organizational control, consider how it helps managers obtain superior efficiency, quality, responsiveness to customers, and innovation—the four building blocks of competitive advantage.

To determine how efficiently they are using their resources, managers must be able to accurately measure how many units of inputs (raw materials, human resources, and so on) are being used to produce a unit of output, such as a Ford or Toyota vehicle. Managers also must be able to measure how many units of outputs (goods and services) are being produced. A control system contains the measures or yardsticks that let managers assess how efficiently the organization is producing goods and services. Moreover, if managers experiment with changing how the organization produces goods and services to find a more efficient way of producing them, these measures tell managers how successful they have been. Without a control system in place, managers have no idea how well their organization is performing and how its performance can be improved—information that is becoming increasingly important in today's highly competitive environment.

Today much of the competition among organizations centers on increasing the quality of goods and services. In the car industry, for example, cars within each price range compete in features, design, and reliability. Thus whether a customer will buy a Ford Focus, Toyota Camry, or Honda Accord depends significantly on the quality of each product. Organizational control is important in determining the quality of goods and services because it gives managers feedback on product quality. If the managers of carmakers consistently measure the number of customer complaints and the number of new cars returned for repairs, or if school principals

From whom would you rather buy a new car? A company that reinforces and rewards employee responsiveness, consistency, and know-how in customer care, or a company that doesn't? Toyota bets you'll pick the former. © Hongqi Zhang/Alamy RF

measure how many students drop out of school or how achievement scores on nationally based tests vary over time, they have a good indication of how much quality they have built into their product—be it an educated student or a car that does not break down. Effective managers create a control system that consistently monitors the quality of goods and services so they can continuously improve quality—an approach to change that gives them a competitive advantage.

Managers can help make their organizations more responsive to customers if they develop a control system that allows them to evaluate how well customer-contact employees perform their jobs. Monitoring employee behavior can help managers find ways to increase employees' performance levels, perhaps by revealing areas in which skill training can help employees or in which new procedures can allow employees to perform their jobs better. Also, when employees know their behaviors are being monitored, they have more incentive to be helpful and consistent in how they act toward customers. To improve customer service, for example, Toyota regularly surveys customers about their experiences with particular Toyota dealers. If a dealership receives too many customer complaints, Toyota's managers investigate the dealership to uncover the sources of the problems and suggest solutions; if necessary, they might even threaten to reduce the number of cars a dealership receives to force the dealer to improve the quality of its customer service.

Finally, controlling can raise the level of innovation in an organization. Successful innovation takes place when managers create an organizational setting in which employees feel empowered to be creative and in which authority is decentralized to employees so they feel free to experiment and take control of their work activities. Deciding on the appropriate control systems to encourage risk taking is an important management challenge; organizational culture is vital in this regard. To encourage work teams at Toyota to perform at a high level, for example, top managers monitored the performance of each team, by examining how each team reduced costs or increased quality—and used a bonus system related to performance to reward each team. The team manager then evaluated each team member's individual performance, and the most innovative employees received promotions and rewards based on their superior performance.

Control Systems and IT

control systems
Formal target-setting, monitoring, evaluation, and feedback systems that provide managers with information about how well the organization's strategy and structure are working.

Control systems are formal target-setting, monitoring, evaluation, and feedback systems that provide managers with information about whether the organization's strategy and structure are working efficiently and effectively.[5] Effective control systems alert managers when something is going wrong and give them time to respond to opportunities and threats. An effective control system has three characteristics: It is flexible enough to allow managers to respond as necessary to unexpected events; it provides accurate information about organizational performance; and it gives managers information in a timely manner because making decisions on the basis of outdated information is a recipe for failure.

New forms of IT have revolutionized control systems because they facilitate the flow of accurate and timely information up and down the organizational hierarchy and between functions and divisions. Today employees at all levels of the organization routinely feed information into a company's information system or network and start the chain of events that affect decision making in some other part of the organization. This could be the retail clerk who scans a tag on a purchased piece of sportswear that tells merchandise managers what items need to be reordered or the salesperson in the field who uses a mobile device to inform marketing about customers' changing wants or needs.

feedforward control Control that allows managers to anticipate problems before they arise.

Control and information systems are developed to measure performance at each stage in the process of transforming inputs into finished goods and services (see Figure 8.1). At the input stage, managers use **feedforward control** to anticipate problems before they arise so problems do not occur later during the conversion process.[6] For example, by giving stringent product specifications to suppliers in advance (a form of performance target), an organization can control the quality of the inputs it receives from its suppliers and thus avoid potential problems during the conversion process. Also, technology can be used to keep in contact with suppliers and to monitor their progress. Similarly, by screening job applicants, often by viewing their résumés electronically and using several interviews to select the most highly skilled people, managers can lessen the chance that they will hire people who lack the necessary skills or experience to perform effectively. In general, the development of management information systems promotes feedforward control that gives managers timely information about changes in the task and general environments that may impact their organization later on. Effective managers always monitor trends and changes in the external environment to try to anticipate problems. (We discuss management information systems in detail in Chapter 13.)

concurrent control Control that gives managers immediate feedback on how efficiently inputs are being transformed into outputs so managers can correct problems as they arise.

At the conversion stage, **concurrent control** gives managers immediate feedback on how efficiently inputs are being transformed into outputs so managers can correct problems as they arise. Concurrent control through IT alerts managers to the need to react quickly to whatever is the source of the problem, be it a defective batch of inputs, a machine that is out of alignment, or a worker who lacks the skills necessary to perform a task efficiently. Concurrent control is at the heart of programs to

Figure 8.1

Three Types of Control

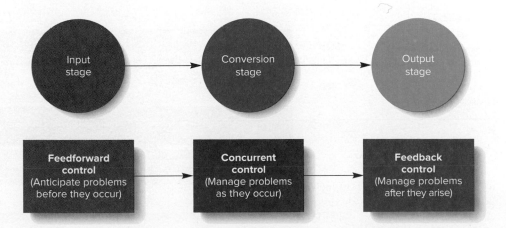

increase quality, in which workers are expected to constantly monitor the quality of the goods or services they provide at every step of the production process and inform managers as soon as they discover problems. One of the strengths of Toyota's production system, for example, is that individual workers have the authority to push a button to stop the assembly line whenever they discover a quality problem. When all problems are corrected, the result is a finished product that is much more reliable.

At the output stage, managers use **feedback control** to provide information about customers' reactions to goods and services so corrective action can be taken if necessary. For example, a feedback control system that monitors the number of customer returns alerts managers when defective products are being produced, and a management information system (MIS) that measures increases or decreases in relative sales of different products alerts managers to changes in customer tastes so they can increase or reduce the production of specific products.

feedback control

Control that gives managers information about customers' reactions to goods and services so corrective action can be taken if necessary.

LO 8-2 Describe the four steps in the control process and the way it operates over time.

The Control Process

The control process, whether at the input, conversion, or output stage, can be broken down into four steps: establishing standards of performance, and then measuring, comparing, and evaluating actual performance (see Figure 8.2).[7]

- Step 1: *Establish the standards of performance, goals, or targets against which performance is to be evaluated.*

At step 1 in the control process managers decide on the standards of performance, goals, or targets that they will use in the future to evaluate the performance of the entire organization or part of it (such as a division, a function, or an individual). The standards of performance that managers select measure efficiency, quality, responsiveness to customers, and innovation.[8] If managers decide to pursue a low-cost strategy, for example, they need to measure efficiency at all levels in the organization.

At the corporate level, a standard of performance that measures efficiency is operating costs, the actual costs associated with producing goods and services, including all employee-related costs. Top managers might set a corporate goal of "reducing operating costs by 10% for the next three years" to increase efficiency. Corporate managers might then evaluate divisional managers for their ability to

Figure 8.2

Four Steps in Organizational Control

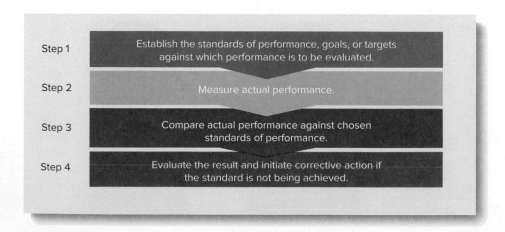

Step 1 — Establish the standards of performance, goals, or targets against which performance is to be evaluated.

Step 2 — Measure actual performance.

Step 3 — Compare actual performance against chosen standards of performance.

Step 4 — Evaluate the result and initiate corrective action if the standard is not being achieved.

reduce operating costs within their respective divisions, and divisional managers might set cost-saving targets for functional managers. Thus performance standards selected at one level affect those at the other levels, and ultimately the performance of individual managers is evaluated in terms of their ability to reduce costs.

The number of standards or indicators of performance that an organization's managers use to evaluate efficiency, quality, and so on can run into the thousands or hundreds of thousands. Managers at each level are responsible for selecting standards that will best allow them to evaluate how well the part of the organization they are responsible for is performing.[9] Managers must be careful to choose standards of performance that let them assess how well they are doing with all four building blocks of competitive advantage. If managers focus on just one standard (such as efficiency), and ignore others (such as determining what customers really want and innovating a new line of products to satisfy them), managers may end up hurting their organization's performance.

- Step 2: *Measure actual performance.*

Once managers have decided which standards or targets they will use to evaluate performance, the next step in the control process is to measure actual performance. In practice, managers can measure or evaluate two things: (1) the actual *outputs* that result from the behavior of their members and (2) the *behaviors* themselves (hence the terms *output control* and *behavior control* used in this chapter).[10]

Sometimes both outputs and behaviors can be easily measured. Measuring outputs and evaluating behavior are relatively easy in a fast-food restaurant, for example, because employees are performing routine tasks. Managers at Home Depot are rigorous in using output control to measure how fast inventory flows through stores. Similarly, managers of a fast-food restaurant can easily measure outputs by counting how many customers their employees serve, the time each transaction takes, and how much money each customer spends. Managers can easily observe each employee's behavior and quickly take action to solve any problems that may arise.

When an organization and its members perform complex, nonroutine activities that are intrinsically hard to measure, it is more challenging for managers to measure outputs or behavior.[11] It is difficult, for example, for managers in charge of R&D departments at Intel or Apple, or at Microsoft or Google, to measure performance or to evaluate the performance of individual members because it can take several years to determine whether the new products that engineers and scientists are developing will be profitable. Moreover, it is impossible for a manager to measure how creative an engineer or scientist is by watching his or her actions.

In general, the more nonroutine or complex organizational activities are, the harder it is for managers to measure outputs or behaviors.[12] Outputs, however, are usually easier to measure than behaviors because they are more tangible and objective. Therefore, the first kind of performance measures that managers tend to use are those that measure outputs. Then managers develop performance measures or standards that allow them to evaluate behaviors to determine whether employees at all levels are working toward organizational goals. Some simple behavior measures are (1) whether employees come to work on time and (2) whether employees consistently follow the established rules for greeting and serving customers. The various types of output and behavior control and how they are used at the different organizational levels—corporate, divisional, functional, and individual—are discussed in detail later.

- Step 3: *Compare actual performance against chosen standards of performance.*

During step 3, managers evaluate whether—and to what extent—performance deviates from the standards of performance chosen in step 1. If performance is higher than expected, managers might decide they set performance standards too low and may raise them for the next period to challenge their subordinates.[13] Managers at successful companies are well known for the way they try to improve performance in manufacturing settings by constantly raising performance standards to motivate managers and workers to find new ways to reduce costs or increase quality.

However, if performance is too low and standards were not reached, or if standards were set so high that employees could not achieve them, managers must decide whether to take corrective action.[14] It is easy to take corrective action when the reasons for poor performance can be identified—for instance, high labor costs. To reduce costs, managers can search for low-cost overseas suppliers, invest more in technology, or implement cross-functional teams. More often, however, the reasons for poor performance are hard to identify. Changes in the environment, such as the emergence of a new global competitor, a recession, or an increase in interest rates, might be the source of the problem. Within an organization, perhaps the R&D function underestimated the problems it would encounter in developing a new product or the extra costs of doing unforeseen research. If managers are to take any form of corrective action, step 4 is necessary.

- Step 4: *Evaluate the result and initiate corrective action (that is, make changes) if the standard is not being achieved.*

The final step in the control process is to evaluate the results and bring about change as appropriate. Whether or not performance standards have been met, managers can learn a great deal during this step. If managers decide the level of performance is unacceptable, they must try to change how work activities are performed to solve the problem. Sometimes performance problems occur because the work standard was too high—for example, a sales target was too optimistic and impossible to achieve. In this case, adopting more realistic standards can reduce the gap between actual performance and desired performance.

However, if managers determine that something in the situation is causing the problem, then to raise performance they will need to change how resources are utilized or shared.[15] Perhaps the latest technology is not being used; perhaps workers lack the advanced training needed to perform at a higher level; perhaps the organization needs to buy its inputs or assemble its products abroad to compete against low-cost rivals; perhaps it needs to restructure itself or reengineer its work processes to increase efficiency. A recent case among forward-deployed troops throughout Afghanistan demonstrates the four steps of the control process. See the accompanying "Management Insight" feature for the details.

MANAGEMENT INSIGHT

The Control Process in Action in Afghanistan

The U.S. Army's research and development team seeks to increase efficiency and performance of power and energy at installations across the globe. The Department of Defense's Project Manager Expeditionary Energy & Sustainment

The mission of Project Manager Expeditionary Energy & Sustainment Systems is to manage the mobile generators used by the military to power modern warfare utilizing the four-step control process. U.S. Army Photo

Systems (formerly known as Project Manager Mobile Electric Power) is the energy behind modern warfare. Two electrical engineers from the Army's Communications, Electronics Research, Development and Engineering Center (CERDEC) deployed to Afghanistan to support the project. The mission of the project was to manage the department's mobile electric power generators. In combat zones, mobile generators supply most of the energy and power. It is policy that all armed forces use the same generator sets as much as possible. Using the same generator sets reduces costs and enhances logistics support and interoperability.[16]

The job of the two engineers deployed to Afghanistan was to assess and improve the energy stability of forward-deployed troops. Their work followed the four steps of the control process.

Step 1: Establish the standards of performance, goals, or targets against which performance is to be evaluated. The two engineers on the project, Noel Pleta and Jennifer Whitmore, outlined the need to know each soldier's energy needs, in addition to figuring out how much energy usage could be reduced.

Step 2: Measure actual performance. The engineers began with collecting data that determined a power profile by surveying all equipment and combining the information with manufacturer data. Data were loaded into a database that could be used to make decisions. A separate planning tool allowed commanders to plan efficient power grids by generating virtual layouts of outposts and bases, along with determining how much energy would be needed based on the number of tents and other energy-using devices.

Step 3: Compare actual performance against chosen standards of performance. The engineers found that much of the current energy and power infrastructure was in bad shape and that the basics needed to be established. "Many of the COPs [combat outposts] were on their last leg of generator power, causing them to shut down their sustainment of life support systems and focus on the tactical support systems," Pleta said. "We found that backup power for tactical operation centers [TOCS] wasn't consistent. If the TOC goes down, the mission is compromised as well as the soldiers' safety, and that's priority. That's why it's so important to do it right the first time."[17]

Step 4: Evaluate the result and initiate corrective action if the standard is not being achieved. The engineers initiated corrective action. More than 30 COPs and 35 village stability platforms were rebuilt. Electrical problems that caused safety concerns were fixed, and new energy plans that improved key facilities for the soldiers, such as dining halls and latrines, were implemented. In 2014, it was reported that the work of the CERDEC engineers under Project Manager Mobile Electric Power lowered fuel consumption by 21% across the fleet. In addition, military units are now set up to do their own quality control by noting trends based on the tracking of energy/fuel consumption and maintenance frequency.

"You just don't get the same experience behind a desk. With each deployment, we increase knowledge regarding the latest challenges," Pleta said. "Most importantly, it allows us to customize user-friendly solutions that will improve safety, reliability, and quality of life for the soldier."[18]

The next step will be to extend the power assessments to individual soldiers. This process will apply the control process to the individual as well as to the squad requirements. In other words, the analysis will begin by establishing the goal for energy consumption by soldiers; it will then measure the actual energy consumption and consider the gap between the two. Engineers will then look to improve energy use by soldiers and squads by eliminating redundancies and finding other ways to reduce energy use.

The simplest example of a control system is the thermostat in a home. By setting the thermostat, you establish the standard of performance with which actual temperature is to be compared. The thermostat contains a sensing or monitoring device, which measures the actual temperature against the desired temperature. Whenever there is a difference between them, the furnace or air-conditioning unit is activated to bring the temperature back to the standard. In other words, corrective action is initiated. This is a simple control system: It is entirely self-contained, and the target (temperature) is easy to measure.

Establishing targets and designing measurement systems are much more difficult for managers because the high level of uncertainty in the organizational environment means managers rarely know what might happen in the future. Thus it is vital for managers to design control systems to alert them to problems quickly so they can be dealt with before they become threatening. Another issue is that managers are not just concerned about bringing the organization's performance up to some predetermined standard; they want to push that standard forward to encourage employees at all levels to find new ways to raise performance. In 2014, Toyota was hit with a $1.2 billion fine by the U.S. Justice Department for not reporting a problem with accelerators in many of its vehicles. In addition to accepting the fine, the company vowed to make changes to its global operations to be more responsive to problems.[19]

In the following sections, we consider three important types of control systems that managers use to coordinate and motivate employees to ensure that they pursue superior efficiency, quality, innovation, and responsiveness to customers: output control, behavior control, and clan control (see Figure 8.3). Managers use all three to shape, regulate, and govern organizational activities, no matter what specific organizational structure is in place.

Figure 8.3
Three Organizational Control Systems

Type of control	Mechanisms of control
Output control	Financial measures of performance Organizational goals Operating budgets
Behavior control	Direct supervision Management by objectives Rules and standard operating procedures
Organizational culture/clan control	Values Norms Socialization

Output Control

All managers develop a system of output control for their organizations. First they choose the goals or output performance standards or targets that they think will best measure efficiency, quality, innovation, and responsiveness to customers. Then they measure to see whether the performance goals and standards are being achieved at the corporate, divisional, functional, and individual employee levels of the organization. The three main mechanisms that managers use to assess output or performance are financial measures, organizational goals, and operating budgets.

LO 8-3 Identify the main output controls, and discuss their advantages and disadvantages as means of coordinating and motivating employees.

Financial Measures of Performance

Top managers are most concerned with overall organizational performance and use various financial measures to evaluate it. The most common are profit ratios, liquidity ratios, leverage ratios, and activity ratios. They are discussed here and summarized in Table 8.1.[20]

- *Profit ratios* measure how efficiently managers are using the organization's resources to generate profits. *Return on investment (ROI)*, an organization's net income before taxes divided by its total assets, is the most commonly used financial performance measure because it allows managers of one organization to

Table 8.1
Four Measures of Financial Performance

Profit Ratios

Return on investment	$= \dfrac{\text{Net profit before taxes}}{\text{Total assets}}$	Measures how well managers are using the organization's resources to generate profits.
Operating margin	$= \dfrac{\text{Total operating profit}}{\text{Sales revenues}}$	A measure of how much percentage profit a company is earning on sales; the higher the percentage, the better a company is using its resources to make and sell the product.

Liquidity Ratios

Current ratio	$= \dfrac{\text{Current assets}}{\text{Current liabilities}}$	Do managers have resources available to meet claims of short-term creditors?
Quick ratio	$= \dfrac{\text{Current assets} - \text{Inventory}}{\text{Current liabilities}}$	Can managers pay off claims of short-term creditors without selling inventory?

Leverage Ratios

Debt-to-assets ratio	$= \dfrac{\text{Total debt}}{\text{Total assets}}$	To what extent have managers used borrowed funds to finance investments?
Times-covered ratio	$= \dfrac{\text{Profit before interest and taxes}}{\text{Total interest charges}}$	Measures how far profits can decline before managers cannot meet interest charges. If this ratio declines to less than 1, the organization is technically insolvent.

Activity Ratios

Inventory turnover	$= \dfrac{\text{Cost of goods sold}}{\text{Inventory}}$	Measures how efficiently managers are turning inventory over so that excess inventory is not carried.
Days sales outstanding	$= \dfrac{\text{Current accounts receivable}}{\text{Sales for period divided by days in period}}$	Measures how efficiently managers are collecting revenues from customers to pay expenses.

compare performance with that of other organizations. ROI lets managers assess an organization's competitive advantage. *Operating margin* is calculated by dividing a company's operating profit (the amount it has left after all the costs of making the product and running the business have been deducted) by sales revenues. This measure tells managers how efficiently an organization is using its resources; every successful attempt to reduce costs will be reflected in increased operating profit, for example. Also, operating margin is a means of comparing one year's performance to another; for example, if managers discover operating margin has improved by 5% from one year to the next, they know their organization is building a competitive advantage.

- *Liquidity ratios* measure how well managers have protected organizational resources to be able to meet short-term obligations. The *current ratio* (current assets divided by current liabilities) tells managers whether they have the resources available to meet the claims of short-term creditors. The *quick ratio* shows whether they can pay these claims without selling inventory.

- *Leverage ratios,* such as the *debt-to-assets ratio* and the *times-covered ratio,* measure the degree to which managers use debt (borrow money) or equity (issue new shares) to finance ongoing operations. An organization is highly leveraged if it uses more debt than equity. Debt can be risky when net income or profit fails to cover the interest on the debt—as some people learn too late when their paychecks do not allow them to pay off their credit cards.

- *Activity ratios* show how well managers are creating value from organizational assets. *Inventory turnover* measures how efficiently managers are turning inventory over so excess inventory is not carried. *Days sales outstanding* reveals how efficiently managers are collecting revenue from customers to pay expenses.

The objectivity of financial measures of performance is the reason why so many managers use them to assess the efficiency and effectiveness of their organizations. When an organization fails to meet performance standards such as ROI, revenue, or stock price targets, managers know they must take corrective action. Thus financial controls tell managers when a corporate reorganization might be necessary, when they should sell off divisions and exit businesses, or when they should rethink their corporate-level strategies. Today, quantitative skills are needed by many job candidates and employees, as the accompanying "Management Insight" box describes.

MANAGEMENT INSIGHT

Wanted: Analysts for Big Data

In today's job market, quantitative skills are important for college graduates. The National Association of Colleges and Employers', *Job Outlook 2015* survey reported that employers highly value an employee's or candidate's ability to analyze quantitative information. Other top skills on the requirements list include the ability to lead, work in a team structure, make decisions, and solve problems; the ability to communicate in writing with persons inside and outside the organization; and the ability to obtain and process information.[21]

These skills will be needed to cope with the flood of data being collected in the global economy. Data are being collected from all types of sources. In addition to collecting information on their own operations, companies are collecting data on their customers, suppliers, and even competitors. Mobile phones and other smart devices create and communicate data. There are even "exhaust data"—data that are by-products of other activities. All this information collectively has been dubbed "big data." It is creating datasets so large that typical database software cannot store or analyze it. So data analysis is no longer the concern of a few well-trained data "geeks," according to McKinsey Global Institute. Big data are now relevant in every sector of the economy.[22]

A study by the McKinsey Global Institute predicts that there will be more jobs for people with strong data analysis skills than there will be people to fill them. There could be as many as 140,000 to 190,000 unfilled positions in the United States by the year 2018. The study also expects a lack of 1.5 million managers who can understand big data well enough to make decisions using them. The gap is so big that the McKinsey report points out it cannot be filled through hiring. Organizations may need to send existing employees back to school to get needed training in data analysis.

That's not to say that soft skills are not in demand as well. Refer back to the list from the National Association of Colleges and Employers', *Job Outlook 2015*. Many of the top attributes include a strong work ethic and initiative.

Although financial information is an important output control, financial information by itself does not tell managers all they need to know about the four building blocks of competitive advantage. Financial results inform managers about the results of decisions they have already made; they do not tell managers how to find new opportunities to build competitive advantage in the future. To encourage a future-oriented approach, top managers must establish organizational goals that encourage middle and first-line managers to achieve superior efficiency, quality, innovation, and responsiveness to customers.

Organizational Goals

Once top managers consult with lower-level managers and set the organization's overall goals, they establish performance standards for the divisions and functions. These standards specify for divisional and functional managers the level at which their units must perform if the organization is to achieve its overall goals.[23] Each division is given a set of specific goals to achieve (see Figure 8.4). We saw in Chapter 6, for example, that Jeffrey Immelt, CEO of GE, has established the goal of

Figure 8.4

Organizationwide Goal Setting

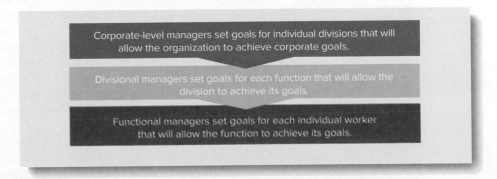

Corporate-level managers set goals for individual divisions that will allow the organization to achieve corporate goals.

Divisional managers set goals for each function that will allow the division to achieve its goals.

Functional managers set goals for each individual worker that will allow the function to achieve its goals.

having each GE division be first or second in its industry in profit. Divisional managers then develop a business-level strategy (based on achieving superior efficiency or innovation) that they hope will allow them to achieve that goal.[24] In consultation with functional managers, they specify the functional goals that the managers of different functions need to achieve to allow the division to achieve its goals. For example, sales managers might be evaluated for their ability to increase sales; materials management managers, for their ability to increase the quality of inputs or lower their costs; R&D managers, for the number of products they innovate or the number of patents they receive. In turn, functional managers establish goals that first-line managers and nonmanagerial employees need to achieve to allow the function to achieve its goals.

Output control is used at every level of the organization, and it is vital that the goals set at each level harmonize with the goals set at other levels so managers and other employees throughout the organization work together to attain the corporate goals that top managers have set.[25] It is also important that goals be set appropriately so managers are motivated to accomplish them. If goals are set at an impossibly high level, managers might work only half-heartedly to achieve them because they are certain they will fail. In contrast, if goals are set so low that they are too easy to achieve, managers will not be motivated to use all their resources as efficiently and effectively as possible. Research suggests that the best goals are specific, difficult goals—goals that challenge and stretch managers' ability but are not out of reach and do not require an impossibly high expenditure of managerial time and energy. Such goals are often called *stretch goals*.

Deciding what is a specific, difficult goal and what is a goal that is too difficult or too easy is a skill that managers must develop. Based on their own judgment and work experience, managers at all levels must assess how difficult a certain task is, and they must assess the ability of a particular subordinate manager to achieve the goal. If they do so successfully, challenging, interrelated goals—goals that reinforce one another and focus on achieving overall corporate objectives—will energize the organization.

Operating Budgets

operating budget A budget that states how managers intend to use organizational resources to achieve organizational goals.

Once managers at each level have been given a goal or target to achieve, the next step in developing an output control system is to establish operating budgets that regulate how managers and workers attain their goals. An **operating budget** is a blueprint that states how managers intend to use organizational resources to achieve organizational goals efficiently. Typically managers at one level allocate to subordinate managers a specific amount of resources to produce goods and services. Once they have been given a budget, these lower-level managers must decide how to allocate money for different organizational activities. They are then evaluated for their ability to stay within the budget and to make the best use of available resources. For example, managers at GE's lighting division might have a budget of $50 million to spend on developing and selling a new line of LED lights. They must decide how much money to allocate to the various functions such as R&D, engineering, and sales so the division generates the most customer revenue and makes the biggest profit.

Large organizations often treat each division as a singular or stand-alone responsibility center. Corporate managers then evaluate each division's contribution to corporate performance. Managers of a division may be given a fixed budget for resources and be evaluated on the amount of goods or services they can produce using those resources (this is a cost or expense budget approach). Alternatively, managers may be asked to maximize the revenues from the sales of goods and services produced (a revenue budget approach). Or managers may be evaluated on the difference between the revenues generated by the sales of goods and services and the budgeted cost of making those goods and services (a profit budget approach). Japanese companies' use of operating budgets and challenging goals to increase efficiency is instructive in this context.

In summary, three components—objective financial measures, challenging goals and performance standards, and appropriate operating budgets—are the essence of effective output control. Most organizations develop sophisticated output control systems to allow managers at all levels to keep accurate account of the organization so they can move quickly to take corrective action as needed.[26] Output control is an essential part of management.

Problems with Output Control

When designing an output control system, managers must be careful to avoid some pitfalls. For example, they must be sure the output standards they create motivate managers at all levels and do not cause managers to behave in inappropriate ways to achieve organizational goals.

Suppose top managers give divisional managers the goal of doubling profits over a three-year period. This goal seems challenging and reachable when it is jointly agreed upon, and in the first two years profits go up by 70%. In the third year, however, an economic recession hits and sales plummet. Divisional managers think it is increasingly unlikely that they will meet their profit goal. Failure will mean losing the substantial monetary bonus tied to achieving the goal. How might managers behave to try to preserve their bonuses?

Perhaps they might find ways to reduce costs because profit can be increased either by raising sales revenues or reducing costs. Thus divisional managers might cut back on expensive research activities, delay machinery maintenance, reduce marketing expenditures, and lay off middle managers and workers to reduce costs so that at the end of the year they will make their target of doubling profits and receive their bonuses. This tactic might help them achieve a short-run goal—doubling profits—but such actions could hurt long-term profitability or ROI (because a cutback in R&D can reduce the rate of product innovation, a cutback in marketing will lead to the loss of customers, and so on).

The message is clear: Although output control is a useful tool for keeping managers and employees at all levels motivated and the organization on track, it is only a guide to appropriate action. Managers must be sensitive in how they use output control and must constantly monitor its effects at all levels in the organization—and on customers and other stakeholders.

Behavior Control

Organizational structure by itself does not provide any mechanism that motivates managers and nonmanagerial employees to behave in ways that make the structure work—or even improve how it works: hence the need for control. Put another way, managers can develop an organizational structure that has the right grouping of divisions and functions, and an effective chain of command, but it will work as designed *only* if managers also establish control systems that motivate and shape employee behavior in ways that *match* this structure.[27] Output control is one method of motivating employees; behavior control is another method. This section examines three mechanisms of behavior control that managers can use to keep subordinates on track and make organizational structures work as they are designed to work: direct supervision, management by objectives, and rules and standard operating procedures (see Figure 8.3).

Direct Supervision

The most immediate and potent form of behavior control is direct supervision by managers who actively monitor and observe the behavior of their subordinates, teach subordinates the behaviors that are appropriate and inappropriate, and intervene to take corrective action as needed. Moreover, when managers personally supervise subordinates, they lead by example and in this way can help subordinates develop and increase their own skill levels. (Leadership is the subject of Chapter 10.)

Direct supervision allows managers at all levels to become personally involved with their subordinates and allows them to mentor subordinates and develop their management skills. Thus control through personal supervision can be an effective way of motivating employees and promoting behaviors that increase efficiency and effectiveness.[28]

Nevertheless, certain problems are associated with direct supervision. First, it is expensive because a manager can personally manage only a relatively small number of subordinates effectively. Therefore, if direct supervision is the main kind of control being used in an organization, a lot of managers will be needed and costs will increase. For this reason, output control is usually preferred to behavior control; indeed, output control tends to be the first type of control that managers at all levels use to evaluate performance. Second, direct supervision can *demotivate* subordinates. This occurs if employees feel they are under such close scrutiny that they are not free to make their own decisions or if they feel they are not being evaluated in an accurate and impartial way. Team members and other employees may start to pass the buck, avoid responsibility, and cease to cooperate with other team members if they feel their manager is not accurately evaluating their performance and is favoring some people over others.

Third, as noted previously, for many jobs personal control through direct supervision is simply not feasible. The more complex a job is, the more difficult it is for a manager to evaluate how well a subordinate is performing. The performance of divisional and functional managers, for example, can be evaluated only over relatively long periods (which is why an output control system is developed), so it makes little sense for top managers to continually monitor their performance. However, managers can still communicate the organization's mission and goals to their subordinates and reinforce the values and norms in the organization's culture through their own personal style.

Management by Objectives

management by objectives (MBO) A goal-setting process in which a manager and each of his or her subordinates negotiate specific goals and objectives for the subordinate to achieve and then periodically evaluate the extent to which the subordinate is achieving those goals.

To provide a framework within which to evaluate subordinates' behavior and, in particular, to allow managers to monitor progress toward achieving goals, many organizations implement some version of management by objectives. **Management by objectives (MBO)** is a formal system of evaluating subordinates on their ability to achieve specific organizational goals or performance standards and to meet operating budgets.[29] Most organizations use some form of MBO system because it is pointless to establish goals and then fail to evaluate whether they are being achieved. Management by objectives involves three specific steps:

- Step 1: *Specific goals and objectives are established at each level of the organization.*

MBO starts when top managers establish overall organizational objectives, such as specific financial performance goals or targets. Then objective setting cascades down throughout the organization as managers at the divisional and functional levels set their goals to achieve corporate objectives.[30] Finally first-level managers and employees jointly set goals that will contribute to achieving functional objectives.

- Step 2: *Managers and their subordinates together determine the subordinates' goals.*

An important characteristic of management by objectives is its participatory nature. Managers at every level sit down with each of the subordinate managers who report directly to them, and together they determine appropriate and feasible goals for the subordinate and bargain over the budget that the subordinate will need to achieve his or her goals. The participation of subordinates in the objective-setting process is a way of strengthening their commitment to achieving their goals and meeting their budgets.[31] Another reason why it is so important for subordinates (both individuals and teams) to participate in goal setting is that doing so enables them to tell managers what they think they can realistically achieve.[32]

- Step 3: *Managers and their subordinates periodically review the subordinates' progress toward meeting goals.*

Once specific objectives have been agreed on for managers at each level, managers are accountable for meeting those objectives. Periodically they sit down with their subordinates to evaluate their progress. Normally salary raises and promotions are linked to the goal-setting process, and managers who achieve their goals receive greater rewards than those who fall short. (The issue of how to design reward systems to motivate managers and other organizational employees is discussed in Chapter 9.)

In the companies that have decentralized responsibility for the production of goods and services to empowered teams and cross-functional teams, management by objectives works somewhat differently. Managers ask each team to develop a set of goals and performance targets that the team hopes to achieve—goals that are consistent with organizational objectives. Managers then negotiate with each team to establish its final goals and the budget the team will need to achieve them. The reward system is linked to team performance, not to the performance of any one team member.

Cypress Semiconductor offers an interesting example of how IT can be used to manage the MBO process quickly and effectively. In the fast-moving semiconductor business, a premium is placed on organizational adaptability. At Cypress, CEO T. J. Rodgers was facing a problem: How could he control his growing 1,500-employee organization without developing a bureaucratic management hierarchy? Rodgers believed that a tall hierarchy hinders the ability of an organization to adapt to changing conditions. He was committed to maintaining a flat and decentralized organizational structure with a minimum of management layers. At the same time he needed to control his employees to ensure that they performed in a manner consistent with the goals of the company.[33] How could he achieve this without resorting to direct supervision and the lengthy management hierarchy that it implies?

To solve this problem, Rodgers implemented an online information system through which he can monitor what every employee and team is doing in his fast-moving and decentralized organization. Each employee maintains a list of 10 to 15 goals, such as "Meet with marketing for new product launch" or "Make sure to check with customer X." Noted next to each goal are when it was agreed upon, when it is due to be finished, and whether it has been finished. All this information is stored on a central computer. Rodgers claims that he can review the goals of all employees in about four hours and that he does so each week.[34] How is this possible? He *manages by exception* and looks only for employees who are falling behind. He then calls them, not to scold but to ask whether there is anything he can do to help them get the job done. It takes only about half an hour each week for employees to review and update their lists. This system allows Rodgers to exercise control over his organization without resorting to the expensive layers of a management hierarchy and direct supervision.

MBO does not always work out as planned, however. Managers and their subordinates at all levels must believe that performance evaluations are accurate and fair. Any suggestion that personal biases and political objectives play a part in the evaluation process can lower or even destroy MBO's effectiveness as a control system. This is why many organizations work so hard to protect the integrity of their systems.

Similarly, when people work in teams, each member's contribution to the team, and each team's contribution to the goals of the organization, must be fairly evaluated. This is no easy thing to do. It depends on managers' ability to create an organizational control system that measures performance accurately and fairly and links performance evaluations to rewards so employees stay motivated and coordinate their activities to achieve the organization's mission and goals.

Bureaucratic Control

bureaucratic control Control of behavior by means of a comprehensive system of rules and standard operating procedures.

When direct supervision is too expensive and management by objectives is inappropriate, managers might turn to another mechanism to shape and motivate employee behavior: bureaucratic control. **Bureaucratic control** is control by means of a comprehensive system of rules and standard operating procedures (SOPs) that shapes and regulates the behavior of divisions, functions, and individuals. In the appendix to Chapter 1, we discussed Weber's theory of bureaucracy and noted that all organizations use bureaucratic rules and procedures but some use them more than others.[35]

Rules and SOPs guide behavior and specify what employees are to do when they confront a problem that needs a solution. It is the responsibility of a manager to develop rules that allow employees to perform their activities efficiently and effectively. When employees follow the rules that managers have developed, their behavior is standardized—actions are performed the same way time and time again—and the outcomes of their work are predictable. And, to the degree that managers can make employees' behavior predictable, there is no need to monitor the outputs of behavior because standardized behavior leads to standardized outputs.

Suppose a worker at Ford comes up with a way to attach exhaust pipes that reduces the number of steps in the assembly process and increases efficiency. Always on the lookout for ways to standardize procedures, managers make this idea the basis of a new rule that says, "From now on, the procedure for attaching the exhaust pipe to the car is as follows." If all workers followed the rule to the letter, every car would come off the assembly line with its exhaust pipe attached in the new way and there would be no need to check exhaust pipes at the end of the line. In practice, mistakes and lapses of attention do happen, so output control is used at the end of the line, and each car's exhaust system is given a routine inspection. However, the number of quality problems with the exhaust system is minimized because the rule (bureaucratic control) is being followed.

Service organizations such as retail stores, fast-food restaurants, and home-improvement stores attempt to standardize the behavior of employees by instructing them on the correct way to greet customers or the appropriate way to serve and bag food. Employees are trained to follow the rules that have proved to be most effective in a particular situation, and the better trained the employees are, the more standardized is their behavior and the more trust managers can have that outputs (such as food quality) will be consistent.

Problems with Bureaucratic Control

All organizations make extensive use of bureaucratic control because rules and SOPs effectively control routine organizational activities. With a bureaucratic control system in place, managers can manage by exception and intervene and take corrective action only when necessary. However, managers need to be aware of a number of problems associated with bureaucratic control, because such problems can reduce organizational effectiveness.

First, establishing rules is always easier than discarding them. Organizations tend to become overly bureaucratic over time as managers do everything according to the rule book. If the amount of red tape becomes too great, decision making slows and managers react slowly to changing conditions. This sluggishness can imperil an organization's survival if agile new competitors emerge.

Second, because rules constrain and standardize behavior and lead people to behave in predictable ways, there is a danger that people become so used to automatically following rules that they stop thinking for themselves. Thus, too much standardization can actually reduce the level of learning taking place in an organization and get the organization off track if managers and workers focus on the wrong issues. An organization thrives when its members are constantly thinking of new ways to increase efficiency, quality, and customer responsiveness. By definition, new ideas do not come from blindly following standardized procedures. Similarly, the pursuit of innovation implies a commitment by managers to discover new ways of doing things; innovation, however, is incompatible with the use of extensive bureaucratic control.

Managers must therefore be sensitive about the way they use bureaucratic control. It is most useful when organizational activities are routine and well understood and when employees are making programmed decisions—for example, in mass-production settings such as Ford or in routine service settings such as stores like Target or Midas Muffler. Bureaucratic control is much less useful in situations where nonprogrammed decisions have to be made and managers have to react quickly to changes in the organizational environment. The accompanying "Management Insight" feature describes how one company has thrived without many bureaucratic rules.

To use output control and behavior control, managers must be able to identify the outcomes they want to achieve and the behaviors they want employees to perform to achieve those outcomes. For many of the most important and significant organizational activities, however, output control and behavior control are inappropriate for several reasons:

- A manager cannot evaluate the performance of workers such as doctors, research scientists, or engineers by observing their behavior on a day-to-day basis.
- Rules and SOPs are of little use in telling a doctor how to respond to an emergency situation or a scientist how to discover something new.
- Output controls such as the amount of time a surgeon takes for each operation or the costs of making a discovery are very crude measures of the quality of performance.

How can managers attempt to control and regulate the behavior of their subordinates when personal supervision is of little use, when rules cannot be developed to tell employees what to do, and when outputs and goals cannot be measured at all or can be measured usefully only over long periods? One source of control increasingly being used by organizations is a strong organizational culture.

MANAGEMENT INSIGHT

Netflix Lacks Bureaucratic Control—On Purpose

Netflix, a company that offers on-demand Internet streaming of movies, TV shows, and original content, as well as DVDs by mail, uses little bureaucratic control within its organizational framework. There are no traditional performance appraisals, no formal tracking of vacation time for managers, and no performance-based bonuses. On its website, the company describes itself this way: "At Netflix we value high performance, freedom, and responsibility. We don't focus on rules, processes, or procedures. We are candid and transparent and seek excellence in everything we do."[36]

Much of this lack of bureaucratic control is captured in a presentation called "Netflix Culture: Freedom & Responsibility," which appears on the Netflix website. Sheryl Sandberg, chief operating officer at Facebook, is quoted as saying the slideshow "may well be the most important document ever to come out of [Silicon] Valley."[37] The presentation's name comes from the Netflix philosophy of allowing employees to make decisions instead of creating a strong command and control environment.

Patty McCord, the former chief talent officer at Netflix, outlined the following five ideas that define Netflix's philosophy in a 2014 *Harvard Business Review* article[38]:

1. "Hire, Reward, and Tolerate Only Fully Formed Adults." Netflix asks employees to rely on their own judgment rather than corporate policies when making decisions. Thus, it is important that Netflix hire people who understand how their actions affect others and who put the best interests of the company first.

2. "Tell the Truth about Performance." The company did away with performance appraisals. It felt they were too infrequent and ritualistic and did not improve performance. Instead, they encourage employees and managers to talk frequently. They also hold informal 360-degree reviews by asking employees to critique each other.

3. "Managers Own the Job of Creating Great Teams." Netflix focuses its energies on making sure the right people are doing the right job for their skill sets. The company places great importance on team building.

4. "Leaders Own the Job of Creating the Company Culture." McCord makes three points about this topic: (a) There should not be a difference between how culture and values are described and how they are carried out in the company. (b) Employees need to understand how the business works so they can support it. (c) There should be awareness that within the culture there will be subcultures to manage.

5. "Good Talent Managers Think Like Businesspeople and Innovators First, and Like HR People Last." She thinks HR is better served to innovate and think of themselves as businesspeople rather than focus on implementing morale improvement plans that don't usually work.

Netflix was founded in 1997, launched its monthly subscription service in 1999, and introduced streaming in 2007. It went from 600,000 members in 2002 to more than 65 million global members in 2015.[39] The company has been successful despite having little bureaucratic control.

Organizational Culture and Clan Control

LO 8-4 Explain how clan control or organizational culture creates an effective organizational architecture.

organizational culture The set of values, norms, and standards of behavior that control the way individuals and groups interact and work together to achieve organizational goals.

clan control The control exerted on individuals and groups by shared organizational values, norms, and standards of behavior.

Organizational culture is another important control system that regulates and governs employee attitudes and behavior. As we discussed in Chapter 2, **organizational culture** is the shared set of beliefs, expectations, values, norms, and work routines that influences how members of an organization relate to one another and work together to achieve organizational goals. **Clan control** is the control exerted on individuals and groups in an organization by shared values, norms, standards of behavior, and expectations. Organizational culture is not an externally imposed system of constraints, such as direct supervision or rules and procedures. Rather, employees internalize organizational values and norms and then let these values and norms guide their decisions and actions. Just as people in society at large generally behave in accordance with socially acceptable values and norms—such as the norm that people should line up at the checkout counters in supermarkets—so are individuals in an organizational setting mindful of the force of organizational values and norms.

Organizational culture functions as a kind of control system because managers can deliberately try to influence the kind of values and norms that develop in an organization—values and norms that specify appropriate and inappropriate behaviors and so determine the way its members behave. An example of using internalized values and norms to guide behavior is described in the accompanying "Management Insight" feature.

MANAGEMENT INSIGHT

How Philanthrofits Help Users Help Charities

The popularity of a new category of fitness apps provides an example of how a control system can use internalized values and norms. "Philanthrofits" are apps that donate money to charity based on the behaviors of their users. For example,

Charity Miles donates 25 cents per mile for walkers and runners to charities including Habitat for Humanity, Wounded Warrior Project, and Autism Speaks.[40] With a $1 million sponsorship pool, the organization hopes that as the number of athletes using the app increases, so will the corporate sponsors, thus providing more money for athletes to donate to charity.[41] Users must share their activity on Facebook for their designated charity to receive the money raised.

Another app, stickK, was developed by Yale University economists based on research about the effectiveness of people making contracts with themselves to achieve their goals. The standard objectives offered by the app include losing weight, exercising regularly, quitting smoking, preparing for a race, and maintaining weight. The user can also choose a custom goal, such as raising his or her grade point average. Next, the user can enter credit card information to wager money on whether he or she will achieve the set goal. If the goal is achieved, the credit card is not charged. If the goal is not achieved, the money the user wagered will go to a charity of the user's choice. The chosen charity can be one the user supports or one the user would prefer not to support. To hold the user accountable, the user chooses a referee to monitor progress. The referee verifies the accuracy of the user's reports. Finally, the user can ask friends and family who also are registered for the app to act as supporters. These supporters can send the user encouraging messages via the app.[42]

There are too many Philanthrofit apps on the market to mention them all here. But Charity Miles and stickK represent two ways of leveraging users' internalized values and norms to influence behavior. Charity Miles allows the user to donate a sponsor's money. StickK has users donate their own money. Charity Miles donates money when users perform their activities, and stickK donates when they do not. But perhaps the biggest difference is that stickK also allows users to donate to either a charity or an "anti-charity" if the user does not live up to the contract.

If a stickK user chooses to send money to a charity, stickK does not inform the user which charity receives the money. The idea is that if the user knew what good cause received the money, he or she might feel OK about breaking the contract. Instead, the stickK web page lists a few reputable charities such as the American Red Cross and Doctors without Borders. Users who chose the charity option are told that their money went to such a charity without providing the charity name.

However, if the user chooses an anti-charity, the user is told which charity got their money. An anti-charity is one with views the user opposes. The stickK website provides a choice of anti-charities from either side of controversial issues, including the political action committees supporting both the Republican and Democratic parties.

Adaptive Cultures versus Inert Cultures

Many researchers and managers believe that employees of some organizations go out of their way to help the organization because it has a strong and cohesive organizational culture—an *adaptive culture* that controls employee attitudes and behaviors. Adaptive cultures are ones whose values and norms help an organization to build momentum and to grow and change as needed to achieve its goals and be effective. By contrast, *inert cultures* are those that lead to values and norms that fail to motivate or inspire employees; they lead to stagnation and often failure over time. What leads to an adaptive or inert culture?

Researchers have found that organizations with strong adaptive cultures, like 3M, UPS, Microsoft, and IBM, invest in their employees. They demonstrate their commitment to their members by, for example, emphasizing the long-term nature of the employment relationship and trying to avoid layoffs. These companies develop long-term career paths for their employees and invest heavily in training and development to increase employees' value to the organization. In these ways, terminal and instrumental values pertaining to the worth of human resources encourage the development of supportive work attitudes and behaviors.

In adaptive cultures employees often receive rewards linked directly to their performance and to the performance of the company as a whole. Sometimes, employee stock ownership plans (ESOPs) are developed in which workers as a group are allowed to buy a significant percentage of their company's stock. Workers who are owners of the company have additional incentive to develop skills that allow them to perform highly and search actively for ways to improve quality, efficiency, and performance.

Some organizations, however, develop cultures with values that do not include protecting and increasing the worth of their human resources as a major goal. Their employment practices are based on short-term employment according to the needs of the organization and on minimal investment in employees who perform simple, routine tasks. Moreover, employees are not often rewarded based on their performance and thus have little incentive to improve their skills or otherwise invest in the organization to help it to achieve goals. If a company has an inert culture, poor working relationships frequently develop between the organization and its employees, and instrumental values of noncooperation, laziness, and loafing and work norms of output restriction are common.

Moreover, an adaptive culture develops an emphasis on entrepreneurship and respect for the employee and allows the use of organizational structures, such as the cross-functional team structure, that empower employees to make decisions and motivate them to succeed. By contrast, in an inert culture, employees are content to be told what to do and have little incentive or motivation to perform beyond minimum work requirements. As you might expect, the emphasis is on close supervision and hierarchical authority, which result in a culture that makes it difficult to adapt to a changing environment.

Organizational Change

As we have discussed, many problems can arise if an organization's control systems are not designed correctly. One of these problems is that an organization cannot change or adapt in response to a changing environment unless it has effective control over its activities. Companies can lose this control over time, or they can change in ways that make them more effective. **Organizational change** is the movement of an organization away from its present state toward some preferred future state to increase its efficiency and effectiveness.

Interestingly enough, there is a fundamental tension or need to balance two opposing forces in the control process that influences the way organizations change. As just noted, organizations and their managers need to be able to control their activities and make their operations routine and predictable. At the same time, however, organizations have to be responsive to the need to change, and managers and employees have to "think on their feet" and realize when they need to depart from routines to be responsive to unpredictable events. In other words, even though adopting the right set of output and behavior controls is essential for improving efficiency, because the environment is dynamic and uncertain, employees also need to feel that they have the autonomy to depart from routines as necessary to increase effectiveness. (See Figure 8.5.)

LO 8-5 Discuss the relationship between organizational control and change, and explain why managing change is a vital management task.

organization change
The movement of an organization away from its present state and toward some desired future state to increase its efficiency and effectiveness.

Figure 8.5

Organizational Control
and Change

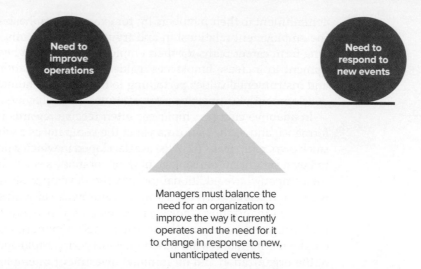

Managers must balance the
need for an organization to
improve the way it currently
operates and the need for it
to change in response to new,
unanticipated events.

For this reason many researchers believe that the highest-performing organizations are those that are constantly changing—and thus become experienced at doing so—in their search to become more efficient and effective. Companies like UPS, Toyota, and Walmart are constantly changing the mix of their activities to move forward even as they seek to make their existing operations more efficient. For example, UPS entered the air express package market, bought a chain of mailbox stores, and began offering consulting services. At the same time, it has been increasing the efficiency of its ground and global air transport network, including the use of handheld computers by its drivers and more than 2,700 alternative fuel and advanced technology vehicles.[43]

The need to constantly search for ways to improve efficiency and effectiveness makes it vital that managers develop the skills necessary to manage change effectively. Several experts have proposed a model that managers can follow to implement change successfully.[44] Figure 8.6 outlines the steps that managers must take to manage change effectively. In the rest of this section we examine each one.

Assessing the Need for Change

Organizational change can affect practically all aspects of organizational functioning, including organizational structure, culture, strategies, control systems, and groups and teams, as well as the human resource management system and critical organizational processes such as communication, motivation, and leadership.

Figure 8.6

Four Steps in the Organizational Change Process

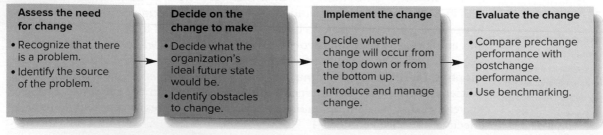

Organizational change can bring alterations in the ways managers carry out the critical tasks of planning, organizing, leading, and controlling and the ways they perform their managerial roles.

Deciding how to change an organization is a complex matter because change disrupts the status quo and poses a threat, prompting employees to resist attempts to alter work relationships and procedures. *Organizational learning,* the process through which managers try to increase organizational members' abilities to understand and appropriately respond to changing conditions, can be an important impetus for change and can help all members of an organization, including managers, effectively make decisions about needed changes.

Assessing the need for change calls for two important activities: recognizing that there is a problem and identifying its source. Sometimes the need for change is obvious, such as when an organization's performance is suffering. Often, however, managers have trouble determining that something is going wrong because problems develop gradually; organizational performance may slip for a number of years before a problem becomes obvious. Thus, during the first step in the change process, managers need to recognize that there is a problem that requires change.

Often the problems that managers detect have produced a gap between desired performance and actual performance. To detect such a gap, managers need to look at performance measures—such as falling market share or profits, rising costs, or employees' failure to meet their established goals or stay within budgets—which indicate whether change is needed. These measures are provided by organizational control systems, discussed earlier in the chapter.

To discover the source of the problem, managers need to look both inside and outside the organization. Outside the organization, they must examine how changes in environmental forces may be creating opportunities and threats that are affecting internal work relationships. Perhaps the emergence of low-cost competitors abroad has led to conflict among different departments that are trying to find new ways to gain a competitive advantage. Managers also need to look within the organization to see whether its structure is causing problems between departments. Perhaps a company does not have integrating mechanisms in place to allow different departments to respond to low-cost competition.

Deciding on the Change to Make

Once managers have identified the source of the problem, they must decide what they think the organization's ideal future state would be. In other words, they must decide where they would like their organization to be in the future—what kinds of goods and services it should be making, what its business-level strategy should be, how the organizational structure should be changed, and so on. During this step, managers also must engage in planning how they are going to attain the organization's ideal future state.

This step in the change process also includes identifying obstacles or sources of resistance to change. Managers must analyze the factors that may prevent the company from reaching its ideal future state. Obstacles to change are found at the corporate, divisional, departmental, and individual levels of the organization.

Corporate-level changes in an organization's strategy or structure, even seemingly trivial changes, may significantly affect how divisional and departmental managers behave. Suppose that to compete with low-cost foreign competitors, top managers decide to increase the resources spent on state-of-the-art machinery and reduce the resources spent on marketing or R&D. The power of manufacturing managers would increase, and the power of marketing and R&D managers would fall. This decision would alter the balance of power among departments and might lead to increased conflict as departments start fighting to retain their status in the organization. An organization's present strategy and structure are powerful obstacles to change.

Whether a company's culture is adaptive or inert facilitates or obstructs change. Organizations with entrepreneurial, flexible cultures, such as high-tech companies, are much easier to change than are organizations with more rigid cultures, such as those sometimes found in large, bureaucratic organizations like the military or GM.

The same obstacles to change exist at the divisional and departmental levels as well. Division managers may differ in their attitudes toward the changes that top managers propose and, if their interests and power seem threatened, will resist those changes. Managers at all levels usually fight to protect their power and control over resources. Given that departments have different goals and time horizons, they may also react differently to the changes that other managers propose. When top managers are trying to reduce costs, for example, sales managers may resist attempts to cut back on sales expenditures if they believe that problems stem from manufacturing managers' inefficiencies.

At the individual level, too, people are often resistant to change because change brings uncertainty and uncertainty brings stress. For example, individuals may resist the introduction of a new technology because they are uncertain about their abilities to learn it and effectively use it.

These obstacles make organizational change a slow process. Managers must recognize the potential obstacles to change and take them into consideration. Some obstacles can be overcome by improving communication so that all organizational members are aware of the need for change and of the nature of the changes being made. Empowering employees and inviting them to participate in the planning for change also can help overcome resistance and allay employees' fears. In addition, managers can sometimes overcome resistance by emphasizing group or shared goals such as increased organizational efficiency and effectiveness. The larger and more complex an organization is, the more complex is the change process.

Implementing the Change

top-down change A fast, revolutionary approach to change in which top managers identify what needs to be changed and then move quickly to implement the changes throughout the organization.

Generally, managers implement—that is, introduce and manage—change from the top down or from the bottom up.[45] **Top-down change** is implemented quickly: Top managers identify the need for change, decide what to do, and then move quickly to implement the changes throughout the organization. For example, top managers may decide to restructure and downsize the organization and then give divisional and departmental managers specific goals to achieve. With top-down change, the emphasis is on making the changes quickly and dealing with problems as they arise; it is revolutionary in nature.

Consider, for example, what happened at the Walt Disney Company when Bob Iger became CEO of the troubled organization. Bob Iger had been COO of Disney under CEO Michael Eisner, and he had noticed that Disney was plagued by slow decision making that had led to many mistakes in putting new business strategies into action. Its Disney retail stores were losing money; its Internet properties were flops; and even its theme parks seemed to have lost their luster as few new rides or attractions were introduced. Iger believed one of the main reasons for Disney's declining performance was that it had become too tall and bureaucratic, and its top managers were following financial rules that did not lead to innovative strategies.

Bob Iger, CEO of the Walt Disney Company, has energized the organization by removing layers of management and returning creative power to the company's employees.
© Chip Somodevilla/Getty Images

One of Iger's first moves to turn around performance was to dismantle Disney's central strategic planning office. In this office, several levels of managers were responsible for sifting through all the new ideas and innovations sent up by Disney's different business divisions—such as theme parks, movies, and gaming—and then deciding which ones to present to the CEO. Iger saw the strategic planning office as a bureaucratic bottleneck that reduced the number of ideas coming from below. So he dissolved the office and reassigned its managers back to the different business units.[46]

The result of eliminating an unnecessary layer in Disney's hierarchy has been the generation of more new ideas by different business units. The level of innovation has increased because managers are more willing to speak out and champion their ideas when they know they are dealing directly with the CEO and a top management team searching for innovative ways to improve performance—rather than a layer of strategic planning bureaucrats concerned only with the bottom line.[47] Disney continues to thrive. Its recent feature, *Frozen,* became the top animated movie of all time, and its other divisions, including theme parks, retail, and cruise ships, continue to be financial successes.[48]

bottom-up change
A gradual or evolutionary approach to change in which managers at all levels work together to develop a detailed plan for change.

Bottom-up change is typically more gradual or evolutionary. Top managers consult with middle and first-line managers about the need for change. Then, over time, managers at all levels work to develop a detailed plan for change. A major advantage of bottom-up change is that it can co-opt resistance to change from employees. Because the emphasis in bottom-up change is on participation and on keeping people informed about what is going on, uncertainty and resistance are minimized.

Evaluating the Change

The last step in the change process is to evaluate how successful the change effort has been in improving organizational performance.[49] Using measures such as changes in market share, in profits, or in the ability of managers to meet their goals, managers compare how well an organization is performing after the change with how well it was performing before. Managers also can use **benchmarking**, comparing their performance on specific dimensions with the performance of high-performing organizations, to decide how successful a change effort has been. For example, when Xerox was doing poorly in the 1980s, it benchmarked the efficiency of its distribution operations against that of L. L. Bean, the efficiency of its central computer operations against that of John Deere, and the efficiency of its marketing abilities against that of Procter & Gamble. Those three companies are renowned for their skills in these different areas, and by studying how they performed, Xerox was able to dramatically increase its own performance. Benchmarking is a key tool in total quality management, an important change program discussed in Chapter 14.

benchmarking The process of comparing one company's performance on specific dimensions with the performance of other, high-performing organizations.

In summary, organizational control and change are closely linked because organizations operate in environments that are constantly changing and so managers must be alert to the need to change their strategies and structures. High-performing organizations are those whose managers are attuned to the need to continually modify the way they operate and adopt techniques like empowered work groups and teams, benchmarking, and global outsourcing to remain competitive in a global world.

Entrepreneurship, Control, and Change

LO 8-6
Understand the role of entrepreneurship in the control and change process.

entrepreneurs
Individuals who notice opportunities and decide how to mobilize the resources necessary to produce new and improved goods and services.

As we discussed in Chapter 1, managers are responsible for supervising the use of human and other resources to achieve effective and efficient organizational goals. **Entrepreneurs**, by contrast, are the people who notice opportunities and take responsibility for mobilizing the resources necessary to produce new and improved goods and services. Essentially, entrepreneurs bring about change to companies and industries because they see new and improved ways to use resources to create products customers will want to buy. At the same time, entrepreneurs who start new business ventures are responsible for all the initial planning, organizing, leading, and controlling necessary to make their idea a reality. If their idea is viable and entrepreneurs do attract customers, then their business grows and then they need to hire managers who will take responsibility for organizing and controlling all the specific functional activities such as marketing, accounting, and manufacturing necessary for a growing organization to be successful.

Typically, entrepreneurs assume the substantial risk associated with starting new businesses (many new businesses fail), and they receive all the returns or profits associated with the new business venture. These people include the likes of Steve Jobs, Mark Zuckerberg, and Tory Burch, all who made vast fortunes when their businesses became successful. Or they are among the millions of people who start new business ventures only to lose their money when their businesses fail. Despite the fact that an estimated 80% of small businesses fail in the first three to five years, by some estimates 38% of men and 50% of women in today's workforce want to start their own companies.

Entrepreneurship does not just end once a new business is founded. Entrepreneurship carries on inside an organization over time, and many people throughout an organization take responsibility for developing innovative goods and services. For example, managers, scientists, or researchers employed by existing companies engage in entrepreneurial activity when they develop new or improved products. To distinguish these individuals from entrepreneurs who found their own businesses, employees of existing organizations who notice opportunities for product or service improvements and are responsible for managing the development process are known as **intrapreneurs**. In general, then, **entrepreneurship** is the mobilization of resources to take advantage of an opportunity to provide customers with new or improved goods and services; intrapreneurs engage in entrepreneurship within an existing company.

intrapreneurs
Employees of existing organizations who notice opportunities to develop new or improved products and better ways to make them.

entrepreneurship
The mobilization of resources to take advantage of an opportunity to provide customers with new or improved goods and services.

An interesting relationship exists between entrepreneurs and intrapreneurs. Many intrapreneurs become dissatisfied when their superiors decide not to support or to fund new product ideas and development efforts that the intrapreneurs think will succeed. What do intrapreneurs do who feel that they are getting nowhere? Very often intrapreneurs decide to leave their employers and start their own organizations to take advantage of their new product ideas. In other words, intrapreneurs become entrepreneurs and found companies that may compete with the companies they left.

Many of the world's most successful organizations have been started by frustrated intrapreneurs who became entrepreneurs. William Hewlett and David

Facebook founder Mark Zuckerberg is among one of the most successful entrepreneurs in the country. Facebook has more than 1.4 billion monthly active users around the globe.
© David Paul Morris/Bloomberg/Getty Images

Packard left Fairchild Semiconductor, an early high-tech industry leader, when managers of that company would not support Hewlett and Packard's ideas; their company now called HP, soon outperformed Fairchild. Compaq Computer was founded by Rod Canion and some of his colleagues, who left Texas Instruments (TI) when managers there would not support Canion's idea that TI should develop its own personal computer, and Compaq was subsequently acquired by HP. To prevent the departure of talented people, organizations need to take steps to promote internal entrepreneurship.

There is also an interesting dynamic between entrepreneurship and management. Very often, it turns out that the entrepreneur who initially founded the business does not have the management skills to successfully control and change the business over time. Entrepreneurs may, for example, lack an understanding of how to create the control structure necessary to manage a successful long-term strategy. Entrepreneurs also may not recognize the need to change their companies because they are so close to them; in other words, they "cannot see the forest for the trees."

Frequently a founding entrepreneur lacks the skills, patience, or experience to engage in the difficult and challenging work of management. Some entrepreneurs find it difficult to delegate authority because they are afraid to risk letting others manage their company. As a result, founding entrepreneurs can become overloaded, and the quality of their decision making declines. Other entrepreneurs lack the detailed knowledge necessary to establish state-of-the-art control systems or to create the organizational culture that is vital to increase organizational effectiveness (discussed in Chapter 14).

In summary, it is necessary to do more than create a new product to succeed. An entrepreneur must hire managers who can create an operating and control system that allows a new venture to survive and prosper. Very often, venture capitalists, the people who provide the capital to fund a new venture, lend entrepreneurs the money only if they agree from the outset to let a professional manager become the CEO of the new company. The entrepreneur then holds a senior planning and advisory role in the company, often chairing its board of directors.

Summary and Review

WHAT IS ORGANIZATIONAL CONTROL? Controlling is the process whereby managers monitor and regulate how efficiently and effectively an organization and its members are performing the activities necessary to achieve organizational goals. Controlling is a four-step process: (1) establishing performance standards, (2) measuring actual performance, (3) comparing actual performance against performance standards, and (4) evaluating the results and initiating corrective action if needed. **[LO 8-1, 8-2]**

OUTPUT CONTROL To monitor output or performance, managers choose goals or performance standards that they think will best measure efficiency, quality, innovation, and responsiveness to customers at the corporate, divisional, departmental or functional, and individual levels. The main mechanisms that managers use to monitor output are financial measures of performance, organizational goals, and operating budgets. [LO 8-3, 8-4]

BEHAVIOR CONTROL In an attempt to shape behavior and induce employees to work toward achieving organizational goals, managers utilize direct supervision, management by objectives, and bureaucratic control by means of rules and standard operating procedures. [LO 8-4]

ORGANIZATIONAL CULTURE AND CLAN CONTROL Organizational culture is the set of values, norms, standards of behavior, and common expectations that control the ways individuals and groups in an organization interact with one another and work to achieve organizational goals. Clan control is the control exerted on individuals and groups by shared values, norms, standards of behavior, and expectations. Organizational culture is transmitted to employees through the values of the founder, the process of socialization, organizational ceremonies and rites, and stories and language. The way managers perform their management functions influences the kind of culture that develops in an organization. [LO 8-4]

ORGANIZATIONAL CONTROL AND CHANGE There is a need to balance two opposing forces in the control process that influences the way organizations change. On the one hand, managers need to be able to control organizational activities and make their operations routine and predictable. On the other hand, organizations have to be responsive to the need to change, and managers must understand when they need to depart from routines to be responsive to unpredictable events. The four steps in managing change are (1) assessing the need for change, (2) deciding on the changes to make, (3) implementing change, and (4) evaluating the results of change. [LO 8-5]

ENTREPRENEURSHIP, CONTROL, AND CHANGE Entrepreneurs are people who notice opportunities and decide how to mobilize the resources necessary to produce new and improved goods and services. Intrapreneurs are employees in existing companies who notice opportunities to develop new or improved products and better ways to make them. Both entrepreneurs and intrapreneurs play important roles in the control and change process. [LO 8-6]

Management *in Action*

 TOPICS FOR DISCUSSION AND ACTION

Discussion

1. What is the relationship between organizing and controlling? [LO 8-1]

2. How do output control and behavior control differ? [LO 8-1, 8-2, 8-3]

3. Why is it important for managers to involve subordinates in the control process? [LO 8-3, 8-4]

4. What kind of controls would you expect to find most used in (a) a hospital, (b) the Navy, (c) a city police force? Why? [LO 8-1, 8-2, 8-3]

5. What is organizational culture, and how does it affect the way employees behave? [LO 8-4]

Action

6. Ask a manager to list the main performance measures that he or she uses to evaluate how well the organization is achieving its goals. [LO 8-1, 8-3, 8-4]

7. Interview some employees of an organization, and ask them about the organization's values, norms, socialization practices, ceremonies and rites, and special language and stories. Referring to this information, describe the organization's culture. [LO 8-3, 8-4, 8-5]

BUILDING MANAGEMENT SKILLS
Understanding Controlling [LO 8-1, 8-3, 8-4]

For this exercise you will analyze the control systems used by a real organization such as a department store, restaurant, hospital, police department, or small business. Your objective is to uncover all the different ways in which managers monitor and evaluate the performance of the organization and employees.

1. At what levels does control take place in this organization?

2. Which output performance standards (such as financial measures and organizational goals) do managers use most often to evaluate performance at each level?

3. Does the organization have a management-by-objectives system in place? If it does, describe it. If it

does not, speculate about why not.

4. How important is behavior control in this organization? For example, how much of managers' time is spent directly supervising employees? How formalized is the organization? Do employees receive a book of rules to instruct them about how to perform their jobs?

5. What kind of culture does the organization have? What are the values and norms? What effect does the organizational culture have on the way employees behave or treat customers?

6. Based on this analysis, do you think there is a fit between the organization's control systems and its culture? What is the nature of this fit? How could it be improved?

MANAGING ETHICALLY [LO 8-4]

Some managers and organizations go to great lengths to monitor their employees' behavior, and they keep extensive records about employees' behavior and performance. Some organizations also seem to possess norms and values that cause their employees to behave in certain ways.

Questions

1. Either by yourself or in a group, think about the ethical implications of organizations' monitoring and collecting information about their employees. What kind of information is it ethical or unethical to collect? Why? Should managers and organizations inform subordinates they are collecting such information?

2. Similarly, some organizations' cultures seem to develop norms and values that cause their members to behave in unethical ways. When and why does a strong norm that encourages high performance become one that can cause people to act unethically? How can organizations keep their values and norms from becoming "too strong"?

SMALL GROUP BREAKOUT EXERCISE [LO 8-3, 8-4, 8-5]
How Best to Control the Sales Force?

Form groups of three or four people, and appoint one member as the spokesperson who will communicate your findings to the whole class when called on by the instructor. Then discuss the following scenario:

You are the regional sales managers of an organization that supplies high-quality windows and doors to building supply centers nationwide. Over the last three years, the rate of sales growth has declined. There is increasing evidence that, to make their jobs easier, salespeople are primarily servicing large customer accounts and ignoring small accounts. In addition, the salespeople are not dealing promptly with customer questions and complaints, and this inattention has resulted in a drop in after-sales service. You have talked about these problems, and you are meeting to design a control system to increase both the amount of sales and the quality of customer service.

1. Design a control system that you think will best motivate salespeople to achieve these goals.

2. What relative importance do you put on (a) output control, (b) behavior control, and (c) organizational culture in this design?

BE THE MANAGER [LO 8-1, 8-5]

You have been asked by your company's CEO to find a way to improve the performance of its teams of web-design and web-hosting specialists and programmers. Each team works on a different aspect of website production, and while each is responsible for the quality of its own performance, its performance also depends on how well the other teams perform. Your task is to create a control system that will help to increase the performance of each team separately and facilitate cooperation among the teams. This is necessary because the various projects are interlinked and affect one another just as the different parts of a car must fit together. Since competition in the website production market is intense, it is imperative that each website be up and running as quickly as possible and incorporate all the latest advances in website software technology.

Questions

1. What kind of output controls will best facilitate positive interactions both within the teams and among the teams?

2. What kind of behavior controls will best facilitate positive interactions both within the teams and among the teams?

3. How would you go about helping managers develop a culture to promote high team performance?

THE WALL STREET JOURNAL CASE IN THE NEWS [LO 8-1, 8-3, 8-4, 8-5]
Behind Ginni Rometty's Plan to Reboot IBM

Big Blue's CEO pushes it toward analytics, mobile, cloud computing

ARMONK, N.Y.—The disconcerting messages started popping up on Virginia Rometty's screen not long after the IBM chief executive began a webcast to explain to her nearly 400,000 employees in 170 countries how she planned to reorganize the tech giant.

"I can't hear."

"I can't see you."

"Is this on?"

When the January presentation ended, Ms. Rometty fumed at colleagues, "We're only the IBM Company—we're better than this," according to people who were there. "Get this fixed now!"

That is a directive Ms. Rometty is giving a lot these days as she tries to reinvent the nearly 104-year-old icon while it continues a years-long slump. International Business Machines Corp.'s sales for 12 straight quarters have fallen from the year-earlier quarter.

The 57-year-old Ms. Rometty, who goes by "Ginni," has spent her three years as CEO trying to revamp slowing businesses like big computers and licensed software. She has shifted toward higher-growth markets she has targeted, like "analytics," which help corporations make sense of their growing data hoards, and "cloud" technologies to manage companies' operations over the Web and mobile devices.

But many of IBM's older businesses continue to drag, while divesting some of them has reduced overall revenue. In finding new revenues, Ms. Rometty hasn't moved fast enough for some investors. The stock is down 9.6% since she became CEO in January 2012, compared with a 67% rise in the S&P 500.

IBM "is at the make-or-break point," says James Lebenthal, a Rometty supporter and CEO of Lebenthal Asset Management LLC, which holds a small IBM stake. "Ginni needs to balance strategic vision with tactical survival."

Ms. Rometty (rhymes with confetti) says IBM is at "an inflection point." But, she says in an interview in her Armonk office last month, she isn't focused solely on the near-term concerns of some Wall Street critics. "My job," she says, "is to balance remaking IBM for the moment with an enduring IBM for the future."

A big shift

Spending time with Ms. Rometty over four recent weeks shows how her task is unlike that of past CEOs, who also remade IBM but mainly by shifting toward new markets it could quickly dominate. Ms. Rometty is overseeing a more fundamental shift, turning IBM into a company that also competes where it isn't in a position of strength.

"I can only change a company this size by making big bets" in new markets, she says.

On Monday, IBM reported $2.33 billion in net income, down from $2.38 billion a year earlier, on $19.6 billion in revenue, down 12%, largely meeting Wall Street expectations. But the company posted earnings per share of $2.91 excluding pension and some other items, beating analyst estimates, up from $2.68 a share from continuing operations in the year-earlier period. Also a bright spot: One of Ms. Rometty's growth pushes, cloud computing, was up 60% in revenue.

Still, with declining revenue and an underperforming stock, the IBM chief remains under pressure to show more progress.

Ms. Rometty recently got a vote of confidence from Warren Buffett, when his Berkshire Hathaway Inc.—IBM's largest shareholder—increased its holdings to 7.8% from 6.3%. Mr. Buffett didn't respond to inquiries.

Apple Inc. CEO Tim Cook, with whom she has begun a partnership to go after the corporate mobile market, says "Ginni is a modern CEO." Mr. Cook, who once worked at IBM, says: "She has the charisma and raw leadership to cut through the thick culture at IBM."

Ms. Rometty has made her goal clear: She wants more than 40% of IBM's revenues in 2018 to be from corporate markets in analytics, cloud computing, cybersecurity, social networking and mobile technologies. Those businesses were 27% of IBM's $92.8 billion in 2014 revenues, up from 15% of $105 billion revenues in 2011.

Computer hardware was 11% of 2014 revenues, versus 16% in 2011. Ms. Rometty sold off low-end servers and divested IBM's chip maker—which her CFO likens to "spinal removal surgery"—once integral elements of its hardware business. These units were producing revenue but not profits, she says, dubbing them "empty calories."

Her challenge is to rejuvenate what's left of IBM's hardware business, such as its newest mainframe rebuilt for mobile transactions. "Hardware was the original soul of this company," she says. Restructuring that business is "probably one of the things I'll be remembered most for," but "we can't hold on to our past."

To get faster-growing businesses to her 40% goal, she has been crisscrossing the globe to pitch them to customers and investors while prodding IBM staff to hurry up.

On trips, she carries a backpack with paperwork, school-sized notebooks and pencils—along with her iPhone. She seldom goes anywhere without a Starbucks Venti Chai Tea Misto in hand and a metallic hair band. Among customers and investors, she is known for her forceful demeanor. She often moves in close to people's faces, touching them to make a point. One day in March found her at BNSF Railway Co.'s Fort Worth, Texas, offices. She swooped into a conference room to bearhug Matt Rose, the railroad's executive chairman, before launching into business.

IBM has been providing analytics technology to help the railroad reduce derailments. With 2,000 sensors checking acoustics, pressure and temperature readings, IBM's analytics detect or predict when readings indicate a railcar component may fail. Analytics are an IBM strong suit that plays well in the era of "big data," the floods of information that companies collect and parse for profits. Ms. Rometty wants to expand that advantage into many industries.

Last week, IBM launched a health-care-analytics platform named "Watson Health," after the Watson artificial-intelligence system, to process data from companies including patient records, research studies and input from wearable devices.

Before leaving BNSF, she recommended Mr. Rose add other IBM offerings, including cloud services that would promise extra security. Mr. Rose says he agreed to migrate to IBM's cloud.

Ms. Rometty's drive into mobile markets was the topic of another meeting that day, with AT&T Inc. CEO Randall Stephenson, at IBM's Austin design lab. The companies together sell IBM's cloud services over AT&T mobile networks.

One topic of discussion: bids to European clients. When the AT&T and IBM managers there said some customers don't want the entire package at once, Ms. Rometty and Mr. Stephenson swung into action around a table, mapping a new strategy on the backside of a document.

At the design lab, IBM's team showed Ms. Rometty a demonstration on a large flat screen showing a real-time view of corporate hacking around the world. IBM is designing a security product, code-named "X-Force," in which businesses share intelligence on security threats. "Fellow CEOs," she told her team, "will see the values I do and want on this platform."

She dropped in on a group of young IBM developers, some with tattoos and piercings, who are responsible for IBM's new email offering, called Verse. A team leader promised to hit a year's-end rollout target.

At that, Ms. Rometty pivoted sharply on her high heels. "No, no, no! Too slow," she interjected. "What can I do to help you move faster?"

Speed is of the essence, she says later, because the industry is fast moving. But remaking a company IBM's size can be complex: "I have trained my life to fly a 747.

That is way different than piloting a two-prop engine plane."

A Chicago native, Ms. Rometty graduated from Northwestern University with electrical-engineering and computer-science majors and joined IBM on the career ground floor as a systems engineer in 1981. She rose quickly, running IBM's consulting business and managing its purchase of Pricewaterhouse Coopers's IT-consulting business in 2002.

Struggling to catch up

As CEO, she followed Sam Palmisano, who himself had remade IBM, selling its PC business in 2005 and expanding into emerging markets.

In her first shareholder letter, in 2012, she described a model of "continuous transformation." It was soon clear IBM was late to some important trends in tech. The corporations that are IBM's main customers were seeking to let employees work from mobile devices and were moving processing and data off in-house computers, handling them through cloud computing. But IBM was struggling in some of these markets. Just before Ms. Rometty became CEO, it launched "SmartCloud," a public cloud service. But sales were anemic, and in early 2013, IBM lost out to Amazon.com Inc. in the Central Intelligence Agency's cloud business—an embarrassment, given IBM's history of federal contracts.

Desperate to jump-start Smart-Cloud, IBM's executive team asked Ms. Rometty for more money and time. She recalls pointing out the window and telling them: "The market is moving too fast. I can't give you more time."

Instead, she spent $2 billion on a cloud-technology company, SoftLayer, and made a $1.2 billion investment in additional data centers.

At the same time, IBM had what many considered a computer-science breakthrough in its analytics business: Watson, the artificial-intelligence computer known for winning "Jeopardy!" in 2011. Some clients were asking to "buy a Watson."

At an operations meeting, senior IBM executives debated how to commercialize Watson, says John Kelly, a senior vice president. Some suggested selling copies of the Watson hardware and software.

Ms. Rometty objected, arguing IBM should sell Watson as a cloud service. In an initial application of Watson analytics, IBM worked with Memorial Sloan Kettering Cancer Center to personalize treatments. That would inspire the Watson health-care platform it unveiled last week.

By 2013, Ms. Rometty was writing checks for acquisitions. She has spent about $8 billion since her ascension buying about 30 companies in her target growth markets.

She has made four major divestitures, taking charges for laying off workers. Head count has shrunk 12% to 380,000 during her tenure.

Last year, she began talking to Apple's Mr. Cook about a broad partnership, starting with putting IBM business apps on Apple mobile devices. Some IBM executives, miffed at working with the some-time rival, called it "Project 30," referring to the 30 years since the 1984 television commercial in which Apple portrayed Big Blue as "Big Brother."

At a July 2014 announcement of the partnership at Apple headquarters, "there was a level of jaw dropping on both sides," Mr. Cook says. He says he is betting Ms. Rometty is on the right track. "It's not the same IBM."

Ms. Rometty has created partnerships with Twitter Inc. in data analytics—allowing companies to analyze Twitter feeds for business clues—and China's Tencent Holdings Ltd. to create cloud services for businesses there.

In July, she invited top executives to a retreat. "Your assignment: one paragraph on what is IBM 10 years from now—no constraints, no sacred cows," she told them. Among their ideas: Ditch the hierarchical structure and form businesses along industry lines.

To redirect funds to new investments, in October 2014 she yanked IBM's longtime promise of $20-a-share profits by 2015—a commitment that forced IBM to buy back shares and cut costs as core-business revenues declined. IBM's share price fell 7.1% in a day. And in January, she unveiled IBM's most sweeping reorganization in three decades, moving it from units defined by hardware, software and services toward a structure of integrated businesses that focus on specific industries.

She's well aware of her Wall Street critics. Emerging from the elevator at IBM's recent investor day, she breezed past people vying for her attention and zeroed in on a tough critic, Bernstein Research analyst Toni Sacconaghi. Looking him in the eye from close range, smiling broadly, she grabbed his elbow and challenged his assertion that IBM had too many lifers in its top ranks.

"They have their backs against the wall," he says afterward. "IBM's future isn't clear."

Later, Ms. Rometty urged patience from the investors, warning that revenue won't improve for another year, partly because of currency headwinds and hardware divestitures.

In the following weeks, IBM invested $3 billion in a new unit dubbed "Internet of Things" to build a business off data from things like factory machines and home appliances. IBM signed a partnership with Weather Channel's parent, Weather Co., to offer weather analyses for businesses. This month, the U.S. Army said IBM's cloud service will power its logistics systems.

Ms. Rometty is relentless in pushing staff. Jeff Smith, an IBM vice president, says he was at a Starbucks with his baseball cap pulled low on a recent Saturday morning and didn't think Ms. Rometty, who lives near him, would notice him. She made a bee-line for him, tea in hand, lifted his cap and asked: "What are we doing to change the company?"

Questions

1. How would you describe Rometty's approach to output control? Provide several examples to support your view.

2. How would you describe Rometty's approach to behavior control? Provide several examples to support your view.

3. What factors should IBM's CEO and other senior managers take into consideration as they shift the focus of the organization going forward? What type of organizational changes do you think could be implemented as part of the plan?

Source: Monica Langley, "Behind Ginni Rometty's Plan to Reboot IBM," *The Wall Street Journal*, April 20, 2105, www.wsj.com.

Endnotes

1. D. Bates, "You've Got (More) Mail: The Average Office Worker Now Spends over a Quarter of Their Day Dealing with Email," *Daily Mail*, accessed April 21, 2015, www.dailymail.co.uk; M. Thomas, "Your Late-Night Emails Are Hurting Your Team," *Harvard Business Review*, accessed April 21, 2015, https://hbr.org.

2. Company website, "About," www.vynamic.com, accessed April 21, 2015; L. Vanderkam, "Should Your Company Use 'Zmail'? The Case for Inbox Curfews," *Fast Company*, accessed April 21, 2015, www.fastcompany.com; "The Five Most Outrageous Company Perks in the World," *Bloomberg Businessweek*, accessed April 21, 2015, www.bloomberg.com; Sathvik Ramanan, "How to Invest in Your Employees' Health—Dan Calista, CEO of Vynamic," *The Work/Life Integration Forum*, accessed April 21, 2015, http://worklife.wharton.upenn.edu.

3. J. Duffy, "Get Organized: 11 Tips for Managing Email," *PC Magazine*, accessed April 21, 2015, www.pcmag.com; S. Green, "8 Ways Not to Manage Your Email (and 5 and a Half Tactics That Work)," *Harvard Business Review*, accessed April 21, 2015, http://blogs.hbr.org.

4. W. G. Ouchi, "Markets, Bureaucracies, and Clans," *Administrative Science Quarterly* 25 (1980), 129–41.

5. P. Lorange, M. Morton, and S. Ghoshal, *Strategic Control* (St. Paul, MN: West, 1986).

6. H. Koontz and R. W. Bradspies, "Managing through Feedforward Control," *Business Horizons*, June 1972, 25–36.

7. E. E. Lawler III and J. G. Rhode, *Information and Control in Organizations* (Pacific Palisades, CA: Goodyear, 1976).

8. C.W.L. Hill and G. R. Jones, *Strategic Management: An Integrated Approach,* 10th ed. (Mason, OH: Cengage Learning, 2012).

9. E. Flamholtz, "Organizational Control Systems as a Management Tool," *California Management Review,* Winter 1979, 50–58.

10. W. G. Ouchi, "The Transmission of Control through Organizational Hierarchy," *Academy of Management Journal* 21 (1978), 173–92.

11. W. G. Ouchi, "The Relationship between Organizational Structure and Organizational Control," *Administrative Science Quarterly* 22 (1977), 95–113.

12. Ouchi, "Markets, Bureaucracies, and Clans."

13. W. H. Newman, *Constructive Control* (Englewood Cliffs, NJ: Prentice-Hall, 1975).

14. J. D. Thompson, *Organizations in Action* (New York: McGraw-Hill, 1967).

15. R. N. Anthony, *The Management Control Function* (Boston: Harvard Business School Press, 1988).

16. "PM Mobile Electric Power," http://peocscss.army.mil, April 23, 2014.

17. T. Clements, "Knowledge Is Power," http://energy.defense.gov, February 14, 2014.

18. Ibid.

19. D. Douglas and M. Fletcher, "Toyota Reaches $1.2 Billion Settlement to End Probe of Accelerator Problems," *The Washington Post,* February 14, 2014, www.washingtonpost.com.

20. Ouchi, "Markets, Bureaucracies, and Clans."

21. Organization website, "The Skills/Qualities Employers Want in New College Graduates," https://www.naceweb.org, accessed April 22, 2015.

22. McKinsey & Company, "Big Data: The Next Frontier for Innovation, Competition, and Productivity," www.mckinsey.com, accessed April 22, 2015.

23. R. Simons, "Strategic Orientation and Top Management Attention to Control Systems," *Strategic Management Journal* 12 (1991), 49–62.

24. G. Schreyogg and H. Steinmann, "Strategic Control: A New Perspective," *Academy of Management Review* 12 (1987), 91–103.

25. B. Woolridge and S. W. Floyd, "The Strategy Process, Middle Management Involvement, and Organizational Performance," *Strategic Management Journal* 11 (1990), 231–41.

26. J. A. Alexander, "Adaptive Changes in Corporate Control Practices," *Academy of Management Journal* 34 (1991), 162–93.

27. Hill and Jones, *Strategic Management.*

28. G.H.B. Ross, "Revolution in Management Control," *Management Accounting* 72 (1992), 23–27.

29. P. F. Drucker, *The Practice of Management* (New York: Harper & Row, 1954).

30. S. J. Carroll and H. L. Tosi, *Management by Objectives: Applications and Research* (New York: Macmillan, 1973).

31. R. Rodgers and J. E. Hunter, "Impact of Management by Objectives on Organizational Productivity," *Journal of Applied Psychology* 76 (1991), 322–26.

32. M. B. Gavin, S. G. Green, and G. T. Fairhurst, "Managerial Control—Strategies for Poor Performance over Time and the Impact on Subordinate Reactions," *Organizational Behavior and Human Decision Processes* 63 (1995), 207–21.

33. www.cypress.com, 2015.

34. B. Dumaine, "The Bureaucracy Busters," *Fortune,* June 17, 1991, 46.

35. D. S. Pugh, D. J. Hickson, C. R. Hinings, and C. Turner, "Dimensions of Organizational Structure," *Administrative Science Quarterly* 13 (1968), 65–91.

36. Company website, "Who We Are," and "Netflix Culture: Freedom & Responsibility," https://jobs.netflix.com, accessed April 22, 2015.

37. A. Shontell, "Sheryl Sandberg: 'The Most Important Document Ever to Come Out of the Valley,'" *Business Insider,* accessed April 22, 2015, www.businessinsider.com.

38. P. McCord, "How Netflix Reinvented HR," *Harvard Business Review,* accessed April 22, 2015, https://hbr.org.

39. Company website, "Company Overview," http://ir.netflix.com, accessed September 4, 2015.

40. J. Herman, "The Latest Fitness Fad (That We Really Like): Philanthrofits," *Cosmopolitan,* accessed April 22, 2015, www.cosmopolitan.com; organization website, "How It Works," www.charitymiles.org, accessed April 22, 2015.

41. Lane Anderson, "Fitness App Lets Charities Cash In on Your Daily Workout," *Deseret News,* accessed April 22, 2015, http://national.deseretnews.com.

42. Organization website, "FAQ—Commitment Contracts—Charities," https://www.stickk.com, accessed April 22, 2015.

43. Company website, "UPS Worldwide," and "UPS Alternative Fuel," www.ups.com, accessed April 23, 2015.

44. L. Brown, "Research Action: Organizational Feedback, Understanding and Change," *Journal of Applied Behavioral Research* 8 (1972), 697–711; P. A. Clark, *Action Research and Organizational Change* (New York: Harper & Row, 1972); N. Margulies and A. P. Raia, eds., *Conceptual Foundations of Organizational Development* (New York: McGraw-Hill, 1978).

45. W. L. French and C. H. Bell, *Organizational Development* (Englewood Cliffs, NJ: Prentice-Hall, 1990).

46. J. McGregor, "The World's Most Innovative Companies," www.businessweek.com, May 4, 2007.

47. Company website, www.waltdisney.com, accessed April 23, 2015.

48. Alex Stedman, "'Frozen' Becomes the Highest Grossing Animated Film Ever," *Variety,* accessed April 23, 2015, http://variety.com.

49. W. L. French, "A Checklist for Organizing and Implementing an OD Effort," in W. L. French, C. H. Bell, and R. A. Zawacki, eds., *Organizational Development and Transformation* (Homewood, IL: Irwin, 1994), 484–95.

PART 5

9 Motivation

Learning Objectives

After studying this chapter, you should be able to:

LO 9-1 Explain what motivation is and why managers need to be concerned about it.

LO 9-2 Describe from the perspectives of expectancy theory and equity theory what managers should do to have a highly motivated workforce.

LO 9-3 Explain how goals and needs motivate people and what kinds of goals are especially likely to result in high performance.

LO 9-4 Identify the motivation lessons that managers can learn from operant conditioning theory and social learning theory.

LO 9-5 Explain why and how managers can use pay as a major motivation tool.

© Yuri Arcurs/Cutcaster RF

Running into your boss's boss in the cafeteria isn't quite so daunting when the food is good, your pay is reasonable, and you know your kids are happily playing in the awesome day care just up the road! SAS knows how to keep its employees engaged in their work by recognizing a broad range of worker needs.
© Jeremy M. Lange/The New York Times/Redux

MANAGEMENT SNAPSHOT

High Motivation at the SAS Institute

How Can Managers Encourage and Maintain High Levels of Employee Motivation?

The SAS Institute is in the enviable position of being listed on *Fortune* magazine's annual ranking of the "100 Best Companies to Work For" for 18 years in a row; in 2015, the SAS Institute was ranked fourth.[1] The SAS Institute is the world's largest privately owned software company, with more than 13,660 employees worldwide and more than $3 billion in revenues.[2] In fact, revenues have increased at SAS every year since the company was founded in 1976. Headquartered in Cary, North Carolina, SAS also has offices in Europe, the Middle East, Africa, Asia Pacific, Latin America, and Canada.[3]

Every indicator suggests that SAS employees are highly motivated and perform well while also working 35-hour weeks. Since its founding, the SAS Institute has strived to ensure that employees enjoy and are motivated by the work they perform. Managers approach motivation from the perspective that all employees should be interested and involved in the work that they are performing and have the sense that they are making meaningful contributions to SAS and SAS' customers. While some software

companies that seek to develop new products buy companies that are already making these products, SAS develops its new products internally, and employees can perform interesting work at the forefront of technology.[4] Creativity is encouraged at SAS, and employees experience the excitement of developing a new product and seeing it succeed.[5] Overall, employees exert high levels of effort and persist in the face of setbacks to develop and provide the outstanding software solutions for businesses that SAS is renowned for.

Recognizing that sometimes employees might lose interest in the type of work they are doing or just need a change of pace, SAS allows employees to change jobs to prevent becoming bored with their work. SAS gives employees any additional training they might need when they change jobs. By encouraging these kinds of lateral moves, managers help to ensure that high levels of motivation at SAS are sustained over time.[6] While annual turnover rates in the software industry are around 15%, SAS's turnover rate in 2013 was 3.6% and average tenure at SAS is around 10 years.[7]

Managers at SAS fairly and equitably reward employees for a job well done. Moreover, Goodnight and other managers recognize that SAS's employees are its biggest asset and go to great lengths to satisfy their needs and create a work environment that will be conducive to creativity, high motivation, and well-being for employees and their families. At headquarters in North Carolina, employees have access to two child care centers that SAS subsidizes, a summer camp, three subsidized cafeterias, a 66,000-square-foot fitness and recreation center including an Olympic-size pool, and all kinds of services ranging from dry cleaning and car detailing to massages and a book exchange. Google (one of SAS's customers) actually used SAS as a prototype when Google was developing its own suite of employee benefits and perks.[8]

An on-campus health care center with an annual budget of $4.5 million and staff of 53 provides SAS employees and their families with free basic care clinic services.[9] SAS estimates that the center saves the company about $5 million per year because employees are not losing valuable time traveling to doctors' offices and waiting a long time to see them. Moreover, employees are more likely to get care when they need it, and SAS can provide the care they need at lower costs.[10]

Wellness and work/life centers offer a variety of programs to help employees achieve a sense of balance in their lives and days. Employees with children are encouraged to have lunch with their kids in the subsidized cafeterias complete with high chairs, and of course they can bring their kids to the health center when they get sick.[11]

Employees have their own offices, and the work environment is rich in pleasant vistas, whether they be artwork on the walls or views of the rolling hills of Cary, North Carolina, at company headquarters. SAS keeps two artists on its staff in the belief that exposure to beautiful artwork and surroundings can spur creativity.[12] Employees and their families are encouraged to use the 200 acres that surround company headquarters for family walks and picnics.[13]

SAS trusts its employees to do what is right for the company. Thus, many employees are able to determine their own work schedules and there are unlimited sick days.[14] And SAS realizes that to maintain high levels of motivation over time, employees need to have a balanced life—hence the 35-hour workweek. Of course, because SAS is a truly global company, sometimes employees on global teams with a tight new product development schedule need to work long hours and some employees check work email at home. Nonetheless, employees at SAS are not expected to work excessive hours as is common at some other companies.[15]

Clearly, motivating employees and helping to satisfy their needs is a win–win situation for SAS. As Bev Brown, a SAS employee in external communications put it, "Some may think that because SAS is family-friendly and has great benefits that we don't work hard . . . But people do work hard here, because they're motivated to take care of a company that takes care of them."[16]

Overview

LO 9-1 Explain what motivation is and why managers need to be concerned about it.

Even with the best strategy in place and an appropriate organizational architecture, an organization will be effective only if its members are motivated to perform at a high level. James Goodnight of SAS in the "Management Snapshot" clearly realizes this. One reason why leading is such an important managerial activity is that it entails ensuring that each member of an organization is motivated to perform highly and help the organization achieve its goals. When managers are effective, the outcome of the leading process is a highly motivated workforce. A key challenge for managers of organizations both large and small is to encourage employees to perform at a high level.

In this chapter, we describe what motivation is, where it comes from, and why managers need to promote high levels of it for an organization to be effective and achieve its goals. We examine important theories of motivation: expectancy theory, need theories, equity theory, goal-setting theory, and learning theories. Each gives managers important insights about how to motivate organizational members. The theories are complementary in that each focuses on a different aspect of motivation. Considering all the theories together helps managers gain a rich understanding of the many issues and problems involved in encouraging high levels of motivation throughout an organization. Last, we consider the use of pay as a motivation tool. By the end of this chapter, you will understand what it takes to have a highly motivated workforce.

The Nature of Motivation

motivation
Psychological forces that determine the direction of a person's behavior in an organization, a person's level of effort, and a person's level of persistence.

Motivation may be defined as psychological forces that determine the direction of a person's behavior in an organization, a person's level of effort, and a person's level of persistence in the face of obstacles.[17] The *direction of a person's behavior* refers to the many possible behaviors a person could engage in. For example, employees at the SAS Institute are encouraged to be creative and develop new software that will meet customers' future needs. *Effort* refers to how hard people work. Employees at the SAS Institute exert high levels of effort to provide superior software solutions for business customers. *Persistence* refers to whether, when faced with roadblocks and obstacles, people keep trying or give up. Setbacks and obstacles are part and parcel of research and development work; at the SAS Institute, employees persist in the face of these difficulties to develop new sophisticated software.

Motivation is central to management because it explains *why* people behave the way they do in organizations[18]—why employees at the SAS Institute continue to develop software that is used by SAS customers around the world. Motivation also explains why a waiter is polite or rude and why a kindergarten teacher really tries to get children to enjoy learning or just goes through the motions. It explains why some managers truly put their organizations' best interests first, whereas others are more concerned with maximizing their salaries and why—more generally—some workers put forth twice as much effort as others.

intrinsically motivated behavior Behavior that is performed for its own sake.

Motivation can come from *intrinsic* or *extrinsic* sources. **Intrinsically motivated behavior** is behavior that is performed for its own sake; the source of motivation is actually performing the behavior, and motivation comes from doing the work itself. Many managers are intrinsically motivated; they derive a sense of accomplishment and achievement from helping the organization achieve its goals and gain competitive advantages. Jobs that are interesting and challenging are more likely to lead to intrinsic motivation than are jobs that are boring or do not use a person's skills and abilities. An elementary school teacher who really enjoys teaching children, a computer programmer who loves solving programming problems, and a commercial photographer who relishes taking creative photographs are all intrinsically motivated. For these individuals, motivation comes from performing their jobs—teaching children, finding bugs in computer programs, and taking pictures.

extrinsically motivated behavior Behavior that is performed to acquire material or social rewards or to avoid punishment.

Extrinsically motivated behavior is behavior that is performed to acquire material or social rewards or to avoid punishment; the source of motivation is the consequences of the behavior, not the behavior itself. A car salesperson who is motivated by receiving a commission on all cars sold, a lawyer who is motivated by the high salary and status that go along with the job, and a factory worker who is motivated by the opportunity to earn a secure income are all extrinsically motivated. Their motivation comes from the consequences they receive as a result of their work behaviors.

People can be intrinsically motivated, extrinsically motivated, or both intrinsically and extrinsically motivated.[19] A top manager who derives a sense of accomplishment and achievement from managing a large corporation and strives to reach year-end

Where are you more likely to find prosocial motivation? Here in the classroom as a teacher walks her student through that tricky math problem. Getting companies to foster this type of motivation is a bit trickier! © LWA/Dann Tardif/Blend Images/ Corbis RF

prosocially motivated behavior Behavior that is performed to benefit or help others.

outcome Anything a person gets from a job or organization.

input Anything a person contributes to his or her job or organization.

targets to obtain a hefty bonus is both intrinsically and extrinsically motivated. Similarly, a nurse who enjoys helping and taking care of patients and is motivated by having a secure job with good benefits is both intrinsically and extrinsically motivated. At the SAS Institute, employees are both extrinsically motivated, because of equitable pay and outstanding benefits, and intrinsically motivated, because of the opportunity to do interesting work. Whether workers are intrinsically motivated, extrinsically motivated, or both depends on a wide variety of factors: (1) workers' own personal characteristics (such as their personalities, abilities, values, attitudes, and needs), (2) the nature of their jobs (such as whether they have been enriched or where they are on the five core characteristics of the job characteristics model), and (3) the nature of the organization (such as its structure, its culture, its control systems, its human resource management system, and the ways in which rewards such as pay are distributed to employees).

In addition to being intrinsically or extrinsically motivated, some people are prosocially motivated by their work.[20] **Prosocially motivated behavior** is behavior that is performed to benefit or help others.[21] Behavior can be prosocially motivated in addition to being extrinsically and/or intrinsically motivated. An elementary school teacher who not only enjoys the process of teaching young children (has high intrinsic motivation) but also has a strong desire to give children the best learning experience possible and help those with learning disabilities overcome their challenges, and who keeps up with the latest research on child development and teaching methods in an effort to continually improve the effectiveness of his teaching, has high prosocial motivation in addition to high intrinsic motivation. A surgeon who specializes in organ transplants, enjoys the challenge of performing complex operations, has a strong desire to help her patients regain their health and extend their lives through successful organ transplants, and is also motivated by the relatively high income she earns has high intrinsic, prosocial, and extrinsic motivation. Recent preliminary research suggests that when workers have high prosocial motivation, also having high intrinsic motivation can be especially beneficial for job performance.[22]

Regardless of whether people are intrinsically, extrinsically, or prosocially motivated, they join and are motivated to work in organizations to obtain certain outcomes. An **outcome** is anything a person gets from a job or organization. Some outcomes, such as autonomy, responsibility, a feeling of accomplishment, and the pleasure of doing interesting or enjoyable work, result in intrinsically motivated behavior. Outcomes such as improving the lives or well-being of other people and doing good by helping others result in prosocially motivated behavior. Other outcomes, such as pay, job security, benefits, and vacation time, result in extrinsically motivated behavior.

Organizations hire people to obtain important inputs. An **input** is anything a person contributes to the job or organization, such as time, effort, education, experience, skills, knowledge, and actual work behaviors. Inputs such as these are necessary for an organization to achieve its goals. Managers strive to motivate members of an organization to contribute inputs—through their behavior, effort,

Figure 9.1

The Motivation Equation

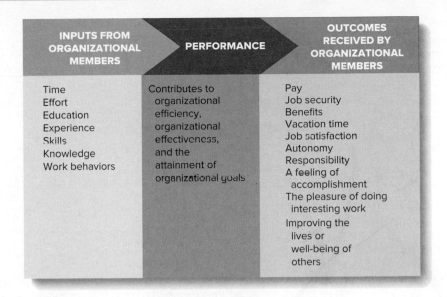

INPUTS FROM ORGANIZATIONAL MEMBERS	PERFORMANCE	OUTCOMES RECEIVED BY ORGANIZATIONAL MEMBERS
Time Effort Education Experience Skills Knowledge Work behaviors	Contributes to organizational efficiency, organizational effectiveness, and the attainment of organizational goals	Pay Job security Benefits Vacation time Job satisfaction Autonomy Responsibility A feeling of accomplishment The pleasure of doing interesting work Improving the lives or well-being of others

and persistence—that help the organization achieve its goals. How do managers do this? They ensure that members of an organization obtain the outcomes they desire when they make valuable contributions to the organization. Managers use outcomes to motivate people to contribute their inputs to the organization. Giving people outcomes when they contribute inputs and perform well aligns the interests of employees with the goals of the organization as a whole because when employees do what is good for the organization, they personally benefit.

This alignment between employees and organizational goals as a whole can be described by the motivation equation depicted in Figure 9.1. Managers seek to ensure that people are motivated to contribute important inputs to the organization, that these inputs are put to good use or focused in the direction of high performance, and that high performance results in workers' obtaining the outcomes they desire.

Each of the theories of motivation discussed in this chapter focuses on one or more aspects of this equation. Each theory focuses on a different set of issues that managers need to address to have a highly motivated workforce. Together the theories provide a comprehensive set of guidelines for managers to follow to promote high levels of employee motivation. Effective managers, such as James Goodnight in the "Management Snapshot," tend to follow many of these guidelines, whereas ineffective managers often fail to follow them and seem to have trouble motivating organizational members.

LO 9-2 Describe from the perspectives of expectancy theory and equity theory what managers should do to have a highly motivated workforce.

expectancy theory The theory that motivation will be high when workers believe that high levels of effort lead to high performance and high performance leads to the attainment of desired outcomes.

Expectancy Theory

Expectancy theory, formulated by Victor H. Vroom in the 1960s, posits that motivation is high when workers believe that high levels of effort lead to high performance and high performance leads to the attainment of desired outcomes. Expectancy theory is one of the most popular theories of work motivation because it focuses on all three parts of the motivation equation: inputs, performance, and outcomes. Expectancy theory identifies three major factors that determine a person's motivation: *expectancy, instrumentality,* and *valence* (see Figure 9.2).[23]

Figure 9.2
Expectancy,
Instrumentality, and
Valence

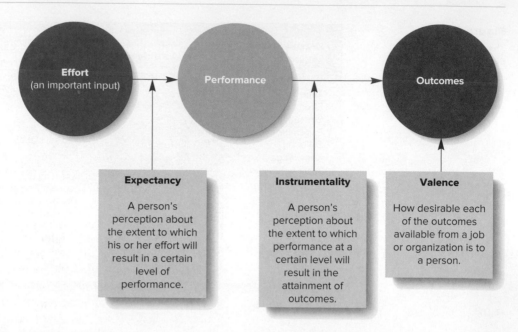

Expectancy

Expectancy is a person's perception about the extent to which effort (an input) results in a certain level of performance. A person's level of expectancy determines whether he or she believes that a high level of effort results in a high level of performance. People are motivated to put forth a lot of effort on their jobs only if they think that their effort will pay off in high performance—that is, if they have high expectancy. Think about how motivated you would be to study for a test if you thought that no matter how hard you tried, you would get a D. Think about how motivated a marketing manager would be who thought that no matter how hard he or she worked, there was no way to increase sales of an unpopular product. In these cases, expectancy is low, so overall motivation is also low.

Members of an organization are motivated to put forth a high level of effort only if they think that doing so leads to high performance.[24] In other words, in order for people's motivation to be high, expectancy must be high. Thus, in attempting to influence motivation, managers need to make sure their subordinates believe that if they do try hard, they can actually succeed. One way managers can boost expectancies is through expressing confidence in their subordinates' capabilities. Managers at The Container Store, for example, express high levels of confidence in their subordinates. As Container Store cofounder Garrett Boone put it, "Everybody we hire, we hire as a leader. Anybody in our store can take an action that you might think of typically being a manager's action."[25]

In addition to expressing confidence in subordinates, other ways for managers to boost subordinates' expectancy levels and motivation are by providing training so people have the expertise needed for high performance and increasing their levels of autonomy and responsibility as they gain experience so they have the freedom to do what it takes to perform at a high level. For example, the Best Buy chain of stores selling electronics, computers, music and movies, and gadgets of all sorts boosts salespeople's expectancies by giving them extensive training in on-site meetings and online. Electronic learning terminals in each department not only help salespeople learn how different systems work and can be sold as an integrated package but also enable them to keep up to date with the latest advances in technology and products.

Salespeople also receive extensive training in how to determine customers' needs.[26] At the SAS Institute in the "Management Snapshot," employees who change jobs receive any additional training they might need to be effective in their new positions, which boosts their expectancy.

Instrumentality

instrumentality In expectancy theory, a perception about the extent to which performance results in the attainment of outcomes.

Expectancy captures a person's perceptions about the relationship between effort and performance. **Instrumentality**, the second major concept in expectancy theory, is a person's perception about the extent to which performance at a certain level results in the attainment of outcomes (see Figure 9.2). According to expectancy theory, employees are motivated to perform at a high level only if they think high performance will lead to (or is *instrumental* for attaining) outcomes such as pay, job security, interesting job assignments, bonuses, or a feeling of accomplishment. In other words, instrumentalities must be high for motivation to be high—people must perceive that because of their high performance they will receive outcomes.[27]

Managers promote high levels of instrumentality when they link performance to desired outcomes. In addition, managers must clearly communicate this linkage to subordinates. By making sure that outcomes available in an organization are distributed to organizational members on the basis of their performance, managers promote high instrumentality and motivation. When outcomes are linked to performance in this way, high performers receive more outcomes than low performers. In the "Management Snapshot," managers raise levels of instrumentality and motivation for SAS employees by rewarding employees for a job well done.

Valence

valence In expectancy theory, how desirable each of the outcomes available from a job or organization is to a person.

Although all members of an organization must have high expectancies and instrumentalities, expectancy theory acknowledges that people differ in their preferences for outcomes. For many people, pay is the most important outcome of working. For others, a feeling of accomplishment or enjoying one's work is more important than pay. The term **valence** refers to how desirable each of the outcomes available from a job or organization is to a person. To motivate organizational members, managers need to determine which outcomes have high valence for them—are highly desired—and make sure that those outcomes are provided when members perform at a high level.

Providing employees with highly valent outcomes not only can contribute to high levels of motivation but also has the potential to reduce turnover, as indicated in the accompanying "Management Insight" feature.

MANAGEMENT INSIGHT

Motivating and Retaining Employees at The Container Store

Kip Tindell and Garrett Boone founded The Container Store in Dallas, Texas, in 1978, and Tindell currently serves as CEO and chairman (Boone is chairman emeritus).[28] When they opened their first store, they were out on the floor trying to sell customers their storage and organization products that would economize on space and time and make purchasers' lives a little less complicated. The Container Store has grown to include 65 stores in 23 U.S. markets from coast to coast; although the original store in Dallas had only 1,600 square feet, the stores today average around 25,000 square feet.[29] The phenomenal growth in the size of the stores has been matched by impressive growth rates in sales and profits.[30] Managers at The

Kip Tindell, founder, CEO, and chairman of the Container Store. The Container Store has seen growth throughout its history which could be partially attributed to the way their managers actively assist customers on the shop floor.
© Brad Swonetz/Redux

Container Store are often found on the shop floor tidying shelves and helping customers carry out their purchases.[31] And that, perhaps, is an important clue to the secret of their success. The Container Store has been consistently ranked among *Fortune* magazine's "100 Best Companies to Work For" for 16 years running.[32] In 2015, The Container Store was 27th on this list.[33]

Early on, Tindell and Boone recognized that people are The Container Store's most valuable asset and that after hiring great people, one of the most important managerial tasks is motivating them. One would think motivating employees might be especially challenging in the retail industry, which has an average annual turnover rate of 100 percent or more.[34] At The Container Store annual voluntary turnover is around 11%, a testament to Tindell's and other managers' ability to motivate.[35]

Tindell and Boone have long recognized the importance of rewarding employees for a job well done with highly valent outcomes. For example, the average annual pay for salespeople is around $48,000, which is significantly higher than retail averages; and employees receive merit pay increases for superior sales performance.[36] To encourage high individual performance as well as teamwork and cooperation, both individual and team-based rewards are given at The Container Store. Some high-performing salespeople earn more than their store managers, which suits the store managers fine as long as equitable procedures are used and rewards are distributed fairly.[37]

Professional development is another valent outcome employees obtain from working at The Container Store. Full-time salespeople receive more than 240 hours of training their first year, and all employees have ongoing opportunities for additional training and development.[38] Employees also have flexible work options and flexible benefits; medical, dental, and 401(k) retirement plans; job security; a casual dress code; and access to a variety of wellness programs ranging from yoga classes and chair massages to a personalized web-based nutrition and exercise planner.[39] Another valent outcome is the opportunity to work with other highly motivated individuals in an environment that exudes enthusiasm and excitement. Not only are The Container Store's employees motivated, but they also look forward to coming to work and feel as if their coworkers and managers are part of their family. Employees feel pride in what they do—helping customers organize their lives, save space and time, and have a better sense of well-being. Hence they not only personally benefit from high performance by receiving highly valent outcomes but also feel good about the products they sell and the help they give customers.[40] Tindell and other managers at The Container Store evidently have never lost sight of the importance of motivation for both organizations and their members.

Bringing It All Together

According to expectancy theory, high motivation results from high levels of expectancy, instrumentality, and valence (see Figure 9.3). If any one of these factors is low, motivation is likely to be low. No matter how tightly desired outcomes are linked to performance, if a person thinks it is practically impossible to perform at

Figure 9.3
Expectancy Theory

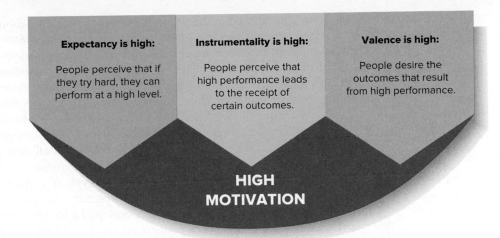

Expectancy is high:	Instrumentality is high:	Valence is high:
People perceive that if they try hard, they can perform at a high level.	People perceive that high performance leads to the receipt of certain outcomes.	People desire the outcomes that result from high performance.

HIGH MOTIVATION

a high level, motivation to perform at a high level will be low. Similarly, if a person does not think outcomes are linked to high performance, or if a person does not desire the outcomes that are linked to high performance, motivation to perform at a high level will be low. Effective managers realize the importance of high levels of expectancy, instrumentality, and valence and take concrete steps to ensure that their employees are highly motivated, as is true at Enterprise Rent-A-Car profiled in the accompanying "Management Insight" feature.

MANAGEMENT INSIGHT

How Enterprise Rent-A-Car Motivates Employees

Enterprise Rent-A-Car was founded by Jack Taylor in 1957 in St. Louis, Missouri, as a very small auto leasing business.[41] Today Enterprise Holdings, which owns and operates Enterprise Rent-A-Car, is the biggest car rental company in the world with over $16 billion in revenues and over 78,000 employees. Enterprise has more than 8,000 locations in the United States, Canada, the United Kingdom, Ireland, and Germany.[42] One of the biggest employers of new college graduates in the United States, Enterprise typically hires over 8,000 college graduates each year.[43] While starting salaries tend to be low and the work can be hard (e.g., four assistant managers once sued the company claiming that they should receive overtime pay), Enterprise has been ranked among the top 50 best companies for new college graduates to launch their careers by *Bloomberg Businessweek* magazine.[44]

One of the keys to Enterprise's success is the way it motivates its employees to provide excellent customer service.[45] Practically all entry-level hires participate in Enterprise's Management Training Program.[46] As part of the program, new hires learn all aspects of the company business, and how to provide excellent customer service. Management trainees first have a four-day training session focused primarily on Enterprise's culture. They are then assigned to a branch office for around 8 to 12 months where they learn all aspects of the business, from negotiating with body shops to helping customers to washing cars. As part of this training, they learn how important high-quality customer service is to Enterprise and how they can personally provide great service, increasing their confidence levels.[47]

All those who do well in the program are promoted after about a year to the position of management assistant. Management assistants who do well are promoted to become assistant branch managers with responsibility for mentoring and supervising employees. Assistant managers who do well can be promoted to become branch managers who are responsible for managing a branch's employees and provision of customer service, rental car fleet, and financial performance. Branch managers with about five years of experience in the position often move on to take up management positions at headquarters or assume the position of area manager overseeing all the branches in a certain geographic region.[48] By training all new hires in all aspects of the business including the provision of excellent customer service, by providing them with valuable experience with increasing levels of responsibility and empowerment, and by providing all new hires who perform well with the opportunity to advance in the company, Enterprise has developed a highly motivated workforce.[49]

In addition to motivating high performance and excellent customer service through training and promotional opportunities, Enterprise also uses financial incentives to motivate employees. Essentially each branch is considered a profit center, and the managers overseeing the branch and in charge of all aspects of its functioning have the autonomy and responsibility for the branch's profitability almost as if the branch was their own small business or franchise.[50] All branch employees at the rank of assistant manager and higher earn incentive compensation whereby their monthly pay depends on the profitability of their branch. Managers at higher levels, such as area managers, have their monthly pay linked to the profitability of the region they oversee. Thus, managers at all levels know that their pay is linked to the profitability of the parts of Enterprise for which they are responsible. And they have the autonomy to make decisions ranging from buying and selling cars to opening new branches.[51]

All in all Enterprise's employees are highly motivated because of their high levels of expectancy, instrumentality, and valence. Contributing to high levels of expectancy is the training all new hires receive in all aspects of the business, including the provision of excellent customer service and the ongoing valuable experiences employees receive with increasing levels of responsibility and empowerment. Linking two highly valent outcomes, pay and promotions, to performance leads to high instrumentality. And highly motivated employees at Enterprise do provide excellent service to their customers.

Need Theories

LO 9-3 Explain how goals and needs motivate people and what kinds of goals are especially likely to result in high performance.

need A requirement or necessity for survival and well-being.

A **need** is a requirement or necessity for survival and well-being. The basic premise of **need theories** is that people are motivated to obtain outcomes at work that will satisfy their needs. Need theory complements expectancy theory by exploring in depth which outcomes motivate people to perform at a high level. Need theories suggest that to motivate a person to contribute valuable inputs to a job and perform at a high level, a manager must determine what needs the person is trying to satisfy at work and ensure that the person receives outcomes that help to satisfy those needs when the person performs at a high level and helps the organization achieve its goals.

There are several need theories. Here we discuss Abraham Maslow's hierarchy of needs, Frederick Herzberg's motivator-hygiene theory, and David McClelland's needs for achievement, affiliation, and power. These theories describe needs that people try to satisfy at work. In doing so, they give managers insights about what outcomes motivate members of an organization to perform at a high level and contribute inputs to help the organization achieve its goals.

need theories Theories of motivation that focus on what needs people are trying to satisfy at work and what outcomes will satisfy those needs.

Maslow's hierarchy of needs An arrangement of five basic needs that, according to Maslow, motivate behavior. Maslow proposed that the lowest level of unmet needs is the prime motivator and that only one level of needs is motivational at a time.

Maslow's Hierarchy of Needs

Psychologist Abraham Maslow proposed that all people seek to satisfy five basic kinds of needs: physiological needs, safety needs, belongingness needs, esteem needs, and self-actualization needs (see Table 9.1).[52] He suggested that these needs constitute a **hierarchy of needs**, with the most basic or compelling needs—physiological and safety needs—at the bottom. Maslow argued that these lowest-level needs must be met before a person strives to satisfy needs higher up in the hierarchy, such as self-esteem needs. Once a need is satisfied, Maslow proposed, it ceases to operate as a source of motivation. The lowest level of *unmet* needs in the hierarchy is the prime motivator of behavior; if and when this level is satisfied, needs at the next highest level in the hierarchy motivate behavior.

Although this theory identifies needs that are likely to be important sources of motivation for many people, research does not support Maslow's contention that there is a need hierarchy or his notion that only one level of needs is motivational at a time.[53] Nevertheless, a key conclusion can be drawn from Maslow's theory: People try to satisfy different needs at work. To have a motivated workforce, managers must determine which needs employees are trying to satisfy in organizations and then make sure that individuals receive outcomes that satisfy

Table 9.1

Maslow's Hierarchy of Needs

	Needs	Description	Examples of How Managers Can Help People Satisfy These Needs at Work
Highest-level needs	**Self-actualization needs**	The needs to realize one's full potential as a human being.	By giving people the opportunity to use their skills and abilities to the fullest extent possible.
	Esteem needs	The needs to feel good about oneself and one's capabilities, to be respected by others, and to receive recognition and appreciation.	By granting promotions and recognizing accomplishments.
	Belongingness needs	Needs for social interaction, friendship, affection, and love.	By promoting good interpersonal relations and organizing social functions such as company picnics and holiday parties.
	Safety needs	Needs for security, stability, and a safe environment.	By providing job security, adequate medical benefits, and safe working conditions.
Lowest-level needs (most basic or compelling)	**Physiological needs**	Basic needs for things such as food, water, and shelter that must be met in order for a person to survive.	By providing a level of pay that enables a person to buy food and clothing and have adequate housing.

The lowest level of unsatisfied needs motivates behavior; once this level of needs is satisfied, a person tries to satisfy the needs at the next level.

No one pumps their fist over their laptop unless it's for a good reason! Clearly, whipping an obnoxious spreadsheet into shape and sending out a calmly worded press release makes for satisfied self-actualization needs. © Jim Esposito/Getty Images RF

their needs when they perform at a high level and contribute to organizational effectiveness. By doing this, managers align the interests of individual members with the interests of the organization as a whole. By doing what is good for the organization (that is, performing at a high level), employees receive outcomes that satisfy their needs.

In our increasingly global economy, managers must realize that citizens of different countries might differ in the needs they seek to satisfy through work.[54] Some research suggests, for example, that people in Greece and Japan are especially motivated by safety needs and that people in Sweden, Norway, and Denmark are motivated by belongingness needs.[55] In less developed countries with low standards of living, physiological and safety needs are likely to be the prime motivators of behavior. As countries become wealthier and have higher standards of living, needs related to personal growth and accomplishment (such as esteem and self-actualization) become important motivators of behavior.

Herzberg's Motivator-Hygiene Theory

Herzberg's motivator-hygiene theory A need theory that distinguishes between motivator needs (related to the nature of the work itself) and hygiene needs (related to the physical and psychological context in which the work is performed) and proposes that motivator needs must be met for motivation and job satisfaction to be high.

Adopting an approach different from Maslow's, Frederick Herzberg focused on two factors: (1) outcomes that can lead to high levels of motivation and job satisfaction and (2) outcomes that can prevent people from being dissatisfied. According to **Herzberg's motivator-hygiene theory**, people have two sets of needs or requirements: motivator needs and hygiene needs.[56] *Motivator needs* are related to the nature of the work itself and how challenging it is. Outcomes such as interesting work, autonomy, responsibility, being able to grow and develop on the job, and a sense of accomplishment and achievement help to satisfy motivator needs. To have a highly motivated and satisfied workforce, Herzberg suggested, managers should take steps to ensure that employees' motivator needs are being met.

Hygiene needs are related to the physical and psychological context in which the work is performed. Hygiene needs are satisfied by outcomes such as pleasant and comfortable working conditions, pay, job security, good relationships with coworkers, and effective supervision. According to Herzberg, when hygiene needs are not met, workers are dissatisfied, and when hygiene needs are met, workers are not dissatisfied. Satisfying hygiene needs, however, does not result in high levels of motivation or even high levels of job satisfaction. For motivation and job satisfaction to be high, motivator needs must be met.

Many research studies have tested Herzberg's propositions, and, by and large, the theory fails to receive support.[57] Nevertheless, Herzberg's formulations have contributed to our understanding of motivation in at least two ways. First, Herzberg helped to focus researchers' and managers' attention on the important distinction between intrinsic motivation (related to motivator needs) and extrinsic motivation (related to hygiene needs), covered earlier in the chapter. Second, his theory prompted researchers and managers to study how jobs could be designed or redesigned so they are intrinsically motivating.

McClelland's Needs for Achievement, Affiliation, and Power

need for achievement The extent to which an individual has a strong desire to perform challenging tasks well and to meet personal standards for excellence.

Psychologist David McClelland extensively researched the needs for achievement, affiliation, and power.[58] The **need for achievement** is the extent to which an individual has a strong desire to perform challenging tasks well and to meet personal standards for excellence. People with a high need for achievement often set clear goals for themselves and like to receive performance feedback. The **need for affiliation** is the extent to which an individual is concerned about establishing and maintaining good interpersonal relations, being liked, and having the people around him or her get along with each other. The **need for power** is the extent to which an individual desires to control or influence others.[59]

need for affiliation The extent to which an individual is concerned about establishing and maintaining good interpersonal relations, being liked, and having the people around him or her get along with each other.

Although each of these needs is present in each of us to some degree, their importance in the workplace depends on the position one occupies. For example, research suggests that high needs for achievement and for power are assets for first-line and middle managers and that a high need for power is especially important for upper managers.[60] One study found that U.S. presidents with a relatively high need for power tended to be especially effective during their terms of office.[61] A high need for affiliation may not always be desirable in managers and other leaders because it might lead them to try too hard to be liked by others (including subordinates) rather than doing all they can to ensure that performance is as high as it can and should be. Although most research on these needs has been done in the United States, some studies suggest that the findings may be applicable to people in other countries as well, such as India and New Zealand.[62]

need for power The extent to which an individual desires to control or influence others.

Other Needs

Clearly, more needs motivate workers than the needs described by these three theories. For example, more and more workers are feeling the need for work–life balance and time to take care of their loved ones while simultaneously being highly motivated at work. Recall how the SAS Institute recognizes and seeks to satisfy these needs from "A Manager's Challenge." Interestingly enough, recent research suggests that being exposed to nature (even just being able to see some trees from an office window) has many salutary effects, and a lack of such exposure can impair well-being and performance.[63] Thus having some time during the day when one can at least see nature may be another important need. Managers of successful companies often strive to ensure that as many of their valued employees' needs as possible are satisfied in the workplace.

 LO 9-2 Describe from the perspectives of expectancy theory and equity theory what managers should do to have a highly motivated workforce.

Equity Theory

equity theory A theory of motivation that focuses on people's perceptions of the fairness of their work outcomes relative to their work inputs.

Equity theory is a theory of motivation that concentrates on people's perceptions of the fairness of their work *outcomes* relative to, or in proportion to, their work *inputs*. Equity theory complements expectancy and need theories by focusing on how people perceive the relationship between the outcomes they receive from their jobs and organizations and the inputs they contribute. Equity theory was formulated in the 1960s by J. Stacy Adams, who stressed that what is important in determining motivation is the *relative* rather than the *absolute* levels of outcomes a person receives and inputs a person contributes. Specifically, motivation is influenced by the comparison of one's own outcome–input ratio with the outcome–input ratio of a referent.[64] The *referent* could be another person or a group of people who are perceived to be similar to oneself; the referent also could be oneself in a previous job or one's expectations about what outcome–input ratios should be. In a comparison of one's own outcome–input

Table 9.2

Equity Theory

Condition	Person		Referent	Example
Equity	$\dfrac{\text{Outcomes}}{\text{Inputs}}$	$=$	$\dfrac{\text{Outcomes}}{\text{Inputs}}$	An engineer perceives that he contributes more inputs (time and effort) and receives proportionally more outcomes (a higher salary and choice job assignments) than his referent.
Underpayment inequity	$\dfrac{\text{Outcomes}}{\text{Inputs}}$	$<$ (less than)	$\dfrac{\text{Outcomes}}{\text{Inputs}}$	An engineer perceives that he contributes more inputs but receives the same outcomes as his referent.
Overpayment inequity	$\dfrac{\text{Outcomes}}{\text{Inputs}}$	$>$ (greater than)	$\dfrac{\text{Outcomes}}{\text{Inputs}}$	An engineer perceives that he contributes the same inputs but receives more outcomes than his referent.

ratio to a referent's ratio, one's *perceptions* of outcomes and inputs (not any objective indicator of them) are key.

Equity

equity The justice, impartiality, and fairness to which all organizational members are entitled.

Equity exists when a person perceives his or her own outcome–input ratio to be equal to a referent's outcome–input ratio. Under conditions of equity (see Table 9.2), if a referent receives more outcomes than you receive, the referent contributes proportionally more inputs to the organization, so his or her outcome–input ratio still equals your ratio. Maria Sanchez and Claudia King, for example, both work in a shoe store in a large mall. Sanchez is paid more per hour than King but also contributes more inputs, including being responsible for some of the store's bookkeeping, closing the store, and periodically depositing cash in the bank. When King compares her outcome–input ratio to Sanchez's (her referent's), she perceives the ratios to be equitable because Sanchez's higher level of pay (an outcome) is proportional to her higher level of inputs (bookkeeping, closing the store, and going to the bank).

Similarly, under conditions of equity, if you receive more outcomes than a referent, your inputs are perceived to be proportionally higher. Continuing with our example, when Sanchez compares her outcome–input ratio to King's (her referent's) ratio, she perceives them to be equitable because her higher level of pay is proportional to her higher level of inputs.

When equity exists, people are motivated to continue contributing their current levels of inputs to their organizations to receive their current levels of outcomes. If people wish to increase their outcomes under conditions of equity, they are motivated to increase their inputs.

Inequity

inequity Lack of fairness.

underpayment inequity The inequity that exists when a person perceives that his or her own outcome–input ratio is less than the ratio of a referent.

Inequity, or lack of fairness, exists when a person's outcome–input ratio is not perceived to be equal to a referent's. Inequity creates pressure or tension inside people and motivates them to restore equity by bringing the two ratios back into balance.

There are two types of inequity: underpayment inequity and overpayment inequity (see Table 9.2). **Underpayment inequity** exists when a person's own outcome–input ratio is perceived to be *less* than that of a referent. In comparing yourself to

overpayment inequity The inequity that exists when a person perceives that his or her own outcome–input ratio is greater than the ratio of a referent.

a referent, you think you are *not* receiving the outcomes you should be, given your inputs. **Overpayment inequity** exists when a person perceives that his or her own outcome–input ratio is *greater* than that of a referent. In comparing yourself to a referent, you think you are receiving *more* outcomes than you should be, given your inputs.

Ways to Restore Equity

According to equity theory, both underpayment inequity and overpayment inequity create tension that motivates most people to restore equity by bringing the ratios back into balance.[65] When people experience *underpayment* inequity, they may be motivated to lower their inputs by reducing their working hours, putting forth less effort on the job, or being absent; or they may be motivated to increase their outcomes by asking for a raise or a promotion. Susan Richie, a financial analyst at a large corporation, noticed that she was working longer hours and getting more work accomplished than a coworker who had the same position, yet they both received the exact same pay and other outcomes. To restore equity, Richie decided to stop coming in early and staying late. Alternatively, she could have tried to restore equity by trying to increase her outcomes, perhaps by asking her boss for a raise.

When people experience underpayment inequity and other means of equity restoration fail, they can change their perceptions of their own or the referent's inputs or outcomes. For example, they may realize that their referent is really working on more difficult projects than they are or that they really take more time off from work than their referent does. Alternatively, if people who feel they are underpaid have other employment options, they may leave the organization. As an example, John Steinberg, an assistant principal in a high school, experienced underpayment inequity when he realized that all the other assistant principals of high schools in his school district had received promotions to the position of principal even though they had been in their jobs for a shorter time than he had. Steinberg's performance had always been appraised as being high, so after his repeated requests for a promotion went unheeded, he found a job as a principal in a different school district.

When people experience *overpayment* inequity, they may try to restore equity by changing their perceptions of their own or their referent's inputs or outcomes. Equity can be restored when people realize they are contributing more inputs than they originally thought. Equity also can be restored by perceiving the referent's inputs to be lower or the referent's outcomes to be higher than one originally thought. When equity is restored in this way, actual inputs and outcomes are unchanged, and the person being overpaid takes no real action. What is changed is how people think about or view their or the referent's inputs and outcomes. For instance, Mary McMann experienced overpayment inequity when she realized she was being paid $2 an hour more than a coworker who had the same job as she did in a health food store and who contributed the same amount of inputs. McMann restored equity by changing her perceptions of her inputs. She realized she worked harder than her coworker and solved more problems that came up in the store.

Experiencing either overpayment or underpayment inequity, you might decide that your referent is not appropriate because, for example, the referent is too different from yourself. Choosing a more appropriate referent may bring the ratios back into balance. Angela Martinez, a middle manager in the engineering department of a chemical company, experienced overpayment inequity when she realized she was being paid quite a bit more than her friend, who was a middle manager in the marketing department of the same company. After thinking about the discrepancy for a while, Martinez decided that engineering and marketing were so different that she should not be comparing her job to her friend's job even though they were both middle managers. Martinez restored equity by changing her referent; she picked a middle manager in the engineering department as a new referent.

Motivation is highest when as many people as possible in an organization perceive that they are being equitably treated—their outcomes and inputs are in balance. Top contributors and performers are motivated to continue contributing a high level of inputs because they are receiving the outcomes they deserve. Mediocre contributors and performers realize that if they want to increase their outcomes, they have to increase their inputs. Managers of effective organizations, like the SAS Institute, realize the importance of equity for motivation and performance and continually strive to ensure that employees believe that they are being equitably treated.

The dot-com boom, its subsequent bust, and two recessions, along with increased global competition, have resulted in some workers putting in longer and longer working hours (increasing their inputs) without any increase in their outcomes. For those whose referents are not experiencing a similar change, perceptions of inequity are likely. According to Jill Andresky Fraser, author of *White Collar Sweatshop*, more than 25 million U.S. workers work more than 49 hours per week in the office, almost 11 million work more than 60 hours per week in the office, and many also put in additional work hours at home. Moreover, advances in information technology, such as email and cell phones, have resulted in work intruding on home time, vacation time, and even special occasions.[66]

Equity and Justice in Organizations

distributive justice A person's perception of the fairness of the distribution of outcomes in an organization.

procedural justice A person's perception of the fairness of the procedures that are used to determine how to distribute outcomes in an organization.

interpersonal justice A person's perception of the fairness of the interpersonal treatment he or she receives from whoever distributes outcomes to him or her.

informational justice A person's perception of the extent to which his or her manager provides explanations for decisions and the procedures used to arrive at them.

Equity theory, given its focus on the fair distribution of outcomes in organizations to foster high motivation, is often labeled a theory of distributive justice.[67] **Distributive justice** refers to an employee's perception of the fairness of the distribution of outcomes (such as promotions, pay, job assignments, and working conditions) in an organization.[68] Employees are more likely to be highly motivated when they perceive distributive justice to be high rather than low.

Three other forms of justice are important for high motivation. **Procedural justice** refers to an employee's perception of the fairness of the procedures used to determine how to distribute outcomes in an organization.[69] For example, if important outcomes such as pay and promotions are distributed based on performance appraisals (see Chapter 12) and an employee perceives that the procedure that is used (i.e., the performance appraisal system) is unfair, then procedural justice is low and motivation is likely to suffer. More generally, motivation is higher when procedural justice is high rather than low.[70] **Interpersonal justice** refers to an employee's perception of the fairness of the interpersonal treatment he or she receives from whoever distributes outcomes to him or her (typically his or her manager).[71] Interpersonal justice is high when managers treat subordinates with dignity and respect and are polite and courteous.[72] Motivation is higher when interpersonal justice is high rather than low. **Informational justice** refers to an employee's perception of the extent to which his or her manager provides explanations for decisions and the procedures used to arrive at them.[73] For example, if a manager explains how performance is appraised and how decisions about the distribution of outcomes are made, informational justice (and motivation) are more likely to be high than if the manager does not do this.[74] All in all, it is most advantageous for distributive, procedural, interpersonal, and informational justice all to be high.

Goal-Setting Theory

LO9-3 Explain how goals and needs motivate people and what kinds of goals are especially likely to result in high performance.

goal-setting theory A theory that focuses on identifying the types of goals that are most effective in producing high levels of motivation and performance and explaining why goals have these effects.

Goal-setting theory focuses on motivating workers to contribute their inputs to their jobs and organizations; in this way, it is similar to expectancy theory and equity theory. But goal-setting theory takes this focus a step further by considering as well how managers can ensure that organizational members focus their inputs in the direction of high performance and the achievement of organizational goals.

Ed Locke and Gary Latham, the leading researchers for goal-setting theory, suggested that the goals organizational members strive to attain are prime determinants of their motivation and subsequent performance. A *goal* is what a person is trying to accomplish through his or her efforts and behaviors.[75] Just as you may have a goal to get a good grade in this course, so do members of an organization have goals they strive to meet. For example, salespeople at Neiman Marcus strive to meet sales goals, while top managers pursue market share and profitability goals.

Goal-setting theory suggests that to stimulate high motivation and performance, goals must be *specific* and *difficult*.[76] Specific goals are often quantitative—a salesperson's goal to sell $500 worth of merchandise per day, a scientist's goal to finish a project in one year, a CEO's goal to reduce debt by 40% and increase revenues by 20%, and a restaurant manager's goal to serve 150 customers per evening. In contrast to specific goals, vague goals such as "doing your best" or "selling as much as you can" do not have much motivational impact.

Difficult goals are hard but not impossible to attain. In contrast to difficult goals, easy goals are those that practically everyone can attain, and moderate goals are goals that about one-half of the people can attain. Both easy and moderate goals have less motivational power than difficult goals.

Regardless of whether specific, difficult goals are set by managers, workers, or teams of managers and workers, they lead to high levels of motivation and performance. When managers set goals for their subordinates, their subordinates must accept the goals or agree to work toward them; also, they should be committed to them or really want to attain them. Some managers find that having subordinates participate in the actual setting of goals boosts their acceptance of and commitment to the goals. In addition, organizational members need to receive *feedback* about how they are doing; feedback can often be provided by the performance appraisal and feedback component of an organization's human resource management system (see Chapter 12).

Specific, difficult goals affect motivation in two ways. First, they motivate people to contribute more inputs to their jobs. Specific, difficult goals cause people to put forth high levels of effort, for example. Just as you would study harder if you were trying to get an A in a course instead of a C, so too will a salesperson work harder to reach a $500 sales goal instead of a $200 sales goal. Specific, difficult goals also cause people to be more persistent than easy, moderate, or vague goals when they run into difficulties. Salespeople who are told to sell as much as possible might stop trying on a slow day, whereas having a specific, difficult goal to reach causes them to keep trying.

Specific, difficult goals can encourage people to exert high levels of effort and to focus efforts in the right direction. © Stockbyte/Punchstock Images RF

A second way in which specific, difficult goals affect motivation is by helping people focus their inputs in the right direction. These goals let people know what they should be focusing their attention on, whether it is increasing the quality of customer service or sales or lowering new product development times. The fact that the goals are specific and difficult also frequently causes people to develop *action plans* for reaching them.[77] Action plans can include the strategies to attain the goals and timetables or schedules for the completion of different activities crucial to goal attainment. Like the goals themselves, action plans also help ensure that efforts are focused in the right direction and that people do not get sidetracked along the way.

Although specific, difficult goals have been found to increase motivation and performance in a wide variety of jobs and organizations both in the United States and abroad, recent research suggests that they may detract from performance under certain conditions. When people are performing complicated and challenging tasks that require them to focus on a considerable amount of learning, specific, difficult goals may actually impair performance.[78] Striving to reach such goals may direct some of a person's attention away from learning about the task and toward trying to figure out how to achieve the goal. Once a person has learned the task and it no longer seems complicated or difficult, then the assignment of specific, difficult goals is likely to have its usual effects. Additionally, for work that is very creative and uncertain, specific, difficult goals may be detrimental.

LO 9-4 Identify the motivation lessons that managers can learn from operant conditioning theory and social learning theory.

Learning Theories

The basic premise of **learning theories** as applied to organizations is that managers can increase employee motivation and performance by how they link the outcomes that employees receive to the performance of desired behaviors and the attainment of goals. Thus, learning theory focuses on the linkage between performance and outcomes in the motivation equation (see Figure 9.1).

learning theories Theories that focus on increasing employee motivation and performance by linking the outcomes that employees receive to the performance of desired behaviors and the attainment of goals.

Learning can be defined as a relatively permanent change in a person's knowledge or behavior that results from practice or experience.[79] Learning takes place in organizations when people learn to perform certain behaviors to receive certain outcomes. For example, a person learns to perform at a higher level than in the past or to come to work earlier because he or she is motivated to obtain the outcomes that result from these behaviors, such as a pay raise or praise from a supervisor. Of the different learning theories, operant conditioning theory and social learning theory provide the most guidance to managers in their efforts to have a highly motivated workforce.

learning A relatively permanent change in knowledge or behavior that results from practice or experience.

Operant Conditioning Theory

According to **operant conditioning theory**, developed by psychologist B. F. Skinner, people learn to perform behaviors that lead to desired consequences and learn not to perform behaviors that lead to undesired consequences.[80] Translated into motivation terms, Skinner's theory means that people will be motivated to perform at a high level and attain their work goals to the extent that high performance and goal attainment allow them to obtain outcomes they desire. Similarly, people avoid performing behaviors that lead to outcomes they do not desire. By linking the performance of *specific behaviors* to the attainment of *specific outcomes*, managers can motivate organizational members to perform in ways that help an organization achieve its goals.

operant conditioning theory The theory that people learn to perform behaviors that lead to desired consequences and learn not to perform behaviors that lead to undesired consequences.

Operant conditioning theory provides four tools that managers can use to motivate high performance and prevent workers from engaging in absenteeism and other behaviors that detract from organizational effectiveness. These tools are positive reinforcement, negative reinforcement, extinction, and punishment.[81]

positive reinforcement
Giving people outcomes they desire when they perform organizationally functional behaviors.

POSITIVE REINFORCEMENT Positive reinforcement gives people outcomes they desire when they perform organizationally functional behaviors. These desired outcomes, called *positive reinforcers,* include any outcomes that a person desires, such as pay, praise, or a promotion. Organizationally functional behaviors are behaviors that contribute to organizational effectiveness; they can include producing high-quality goods and services, providing high-quality customer service, and meeting deadlines. By linking positive reinforcers to the performance of functional behaviors, managers motivate people to perform the desired behaviors.

negative reinforcement
Eliminating or removing undesired outcomes when people perform organizationally functional behaviors.

NEGATIVE REINFORCEMENT Negative reinforcement also can encourage members of an organization to perform desired or organizationally functional behaviors. Managers using negative reinforcement actually eliminate or remove undesired outcomes once the functional behavior is performed. These undesired outcomes, called *negative reinforcers,* can range from a manager's constant nagging or criticism to unpleasant assignments or the ever-present threat of losing one's job. When negative reinforcement is used, people are motivated to perform behaviors because they want to stop receiving or avoid undesired outcomes. Managers who try to encourage salespeople to sell more by threatening them with being fired are using negative reinforcement. In this case, the negative reinforcer is the threat of job loss, which is removed once the functional behavior is performed.

Whenever possible, managers should try to use positive reinforcement. Negative reinforcement can create a very unpleasant work environment and even a negative culture in an organization. No one likes to be nagged, threatened, or exposed to other kinds of negative outcomes. The use of negative reinforcement sometimes causes subordinates to resent managers and try to get back at them.

IDENTIFYING THE RIGHT BEHAVIORS FOR REINFORCEMENT Even managers who use positive reinforcement (and refrain from using negative reinforcement) can get into trouble if they are not careful to identify the right behaviors to reinforce—behaviors that are truly functional for the organization. Doing this is not always as straightforward as it might seem. First, it is crucial for managers to choose behaviors over which subordinates have control; in other words, subordinates must have the freedom and opportunity to perform the behaviors that are being reinforced. Second, it is crucial that these behaviors contribute to organizational effectiveness.

EXTINCTION Sometimes, members of an organization are motivated to perform behaviors that detract from organizational effectiveness. According to operant conditioning theory, all behavior is controlled or determined by its consequences; one way for managers to curtail the performance of dysfunctional behaviors is to eliminate whatever is reinforcing the behaviors. This process is called **extinction**.

extinction Curtailing the performance of dysfunctional behaviors by eliminating whatever is reinforcing them.

Suppose a manager has a subordinate who frequently stops by his office to chat—sometimes about work-related matters but at other times about various topics ranging from politics to last night's football game. The manager and the subordinate share certain interests and views, so these conversations can get quite involved, and both seem to enjoy them. The manager, however, realizes that these frequent and sometimes lengthy conversations are causing him to stay at work later in the evenings to make up for the time he loses during the day. The manager also realizes that he is reinforcing his subordinate's behavior by acting interested in the topics the subordinate brings up and responding at length to them. To extinguish this behavior, the manager stops acting interested in these non-work-related conversations and keeps his responses polite and friendly but brief. No longer being reinforced with a pleasurable conversation, the subordinate eventually ceases to be motivated to interrupt the manager during working hours to discuss non-work-related issues.

punishment
Administering an undesired or negative consequence when dysfunctional behavior occurs.

PUNISHMENT Sometimes, managers cannot rely on extinction to eliminate dysfunctional behaviors because they do not have control over whatever is reinforcing the behavior or because they cannot afford the time needed for extinction to work. When employees are performing dangerous behaviors or behaviors that are illegal or unethical, the behavior needs to be eliminated immediately. Sexual harassment, for example, is an organizationally dysfunctional behavior that cannot be tolerated. In such cases, managers often rely on **punishment**, which is administering an undesired or negative consequence to subordinates when they perform the dysfunctional behavior. Punishments used by organizations range from verbal reprimands to pay cuts, temporary suspensions, demotions, and firings. Punishment, however, can have some unintended side effects—resentment, loss of self-respect, a desire for retaliation—and should be used only when necessary.

To avoid the unintended side effects of punishment, managers should keep in mind these guidelines:

- Downplay the emotional element involved in punishment. Make it clear that you are punishing a person's performance of a dysfunctional behavior, not the person himself or herself.

- Try to punish dysfunctional behaviors as soon as possible after they occur and make sure that the negative consequence is a source of punishment for the individuals involved. Be certain that organizational members know exactly why they are being punished.

- Try to avoid punishing someone in front of others because this can hurt a person's self-respect and lower esteem in the eyes of coworkers as well as make coworkers feel uncomfortable.[82] Even so, making organizational members aware that an individual who has committed a serious infraction has been punished can sometimes be effective in preventing future infractions and teaching all members of the organization that certain behaviors are unacceptable. For example, when organizational members are informed that a manager who has sexually harassed subordinates has been punished, they learn or are reminded of the fact that sexual harassment is not tolerated in the organization.

Managers and students alike often confuse negative reinforcement and punishment. To avoid such confusion, keep in mind the two major differences between them. First, negative reinforcement is used to promote the performance of functional behaviors in organizations; punishment is used to stop the performance of dysfunctional behaviors. Second, negative reinforcement entails the *removal* of a negative consequence when functional behaviors are performed; punishment entails the *administration* of negative consequences when dysfunctional behaviors are performed.

social learning theory A theory that takes into account how learning and motivation are influenced by people's thoughts and beliefs and their observations of other people's behavior.

Social Learning Theory

Social learning theory proposes that motivation results not only from direct experience of rewards and punishments but also from a person's thoughts and beliefs. Social learning theory extends operant conditioning's contribution to managers' understanding of motivation by explaining (1) how people can be motivated by observing other people performing a behavior and being reinforced for doing so (*vicarious learning*), (2) how people can be motivated to control their behavior themselves (*self-reinforcement*), and (3) how people's beliefs about their ability to successfully perform a behavior affect motivation (*self-efficacy*).[83] We look briefly at each of these motivators.

vicarious learning Learning that occurs when the learner becomes motivated to perform a behavior by watching another person performing it and being reinforced for doing so; also called *observational learning.*

VICARIOUS LEARNING Vicarious learning, often called *observational learning,* occurs when a person (the learner) becomes motivated to perform a behavior by watching another person (the model) performing the behavior and being positively reinforced for doing so. Vicarious learning is a powerful source of motivation on many jobs in which people learn to perform functional behaviors by watching others. Salespeople learn how to help customers, medical school students learn how to treat patients, law clerks learn how to practice law, and nonmanagers learn how to be managers, in part, by observing experienced members of an organization perform these behaviors properly and be reinforced for them. In general, people are more likely to be motivated to imitate the behavior of models who are highly competent, are (to some extent) experts in the behavior, have high status, receive attractive reinforcers, and are friendly or approachable.[84]

To promote vicarious learning, managers should strive to have the learner meet the following conditions:

- The learner observes the model performing the behavior.
- The learner accurately perceives the model's behavior.
- The learner remembers the behavior.
- The learner has the skills and abilities needed to perform the behavior.
- The learner sees or knows that the model is positively reinforced for the behavior.[85]

self-reinforcer Any desired or attractive outcome or reward that a person gives to himself or herself for good performance.

SELF-REINFORCEMENT Although managers are often the providers of reinforcement in organizations, sometimes people motivate themselves through self-reinforcement. People can control their own behavior by setting goals for themselves and then reinforcing themselves when they achieve the goals.[86] **Self-reinforcers** are any desired or attractive outcomes or rewards that people can give to themselves for good performance, such as a feeling of accomplishment, going to a movie, having dinner out, buying a new CD, or taking time out for a golf game. When members of an organization control their own behavior through self-reinforcement, managers do not need to spend as much time as they ordinarily would trying to motivate and control behavior through the administration of consequences because subordinates are controlling and motivating themselves. In fact, this self-control is often referred to as the *self-management of behavior.*

When employees are highly skilled and are responsible for creating new goods and services, managers typically rely on self-control and self-management of

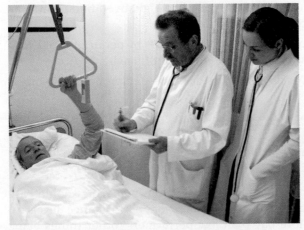

How do you treat that? When medical students enter residency, they learn vicariously by shadowing a full physician on his or her rounds. © vario images GmbH & Co.KG/Alamy

behavior, as is the case at Google. Employees at Google are given the flexibility and autonomy to experiment, take risks, and sometimes fail as they work on new projects. They are encouraged to learn from their failures and apply what they learn to subsequent projects.[87] Google's engineers are given one day a week to work on their own projects that they are highly involved with, and new products such as Google News often emerge from these projects.[88]

SELF-EFFICACY

self-efficacy A person's belief about his or her ability to perform a behavior successfully.

Self-efficacy is a person's belief about his or her ability to perform a behavior successfully.[89] Even with all the most attractive consequences or reinforcers hinging on high performance, people are not going to be motivated if they do not think they can actually perform at a high level. Similarly, when people control their own behavior, they are likely to set for themselves difficult goals that will lead to outstanding accomplishments only if they think they can reach those goals. Thus, self-efficacy influences motivation both when managers provide reinforcement and when workers themselves provide it.[90] The greater the self-efficacy, the greater is the motivation and performance. Verbal persuasion such as a manager expressing confidence in an employee's ability to reach a challenging goal, as well as a person's own past performance and accomplishments and the accomplishments of other people, plays a role in determining a person's self-efficacy.

Pay and Motivation

In Chapter 12, we discuss how managers establish a pay level and structure for an organization as a whole. Here we focus on how, once a pay level and structure are in place, managers can use pay to motivate employees to perform at a high level and attain their work goals. Pay is used to motivate entry-level workers, first-line and middle managers, and even top managers such as CEOs. Pay can motivate people to perform behaviors that help an organization achieve its goals, and it can motivate people to join and remain with an organization.

LO 9-5 Explain why and how managers can use pay as a major motivation tool.

Each of the theories described in this chapter alludes to the importance of pay and suggests that pay should be based on performance:

- *Expectancy theory:* Instrumentality, the association between performance and outcomes such as pay, must be high for motivation to be high. In addition, pay is an outcome that has high valence for many people.

- *Need theories:* People should be able to satisfy their needs by performing at a high level; pay can be used to satisfy several different kinds of needs.

- *Equity theory:* Outcomes such as pay should be distributed in proportion to inputs (including performance levels).

- *Goal-setting theory:* Outcomes such as pay should be linked to the attainment of goals.

- *Learning theories:* The distribution of outcomes, such as pay, should be contingent on the performance of organizationally functional behaviors.

merit pay plan A compensation plan that bases pay on performance.

As these theories suggest, to promote high motivation, managers should base the distribution of pay to organizational members on performance levels so that high performers receive more pay than low performers (other things being equal).[91] A compensation plan basing pay on performance is often called a **merit pay plan**.

In tough economic times, when organizations lay off employees and pay levels and benefits of those who are at least able to keep their jobs may be cut while their responsibilities are often increased,[92] managers are often limited in the extent to which they can use merit pay, if at all.[93] Nonetheless, in such times, managers can still try to recognize top performers. Jenny Miller, manager of 170 engineers in the commercial systems engineering department at Rockwell Collins, an aerospace electronics company in Cedar Rapids, Iowa, experienced firsthand the challenge of not being able to recognize top performers with merit pay during tough economic times.[94] Rockwell Collins laid off 8% of its workforce, and the workloads for the engineers Miller managed increased by about 15%. The engineers were working longer hours without receiving any additional pay; there was a salary freeze, so they knew raises were not in store. With a deadline approaching for flight deck software for a customer, she needed some engineers to work over the Thanksgiving holiday and so sent out an email request for volunteers. Approximately 20 employees volunteered. In recognition of their contributions, Miller gave them each a $100 gift card.[95]

A $100 gift card might not seem like much for an employee who is already working long hours to come to work over the Thanksgiving holiday for no additional pay or time off. Yet Steve Nieuwsma, division vice president at Rockwell Collins, indicates that the gift cards at least signaled that managers recognized and appreciated employees' efforts and sought to thank them for it. Not being able to give his employees raises at that time, Nieuwsma also gave gift cards to recognize contributions and top performers in amounts varying between $25 and $500.[96]

Once managers have decided to use a merit pay plan, they face two important choices: whether to base pay on individual, group, or organizational performance and whether to use salary increases or bonuses.

Basing Merit Pay on Individual, Group, or Organizational Performance

Managers can base merit pay on individual, group, or organizational performance. When individual performance (such as the dollar value of merchandise a salesperson sells, the number of loudspeakers a factory worker assembles, and a lawyer's billable hours) can be accurately determined, individual motivation is likely to be highest when pay is based on individual performance.[97] When members of an organization work closely together and individual performance cannot be accurately determined (as in a team of computer programmers developing a single software package), pay cannot be based on individual performance, and a group- or organization-based plan must be used. When the attainment of organizational goals hinges on members' working closely together and cooperating with each other (as in a small construction company that builds custom homes), group- or organization-based plans may be more appropriate than individual-based plans.[98]

It is possible to combine elements of an individual-based plan with a group- or organization-based plan to motivate each individual to perform highly and, at the same time, motivate all individuals to work well together, cooperate with one another, and help one another as needed. Lincoln Electric, a very successful company and a leading manufacturer of welding machines, uses a combination individual- and organization-based plan.[99] Pay is based on individual performance. In addition, each year the size of a bonus fund depends on organizational performance. Money from the bonus fund is distributed to people on the basis of their contributions to the organization, attendance, levels of cooperation, and other indications of performance. Employees of Lincoln Electric are motivated to cooperate and help one another because when the firm as a whole performs well, everybody benefits by having a larger bonus fund. Employees also are motivated to contribute their inputs to the organization because their contributions determine their share of the bonus fund.

Salary Increase or Bonus?

Managers can distribute merit pay to people in the form of a salary increase or a bonus on top of regular salaries. Although the dollar amount of a salary increase or bonus might be identical, bonuses tend to have more motivational impact for at least three reasons. First, salary levels are typically based on performance levels, cost-of-living increases, and so forth, from the day people start working in an organization, which means the absolute level of the salary is based largely on factors unrelated to *current* performance. A 5 percent merit increase in salary, for example, may seem relatively small in comparison to one's total salary. Second, a current salary increase may be affected by other factors in addition to performance, such as cost-of-living increases or across-the-board market adjustments. Third, because organizations rarely reduce salaries, salary levels tend to vary less than performance levels do. Related to this point is the fact that bonuses give managers more flexibility in distributing outcomes. If an organization is doing well, bonuses can be relatively high to reward employees for their contributions. However, unlike salary increases, bonus levels can be reduced when an organization's performance lags. All in all, bonus plans have more motivational impact than salary increases because the amount of the bonus can be directly and exclusively based on performance.[100]

Consistent with the lessons from motivation theories, bonuses can be linked directly to performance and vary from year to year and employee to employee, as at Gradient Corporation, a Cambridge, Massachusetts, environmental consulting firm.[101] Another organization that successfully uses bonuses is Nucor Corporation. Steelworkers at Nucor tend to be much more productive than steelworkers in other companies—probably because they can receive bonuses tied to performance and quality that can range from 130% to 150% of their regular base pay.[102] During the economic downturn in 2007–2009, Nucor struggled as did many other companies, and bonus pay for steelworkers dropped considerably. However, managers at Nucor avoided having to lay off employees by finding ways to cut costs and having employees work on maintenance activities and safety manuals, along with taking on tasks that used to be performed by independent contractors, such as producing specialty parts and mowing the grass.[103]

employee stock option A financial instrument that entitles the bearer to buy shares of an organization's stock at a certain price during a certain period or under certain conditions.

In addition to receiving pay raises and bonuses, high-level managers and executives are sometimes granted employee stock options. **Employee stock options** are financial instruments that entitle the bearer to buy shares of an organization's stock at a certain price during a certain period or under certain conditions.[104] For example, in addition to salaries, stock options are sometimes used to attract high-level managers. The exercise price is the stock price at which the bearer can buy the stock, and the vesting conditions specify when the bearer can actually buy the stock at the exercise price. The option's exercise price is generally set equal to the market price of the stock on the date it is granted, and the vesting conditions might specify that the manager has to have worked at the organization for 12 months or perhaps met some performance target (perhaps an increase in profits) before being able to exercise the option. In high-technology firms and start-ups, options are sometimes used in a similar fashion for employees at various levels in the organization.[105]

From a motivation standpoint, stock options are used not so much to reward past individual performance but, rather, to motivate employees to work in the future for the good of the company as a whole. This is true because stock options issued at current stock prices have value in the future only if an organization does well and its stock price appreciates; thus giving employees stock options should encourage them to help the organization improve its performance over time.[106] At high-technology start-ups and dot-coms, stock options have often motivated potential employees to leave promising jobs in larger companies and work for the start-ups. In the late 1990s and early 2000s, many dot-commers were devastated to learn not only that their stock options were worthless, because their companies went out of business or were doing poorly, but also that they were unemployed. Unfortunately stock options have also led to unethical behavior; for example, sometimes individuals seek to artificially inflate the value of a company's stock to increase the value of stock options.

Examples of Merit Pay Plans

Managers can choose among several merit pay plans, depending on the work that employees perform and other considerations. Using *piece-rate pay,* an individual-based merit plan, managers base employees' pay on the number of units each employee produces, whether televisions, computer components, or welded auto parts. Managers at Lincoln Electric use piece-rate pay to determine individual pay levels. Advances in information technology have dramatically simplified the administration of piece-rate pay in a variety of industries.

Using *commission pay,* another individual-based merit pay plan, managers base pay on a percentage of sales. Managers at the successful real estate company Re/Max International Inc. use commission pay for their agents, who are paid a percentage of their sales. Some department stores, such as Neiman Marcus, use commission pay for their salespeople.

Examples of organizational-based merit pay plans include the Scanlon plan and profit sharing. The *Scanlon plan* (developed by Joseph Scanlon, a union leader in a steel and tin plant in the 1920s) focuses on reducing expenses or cutting costs; members of an organization are motivated to propose and implement cost-cutting strategies because a percentage of the cost savings achieved during a specified time is distributed to the employees.[107] Under *profit sharing,* employees receive a share of an organization's profits. Regardless of the specific kind of plan that is used, managers should always strive to link pay to the performance of behaviors that help an organization achieve its goals.

Japanese managers in large corporations have long shunned merit pay plans in favor of plans that reward seniority. However, more and more Japanese companies are adopting merit-based pay due to its motivational benefits; among such companies are SiteDesign,[108] Tokio Marine and Fire Insurance, and Hissho Iwai, a trading organization.[109]

Summary and Review

THE NATURE OF MOTIVATION Motivation encompasses the psychological forces within a person that determine the direction of the person's behavior in an organization, the person's level of effort, and the person's level of persistence in the face of obstacles. Managers strive to motivate people to contribute their inputs to an organization, to focus these inputs in the direction of high performance, and to ensure that people receive the outcomes they desire when they perform at a high level. **LO 9-1**

EXPECTANCY THEORY According to expectancy theory, managers can promote high levels of motivation in their organizations by taking steps to ensure that expectancy is high (people think that if they try, they can perform at a high level), instrumentality is high (people think that if they perform at a high level, they will receive certain outcomes), and valence is high (people desire these outcomes). **LO 9-2**

NEED THEORIES Need theories suggest that to motivate their workforces, managers should determine what needs people are trying to satisfy in organizations and then ensure that people receive outcomes that satisfy these needs when they perform at a high level and contribute to organizational effectiveness. **LO 9-3**

EQUITY THEORY According to equity theory, managers can promote high levels of motivation by ensuring that people perceive that there is equity in the organization or that outcomes are distributed in proportion to inputs. Equity exists when a person perceives that his or her own outcome–input ratio equals the outcome–input ratio of a referent. Inequity motivates people to try to restore equity. Equity theory is a theory of distributive justice. It is most advantageous for distributive, procedural, interpersonal, and informational justice all to be high. **LO 9-2**

GOAL-SETTING THEORY Goal-setting theory suggests that managers can promote high motivation and performance by ensuring that people are striving to achieve specific, difficult goals. It is important for people to accept the goals, be committed to them, and receive feedback about how they are doing. **LO 9-3**

LEARNING THEORIES Operant conditioning theory suggests that managers can motivate people to perform highly by using positive reinforcement or negative reinforcement (positive reinforcement being the preferred strategy). Managers can motivate people to avoid performing dysfunctional behaviors by using extinction or punishment. Social learning theory suggests that people can also be motivated by observing how others perform behaviors and receive rewards, by engaging in self-reinforcement, and by having high levels of self-efficacy. **LO 9-4**

PAY AND MOTIVATION Each of the motivation theories discussed in this chapter alludes to the importance of pay and suggests that pay should be based on performance. Merit pay plans can be individual-, group-, or organization-based and can entail the use of salary increases or bonuses. **LO 9-5**

Management *in Action*

TOPICS FOR DISCUSSION AND ACTION

Discussion

1. Discuss why two people with similar abilities may have very different expectancies for performing at a high level. [LO 9-2]

2. Describe why some people have low instrumentalities even when their managers distribute outcomes based on performance. [LO 9-2]

3. Analyze how professors try to promote equity to motivate students. [LO 9-2]

4. Describe three techniques or procedures that managers can use to determine whether a goal is difficult. [LO 9-3]

5. Discuss why managers should always try to use positive reinforcement instead of negative reinforcement. [LO 9-4]

Action

6. Interview three people who have the same kind of job (such as salesperson, waiter/waitress, or teacher), and determine what kinds of needs each is trying to satisfy at work. [LO 9-3]

7. Interview a manager in an organization in your community to determine the extent to which the manager takes advantage of vicarious learning to promote high motivation among subordinates. [LO 9-3]

BUILDING MANAGEMENT SKILLS

Diagnosing Motivation [LO 9-1, 9-2, 9-3, 9-4]

Think about the ideal job that you would like to obtain after graduation. Describe this job, the kind of manager you would like to report to, and the kind of organization you would be working in. Then answer the following questions:

1. What would be your levels of expectancy and instrumentality on this job? Which outcomes would have high valence for you on this job? What steps would your manager take to influence your levels of expectancy, instrumentality, and valence?

2. Whom would you choose as a referent on this job? What steps would your manager take to make you feel that you were being equitably treated? What would you do if, after a year on the job, you experienced underpayment inequity?

3. What goals would you strive to achieve on this job? Why? What role would your manager play in determining your goals?

4. What needs would you strive to satisfy on this job? Why? What role would your manager play in helping you satisfy these needs?

5. What behaviors would your manager positively reinforce on this job? Why? What positive reinforcers would your manager use?

6. Would there be any vicarious learning on this job? Why or why not?

7. To what extent would you be motivated by self-control on this job? Why?

8. What would be your level of self-efficacy on this job? Why would your self-efficacy be at this level? Should your manager take steps to boost your self-efficacy? If not, why not? If so, what would these steps be?

Sometimes pay is so contingent upon performance that it creates stress for employees. Imagine a salesperson who knows that if sales targets are not met, she or he will not be able to make a house mortgage payment or pay the rent.

Questions

1. Either individually or in a group, think about the ethical implications of closely linking pay to performance.

2. Under what conditions might contingent pay be most stressful, and what steps can managers take to try to help their subordinates perform effectively and not experience excessive amounts of stress?

👥 SMALL GROUP BREAKOUT EXERCISE [LO 9-1, 9-2, 9-3, 9-4, 9-5]
Increasing Motivation

Form groups of three or four people, and appoint one member as the spokesperson who will communicate your findings to the class when called on by the instructor. Then discuss the following scenario:

You and your partners own a chain of 15 dry-cleaning stores in a medium-size town. All of you are concerned about a problem in customer service that has surfaced recently. When any one of you spends the day, or even part of the day, in a particular store, clerks seem to provide excellent customer service, spotters make sure that all stains are removed from garments, and pressers do a good job of pressing difficult items such as silk blouses. Yet during those same visits customers complain to you about such things as stains not being removed and items being poorly pressed in some of their previous orders; indeed, several customers have brought garments in to be redone. Customers also sometimes comment on having waited too long for service on previous visits. You and your partners are meeting today to address this problem.

1. Discuss the extent to which you believe that you have a motivation problem in your stores.

2. Given what you have learned in this chapter, design a plan to increase the motivation of clerks to provide prompt service to customers even when they are not being watched by a partner.

3. Design a plan to increase the motivation of spotters to remove as many stains as possible even when they are not being watched by a partner.

4. Design a plan to increase the motivation of pressers to do a top-notch job on all clothes they press, no matter how difficult.

💡 BE THE MANAGER [LO 9-1, 09-2, 9-3, 9-4, 9-5]

You supervise a team of marketing analysts who work on different snack products in a large food products company. The marketing analysts have recently received undergraduate degrees in business or liberal arts and have been on the job between one and three years. Their responsibilities include analyzing the market for their respective products, including competitors; tracking current marketing initiatives; and planning future marketing campaigns. They also need to prepare quarterly sales and expense reports for their products and estimated budgets for the next three quarters; to prepare these reports, they need to obtain data from financial and accounting analysts assigned to their products.

When they first started on the job, you took each marketing analyst through the reporting cycle, explaining what needs to be done and how to accomplish it and emphasizing the need for timely reports. Although preparing the reports can be tedious, you think the task is pretty straightforward and easily accomplished if the analysts plan ahead and allocate sufficient time for it.

When reporting time approaches, you remind the analysts through email messages and emphasize the need for accurate and timely reports in team meetings.

You believe this element of the analysts' jobs couldn't be more straightforward. However, at the end of each quarter, the majority of the analysts submit their reports a day or two late, and, worse yet, your own supervisor (to whom the reports are eventually given) has indicated that information is often missing and sometimes the reports contain errors. Once you started getting flak from your supervisor about this problem, you decided you had better fix things quickly. You met with the marketing analysts, explained the problem, told them to submit the reports to you a day or two early so you could look them over, and more generally emphasized that they really needed to get their act together. Unfortunately, things have not improved much and you are spending more and more of your own time doing the reports. What are you going to do?

THE WALL STREET JOURNAL CASE IN THE NEWS [LO 9-1, 9-2, 9-3, 9-4]

Bright Future in Sales? Millennials Are Hesitant

Some companies are having a hard time selling people on a career in sales.

As the U.S. economy gains momentum, companies selling technology and other services to corporate customers are struggling to fill potentially lucrative sales jobs.

Sales reps who peddle technical and scientific products earned a median annual wage of $74,970 in 2012, more than twice the median for all workers, according to the Labor Department. A competitive hiring market for science and tech workers is part of the reason, but employers also say young workers are uninterested in sales—a field they perceive as risky and defined by competition.

Technical sales and sales-management positions play a critical role for U.S. businesses, but they are among the hardest to fill, according to a 2014 report from Harvard Business School's U.S. Competitiveness Project. Employers spent an average of 41 days trying to fill technical sales jobs, compared with an average of 33 days for all jobs for the 12-month period ending in September 2014, according to Burning Glass, a labor-market analysis firm that worked with Harvard Business School on the report.

Paycor Inc., which sells cloud-based software for human-resources and payroll management, said it would have forecast $2 million more in 2015 revenue if it had hit its 2014 hiring goals for new sales reps in 2014. The time spent bringing new reps up to speed means the company doesn't see the full benefit of their productivity until 12 to 18 months into their tenure.

"That wakes you up," said Bob Coughlin, chief executive Paycor, which has about $130 million in annual revenue. In the past few years, the Cincinnati-based company has added seven dedicated sales recruiters, hired a director of learning to boost training and support for the sales team, and modernized its sales software.

Paycor's sales staff has since grown to 240 people from 125 three or four years ago, Mr. Coughlin said. Even so, he said persuading young people to enter the field remains a challenge.

The youngest generation of workers, having lived through the financial crisis and recession, is more risk-averse, say sales executives, adding that young prospects are reluctant to enter a hard-charging work environment where success often boils down to a number.

In addition, "there's a huge stereotype that sales isn't really a career—that either anyone can do it or you're born to it," said Suzanne Fogel, chair of the marketing department at DePaul University's Driehaus College of Business. Parents share some of those misconceptions, and often dissuade their children from pursuing sales careers, she added. (They change their tune once their children start getting job offers, Ms. Fogel said.)

Selling technical and scientific products in a business-to-business environment differs from the stereotypes in "Death of a Salesman" or David Mamet's Pulitzer Prize-winning "Glengarry Glen Ross," in which a real estate salesman famously declares that "first prize is a Cadillac El Dorado. . . Second prize is a set of steak knives. Third prize is you're fired."

As companies become savvier about the products they buy, wheeler-dealers are out, and problem-solvers are in. Sales organizations today are more commonly structured as teams, with lower-ranking members identifying prospects and developing early interest, someone else running, through the specs or demos on highly technical products, and field reps negotiating and closing deals, employers say.

Curiously, few employers have realized they need a different sales pitch to attract a younger cohort, said Nick Toman, a managing director who oversees the sales practice at business advisory firm CEB, pointing to sales-job postings that use phrases like "competitive environment," and "tremendous variable compensation packages."

"Those things become huge turnoffs to a lot of potential applicants," he added. "People today want to be part of a team, they want stable pay."

They also want a clear career path, along with support to work their way up. Business-software giant **Oracle** Corp., which has a famously competitive sales culture, began recruiting reps on college campuses a few years ago. Students frequently show a "lack of awareness" about sales roles, said Sharon Prosser, group vice president of Oracle Direct, but then interest is piqued when they learn that the field is well-suited to "continuous learners and that there's training and career progression built into the program."

To find job candidates, **Acquia** Inc., a cloud-based open-source software company in Burlington, Mass., last fall sponsored a sales contest at Bryant University in Rhode Island.

At Bryant, 140 students presented mock sales pitches, and about five recruiters were on hand, said Tim Bertrand, an Acquia sales executive.

"Every candidate that looked really good, we were going up and saying 'We'd like to interview you now for a June job.'" The company intends to hire seven to nine contest participants.

The contest winner, Tom Keenan, a 21-year-old senior at Bryant, says his mother urged him to enter. Days later, he interviewed for a job as a business development rep at Acquia; he starts in June.

"If you asked me six months ago if I'd become a salesman, I would've said absolutely not," he said, noting that he had assumed that "salespeople only sold products to take the consumers' money—and that bothered me."

Companies are rethinking their compensation strategies to appeal to young people who want more of a financial safety net, favoring a higher base pay with a lower proportion of the riskier commission pay. In the pay mix for sales jobs, the base portion has increased 11.7% from 2010 through 2014 while the variable amount has remained steady, according to **Xactly** Corp., a firm whose software tracks sales compensation and helps companies formulate incentive strategies.

"People don't want super high-risk jobs," said Christopher Cabrera, Xactly's CEO. Companies typically offer a 50-50 split of base and variable pay for entry-level jobs, he said.

As much as companies are eager to fill sales-rep jobs, the heavy investment to get new hires up to speed has made employers careful about bringing on new blood, says Alan Benson, a professor at the University of Minnesota Carlson School of Management who studies sales organizations.

"To get someone through the door means you also have to train them, and that can be extremely expensive. There's usually a ramp-up of six months before they're productive, so you can't really take a risk."

To hedge their bets, more employers are requiring new hires arrive with a college degree. Some 56% of job postings for wholesale and technical sales reps ads now require a bachelor's degree, but only 43% of current sales workers have that degree, according to an analysis by **Burning Glass Technologies.**

Universities are getting the message. DePaul has revised its sales courses to reflect the new reality of sales jobs, emphasizing critical thinking and collaboration, said Ms. Fogel. A biannual DePaul survey found that 101 U.S. colleges offered sales curricula in 2011, up from 44 in 2007.

"These are great jobs that are going begging," said Ms. Fogel. "It's a field that may finally be getting a little respect."

Questions

1. Why are some millennials unmotivated by the prospect of a job and career in sales?

2. From an expectancy theory perspective, what steps can managers take to make sales positions attractive and motivating for millennials?

3. From a need theory perspective, what steps can managers take to make sales positions attractive and motivating for millennials?

4. From a learning theory perspective, what steps can managers take to make sales positions attractive and motivating for millennials?

Source: "Bright Future in Sales? Millenials Are Hesitant" by L. Weber. *The Wall Street Journal,* February 4, 2015, pp. B1, B7.

Endnotes

1. J. Schlosser and J. Sung, "The 100 Best Companies to Work For," *Fortune,* January 8, 2001, 148–68; R. Levering, M. Moskowitz, and S. Adams,"The 100 Best Companies to Work For," *Fortune* 149, no. 1 (2004), 56–78; "*Fortune* 100 Best Companies to Work For 2006, CNNMoney.com, June 5, 2006 (www.money .cnn.com/magazines/fortune/ bestcompanies/snapshots/1181 .html; "Awards," *SAS,* www.sas.com/ awards/index.html, April 1, 2008; R. Levering and M. Moskowitz, "100 Best Companies to Work For: The Rankings," *Fortune,* February 4, 2008, 75–94; "100 Best Companies to Work For 2012 : Full List," *Fortune,* http://money.cnn.com/magazines/ fortune/best-companies/2012/ full_list/, April 30, 2012.; "Inside Story at SAS Institute Inc.—Great Rated!" http://us.greatrated. com/sas, April 29, 2014.; "Best Companies to Work For 2014," *Fortune,* http://money.cnn.com/ magazines/fortune/best-companies/, April 29, 2014.; "SAS Ranks No. 2 on 2014 Fortune List of Best Companies to Work For in the US," January 16, 2014, www.sas.com/ en_us/news/press-releases/2014/ january/great-workplace-US- Fortune-2014.html, April 29, 2014.; "SAF—100 Best Companies to Work For 2014," *Fortune,* http:// money.cnn.com/magazines/ fortune/best-companies/2014/ snapshots/2.html?iid=BC14_sp_list, April 29, 2014; M. Moskowitz and R. Levering, "The 100 Best Companies to Work For." *Fortune,* March 5, 2015, 140–54.

2. E.P. Dalesio, "Quiet Giant Ready to Raise Its Profits," *Houston Chronicle,* May 6, 2001, 4D; Levering et al., "The 100 Best Companies to Work For"; J. Goodnight, "Welcome to SAS," www.sas.com/corporate/ index.html, August 26, 2003; "SAS Press Center: SAS Corporate Statistics," www.sas.com/bin/ pfp.pl?=fi, April 18, 2006; "SAS Continues Annual Revenue Growth Streak," www.sas.com/ news/prelease/031003/newsl.html,

August 28, 2003; R. Levering and M. Moskowitz, "100 Best Companies to Work For: The Rankings"; L. Buchanan, "No Doubt about It," *Inc.,* September 2011, 104–110; 'SAS Institute—Best Companies to Work For 2012," *Fortune,* http://money .cnn.com/magazines/fortune/best- companies/2012/snapshots/3.html, April 30, 2012., "SAS Surpasses $3 Billion in 2013 Revenue, Growing 5.2% Over 2012 Results," January 23, 2014, www.sas.com/en_us/news/ press-release/2014/january/2013- financials.html, April 29, 2014.; "SAS Overview and Annual Report – 2013," www.sas.com/content/ dam/SAS/en_us/doc/other1/2013- annual-report.pdf, April 29, 2014; "About SAS," www.sas.com/ en_us/company-information.html, February 25, 2015.

3. "About SAS," SAS, www.sas.com/ corporate/overview/index.html, March 1, 2010; "Corporate Statistics," SAS, Updated February 2010, www. sas.com/presscenter/bgndr_statistics. html, March 1, 2010.; "About SAS," SAS, www.sas.com/en_us/company- information.html, April 29, 2014.; M. Crowley, "How SAS Became the World's Best Place to Work," www. fastcompany.com/3004953/how- sas-became-worlds-best-place-work, April 29, 2014.

4. J. Pfeffer, "SAS Institute: A Different Approach to Incentives and People Management Practices in the Software Industry," (January 1998), *Harvard Business School* Case HR-6.

5. "Saluting the Global Awards Recipients of Arthur Andersen's Best Practices Awards 2000," www. fortune.com, September 6, 2000; N. Stein, "Winning the War to Keep Top Talent," www.fortune.com, September 6, 2000.

6. J. Pfeffer, "SAS Institute: A Different Approach to Incentives and People Management Practices in the Software Industry," January 1998, *Harvard Business School* Case HR-6; D.A. Kaplan, "The Best Company to Work For," *Fortune,* February 8, 2010, 57–64.

7. Kaplan, "The Best Company to Work For"; "SAS Ranks No. 2 on 2014 Fortune List of Best Companies to Work For in the US," January 16, 2014, www.sas.com/en_us/news/ press-releases/2014/january/great- workplace-US-Fortune-2014.html, April 29, 2014.

8. Kaplan, "The Best Company to Work For"; S. Lahr, "At a Software Powerhouse, the Good Life Is Under Siege," *The New York Times,* November 22, 2009, BU1, BU6.

9. Ibid.; "SAF—100 Best Companies to Work For 2014," *Fortune,* http:// money.cnn.com/magazines/fortune/ best-companies/2014/snapshots/2 .html?iid=BC14_sp_list, April 29, 2014.

10. Ibid.

11. Kaplan, "The Best Company to Work For."

12. Ibid.

13. "Saluting the Global Awards Recipients of Arthur Andersen's Best Practices Awards 2000," www. fortune.com, September 6, 2000; N. Stein, "Winning the War to Keep Top Talent," www.fortune.com, September 6, 2000.

14. Kaplan, "The Best Company to Work For"; Lahr, "At a Software Powerhouse, the Good Life Is Under Siege"; J. Pfeffer, "SAS Institute: A Different Approach to Incentives and People Management Practices in the Software Industry," January 1998, *Harvard Business School* Case HR-6.

15. Kaplan, "The Best Company to Work For"; Lahr, "At a Software Powerhouse, the Good Life Is Under Siege."

16. Kaplan, "The Best Company to Work For."

17. R. Kanfer, "Motivation Theory and Industrial and Organizational Psychology," in M.D. Dunnette and L.M. Hough, eds., *Handbook of Industrial and Organizational Psychology,* 2nd ed., vol. 1 (Palo Alto, CA: Consulting Psychologists Press, 1990), 75–170.

18. G.P. Latham and M.H. Budworth, "The Study of Work Motivation in

the 20th Century," in L.L. Koppes, ed., *Historical Perspectives in Industrial and Organizational Psychology* (Hillsdale, NJ: Laurence Erlbaum, 2006).

19. N. Nicholson, "How to Motivate Your Problem People," *Harvard Business Review,* January 2003, 57–65.

20. A.M. Grant, "Does Intrinsic Motivation Fuel the Prosocial Fire? Motivational Synergy in Predicting Persistence, Performance, and Productivity," *Journal of Applied Psychology* 93, no. 1 (2008), 48–58.

21. Grant, "Does Intrinsic Motivation Fuel the Prosocial Fire?"; C.D. Batson, "Prosocial Motivation: Is It Ever Truly Altruistic?" in L. Berkowitz, ed., *Advances in Experimental Social Psychology,* vol. 20 (New York: Academic Press, 1987), 65–122.

22. Ibid.

23. J.P. Campbell and R.D. Pritchard, "Motivation Theory in Industrial and Organizational Psychology," in M.D. Dunnette, ed., *Handbook of Industrial and Organizational Psychology* (Chicago: Rand McNally, 1976), 63–130; T.R. Mitchell, "Expectancy Value Models in Organizational Psychology," in N.T. Feather, ed., *Expectations and Actions: Expectancy Value Models in Psychology* (Hillsdale, NJ: Erlbaum, 1982), 293–312; V.H. Vroom, *Work and Motivation* (New York: Wiley, 1964).

24. N. Shope Griffin, "Personalize Your Management Development," *Harvard Business Review* 8, no. 10 (2003), 113–119.

25. T.A. Stewart, "Just Think: No Permission Needed," *Fortune,* January 8, 2001(www.fortune.com, June 26, 2001).

26. M. Copeland, "Best Buy's Selling Machine," *Business 2.0,* July 2004, 91–102; L. Heller, "Best Buy Still Turning on the Fun," *DSN Retailing Today* 43, no. 13 (July 5, 2004), 3; S. Pounds, "Big-Box Retailers Cash In on South Florida Demand for Home Computer Repair," *Knight Ridder Tribune Business News,* July 5, 2004 (gateway.proquest.com); J. Bloom, "Best Buy Reaps the Rewards of Risking Marketing Failure," *Advertising Age* 75, no. 25 (June 21, 2004), 16; L. Heller, "Discount Turns Up the Volume: PC Comeback, iPod Popularity Add Edge," *DSN Retailing Today* 43, no. 13 (July 5, 2004), 45; www.bestbuy.com, June 8, 2006.

27. T.J. Maurer, E.M. Weiss, and F.G. Barbeite, "A Model of Involvement in Work-Related Learning and Development Activity: The Effects of Individual, Situational, Motivational, and Age Variables," *Journal of Applied Psychology* 88, no. 4 (2003), 707–24.

28. "Learn about Us"; The Container Store, "Welcome from Kip Tindell, Chairman & CEO," http://standfor.containerstore.com, March 3, 2010.; "The Container Store—Corporate Governance—Management," http://investor.containerstore.com/corporate-governance/management/default.aspx, May 2, 2014; "Management," http://investor.containerstore.com/corporate-governance/management/default.aspx, February 25, 2105.

29. M. Duff, "Top-Shelf Employees Keep Container Store on Track," www.looksmart.com, www.findarticles.com, March 8, 2004; M.K. Ammenheuser, "The Container Store Helps People Think inside the Box," www.icsc.org, May 2004; "The Container Store: Store Location," www.containerstore.com/find/index/jhtml, June 5, 2006; "Store Locations," *The Container Store,* www.containerstore.com/find/index.jhtml, April 1, 2008; "The Container Store—What We Stand For—Our Story," http:/standfor.containerstore.com/our-story/, March 3, 2010; "CEO Maxine Clark, of Build-a-Bear, Traded in Her Kid-Filled Existence for a Day in the Orderly Aisles of the Container Store, Doing the 'Closet Dance,'" *Fortune,* February 8, 2010, 68–72; "Store Locator," *The Container Store,* www.containerstore.com/locations/index.htm, May 3, 2012.; "The Container Store Group, Inc. Announces Fourth Quarter and Full Fiscal 2013 Financial Results," April 28, 2014, http://investor.containerstore.com/press-releases/press-release-details/2014/The-Container-Store-Group-Inc-Announces-Fourth-Quarter-and-Full-Fiscal-2013-Financial-Results/default.aspx, May 2, 2014.

30. "Learn about Us," www.containerstore.com, June 26, 2001.

31. Ibid.

32. J. Schlosser and J. Sung, "The 100 Best Companies to Work For," *Fortune,* January 8, 2001, 148–168; "Fortune 100 Best Companies to Work For 2006," cnn.com, June 5, 2006 (http://money.cnn.com/magazines/fortune/bestcompanies/snapshots/359.html); "Learn about Us"; "A Career at The Container Store," *The Container Store,* www.containerstore.com/careers/index.html, May 3, 2012.; "The Container Store Organizes Stakeholders to Talk Conscious Capitalism in New Purpose-Focused Marketing Campaign," January 16, 2014, http://investor.containerstore.com/press-releases/press-release-details/2014/The-Container-Store-Organizes-Stakeholders-to-Talk-Conscious-Capitalism-in-New-Purpose-Focused-Marketing-Campaign/default.aspx, May 2, 2014.

33. "The Container Store," www.careerbuilder.com, July 13, 2004; "Tom Takes Re-imagineto PBS," Case Studies, www.tompeters.com, March 15, 2004; "2004 Best Companies to Work For," www.fortune.com, July 12, 2004; *Fortune* 100 Best Companies to Work For 2006"; Levering and Moskowitz, "100 Best Companies to Work For: The Rankings"; Moskowitz, Levering, and Tkacyzk, "The List"; "100 Best Companies to Work for 2012," *Fortune,* http://money.cnn.com/magazines/fortune/best-companies/2012/snapshots/22.html, May 3, 2012.; "The Container Store—100 Best Companies to Work For 2014," *Fortune,* http://money.cnn.com/magazines/fortune/best-companies/2014/snapshots/28.html, May 2, 2014; Moskowitz and Levering, "The 100 Best Companies to Work For."

34. "The Container Store—What We Stand For."

35. D. Roth, "My Job at The Container Store," *Fortune,* January 10, 2000 (www.fortune.com, June 26, 2001); "*Fortune* 2004: 100 Best Companies to Work For," www.containerstore.com/careers/FortunePR_2004.jhtml?message=/repository/messages/fortuneCareer.jhtml, January 12, 2004; Levering,

Moskowitz, and Adams, "The 100 Best Companies to Work For"; www.containerstore.com/careers/FortunePR_2004.jhtml?message=/repository/messages/fortuneCareer.jhtml, January 12, 2004.; "The Container Store—100 Best Companies to Work For 2014," *Fortune,* http://money.cnn.com/magazines/fortune/best-companies/2014/snapshots/28.html, May 2, 2014.

36. "The Container Store—100 Best Companies to Work For 2014," *Fortune,* http://money.cnn.com/magazines/fortune/best-companies/2014/snapshots/28.html, May 2, 2014.

37. Roth, "My Job at The Container Store."

38. "Learn about Us," www.containerstore.com, June 26, 2001.

39. R. Yu, "Some Texas Firms Start Wellness Programs to Encourage Healthier Workers," *Knight Ridder Tribune Business News,* July 7, 2004 (gateway.proquest.com); Levering et al., "The 100 Best Companies to Work For."

40. Roth, "My Job at The Container Store"; "The Foundation Is Organization," *The Container Store,* June 5, 2006 (www.containerstore.com/careers/foundation.html).

41. C.J. Loomis, "The Big Surprise Is Enterprise," *Fortune,* July 14, 2006, http://cnnmoney.printthis.clickability.com/pt/cpt?action=cpt&title=Fortune%3A+The+big..., March 31, 2008; "About Enterprise," http://aboutus.enterprise.com, February 26, 2015.

42. "Overview," *Enterprise Rent-A-Car Careers—Overview,* www.erac.com/recruit/about_enterprise.asp?navID=overview, March 27, 2008; "Enterprise Rent-A-Car Looks to Hire Student-Athletes, Partners with Career Athletes," April 25, 2012, www.enterpriseholdings.com/press-room/enterprise-rent-a-car-looks-to-hire-student-..., April 30, 2012.; EnterpriseHoldings, World Headquarters, Highlights, www.enterpriseholdings.com/, April 29, 2014.; EnterpriseHoldings – Alamo, Enterprise, National, Enterprise CarShare, www.enterpriseholdings.com/, April 29, 2014.

43. A. Fisher, "Who's Hiring New College Grads Now," *CNNMoney*

.com, http://cnnmoney.printthis.clickability.com/pt/cpt?action=cpt&title=Who%27s+hiring+coll..., March 31, 2008; Francesca Di Meglio, "A Transcript for Soft Skills, Wisconsin Is Considering a Dual Transcript—One for Grades and One to Assess Critical Areas Such As Leadership and Communication," www.businessweek.com/print/bschools/content/feb2008/bs20080221_706663.htm, March 28, 2008; "Enterprise Rent-A-Car Career Site," www.erac.com/opportunities/default.aspx, May 1, 2012.

44. "Enterprise Ranked in Top 10 of Business Week's 'Customer Service Champs,'" February 22, 2007, *Enterprise Rent-A-Car Careers—* Enterprise in the News, www.erac.com/recruit/news_detail.asp?navID=frontpage&RID=211, March 27, 2008; L. Gerdes, "The Best Places to Launch a Career, *Business Week,* September 24, 2007, 49–60; P. Lehman, "A Clear Road to the Top," *Businessweek,* September 18, 2006, 72–82.

45. "Enterprise Ranked in Top 10"; L. Gerdes, "The Best Places to Launch a Career."

46. "It's Running a Business . . . Not Doing a Job," *Enterprise Rent-A-Car Careers—Opportunities,* www.erac.com/recruit/opportunities.asp, March 27, 2008.

47. Loomis, "The Big Surprise Is Enterprise"; Lehman, "A Clear Road to the Top."

48. Ibid.

49. Lehman, "A Clear Road to the Top."

50. Loomis, "The Big Surprise Is Enterprise."

51. Loomis, "The Big Surprise Is Enterprise"; Lehman, "A Clear Road to the Top."

52. A.H. Maslow, *Motivation and Personality* (New York: Harper & Row, 1954); Campbell and Pritchard, "Motivation Theory in Industrial and Organizational Psychology."

53. Kanfer, "Motivation Theory and Industrial and Organizational Psychology."

54. S. Ronen, "An Underlying Structure of Motivational Need Taxonomies: A Cross-Cultural Confirmation," in H.C. Triandis, M.D. Dunnette, and L.M. Hough, eds., *Handbook of Industrial and Organizational*

Psychology, vol. 4 (Palo Alto, CA: Consulting Psychologists Press, 1994), 241–69.

55. N.J. Adler, *International Dimensions of Organizational Behavior,* 2nd ed. (Boston: P.W.S. Kent, 1991); G. Hofstede, "Motivation, Leadership, and Organization: Do American Theories Apply Abroad?" *Organizational Dynamics,* Summer 1980, 42–63.

56. Kanfer, "Motivation Theory and Industrial and Organizational Psychology."

57. F. Herzberg, *Work and the Nature of Man* (Cleveland: World, 1966).

58. N. King, "Clarification and Evaluation of the Two-Factor Theory of Job Satisfaction," *Psychological Bulletin* 74 (1970), 18–31; E.A. Locke, "The Nature and Causes of Job Satisfaction," in Dunnette, *Handbook of Industrial and Organizational Psychology,* 1297–1349.

59. D.C. McClelland, *Human Motivation* (Glenview, IL: Scott, Foresman, 1985); D.C. McClelland, "How Motives, Skills, and Values Determine What People Do," *American Psychologist* 40 (1985), 812–25; D.C. McClelland, "Managing Motivation to Expand Human Freedom," *American Psychologist* 33 (1978), 201–10.

60. D.G. Winter, *The Power Motive* (New York: Free Press, 1973).

61. M.J. Stahl, "Achievement, Power, and Managerial Motivation: Selecting Managerial Talent with the Job Choice Exercise," *Personnel Psychology* 36 (1983), 775–89; D.C. McClelland and D.H. Burnham, "Power Is the Great Motivator," *Harvard Business Review* 54 (1976), 100–10.

62. R.J. House, W.D. Spangler, and J. Woycke, "Personality and Charisma in the U.S. Presidency: A Psychological Theory of Leader Effectiveness," *Administrative Science Quarterly* 36 (1991), 364–96.

63. G.H. Hines, "Achievement, Motivation, Occupations, and Labor Turnover in New Zealand," *Journal of Applied Psychology* 58 (1973), 313–17; P.S. Hundal, "A Study of Entrepreneurial Motivation: Comparison of Fast- and Slow-Progressing Small Scale Industrial Entrepreneurs in Punjab, India,"

Journal of Applied Psychology 55 (1971), 317–23.

64. R.A. Clay, "Green Is Good for You," *Monitor on Psychology,* April 2001, 40–42.

65. J.S. Adams, "Toward an Understanding of Inequity," *Journal of Abnormal and Social Psychology* 67 (1963), 422–36.

66. Ibid.; J. Greenberg, "Approaching Equity and Avoiding Inequity in Groups and Organizations," in J. Greenberg and R.L. Cohen, eds., *Equity and Justice in Social Behavior* (New York: Academic Press, 1982), 389–435; J. Greenberg, "Equity and Workplace Status: A Field Experiment," *Journal of Applied Psychology* 73 (1988), 606–13; R.T. Mowday, "Equity Theory Predictions of Behavior in Organizations," in R.M. Steers and L.W. Porter, eds., *Motivation and Work Behavior* (New York: McGraw-Hill, 1987), 89–110.

67. A. Goldwasser, "Inhuman Resources," Ecompany.com, March 2001, 154–55. L.J. Skitka and F.J. Crosby, "Trends in the Social Psychological Study of Justice," *Personality and Social Psychology Review* 7 (April 2003), 282–85.

68. J.A. Colquitt, J. Greenbery, and C.P. Zapata-Phelan, "What Is Organizational Justice? A Historical Overview," in J. Greenberg and J.A. Colquitt (eds.), *Handbook of Organizational Justice* (Mahwah, NJ: Erlbaum, 2005), 12–45; J.A. Colquitt, "On the Dimensionality of Organizational Justice: A Construct Validation of a Measure," *Journal of Applied Psychology* 86 (March 2001), 386–400.

69. R. Folger and M.A. Konovsky, "Effects of Procedural and Distributive Justice on Reactions to Pay Raise Decisions," *Academy of Management Journal* 32 (1989), 115–30; J. Greenberg, "Organizational Justice: Yesterday, Today, and Tomorrow," *Journal of Management* 16 (1990), 339–432; M.L. Ambrose and A. Arnaud, "Are Procedural Justice and Distributive Justice Conceptually Distinct?" in J. Greenberg and J.A. Colquitt (eds.), *Handbook of Organizational Justice* (Mahwah, NJ: Erlbaum, 2005), 60–78.

70. M.L. Ambrose and M. Schminke, "Organization Structure as a Moderator of the Relationship Between Procedural Justice, Interactional Justice, Perceived Organizational Support, and Supervisory Trust," *Journal of Applied Psychology* 88 (February 2003), 295–305.

71. J.A. Colquitt, "On the Dimensionality of Organizational Justice: A Construct Validation of a Measure," *Journal of Applied Psychology* 86 (March 2001), 386–400.

72. Greenberg, "Organizational Justice: Yesterday, Today, and Tomorrow"; E.A. Lind and T. Tyler, *The Social Psychology of Procedural Justice* (New York: Plenum, 1988).

73. R.J. Bies, "The Predicament of Injustice: The Management of Moral Outrage," in L.L. Cummings and B.M. Staw (eds.), *Research in Organizational Behavior,* vol. 9 (Greenwich, CT: JAI Press, 1987), 289–319; R.J. Bies and D.L. Shapiro, "Interactional Fairness Judgments: The Influence of Casual Accounts," *Social Justice Research* 1 (1987), 199–218; J. Greenberg, "Looking Fair vs. Being Fair: Managing Impression of Organizational Justice," in B.M. Staw and L.L. Cummings (eds.), *Research in Organizational Behavior,* vol. 12 (Greenwich, CT: JAI Press, 1990), 111–57; T.R. Tyler and R. J. Bies, "Beyond Formal Procedures: The Interpersonal Context of Procedural Justice," in J. Carroll (ed.), *Advances in Applied Social Psychology: Business Settings* (Hillsdale, NJ: Erlbaum, 1989), 77–98; Colquitt, "On the Dimensionality of Organizational Justice."

74. Colquitt, "On the Dimensionality of Organizational Justice"; J.A. Colquitt and J.C. Shaw, "How Should Organizational Justice Be Measured?" in J. Greenberg and J.A. Colquitt (eds.), *Handbook of Organizational Justice* (Mahwah, NJ: Erlbaum, 2005), 115–41.

75. E.A. Locke and G.P. Latham, *A Theory of Goal Setting and Task Performance* (Englewood Cliffs, NJ: Prentice-Hall, 1990).

76. Ibid.; J.J. Donovan and D.J. Radosevich, "The Moderating Role of Goal Commitment on the Goal Difficulty–Performance Relationship: A Meta-Analytic Review and Critical Analysis," *Journal of Applied Psychology* 83 (1998), 308–15; M.E. Tubbs, "Goal Setting: A Meta Analytic Examination of the Empirical Evidence," *Journal of Applied Psychology* 71 (1986), 474–83.

77. E.A. Locke, K.N. Shaw, L.M. Saari, and G.P. Latham, "Goal Setting and Task Performance: 1969–1980," *Psychological Bulletin* 90 (1981), 125–52.

78. P.C. Earley, T. Connolly, and G. Ekegren, "Goals, Strategy Development, and Task Performance: Some Limits on the Efficacy of Goal Setting," *Journal of Applied Psychology* 74 (1989), 24–33; R. Kanfer and P.L. Ackerman, "Motivation and Cognitive Abilities: An Integrative/Aptitude–Treatment Interaction Approach to Skill Acquisition," *Journal of Applied Psychology* 74 (1989), 657–90.

79. W.C. Hamner, "Reinforcement Theory and Contingency Management in Organizational Settings," in H. Tosi and W.C. Hamner, eds., *Organizational Behavior and Management: A Contingency Approach* (Chicago: St. Clair Press, 1974).

80. B.F. Skinner, *Contingencies of Reinforcement* (New York: Appleton-Century-Crofts, 1969).

81. H.W. Weiss, "Learning Theory and Industrial and Organizational Psychology," in Dunnette and Hough, *Handbook of Industrial and Organizational Psychology,* 171–221.

82. Hamner, "Reinforcement Theory and Contingency Management."

83. A. Bandura, *Principles of Behavior Modification* (New York: Holt, Rinehart and Winston, 1969); A. Bandura, *Social Learning Theory* (Englewood Cliffs, NJ: Prentice-Hall, 1977); T.R.V. Davis and F. Luthans, "A Social Learning Approach to Organizational Behavior," *Academy of Management Review* 5 (1980), 281–90.

84. A.P. Goldstein and M. Sorcher, *Changing Supervisor Behaviors* (New York: Pergamon Press, 1974); Luthans and Kreitner, *Organizational Behavior Modification and Beyond.*

85. Bandura, *Social Learning Theory;* Davis and Luthans, "A Social Learning Approach to Organizational Behavior"; Luthans and Kreitner, *Organizational Behavior Modification and Beyond.*

86. A. Bandura, "Self-Reinforcement: Theoretical and Methodological

Considerations," *Behaviorism* 4 (1976), 135–55.

87. K.H. Hammonds, "Growth Search," *Fast Company,* April, 2003, 74–81.

88. B. Elgin, "Managing Google's Idea Factory," *BusinessWeek,* October 3, 2005, 88–90.

89. A. Bandura, *Self-Efficacy: The Exercise of Control* (New York: W.H. Freeman, 1997); J.B. Vancouver, K.M. More, and R.J. Yoder, "Self-Efficacy and Resource Allocation: Support for a Nonmonotonic, Discontinuous Model," *Journal of Applied Psychology* 93, no. 1 (2008), 35–47.

90. A. Bandura, "Self-Efficacy Mechanism in Human Agency," *American Psychologist* 37 (1982), 122–27; M.E. Gist and T.R. Mitchell, "Self-Efficacy: A Theoretical Analysis of Its Determinants and Malleability," *Academy of Management Review* 17 (1992), 183–211.

91. E.E. Lawler III, *Pay and Organization Development* (Reading, MA: Addison-Wesley, 1981).

92. P. Dvorak and S. Thurm, "Slump Prods Firms to Seek New Compact with Workers," *The Wall Street Journal,* October 19, 2009, A1, A18.

93. D. Mattioli, "Rewards for Extra Work Come Cheap in Lean Times,"

The Wall Street Journal, January 4, 2010, B7.

94. Ibid.; www.rockwellcollins.com/, March 3, 2010.

95. Mattioli, "Rewards for Extra Work Come Cheap."

96. Ibid.

97. Lawler, *Pay and Organization Development.*

98. Ibid.

99 J.F. Lincoln, *Incentive Management* (Cleveland: Lincoln Electric Company, 1951); R. Zager, "Managing Guaranteed Employment," *Harvard Business Review* 56 (1978), 103–15.

100. Lawler, *Pay and Organization Development.*

101. M. Gendron, "Gradient Named 'Small Business of Year,' " *Boston Herald,* May 11, 1994, 35; "Gradient—Environmental Consulting," www.gradientcorp.com/index.php, March 3, 2010.

102. W. Zeller, R.D. Hof, R. Brandt, S. Baker, and D. Greising, "Go-Go Goliaths," *BusinessWeek,* February 13, 1995, 64–70.

103. N. Byrnes, "A Steely Resolve" *BusinessWeek,* April 6, 2009, 54.

104. "Stock Option," *Encarta World English Dictionary,* June 28, 2001 (www.

dictionary.msn.com); personal interview with Professor Bala Dharan, Jones Graduate School of Business, Rice University, June 28, 2001.

105. Personal interview with Professor Bala Dharan.

106. Ibid.

107. C.D. Fisher, L.F. Schoenfeldt, and J.B. Shaw, *Human Resource Management* (Boston: Houghton Mifflin, 1990); B.E. Graham-Moore and T.L. Ross, *Productivity Gainsharing* (Englewood Cliffs, NJ: Prentice-Hall, 1983); A.J. Geare, "Productivity from Scanlon Type Plans," *Academy of Management Review* 1 (1976), 99–108.

108. K. Belson, "Japan's Net Generation," *BusinessWeek,* March 19, 2001 (*BusinessWeek* Archives, June 27, 2001).

109. K. Belson, "Taking a Hint from the Upstarts," *BusinessWeek,* March 19, 2001 (*BusinessWeek* Archives, June 27, 2001); "Going for the Gold," *BusinessWeek,* March 19, 2001 (*BusinessWeek* Archives, June 27, 2001); "What the Government Can Do to Promote a Flexible Workforce," *BusinessWeek,* March 19, 2001 (*BusinessWeek* Archives, June 27, 2001).

10 Leaders and Leadership

Learning Objectives

After studying this chapter, you should be able to:

LO 10-1 Explain what leadership is, when leaders are effective and ineffective, and the sources of power that enable managers to be effective leaders.

LO 10-2 Identify the traits that show the strongest relationship to leadership, the behaviors leaders engage in, and the limitations of the trait and behavior models of leadership.

LO 10-3 Explain how contingency models of leadership enhance our understanding of effective leadership and management in organizations.

LO 10-4 Describe what transformational leadership is, and explain how managers can engage in it.

LO 10-5 Characterize the relationship between gender and leadership, and explain how emotional intelligence may contribute to leadership effectiveness.

© Joshua Hodge Photography/Getty Images RF

Jim Whitehurst, president and CEO of Red Hat, Inc., has a broad base of experience to draw upon in his leadership role at Red Hat. He has been COO of Delta Airlines, managing director and partner at Boston Consulting Group, and has degrees in computer science and economics as well as an MBA from Harvard. © Tony Kurdzuk/Star Ledger/Corbis

Whitehurst Leads Red Hat

How Can a Manager Foster Creativity In a Rapidly Changing Environment?

Jim Whitehurst, president and CEO of Red Hat, Inc., the world's largest open-source software company with more than $1 billion in revenues,[1] recognizes the vital role that creativity plays in organizations in rapidly changing arenas like open-source software. As he puts it, "In today's workforce, creativity is a critical skill. I strive every day at Red Hat to be a catalyst with our associates to fuel and spark their creativity and not stifle it by simply telling people what to do."[2]

Red Hat, headquartered in Raleigh, North Carolina, fully embraces the open source development model, which relies on global communities of contributors to develop, service, and improve software. Red Hat earns revenues through a variety of sources from its business and organizational customers. For example, software is provided via subscriptions (annual or multiyear) that include software support, new editions and updates of software, security upgrades, improvements and solutions to problems, advances in technology, functionality upgrades, and other services.[3] Red Hat also offers paid technical support to help clients most effectively utilize software as well as keep up-to-date with latest developments and

integrate software offerings with other applications. Consulting services are also offered by Red Hat. Thus, Red Hat provides its customers with the benefits of having a global community develop and improve open-source software while at the same time having expert software support and assistance to fully utilize the software to meet business needs while keeping up-to-date with the latest developments and improvements.[4]

Jim Whitehurst has been CEO and president of Red Hat for over seven years. Prior to joining Red Hat, he was the chief operating officer for Delta Airlines.[5] Before joining Delta, he was a managing director at the Boston Consulting Group. He has a bachelor's degree from Rice University in economics and computer science and an MBA from the Harvard Business School.[6] Thus, his prior education and work experience have given him a broad base of expertise to draw upon in his leadership role at Red Hat.

At Red Hat, Whitehurst emphasizes that respect is earned by everyone (including top managers like himself) by what they do and how they contribute. In fact, Whitehurst believes that in order for leaders to be effective, they need to be respected by organizational members for their words and deeds and not just their titles. According to Whitehurst, three important means by which leaders like himself can gain the respect of organizational members is by being passionate about their mission and vision, being confident, and engaging other organizational members.[7] At Red Hat, Whitehurst is passionate about creatively developing better technology and software in an open-source manner involving communities of contributors, partners, and customers. Whitehurst is very competent and confident both in his own abilities and in the capabilities of teams at Red Hat. Whitehurst engages Red Hat employees by encouraging and supporting their creative ideas and perspectives and being inspirational, open, and honest. Mutual trust and respect are important to Whitehurst (and at Red Hat) as are honesty, integrity, and open communication.[8]

A strong believer in empowerment and trusting employees to do what they think is right, Whitehurst also thinks that leaders and all employees must feel accountable to each other. Whitehurst holds himself accountable to employees by his performance, by the ways in which he provides explanations for his decisions and for Red Hat's performance, and for his sincere apologies when things don't go as planned.[9] In fact, Whitehurst often asks employees for feedback before he makes decisions so as to make the best decisions possible. Whitehurst strives to create an environment in which employees will be creative, motivated, energetic, inspired, enthusiastic, and excited and use these sentiments to help Red Hat achieve its mission. Importantly, Whitehurst empowers employees and gives them the freedom to be creative in the ways in which they contribute to Red Hat's mission.[10]

Red Hat has performed well under Whitehurst's leadership. Thus, it's not surprising that he has received recognition for his accomplishments. For example, in April 2014, Whitehurst gave the keynote address at The Cloud Factory conference in Banff, Alberta, Canada.[11] The Cloud Factory is a major enterprise technology conference.[12] All in all, Whitehurst certainly seems to be effectively leading Red Hat.

LO 10-1 Explain what leadership is, when leaders are effective and ineffective, and the sources of power that enable managers to be effective leaders.

Overview Jim Whitehurst exemplifies the many facets of effective leadership. In Chapter 1, we explained that one of the four primary tasks of managers is leading. Thus, it should come as no surprise that leadership is a key ingredient in effective management. When leaders are effective, their subordinates or followers are highly motivated, committed, and high-performing. When leaders are ineffective, chances are good that their subordinates do not perform up to their capabilities, are demotivated, and may be dissatisfied as well. Jim Whitehurst is a leader at the top of an organization, but leadership is an important ingredient for managerial success at all levels of organizations: top management, middle management, and first-line management. Moreover, leadership is a key ingredient of managerial success for organizations large and small.

In this chapter, we describe what leadership is and examine the major leadership models that shed light on the factors that contribute to a manager being an effective leader. We look at trait and behavior models, which focus on what leaders are like and what they do, and contingency models—Fiedler's contingency model, path–goal theory, and the leader substitutes model—each of which takes into account the complexity surrounding leadership and the role of the situation in leader effectiveness. We also describe how managers can use transformational leadership to dramatically affect their organizations. By the end of this chapter, you will appreciate the many factors and issues that managers face in their quest to be effective leaders.

The Nature of Leadership

leadership The process by which an individual exerts influence over other people and inspires, motivates, and directs their activities to help achieve group or organizational goals.

leader An individual who is able to exert influence over other people to help achieve group or organizational goals.

Leadership is the process by which a person exerts influence over other people and inspires, motivates, and directs their activities to help achieve group or organizational goals.[13] The person who exerts such influence is a **leader**. When leaders are effective, the influence they exert over others helps a group or organization achieve its performance goals. When leaders are ineffective, their influence does not contribute to, and often detracts from, goal attainment. As the "Management Snapshot" makes clear, Jim Whitehurst is taking multiple steps to inspire and motivate Red Hat's employees so they help Red Hat achieve its goals.

Beyond facilitating the attainment of performance goals, effective leadership increases an organization's ability to meet all the contemporary challenges discussed throughout this book, including the need to obtain a competitive advantage, the need to foster ethical behavior, and the need to manage a diverse workforce fairly and equitably. Leaders who exert influence over organizational members to help meet these goals increase their organizations' chances of success.

In considering the nature of leadership, we first look at leadership styles and how they affect managerial tasks and at the influence of culture on leadership styles. We then focus on the key to leadership, *power,* which can come from a variety of sources. Finally, we consider the contemporary dynamic of empowerment and how it relates to effective leadership.

Personal Leadership Style and Managerial Tasks

A manager's *personal leadership style*—that is, the specific ways in which a manager chooses to influence other people—shapes how that manager approaches planning, organizing, and controlling (the other principal tasks of managing). Consider Jim Whitehouse's personal leadership style in the "Management Snapshot": He empowers employees, emphasizes being open and honest, and really cares about the well-being of employees and fostering their creativity and passion.

Managers at all levels and in all kinds of organizations have their own personal leadership styles that determine not only how they lead their subordinates but also how they perform the other management tasks. Michael Kraus, owner and manager of a dry cleaning store in the northeastern United States, for example, takes a hands-on approach to leadership. He has the sole authority for determining work schedules and job assignments for the 15 employees in his store (an organizing task), makes all important decisions by himself (a planning task), and closely monitors his employees' performance and rewards top performers with pay increases (a control task). Kraus's personal leadership style is effective in his organization. His employees generally are motivated, perform highly, and are satisfied; and his store is highly profitable.

Developing an effective personal leadership style often is a challenge for managers at all levels in an organization. This challenge is often exacerbated when times are tough, due, for example, to an economic downturn or a decline in customer demand. The recession in the late 2000s provided many managers with just such a challenge.

Although leading is one of the four principal tasks of managing, a distinction is often made between managers and leaders. When this distinction is made, managers are thought of as those organizational members who establish and implement procedures and processes to ensure smooth functioning and are accountable for goal accomplishment.[14] Leaders look to the future, chart the course for the organization, and attract, retain, motivate, inspire, and develop relationships with employees based on trust and mutual respect.[15] Leaders provide meaning and purpose, seek innovation rather than stability, and impassion employees to work together to achieve the leaders' vision.[16]

As part of their personal leadership style, some leaders strive to truly serve others. Robert Greenleaf, who was director of management research at AT&T and upon his retirement in 1964 embarked on a second career focused on writing, speaking, and consulting, came up with the term *servant leadership* to describe these leaders.[17] **Servant leaders**, above all else, have a strong desire to serve and work for the benefit of others.[18] Servant leaders share power with followers and strive to ensure that followers' most important needs are met, that they are able to develop as individuals, and that their well-being is enhanced, and that attention is paid to those who are least well-off in a society.[19] Greenleaf founded a nonprofit organization called the Greenleaf Center for Servant Leadership (formerly called the Center for Applied Ethics) to foster leadership focused on service to others, power sharing, and a sense of community between organizations and their multiple stakeholders.[20]

servant leader A leader who has a strong desire to serve and work for the benefit of others.

Leadership Styles across Cultures

Some evidence suggests that leadership styles vary not only among individuals but also among countries or cultures. Some research indicates that European managers tend to be more humanistic or people-oriented than both Japanese and American managers. The collectivistic culture in Japan places prime emphasis on the group rather than the individual, so the importance of individuals' own personalities, needs, and desires is minimized. Organizations in the United States tend to be very profit-oriented and thus tend to downplay the importance of individual employees' needs and desires. Many countries in Europe have a more individualistic perspective than Japan and a more humanistic perspective than the United States, and this may result in some European managers' being more people-oriented than their Japanese or American counterparts. European managers, for example, tend to be reluctant to lay off employees, and when a layoff is absolutely necessary, they take careful steps to make it as painless as possible.[21]

Another cross-cultural difference occurs in time horizons. While managers in any one country often differ in their time horizons, there are also national differences. For example, U.S. organizations tend to have a short-term profit orientation, and thus U.S. managers' personal leadership styles emphasize short-term performance. Japanese organizations tend to have a long-term growth orientation, so Japanese managers' personal leadership styles emphasize long-term performance. Justus Mische, a personnel manager at the European organization Hoechst, suggested that "Europe, at least the big international firms in Europe, have a philosophy between the Japanese, long term, and the United States, short term."[22] Research on these and other global aspects of leadership is ongoing; as it continues, more cultural differences in managers' personal leadership styles may be discovered.

Power: The Key to Leadership

No matter what one's leadership style, a key component of effective leadership is found in the *power* the leader has to affect other people's behavior and get them to act in certain ways.[23] There are several types of power: legitimate, reward, coercive, expert, and referent power (see Figure 10.1).[24] Effective leaders take steps to ensure

Figure 10.1

Sources of Managerial Power

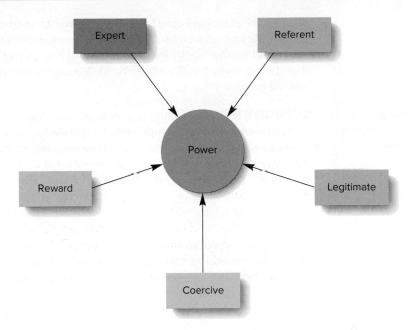

that they have sufficient levels of each type and that they use the power they have in beneficial ways.

legitimate power The authority that a manager has by virtue of his or her position in an organization's hierarchy.

LEGITIMATE POWER **Legitimate power** is the authority a manager has by virtue of his or her position in an organization's hierarchy. Personal leadership style often influences how a manager exercises legitimate power. Take the case of Carol Loray, who is a first-line manager in a greeting card company and leads a group of 15 artists and designers. Loray has the legitimate power to hire new employees, assign projects to the artists and designers, monitor their work, and appraise their performance. She uses this power effectively. She always makes sure her project assignments match the interests of her subordinates as much as possible so they will enjoy their work. She monitors their work to make sure that they are on track but does not engage in close supervision, which can hamper creativity. She makes sure her performance appraisals are developmental, providing concrete advice for areas where improvements could be made. Recently, Loray negotiated with her manager to increase her legitimate power so she can now initiate and develop proposals for new card lines.

reward power The ability of a manager to give or withhold tangible and intangible rewards.

REWARD POWER **Reward power** is the ability of a manager to give or withhold tangible rewards (pay raises, bonuses, choice job assignments) and intangible rewards (verbal praise, a pat on the back, respect). As you learned in Chapter 9, members of an organization are motivated to perform at a high level by a variety of rewards. Being able to give or withhold rewards based on performance is a major source of power that allows managers to have a highly motivated workforce. Managers of salespeople in retail organizations such as Neiman Marcus, Nordstrom, and Macy's[25] and in car dealerships such as Mazda, Ford, and Volvo often use their reward power to motivate their subordinates. Subordinates in organizations such as these often receive commissions on whatever they sell and rewards for the quality of their customer service, which motivate them to do the best they can.

Effective managers use their reward power to show appreciation for subordinates' good work and efforts. Ineffective managers use rewards in a more controlling manner (wielding the "stick" instead of offering the "carrot") that signals to subordinates that the manager has the upper hand. Managers also can take steps to increase their reward power.

coercive power The ability of a manager to punish others.

COERCIVE POWER Coercive power is the ability of a manager to punish others. Punishment can range from verbal reprimands to reductions in pay or working hours to actual dismissal. In the previous chapter, we discussed how punishment can have negative side effects, such as resentment and retaliation, and should be used only when necessary (for example, to curtail a dangerous behavior). Managers who rely heavily on coercive power tend to be ineffective as leaders and sometimes even get fired themselves. William J. Fife is one example; he was fired from his position as CEO of Giddings and Lewis Inc., a manufacturer of factory equipment, because of his overreliance on coercive power. In meetings Fife often verbally criticized, attacked, and embarrassed top managers. Realizing how destructive Fife's use of punishment was for them and the company, these managers complained to the board of directors, who, after a careful consideration of the issues, asked Fife to resign.[26]

Excessive use of coercive power seldom produces high performance and is questionable ethically. Sometimes, it amounts to a form of mental abuse, robbing workers of their dignity and causing excessive levels of stress. Overuse of coercive power can even result in dangerous working conditions. Better results and, importantly, an ethical workplace that respects employee dignity can be obtained by using reward power.

expert power Power that is based on the special knowledge, skills, and expertise that a leader possesses.

EXPERT POWER Expert power is based on the special knowledge, skills, and expertise that a leader possesses. The nature of expert power varies, depending on the leader's level in the hierarchy. First-level and middle managers often have technical expertise relevant to the tasks their subordinates perform. Their expert power gives them considerable influence over subordinates. Jim Whitehurst in the "Management Snapshot" has expert power from the prior leadership positions he has had and from his educational background.

Some top managers derive expert power from their technical expertise. Other top-level managers lack technical expertise and derive their expert power from their abilities as decision makers, planners, and strategists. Jack Welch, the former well-known leader and CEO of General Electric, summed it up this way: "The basic thing that we at the top of the company know is that we don't know the business. What we have, I hope, is the ability to allocate resources, people, and dollars."[27]

Effective leaders take steps to ensure that they have an adequate amount of expert power to perform their leadership roles. They may obtain additional training or education in their fields, make sure that they keep up with the latest developments and changes in technology, stay abreast of changes in their fields through involvement in professional associations, and read widely to be aware of momentous changes in the organization's task and general environments. Expert power tends to be best used in a guiding or coaching manner rather than in an arrogant, high-handed manner.

referent power Power that comes from subordinates' and coworkers' respect, admiration, and loyalty.

REFERENT POWER Referent power is more informal than the other kinds of power. Referent power is a function of the personal characteristics of a leader; it is the power that comes from subordinates' and coworkers' respect, admiration, and loyalty. Leaders who are likable and whom subordinates wish to use as a role model are especially likely to possess referent power, as is true of Jim Whitehurst in the "Management Snapshot."

The Chrysler Jefferson North Assembly plant in Detroit. Empowered employees make some decisions that managers or other leaders used to make. © Paul Sancya/AP Images

In addition to being a valuable asset for top managers like Whitehurst, referent power can help first-line and middle managers be effective leaders as well. Sally Carruthers, for example, is the first-level manager of a group of secretaries in the finance department of a large state university. Carruthers's secretaries are known to be among the best in the university. Much of their willingness to go above and beyond the call of duty has been attributed to Carruthers's warm and caring nature, which makes each of them feel important and valued. Managers can take steps to increase their referent power, such as taking time to get to know their subordinates and showing interest in and concern for them.

Empowerment: An Ingredient in Modern Management

empowerment The expansion of employees' knowledge, tasks, and decision-making responsibilities.

More and more managers today are incorporating into their personal leadership styles an aspect that at first glance seems to be the opposite of being a leader. In Chapter 1, we described how **empowerment**—the process of giving employees at all levels the authority to make decisions, be responsible for their outcomes, improve quality, and cut costs—is becoming increasingly popular in organizations. When leaders empower their subordinates, the subordinates typically take over some responsibilities and authority that used to reside with the leader or manager, such as the right to reject parts that do not meet quality standards, the right to check one's own work, and the right to schedule work activities. Empowered subordinates are given the power to make some decisions that their leaders or supervisors used to make.

Empowerment might seem to be the opposite of effective leadership because managers are allowing subordinates to take a more active role in leading themselves. In actuality, however, empowerment can contribute to effective leadership for several reasons:

- Empowerment increases a manager's ability to get things done because the manager has the support and help of subordinates who may have special knowledge of work tasks.

- Empowerment often increases workers' involvement, motivation, and commitment; and this helps ensure that they are working toward organizational goals.

- Empowerment gives managers more time to concentrate on their pressing concerns because they spend less time on day-to-day supervision.

Effective managers like Jim Whitehurst realize the benefits of empowerment. The personal leadership style of managers who empower subordinates often entails developing subordinates' ability to make good decisions as well as being their guide, coach, and source of inspiration. Empowerment is a popular trend in the United States and is a part of servant leadership. Empowerment is also taking off around the world.[28] For instance, companies in South Korea (such as Samsung, Hyundai, and Daewoo), in which decision making typically was centralized with the founding families, are now empowering managers at lower levels to make decisions.[29]

Trait and Behavior Models of Leadership

Leading is such an important process in all organizations—nonprofit organizations, government agencies, and schools, as well as for-profit corporations—that it has been researched for decades. Early approaches to leadership, called the *trait model* and the *behavior model,* sought to determine what effective leaders are like as people and what they do that makes them so effective.

The Trait Model

LO 10-2 Identify the traits that show the strongest relationship to leadership, the behaviors leaders engage in, and the limitations of the trait and behavior models of leadership.

The trait model of leadership focused on identifying the personal characteristics that cause effective leadership. Researchers thought effective leaders must have certain personal qualities that set them apart from ineffective leaders and from people who never become leaders. Decades of research (beginning in the 1930s) and hundreds of studies indicate that certain personal characteristics do appear to be associated with effective leadership. (See Table 10.1 for a list of these.)[30] Notice that although this model is called the "trait" model, some of the personal characteristics that it identifies are not personality traits per se but, rather, are concerned with a leader's skills, abilities, knowledge, and expertise. As the "Management Snapshot" shows, Jim Whitehurst certainly appears to possess many of these characteristics (such as intelligence, knowledge and expertise, self-confidence, high energy, and integrity and honesty). Leaders who do not possess these traits may be ineffective.

Traits alone are not the key to understanding leader effectiveness, however. Some effective leaders do not possess all these traits, and some leaders who possess them are not effective in their leadership roles. This lack of a consistent relationship between leader traits and leader effectiveness led researchers to shift their attention away from traits and to search for new explanations for effective leadership. Rather than focusing on what leaders are like (the traits they possess), researchers began looking at what effective leaders actually do—in other words, at the behaviors that allow effective leaders to influence their subordinates to achieve group and organizational goals.

Table 10.1

Traits and Personal Characteristics Related to Effective Leadership

Trait	Description
Intelligence	Helps managers understand complex issues and solve problems.
Knowledge and expertise	Help managers make good decisions and discover ways to increase efficiency and effectiveness.
Dominance	Helps managers influence their subordinates to achieve organizational goals.
Self-confidence	Contributes to managers' effectively influencing subordinates and persisting when faced with obstacles or difficulties.
High energy	Helps managers deal with the many demands they face.
Tolerance for stress	Helps managers deal with uncertainty and make difficult decisions.
Integrity and honesty	Help managers behave ethically and earn their subordinates' trust and confidence.
Maturity	Helps managers avoid acting selfishly, control their feelings, and admit when they have made a mistake.

The Behavior Model

After extensive study in the 1940s and 1950s, researchers at The Ohio State University identified two basic kinds of leader behaviors that many leaders in the United States, Germany, and other countries engaged in to influence their subordinates: *consideration* and *initiating structure*.[31]

consideration

Behavior indicating that a manager trusts, respects, and cares about subordinates.

CONSIDERATION Leaders engage in **consideration** when they show their subordinates that they trust, respect, and care about them. Managers who truly look out for the well-being of their subordinates, and do what they can to help subordinates feel good and enjoy their work, perform consideration behaviors. In the "Management Snapshot," Jim Whitehurst engages in consideration when he looks out for the well-being of his employees, shows them that he trusts them, and fosters an environment in which they will be engaged and passionate about their work.

At Costco Wholesale Corporation, cofounder and director Jim Senegal believes that consideration not only is an ethical imperative but also makes good business sense,[32] as indicated in the accompanying "Management Insight" feature.

MANAGEMENT INSIGHT

Consideration at Costco

Managers at Costco, including cofounder and director Jim Senegal and CEO Craig Jelinek, believe consideration is so important that one of the principles in Costco's code of ethics is "Take Care of Our Employees."[33] Costco Wholesale Corporation is the third largest retailer and the top warehouse retailer in the United States.[34] Wages at Costco are an average of $17 per hour—more than 40% higher than the average hourly wage at Walmart, Costco's major competitor.[35] Costco pays the majority of health insurance costs for its employees (employees pay around 8% of health insurance costs compared to an industry average of around 25%), and part-time employees receive health insurance after they have been with the company six months. Overall, about 85% of Costco employees are covered by health insurance, compared with fewer than 45% of employees at Target and Walmart.[36]

Jim Senegal and Craig Jelinek believe that caring about the well-being of employees is a win-win proposition because Costco's employees are satisfied, committed, loyal, and motivated. Additionally, turnover and employee theft rates at Costco are much lower than industry averages.[37] In the retail industry, turnover tends to be high and costly because for every employee who quits, a new hire needs to be recruited, tested, interviewed, and trained. Even though pay and benefits are higher at Costco than at rival Walmart, Costco actually has lower labor costs as a percentage of sales and higher sales per square foot of store space than Walmart.[38]

Loyal Costco customers like these know that their bargains don't come at the expense of employees' paychecks and benefits.
© Tim Boyle/Getty Images

Additionally, treating employees well helps build customer loyalty at Costco. Surely customers enjoy the bargains and low prices that come from shopping in a warehouse store, the relatively high quality of the goods Costco stocks, and Costco's policy of not marking up prices by more than 14% to 15% (relatively low markups for retail) even if the goods would sell with higher markups. However, customers are also loyal to Costco because they know the company treats its employees well and their bargains are not coming at the expense of employees' paychecks and benefits.[39]

Costco started out as a single warehouse store in Seattle, Washington, in 1983. Now the company has 664 stores (including stores in Puerto Rico, South Korea, Taiwan, Japan, Australia, Mexico, Canada, and Britain) and tens of millions of members who pay an annual fee to shop at Costco stores.[40] Costco's growth and financial performance are enviable.[41] For example, net sales for the 2014 fiscal year were $110.21 billion.[42] Clearly, consideration has paid off for Costco and for its employees.[43]

True to caring for the well-being of employees, Costco did not lay off any employees during the recession in the late 2000s.[44] However, some female employees filed a class action lawsuit alleging gender discrimination at Costco.[45] The lawsuit started when Shirley Ellis filed a discrimination complaint and a later lawsuit in the early 2000s.[46] In December 2013, the lawsuit was tentatively settled for $8 million to compensate women who were inappropriately blocked from promotions to positions of assistant general manager and general manager.[47] The settlement also entails Costco having its promotion procedures for assistant general managers and general managers reviewed by an industrial organizational psychologist. Additionally, Costco will post assistant general manager openings and have a system for employees to indicate their interest in general manager positions. In terms of the settlement, Ellis indicated that, "I believe this to be a fair settlement to both parties. . . . Even though this process has taken much longer than anticipated initially, I'm encouraged by Costco's efforts to welcome women and all they have to offer in the ranks of GM and AGM companywide."[48]

initiating structure Behavior that managers engage in to ensure that work gets done, subordinates perform their jobs acceptably, and the organization is efficient and effective.

LO10-3 Explain how contingency models of leadership enhance our understanding of effective leadership and management in organizations.

INITIATING STRUCTURE Leaders engage in **initiating structure** when they take steps to make sure that work gets done, subordinates perform their jobs acceptably, and the organization is efficient and effective. Assigning tasks to individuals or work groups, letting subordinates know what is expected of them, deciding how work should be done, making schedules, encouraging adherence to rules and regulations, and motivating subordinates to do a good job are all examples of initiating structure.[49]

Michael Teckel, the manager of an upscale store selling imported men's and women's shoes in a Midwestern city, engages in initiating structure when he establishes weekly work, lunch, and break schedules to ensure that the store has enough salespeople on the floor. Teckel also initiates structure when he discusses the latest shoe designs with his subordinates so they are knowledgeable with customers, when he encourages adherence to the store's refund and exchange policies, and when he encourages his staff to provide high-quality customer service and to avoid a hard-sell approach.

Initiating structure and consideration are independent leader behaviors. Leaders can be high on both, low on both, or high on one and low on the other. Many effective leaders, like Jim Whitehurst of Red Hat, engage in both of these behaviors.

You might expect that effective leaders and managers would perform both kinds of behaviors, but research has found that this is not necessarily the case. The relationship between performance of consideration and initiating-structure behaviors and leader effectiveness is not clear-cut. Some leaders are effective even when they do not perform consideration or initiating-structure behaviors, and some leaders are ineffective even when they perform both kinds of behaviors. Like the trait model of leadership, the behavior model alone cannot explain leader effectiveness. Realizing this, researchers began building more complicated models of leadership, focused not only on the leader and what he or she does but also on the situation or context in which leadership occurs.

Contingency Models of Leadership

Simply possessing certain traits or performing certain behaviors does not ensure that a manager will be an effective leader in all situations calling for leadership. Some managers who seem to possess the right traits and perform the right behaviors turn out to be ineffective leaders. Managers lead in a wide variety of situations and organizations and have various kinds of subordinates performing diverse tasks in a multiplicity of environmental contexts. Given the wide variety of situations in which leadership occurs, what makes a manager an effective leader in one situation (such as certain traits or behaviors) is not necessarily what that manager needs to be equally effective in a different situation. An effective army general might not be an effective university president; an effective restaurant manager might not be an effective clothing store manager; an effective football team coach might not be an effective fitness center manager; and an effective first-line manager in a manufacturing company might not be an effective middle manager. The traits or behaviors that may contribute to a manager's being an effective leader in one situation might actually result in the same manager being an ineffective leader in another situation.

Contingency models of leadership take into account the situation or context within which leadership occurs. According to contingency models, whether or not a manager is an effective leader is the result of the interplay between what the manager is like, what he or she does, and the situation in which leadership takes place. Contingency models propose that whether a leader who possesses certain traits or performs certain behaviors is effective depends on, or is contingent on, the situation or context. In this section, we discuss three prominent contingency models developed to shed light on what makes managers effective leaders: Fred Fiedler's contingency model, Robert House's path–goal theory, and the leader substitutes model. As you will see, these leadership models are complementary; each focuses on a somewhat different aspect of effective leadership in organizations.

Fiedler's Contingency Model

Fred E. Fiedler was among the first leadership researchers to acknowledge that effective leadership is contingent on, or depends on, the characteristics of the leader *and* of the situation. Fiedler's contingency model helps explain why a manager may be an effective leader in one situation and ineffective in another; it also suggests which kinds of managers are likely to be most effective in which situations.[50]

LEADER STYLE As with the trait approach, Fiedler hypothesized that personal characteristics can influence leader effectiveness. He used the term *leader style* to refer to a manager's characteristic approach to leadership and identified two basic leader styles: *relationship–oriented* and *task-oriented.* All managers can be described as having one style or the other.

relationship-
oriented
leaders Leaders
whose primary concern
is to develop good
relationships with their
subordinates and to be
liked by them.

Relationship-oriented leaders are primarily concerned with developing good relationships with their subordinates and being liked by them. Relationship-oriented managers focus on having high-quality interpersonal relationships with subordinates. This does not mean, however, that the job does not get done when such leaders are at the helm. But it does mean that the quality of interpersonal relationships with subordinates is a prime concern for relationship-oriented leaders.

task-oriented
leaders Leaders
whose primary concern
is to ensure that
subordinates perform at
a high level.

Task-oriented leaders are primarily concerned with ensuring that subordinates perform at a high level and focus on task accomplishment. While task-oriented leaders also may be concerned about having good interpersonal relationships with their subordinates, task accomplishment is their prime concern.

SITUATIONAL CHARACTERISTICS According to Fiedler, leadership style is an enduring characteristic; managers cannot change their style, nor can they adopt different styles in different kinds of situations. With this in mind, Fiedler identified three situational characteristics that are important determinants of how favorable a situation is for leading: leader–member relations, task structure, and position power. When a situation is favorable for leading, it is relatively easy for a manager to influence subordinates so they perform at a high level and contribute to organizational efficiency and effectiveness. In a situation unfavorable for leading, it is much more difficult for a manager to exert influence.

LEADER–MEMBER RELATIONS The first situational characteristic Fiedler described, **leader–member relations**, is the extent to which followers like, trust, and are loyal to their leader. Situations are more favorable for leading when leader–member relations are good.

leader–member
relations The extent
to which followers
like, trust, and are
loyal to their leader;
a determinant of how
favorable a situation is
for leading.

TASK STRUCTURE The second situational characteristic Fiedler described, **task structure**, is the extent to which the work to be performed is clear-cut so that a leader's subordinates know what needs to be accomplished and how to go about doing it. When task structure is high, the situation is favorable for leading. When task structure is low, goals may be vague, subordinates may be unsure of what they should be doing or how they should do it, and the situation is unfavorable for leading.

task structure The
extent to which the
work to be performed
is clear-cut so that a
leader's subordinates
know what needs to be
accomplished and how
to go about doing it;
a determinant of how
favorable a situation is
for leading.

Task structure was low for Geraldine Laybourne when she was a top manager at Nickelodeon, the children's television network. It was never precisely clear what would appeal to her young viewers, whose tastes can change dramatically, or how to motivate her subordinates to come up with creative and novel ideas.[51] In contrast, Herman Mashaba, founder of Black Like Me, a hair care products company based in South Africa, seemed to have relatively high task structure when he started his company. His company's goals were to produce and sell inexpensive hair care products to native Africans, and managers accomplished these goals by using simple yet appealing packaging and distributing the products through neighborhood beauty salons.[52]

position power The
amount of legitimate,
reward, and coercive
power that a leader
has by virtue of his
or her position in
an organization; a
determinant of how
favorable a situation is
for leading.

POSITION POWER The third situational characteristic Fiedler described, **position power**, is the amount of legitimate, reward, and coercive power a leader has by virtue of his or her position in an organization. Leadership situations are more favorable for leading when position power is strong.

COMBINING LEADER STYLE AND THE SITUATION By considering all possible combinations of good and poor leader–member relations, high and low task structure, and strong and weak position power, Fiedler identified eight leadership situations, which vary in their favorability for leading (see Figure 10.2). After extensive research, he

Figure 10.2

Fiedler's Contingency Theory of Leadership

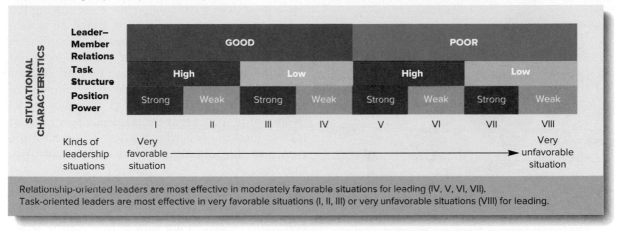

Relationship-oriented leaders are most effective in moderately favorable situations for leading (IV, V, VI, VII).
Task-oriented leaders are most effective in very favorable situations (I, II, III) or very unfavorable situations (VIII) for leading.

determined that relationship-oriented leaders are most effective in moderately favorable situations (IV, V, VI, and VII in Figure 10.2) and task-oriented leaders are most effective in situations that are either very favorable (I, II, and III) or very unfavorable (VIII).

PUTTING THE CONTINGENCY MODEL INTO PRACTICE Recall that, according to Fiedler, leader style is an enduring characteristic that managers cannot change. This suggests that for managers to be effective, either managers need to be placed in leadership situations that fit their style or situations need to be changed to suit the managers. Situations can be changed, for example, by giving a manager more position power or taking steps to increase task structure, such as by clarifying goals.

Take the case of Mark Compton, a relationship-oriented leader employed by a small construction company, who was in a very unfavorable situation and was having a rough time leading his construction crew. His subordinates did not trust him to look out for their well-being (poor leader–member relations); the construction jobs he supervised tended to be novel and complex (low task structure); and he had no control over the rewards and disciplinary actions his subordinates received (weak position power). Recognizing the need to improve matters, Compton's supervisor gave him the power to reward crew members with bonuses and overtime work as he saw fit and to discipline crew members for poor-quality work and unsafe on-the-job behavior. As his leadership situation improved to moderately favorable, so too did Compton's effectiveness as a leader and the performance of his crew.

Research studies tend to support some aspects of Fiedler's model but also suggest that, like most theories, it needs some modifications.[53] Some researchers have questioned what the LPC scale really measures. Others find fault with the model's premise that leaders cannot alter their styles. That is, it is likely that at least some leaders can diagnose the situation they are in and, when their style is inappropriate for the situation, modify their style so that it is more in line with what the leadership situation calls for.

House's Path–Goal Theory

In what he called **path–goal theory**, leadership researcher Robert House focused on what leaders can do to motivate their subordinates to achieve group and

path-goal theory
A contingency model of leadership proposing that leaders can motivate subordinates by identifying their desired outcomes, rewarding them for high performance and the attainment of work goals with these desired outcomes, and clarifying for them the paths leading to the attainment of work goals.

You could stand over your subordinate and berate him or you could empower him to find the solution by working to see where the issue developed. Supportive managers make a world of difference in retaining and motivating employees.
© Stockbyte/Getty Images RF

organizational goals.[54] The premise of path–goal theory is that effective leaders motivate subordinates to achieve goals by (1) clearly identifying the outcomes that subordinates are trying to obtain from the workplace, (2) rewarding subordinates with these outcomes for high performance and the attainment of work goals, and (3) clarifying for subordinates the *paths* leading to the attainment of work *goals*. Path–goal theory is a contingency model because it proposes that the steps managers should take to motivate subordinates depend on both the nature of the subordinates and the type of work they do.

Path–goal theory identifies four kinds of leadership behaviors that motivate subordinates:

- *Directive behaviors* are similar to initiating structure and include setting goals, assigning tasks, showing subordinates how to complete tasks, and taking concrete steps to improve performance.

- *Supportive behaviors* are similar to consideration and include expressing concern for subordinates and looking out for their best interests.

- *Participative behaviors* give subordinates a say in matters and decisions that affect them.

- *Achievement-oriented behaviors* motivate subordinates to perform at the highest level possible by, for example, setting challenging goals, expecting that they be met, and believing in subordinates' capabilities.

Which of these behaviors should managers use to lead effectively? The answer to this question depends, or is contingent on, the nature of the subordinates and the kind of work they do.

Directive behaviors may be beneficial when subordinates are having difficulty completing assigned tasks, but they might be detrimental when subordinates are independent thinkers who work best when left alone. *Supportive* behaviors are often advisable when subordinates are experiencing high levels of stress. *Participative* behaviors can be particularly effective when subordinates' support of a decision is required. *Achievement-oriented* behaviors may increase motivation levels of highly capable subordinates who are bored from having too few challenges, but they might backfire if used with subordinates who are already pushed to their limit.

leadership substitute A characteristic of a subordinate or of a situation or context that acts in place of the influence of a leader and makes leadership unnecessary.

The Leader Substitutes Model

The leader substitutes model suggests that leadership is sometimes unnecessary because substitutes for leadership are present. A **leadership substitute** is something that acts in place of the influence of a leader and makes leadership unnecessary. This model suggests that under certain conditions managers do not have to play a leadership role—members of an organization sometimes can perform at a high level without a manager exerting influence over them.[55] The leader substitutes model is a contingency model because it suggests that in some situations leadership is unnecessary.

Take the case of David Cotsonas, who teaches English at a foreign language school in Cyprus, an island in the Mediterranean Sea. Cotsonas is fluent in Greek, English, and French; is an excellent teacher; and is highly motivated. Many of his students are businesspeople who have some rudimentary English skills and wish to increase their fluency to be able to conduct more of their business in English. He enjoys not only teaching them English but also learning about the work they do, and he often keeps in touch with his students after they finish his classes. Cotsonas meets with the director of the school twice a year to discuss semiannual class schedules and enrollments.

With practically no influence from a leader, Cotsonas is a highly motivated top performer at the school. In his situation, leadership is unnecessary because substitutes for leadership are present. Cotsonas's teaching expertise, his motivation, and his enjoyment of his work are substitutes for the influence of a leader—in this case the school's director. If the school's director were to try to influence how Cotsonas performs his job, Cotsonas would probably resent this infringement on his autonomy, and it is unlikely that his performance would improve because he is already one of the school's best teachers.

As in Cotsonas's case, *characteristics of subordinates*—such as their skills, abilities, experience, knowledge, and motivation—can be substitutes for leadership.[56] *Characteristics of the situation or context*—such as the extent to which the work is interesting and enjoyable—also can be substitutes. When work is interesting and enjoyable, as it is for Cotsonas, jobholders do not need to be coaxed into performing because performing is rewarding in its own right. Similarly, when managers *empower* their subordinates or use *self-managed work teams* (discussed in detail in Chapter 15), the need for leadership influence from a manager is decreased because team members manage themselves.

Substitutes for leadership can increase organizational efficiency and effectiveness because they free up some of managers' valuable time and allow managers to focus their efforts on discovering new ways to improve organizational effectiveness. The director of the language school, for example, was able to spend much of his time making arrangements to open a second school in Rhodes, an island in the Aegean Sea, because of the presence of leadership substitutes, not only for Cotsonas but for most other teachers at the school as well.

Bringing It All Together

Effective leadership in organizations occurs when managers take steps to lead in a way that is appropriate for the situation or context in which leadership occurs and for the subordinates who are being led. The three contingency models of leadership just discussed help managers focus on the necessary ingredients for effective leadership. They are complementary in that each one looks at the leadership question from a different angle. Fiedler's contingency model explores how a manager's leadership style needs to be matched to that person's leadership situation for maximum effectiveness. House's path–goal theory focuses on how managers should motivate subordinates and describes the specific kinds of behaviors managers can engage in to have a highly motivated workforce. The leadership substitutes model alerts managers to the fact that sometimes they do not need to exert influence over subordinates and thus can free up their time for other important activities. Table 10.2 recaps these three contingency models of leadership.

Table 10.2

Contingency Models of Leadership

Model	Focus	Key Contingencies
Fiedler's contingency model	Describes two leader styles, relationship-oriented and task-oriented, and the kinds of situations in which each kind of leader will be most effective.	Whether a relationship-oriented or a task-oriented leader is effective is contingent on the situation.
House's path–goal theory	Describes how effective leaders motivate their followers.	The behaviors that managers should engage in to be effective leaders are contingent on the nature of the subordinates and the work they do.
Leader substitutes model	Describes when leadership is unnecessary.	Whether leadership is necessary for subordinates to perform highly is contingent on characteristics of the subordinates and the situation.

Transformational Leadership

LO 10-4
Describe what transformational leadership is, and explain how managers can engage in it.

transformational leadership
Leadership that makes subordinates aware of the importance of their jobs and performance to the organization and aware of their own needs for personal growth and that motivates subordinates to work for the good of the organization.

Time and time again, throughout business history, certain leaders seem to literally transform their organizations, making sweeping changes to revitalize and renew operations. For example, when Sue Nokes became senior vice president of sales and customer service at T-Mobile USA in 2002, the quality of T-Mobile's customer service was lower than that of its major competitors; on average, 12% of employees were absent on any day; and annual employee turnover was more than 100%.[57] T-Mobile USA is a subsidiary of Deutsche Telekom; has approximately 38,000 employees; and provides wireless voice, messaging, and data services.[58] When Nokes arrived at T-Mobile, valuable employees were quitting their jobs and customers weren't receiving high-quality service; neither employees nor customers were satisfied with their experience with the company.[59] However, by the late 2000s T-Mobile was regularly receiving highest rankings for customer care and satisfaction in the wireless category by J. D. Power and Associates, absence and turnover rates substantially declined, and around 80% of employees indicated that they were satisfied with their jobs.[60] In fact, when Nokes visited call centers, it was not uncommon for employees to greet her with cheers and accolades.[61]

Nokes transformed T-Mobile into a company in which satisfied employees provide excellent service to customers.[62] When managers have such dramatic effects on their subordinates and on an organization as a whole, they are engaging in transformational leadership. **Transformational leadership** occurs when managers change (or transform) their subordinates in three important ways:[63]

1. *Transformational managers make subordinates aware of how important their jobs are for the organization and how necessary it is for them to perform those jobs as best they can so the organization can attain its goals.* At T-Mobile, Nokes visited call centers, conducted focus groups, and had town hall meetings to find out what employees and customers were unhappy with and what steps she could take to improve matters.[64] Her philosophy was that when employees are satisfied with their jobs and view their work as important, they are much more likely to provide high-quality customer service. She made employees aware of how important their jobs were by the many steps she took to improve their working conditions, ranging from providing them with their own workspaces to substantially raising their salaries.[65] She emphasized the importance of providing excellent customer

Sue Nokes exhibited transformational leadership at T-Mobile.
© IPON-BONESS/SIPA/ Newscom

service by periodically asking employees what was working well and what was not working well, asking them what steps could be taken to improve problem areas, and taking actions to ensure that employees were able to provide excellent customer service. Nokes also instituted a performance measurement system to track performance in key areas such as quality of service and speed of problem resolution.[66] She sincerely told employees, "You are No. 1, and the customer is why."[67]

2. *Transformational managers make their subordinates aware of the subordinates' own needs for personal growth, development, and accomplishment.* Nokes made T-Mobile's employees aware of their own needs in this regard by transforming training and development at T-Mobile and increasing opportunities for promotions to more responsible positions. Employees now spend more than 130 hours per year in training and development programs and team meetings. Nokes also instituted a promote-from-within policy, and around 80% of promotions are given to current employees.[68]

3. *Transformational managers motivate their subordinates to work for the good of the organization as a whole, not just for their own personal gain or benefit.* Nokes emphasized that employees should focus on what matters to customers, coworkers, and T-Mobile as a whole. She let employees know that when they were unnecessarily absent from their jobs, they were not doing right by their coworkers. And she emphasized the need to try to resolve customer problems in a single phone call so customers can get on with their busy lives.[69]

When managers transform their subordinates in these three ways, subordinates trust the managers, are highly motivated, and help the organization achieve its goals. How do managers such as Nokes transform subordinates and produce dramatic effects in their organizations? There are at least three ways in which transformational leaders can influence their followers: by being a charismatic leader, by intellectually stimulating subordinates, and by engaging in developmental consideration (see Table 10.3).

Being a Charismatic Leader

charismatic leader
An enthusiastic, self-confident leader who is able to clearly communicate his or her vision of how good things could be.

Transformational managers such as Nokes are **charismatic leaders**. They have a vision of how good things could be in their work groups and organizations that is in contrast with the status quo. Their vision usually entails dramatic improvements in group and organizational performance as a result of changes in the organization's structure, culture, strategy, decision making, and other critical processes and factors. This vision paves the way for gaining a competitive advantage.

Table 10.3

Transformational Leadership

Transformational managers
- Are charismatic.
- Intellectually stimulate subordinates.
- Engage in developmental consideration.

Subordinates of transformational managers
- Have increased awareness of the importance of their jobs and high performance.
- Are aware of their own needs for growth, development, and accomplishment.
- Work for the good of the organization and not just their own personal benefit.

Charismatic leaders are excited and enthusiastic about their vision and clearly communicate it to their subordinates. The excitement, enthusiasm, and self-confidence of a charismatic leader contribute to the leader's being able to inspire followers to enthusiastically support his or her vision.[70] People often think of charismatic leaders or managers as being "larger than life." The essence of charisma, however, is having a vision and enthusiastically communicating it to others. Thus, managers who appear to be quiet and earnest can also be charismatic.

Stimulating Subordinates Intellectually

intellectual stimulation Behavior a leader engages in to make followers aware of problems and view these problems in new ways, consistent with the leader's vision.

Transformational managers openly share information with their subordinates so they are aware of problems and the need for change. The manager causes subordinates to view problems in their groups and throughout the organization from a different perspective, consistent with the manager's vision. Whereas in the past subordinates might not have been aware of some problems, may have viewed problems as a "management issue" beyond their concern, or may have viewed problems as insurmountable, the transformational manager's **intellectual stimulation** leads subordinates to view problems as challenges that they can and will meet and conquer. The manager engages and empowers subordinates to take personal responsibility for helping to solve problems, as did Nokes at T-Mobile.[71]

Engaging in Developmental Consideration

developmental consideration Behavior a leader engages in to support and encourage followers and help them develop and grow on the job.

When managers engage in **developmental consideration**, they not only perform the consideration behaviors described earlier, such as demonstrating true concern for the well-being of subordinates, but go one step further. The manager goes out of his or her way to support and encourage subordinates, giving them opportunities to enhance their skills and capabilities and to grow and excel on the job.[72] As mentioned earlier, Nokes did this in numerous ways. In fact, after she first met with employees in a call center in Albuquerque, New Mexico, Karen Viola, the manager of the call center, said, "Everyone came out crying. The people said that they had never felt so inspired in their lives, and that they had never met with any leader at that level who [they felt] cared."[73]

All organizations, no matter how large or small, successful or unsuccessful, can benefit when their managers engage in transformational leadership. Moreover, while the benefits of transformational leadership are often most apparent when an organization is in trouble, transformational leadership can be an enduring approach to leadership, leading to long-term organizational effectiveness.

The Distinction between Transformational and Transactional Leadership

transactional leadership Leadership that motivates subordinates by rewarding them for high performance and reprimanding them for low performance.

Transformational leadership is often contrasted with transactional leadership. In **transactional leadership**, managers use their reward and coercive powers to encourage high performance. When managers reward high performers, reprimand or otherwise punish low performers, and motivate subordinates by reinforcing desired behaviors and extinguishing or punishing undesired ones, they are engaging in transactional leadership.[74] Managers who effectively influence their subordinates to achieve goals, yet do not seem to be making the kind of dramatic changes that are part of transformational leadership, are engaging in transactional leadership.

Many transformational leaders engage in transactional leadership. They reward subordinates for a job well done and notice and respond to substandard performance. But they also have their eyes on the bigger picture of how much better things could be in their organizations, how much more their subordinates are capable of achieving, and how important it is to treat their subordinates with respect and help them reach their full potential.

Research has found that when leaders engage in transformational leadership, their subordinates tend to have higher levels of job satisfaction and performance.[75] Additionally, subordinates of transformational leaders may be more likely to trust their leaders and their organizations and feel that they are being fairly treated, and this, in turn, may positively influence their work motivation (see Chapter 9).[76]

Gender and Leadership

The increasing number of women entering the ranks of management, as well as the problems some women face in their efforts to be hired as managers or promoted into management positions, has prompted researchers to explore the relationship between gender and leadership. Although there are relatively more women in management positions today than there were 10 years ago, there are still relatively few women in top management and, in some organizations, even in middle management.

When women do advance to top management positions, special attention often is focused on them and the fact that they are women. For example, women CEOs of large companies are still rare; those who make it to the top post, such as Indra Nooyi of PepsiCo[77] and Meg Whitman of Hewlett-Packard, are salient. As business writer Linda Tischler puts it, "In a workplace where women CEOs of major companies are so scarce . . . they can be identified, like rock stars, by first name only."[78] Although women have certainly made inroads into leadership positions in organizations, they continue to be underrepresented in top leadership posts. For example, as was indicated in Chapter 3, while around 51.5% of the employees in managerial and professional jobs in the United States are women, only about 14.6% of corporate officers in the *Fortune* 500 are women, and only 8.1% of the top earners are women.[79]

A widespread stereotype of women is that they are nurturing, supportive, and concerned with interpersonal relations. Men are stereotypically viewed as being directive and focused on task accomplishment. Such stereotypes suggest that women tend to be more relationship-oriented as managers and engage in more consideration behaviors, whereas men are more task-oriented and engage in more initiating-structure behaviors. Does the behavior of actual male and female managers bear out these stereotypes? Do women managers lead in different ways than men do? Are male or female managers more effective as leaders?

Research suggests that male and female managers who have leadership positions in organizations behave in similar ways.[80] Women do not engage in more consideration than men, and men do not engage in more initiating structure than women. Research does suggest, however, that leadership style may vary between women and men. Women tend to be somewhat more participative as leaders than are men, involving subordinates in decision making and seeking their input.[81] Male managers tend to be less participative than are female managers, making more decisions on their own and wanting to do things their own way. Moreover, research suggests that men tend to be harsher when they punish their subordinates than do women.[82]

LO 10-5 Characterize the relationship between gender and leadership, and explain how emotional intelligence may contribute to leadership effectiveness.

There are at least two reasons why female managers may be more participative as leaders than are male managers.[83] First, subordinates may try to resist the influence of female managers more than they do the influence of male managers. Some subordinates may never have reported to a woman before; some may incorrectly see a management role as being more appropriate for a man than for a woman; and some may just resist being led by a woman. To overcome this resistance and encourage subordinates' trust and respect, women managers may adopt a participative approach.

A second reason why female managers may be more participative is that they sometimes have better interpersonal skills than male managers.[84] A participative approach to leadership requires high levels of interaction and involvement between a manager and his or her subordinates, sensitivity to subordinates' feelings, and the ability to make decisions that may be unpopular with subordinates but necessary for goal attainment. Good interpersonal skills may help female managers have the effective interactions with their subordinates that are crucial to a participative approach.[85] To the extent that male managers have more difficulty managing interpersonal relationships, they may shy away from the high levels of interaction with subordinates necessary for true participation.

The key finding from research on leader behaviors, however, is that male and female managers do *not* differ significantly in their propensities to perform different leader behaviors. Even though they may be more participative, female managers do not engage in more consideration or less initiating structure than male managers.

Perhaps a question even more important than whether male and female managers differ in the leadership behaviors they perform is whether they differ in effectiveness. Consistent with the findings for leader behaviors, research suggests that across different kinds of organizational settings, male and female managers tend to be *equally effective* as leaders.[86] Thus, there is no logical basis for stereotypes favoring male managers and leaders or for the existence of the "glass ceiling" (an invisible barrier that seems to prevent women from advancing as far as they should in some organizations). Because women and men are equally effective as leaders, the increasing number of women in the workforce should result in a larger pool of highly qualified candidates for management positions in organizations, ultimately enhancing organizational effectiveness.[87]

Emotional Intelligence and Leadership

Do the moods and emotions leaders experience on the job influence their behavior and effectiveness as leaders? Research suggests that this is likely to be the case. For example, one study found that when store managers experienced positive moods at work, salespeople in their stores provided high-quality customer service and were less likely to quit.[88] Another study found that groups whose leaders experienced positive moods had better coordination, whereas groups whose leaders experienced negative moods exerted more effort; members of groups with leaders in positive moods also tended to experience more positive moods themselves; and members of groups with leaders in negative moods tended to experience more negative moods.[89]

A leader's level of emotional intelligence (see Chapter 2) may play a particularly important role in leadership effectiveness.[90] For example, emotional intelligence may help leaders develop a vision for their organizations, motivate their subordinates to commit to this vision, and energize them to enthusiastically work to achieve this vision. Moreover, emotional intelligence may enable leaders to develop a significant identity for their organization and instill high levels of trust and cooperation throughout the organization while maintaining the flexibility needed to respond to changing conditions.[91]

Emotional intelligence also plays a crucial role in how leaders relate to and deal with their followers, particularly when it comes to encouraging followers to be creative.[92] Creativity in organizations is an emotion-laden process; it often entails challenging the status quo, being willing to take risks and accept and learn from failures, and doing much hard work to bring creative ideas to fruition in terms of new products, services, or procedures and processes when uncertainty is bound to be high.[93] Leaders who are high on emotional intelligence are more likely to understand all the emotions surrounding creative endeavors, to be able to awaken and support the creative pursuits of their followers, and to provide the kind of support that enables creativity to flourish in organizations.[94]

Leaders, like people everywhere, sometimes make mistakes. Emotional intelligence may also help leaders respond appropriately when they realize they have made a mistake. Recognizing, admitting, and learning from mistakes can be especially important for entrepreneurs who start their own businesses, as profiled in the accompanying "Focus on Diversity" feature.

FOCUS ON DIVERSITY

Admitting a Mistake Helps Small Business Leader

Things seemed to be going well for Maureen Borzacchiello, CEO of Creative Display Solutions, located in Garden City, New York.[95] She founded her small business in 2001 to provide displays, graphics, and exhibits for use in trade shows and at events for companies ranging from American Express, FedEx, and General Electric to JetBlue Airways, AIG, and The Weather Channel.[96] Her company was growing, and she had received an award from the nonprofit organization, Count Me In for Women's Economic Independence.[97]

However, in 2006, she realized she had overextended her business financially. A large investment in inventory coupled with a sizable lease commitment, the need for office space renovations, the purchase of new furniture, and the addition of three new employees brought her to the point where she lacked the cash to pay her employees their regular salaries. When she had made these decisions, she thought she and her husband (who also works in the company) would be able to generate the revenues to cover the expenditures. But her brother-in-law unexpectedly passed away, and their involvement in family matters meant they weren't able to get new accounts as quickly as she had thought they would.[98]

Still confident that if she could get through this tough period, she would be able to get her business back on track, Borzacchiello decided to be honest with her employees about the company's current financial problems, why they occurred, and how she would strive to prevent such problems in the future. She met with her employees and told them, "All I can tell you is that I apologize. . . . We were so focused on accelerating growth that I didn't see it coming."[99] She admitted she needed to better understand her company's financial situation and daily cash flow, reassured employees that the company would be back on square footing in two to three months, and promised she would pay much more attention to ongoing financial performance and cash flow in the future.[100]

Borzacchiello also told employees that she and her husband would take no money out of the business for their own salaries until the financial problems were resolved. By being honest and open with employees, Borzacchiello gained their commitment and support. All employees decided to work shorter hours, and two employees were willing to have their hourly pay rates cut.[101] True to her promise, within two months, all employees were able to return to their regular work hours; and by the beginning of 2007, Creative Display Solutions had more than $1 million in revenues (which was more than double its revenues at the time of the financial problems).[102] Today, Creative Display Solutions is a profitable multimillion-dollar business with hundreds of clients.[103] Clearly Borzacchiello effectively handled the temporary crisis her company faced by admitting and apologizing for her mistake and being open and honest with employees about her company's future prospects.[104]

Summary and Review

THE NATURE OF LEADERSHIP Leadership is the process by which a person exerts influence over other people and inspires, motivates, and directs their activities to help achieve group or organizational goals. Leaders can influence others because they possess power. The five types of power available to managers are legitimate power, reward power, coercive power, expert power, and referent power. Many managers are using empowerment as a tool to increase their effectiveness as leaders. **LO 10-1**

TRAIT AND BEHAVIOR MODELS OF LEADERSHIP The trait model of leadership describes personal characteristics or traits that contribute to effective leadership. However, some managers who possess these traits are not effective leaders, and some managers who do not possess all the traits are nevertheless effective leaders. The behavior model of leadership describes two kinds of behavior that most leaders engage in: consideration and initiating structure. **LO 10-2**

CONTINGENCY MODELS OF LEADERSHIP Contingency models take into account the complexity surrounding leadership and the role of the situation in determining whether a manager is an effective leader. Fiedler's contingency model explains why managers may be effective leaders in one situation and ineffective in another. According to Fiedler's model, relationship-oriented leaders are most effective in situations that are moderately favorable for leading, and task-oriented leaders are most effective in situations that are very favorable or very unfavorable for leading. House's path–goal theory describes how effective managers motivate their subordinates by determining what outcomes their subordinates want, rewarding subordinates with these outcomes when they achieve their goals and perform at a high level, and clarifying the paths to goal attainment. Managers can engage in four kinds of behaviors to motivate subordinates: directive, supportive, participative, and achievement-oriented behaviors. The leader substitutes model suggests that sometimes managers do not have to play a leadership role because their subordinates perform at a high level without the manager having to exert influence over them. **LO 10-3**

TRANSFORMATIONAL LEADERSHIP Transformational leadership occurs when managers have dramatic effects on their subordinates and on the organization as a whole, and inspire and energize subordinates to solve problems and improve performance. These effects include making subordinates aware of the importance of their own jobs and high performance; making subordinates aware of their own needs for personal growth, development, and accomplishment; and motivating subordinates to work for the good of the organization and not just their own personal gain. Managers can engage in transformational leadership by being charismatic leaders, by intellectually stimulating subordinates, and by engaging in developmental consideration. Transformational managers also often engage in transactional leadership by using their reward and coercive powers to encourage high performance. **LO 10-4**

GENDER AND LEADERSHIP Female and male managers do not differ in the leadership behaviors they perform, contrary to stereotypes suggesting that women are more relationship-oriented and men more task-oriented. Female managers sometimes are more participative than male managers, however. Research has found that women and men are equally effective as managers and leaders. **LO 10-5**

EMOTIONAL INTELLIGENCE AND LEADERSHIP The moods and emotions leaders experience on the job, and their ability to effectively manage these feelings, can influence their effectiveness as leaders. Moreover, emotional intelligence can contribute to leadership effectiveness in multiple ways, including encouraging and supporting creativity among followers. **LO 10-5**

Management *in Action*

 TOPICS FOR DISCUSSION AND ACTION

Discussion

1. Describe the steps managers can take to increase their power and ability to be effective leaders. [LO 10-1]

2. Think of specific situations in which it might be especially important for a manager to engage in consideration and in initiating structure. [LO 10-2]

3. Discuss why managers might want to change the behaviors they engage in, given their situation, their subordinates, and the nature of the work being done. Do you think managers can readily change their leadership behaviors? Why or why not? [LO 10-3]

4. Discuss why substitutes for leadership can contribute to organizational effectiveness. [LO 10-3]

5. Describe what transformational leadership is, and explain how managers can engage in it. [LO 10-4]

6. Imagine that you are working in an organization in an entry-level position after graduation and have come up with what you think is a great idea for improving a critical process in the organization that relates to your job. In what ways might your supervisor encourage you to implement your idea? How might your supervisor discourage you from even sharing your idea with others? [LO 10-4, 10-5]

Action

7. Interview a manager to find out how the three situational characteristics that Fiedler identified affect his or her ability to provide leadership. [LO 10-3]

8. Find a company that has dramatically turned around its fortunes and improved its performance. Determine whether a transformational manager was behind the turnaround and, if one was, what this manager did. [LO 10-4]

BUILDING MANAGEMENT SKILLS

Analyzing Failures of Leadership [LO 10-1, 10-2, 10-3, 10-4]

Think about a situation you are familiar with in which a leader was very ineffective. Then answer the following questions:

1. What sources of power did this leader have? Did the leader have enough power to influence his or her followers?

2. What kinds of behaviors did this leader engage in? Were they appropriate for the situation? Why or why not?

3. From what you know, do you think this leader was a task-oriented leader or a relationship-oriented leader? How favorable was this leader's situation for leading?

4. What steps did this leader take to motivate his or her followers? Were these steps appropriate or inappropriate? Why?

5. What signs, if any, did this leader show of being a transformational leader?

MANAGING ETHICALLY [LO 10-1]

Managers who verbally criticize their subordinates, put them down in front of their coworkers, or use the threat of job loss to influence behavior are exercising coercive power. Some employees subject to coercive power believe that using it is unethical.

Questions

1. Either alone or in a group, think about the ethical implications of the use of coercive power.

2. To what extent do managers and organizations have an ethical obligation to put limits on the amount of coercive power that is exercised?

SMALL GROUP BREAKOUT EXERCISE [LO 10-1, 10-2, 10-3, 10-4]

Improving Leadership Effectiveness

Form groups of three to five people, and appoint one member as the spokesperson who will communicate your findings and conclusions to the class when called on by the instructor. Then discuss the following scenario:

You are a team of human resource consultants who have been hired by Carla Caruso, an entrepreneur who has started her own interior decorating business. A highly competent and creative interior decorator, Caruso has established a working relationship with most of the major home builders in her community. At first she worked on her own as an independent contractor. Then because of a dramatic increase in the number of new homes being built, she became swamped with requests for her services and decided to start her own company.

She hired a secretary–bookkeeper and four interior decorators, all of whom are highly competent. Caruso still does decorating jobs herself and has adopted a hands-off approach to leading the four decorators who report to her because she feels that interior design is a very personal, creative endeavor. Rather than pay the decorators on some kind of commission basis (such as a percentage of their customers' total billings), she pays them a premium salary, higher than average, so they are motivated to do what's best for a customer's needs and not what will result in higher billings and commissions.

Caruso thought everything was going smoothly until customer complaints started coming in. The complaints ranged from the decorators' being hard to reach, promising unrealistic delivery times, and being late for or failing to keep appointments to their being impatient and rude when customers had trouble making up their minds. Caruso knows her decorators are competent and is concerned that she is not effectively leading and managing them. She wonders, in particular, if her hands-off approach is to blame and if she should change the manner in which she rewards or pays her decorators. She has asked for your advice.

1. Analyze the sources of power that Caruso has available to her to influence the decorators. What advice can you give her to either increase her power base or use her existing power more effectively?

2. Given what you have learned in this chapter (for example, from the behavior model and path–goal theory), does Caruso seem to be performing appropriate leader behaviors in this situation? What advice can you give her about the kinds of behaviors she should perform?

3. What steps would you advise Caruso to take to increase the decorators' motivation to deliver high-quality customer service?

4. Would you advise Caruso to try to engage in transformational leadership in this situation? If not, why not? If so, what steps would you advise her to take?

BE THE MANAGER [LO 10-1, 10-2, 10-3, 10-4, 10-5]

You are the CEO of a medium-size company that makes window coverings similar to Hunter Douglas blinds and duettes. Your company has a real cost advantage in terms of being able to make custom window coverings at costs that are relatively low in the industry. However, the performance of your company has been lackluster. To make needed changes and improve performance, you met with the eight other top managers in your company and charged them with identifying problems and missed opportunities in each of their areas and coming up with an action plan to address the problems and take advantage of opportunities.

Once you gave the managers the okay, they were charged with implementing their action plans in a timely fashion and monitoring the effects of their initiatives monthly for the next 8 to 12 months.

You approved each of the managers' action plans, and a year later most of the managers were reporting that their initiatives had been successful in addressing the problems and opportunities they had identified a year ago. However, overall company performance continues to be lackluster and shows no signs of improvement. You are confused and starting to question your leadership capabilities and approach to change. What are you going to do to improve the performance and effectiveness of your company?

THE WALL STREET JOURNAL CASE IN THE NEWS [LO 10-1, 10-2, 10-4, 10-5]
Managers Need to Make Time for Face Time

Alan Buckelew, chief operations officer of **Carnival** Corp., moved to Shanghai last September so he could help the world's biggest cruise-ship company expand in China. He still supervises five executives at its Miami headquarters.

A heavy workload forced Mr. Buckelew to conduct year-end performance reviews for three of those deputies via videoconference but he wasn't happy about it.

"A review is probably the one time when you want to be physically present," Mr. Buckelew says.

He says he apologized to them about his Miami absence, and vows to evaluate every lieutenant face-to-face this year.

As businesses expect more senior leaders to both manage more far-flung teams and spend more time with distant clients, face time has become a precious commodity—and a source of professional agita. Technologies like videoconferencing and enterprise social networks claim to enable true connection over great distances, but the reality is often is far from perfect.

When it comes down to it, there is still no good substitute for being in the same room with a direct report or a high-level boss, many executives say. Yet there is little consensus about how much face time it takes to manage effectively.

"Few executives can deliver business results quickly and engage their people at the same time/," says Matt Paese, vice president of succession management and C-suite services for leadership consultants Development Dimensions International. "But increasingly, our corporate clients try to hire or grow ones who can," because they recognize "they can't sustain business growth without a healthy culture."

Hands-off leadership carries career risks. Take, for example, Louis Chenevert, who abruptly relinquished command of conglomerate **United Technologies** Corp. in November 2014 amid criticism that he was too detached from his top team.

Traveling frequently for work can leave employees without adequate feedback or a boss wondering whether you manage well, suggests Bruce Tulgan, author and chief executive of **Rainmaker Thinking** Inc., a management research and training firm. "You have to be there to problem-solve."

Ramesh Tainwala, CEO of luggage maker **Samonite International S.A.,** says that after advancing into the top job in October, he quickly replaced its head of Latin America because the man ran the region from Denver and spent only 40 days a year in Latin America. (Sam-sonite previously had been based in Denver.)

"Unless you are in the field with your people, it's difficult for you to manage it," he adds.

The new head of Latin America is based in Chile but is almost constantly on the road. Mr. Tainwala told him, "You need to be traveling 20 to 25 days a month" in the new role.

Mr. Tainwala himself travels 25 days a month for **Samsonite** from his base in Hong Kong. Since becoming CEO last fall, he has held four face-to-face sessions with his senior management team, stationed in four regions world-wide. An April 13 session in Mansfield, Mass., will be his third far from Hong Kong.

"A conference call cannot substitute for face-to-face interactions," Mr. Tainwala continues. "When we meet in person, we almost hear each other's thoughts."

Yet a distant boss with a sudden yen for face time may encounter resistance from subordinates. That happened to a senior manager at an environmental consulting firm in 2012.

The manager realized she had been too hands-off with her team, missing meetings due to conflicting client demands, she told Mr. Tulgan of Rainmaker Thinking after attending his seminar about being a highly engaged boss. She soon scheduled half-hour sessions with each team member.

Several staffers bristled at the sudden outreach, complaining that she was micromanaging them, according to Mr. Tulgan. She convened a meeting to explain how her increased engagement could be helpful. "I want you to help me help you," she said. Her team adjusted over time, and that helped her land a higher-level role at a larger rival early last year, Mr. Tulgan says.

Even when the team is nearby, isolated bosses must find ways to appear present. When Rick Russell managed 1,100 people as chief commercial officer of Sunovian Pharmaceuticals Inc., a small drug maker in Marlborough, Mass., his dozen deputies occupied the second floor at headquarters. He toiled behind closed doors in the executive suite two floors above.

After a 2012 employee survey concluded that people felt walled off from their leaders, he decided to make himself more visible. He created a second-floor satellite office surrounded by glass on three sides. Dubbed his "fish-bowl," he worked from the office nearly every Friday, with a deliberately light schedule and no executive assistant.

Wary colleagues gradually grew comfortable about dropping by, Mr. Russell recalls. The chief medical officer adopted the satellite-office idea, too.

The next year's poll showed Sunovian employees' trust for the top brass improved a lot.

"You have to rally the troops. You can't do it from a memo," says Mr. Russell, now CEO of **Greer Laboratories** Inc., a midsize biologies concern.

Mel Berning, chief revenue officer at A+E Networks in New York, takes a different approach. He travels two weeks a month for the cable network. While at headquarters, he says he tries to, avoid "antiseptic" formal meetings and calls with his six direct reports.

Instead, he breezes into somebody's office at 8:30 a.m. "You have a conversation that is less hurried and less guarded," Mr. Berning notes. "Face-to-face encounters are so much more revealing than a text or an email."

Questions

1. Why might making sure to incorporate time for face-to-face interactions be an important component for many managers' personal leadership styles?

2. How might face-to-face interactions contribute to managers effectively engaging in consideration and initiating structure?

3. How might face-to-face interactions help managers effectively engage in transformational leadership?

4. How might emotional intelligence help managers to ensure that they have effective face-to-face interactions?

Source: "Managers Need to Make Time for Face Time" by J. S. Lublin. *The Wall Street Journal*, March 18, 2015, p. B6.

Endnotes

1. I. Faletski, "Yes, You Can Make Money with Open Source," *Harvard Business Review,* http://blogs.hbr .org/2013/01/yes-you-can-make-money-with-op/, May 5, 2014; "The Open Source CEO: Jim Whitehurst," *TechCrunch,* http:// techcrunch.com/2012/04/27/i-would-like-to-work-at-red-hat/, May 5, 2014; Red Hat, Our Company," www.redhat.com/en/about/ company, March 10, 2015.

2. "Great Leaders Are Comfortable with Who They Are," Opensource .com, http://opensource.com/14/3/ leadership-tips-red-hat-earn-respect, May 5, 2014.

3. Faletski, "Yes, You Can Make Money with Open Source."

4. Faletski, "Yes, You Can Make Money with Open Source"; "Red Hat—About Red Hat," www. redhat.com/about/, May 5, 2014; "Red Hat Inc—Form 10-K," EDGAR Online, http://files.shareholders. com/downloads/RHAT/314972675 9x0x51193125-14157171/1087423/ final.pdf, May 6, 2014.

5. "James Whitehurst: Executive Profile & Biography," *Businessweek,* http://investing.businessweek.com/ research/stocks/people/person. asp?personId=1474206&ticker= RHT, May 5, 2014; "Red Hat—Jim Whitehurst," www.redhat.com/ about/company/management/bios/ management-team-jim-whitehurst-bio, May 5, 2014.

6. "James Whitehurst: Executive Profile & Biography."

7. J. Haden, "What's Your Mission?" *Inc.,* April 12, 2013; "Great Leaders Are Comfortable with Who They Are"; J. Bort, "Red Hat CEO: My Employees and I Cuss at Each Other," *Business Insider,* www.businessinsider .com/red-hat-ceo-cussing-at-employees-2013-9, May 5, 2014.

8. Haden, "What's Your Mission?"; "Great Leaders Are Comfortable with Who They Are"; Bort, "Red Hat CEO: My Employees and I Cuss at Each Other"; L.K. Ohnesorge, "Red Hat CEO Jim Whitehurst Doubles as a Cloud Computing Evangelist and Entrepreneur Advisor," http://upstart .bizjournals.com/entrepreneurs/ hot-shots/2014/05/04/passion-drives-red-hat-jim-whitehurst. html?page=all, May 5, 2014.

9. Haden, "What's Your Mission?"; "Great Leaders Are Comfortable with Who They Are"; Bort, "Red Hat CEO: My Employees and I Cuss at Each Other."

10. Haden, "What's Your Mission?"; "Great Leaders Are Comfortable with Who They Are"; Bort, "Red Hat CEO: My Employees and I Cuss at Each Other"; P. High, "Red Hat CEO Jim Whitehurst Opens Up," *Forbes,* www.forbes.com/sites/ peterhigh/2012/12/11/red-hat-ceo-jim-whitehurst-opens-up/, May 5, 2014.

11. "Red Hat CEO Jim Whitehurst to Deliver Keynote Address at the Cloud Factory," www.redhat.com/ about/news/press-archive/2014/4/ red-hat-ceo-jim-whitehurst-to-deliver-keynote-address-at-the-cloud-factory, May 5, 20104.

12. "Planet Earth's Premiere Enterprise Technology Conference," The Cloud Factory, http://thecloudfactory.io/ story/, May 6, 2014.

13. G. Yukl, *Leadership in Organizations,* 2nd ed. (New York: Academic Press, 1989); R.M. Stogdill, *Handbook of Leadership: A Survey of the Literature* (New York: Free Press, 1974).

14. W.D. Spangler, R.J. House, and R. Palrecha, "Personality and Leadership," in B. Schneider and D.B. Smith, eds., *Personality and Organizations* (Mahwah, NJ: Lawrence Erlbaum, 2004), 251–90.

15. Ibid.; "Leaders vs. Managers: Leaders Master the Context of Their Mission, Managers Surrender to It," www.msue.msu.edu/msue/ imp/modtd/visuals/tsld029. htm, July 28, 2004; "Leadership," Leadership Center at Washington State University; M. Maccoby, "Understanding the Difference between Management and Leadership," *Research Technology Management* 43, no. 1 (January–February2000), 57–59, www .maccoby.com/articles/UtD–BMaL. html; P. Coutts, "Leadership vs. Management," www.telusplanet .net/public/pdcoutts/leadership/ LdrVsMgnt.htm, October 1, 2000; S. Robbins, "The Difference between Managing and Leading," www.Entrepreneur.com/ article/0,4621,304743,00.html, November 18, 2002; W. Bennis, "The Leadership Advantage," *Leader to Leader* 12 (Spring 1999), www.pfdf .org/leaderbooks/121/spring99/ bennis/html.

16. Spangler et al., "Personality and Leadership"; "Leaders vs.

Managers"; "Leadership"; Maccoby, "Understanding the Difference between Management and Leadership"; Coutts, "Leadership vs. Management"; Robbins, "The Difference between Managing and Leading"; Bennis, "The Leadership Advantage."

17. "Greenleaf: Center for Servant Leadership: History," *Greenleaf Center for Servant Leadership,* www.greenleaf.org/aboutus/history.html, April 7, 2008.

18. "What Is Servant Leadership?" *Greenleaf: Center for Servant Leadership,* www.greenleaf.org/whatissl/index.html, April 2, 2008.

19. "What Is Servant Leadership?"; Review by F. Hamilton of L. Spears and M. Lawrence, *Practicing Servant Leadership: Succeeding through Trust, Bravery, and Forgiveness* (San Francisco: Jossey-Bass, 2004), in *Academy of Management Review* 30 (October 2005), 875–87; R.R. Washington, "Empirical Relationships between Theories of Servant, Transformational, and Transactional Leadership," *Academy of Management,* Best Paper Proceedings, 2007, 1–6.

20. "Greenleaf: Center for Servant Leadership: History"; "What Is Servant Leadership?"; "Greenleaf: Center for Servant Leadership: Our Mission," *Greenleaf Center for Servant Leadership,* www.greenleaf.org/aboutus/mission.html, April 7, 2008.

21. R. Calori and B. Dufour, "Management European Style," *Academy of Management Executive* 9, no. 3 (1995), 61–70.

22. Ibid.

23. H. Mintzberg, *Power in and around Organizations* (Englewood Cliffs, NJ: Prentice-Hall, 1983); J. Pfeffer, *Power in Organizations* (Marshfield, MA: Pitman, 1981).

24. R.P. French, Jr., and B. Raven, "The Bases of Social Power," in D. Cartwright and A.F. Zander, eds., *Group Dynamics* (Evanston, IL: Row, Peterson, 1960), 607–23.

25. C. Frey, "Nordstrom Salesman's Million-Dollar Secret Is in His Treasured Client List," *Seattle Post-Intelligencer,* Saturday, March 27, 2004, www.seattlepi.com/business/166571_retail27.html, March 5, 2010; "Macy's Herald

Square, New York, NY: Retail Commission Sales Associate—Women's Shoes," http://jobview.monster.com/Macy's-Herald-Square-New-York-NY-Retail-Commission-Sale . . ., March 5, 2010.

26. R.L. Rose, "After Turning Around Giddings and Lewis, Fife Is Turned Out Himself," *The Wall Street Journal,* June 22, 1993, A1.

27. M. Loeb, "Jack Welch Lets Fly on Budgets, Bonuses, and Buddy Boards," *Fortune,* May 29, 1995, 146.

28. T.M. Burton, "Visionary's Reward: Combine 'Simple Ideas' and Some Failures; Result: Sweet Revenge," *The Wall Street Journal,* February 3, 1995, A1, A5.

29. L. Nakarmi, "A Flying Leap toward the 21st Century? Pressure from Competitors and Seoul May Transform the Chaebol," *BusinessWeek,* March 20, 1995, 78–80.

30. B.M. Bass, *Bass and Stogdill's Handbook of Leadership: Theory, Research, and Managerial Applications,* 3rd ed. (New York: Free Press, 1990); R.J. House and M.L. Baetz, "Leadership: Some Empirical Generalizations and New Research Directions," in B.M. Staw and L.L. Cummings, eds., *Research in Organizational Behavior,* vol. 1 (Greenwich, CT: JAI Press, 1979), 341–423; S. A. Kirpatrick and E.A. Locke, "Leadership: Do Traits Matter?" *Academy of Management Executive* 5, no. 2 (1991), 48–60; Yukl, *Leadership in Organizations;* G. Yukl and D.D. Van Fleet, "Theory and Research on Leadership in Organizations," in M.D. Dunnette and L.M. Hough, eds., *Handbook of Industrial and Organizational Psychology,* 2nd ed., vol. 3 (Palo Alto, CA: Consulting Psychologists Press, 1992), 147–97.

31. E.A. Fleishman, "Performance Assessment Based on an Empirically Derived Task Taxonomy," *Human Factors* 9 (1967), 349–66; E.A. Fleishman, "The Description of Supervisory Behavior," *Personnel Psychology* 37 (1953), 1–6; A.W. Halpin and B.J. Winer, "A Factorial Study of the Leader Behavior Descriptions," in R.M. Stogdill and A.I. Coons, eds., *Leader Behavior: Its Description and Measurement* (Columbus Bureau of Business Research, Ohio State University,

1957); D. Tscheulin, "Leader Behavior Measurement in German Industry," *Journal of Applied Psychology* 56 (1971), 28–31.

32. S. Greenhouse, "How Costco Became the Anti-Wal-Mart," *The New York Times,* July 17, 2005, BU1, BU8; "Directors," *Costco Wholesale, Investors Relations,* http://phx.corporate-ir.net/phoenix.zhtml?c=83830&p=irol-govBoard, April 8, 2008; "Company Profile," *Costco Wholesale, Investor Relations,* http://phx.corporate-ir.net/phoenix.zhtml?c=83830&p=irol-homeprofile, May 17, 2012.

33. "Corporate Governance," *Costco Wholesale, Investor Relations,* April 28, 2006, http://phx.corporate-ir.net/phoenix.zhtml?c=83830&p=irol-govhighlights; J. Wohl, "Costco CEO's Legacy Continues as He Steps Down," September 1, 2011, Business & Financial News, Breaking US & International News, *Reuters.com,* http://www.reuters.com/assets/print?aid=USTRE7805VW20110901, May 10, 2012.; A. Gonzalez, "Costco Cofounder Sinegal Honored with Top Retail Award," *The Seattle Times,* January 8, 2014, http://seattletimes.com/html/businesstechnology/2022616694_costcoawardxml.html, May 14, 2014; Costco—Biography," http://phx.corporate-ir.net/phoenix.zhtml?c=83830&p=irol-govBio&ID=202690, May 14, 2014; "Costco—Directors," http://phx.corporate-ir.net/phoenix.zhtml?c=8380&p=irol-govBoard, May 14, 2014; "Costco Wholesale Corporation—Investor Relations, Board of Directors," http://phx.corporate.ir.net/phoenix.zhtml?c=83830&p=irol-govboard, March 10, 2015.

34. Greenhouse, "How Costco Became the Anti-Wal-Mart;" M. Allison, "Costco's Colorful CEO, Cofounder Jim Sinegal to Retire," *The Seattle Times,* August 31, 2011, http://seattletimes.nwsource.com/html/businesstechnology/2016072309_costco01.html, May 10, 2012.

35. Greenhouse, "How Costco Became the Anti-Wal-Mart."

36. Ibid.

37. Ibid.; S. Clifford, "Because Who Knew a Big-Box Chain Could Have a Generous Soul," *Inc.,* April 2005, 88.

38. S. Holmes and W. Zellner, "Commentary: The Costco Way," *BusinessWeek Online,* April 12, 2004, www.businessweek.com/print/magazine/content/04_15/b3878084_mz021.htm? chan . . .; M. Herbst, "The Costco Challenge: An Alternative to Wal-Martization?" *LRA Online,* July 5, 2005, www.laborresearch.org/print.php?id=391.

39. Greenhouse, "How Costco Became the Anti-Wal-Mart."

40. Ibid.; "Company Profile," *Costco Wholesale, Investor Relations,* http://phx.corporate-ir.net/phoenix.zhtml?c=83830&p=irol-homeprofile, April 8, 2008; "Costco—Company Profile," http://phx.corporate-ir.net/phoenix.zhtml?c=83830&p=irol-homeprofile, March 5, 2010; "Company Profile," *Costco Wholesale, Investor Relations,* http://phx.corporate-ir.net/phoenix.zhtml?c=83830&p=irol-homeprofile, May 17, 2012; "Costco—News Release," Costco Wholesale Corporation Reports April Sales Results, http://phx.corporate-ir.net/phoenix.zhtml?c=83830&p=irol-newsArticle&ID=1928586&highlight=, May14, 2014; "Costco Wholesale Corporation Reports Fourth Quarter and Fiscal Year 2014 Operating Results and September Sales Results," http://phx.corporate.ir.net/phoenix.zhtml?c=83830&p=irol-newsArticle&ID=1975151, March 10, 2015.

41. A. Martinez and M. Allison, "Costco, Other Warehouse Clubs Holding Their Own during Recession," *The Seattle Times,* February 1, 2010, http://seattletimes.nwsource.com/cgi-bin/PrintStory.pl?document_id=2010922094&zsection . . ., March 3, 2010; S. Skidmore, "Wholesale Clubs' Profit Grows as Grocery Supermarkets Slide," *USA TODAY,* www.usatoday.com/cleanprint/?1267669249262, March 3, 2010.

42. Costco—Company Profile; "Company Profile," *Costco Wholesale, Investor Relations;* "Costco—News Release: Costco Wholesale Corporation Reports Second Quarter and Year-to-Date Operating Results for Fiscal 2014 and February Sales Results," http://phx.corporate-ir.net/phoenix.zhtml?c=83830&p=irol-newsArticle&ID=1906628&highlight=, May 14, 2014; "Costco Wholesale Corporation Reports Fourth Quarter and Fiscal Year 2014 Operating Results and September Sales Results."

43. "Costco Wholesale Corporation Reports Second Quarter and Year-to-Date Operating Results Fiscal 2006 and February Sales Results," *Costco Wholesale, Investor Relations: News Release,* April 28, 2006, http://phx.corporate-ir.net/phoenix.zhtml?c=83830&p=irol-newsArticle&ID=824344&highlight=; "Costco Wholesale Corporation Reports March Sales Results and Plans for Membership Fee Increase," *Costco Wholesale, Investor Relations: News Release,* April 28, 2006, http://phx.corporate-ir.net/phoenix.zhtml?c=83830&p=irol-newsArticle&ID=839605&highlight=; "Wal-Mart Stores Post Higher January Sales," *BusinessWeek Online,* February 2, 2006, www.businessweek.com/print/investor/conent/feb2006/pi2006022_0732_pi004.htm.

44. Martinez and Allison, "Costco, Other Warehouse Clubs Holding Their Own"; M. Allison, "Costco's Colorful CEO, Co-Founder Jim Sinegal to Retire."

45. "Costco Class Action Discrimination Lawsuit: Women Sue Costco," http://genderclassactionagainstcostco.com/costco94.pl, March 3, 2010; M.C. Fisk and K. Gullo, "Costco Ignored Sex Bias Warnings, Employees Say," www.seattlepi.com/business/284317_costcobias08.html, March 3, 2010; "Costco Job-Bias Lawsuit Advances," *Los Angeles Times,* January 12, 2007, http://articles.latimes.com/2007/jan/12/business/fi-costco12, March 3, 2010.

46. A. Gonzalez, "Costco Settles Promotion Lawsuit for $8M, Vows Reforms," *The Seattle Times,* December 18, 2013, http://seattletimes.com/html/businesstechnology/2022479586_costcosettlementxml.html, May 14, 2014.

47. Ibid.

48. Ibid.

49. E.A. Fleishman and E.F. Harris, "Patterns of Leadership Behavior Related to Employee Grievances and Turnover," *Personnel Psychology* 15 (1962), 43–56.

50. F.E. Fiedler, *A Theory of Leadership Effectiveness* (New York: McGraw-Hill, 1967); F.E. Fiedler, "The Contingency Model and the Dynamics of the Leadership Process," in L. Berkowitz, ed., *Advances in Experimental Social Psychology* (New York: Academic Press, 1978).

51. J. Fierman, "Winning Ideas from Maverick Managers," *Fortune,* February 6, 1995, 66–80; "Laybourne, Geraldine, U.S. Media Executive," *Laybourne, Geraldine,* http://museum.tv/archives/etv/L/htmlL/laybournege/laybournege.htm, April 8, 2008.

52. M. Schuman, "Free to Be," *Forbes,* May 8, 1995, 78–80; "Profile—Herman Mashaba," *SAIE—Herman Mashaba,* www.entrepreneurship.co.za/page/herman_mashaba, April 8, 2008.

53. House and Baetz, "Leadership"; L.H. Peters, D.D. Hartke, and J.T. Pohlmann, "Fiedler's Contingency Theory of Leadership: An Application of the Meta-Analysis Procedures of Schmidt and Hunter," *Psychological Bulletin* 97 (1985), 274–85; C.A. Schriesheim, B.J. Tepper, and L.A. Tetrault, "Least Preferred Co-Worker Score, Situational Control, and Leadership Effectiveness: A Meta-Analysis of Contingency Model Performance Predictions," *Journal of Applied Psychology* 79 (1994), 561–73.

54. M.G. Evans, "The Effects of Supervisory Behavior on the Path–Goal Relationship," *Organizational Behavior and Human Performance* 5 (1970), 277–98; R.J. House, "A Path–Goal Theory of Leader Effectiveness," *Administrative Science Quarterly* 16 (1971), 321–38; J.C. Wofford and L.Z. Liska, "Path–Goal Theories of Leadership: A Meta-Analysis," *Journal of Management* 19 (1993), 857–76.

55. S. Kerr and J.M. Jermier, "Substitutes for Leadership: Their Meaning and Measurement," *Organizational Behavior and Human Performance* 22 (1978), 375–403; P.M. Podsakoff, B.P. Niehoff, S.B. MacKenzie, and M.L. Williams,

"Do Substitutes for Leadership Really Substitute for Leadership? An Empirical Examination of Kerr and Jermier's Situational Leadership Model," *Organizational Behavior and Human Decision Processes* 54 (1993), 1–44.

56. Kerr and Jermier, "Substitutes for Leadership"; Podsakoff et al., "Do Substitutes for Leadership Really Substitute for Leadership?"

57. J. Reingold, "You Got Served," *Fortune,* October 1, 2007, 55–58; "News on Women," *News on Women: Sue Nokes SVP at T-Mobile,* http://newsonwomen.typepad.com/news_on_women/2007/09/sue-nokes-svp-a.html, April 8, 2008.

58. "Company Information," "T-Mobile Cell Phone Carrier Quick Facts," www.t-mobile/Company/CompanyInfo.aspx?tp=Abt_Tab_CompanyOverview, April 8, 2008; "T-Mobile Cell Phone Carrier Quick Facts," www.t-mobile.com/Company/CompanyInfo.aspx?tp=Abt_Tab_CompanyOverview, March 5, 2010; "T-Mobile Company Information/Quick Facts," www.t-mobile.com/Company/CompanyInfo.aspx?tp=Abt_Tab_CompanyOverview, May 17, 2012; T-Mobile Company Information–Quick Facts, www.t-mobile.com/Company/CompanyInfo.aspx?tp=Abt_Tab_CompanyOverview, May 15, 2014.

59. Reingold, "You Got Served."

60. Ibid; "Company Information," "Highest Customer Satisfaction & Wireless Call Quality—J.D. Power Awards," www.t-mobile.com/Company/CompanyInfo.aspx?tp=Abt_Tab_Awards, April 8, 2008.

61. Reingold, "You Got Served."

62. Ibid.

63. B.M. Bass, *Leadership and Performance beyond Expectations* (New York: Free Press, 1985); Bass, *Bass and Stogdill's Handbook of Leadership;* Yukl and Van Fleet, "Theory and Research on Leadership."

64. Reingold, "You Got Served."

65. Ibid.

66. Ibid.

67. Ibid.

68. Ibid.

69. Ibid.

70. J.A. Conger and R.N. Kanungo, "Behavioral Dimensions of Charismatic Leadership," in J.A. Conger, R.N. Kanungo, and Associates, *Charismatic Leadership* (San Francisco: Jossey-Bass, 1988).

71. Bass, *Leadership and Performance beyond Expectations;* Bass, *Bass and Stogdill's Handbook of Leadership;* Yukl and Van Fleet, "Theory and Research on Leadership;" Reingold, "You Got Served."

72. Ibid.

73. Reingold, "You Got Served."

74. Bass, *Leadership and Performance beyond Expectations.*

75. Bass, *Bass and Stogdill's Handbook of Leadership;* B.M. Bass and B.J. Avolio, "Transformational Leadership: A Response to Critiques," in M.M. Chemers and R. Ayman, eds., *Leadership Theory and Research: Perspectives and Directions* (San Diego: Academic Press, 1993), 49–80; B.M. Bass, B.J. Avolio, and L. Goodheim, "Biography and the Assessment of Transformational Leadership at the World Class Level," *Journal of Management* 13 (1987), 7–20; J.J. Hater and B.M. Bass, "Supervisors' Evaluations and Subordinates' Perceptions of Transformational and Transactional Leadership," *Journal of Applied Psychology* 73 (1988), 695–702; R. Pillai, "Crisis and Emergence of Charismatic Leadership in Groups: An Experimental Investigation," *Journal of Applied Psychology* 26 (1996), 543–62; J. Seltzer and B.M. Bass, "Transformational Leadership: Beyond Initiation and Consideration," *Journal of Management* 16 (1990), 693–703; D.A. Waldman, B.M. Bass, and W.O. Einstein, "Effort, Performance, Transformational Leadership in Industrial and Military Service," *Journal of Occupation Psychology* 60 (1987), 1–10.

76. R. Pillai, C.A. Schriesheim, and E.S. Williams, "Fairness Perceptions and Trust as Mediators of Transformational and Transactional Leadership: A Two-Sample Study," *Journal of Management* 25 (1999), 897–933; "About Us," HP, www8.hp.com/us/en/hp-information/about-hp/index.html, May 14, 2012.

77. "50 Most Powerful Women—1. Indra Nooyi (1)—*Fortune,*" http://money.cnn.com/galleries/2009/fortune/0909/gallery.most_powerful_women.fortune/i . . ., March 5, 2010.

78. L. Tischler, "Where Are the Women?" *Fast Company,* February 2004, 52–60.

79. "2000 Catalyst Census of Women Corporate Officers and Top Earners of the *Fortune* 500," www.catalystwomen.org, October 21, 2001; S. Wellington, M. Brumit Kropf, and P.R. Gerkovich, "What's Holding Women Back?" *Harvard Business Review,* June 2003, 18–19; D. Jones, "The Gender Factor," USA *Today.com,* December 30, 2003; "2002 Catalyst Census of Women Corporate Officers and Top Earners in the *Fortune* 500," www.catalystwomen.org, August 17, 2004; "2007 Catalyst Census of Women Corporate Officers and Top Earners of the *Fortune* 500," www.catalyst.org/knowledge/titles/title/php?page=cen_COTE_07, February 8, 2008; "No News Is Bad News: Women's Leadership Still Stalled in Corporate America," December 14, 2011, *Catalyst,* www.catalyst.org/press-release/199/no-news-is-bad-news-womens-leadership-still-sta . . ., April 5, 2012; Knowledge Center – Catalyst.org, Statistical Overview of Women in the Workplace, March 3, 2014, www.catalyst.org/knowledge/statistical-overview-women-workplace, April 1, 2014; "Knowledge Center—Catalyst.org, *Fortune* 500 Executive Officer Top Earner Positions Held by Women," www.catlyst.org/knowledge/women-executive-officer-top-earners-fortune-500-0, April 1, 2014.

80. A.H. Eagly and B.T. Johnson, "Gender and Leadership Style: A Meta-Analysis," *Psychological Bulletin* 108 (1990), 233–56.

81. Ibid.

82. The Economist, "Workers Resent Scoldings from Female Bosses," *Houston Chronicle,* August 19, 2000, 1C.

83. Ibid.

84. Ibid.

85. Ibid.

86. A.H. Eagly, S.J. Karau, and M.G. Makhijani, "Gender and the Effectiveness of Leaders: A

Meta-Analysis," *Psychological Bulletin* 117 (1995), 125–45.

87. Eagly, Karau, and Makhijani, "Gender and the Effectiveness of Leaders: A Meta-Analysis."

88. J.M. George and K. Bettenhausen, "Understanding Prosocial Behavior, Sales Performance, and Turnover: A Group-Level Analysis in a Service Context," *Journal of Applied Psychology* 75 (1990), 698–709.

89. T. Sy, S. Cote, and R. Saavedra, "The Contagious Leader: Impact of the Leader's Mood on the Mood of Group Members, Group Affective Tone, and Group Processes," *Journal of Applied Psychology* 90(2), (2005), 295–305.

90. J.M. George, "Emotions and Leadership: The Role of Emotional Intelligence," *Human Relations* 53 (2000), 1027–55.

91. Ibid.

92. J. Zhou and J.M. George, "Awakening Employee Creativity: The Role of Leader Emotional Intelligence," *The Leadership Quarterly* 14, no. 45 (August–October 2003), 545–68.

93. Ibid.

94. Ibid.

95. D. Fenn, "My Bad," *Inc.*, October 2007, 37–38; *Creative Display Solutions: About Us*, www.creativedisplaysolutions.com/pages/about/about.html, April 4, 2008; *Creative Display Solutions: About Us*, www.creativedisplaysolutions.com/pages/about/about.html, March 5, 2010; "Maureen Borzacchiello—Creative Display Solutions, Inc.," www.savorthesuccess.com/member/maureen-borzacchiello, May 15, 2014; "What We DoTrade Show Marketing Event Services," http://creativedisplaysolutions.com/what-we-do, May 15, 2014; "Who We Are," http://creativedisplaysolutions.com/who-we-are.shtml, March 11, 2015.

96. Fenn, "My Bad"; *Creative Display Solutions: About Us*, www.creativedisplay solutions.com/pages/about/about.html, April 4, 2008.

97. Ibid.

98. Ibid.

99. Ibid.

100. Ibid.

101. Ibid.

102. Ibid.; C. Mason-Draffen, "Inside Stories," "Feeling Like a Million," *Creative Display Solutions: CDS News*, www.creativedisplaysolutions.com/pages/about/news6.html, April 4, 2008.

103. D. Sonnenberg, "Mother Load: How to Balance Career and Family," July 30, 2007, *Creative Display Solutions: CDS News*, www.creativedisplay solutions.com/pages/about/news8.html, April 4, 2008; C. Mason-Draffen, "Partnership at Work: Couples in Business Together Have Their Share of Sweet Rewards and Unique Challenges," February 13, 2007, *Creative Display Solutions, CDS News*, www.creativedisplaysolutions.com/pages/about/news7.html, April 4, 2008; "Client List," *Creative Display Solutions: About Us*, www.creativedisplaysolutions.com/pages/about/clients.html, April 8, 2008; Fenn, "My Bad;" "Client List," *Creative*, www.creativedisplaysolutions.com/pages/about/clients.html, March 5, 2010; "Creative Display Solutions—Who We Are," www.creativedisplaysolutions.com/who-we-are.shtml, May 17, 2012; "What We Do—Trade Show Marketing Event Services," http://creativedisplaysolutions.com/what-we-do, May 15, 2014.

104. Fenn, "My Bad."

11 Effective Team Management

Learning Objectives

After studying this chapter, you should be able to:

LO 11-1 Explain why groups and teams are key contributors to organizational effectiveness.

LO 11-2 Identify the different types of groups and teams that help managers and organizations achieve their goals.

LO 11-3 Explain how different elements of group dynamics influence the functioning and effectiveness of groups and teams.

LO 11-4 Explain why it is important for groups and teams to have a balance of conformity and deviance and a moderate level of cohesiveness.

LO 11-5 Describe how managers can motivate group members to achieve organizational goals and reduce social loafing in groups and teams.

© Digital Vision/Getty Images RF

Gore uses teams to develop new products rather than a hierarchy of managers. Its best-known product is the waterproof fabric Gore-Tex.
© Ruaridh Stewart/ZUMA Press, Inc./ Alamy

MANAGEMENT SNAPSHOT

Teams Innovate at W.L. Gore

How Can Managers Promote High Motivation, Performance, and Innovation?

W. L. Gore & Associates was founded by Wilbert ("Bill") Gore and his wife Genevieve ("Vieve") in the basement of their house in 1958, and the rest has literally been history.[1] Widely recognized for its diverse and innovative products, Gore has more than $3 billion in annual sales and more than 10,000 employees (who are called associates) worldwide.[2] Headquartered in Newark, Delaware, Gore's most widely recognized product is the waterproof fabric Gore-Tex. Gore makes a wide array of products including fabrics for outerwear, medical products used in surgeries, fibers for astronauts' space suits, and Elexir strings for acoustic guitars. While Gore has thousands of products and more than 2,000 worldwide patents, most of Gore's products are based on a very adaptable material, expanded polytetrafluoroethylene (ePTFE), a polymer invented by the Gores' son in 1969.[3] A key ingredient to Gore's enduring success is its use of teams to innovate and motivate rather than relying on a hierarchy of managers.[4]

The Gores were 45 years old and the parents of five children when they took the plunge.[5] Prior to starting his own company, Bill Gore worked at DuPont, which helped him realize how teams can be powerful sources of innovation and high performance. As a member of small R&D teams at DuPont, Gore experienced firsthand how inspiring and motivating it can be to work on a self-managed team with the objective to create and innovate and having high levels of autonomy to do so. He reasoned that innovation and high motivation and performance would likely result when as many people as possible in an organization were members of self-managed teams tasked to be innovative with high levels of autonomy. And that is what he set out to accomplish by founding W. L. Gore. Thus, many teams at Gore have the goal of developing innovative new products.[6]

While Gore has a CEO (Terri Kelly) and four divisions (electronics, fabrics, industrial, and medical), there are few managers, and associates do not have supervisors. Gore is structured around a lattice of self-managed teams in which associates and their teams communicate directly with each other whenever the need or desire arises and are tasked with the mission to innovate, perform highly, and to enjoy their work.[7] Personal initiative and high motivation are greatly valued at Gore, and working in self-managed teams with high levels of autonomy fuels new product innovations.[8] Associates working in manufacturing are also empowered to work in self-managed teams.[9]

At Gore, associates recognize leaders who are especially proficient at building great teams and accomplishing goals and willingly become their followers.[10] New hires at Gore are assigned into broad areas—such as R&D, engineering, sales and marketing, information technology, operations management, and human resources—and assigned a sponsor.[11] Sponsors are experienced associates who help newcomers learn the ropes, meet other associates, and acclimatize to Gore's unique culture and values centered around high trust and motivation. When Jim Grigsby, an electrical engineer, was hired by Gore around 15 years ago, his sponsor told him to spend some time meeting other associates and gave him a list of associates it would be good for him to talk with.[12] Having worked for more traditional and hierarchical companies, Grigsby was surprised by this advice. His thinking: "Am I really getting paid just to meet people?" After gaining an appreciation for Gore's collaborative lattice structure and extensive use of self-managed teams weeks later, Grigsby realized that he had received good advice. As he put it, "It becomes apparent that you need these people to get project work done."[13] Ultimately sponsors help newcomers find a team for which they are a good fit. Teams are truly self-managing, so it is up to the team to decide if they want to have newcomers join them, and the newcomers are responsible to the teams they join. Experienced associates are typically members of multiple self-managed teams.[14]

One of the largest 200 privately held companies in the United States, Gore is owned by the Gore family and associates.[15] Associates are awarded a percentage of their salary in shares of the company and also participate in a profit-sharing program. The shares become vested after a certain time period elapses, and associates who leave the company can sell their shares back for cash payouts.[16]

At Gore, associates are accountable to each other and the teams they are members of. Thus, perhaps it is not surprising that associates are reviewed by their peers. Each year information is gathered from around 20 colleagues of each associate and given to a compensation committee in their work unit that determines relative contributions and compensation levels for members of the unit.[17]

Associates thrive in Gore's collaborative and team-based structure. Thus, it is not surprising that Gore has received recognition for being a top employer. For example, Gore has been on *Fortune* magazine's list of the "100 Best Companies to Work For" for 18 years in a row; in 2015 Gore was 17th on the list.[18] As Gore CEO Terri Kelly indicates, ". . . we take great pride in our continued recognition as a top workplace in the United States and around the world, and we also continue to focus on cultivating an environment where creativity and innovation thrive."[19]

LO11-1 Explain why groups and teams are key contributors to organizational effectiveness.

Overview

W. L. Gore is not alone in using groups and teams to innovate and improve organizational effectiveness. Managers in companies large and small are using groups and teams to enhance performance, increase responsiveness to customers, spur innovation, and motivate employees. In this chapter, we look in detail at how groups and teams can contribute to organizational effectiveness and the types of groups and teams used in organizations. We discuss how different elements of group dynamics influence the functioning and effectiveness of groups, and we describe how managers can motivate group members to achieve organizational goals and reduce social loafing in groups and teams. By the end of this chapter, you will appreciate why the effective management of groups and teams is a key ingredient for organizational performance and effectiveness.

Groups, Teams, and Organizational Effectiveness

A **group** may be defined as two or more people who interact with each other to accomplish certain goals or meet certain needs.[20] A **team** is a group whose members work *intensely* with one another to achieve a specific common goal or objective. As these definitions imply, all teams are groups, but not all groups are teams. The two characteristics that distinguish teams from groups are the *intensity* with which team members work together and the presence of a *specific, overriding team goal or objective.*

group Two or more people who interact with each other to accomplish certain goals or meet certain needs.

team A group whose members work intensely with one another to achieve a specific common goal or objective.

Recall from the "Management Snapshot" how teams at Gore have the goal of developing innovative new products. In contrast, the accountants who work in a small CPA firm are a group: They may interact with one another to achieve goals such as keeping up-to-date on the latest changes in accounting rules and regulations, maintaining a smoothly functioning office, satisfying clients, and attracting new clients. But they are not a team because they do not work intensely with one another. Each accountant concentrates on serving the needs of his or her own clients.

Because all teams are also groups, whenever we use the term *group* in this chapter, we are referring to both groups *and* teams. As you might imagine, because members of teams work intensely together, teams can sometimes be difficult to form, and it may take time for members to learn how to effectively work together. Groups and teams can help an organization gain a competitive advantage because they can (1) enhance its performance, (2) increase its responsiveness to customers, (3) increase innovation, and (4) increase employees' motivation and satisfaction (see Figure 11.1). In this section, we look at each of these contributions in turn.

Groups and Teams as Performance Enhancers

synergy Performance gains that result when individuals and departments coordinate their actions.

One of the main advantages of using groups is the opportunity to obtain a type of **synergy**: People working in a group can produce more or higher-quality outputs than would have been produced if each person had worked separately and all their individual efforts were later combined. The essence of synergy is captured in the saying "The whole is more than the sum of its parts." Factors that can contribute to synergy in groups include the ability of group members to bounce ideas off one another, to correct one another's mistakes, to solve problems immediately as they arise, to bring a diverse knowledge base to bear on a problem or goal, and to accomplish work that is too vast or all-encompassing for any individual to achieve on his or her own.

To take advantage of the potential for synergy in groups, managers need to make sure that groups are composed of members who have complementary skills and knowledge relevant to the group's work. For example, at Hallmark Cards, synergies are created by bringing together all the different functions needed to create and produce a greeting card in a cross-functional team (a team composed of members from different departments or functions). For instance, artists, writers, designers, and marketing experts work together as team members to develop new cards.[21]

Figure 11.1

Groups' and Teams' Contributions to Organizational Effectiveness

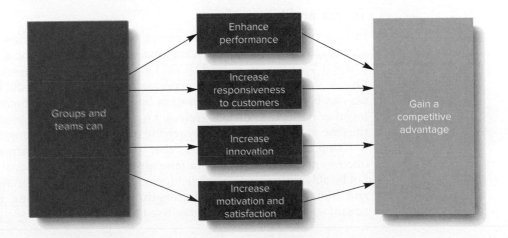

Groups and teams can → Enhance performance → Gain a competitive advantage

Increase responsiveness to customers

Increase innovation

Increase motivation and satisfaction

At Hallmark, the skills and expertise of the artists complement the contributions of the writers and vice versa. Managers also need to give groups enough autonomy so that the groups, rather than the manager, are solving problems and determining how to achieve goals and objectives, as is true in the cross-functional teams at Hallmark and the teams at Gore in the "Management Snapshot." To promote synergy, managers need to empower their subordinates and to be coaches, guides, and resources for groups while refraining from playing a more directive or supervisory role. The potential for synergy in groups may be why more and more managers are incorporating empowerment into their personal leadership styles (see Chapter 10).

Groups, Teams, and Responsiveness to Customers

Being responsive to customers is not always easy. In manufacturing organizations, for example, customers' needs and desires for new and improved products have to be balanced against engineering constraints, production costs and feasibilities, government safety regulations, and marketing challenges. In service organizations such as health maintenance organizations (HMOs), being responsive to patients' needs and desires for prompt, high-quality medical care and treatment has to be balanced against meeting physicians' needs and desires and keeping health care costs under control. Being responsive to customers often requires the wide variety of skills and expertise found in different departments and at different levels in an organization's hierarchy. Sometimes, for example, employees at lower levels in an organization's hierarchy, such as sales representatives for a computer company, are closest to its customers and the most attuned to their needs. However, lower-level employees like salespeople often lack the technical expertise needed for new product ideas; such expertise is found in the research and development department. Bringing salespeople, research and development experts, and members of other departments together in a group or cross-functional team can enhance responsiveness to customers. Consequently, when managers form a team, they must make sure that the diversity of expertise and knowledge needed to be responsive to customers exists within the team; this is why cross-functional teams are so popular.

In a cross-functional team, the expertise and knowledge in different organizational departments are brought together in the skills and knowledge of the team members. Managers of high-performing organizations are careful to determine which types of expertise and knowledge are required for teams to be responsive to customers, and they use this information in forming teams.

Teams and Innovation

Innovation—the creative development of new products, new technologies, new services, or even new organizational structures—is a topic we introduced in Chapter 1. Often, an individual working alone does not possess the extensive and diverse skills, knowledge, and expertise required for successful innovation. Managers can better encourage innovation by creating teams of diverse individuals who together have the knowledge relevant to a particular type of innovation, as has been the case at Gore, rather than by relying on individuals working alone.

Using teams to innovate has other advantages. First, team members can often uncover one another's errors or false assumptions; an individual acting alone would not be able to do this. Second, team members can critique one another's approaches and build off one another's strengths while compensating for weaknesses—an advantage of devil's advocacy discussed in Chapter 5.

To further promote innovation, managers can empower teams and make their members fully responsible and accountable for the innovation process. The manager's role is to provide guidance, assistance, coaching, and the resources that team members need and *not* to closely direct or supervise their activities. To speed innovation, managers also need to form teams in which each member brings some unique resource to the team, such as engineering prowess, knowledge of production, marketing expertise, or financial savvy. Successful innovation sometimes requires that managers form teams with members from different countries and cultures.

Groups and Teams as Motivators

Managers often form groups and teams to accomplish organizational goals and then find that using groups and teams brings additional benefits. Members of groups, and especially members of teams (because of the higher intensity of interaction in teams), are likely to be more satisfied than they would have been if they were working on their own. The experience of working alongside other highly charged and motivated people can be stimulating and motivating: Team members can see how their efforts and expertise directly contribute to the achievement of team and organizational goals, and they feel personally responsible for the outcomes or results of their work. This has been the case at Hallmark Cards.

The increased motivation and satisfaction that can accompany the use of teams can also lead to other outcomes, such as lower turnover. This has been Frank B. Day's experience as founder and chairman of the board of Rock Bottom Restaurants Inc.[22] To provide high-quality customer service, Day has organized the restaurants' employees into waitstaff teams, whose members work together to refill beers, take orders, bring hot chicken enchiladas to the tables, or clear off the tables. Team members share the burden of undesirable activities and unpopular shift times, and customers no longer have to wait until a particular waitress or waiter is available. Motivation and satisfaction levels in Rock Bottom restaurants seem to be higher than in other restaurants, and turnover is about half that experienced in other U.S. restaurant chains.[23]

Working in a group or team can also satisfy organizational members' needs for engaging in social interaction and feeling connected to other people. For workers who perform highly stressful jobs, such as hospital emergency and operating room staff, group membership can be an important source of social support and motivation. Family members or friends may not be able to fully understand or appreciate some sources of work stress that these group members experience firsthand. Moreover, group members may cope better with work stressors when they can share them with other members of their group. In addition, groups often devise techniques to relieve stress, such as the telling of jokes among hospital operating room staff.

LO11-2 Identify the different types of groups and teams that help managers and organizations achieve their goals.

Why do managers in all kinds of organizations rely so heavily on groups and teams? Effectively managed groups and teams can help managers in their quest for high performance, responsiveness to customers, and employee motivation. Before explaining how managers can effectively manage groups, however, we will describe the types of groups that are formed in organizations.

Types of Groups and Teams

To achieve their goals of high performance, responsiveness to customers, innovation, and employee motivation, managers can form various types of groups and teams (see Figure 11.2). **Formal groups** are those that managers

Figure 11.2

Types of Groups and Teams in Organizations

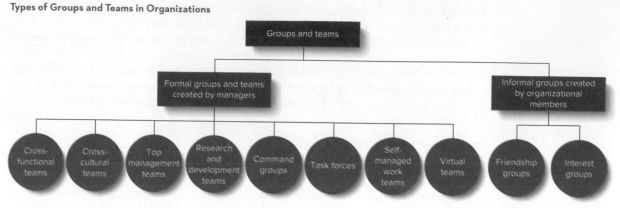

formal group
A group that managers establish to achieve organizational goals.

establish to achieve organizational goals. The formal work groups are *cross-functional* teams composed of members from different departments, such as those at Hallmark Cards, and *cross-cultural* teams composed of members from different cultures or countries, such as the teams at global carmakers. As you will see, some of the groups discussed in this section also can be considered to be cross-functional (if they are composed of members from different departments) or cross-cultural (if they are composed of members from different countries or cultures).

Sometimes organizational members, managers or nonmanagers, form groups because they feel that groups will help them achieve their own goals or meet their own needs (for example, the need for social interaction). Groups formed in this way are **informal groups**. Four nurses who work in a hospital and have lunch together twice a week constitute an informal group.

informal group A group that managers or nonmanagerial employees form to help achieve their own goals or meet their own needs.

The Top Management Team

A central concern of the CEO and president of a company is to form a **top management team** to help the organization achieve its mission and goals. Top management teams are responsible for developing the strategies that result in an organization's competitive advantage; most have between five and seven members. In forming their top management teams, CEOs are well advised to stress diversity in expertise, skills, knowledge, and experience. Thus, many top management teams are also cross-functional teams: They are composed of members from different departments, such as finance, marketing, production, and engineering. Diversity helps ensure that the top management team will have all the background and resources it needs to make good decisions. Diversity also helps guard against *groupthink*—faulty group decision making that results when group members strive for agreement at the expense of an accurate assessment of the situation (see Chapter 5).

top management team A group composed of the CEO, the president, and the heads of the most important departments.

Research and Development Teams

Managers in pharmaceuticals, computers, electronics, electronic imaging, and other high-tech industries often create **research and development teams** to develop new products. Managers select R&D team members on the basis of their expertise and experience in a certain area. Sometimes R&D teams are cross-functional teams with

research and development team
A team whose members have the expertise and experience needed to develop new products.

members from departments such as engineering, marketing, and production in addition to members from the research and development department.

Command Groups

command group A group composed of subordinates who report to the same supervisor; also called *department* or *unit.*

Subordinates who report to the same supervisor compose a **command group**. When top managers design an organization's structure and establish reporting relationships and a chain of command, they are essentially creating command groups. Command groups, often called *departments* or *units,* perform a significant amount of the work in many organizations. In order to have command groups that help an organization gain a competitive advantage, managers not only need to motivate group members to perform at a high level but also need to be effective leaders.

Task Forces

task force A committee of managers or nonmanagerial employees from various departments or divisions who meet to solve a specific, mutual problem; also called an *ad hoc committee.*

Managers form **task forces** to accomplish specific goals or solve problems in a certain time period; task forces are sometimes called *ad hoc committees.* For example, Michael Rider, owner and top manager of a chain of six gyms and fitness centers in the Midwest, created a task force composed of the general managers of the six gyms to determine whether the fitness centers should institute a separate fee schedule for customers who wanted to use the centers only for aerobics classes (and not use other facilities such as weights, steps, tracks, and swimming pools). The task force was given three months to prepare a report summarizing the pros and cons of the proposed change in fee schedules. After the task force completed its report and reached the conclusion that the change in fee structure probably would reduce revenues rather than increase them and thus should not be implemented, it was disbanded. As in Rider's case, task forces can be a valuable tool for busy managers who do not have the time to personally explore an important issue in depth.

Self-Managed Work Teams

self-managed work team A group of employees who supervise their own activities and monitor the quality of the goods and services they provide.

Self-managed work teams are teams in which members are empowered and have the responsibility and autonomy to complete identifiable pieces of work, as is true at W. L. Gore in the "Management Snapshot." On a day-to-day basis, team members decide what the team will do, how it will do it, and which members will perform which specific tasks.[24] Managers can assign self-managed work teams' overall goals (such as assembling defect-free computer keyboards) but let team members decide how to meet those goals. Managers usually form self-managed work teams to improve quality, increase motivation and satisfaction, and lower costs. Often, by creating self-managed work teams, they combine tasks that individuals working separately used to perform, so the team is responsible for the whole set of tasks that yields an identifiable output or end product.

Managers can take a number of steps to ensure that self-managed work teams are effective and help an organization achieve its goals:[25]

- Give teams enough responsibility and autonomy to be truly self-managing. Refrain from telling team members what to do or solving problems for them even if you (as a manager) know what should be done.

- Make sure that a team's work is sufficiently complex so that it entails a number of different steps or procedures that must be performed and results in some kind of finished end product.

- Carefully select members of self-managed work teams. Team members should have the diversity of skills needed to complete the team's work, have the ability to work with others, and want to be part of a team.

- As a manager, realize that your role with self-managed work teams calls for guidance, coaching, and supporting, not supervising. You are a resource for teams to turn to when needed.

- Analyze what type of training team members need and provide it. Working in a self-managed work team often requires that employees have more extensive technical and interpersonal skills.

Managers in a wide variety of organizations have found that self-managed work teams help the organization achieve its goals.[26]

Sometimes, employees not only have individual jobs but also are part of a self-managed team that is formed to accomplish a specific goal or work on an important project. Employees need to perform their own individual job tasks and also actively contribute to the self-managed team so that the team achieves its goal.

Like all groups, self-managed work teams can sometimes run into trouble. Members may be reluctant to discipline one another by withholding bonuses from members who are not performing up to par or by firing members.[27] Buster Jarrell, a manager who oversaw self-managed work teams in AES Corporation's Houston plant, found that although the self-managed work teams were highly effective, they had a difficult time firing team members who were performing poorly.[28]

Virtual Teams

virtual team A team whose members rarely or never meet face-to-face but, rather, interact by using various forms of information technology such as e-mail, computer networks, telephone, fax, and videoconferences.

Virtual teams are teams whose members rarely or never meet face-to-face but, rather, interact by using various forms of information technology such as email, text messaging, computer networks, telephone, fax, and videoconferences. As organizations become increasingly global, and as the need for specialized knowledge increases due to advances in technology, managers can create virtual teams to solve problems or explore opportunities without being limited by team members needing to work in the same geographic location.[29]

Take the case of an organization that has manufacturing facilities in Australia, Canada, the United States, and Mexico and is encountering a quality problem in a complex manufacturing process. Each of its facilities has a quality control team headed by a quality control manager. The vice president for production does not try to solve the problem by forming and leading a team at one of the four manufacturing facilities; instead she forms and leads a virtual team composed of the quality control managers of the four plants and the plants' general managers. When these team members communicate via email, the company's networking site, and videoconferencing, a wide array of knowledge and experience is brought to solve the problem.

The principal advantage of virtual teams is that they enable managers to disregard geographic distances and form teams whose members have the knowledge, expertise, and experience to tackle a particular problem or take advantage of a specific opportunity.[30] Virtual teams also can include members who are not actually employees of the organization itself; a virtual team might include members of a company that is used for outsourcing. More and more companies, including BP PLC, Nokia Corporation, and Ogilvy & Mather, are using virtual teams.[31]

Members of virtual teams rely on two forms of information technology: synchronous technologies and asynchronous technologies.[32] *Synchronous technologies* let virtual team members communicate and interact with one another in real time simultaneously and include videoconferencing, teleconferencing, and electronic meetings. *Asynchronous technologies* delay communication and include email, electronic bulletin boards, and Internet websites. Many virtual teams use both kinds of technology depending on what projects they are working on.

Increasing globalization is likely to result in more organizations relying on virtual teams to a greater extent.[33] One challenge members of virtual teams face is building a sense of camaraderie and trust among team members who rarely, if ever, meet face-to-face. To address this challenge, some organizations schedule recreational activities, such as ski trips, so virtual team members can get together. Other organizations make sure that virtual team members have a chance to meet in person soon after the team is formed and then schedule periodic face-to-face meetings to promote trust, understanding, and cooperation in the teams.[34] The need for such meetings is underscored by research suggesting that while some virtual teams can be as effective as teams that meet face-to-face, virtual team members might be less satisfied with teamwork efforts and have fewer feelings of camaraderie or cohesion. (Group cohesiveness is discussed in more detail later in the chapter.)[35]

Research also suggests that it is important for managers to keep track of virtual teams and intervene when necessary by, for example, encouraging members of teams who do not communicate often enough to monitor their team's progress and making sure that team members actually have the time, and are recognized for, their virtual teamwork.[36] Additionally, when virtual teams are experiencing downtime or rough spots, managers might try to schedule face-to-face team time to bring team members together and help them focus on their goals.[37]

Researchers at the London Business School, including Professor Lynda Gratton, studied global virtual teams to try to identify factors that might help such teams be effective.[38] Based on their research, Gratton suggests that when forming virtual teams, it is helpful to include a few members who already know each other, other members who are well connected to people outside the team, and when possible, members who have volunteered to be a part of the team.[39] It is also advantageous for companies to have some kind of online site where team members can learn more about each other and the kinds of work they are engaged in, and in particular, a shared online workspace that team members can access around the clock.[40] Frequent communication is beneficial. Additionally, virtual team projects should be perceived as meaningful, interesting, and important by their members to promote and sustain their motivation.[41]

Friendship Groups

friendship group
An informal group composed of employees who enjoy one another's company and socialize with one another.

The groups described so far are formal groups created by managers. **Friendship groups** are informal groups composed of employees who enjoy one another's company and socialize with one another. Members of friendship groups may have lunch together, take breaks together, or meet after work for meals, sports, or other activities. Friendship groups help satisfy employees' needs for interpersonal interaction, can provide needed social support in times of stress, and can contribute to people's feeling good at work and being satisfied with their jobs. Managers themselves often form friendship groups. The informal relationships that managers build in friendship groups can often help them solve work-related problems because members of these groups typically discuss work-related matters and offer advice.

Interest Groups

interest group An informal group composed of employees seeking to achieve a common goal related to their membership in an organization.

Employees form informal **interest groups** when they seek to achieve a common goal related to their membership in an organization. Employees may form interest groups, for example, to encourage managers to consider instituting flexible working hours, providing on-site child care, improving working conditions, or more proactively supporting environmental protection. Interest groups can give managers valuable insights into the issues and concerns that are foremost in employees' minds. They also can signal the need for change.

Group Dynamics

How groups function and, ultimately, their effectiveness hinge on group characteristics and processes known collectively as *group dynamics.* In this section, we discuss five key elements of group dynamics: group size and roles, group leadership, group development, group norms, and group cohesiveness.

Group Size and Roles

LO11-3 Explain how different elements of group dynamics influence the functioning and effectiveness of groups and teams.

Managers need to take group size and group roles into account as they create and maintain high-performing groups and teams.

GROUP SIZE The number of members in a group can be an important determinant of members' motivation and commitment and group performance. There are several advantages to keeping a group relatively small—between two and nine members. Compared with members of large groups, members of small groups tend to (1) interact more with each other and find it easier to coordinate their efforts, (2) be more motivated, satisfied, and committed, (3) find it easier to share information, and (4) be better able to see the importance of their personal contributions for group success. A disadvantage of small rather than large groups is that members of small groups have fewer resources available to accomplish their goals.

Large groups—with 10 or more members—also offer some advantages. They have more resources at their disposal to achieve group goals than small groups do. These resources include the knowledge, experience, skills, and abilities of group members as well as their actual time and effort. Large groups also let managers obtain the advantages stemming from the **division of labor**—splitting the work to be performed into particular tasks and assigning tasks to individual workers. Workers who specialize in particular tasks are likely to become skilled at performing those tasks and contribute significantly to high group performance.

division of labor Splitting the work to be performed into particular tasks and assigning tasks to individual workers.

The disadvantages of large groups include the problems of communication and coordination and the lower levels of motivation, satisfaction, and commitment that members of large groups sometimes experience. It is clearly more difficult to share information with, and coordinate the activities of, 16 people rather than 8 people. Moreover, members of large groups might not think their efforts are really needed and sometimes might not even feel a part of the group.

In deciding on the appropriate size for any group, managers attempt to gain the advantages of small group size and, at the same time, form groups with sufficient resources to accomplish their goals and have a well-developed division of labor. As a general rule of thumb, groups should have no more members than necessary to achieve a division of labor and provide the resources needed to achieve group goals. In R&D teams, for example, group size is too large when (1) members spend more time communicating what they know to others than applying what they know to solve problems and create new products, (2) individual productivity decreases, and (3) group performance suffers.[42]

group role A set of behaviors and tasks that a member of a group is expected to perform because of his or her position in the group.

GROUP ROLES A **group role** is a set of behaviors and tasks that a member of a group is expected to perform because of his or her position in the group. Members of cross-functional teams, for example, are expected to perform roles relevant to their special areas of expertise. In our earlier example of cross-functional teams at Hallmark Cards, it is the role of writers on the teams to create verses for new cards, the role of artists to draw illustrations, and the role of designers to put verse and artwork together in an attractive and appealing card design. The roles of members of top management teams are shaped primarily by their areas of expertise—production, marketing, finance, research and development—but members of top management teams also typically draw on their broad expertise as planners and strategists.

In forming groups and teams, managers need to clearly communicate to group members the expectations for their roles in the group, what is required of them, and how the different roles in the group fit together to accomplish group goals. Managers also need to realize that group roles often change and evolve as a group's tasks and goals change and as group members gain experience and knowledge. Thus, to get the performance gains that come from experience or "learning by doing," managers should encourage group members to take the initiative to assume additional responsibilities as they see fit and modify their assigned roles. This process, called **role making**, can enhance individual and group performance.

role making Taking the initiative to modify an assigned role by assuming additional responsibilities.

In self-managed work teams and some other groups, group members themselves are responsible for creating and assigning roles. Many self-managed work teams also pick their own team leaders. When group members create their own roles, managers should be available to group members in an advisory capacity, helping them effectively settle conflicts and disagreements. At Johnsonville Foods, for example, the position titles of first-line managers were changed to "advisory coach" to reflect the managers' role with the self-managed work teams they oversaw.[43]

Group Leadership

All groups and teams need leadership. Indeed, as we discussed in detail in Chapter 10, effective leadership is a key ingredient for high-performing groups, teams, and organizations. Sometimes, managers assume the leadership role in groups and teams, as is the case in many command groups and top management teams. Or a manager may appoint a member of a group who is not a manager to be group leader or chairperson, as is the case in a task force or standing committee. In other cases, group or team members may choose their own leaders, or a leader may emerge naturally as group members work together to achieve group goals. When managers empower members of self-managed work teams, they often let group members choose their own leaders. Some self-managed work teams find it effective to rotate the leadership role among their members. Whether or not leaders of groups and teams are managers, and whether they are appointed by managers (often referred to as *formal leaders*) or emerge naturally in a group (often referred to as *informal leaders*), they play an important role in ensuring that groups and teams perform up to their potential.

When teams do not live up to their promise, sometimes the problem is a lack of team leadership, as illustrated in the accompanying "Ethics in Action" feature.

ETHICS IN ACTION

Leadership in Teams at ICU Medical

Dr. George Lopez, an internal medicine physician, founded ICU Medical in San Clemente, California, in 1984, after a patient of his accidentally died when an intravenous (IV) line became inadvertently disconnected.[44] Lopez thought there must be a better way to design components of IV lines so that these kinds of tragic accidents don't happen. He developed a product called the Click Lock, which has both a locking mechanism for IV systems and also a protected needle so that health care workers are protected from accidental needle pricks.[45] Today, ICU Medical has more than 2,260 employees and revenues more than $313 million.[46] Lopez is a member of the board of directors, and ICU Medical made *Forbes* magazine's list of "The 200 Best Small Companies."[47] ICU Medical continues to focus on the development and manufacture of products that improve the functioning of IV lines and systems while protecting health care workers from accidental needle pricks.[48] For example, the CLAVE NeedleFree Connector for IV lines is one of ICU Medical's top-selling products.[49]

In the early 1990s, Lopez experienced something not uncommon to successful entrepreneurs as their businesses grow. As the entrepreneur–CEO, he continued to make the majority of important decisions himself; yet he had close to 100 employees, demand for the CLAVE was very high, and he was starting to feel overloaded to the point where he would often sleep at nights in the office.[50] After watching one of his son's hockey games, he realized that a well-functioning team could work wonders; in the case of the hockey game, although the opposing team had an outstanding player, his son's team really pulled together as a team and was able to win the game despite the rival team's outstanding member. Lopez decided to empower employees to form teams to work on a pressing goal for ICU Medical: increasing production.[51] While employees did form teams and spent a lot of time in team interactions, the teams did not seem to come up with any real tangible results, perhaps because there were no team leaders in place and the teams had no guidelines to help them accomplish their goals.[52]

In an effort to improve team effectiveness, Lopez told employees that teams should elect team leaders. And together with Jim Reitz, ICU Medical's director of human resources at the time, Lopez came up with rules or guidelines teams should follow, such as "challenge the issue, not the person" and "stand up for your position, but never argue against the facts."[53] ICU Medical also started to reward team members for their team's contributions to organizational effectiveness. With these changes, Reitz and Lopez were striving to ensure that teams had leaders, had some guidelines for team member behavior, and were rewarded for their contributions to organizational effectiveness but, at the same time, were not bogged down by unnecessary constraints and structures and were truly self-managing.[54]

With these changes in place, teams at ICU Medical began to live up to their promise. Today, any ICU Medical employee can create a team to address a problem, seize an opportunity, or work on a project ranging from developing a new product to making improvements in the physical work environment.[55] The teams have leaders and are self-managing.

Recognizing that self-managed teams still need rules, guidelines, leadership, and structure, a team of employees developed a 25-page guidebook for effective team functioning. And to ensure that teams learn from each other as well as get feedback, teams are required to put up notes from each of their meetings on ICU Medical's intranet, and any employee can provide feedback to any of the teams.[56] All in all, effectively led teams have helped ICU Medical prosper in its efforts to develop and manufacture products that protect the safety of both patients and health care workers.

Group Development over Time

As many managers overseeing self-managed teams have learned, it sometimes takes a self-managed work team two or three years to perform up to its true capabilities.[57] As their experience suggests, what a group is capable of achieving depends in part on its stage of development. Knowing that it takes considerable time for self-managed work teams to get up and running has helped managers have realistic expectations for new teams and know that they need to give new team members considerable training and guidance.

Although every group's development over time is unique, researchers have identified five stages of group development that many groups seem to pass through (see Figure 11.3).[58] In the first stage, *forming,* members try to get to know one another and reach a common understanding of what the group is trying to accomplish and how group members should behave. During this stage, managers should strive to make each member feel that he or she is a valued part of the group.

In the second stage, *storming,* group members experience conflict and disagreements because some members do not wish to submit to the demands of other group members. Disputes may arise over who should lead the group. Self-managed work teams can be particularly vulnerable during the storming stage. Managers need to keep an eye on groups at this stage to make sure conflict does not get out of hand.

During the third stage, *norming,* close ties between group members develop, and feelings of friendship and camaraderie emerge. Group members arrive at a consensus about what goals they should seek to achieve and how group members should behave toward one another. In the fourth stage, *performing,* the real work of the group gets accomplished. Depending on the type of group in question, managers need to take different steps at this stage to help ensure that groups are effective. Managers of command groups need to make sure that group members are motivated and that they are effectively leading group members. Managers overseeing self-managed work teams have to empower team members and make sure that teams are given enough responsibility and autonomy at the performing stage.

The last stage, *adjourning,* applies only to groups that eventually are disbanded, such as task forces. During adjourning a group is dispersed. Sometimes, adjourning takes place when a group completes a finished product, such as when a task force evaluating the pros and cons of providing on-site child care produces a report supporting its recommendation.

Managers should have a flexible approach to group development and should keep attuned to the different needs and requirements of groups at the various stages.[59] Above all else, and regardless of the stage of development, managers need to think

LO11-4 Explain why it is important for groups and teams to have a balance of conformity and deviance and a moderate level of cohesiveness.

Figure 11.3

Five Stages of Group Development

Forming → Storming → Norming → Performing → Adjourning

of themselves as *resources* for groups. Thus, managers always should strive to find ways to help groups and teams function more effectively.

Group Norms

All groups, whether top management teams, self-managed work teams, or command groups, need to control their members' behaviors to ensure that the group performs at a high level and meets its goals. Assigning roles to each group member is one way to control behavior in groups. Another important way in which groups influence members' behavior is through the development and enforcement of group norms.[60] **Group norms** are shared guidelines or rules for behavior that most group members follow. Groups develop norms concerning a wide variety of behaviors, including working hours, the sharing of information among group members, how certain group tasks should be performed, and even how members of a group should dress.

group norms Shared guidelines or rules for behavior that most group members follow.

Managers should encourage members of a group to develop norms that contribute to group performance and the attainment of group goals. For example, group norms dictating that each member of a cross-functional team should always be available for the rest of the team when his or her input is needed, return phone calls as soon as possible, inform other team members of travel plans, and give team members a phone number at which he or she can be reached when traveling on business help to ensure that the team is efficient, performs at a high level, and achieves its goals. A norm in a command group of secretaries that dictates that secretaries who happen to have a light workload in any given week should help out secretaries with heavier workloads helps to ensure that the group completes all assignments in a timely and efficient manner. And a norm in a top management team that dictates that team members should always consult with one another before making major decisions helps to ensure that good decisions are made with a minimum of errors.

CONFORMITY AND DEVIANCE Group members conform to norms for three reasons: (1) They want to obtain rewards and avoid punishments. (2) They want to imitate group members whom they like and admire. (3) They have internalized the norm and believe it is the right and proper way to behave.[61] Consider the case of Robert King, who conformed to his department's norm of attending a fund-raiser for a community food bank. King's conformity could be due to (1) his desire to be a member of the group in good standing and to have friendly relationships with other group members (rewards), (2) his copying the behavior of other members of the department whom he respects and who always attend the fund-raiser (imitating other group members), or (3) his belief in the merits of supporting the activities of the food bank (believing that is the right and proper way to behave).

Failure to conform, or deviance, occurs when a member of a group violates a group norm. Deviance signals that a group is not controlling one of its member's behaviors. Groups generally respond to members who behave defiantly in one of three ways:[62]

1. The group might try to get the member to change his or her deviant ways and conform to the norm. Group members might try to convince the member of the need to conform, or they might ignore or even punish the deviant. For example, in a Jacksonville Foods plant, Liz Senkbiel, a member of a self-managed work team responsible for weighing sausages, failed to conform to a group norm dictating that group members should periodically clean up an untidy interview room. Because Senkbiel refused to take part in the team's cleanup efforts, team

members reduced her monthly bonus by about \$225 for a two-month period.[63] Senkbiel clearly learned the costs of deviant behavior in her team.

2. The group might expel the member.

3. The group might change the norm to be consistent with the member's behavior.

This last alternative suggests that some deviant behavior can be functional for groups. Deviance is functional for a group when it causes group members to evaluate norms that may be dysfunctional but are taken for granted by the group. Often, group members do not think about why they behave in a certain way or why they follow certain norms. Deviance can cause group members to reflect on their norms and change them when appropriate.

Consider a group of receptionists in a beauty salon who followed the norm that all appointments would be handwritten in an appointment book and, at the end of each day, the receptionist on duty would enter the appointments into the salon's computer system, which printed out the hairdressers' daily schedules. One day a receptionist decided to enter appointments directly into the computer system when they were being made, bypassing the appointment book. This deviant behavior caused the other receptionists to think about why they were using the appointment book at all. After consulting with the owner of the salon, the group changed its norm. Now appointments are entered directly into the computer, which saves time and reduces scheduling errors.

ENCOURAGING A BALANCE OF CONFORMITY AND DEVIANCE To effectively help an organization gain a competitive advantage, groups and teams need the right balance of conformity and deviance (see Figure 11.4). A group needs a certain level of conformity to ensure that it can control members' behavior and channel it in the direction of high performance and group goal accomplishment. A group also needs a certain level of deviance to ensure that dysfunctional norms are discarded and replaced with functional ones. Balancing conformity and deviance is a pressing concern for all groups, whether they are top management teams, R&D teams, command groups, or self-managed work teams.

The extent of conformity and reactions to deviance within groups are determined by group members themselves. The three bases for conformity just described are powerful forces that more often than not result in group members' conforming to norms. Sometimes, these forces are so strong that deviance rarely occurs in groups, and when it does, it is stamped out.

Managers can take several steps to ensure adequate tolerance of deviance in groups so that group members are willing to deviate from dysfunctional norms and, when deviance occurs in their group, reflect on the appropriateness of the violated norm and change the norm if necessary. First, managers can be role models for the groups and teams they oversee. When managers encourage and accept employees' suggestions for changes in procedures, do not rigidly insist that tasks be accomplished in a certain way, and admit when a norm they once supported is no longer functional, they signal to group members that conformity should not come at the expense of needed changes and improvements. Second, managers should let employees know that there are always ways to improve group processes and performance levels and thus opportunities to replace existing norms with norms that will better enable a group to achieve its goals and perform at a high level. Third, managers should encourage members of groups and teams to periodically assess the appropriateness of their norms.

Figure 11.4
Balancing Conformity
and Deviance in Groups

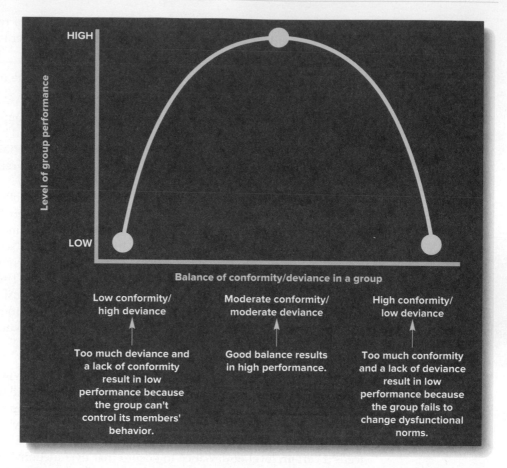

Managers in the innovative design firm IDEO, based in Palo Alto, California (IDEO's culture is described in Chapter 2), have excelled at ensuring that design teams have the right mix of conformity and deviance, resulting in IDEO's designing products in fields ranging from medicine to space travel to computing and personal hygiene, as indicated in the accompanying "Management Insight" feature.

MANAGEMENT INSIGHT

Teams Benefit from Deviance and Conformity at IDEO

IDEO has designed many products we now take for granted: the first Apple mouse, stand-up toothpaste containers, flexible shelving for offices, self-sealing drink bottles for sports, blood analyzers, and even equipment used in space travel.[64] Managers and designers at IDEO take pride in being experts at the process of innovation in general, rather than in any particular domain. Of course, the company has technical design experts, such as mechanical and electrical engineers, who work on products requiring specialized knowledge; but on the same teams with the engineers might be an anthropologist, a biologist, and a social scientist.[65]

A guiding principle at IDEO is that innovation comes in many shapes and sizes, and it is only through diversity in thought that people can recognize opportunities for innovation. To promote such diversity in thought, new product development at IDEO is a team effort.[66] Moreover, both conformity and deviance are encouraged on IDEO teams.

Deviance, thinking differently, and not conforming to expected ways of doing things and mind-sets are encouraged at IDEO. In fact, innovative ideas often flow when designers try to see things as they really are and are not blinded by thoughts of what is appropriate, what is possible, or how things should be. Often, constraints on new product design are created by designers themselves conforming to a certain mind-set about the nature of a product or what a product can or should do and look like. IDEO designers are encouraged to actively break down these constraints in their design teams.[67]

Managers at IDEO realize the need for a certain amount of conformity so members of design teams can work effectively together and achieve their goals. Thus, conformity to a few central norms is emphasized in IDEO teams. These norms include understanding

Both conformity and deviance are encouraged within teams at IDEO, which makes it easier to recognize opportunities for innovation. IDEO has developed many successful products including the first Apple mouse. © OJO Images Ltd/Alamy RF

what the team is working on (the product, market, or client need), observing real people in their natural environments, visualizing how new products might work and be used, evaluating and refining product prototypes, encouraging wild ideas, and never rejecting an idea simply because it sounds too crazy.[68] As long as these norms are followed, diversity of thought and even deviance promote innovation at IDEO. In fact, another norm at IDEO is to study "rule breakers"—people who don't follow instructions for products, for example, or who try to put products to different uses—because these individuals might help designers identify problems with existing products and unmet consumer needs.[69] All in all, IDEO's focus on encouraging both deviance and conformity in design teams has benefited all of us—we use IDEO-designed products that seem so familiar we take them for granted. We forget that these products did not exist until a design team at IDEO was called on by a client to develop a new product or improve an existing one.[70]

Group Cohesiveness

Another important element of group dynamics that affects group performance and effectiveness is **group cohesiveness**, which is the degree to which members are attracted to or loyal to their group or team.[71] When group cohesiveness is high, individuals strongly value their group membership, find the group appealing, and have strong desires to remain a part of the group. When group cohesiveness is low, group members do not find their group particularly appealing and have little desire to retain their group membership. Research suggests that managers should strive to have a moderate level of cohesiveness in the groups and teams they manage because that is most likely to contribute to an organization's competitive advantage.

group cohesiveness The degree to which members are attracted to or loyal to their group.

CONSEQUENCES OF GROUP COHESIVENESS There are three major consequences of group cohesiveness: level of participation within a group, level of conformity to group norms, and emphasis on group goal accomplishment (see Figure 11.5).[72]

LEVEL OF PARTICIPATION WITHIN A GROUP As group cohesiveness increases, the extent of group members' participation within the group increases. Participation contributes to group effectiveness because group members are actively involved in the group, ensure that group tasks get accomplished, readily share information with each other, and have frequent and open communication (the important topic of communication is covered in depth in Chapter 13).

A moderate level of group cohesiveness helps ensure that group members actively participate in the group and communicate effectively with one another. The reason why managers may not want to encourage high levels of cohesiveness is illustrated by the example of two cross-functional teams responsible for developing new toys. Members of the highly cohesive Team Alpha often have lengthy meetings that usually start with nonwork-related conversations and jokes, meet more often than most of the other cross-functional teams in the company, and spend a good portion of their time communicating the ins and outs of their department's contribution to toy development to other team members. Members of the moderately cohesive Team Beta generally have efficient meetings in which ideas are communicated and discussed as needed, do not meet more often than necessary, and share the ins and outs of their expertise with one another to the extent needed for the development process. Teams Alpha and Beta have both developed some top-selling toys. However, it generally takes Team Alpha 30% longer to do so than Team Beta. This is why too much cohesiveness can be too much of a good thing.

LEVEL OF CONFORMITY TO GROUP NORMS Increasing levels of group cohesiveness result in increasing levels of conformity to group norms, and when cohesiveness becomes high, there may be so little deviance in groups that group members conform to norms even when they are dysfunctional. In contrast, low cohesiveness can result in too much deviance and undermine the ability of a group to control its members' behaviors to get things done.

Figure 11.5

Sources and Consequences of Group Cohesiveness

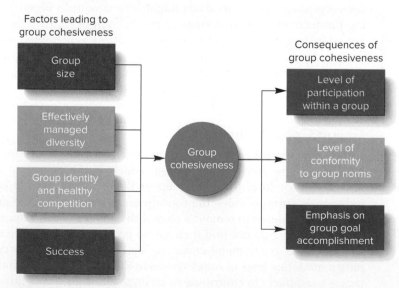

How much cohesiveness is too much? You can answer that question when you evaluate whether a group actually gets something done in its meetings or whether most of the conversation drifting out of the room consists of jokes, life experiences, or comparisons of the last company dinner's entrees. © Associated Press/AP Images RF

Teams Alpha and Beta in the toy company both had the same norm for toy development. It dictated that members of each team would discuss potential ideas for new toys, decide on a line of toys to pursue, and then have the team member from R&D design a prototype. Recently a new animated movie featuring a family of rabbits produced by a small film company was an unexpected hit, and major toy companies were scrambling to reach licensing agreements to produce toy lines featuring the rabbits. The top management team in the toy company assigned Teams Alpha and Beta to develop the new toy lines quickly to beat the competition.

Members of Team Alpha followed their usual toy development norm even though the marketing expert on the team believed that the process could have been streamlined to save time. The marketing expert on Team Beta urged the team to deviate from its toy development norm. She suggested that the team not have R&D develop prototypes but, instead, modify top-selling toys the company already made to feature rabbits and then reach a licensing agreement with the film company based on the high sales potential (given the company's prior success). Once the licensing agreement was signed, the company could take the time needed to develop innovative and unique rabbit toys with more input from R&D.

As a result of the willingness of the marketing expert on Team Beta to deviate from the norm for toy development, the toy company obtained an exclusive licensing agreement with the film company and had its first rabbit toys on the shelves of stores in a record three months. Groups need a balance of conformity and deviance, so a moderate level of cohesiveness often yields the best outcome, as it did in the case of Team Beta.

EMPHASIS ON GROUP GOAL ACCOMPLISHMENT As group cohesiveness increases, the emphasis placed on group goal accomplishment also increases within a group. A strong emphasis on group goal accomplishment, however, does not always lead to organizational effectiveness. For an organization to be effective and gain a competitive advantage, the different groups and teams in the organization must cooperate with one another and be motivated to achieve *organizational goals*, even if doing so sometimes comes at the expense of the achievement of group goals. A moderate level of cohesiveness motivates group members to accomplish both group and organizational goals. High levels of cohesiveness can cause group members to be so focused on group goal accomplishment that they may strive to achieve group goals no matter what—even when doing so jeopardizes organizational performance.

At the toy company, the major goal of the cross-functional teams was to develop new toy lines that were truly innovative, utilized the latest in technology, and were in some way fundamentally distinct from other toys on the market. When it came to the rabbit project, Team Alpha's high level of cohesiveness contributed to its continued emphasis on its group goal of developing an innovative line of toys; thus, the team stuck with its usual design process. Team Beta, in contrast, realized that developing the new line of toys quickly was an important organizational goal that should take precedence over the group's goal of developing groundbreaking new toys, at least in the short term. Team Beta's moderate level of cohesiveness contributed to team members' doing what was best for the toy company in this case.

FACTORS LEADING TO GROUP COHESIVENESS Four factors contribute to the level of group cohesiveness (see Figure 11.5).[73] By influencing these *determinants of group cohesiveness,* managers can raise or lower the level of cohesiveness to promote moderate levels of cohesiveness in groups and teams.

Group Size As we mentioned earlier, members of small groups tend to be more motivated and committed than members of large groups. Thus to promote cohesiveness in groups, when feasible, managers should form groups that are small to medium in size (about 2 to 15 members). If a group is low in cohesiveness and large in size, managers might want to consider dividing the group in half and assigning different tasks and goals to the two newly formed groups.

Effectively Managed Diversity In general, people tend to like and get along with others who are similar to themselves. It is easier to communicate with someone, for example, who shares your values, has a similar background, and has had similar experiences. However, as discussed in Chapter 3, diversity in groups, teams, and organizations can help an organization gain a competitive advantage. Diverse groups often come up with more innovative and creative ideas. One reason why cross-functional teams are so popular in organizations like Hallmark Cards is that the diverse expertise represented in the teams results in higher levels of team performance.

In forming groups and teams, managers need to make sure that the diversity in knowledge, experience, expertise, and other characteristics necessary for group goal accomplishment is represented in the new groups. Managers then have to make sure that this diversity in group membership is effectively managed so groups will be cohesive (see Chapter 3).

Group Identity And Healthy Competition When group cohesiveness is low, managers can often increase it by encouraging groups to develop their own identities or personalities and engage in healthy competition. This is precisely what managers at Eaton Corporation's manufacturing facility in Lincoln, Illinois, did. Eaton's employees manufacture products such as engine valves, gears, truck axles, and circuit breakers. Managers at Eaton created self-managed work teams to cut costs and improve performance. They realized, however, that the teams would have to be cohesive to ensure that they would strive to achieve their goals. Managers promoted group identity by having the teams give themselves names such as "The Hoods," "The Worms," and "Scrap Attack" (a team striving to reduce costly scrap metal waste by 50%). Healthy competition among groups was promoted by displaying measures of each team's performance and the extent to which teams met their goals on a large TV screen in the cafeteria and by rewarding team members for team performance.[74]

If groups are too cohesive, managers can try to decrease cohesiveness by promoting organizational (rather than group) identity and making the organization as a whole the focus of the group's efforts. Organizational identity can be promoted by making group members feel that they are valued members of the organization and by stressing cooperation across groups to promote the achievement of organizational goals. Excessive levels of cohesiveness also can be reduced by reducing or eliminating competition among groups and rewarding cooperation.

Success When it comes to promoting group cohesiveness, there is more than a grain of truth to the saying "Nothing succeeds like success." As groups become more successful, they become increasingly attractive to their members, and their cohesiveness tends to increase. When cohesiveness is low, managers can increase cohesiveness by making sure that a group can achieve some noticeable and visible successes.

Consider a group of salespeople in the housewares department of a medium-size department store. The housewares department was recently moved to a corner of the store's basement. Its remote location resulted in low sales because of infrequent customer traffic in that part of the store. The salespeople, who were generally evaluated favorably by their supervisors and were valued members of the store, tried various initiatives to boost sales, but to no avail. As a result of this lack of success and the poor performance of their department, their cohesiveness started to plummet. To increase and preserve the cohesiveness of the group, the store manager implemented a group-based incentive across the store. In any month, members of the group with the best attendance and punctuality records would have their names and pictures posted on a bulletin board in the cafeteria and would each receive a $50 gift certificate. The housewares group frequently had the best records, and their success on this dimension helped to build and maintain their cohesiveness. Moreover, this initiative boosted attendance and discouraged lateness throughout the store.

Managing Groups and Teams for High Performance

Now that you understand why groups and teams are so important for organizations, the types of groups managers create, and group dynamics, we consider some additional steps managers can take to make sure groups and teams perform at a high level and contribute to organizational effectiveness. Managers striving to have top-performing groups and teams need to motivate group members to work toward the achievement of organizational goals and reduce social loafing.

LO11-5 Describe how managers can motivate group members to achieve organizational goals and reduce social loafing in groups and teams.

Motivating Group Members to Achieve Organizational Goals

When work is difficult, tedious, or requires a high level of commitment and energy, managers cannot assume that group members will always be motivated to work toward the achievement of organizational goals. Consider a group of house painters who paint the interiors and exteriors of new homes for a construction company and are paid on an hourly basis. Why should they strive to complete painting jobs quickly and efficiently if doing so will just make them feel more tired at the end of the day and they will not receive any tangible benefits? It makes more sense for the painters to adopt a relaxed approach, to take frequent breaks, and to work at a leisurely pace. This relaxed approach, however, impairs the construction company's ability to gain a competitive advantage because it raises costs and increases the time needed to complete a new home.

Managers can motivate members of groups and teams to achieve organizational goals by making sure that the members themselves benefit when the group or team performs highly. For example, if members of a self-managed work team know they will receive a weekly bonus based on team performance, they will be motivated to perform at a high level.

Managers often rely on some combination of individual and group-based incentives to motivate members of groups and teams to work toward the achievement of organizational goals. When individual performance within a group can be assessed, pay is often determined by individual performance or by both individual and group performance. When individual performance within a group cannot be accurately assessed, group performance should be the key determinant of pay levels. Many companies, that use self-managed work teams, base team members' pay in part on team performance.[75] A major challenge for managers is to develop a fair pay system that will lead to both high individual motivation and high group or team performance.

Other benefits managers can make available to high-performing group members—in addition to monetary rewards—include extra resources such as equipment and computer software, awards and other forms of recognition, and choice of future work assignments. For example, members of self-managed work teams that develop new software at companies such as Microsoft often value working on interesting and important projects; members of teams that have performed at a high level are rewarded by being assigned to interesting and important new projects.

At IDEO (profiled earlier in a "Management Insight" feature), managers motivate team members by making them feel important. As Tom Kelley, a partner at IDEO, put it, "When people feel special, they'll perform beyond your wildest dreams."[76] To make IDEO team members feel special, IDEO managers plan unique and fun year-end parties, give teams the opportunity to take time off if they feel they need or want to, encourage teams to take field trips, and see pranks as a way to incorporate fun into the workplace.[77]

Reducing Social Loafing in Groups

social loafing The tendency of individuals to put forth less effort when they work in groups than when they work alone.

We have been focusing on the steps managers can take to encourage high levels of performance in groups. Managers, however, need to be aware of an important downside to group and team work: the potential for social loafing, which reduces group performance. **Social loafing** is the tendency of individuals to put forth less effort when they work in groups than when they work alone.[78] Have you ever worked on a group project in which one or two group members never seemed to be pulling their weight? Have you ever worked in a student club or committee in which some members always seemed to be missing meetings and never volunteered for activities? Have you ever had a job in which one or two of your coworkers seemed to be slacking off because they knew you or other members of your work group would make up for their low levels of effort? If so, you have witnessed social loafing in action.

Social loafing can occur in all kinds of groups and teams and in all kinds of organizations. It can result in lower group performance and may even prevent a group from attaining its goals. Fortunately, managers can take steps to reduce social loafing and sometimes completely eliminate it; we will look at three (see Figure 11.6):

1. *Make individual contributions to a group identifiable.* Some people may engage in social loafing when they work in groups because they think they can hide in the crowd—no one will notice if they put forth less effort than they should. Other people may think if they put forth high levels of effort and make substantial contributions to the group, their contributions will not be noticed and they will receive no rewards for their work—so why bother?[79]

One way that managers can effectively eliminate social loafing is by making individual contributions to a group identifiable so that group members perceive that low and high levels of effort will be noticed and individual contributions evaluated.[80] Managers can accomplish this by assigning specific tasks to group members and holding them accountable for their completion. Take the case of a group of eight

Figure 11.6

Three Ways to Reduce Social Loafing

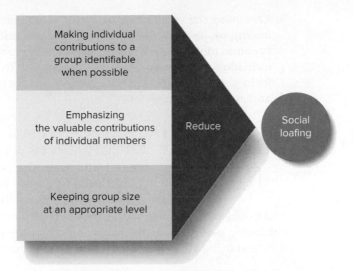

employees responsible for reshelving returned books in a large public library in New York. The head librarian was concerned that there was always a backlog of seven or eight carts of books to be reshelved, even though the employees never seemed to be particularly busy and some even found time to sit down and read newspapers and magazines. The librarian decided to try to eliminate the apparent social loafing by assigning each employee sole responsibility for reshelving a particular section of the library. Because the library's front desk employees sorted the books by section on the carts as they were returned, holding the shelvers responsible for particular sections was easily accomplished. Once the shelvers knew the librarian could identify their effort or lack thereof, there were rarely any backlogs of books to be reshelved.

Sometimes, the members of a group can cooperate to eliminate social loafing by making individual contributions identifiable. For example, in a small security company, members of a self-managed work team who assemble control boxes for home alarm systems start each day by deciding who will perform which tasks that day and how much work each member and the group as a whole should strive to accomplish. Each team member knows that, at the end of the day, the other team members will know exactly how much he or she has accomplished. With this system in place, social loafing never occurs in the team. Remember, however, that in some teams, individual contributions cannot be made identifiable.

2. *Emphasize the valuable contributions of individual members.* Another reason why social loafing may occur is that people sometimes think their efforts are unnecessary or unimportant when they work in a group. They feel the group will accomplish its goals and perform at an acceptable level whether or not they personally perform at a high level. To counteract this belief, when managers form groups, they should assign individuals to a group on the basis of the valuable contributions that *each* person can make to the group as a whole. Clearly communicating to group members why each person's contributions are valuable to the group is an effective means by which managers and group members themselves can reduce or eliminate social loafing.[81] This is most clearly illustrated in cross-functional teams, where each member's valuable contribution to the team derives from a personal area of expertise. By emphasizing why each member's skills are important, managers can reduce social loafing in such teams.

3. *Keep group size at an appropriate level.* Group size is related to the causes of social loafing we just described. As size increases, identifying individual contributions becomes increasingly difficult, and members are increasingly likely to think their individual contributions are not important. To overcome this, managers should form groups with no more members than are needed to accomplish group goals and perform at a high level.[82]

Summary and Review

GROUPS, TEAMS, AND ORGANIZATIONAL EFFECTIVENESS A group is two or more people who interact with each other to accomplish certain goals or meet certain needs. A team is a group whose members work intensely with one another to achieve a specific common goal or objective. Groups and teams can contribute to organizational effectiveness by enhancing performance, increasing responsiveness to customers, increasing innovation, and being a source of motivation for their members. [LO11-1]

TYPES OF GROUPS AND TEAMS Formal groups are groups that managers establish to achieve organizational goals; they include cross-functional teams, cross-cultural teams, top management teams, research and development teams, command groups, task forces, self-managed work teams, and virtual teams. Informal groups are groups that employees form because they believe that the groups will help them achieve their own goals or meet their needs; they include friendship groups and interest groups. [LO11-2]

GROUP DYNAMICS Key elements of group dynamics are group size and roles, group leadership, group development, group norms, and group cohesiveness. The advantages and disadvantages of large and small groups suggest that managers should form groups with no more members than are needed to provide the group with the human resources it needs to achieve its goals and use a division of labor. A group role is a set of behaviors and tasks that a member of a group is expected to perform because of his or her position in the group. All groups and teams need leadership. [LO11-3]

Five stages of development that many groups pass through are forming, storming, norming, performing, and adjourning. Group norms are shared rules for behavior that most group members follow. To be effective, groups need a balance of conformity and deviance. Conformity allows a group to control its members' behavior to achieve group goals; deviance provides the impetus for needed change. [LO11-3, 11-4]

Group cohesiveness is the attractiveness of a group or team to its members. As group cohesiveness increases, so do the level of participation and communication within a group, the level of conformity to group norms, and the emphasis on group goal accomplishment. Managers should strive to achieve a moderate level of group cohesiveness in the groups and teams they manage. [LO11-4]

MANAGING GROUPS AND TEAMS FOR HIGH PERFORMANCE To make sure that groups and teams perform at a high level, managers need to motivate group members to work toward the achievement of organizational goals and reduce social loafing. Managers can motivate members of groups and teams to work toward the achievement of organizational goals by making sure that members personally benefit when the group or team performs at a high level. [LO11-5]

Management *in Action*

TOPICS FOR DISCUSSION AND ACTION

Discussion

1. Why do all organizations need to rely on groups and teams to achieve their goals and gain a competitive advantage? [LO11-1]

2. What kinds of employees would prefer to work in a virtual team? What kinds of employees would prefer to work in a team that meets face-to-face? [LO11-2]

3. Think about a group that you are a member of, and describe that group's current stage of development. Does the development of this group seem to be following the forming, storming, norming, performing, and adjourning stages described in the chapter? [LO11-3]

4. Discuss the reasons why too much conformity can hurt groups and their organizations. [LO11-4]

5. Why do some groups have very low levels of cohesiveness? [LO11-4]

6. Imagine that you are the manager of a hotel. What steps will you take to reduce social loafing by members of the cleaning staff who are responsible for keeping all common areas and guest rooms spotless? [LO11-5]

Action

7. Interview one or more managers in an organization in your local community to identify the types of groups and teams that the organization uses to achieve its goals. What challenges do these groups and teams face? [LO11-2]

BUILDING MANAGEMENT SKILLS

Diagnosing Group Failures [LO11-1, 11-2, 11-3, 11-4, 11-5]

Think about the last dissatisfying or discouraging experience you had as a member of a group or team. Perhaps the group did not accomplish its goals, perhaps group members could agree about nothing, or perhaps there was too much social loafing. Now answer the following questions:

1. What type of group was this?

2. Were group members motivated to achieve group goals? Why or why not?

3. How large was the group, and what group roles did members play?

4. What were the group's norms? How much conformity and deviance existed in the group?

5. How cohesive was the group? Why do you think the group's cohesiveness was at this level? What consequences did this level of group cohesiveness have for the group and its members?

6. Was social loafing a problem in this group? Why or why not?

7. What could the group's leader or manager have done differently to increase group effectiveness?

8. What could group members have done differently to increase group effectiveness?

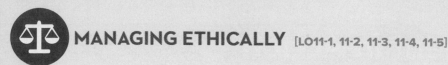

MANAGING ETHICALLY [LO11-1, 11-2, 11-3, 11-4, 11-5]

Some self-managed teams encounter a vexing problem: One or more members engage in social loafing, and other members are reluctant to try to rectify the situation. Social loafing can be especially troubling if team members' pay is based on team performance and social loafing reduces the team's performance and thus the pay of all members (even the highest performers). Even if managers are aware of the problem, they may be reluctant to take action because the team is supposedly self-managing.

Questions

1. Either individually or in a group, think about the ethical implications of social loafing in a self-managed team.

2. Do managers have an ethical obligation to step in when they are aware of social loafing in a self-managed team? Why or why not? Do other team members have an obligation to try to curtail the social loafing? Why or why not?

SMALL GROUP BREAKOUT EXERCISE [LO11-1, 11-2, 11-3, 11-4, 11-5]
Creating a Cross-Functional Team

Form groups of three or four people, and appoint one member as the spokesperson who will communicate your findings to the class when called on by the instructor. Then discuss the following scenario:

You are a group of managers in charge of food services for a large state university in the Midwest. Recently, a survey of students, faculty, and staff was conducted to evaluate customer satisfaction with the food services provided by the university's eight cafeterias. The results were disappointing, to put it mildly. Complaints ranged from dissatisfaction with the type and range of meals and snacks provided, operating hours, and food temperature to frustration about unresponsiveness to current concerns about healthful diets and the needs of vegetarians. You have decided to form a cross-functional team that will further evaluate reactions to the food services and will develop a proposal for changes to be made to increase customer satisfaction.

1. Indicate who should be on this important cross-functional team, and explain why.

2. Describe the goals the team should strive to achieve.

3. Describe the different roles that will need to be performed on this team.

4. Describe the steps you will take to help ensure that the team has a good balance between conformity and deviance and has a moderate level of cohesiveness.

BE THE MANAGER [LO11-1, 11-2, 11-3, 11-4, 11-5]

You were recently hired in a boundary-spanning role for the global unit of an educational and professional publishing company. The company is headquartered in New York (where you work) and has divisions in multiple countries. Each division is responsible for translating, manufacturing, marketing, and selling a set of books in its country. Your responsibilities include interfacing with managers in each of the divisions in your region (Central and South America), overseeing their budgeting and financial reporting to headquarters, and leading a virtual team consisting of the top managers in charge of each of the divisions in your region. The virtual team's mission is to promote global learning, explore new potential opportunities and markets, and address ongoing problems. You communicate directly with division managers via telephone and email, as well as written reports, memos, and faxes. When virtual team meetings are convened, video-conferencing is often used.

After your first few virtual team meetings, you noticed that the managers seemed to be reticent about speaking up. Interestingly enough, when each manager communicates with you individually, primarily in telephone conversations and e-mails, she or he tends to be forthcoming and frank, and you feel you have a good rapport with each of them. However, getting the managers to communicate with one another as a virtual team has been a real challenge. At the last meeting you tried to prompt some of the managers to raise issues relevant to the agenda that you knew were on their minds from your individual conversations with them. Surprisingly, the managers skillfully avoided informing their teammates about the heart of the issues in question. You are confused and troubled. Although you feel your other responsibilities are going well, you know your virtual team is not operating like a team at all; and no matter what you try, discussions in virtual team meetings are forced and generally unproductive. What are you going to do to address this problem?

THE WALL STREET JOURNAL CASE IN THE NEWS [LO11-3, 11-4, 11-5]

Thinking of Quitting? The Boss Knows

Employers want to know who has one foot out the door.

As turnover becomes a bigger worry—and expense—in a tightening labor market, companies including Wal-Mart Stores Inc., Credit Suisse Group AG and Box Inc. are analyzing a vast array of data points to determine who is likely to leave.

The idea, say people who run analytics teams, is to give managers early warning so they can take action before employees jump ship.

Corporate data crunchers play with dozens of factors, which may include job tenure, geography, performance reviews, employee surveys, communication patterns and even personality tests to identify flight risks, a term human-resources departments sometimes use for people likely to leave.

The data often reveal a complex picture of what motivates workers to stay—and what causes them to look elsewhere.

At Box, for example, a worker's pay or relationship with his boss matters far less than how connected the worker feels to his team, according to an analysis from human-resources analytics firm Culture Amp. At Credit Suisse, managers' performance and team size turn out to be surprisingly powerful influences, with a spike in attrition among employees working on large teams with low-rated managers.

Human-resources software company Ultimate Software Group Inc. has a product that assigns clients' employees, and even its own workers, individual "retention predictor" numbers, similar to a credit score, to indicate the likelihood that a worker will leave.

As the employment picture improves, companies are focusing more on retaining workers, largely because replacing them is costly. The median cost of turnover for most jobs is about 21% of an employee's annual salary, according to the Center for American Progress, a liberal-leaning think tank.

William Wolf, Credit Suisse's global head of talent acquisition and development, says a one-point reduction in unwanted attrition rates saves the bank $75 million to $100 million a year.

No single piece of data predicts whether an employee will stay or go, though many employers wish it were so. Data scientists create models to predict which workers might leave a company in the near future, combining a range of variables and testing the predictions over time.

"One of the things that people want to find is that one nugget, that key thing that correlates with someone leaving, but it is never that simple," says Thomas Daglis, a data scientist at Ultimate Software.

Employers may not mind that some employees are at risk of leaving, though companies stress that they are using the data to find ways to improve retention, and not nudge people out.

Those caveats aside, data scientists who study retention say they have found some meaningful correlations.

VoloMetrix Inc., which examines HR data as well as anonymized employee email and calendar data, found that it could predict flight risk up to a year in advance for employees who were spending less time interacting with certain colleagues or attending events beyond required meetings. And Ultimate Software found a correlation between a client's employees who waived their benefits coverage and those who left the company.

The big challenge for employers is what, exactly, to do with the information. Some aren't sure how to approach employees at risk of leaving.

"Our goal is to never say the only reason we are coming to talk to you is because an algorithm told us to do so," says John Callery, director of people analytics at AOL Inc., which recently started working with workforce analytics firm Visier Inc. on a program to help predict attrition down to the individual employee.

For the past three years, Credit Suisse has studied what happens to employees over time, including raises, promotions, and life transitions, to predict whether they will choose to stay or leave the bank in the subsequent year. Changing jobs makes people "sticky," or likely to stay on, says Mr. Wolf, who oversees the bank's people analytics team. Yet as recently as five years ago, fewer than half of open jobs at the bank were posted, and most went to outsiders.

About a year and a half ago, the bank launched a global effort allowing its workers to raise their hands for internal moves. Credit Suisse recruiters now post 80% of open jobs, and cold-call employees when jobs open up.

After observing that some who volunteered to be considered for internal moves ended up leaving for jobs elsewhere, bank recruiters began using attrition probability estimates in deciding which employees to target when positions opened up.

Some 300 people have been promoted through the internal program; many of those people, Mr. Wolf says, might have left otherwise. "We believe we've saved a number of them from taking jobs at other banks."

To kindle closeness among team members, and help forestall attrition, Box has encouraged managers to throw more social events, recognize team-based work and hold more mentoring meetings between senior leaders and newer employees. Since workers were more likely to leave if they didn't see clear career opportunities at the company, it has sought to improve at pointing out career possibilities for individual workers and encouraging "stretch" assignments.

Semiconductor maker Micron Technology Inc. is using data in its efforts to reduce turnover among first-year employees, who have about a 20% world-wide attrition rate, largely driven by manufacturing personnel.

Among its early findings, Micron discovered that workers were more likely to leave if they felt their job hadn't been accurately described when they were hired, so the company is trying to create clearer job descriptions. Micron also found that people who relocated for a job were more likely to leave, but it isn't sure why.

"It's very delicate how you approach things," says Timothy Long, the company's director of workforce analytics and systems. "The idea is to determine, what can we do to get [people] to stay?"

Companies also are trying to predict when workers might leave their positions, but not necessarily the company. Wal-Mart is trying to determine in advance which employees are likely to get promoted so that it can line up replacements more quickly. The company says it promotes some 160,000 to 170,000 people a year.

"If we can tell three months in advance [that a position is going to be open], we can start hiring and training people. You don't want the jobs vacant for that long a time," says Elpida Ormanidou, Wal-Mart's vice president of global people analytics.

Questions

1. How might different aspects of teams and teamwork contribute to team members thinking about quitting their jobs?

2. Why might low feelings of connectedness to one's team lead a team member to think about quitting?

3. What steps has Box taken to increase cohesiveness in teams?

4. Why might working in a large team with a poorly rated manager make a team member more likely to think about quitting?

Source: Rachel Emma Silverman and Nikki Walker, "Thinking of Quitting? The Boss Knows," *The Wall Street Journal*, March 14, 2015, pp. A1–A2.

Endnotes

1. G. Hamel, *The Future of Management* (Boston, MA: Harvard Business School Press, 2007); "Our History," http://gore.com/en_xx/aboutus/timeline/index.html, May 20, 2014.

2. "About Gore," www.gore.com/en_xx/aboutus/index.html, March 19, 2015.

3. Hamel, *The Future of Management;* "Our History."

4. Ibid.

5. Ibid.

6. Ibid.

7. "Gore Culture," www.gore.com/en_xx/aboutus/culture/index.html, May 19, 2014.

8. Hamel, *The Future of Management;* "Our History."

9. R.E. Silverman, "Who's the Boss? There Isn't One," *The Wall Street Journal,* sec. Careers, June 20, 2012, B1, B8.

10. Hamel, *The Future of Management;* "Our History."

11. Ibid.; "Opportunities for Professionals at Gore," www.gore.com/en_xx/careers/professionals/index.html, May 20, 2014.

12. Silverman, "Who's the Boss? There Isn't One."

13. Ibid.

14. Hamel, *The Future of Management;* "Our History."

15. "Our History."

16. Hamel, *The Future of Management;* "Our History."

17. Hamel, *The Future of Management.*

18. "W.L. Gore & Associates Named a Top U.S. Workplace in 2014," www.gore.com/en_xx/news/FORTUNE-2014.html_May 19, 2014; M. Moskowitz and R. Levering, "The Best 100 Companies to Work For," *Fortune,* March 15, 2105, 140–54.

19. "W.L. Gore & Associates Named a Top U.S. Workplace in 2014," www.gore.com/en_xx/news/FORTUNE-2014.html_May 19, 2014.

20. T.M. Mills, *The Sociology of Small Groups* (Englewood Cliffs, NJ: Prentice-Hall, 1967); M.E. Shaw, *Group Dynamics* (New York: McGraw-Hill, 1981).

21. R.S. Buday, "Reengineering One Firm's Product Development and Another's Service Delivery," *Planning Review,* March–April 1993, 14–19; J.M. Burcke, "Hallmark's Quest for Quality Is a Job Never Done," *Business Insurance,* April 26, 1993, 122; M. Hammer and J. Champy, *Reengineering the Corporation* (New York: HarperBusiness, 1993); T.A. Stewart, "The Search for the Organization of Tomorrow," *Fortune,* May 18, 1992, 92–98; "Hallmark Corporate Information/About Hallmark," http://corporate.hallmark.com/Company, March 15, 2010; "Hallmark Corporate Information / Hallmark Facts," http://corporate.hallmark.com/ Company/Hallmark-Facts, May 24, 2012.

22. "RockBottom Restaurants," www.rockbottom.com/RockBottomWeb/RBR/index.aspx?PageName5/RockBottom. . ., April 15, 2008; "Craft Works Restaurants & Breweries Inc.," www.craftworksrestaurants.com/executive.html, May 24, 2012; "Rock Bottom Restaurants, Inc. – Franchising.com," www.franchising.com/rockbottomrestaurant/, May 21, 2014.

23. S. Dallas, "Rock Bottom Restaurants: Brewing Up Solid Profits," *BusinessWeek,* May 22, 1995, 74.

24. J.A. Pearce II and E.C. Ravlin, "The Design and Activation of Self-Regulating Work Groups," *Human Relations* 11 (1987), 751–82.

25. B. Dumaine, "Who Needs a Boss?" *Fortune,* May 7, 1990, 52–60; Pearce and Ravlin, "The Design and Activation of Self-Regulating Work Groups."

26. Dumaine, "Who Needs a Boss?"; A.R. Montebello and V.R. Buzzotta, "Work Teams That Work," *Training and Development,* March 1993, 59–64.

27. T.D. Wall, N.J. Kemp, P.R. Jackson, and C.W. Clegg, "Outcomes of Autonomous Work Groups: A Long-Term Field Experiment," *Academy of Management Journal* 29 (1986), 280–304.

28. A. Markels, "A Power Producer Is Intent on Giving Power to Its People," *The Wall Street Journal,* July 3, 1995, A1, A12; "AES Corporation/The Power of Being Global," www.aes.com/aes/index?page=home, April 15, 2008.

29. W.R. Pape, "Group Insurance," *Inc.* (Technology Supplement), June 17, 1997, 29–31; A.M. Townsend, S.M. DeMarie, and A.R. Hendrickson, "Are You Ready for Virtual Teams?" *HR Magazine,* September 1996, 122–126; A.M. Townsend, S.M. DeMarie, and A.M. Hendrickson, "Virtual Teams: Technology and the Workplace of the Future," *Academy of Management Executive* 12, no. 3 (1998), 17–29.

30. Townsend et al., "Virtual Teams."

31. Pape, "Group Insurance"; Townsend et al., "Are You Ready for Virtual Teams?"; L. Gratton, "Working Together . . . When Apart," *The Wall Street Journal,* June 16–17, 2007, R4.

32. D.L. Duarte and N.T. Snyder, *Mastering Virtual Teams* (San Francisco: Jossey-Bass, 1999); K A. Karl, "Book Reviews: *Mastering Virtual Teams,*" *Academy of Management Executive,* August 1999, 118–19.

33. B. Geber, "Virtual Teams," *Training* 32, no. 4 (August 1995), 36–40; T. Finholt and L.S. Sproull, "Electronic Groups at Work," *Organization Science* 1 (1990), 41–64.

34. Geber, "Virtual Teams."

35. E.J. Hill, B.C. Miller, S.P. Weiner, and J. Colihan, "Influences of the Virtual Office on Aspects of Work and Work/Life Balance," *Personnel Psychology* 31 (1998), 667–83; S.G. Strauss, "Technology, Group Process, and Group Outcomes: Testing the Connections in Computer-Mediated and Face-to-Face Groups," *Human Computer Interaction,* 12 (1997), 227–66; M.E. Warkentin, L. Sayeed, and R. High-tower, "Virtual Teams versus Face-to-Face Teams: An Exploratory Study of a Web-Based Conference System," *Decision Sciences* 28, no. 4 (Fall 1997), 975–96.

36. S.A. Furst, M. Reeves, B. Rosen, and R.S. Blackburn, "Managing the Life Cycle of Virtual Teams," *Academy of Management Executive* 18, no. 2 (May 2004), 6–20.

37. Ibid.

38. Gratton, "Working Together . . . When Apart."

39. Ibid.

40. Ibid.

41. Ibid.

42. A. Deutschman, "The Managing Wisdom of High-Tech Superstars," *Fortune,* October 17, 1994, 197–206.

43. Lublin, "My Colleague, My Boss."

44. "About ICU Medical, Inc.," www.icumed.com/about.asp, April 11, 2008.

45. "About ICU Medical, Inc."

46. "ICU Medical, Inc.—Fundamentals," http://phx.corporate-ir.net/phoenix.zhtml?c=86695&p=irol-fundamentals, April 11, 2008; "ICU Medical Inc. (ICUI): Stock Quote & Company Profile—BusinessWeek," *BusinessWeek,* http://investing.businessweek.com/research/stocks/snapshot/snapshot_article.asp?symbol5. . ., April 11, 2008; "The 200 Best Small Companies \#80 ICU Medical," *Forbes*

.com, www.forbes.com/lists/2009/23/small-companies-09_ICU-Medical_J1UO.html, March 14, 2010; "2011 Annual Report to Shareholders and Form 10-K," ICU Medical, http://files.shareholder.com/downloads/ICUI/0x0x563714/664702F0-84A0-41B4-B90B-B8204D2437EC/ICU_WEB_READY_PDF.pdf, May 24, 2012; "People at ICUI – Executives, Board, & Key Employees at ICU Medical Inc.–WSJ.com," http://quotes.wsj.com/ICUI/company-people, May 22, 2014.

47. "ICU Medical, Inc.–Investor Relations Home," http://phx.corporate-ir.net/phoenix.zhtml?c=86695&p=irol-IRHome, April 11, 2008; "The 200 Best Small Companies \#80 ICU Medical"; "People at ICUI – Executives, Board, & Key Employees at ICU Medical Inc.–WSJ.com," http://quotes.wsj.com/ICUI/company-people, May 22, 2014; "Board of Directors–ICU Medical," http://ic.icumed.com/directors.cfm, March 23, 2015.

48. "About ICU Medical, Inc."

49. "Clave Connector," ICU Medical, Inc., www.icumend.com, April 11, 2008; "2011 Annual Report to Shareholders and Form 10-K," *ICU Medical,* http://files.shareholder.com/downloads/ICUI/0x0x563714/664702F0-84A0-41B4-B90B-B8204D2437EC/ICU_WEB_READY_PDF.pdf, May 24, 2012.

50. E. White, "How a Company Made Everyone a Team Player," *The Wall Street Journal,* August 13, 2007, B1, B7.

51. Ibid.

52. Ibid.

53. Ibid.

54. Ibid.

55. Ibid.

56. Ibid.

57. R.G. LeFauve and A.C. Hax, "Managerial and Technological Innovations at Saturn Corporation," *MIT Management,* Spring 1992, 8–19.

58. B.W. Tuckman, "Developmental Sequences in Small Groups," *Psychological Bulletin* 63 (1965), 384–99; B.W. Tuckman and M.C. Jensen, "Stages of Small Group Development," *Group and Organizational Studies* 2 (1977), 419–27.

59. C.J.G. Gersick, "Time and Transition in Work Teams: Toward a New Model of Group Development," *Academy of Management Journal* 31 (1988), 9–41; C.J.G. Gersick, "Marking Time: Predictable Transitions in Task Groups," *Academy of Management Journal* 32 (1989), 274–309.

60. J.R. Hackman, "Group Influences on Individuals in Organizations," in M.D. Dunnette and L.M. Hough, eds., *Handbook of Industrial and Organizational Psychology,* 2nd ed., vol. 3 (Palo Alto, CA: Consulting Psychologists Press, 1992), 199–267.

61. Ibid.

62. Ibid.

63. Lublin, "My Colleague, My Boss."

64. T. Kelley and J. Littman, *The Art of Innovation* (New York: Doubleday, 2001); "ideo.com: Our Work," www.ideo.com/portfolio, June 19, 2006; "About IDEO," *IDEO,* www.ideo.com/about/, May 24, 2012; "IDEO – A Design and Innovation Consulting Firm," www.ideo.com/, May 22, 2014; www.ideo.com, March 23, 2015.

65. B. Nussbaum, "The Power of Design," *BusinessWeek,* May 17, 2004, 86–94; "ideo.com: About Us: Teams," www.ideo.com/about/index.asp?x=1&y=1, June 19, 2006.

66. "ideo.com: About Us: Teams," www.ideo.com/about/index.asp?x=1&y=1, June 19, 2006; "ideo.com: About Us: Teams," www.ideo.com/about/index.asp?x=1&y=1, April 18, 2008; "Teams–IDEO," www.ideo.com/culture/teams/ March 15, 2010.

67. Nussbaum, "The Power of Design."

68. Kelley and Littman, *The Art of Innovation.*

69. Ibid.; www.ideo.com; "1999 Idea Winners," *BusinessWeek,* June 7, 1999, *BusinessWeek* Archives.

70. Nussbaum, "The Power of Design; "ideo.com: About Us: Teams;" "About IDEO," IDEO, www.ideo.com/about/, May 24, 2012.

71. L. Festinger, "Informal Social Communication," *Psychological Review* 57 (1950), 271–82; Shaw, *Group Dynamics.*

72. Hackman, "Group Influences on Individuals in Organizations"; Shaw, *Group Dynamics.*

73. D. Cartwright, "The Nature of Group Cohesiveness," in D. Cartwright and A. Zander, eds., *Group Dynamics,* 3rd ed. (New York: Harper & Row, 1968); L. Festinger, S. Schacter, and K. Black, *Social Pressures in Informal Groups* (New York: Harper & Row, 1950); Shaw, *Group Dynamics.*

74. T.F. O'Boyle, "A Manufacturer Grows Efficient by Soliciting Ideas from Employees," *The Wall Street Journal,* June 5, 1992, A1, A5.

75. Lublin, "My Colleague, My Boss."

76. Kelley and Littman, "The Art of Innovation," 93; "People—Tom Kelley—IDEO," www.ideo.com/people/tom-kelley, May 22, 2014.

77. Kelley and Littman, "The Art of Innovation."

78. P.C. Earley, "Social Loafing and Collectivism: A Comparison of the United States and the People's Republic of China," *Administrative Science Quarterly* 34 (1989), 565–81; J.M. George, "Extrinsic and Intrinsic Origins of Perceived Social Loafing in Organizations," *Academy of Management Journal* 35 (1992), 191–202; S.G. Harkins, B. Latane, and K. Williams, "Social Loafing: Allocating Effort or Taking It Easy," *Journal of Experimental Social Psychology* 16 (1980), 457–65; B. Latane, K.D. Williams, and S. Harkins, "Many Hands Make Light the Work: The Causes and Consequences of Social Loafing," *Journal of Personality and Social Psychology* 37 (1979), 822–32; J.A. Shepperd, "Productivity Loss in Performance Groups: A Motivation Analysis," *Psychological Bulletin* 113 (1993), 67–81.

79. George, "Extrinsic and Intrinsic Origins"; G.R. Jones, "Task Visibility, Free Riding, and Shirking: Explaining the Effect of Structure and Technology on Employee Behavior," *Academy of Management Review* 9 (1984), 684–95; K. Williams, S. Harkins, and B. Latane, "Identifiability as a Deterrent to Social Loafing: Two Cheering Experiments," *Journal of Personality and Social Psychology* 40 (1981), 303–11.

80. S. Harkins and J. Jackson, "The Role of Evaluation in Eliminating Social Loafing," *Personality and Social Psychology Bulletin* 11 (1985), 457–65; N.L. Kerr and S.E. Bruun, "Ringelman Revisited: Alternative Explanations for the Social Loafing Effect," *Personality and Social Psychology Bulletin* 7 (1981), 224–31;

Williams et al., "Identifiability as a Deterrent to Social Loafing"; Harkins and Jackson, "The Role of Evaluation in Eliminating Social Loafing."

81. M.A. Brickner, S.G. Harkins, and T.M. Ostrom, "Effects of Personal Involvement: Thought-Provoking Implications for Social Loafing," *Journal of Personality and Social Psychology* 51 (1986), 763–69; S.G. Harkins and R.E. Petty, "The Effects of Task Difficulty and Task Uniqueness on Social Loafing," *Journal of Personality and Social Psychology* 43 (1982), 1214–29.

82. B. Latane, "Responsibility and Effort in Organizations," in P.S. Goodman, ed., *Designing Effective Work Groups* (San Francisco: Jossey-Bass, 1986); Latane et al., "Many Hands Make Light the Work"; I.D. Steiner, *Group Process and Productivity* (New York: Academic Press, 1972).

12 Building and Managing Human Resources

Learning Objectives

After studying this chapter, you should be able to:

LO 12-1 Explain why strategic human resource management can help an organization gain a competitive advantage.

LO 12-2 Describe the steps managers take to recruit and select organizational members.

LO 12-3 Discuss the training and development options that ensure organizational members can effectively perform their jobs.

LO 12-4 Explain why performance appraisal and feedback are such crucial activities, and list the choices managers must make in designing effective performance appraisal and feedback procedures.

LO 12-5 Explain the issues managers face in determining levels of pay and benefits.

LO 12-6 Understand the role that labor relations play in the effective management of human resources.

© David Lees/Getty Images RF

At the Four Seasons, treating employees well leads to satisfied customers. Everyone wins!
© Mark Peterson/Redux

Effectively Managing Human Resources at the Four Seasons

How Can Managers Promote Excellent Customer Service In an Industry Known for High Employee Turnover?

Four Seasons Hotels and Resorts is one of only 12 companies to be ranked one of the "100 Best Companies to Work For" every year since *Fortune* magazine started this annual ranking of companies (from 1998 to 2015).[1] And the Four Seasons often receives other awards and recognition.[2] In an industry in which annual turnover rates are relatively high, the Four Seasons' turnover rate for full-time employees is 12.7%, which is among the lowest in the industry.[3] Evidently employees and customers alike are satisfied with how they are treated at the Four Seasons. Understanding that the two are causally linked is perhaps the key to the Four Seasons' success. As the Four Seasons' founder and Chairman of the Board Isadore Sharp[4] suggested, "How you treat your employees is how you expect them to treat the customer."[5]

The Four Seasons was founded by Sharp in 1961 when he opened his first hotel called the Four Seasons Motor Hotel outside downtown Toronto. Whereas his first hotel had 125 inexpensively priced rooms appealing to the individual traveler, his fourth hotel was built to appeal to business travelers and conventions with 1,600 rooms and conference facilities. Both these hotels were successful, but Sharp decided he could provide customers with a different kind of hotel experience by combining the best features of both kinds of hotel experiences—the sense of closeness and personal attention that a small hotel brings with the amenities of a big hotel to suit the needs of business travelers.[6]

Sharp sought to provide the kind of personal service that would really help business travelers on the road. Thus, the Four Seasons was the first hotel chain to provide bathrobes, shampoo, round-the-clock room service, laundry and dry cleaning services, large desks, two-line phones, and round-the-clock secretarial assistance.[7] While these are relatively concrete ways of personalizing the hotel experience, Sharp realized that how employees treat customers is just as important. When employees view each customer as an individual with his or her own needs and desires a hotel can indeed serve the purposes of a home away from home (and an office away from the office), and customers are likely to be both loyal and highly satisfied.[8]

Sharp always realized that for employees to treat customers well, the Four Seasons needs to treat its employees well. Salaries are relatively high at the

Four Seasons by industry standards; employees participate in a profit-sharing plan; and the company contributes to their 401(k) plans. Four Seasons pays 78% of employees' health insurance premiums and provides free dental insurance.[9] All employees get free meals in the cafeteria, have access to staff showers and a locker room, and receive an additional highly attractive benefit—once a new employee has worked for the Four Seasons for six months, he or she can stay for three nights free at any Four Seasons hotel or resort in the world. After a year of employment, this benefit increases to six free nights, and it continues to grow as tenure with the company increases.[10]

All aspects of human resource management at the Four Seasons are oriented around ensuring that the guiding principle behind all Four Seasons operations is upheld.[11] As Nick Mutton, executive vice president for human resources, indicated, "Our strong culture has always been based on the Golden Rule—the simple idea of treating others as you would have them treat you."[12]

All job applicants to the Four Seasons have a minimum of four interviews, one of which is with the general manager of the property.[13] The human resources department interviews many of the applicants because the philosophy at the Four Seasons is that employees need to be helpful and have a positive approach or perspective. Given the reputation that the Four Seasons has for treating employees well and providing them with great benefits, it often has many applicants for job openings. The Four Seasons devotes so much attention to hiring the right people because of the importance of each and every employee providing a consistently high level of empathetic and responsive customer service.[14]

New hires participate in a three-month training program that includes improvisation activities to help new hires learn how to anticipate guests' needs and appropriately respond to them.[15] The aim of training is to help ensure that all employees provide consistently high quality and highly responsive customer service. Since customer service is everyone's responsibility, the Four Seasons has no separate customer service department per se. Training is ongoing at the Four Seasons and never really stops.[16]

The Four Seasons also tends to promote from within.[17] For example, while recent college graduates may start out as assistant managers, those who do well and have high aspirations could potentially become general managers in less than 15 years. This helps to ensure that managers have empathy and respect for those in lower-level positions as well as the ingrained ethos of treating others as they would like to be treated. All in all, treating employees well leads to satisfied customers at the Four Seasons.[18]

LO 12-1 Explain why strategic human resource management can help an organization gain a competitive advantage.

Overview

Managers are responsible for acquiring, developing, protecting, and utilizing the resources an organization needs to be efficient and effective. One of the most important resources in all organizations is human resources—the people involved in producing and distributing goods and services. Human resources include all members of an organization, ranging from top managers to entry-level employees. Effective managers like Isadore Sharp and Nick Mutton in the "Management Snapshot" realize how valuable human resources are and take active steps to make sure that their organizations build and fully utilize their human resources to gain a competitive advantage.

This chapter examines how managers can tailor their human resource management system to their organization's strategy and structure. We discuss in particular the major components of human resource management: recruitment and selection, training and development, performance appraisal, pay and benefits, and labor relations. By the end of this chapter, you will understand the central role human resource management plays in creating a high-performing organization.

Strategic Human Resource Management

Human resource management (HRM) includes all the activities managers engage in to attract and retain employees and to ensure that they perform at a high level and contribute to the accomplishment of organizational goals. These activities make up an organization's human resource management system, which has five major components: recruitment and selection, training and development, performance appraisal and feedback, pay and benefits, and labor relations (see Figure 12.1).

human resource management (HRM) Activities that managers engage in to attract and retain employees and to ensure that they perform at a high level and contribute to the accomplishment of organizational goals.

strategic human resource management The process by which managers design the components of an HRM system to be consistent with each other, with other elements of organizational architecture, and with the organization's strategy and goals.

Strategic human resource management is the process by which managers design the components of an HRM system to be consistent with each other, with other elements of organizational architecture, and with the organization's strategy and goals.[19] The objective of strategic HRM is the development of an HRM system that enhances an organization's efficiency, quality, innovation, and responsiveness to customers—the four building blocks of competitive advantage. At the Four Seasons in the "Management Snapshot," HRM practices ensure that all employees provide excellent customer service.

As part of strategic human resource management, some managers have adopted Six Sigma quality improvement plans. These plans ensure that an organization's products and services are as free of errors or defects as possible through a variety of human resource–related initiatives. Jack Welch, former CEO of General Electric Company (GE), indicated that these initiatives saved GE millions of dollars; and other companies, such as Whirlpool and Motorola, also have implemented Six Sigma initiatives. For such initiatives to be effective, however, top managers have to be committed to Six Sigma, employees must be motivated, and there must be demand for the products or services of the organization in the first place. David Fitzpatrick, former head of Deloitte Consulting's Lean Enterprise Practice and currently a managing director at AlixPartners Professionals,[20] estimated that most Six Sigma plans are not effective because the conditions for effective Six Sigma are not in place. For example, if top managers are not committed to the quality initiative,

Figure 12.1

Components of a Human Resource Management System

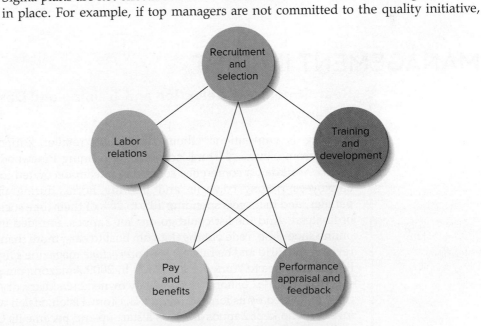

Each component of an HRM system influences the others, and all five must fit together.

they may not devote the necessary time and resources to make it work and may lose interest in it prematurely.[21]

Overview of the Components of HRM

Managers use *recruitment and selection,* the first component of an HRM system, to attract and hire new employees who have the abilities, skills, and experiences that will help an organization achieve its goals. Microsoft Corporation, for example, has the goal of remaining the premier computer software company in the world. To achieve this goal, managers at Microsoft realize the importance of hiring only the best software designers: hundreds of highly qualified candidates are interviewed and rigorously tested. This careful attention to selection has contributed to Microsoft's competitive advantage. Microsoft has little trouble recruiting top programmers because candidates know they will be at the forefront of the industry if they work for Microsoft.[22]

After recruiting and selecting employees, managers use the second component, *training and development,* to ensure that organizational members develop the skills and abilities that will enable them to perform their jobs effectively in the present and the future. Training and development are an ongoing process; changes in technology and the environment, as well as in an organization's goals and strategies, often require that organizational members learn new techniques and ways of working. At Microsoft, newly hired program designers receive on-the-job training by joining small teams that include experienced employees who serve as mentors or advisers. New recruits learn firsthand from team members how to develop computer systems that are responsive to customers' programming needs.[23]

Recruiting and selecting employees and providing training and development often go hand-in-hand, as is true at Zappos, profiled in the accompanying "Management Insight" feature.

MANAGEMENT INSIGHT

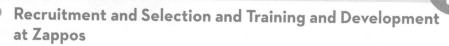

Recruitment and Selection and Training and Development at Zappos

Nothing is conventional about the online retailer Zappos, headquartered in Henderson, Nevada.[24] Think accountants running Pinewood Derby car races during the workday, a conference room that a team decorated to simulate a log cabin, employees ringing cowbells and blowing horns during visitor tours, costume parades, and managers spending 10% to 20% of their time socializing with their subordinates.[25] And the list could go on. Yet Zappos, founded in 1999 as a struggling online shoe shop, rode out the dot-com bust to earn more than $1.6 billion in annual revenues in 2010 and be ranked 86th on *Fortune* magazine's list of the One Hundred Best Companies to Work For in 2015.[26] In 2009 Amazon.com purchased Zappos for shares worth $1.2 billion.[27] As a wholly owned subsidiary of Amazon, Zappos continues to be led by its long-standing CEO Tony Hsieh; Hsieh was the initial primary investor who kept Zappos afloat as a start-up and became its CEO in 2000.[28]

Zappos has expanded from selling shoes to selling a wide range of products ranging from clothing and handbags to housewares, watches, and jewelry.[29] What

Training at Zappos for new employees of the Customer Loyalty Team. Zappos' careful attention to recruitment, selection, and training have contributed to the company's success, as has a work environment geared toward making employees happy. © Jared McMillen/Aurora Photos/Corbis

is distinctive about Zappos is not so much the products it sells but rather the exceptional service it provides customers.[30] In fact, central to the guiding philosophy at Zappos is having a happy workforce of satisfied employees who actually want to come to work each day and have fun on and off the job.[31] Thus, Hsieh and other managers at Zappos go to great lengths to ensure that the Zappos core values and unique culture are maintained and strengthened. The core values of Zappos are these: "1. Deliver WOW through Service; 2. Embrace and Drive Change; 3. Create Fun and a Little Weirdness; 4. Be Adventurous, Creative, and Open-Minded; 5. Pursue Growth and Learning; 6. Build Open and Honest Relationships with Communication; 7. Build a Positive Team and Family Spirit; 8. Do More with Less; 9. Be Passionate and Determined; 10. Be Humble."[32]

Because of the importance of having happy employees, Zappos goes to great lengths to effectively manage human resources. Potential new hires are interviewed by human resources, to make sure they will work well in Zappos's culture and support its values, as well as by the department doing the hiring, to determine their suitability for the position they are interviewing for. If human resources and the hiring manager disagree in their assessments of an applicant, Hsieh interviews the applicant himself and makes the final decision.[33]

Newly hired employees receive extensive training. For example, the Customer Loyalty Team (CLT) new hires who answer calls have two weeks of classroom training followed by two weeks of training in answering calls. Once the training is completed, they are given the opportunity to receive $2,000 and pay for the time they spent in training if they want to quit.[34] This way only new hires who want to stay with the company remain.

Experienced employees are encouraged to continue to grow and develop on the job. For example, employees who have worked at Zappos for two or fewer years have over 200 hours of classroom training and development during their work hours and are required to read nine books about business. More experienced employees receive training and development in areas such as financial planning and speaking in public. Zappos has a company library well stocked with multiple copies of business books and books about personal growth and development for employees to borrow and read. Training and development at Zappos not only help to keep employees happy but also help them gain the skills and abilities needed to advance to higher-level positions in the company.[35] All in all, careful attention to recruitment and selection and training and development have certainly contributed to Zappo's ongoing success story.

The third component, *performance appraisal and feedback,* serves two different purposes in HRM. First, performance appraisal can give managers the information they need to make good human resources decisions—decisions about how to train, motivate, and reward organizational members.[36] Second, feedback from performance appraisal serves a developmental purpose for members of an organization. When managers regularly evaluate their subordinates' performance, they can give employees valuable information about their strengths and weaknesses and the areas in which they need to concentrate.

On the basis of performance appraisals, managers distribute *pay* to employees, which is part of the fourth component of an HRM system. By rewarding high-performing organizational members with pay raises, bonuses, and the like, managers increase the likelihood that an organization's most valued human resources will be motivated to continue their high levels of contribution to the organization. Moreover, if pay is linked to performance, high-performing employees are more likely to stay with the organization, and managers are more likely to fill positions that become open with highly talented individuals. *Benefits* such as health insurance are important outcomes that employees receive by virtue of their membership in an organization.

Last but not least, *labor relations* encompass the steps that managers take to develop and maintain good working relationships with the labor unions that may represent their employees' interests. For example, an organization's labor relations component can help managers establish safe working conditions and fair labor practices in their offices and plants.

Managers must ensure that all five of these components fit together and complement their company's structure and control systems.[37] For example, if managers decide to decentralize authority and empower employees, they need to invest in training and development to ensure that lower-level employees have the knowledge and expertise they need to make the decisions that top managers would make in a more centralized structure.

Each of the five components of HRM influences the others (see Figure 12.1).[38] The kinds of people that the organization attracts and hires through recruitment and selection, for example, determine (1) the kinds of training and development that are necessary, (2) the way performance is appraised, and (3) the appropriate levels of pay and benefits. Managers at Microsoft ensure that their organization has highly qualified program designers by (1) recruiting and selecting the best candidates, (2) guiding new hires with experienced team members, (3) appraising program designers' performance in terms of their individual contributions and their teams' performance, and (4) basing programmers' pay on individual and team performance.

Effectively managing human resources helps ensure that both customers and employees are satisfied and loyal, as illustrated in the accompanying "Managing Globally" feature.

MANAGING GLOBALLY

Managing Human Resources at Semco

Ricardo Semler was 21 years old (and one of the youngest graduates from the Harvard Business School MBA program) when he took his father's place as head of the family business, Semco, based in São Paolo, Brazil, in 1984.[39] His father Antonio had founded Semco in 1954 as a machine shop; the company went on to become a manufacturer of marine pumps for the shipbuilding industry, with $4 million a year in revenues when Ricardo Semler took over. Today, Semco's revenues are more than $200 million a year from a diverse set of businesses ranging from the development and manufacture of industrial mixing and refrigeration equipment to the provision of systems to manage communication, correspondence, and goods exchanges between an organization and its suppliers, customers, and partners.[40] Semco prides itself on being a premier provider of goods and services in its markets and has loyal customers.[41]

Semler is the first to admit that Semco's track record of success is due to its human resources—its employees. In fact, Semler so firmly believes in Semco's employees that he and the other top managers are reluctant to tell employees what to do. Semco has no rules, regulations, or organizational charts; hierarchy is eschewed; and workplace democracy rules the day. Employees have levels of autonomy unheard of in other companies, and flexibility and trust are built into every aspect of human resource management at Semco.[42]

Human resource practices at Semco revolve around maximizing the contributions employees make to the company, and this begins by hiring individuals who want to, can, and will contribute. Semco strives to ensure that all selection decisions are based on relevant and complete information. Job candidates are first interviewed as a group; the candidates meet many employees, receive a tour of the company, and interact with potential coworkers. This gives Semco a chance to size up candidates in ways more likely to reveal their true natures, and it gives the candidates a chance to learn about Semco. When finalists are identified from the pool, multiple Semco employees interview each finalist five or six more times to choose the best person(s) to be hired. The result is that both Semco and new hires make informed decisions and are mutually committed to making the relationship a success.[43]

Once hired, entry-level employees participate in the Lost in Space program, in which they rotate through different positions and units of their own choosing for about a year.[44] In this way, the new hires learn about their options and can decide where their interests lie, and the units they work in learn about the new hires. At the end of the year, the new employees may be offered a job in one of the units in which they worked, or they may seek a position elsewhere in Semco. Seasoned Semco employees are also encouraged to rotate positions and work in different parts of the company to keep them fresh, energized, and motivated and to give them the opportunity to contribute in new ways as their interests change.[45]

Performance is appraised at Semco in terms of results; all employees and managers must demonstrate that they are making valuable contributions and deserve to be "rehired." For example, each manager's performance is anonymously appraised by all the employees who report to him or her, and the appraisals are made publicly available in Semco. Employees also can choose how they are paid from a combination of 11 different compensation options, ranging from fixed salaries, bonuses, and profit sharing to royalties on sales or profits and arrangements based on meeting annual self-set goals. Flexibility in compensation promotes risk taking and innovation, according to Semler, and maximizes returns to employees in terms of their pay and to the company in terms of revenues and profitability.[46] Flexibility, autonomy, the ability to change jobs often, and control of working hours and even compensation are some of the ways by which Semler strives to ensure that employees are loyal and involved in their work because they *want* to be; turnover at Semco is less than 1% annually.[47] And with human resource practices geared toward maximizing contributions and performance, Semco is well poised to continue to provide value to its customers.

The Legal Environment of HRM

In the rest of this chapter, we focus in detail on the choices managers must make in strategically managing human resources to attain organizational goals and gain a competitive advantage. Effectively managing human resources is a complex undertaking for managers, and we provide an overview of some major issues they face. First, however, we need to look at how the legal environment affects human resource management.

The local, state, and national laws and regulations that managers and organizations must abide by add to the complexity of HRM. For example, the U.S. government's commitment to **equal employment opportunity (EEO)** has resulted in the creation and enforcement of a number of laws that managers must abide by. The goal of EEO is to ensure that all citizens have an equal opportunity to obtain employment regardless of their gender, race, country of origin, religion, age, or disabilities. Table 12.1 summarizes some of the major EEO laws affecting HRM. Other laws, such as the Occupational Safety and Health Act of 1970, require that managers ensure that employees are protected from workplace hazards and safety standards are met.

In Chapter 3, we explained how effectively managing diversity is an ethical and business imperative, and we discussed the many issues surrounding diversity. EEO laws and their enforcement make the effective management of diversity a legal imperative as well. The Equal Employment Opportunity Commission (EEOC) is the division of the Department of Justice that enforces most EEO laws and handles discrimination complaints. In addition, the EEOC issues guidelines for managers to follow to ensure that they are abiding by EEO laws. For example, the Uniform Guidelines on Employee Selection Procedures issued by the EEOC (in conjunction

equal employment opportunity (EEO)
The equal right of all citizens to the opportunity to obtain employment regardless of their gender, age, race, country of origin, religion, or disabilities.

Table 12.1

Major Equal Employment Opportunity Laws Affecting HRM

Year	Law	Description
1963	Equal Pay Act	Requires that men and women be paid equally if they are performing equal work.
1964	Title VII of the Civil Rights Act	Prohibits employment discrimination on the basis of race, religion, sex, color, or national origin; covers a wide range of employment decisions, including hiring, firing, pay, promotion, and working conditions.
1967	Age Discrimination in Employment Act	Prohibits discrimination against workers over the age of 40 and restricts mandatory retirement.
1978	Pregnancy Discrimination Act	Prohibits employment discrimination against women on the basis of pregnancy, childbirth, and related medical decisions.
1990	Americans with Disabilities Act	Prohibits employment discrimination against individuals with disabilities and requires that employers make accommodations for such workers to enable them to perform their jobs.
1991	Civil Rights Act	Prohibits discrimination (as does Title VII) and allows the awarding of punitive and compensatory damages, in addition to back pay, in cases of intentional discrimination.
1993	Family and Medical Leave Act	Requires that employers provide 12 weeks of unpaid leave for medical and family reasons, including paternity and illness of a family member.

with the Departments of Labor and Justice and the Civil Service Commission) guide managers on how to ensure that the recruitment and selection component of human resource management complies with Title VII of the Civil Rights Act (which prohibits discrimination based on gender, race, color, religion, and national origin).[48]

Contemporary challenges that managers face related to the legal environment include how to eliminate sexual harassment (see Chapter 3 for an in-depth discussion of sexual harassment), how to accommodate employees with disabilities, how to deal with employees who have substance abuse problems, and how to manage HIV-positive employees and employees with AIDS.[49] HIV-positive employees are infected with the virus that causes AIDS but may show no AIDS symptoms and may not develop AIDS in the near future. Often such employees are able to perform their jobs effectively, and managers must take steps to ensure that they are allowed to do so and are not discriminated against in the workplace.[50] Employees with AIDS may or may not be able to perform their jobs effectively, and, once again, managers need to ensure that they are not unfairly discriminated against.[51] Many organizations have instituted AIDS awareness training programs to educate organizational members about HIV and AIDS, dispel myths about how HIV is spread, and ensure that individuals infected with the HIV virus are treated fairly and are able to be productive as long as they can be while not putting others at risk.[52]

LO 12-2 Describe the steps managers take to recruit and select organizational members.

Recruitment and Selection

recruitment
Activities that managers engage in to develop a pool of qualified candidates for open positions.

selection The process that managers use to determine the relative qualifications of job applicants and their potential for performing well in a particular job.

human resource planning Activities that managers engage in to forecast their current and future needs for human resources.

outsource To use outside suppliers and manufacturers to produce goods and services.

Recruitment includes all the activities managers engage in to develop a pool of qualified candidates for open positions.[53] **Selection** is the process by which managers determine the relative qualifications of job applicants and their potential for performing well in a particular job. Before actually recruiting and selecting employees, managers need to engage in two important activities: human resource planning and job analysis (Figure 12.2).

Human Resource Planning

Human resource planning includes all the activities managers engage in to forecast their current and future human resource needs. Current human resources are the employees an organization needs today to provide high-quality goods and services to customers. Future human resource needs are the employees the organization will need at some later date to achieve its longer-term goals.

As part of human resource planning, managers must make both demand forecasts and supply forecasts. *Demand forecasts* estimate the qualifications and numbers of employees an organization will need given its goals and strategies. *Supply forecasts* estimate the availability and qualifications of current employees now and in the future, as well as the supply of qualified workers in the external labor market.

As a result of their human resource planning, managers sometimes decide to **outsource** to fill some of their human resource needs. Instead of recruiting and selecting employees to produce goods and services, managers contract with people who are not members of their organization to produce goods and services. Managers in publishing companies, for example, frequently contract with freelance editors to copyedit books that they intend to publish. Kelly Services is an organization that provides the services of technical and professional employees to managers who want to use outsourcing to fill some of their human resource requirements in these areas.[54]

Figure 12.2

The Recruitment and Selection System

Two reasons why human resource planning sometimes leads managers to outsource are flexibility and cost. First, outsourcing can give managers increased flexibility, especially when accurately forecasting human resource needs is difficult, human resource needs fluctuate over time, or finding skilled workers in a particular area is difficult. Second, outsourcing can sometimes allow managers to use human resources at a lower cost. When work is outsourced, costs can be lower for a number of reasons: The organization does not have to provide benefits to workers; managers can contract for work only when the work is needed; and managers do not have to invest in training. Outsourcing can be used for functional activities such as after-sales service on appliances and equipment, legal work, and the management of information systems.[55]

Outsourcing has disadvantages, however.[56] When work is outsourced, managers may lose some control over the quality of goods and services. Also, individuals performing outsourced work may have less knowledge of organizational practices, procedures, and goals and less commitment to an organization than regular employees. In addition, unions resist outsourcing because it has the potential to eliminate some of their members. To gain some of the flexibility and cost savings of outsourcing and avoid some of its disadvantages, a number of organizations, such as Microsoft and IBM, rely on a pool of temporary employees to, for example, debug programs.

A major trend reflecting the increasing globalization of business is the outsourcing of office work, computer programming, and technical jobs from the United States and countries in western Europe, with high labor costs, to countries like India and China, with low labor costs.[57] For example, computer programmers in India and China earn a fraction of what their U.S. counterparts earn. Outsourcing (or *offshoring*, as it is also called when work is outsourced to other countries) has also expanded into knowledge-intensive work such as engineering, research and development, and the development of computer software. According to a study conducted by The Conference Board and Duke University's Offshoring Research Network, more than half of U.S. companies surveyed have some kind of offshoring strategy related to knowledge-intensive work and innovation.[58] Why are so many companies engaged in offshoring, and why are companies that already offshore work planning to increase the extent of offshoring? While cost savings continue to be a major motivation for offshoring, managers also want to take advantage of an increasingly talented global workforce and be closer to the growing global marketplace for goods and services.[59]

Major U.S. companies often earn a substantial portion of their revenues overseas. For example, Hewlett-Packard, Caterpillar, and IBM earn more than 60% of their revenues from overseas markets. And many large companies employ thousands of workers overseas. For example, IBM employs close to 100,000 workers in India and Hewlett-Packard, over 25,000.[60] Managers at some smaller companies have offshored work to Sri Lanka, Russia, and Egypt.[61] Key challenges for managers who offshore are retaining sufficient managerial control over activities and employee turnover.[62]

Job Analysis

job analysis

Identifying the tasks, duties, and responsibilities that make up a job and the knowledge, skills, and abilities needed to perform the job.

Job analysis is a second important activity that managers need to undertake prior to recruitment and selection.[63] **Job analysis** is the process of identifying (1) the tasks, duties, and responsibilities that make up a job (the *job description*) and (2) the knowledge, skills, and abilities needed to perform the job (the *job specifications*).[64] For each job in an organization, a job analysis needs to be done.

Job analysis can be done in a number of ways, including observing current employees as they perform the job or interviewing them. Often managers rely on questionnaires compiled by jobholders and their managers. The questionnaires ask about the skills and abilities needed to perform the job, job tasks and the amount of time spent on them, responsibilities, supervisory activities, equipment used, reports prepared, and decisions made.[65] A trend, in some organizations, is toward more flexible jobs in which tasks and responsibilities change and cannot be clearly specified in advance. For these kinds of jobs, job analysis focuses more on determining the skills and knowledge workers need to be effective and less on specific duties.

After managers have completed human resource planning and job analyses for all jobs in an organization, they will know their human resource needs and the jobs they need to fill. They will also know what knowledge, skills, and abilities potential employees need to perform those jobs. At this point, recruitment and selection can begin.

External and Internal Recruitment

As noted earlier, recruitment is what managers do to develop a pool of qualified candidates for open positions.[66] They traditionally have used two main types of recruiting, external and internal, which are now supplemented by recruiting over the Internet.

EXTERNAL RECRUITING When managers recruit externally to fill open positions, they look outside the organization for people who have not worked for the organization previously. There are multiple means through which managers can recruit externally: advertisements in newspapers and magazines, open houses for students and career counselors at high schools and colleges or on-site at the organization, career fairs at colleges, and recruitment meetings with groups in the local community.

Many large organizations send teams of interviewers to college campuses to recruit new employees. External recruitment can also take place through informal networks, as occurs when current employees inform friends about open positions in their companies or recommend people they know to fill vacant spots. Some organizations use employment agencies for external recruitment, and some external recruitment takes place simply through walk-ins—job hunters coming to an organization and inquiring about employment possibilities.

With all the downsizing and corporate layoffs that have taken place in recent years, you might think external recruiting would be a relatively easy task for managers. However, it often is not, because even though many people may be looking for jobs, many jobs that are open require skills and abilities that these job hunters do not have. Managers needing to fill vacant positions and job hunters seeking employment opportunities are increasingly relying on the Internet to connect with each other through employment websites such as Monster.com[67] and JobLine International.[68] Major corporations such as Coca-Cola, Cisco, Ernst & Young, Canon, and Telia have relied on JobLine to fill global positions.[69]

External recruiting has both advantages and disadvantages for managers. Advantages include having access to a potentially large applicant pool, being able to attract people who have the skills, knowledge, and abilities that an organization needs to achieve its goals, and being able to bring in newcomers who may have a fresh approach to problems and be up to date on the latest technology. These advantages have to be weighed against the disadvantages, including the relatively high costs of external recruitment. Employees recruited externally lack knowledge about the inner workings of the organization and may need to receive more training than those recruited internally. Finally, when employees are recruited externally, there is always uncertainty concerning whether they will actually be good performers. Nonetheless, managers can take steps to reduce some of the uncertainty surrounding external recruitment.

INTERNAL RECRUITING When recruiting is internal, managers turn to existing employees to fill open positions. Employees recruited internally are either seeking **lateral moves** (job changes that entail no major changes in responsibility or authority levels) or promotions. Internal recruiting has several advantages. First, internal applicants are already familiar with the organization (including its goals, structure, culture, rules, and norms). Second, managers already know the candidates; they have considerable information about their skills and abilities and actual behavior on the job. Third, internal recruiting can help boost levels of employee motivation and morale, both for the employee who gets the job and for other workers. Those who are not seeking a promotion or who may not be ready for one can see that promotion is a possibility in the future; or a lateral move can alleviate boredom once a job has been fully mastered and can also be a useful way to learn new skills. Finally, internal recruiting is normally less time-consuming and expensive than external recruiting.

Given the advantages of internal recruiting, why do managers rely on external recruiting as much as they do? The answer lies in the disadvantages of internal recruiting—among them, a limited pool of candidates and a tendency among those candidates to be set in the organization's ways. Often the organization simply does not have suitable internal candidates. Sometimes, even when suitable internal applicants are available, managers may rely on external recruiting to find the very best candidate or to help bring new ideas and approaches into their organization. When organizations are in trouble and performing poorly, external recruiting is often relied on to bring in managerial talent with a fresh approach.

The Selection Process

Once managers develop a pool of applicants for open positions through the recruitment process, they need to find out whether each applicant is qualified for the position and likely to be a good performer. If more than one applicant meets these two conditions, managers must further determine which applicants are likely to be better performers than others. They have several selection tools to help them sort out the relative qualifications of job applicants and appraise their potential for being good performers in a particular job. These tools include background information, interviews, paper-and-pencil tests, physical ability tests, performance tests, and references (see Figure 12.3).[70]

BACKGROUND INFORMATION To aid in the selection process, managers obtain background information from job applications and from résumés. Such information might include the highest levels of education obtained, college majors and minors,

---

lateral move
A job change that entails no major changes in responsibility or authority levels.

Figure 12.3

Selection Tools

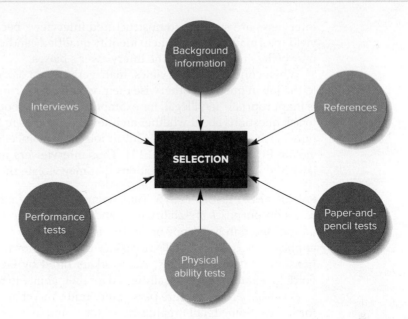

type of college or university attended, years and type of work experience, and mastery of foreign languages. Background information can be helpful both to screen out applicants who are lacking key qualifications (such as a college degree) and to determine which qualified applicants are more promising than others. For example, applicants with a BS may be acceptable, but those who also have an MBA may be preferable.

Increasing numbers of organizations are performing background checks to verify the background information prospective employees provide (and also to uncover any negative information such as crime convictions).[71] According to Automatic Data Processing, Inc. (ADP), an outsourcing company that performs payroll and human resource functions for organizations, more and more companies are performing background checks on prospective employees and are uncovering inaccuracies, inconsistencies, and negative information not reported on applications.[72] According to ADP, about 30% of applicants provide some form of false information about their employment history.[73] And in some cases, background checks reveal prior convictions.[74]

INTERVIEWS Virtually all organizations use interviews during the selection process, as is true at the Four Seasons in the "Management Snapshot." Interviews may be structured or unstructured. In a *structured interview,* managers ask each applicant the same standard questions (such as "What are your unique qualifications for this position?" and "What characteristics of a job are most important to you?"). Particularly informative questions may be those that prompt an interviewee to demonstrate skills and abilities needed for the job by answering the question. Sometimes called *situational interview questions,* these often present interviewees with a scenario they would likely encounter on the job and ask them to indicate how they would handle it.[75] For example, applicants for a sales job may be asked to indicate how they would respond to a customer who complains about waiting too long for service, a customer who is indecisive, and a customer whose order is lost.

An *unstructured interview* proceeds more like an ordinary conversation. The interviewer feels free to ask probing questions to discover what the applicant is like and does not ask a fixed set of questions determined in advance. In general, structured interviews are superior to unstructured interviews because they are more likely to yield information that will help identify qualified candidates, are less subjective, and may be less influenced by the interviewer's biases.

When conducting interviews, managers cannot ask questions that are irrelevant to the job in question; otherwise their organizations run the risk of costly lawsuits. It is inappropriate and illegal, for example, to inquire about an interviewee's spouse or to ask questions about whether an interviewee plans to have children. Because questions such as these are irrelevant to job performance, they are discriminatory and violate EEO laws (see Table 12.1). Thus interviewers need to be instructed in EEO laws and informed about questions that may violate those laws.

PAPER-AND-PENCIL TESTS The two main kinds of paper-and-pencil tests used for selection purposes are ability tests and personality tests; both kinds of tests can be administered in hard copy or electronic form. *Ability tests* assess the extent to which applicants possess the skills necessary for job performance, such as verbal comprehension or numerical skills. Autoworkers hired by General Motors, Chrysler, and Ford, for example, are typically tested for their ability to read and to do mathematics.[76]

Personality tests measure personality traits and characteristics relevant to job performance. Some retail organizations, for example, give job applicants honesty tests to determine how trustworthy they are. The use of personality tests (including honesty tests) for hiring purposes is controversial. Some critics maintain that honesty tests do not really measure honesty (that is, they are not valid) and can be faked by job applicants. Before using any paper-and-pencil tests for selection purposes, managers must have sound evidence that the tests are actually good predictors of performance on the job in question. Managers who use tests without such evidence may be subject to costly discrimination lawsuits.

PHYSICAL ABILITY TESTS For jobs requiring physical abilities, such as firefighting, garbage collecting, and package delivery, managers use physical ability tests that measure physical strength and stamina as selection tools. Autoworkers are typically tested for mechanical dexterity because this physical ability is an important skill for high job performance in many auto plants.[77]

PERFORMANCE TESTS *Performance tests* measure job applicants' performance on actual job tasks. Applicants for secretarial positions, for example, typically are required to complete a keyboarding test that measures how quickly and accurately they type. Applicants for middle and top management positions are sometimes given short-term projects to complete—projects that mirror the kinds of situations that arise in the job being filled—to assess their knowledge and problem-solving capabilities.[78]

Assessment centers, first used by AT&T, take performance tests one step further. In a typical assessment center, about 10 to 15 candidates for managerial positions participate in a variety of activities over a few days. During this time they are assessed for the skills an effective manager needs—problem-solving, organizational, communication, and conflict resolution skills. Some of the activities are performed individually; others are performed in groups. Throughout the process, current managers observe the candidates' behavior and measure performance. Summary evaluations are then used as a selection tool.

REFERENCES Applicants for many jobs are required to provide references from former employers or other knowledgeable sources (such as a college instructor or adviser) who know the applicants' skills, abilities, and other personal characteristics. These individuals are asked to provide candid information about the applicant. References are often used at the end of the selection process to confirm a decision to hire. Yet the fact that many former employers are reluctant to provide negative information in references sometimes makes it difficult to interpret what a reference is really saying about an applicant.

In fact, several recent lawsuits filed by applicants who felt that they were unfairly denigrated or had their privacy invaded by unfavorable references from former employers have caused managers to be increasingly wary of providing any negative information in a reference, even if it is accurate. For jobs in which the jobholder is responsible for the safety and lives of other people, however, failing to provide accurate negative information in a reference does not just mean that the wrong person might get hired; it may also mean that other people's lives will be at stake.

THE IMPORTANCE OF RELIABILITY AND VALIDITY Whatever selection tools a manager uses need to be both reliable and valid. **Reliability** is the degree to which a tool or test measures the same thing each time it is administered. Scores on a selection test should be similar if the same person is assessed with the same tool on two different days; if there is quite a bit of variability, the tool is unreliable. For interviews, determining reliability is more complex because the dynamic is personal interpretation. That is why the reliability of interviews can be increased if two or more different qualified interviewers interview the same candidate. If the interviews are reliable, the interviewers should come to similar conclusions about the interviewee's qualifications.

Validity is the degree to which a tool measures what it purports to measure—for selection tools, it is the degree to which the test predicts performance on the tasks or job in question. Does a physical ability test used to select firefighters, for example, actually predict on-the-job performance? Do assessment center ratings actually predict managerial performance? Do keyboarding tests predict secretarial performance? These are all questions of validity. Honesty tests, for example, are controversial because it is not clear that they validly predict honesty in such jobs as retailing and banking.

Managers have an ethical and legal obligation to use reliable and valid selection tools. Yet reliability and validity are matters of degree rather than all-or-nothing characteristics. Thus managers should strive to use selection tools in such a way that they can achieve the greatest degree of reliability and validity. For ability tests of a particular skill, managers should keep up to date on the latest advances in the development of valid paper-and-pencil tests and use the test with the highest reliability and validity ratings for their purposes. Regarding interviews, managers can improve reliability by having more than one person interview job candidates.

reliability The degree to which a tool or test measures the same thing each time it is used.

validity The degree to which a tool or test measures what it purports to measure.

training Teaching organizational members how to perform their current jobs and helping them acquire the knowledge and skills they need to be effective performers.

development Building the knowledge and skills of organizational members so they are prepared to take on new responsibilities and challenges.

LO 12-3 Discuss the training and development options that ensure organizational members can effectively perform their jobs.

Training and Development

Training and development help to ensure that organizational members have the knowledge and skills needed to perform jobs effectively, take on new responsibilities, and adapt to changing conditions. **Training** focuses primarily on teaching organizational members how to perform their current jobs and helping them acquire the knowledge and skills they need to be effective performers. **Development** focuses on building the knowledge and skills of organizational members so they are prepared to take on new responsibilities and challenges. Training tends to be used more frequently at lower levels of an organization; development tends to be used more frequently with professionals and managers.

Before creating training and development programs, managers should perform a **needs assessment** to determine which employees need training or development and what type of skills or knowledge they need to acquire (see Figure 12.4).[79]

needs assessment
An assessment of which employees need training or development and what type of skills or knowledge they need to acquire.

Types of Training

There are two types of training: classroom instruction and on-the-job training.

CLASSROOM INSTRUCTION Through classroom instruction, employees acquire knowledge and skills in a classroom setting. This instruction may take place within the organization or outside it, such as through courses at local colleges and universities. Many organizations establish their own formal instructional divisions—some are even called "colleges"—to provide needed classroom instruction. For example, at Disney, classroom instruction and other forms of training and developing are provided to employees at Disney University.[80]

Classroom instruction frequently uses videos and role playing in addition to traditional written materials, lectures, and group discussions. *Videos* can demonstrate appropriate and inappropriate job behaviors. For example, by watching an experienced salesperson effectively deal with a loud and angry customer, inexperienced salespeople can develop skills in handling similar situations. During *role playing*, trainees either directly participate in or watch others perform actual job activities in a simulated setting. At McDonald's Hamburger University, for example, role playing helps franchisees acquire the knowledge and skills they need to manage their restaurants.

Simulations also can be part of classroom instruction, particularly for complicated jobs that require an extensive amount of learning and in which errors carry a high cost. In a simulation, key aspects of the work situation and job tasks are duplicated as closely as possible in an artificial setting. For example, air traffic controllers are trained by simulations because of the complicated nature of the work, the extensive amount of learning involved, and the very high costs of air traffic control errors.

on-the-job training
Training that takes place in the work setting as employees perform their job tasks.

ON-THE-JOB TRAINING In **on-the-job training**, learning occurs in the work setting as employees perform their job tasks. On-the-job training can be provided by

Figure 12.4
Training and Development

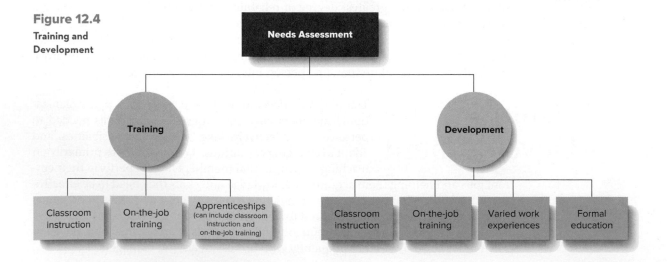

coworkers or supervisors or can occur simply as jobholders gain experience and knowledge from doing the work. Newly hired waiters and waitresses in chains such as Red Lobster or the Olive Garden often receive on-the-job training from experienced employees. The supervisor of a new bus driver for a campus bus system may ride the bus for a week to ensure that the driver has learned the routes and follows safety procedures. For all on-the-job training, employees learn by doing.

Managers often use on-the-job training on a continuing basis to ensure that their subordinates keep up to date with changes in goals, technology, products, or customer needs and desires. For example, sales representatives at Mary Kay Cosmetics Inc. receive ongoing training so they not only know about new cosmetic products and currently popular colors but also are reminded of Mary Kay's guiding principles. Mary Kay's expansion into Russia has succeeded in part because of the ongoing training that Mary Kay's Russian salespeople receive.[81]

Types of Development

Although both classroom instruction and on-the-job training can be used for development as well as training, development often includes additional activities such as varied work experiences and formal education.

VARIED WORK EXPERIENCES Top managers need to develop an understanding of, and expertise in, a variety of functions, products and services, and markets. To develop executives who will have this expertise, managers frequently make sure that employees with high potential have a wide variety of different job experiences, some in line positions and some in staff positions. Varied work experiences broaden employees' horizons and help them think about the big picture. For example, one- to three-year stints overseas are being used increasingly to provide managers with international work experiences. With organizations becoming more global, managers need to understand the different values, beliefs, cultures, regions, and ways of doing business in different countries.

Another development approach is mentoring. (A *mentor* is an experienced member of an organization who provides advice and guidance to a less experienced member, called a *protégé*.) Having a mentor can help managers seek out work experiences and assignments that will contribute to their development and can enable them to gain the most possible from varied work experiences.[82] Although some mentors and protégés hook up informally, organizations have found that formal mentoring programs can be valuable ways to contribute to the development of managers and all employees. For example, Goldman Sachs, Deloitte, and Time Inc. all have formal (and mandatory) mentoring programs.[83]

Formal mentoring programs ensure that mentoring takes place in an organization and structure the process. Participants receive training, efforts are focused on matching mentors and protégés so meaningful developmental relationships ensue, and organizations can track reactions and assess the potential benefits of

At many restaurants, new employees receive on-the-job training by shadowing more experienced waiters and waitresses as they go about their work. © Reza Estakhrian/Photographer's Choice/Getty Images

mentoring. Formal mentoring programs can also ensure that diverse members of an organization receive the benefits of mentoring. A study conducted by David A. Thomas, a professor at the Harvard Business School, found that members of racial minority groups at three large corporations who were very successful in their careers had the benefit of mentors. Formal mentoring programs help organizations make this valuable development tool available to all employees.[84]

When diverse members of an organization lack mentors, their progress in the organization and advancement to high-level positions can be hampered. Ida Abott, a lawyer and consultant on work-related issues, presented a paper to the Minority Corporate Counsel Association in which she concluded, "The lack of adequate mentoring has held women and minority lawyers back from achieving professional success and has led to high rates of career dissatisfaction and attrition."[85]

Mentoring can benefit all kinds of employees in all kinds of work.[86] John Washko, a manager at the Four Seasons hotel chain, benefited from the mentoring he received from Stan Bromley on interpersonal relations and how to deal with employees; mentor Bromley, in turn, found that participating in the Four Seasons' mentoring program helped him develop his own management style.[87] More generally, development is an ongoing process for all managers, and mentors often find that mentoring contributes to their own personal development.

FORMAL EDUCATION Many large corporations reimburse employees for tuition expenses they incur while taking college courses and obtaining advanced degrees. This is not just benevolence on the part of the employer or even a simple reward given to the employee; it is an effective way to develop employees who can take on new responsibilities and more challenging positions. For similar reasons, corporations spend thousands of dollars sending managers to executive development programs such as executive MBA programs. In these programs, experts teach managers the latest in business and management techniques and practices.

To save time and travel costs, some managers rely on *long-distance learning* to formally educate and develop employees. Using videoconferencing technologies, business schools such as the Harvard Business School, the University of Michigan, and Babson College teach courses on video screens in corporate conference rooms. Business schools also customize courses and degrees to fit the development needs of employees in a particular company and/or a particular geographic region.[88] Moreover, some employees and managers seek to advance their educations though online degree programs.[89]

> **LO 12-4** Explain why performance appraisal and feedback are such crucial activities, and list the choices managers must make in designing effective performance appraisal and feedback procedures.

Transfer of Training and Development

Whenever training and development take place off the job or in a classroom setting, it is vital for managers to promote the transfer of the knowledge and skills acquired *to the actual work situation.* Trainees should be encouraged and expected to use their newfound expertise on the job.

> **performance appraisal** The evaluation of employees' job performance and contributions to their organization.

Performance Appraisal and Feedback

The recruitment/selection and training/development components of a human resource management system ensure that employees have the knowledge and skills needed to be effective now and in the future. Performance appraisal and feedback complement recruitment, selection, training, and development. **Performance appraisal** is the evaluation

performance feedback

The process through which managers share performance appraisal information with subordinates, give subordinates an opportunity to reflect on their own performance, and develop, with subordinates, plans for the future.

of employees' job performance and contributions to the organization. **Performance feedback** is the process through which managers share performance appraisal information with their subordinates, give subordinates an opportunity to reflect on their own performance, and develop, with subordinates, plans for the future. Before performance feedback, performance appraisal must take place. Performance appraisal could take place without providing performance feedback, but wise managers are careful to provide feedback because it can contribute to employee motivation and performance.

Performance appraisal and feedback contribute to the effective management of human resources in several ways. Performance appraisal gives managers important information on which to base human resource decisions.[90] Decisions about pay raises, bonuses, promotions, and job moves all hinge on the accurate appraisal of performance. Performance appraisal can also help managers determine which workers are candidates for training and development and in what areas. Performance feedback encourages high levels of employee motivation and performance. It lets good performers know that their efforts are valued and appreciated. It also lets poor performers know that their lackluster performance needs improvement. Performance feedback can give both good and poor performers insight on their strengths and weaknesses and ways in which they can improve their performance in the future.

Types of Performance Appraisal

Performance appraisal focuses on the evaluation of traits, behaviors, and results.[91]

TRAIT APPRAISALS When trait appraisals are used, managers assess subordinates on personal characteristics that are relevant to job performance, such as skills, abilities, or personality. A factory worker, for example, may be evaluated based on her ability to use computerized equipment and perform numerical calculations. A social worker may be appraised based on his empathy and communication skills.

Three disadvantages of trait appraisals often lead managers to rely on other appraisal methods. First, possessing a certain personal characteristic does not ensure that the personal characteristic will actually be used on the job and result in high performance. For example, a factory worker may possess superior computer and numerical skills but be a poor performer due to low motivation. The second disadvantage of trait appraisals is linked to the first. Because traits do not always show a direct association with performance, workers and courts of law may view them as unfair and potentially discriminatory. The third disadvantage of trait appraisals is that they often do not enable managers to give employees feedback they can use to improve performance. Because trait appraisals focus on relatively enduring human characteristics that change only over the long term, employees can do little to change their behavior in response to performance feedback from a trait appraisal. Telling a social worker that he lacks empathy says little about how he can improve his interactions with clients, for example. These disadvantages suggest that managers should use trait appraisals only when they can demonstrate that the assessed traits are accurate and important indicators of job performance.

BEHAVIOR APPRAISALS Through behavior appraisals, managers assess how workers perform their jobs—the actual actions and behaviors that workers exhibit on the job. Whereas trait appraisals assess what workers *are like,* behavior appraisals assess what workers *do.* For example, with a behavior appraisal, a manager might evaluate a social worker on the extent to which he looks clients in the eye when talking with them, expresses sympathy when they are upset, and refers them to community counseling and support groups geared toward the specific problems they are encountering. Behavior appraisals are especially useful when *how* workers perform their jobs is important. In educational organizations such as high schools, for example, the numbers of classes and students taught are important, but also important is how they are taught or the methods teachers use to ensure that learning takes place.

Behavior appraisals have the advantage of giving employees clear information about what they are doing right and wrong and how they can improve their performance. And because behaviors are much easier for employees to change than traits, performance feedback from behavior appraisals is more likely to lead to improved performance.

RESULTS APPRAISALS For some jobs, *how* people perform the job is not as important as *what* they accomplish or the results they obtain. With results appraisals, managers appraise performance by the results or the actual outcomes of work behaviors. Take the case of two new car salespeople. One salesperson strives to develop personal relationships with her customers. She spends hours talking to them and frequently calls them to see how their decision-making process is going. The other salesperson has a much more hands-off approach. He is very knowledgeable, answers customers' questions, and then waits for them to come to him. Both salespersons sell, on average, the same number of cars, and the customers of both are satisfied with the service they receive, according to postcards the dealership mails to customers asking for an assessment of their satisfaction. The manager of the dealership appropriately uses results appraisals (sales and customer satisfaction) to evaluate the salespeople's performance because it does not matter which behavior salespeople use to sell cars as long as they sell the desired number and satisfy customers. If one salesperson sells too few cars, however, the manager can give that person performance feedback about his or her low sales.

OBJECTIVE AND SUBJECTIVE APPRAISALS Whether managers appraise performance in terms of traits, behaviors, or results, the information they assess is either *objective* or *subjective*. **Objective appraisals** are based on facts and are likely to be numerical—the number of cars sold, the number of meals prepared, the number of times late, the number of audits completed. Managers often use objective appraisals when results are being appraised because results tend to be easier to quantify than traits or behaviors. When *how* workers perform their jobs is important, however, subjective behavior appraisals are more appropriate than results appraisals.

Subjective appraisals are based on managers' perceptions of traits, behaviors, or results. Because subjective appraisals rest on managers' perceptions, there is always the chance that they are inaccurate. This is why both researchers and managers have spent considerable time and effort on determining the best way to develop reliable and valid subjective measures of performance.

objective appraisal An appraisal that is based on facts and is likely to be numerical.

subjective appraisal An appraisal that is based on perceptions of traits, behaviors, or results.

Who Appraises Performance?

We have been assuming that managers or the supervisors of employees evaluate performance. This is a reasonable assumption: supervisors are the most common appraisers of performance.[92] Performance appraisal is an important part of most managers' job duties. Managers are responsible for not only motivating their subordinates to perform at a high level but also making many decisions hinging on performance appraisals, such as pay raises or promotions. Appraisals by managers can be usefully augmented by appraisals from other sources (see Figure 12.5).

SELF, PEERS, SUBORDINATES, AND CLIENTS When self-appraisals are used, managers supplement their evaluations with an employee's assessment of his or her own performance. Peer appraisals are provided by an employee's coworkers. Especially when subordinates work in groups or teams, feedback from peer appraisals can motivate team members while giving managers important information for decision making. A growing number of companies are having subordinates appraise their managers' performance and leadership as well. And sometimes customers or clients assess employee performance in terms of responsiveness to customers and quality of service. Although appraisals from these sources can be useful, managers need to be aware of potential issues that may arise when they are used. Subordinates sometimes may be inclined to inflate self-appraisals, especially if organizations are downsizing and they are worried about job security. Managers who are appraised by their subordinates may fail to take needed but unpopular actions out of fear that their subordinates will appraise them negatively. Some of these potential issues can be mitigated to the extent that there are high levels of trust in an organization.

360-DEGREE PERFORMANCE APPRAISALS To improve motivation and performance, some organizations include 360-degree appraisals and feedback in their performance appraisal systems, especially for managers. In a **360-degree appraisal** a variety of people, beginning with the manager and including peers or coworkers, subordinates, superiors, and sometimes even customers or clients, appraise a manager's performance. The manager receives feedback based on evaluations from these multiple sources.

Companies in a variety of industries rely on 360-degree appraisals and feedback.[93] For 360-degree appraisals and feedback to be effective, there has to be trust throughout an organization. More generally, trust is a critical ingredient in any performance appraisal and feedback procedure. In addition, research suggests that 360-degree appraisals should focus on behaviors rather than traits or results and that managers need to carefully select appropriate raters. Moreover, appraisals tend to be more honest when made anonymously and when raters have been trained in how to use

360-degree appraisal

A performance appraisal by peers, subordinates, superiors, and sometimes clients who are in a position to evaluate a manager's performance.

Figure 12.5

Who Appraises Performance?

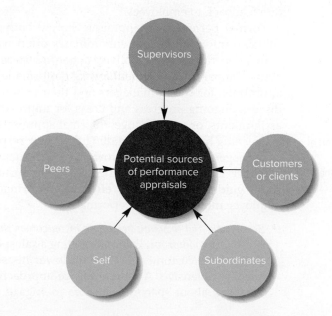

360-degree appraisal forms.[94] Additionally, managers need to think carefully about the extent to which 360-degree appraisals are appropriate for certain jobs and be willing to modify any appraisal system they implement if they become aware of unintended problems it creates.[95]

Even when 360-degree appraisals are used, it is sometimes difficult to design an effective process by which subordinates' feedback can be communicated to their managers; but advances in information technology can solve this problem. For example, ImproveNow.com has online questionnaires that subordinates fill out to evaluate the performance of their managers and give the managers feedback. Each subordinate of a particular manager completes the questionnaire independently, all responses are tabulated, and the manager is given specific feedback on behaviors in a variety of areas, such as rewarding good performance, looking out for subordinates' best interests and being supportive, and having a vision for the future.[96]

Effective Performance Feedback

For the appraisal and feedback component of a human resource management system to encourage and motivate high performance, managers must give their subordinates feedback. To generate useful information to feed back to their subordinates, managers can use both formal and informal appraisals. **Formal appraisals** are conducted at set times during the year and are based on performance dimensions and measures that have been specified in advance.

formal appraisal
An appraisal conducted at a set time during the year and based on performance dimensions and measures that were specified in advance.

Managers in most large organizations use formal performance appraisals on a fixed schedule dictated by company policy, such as every six months or every year. An integral part of a formal appraisal is a meeting between the manager and the subordinate in which the subordinate is given feedback on performance. Performance feedback lets subordinates know which areas they are excelling in and which areas need improvement; it should also tell them *how* they can improve their performance. Realizing the value of formal appraisals, managers in many large corporations have committed substantial resources to updating their performance appraisal procedures and training low-level managers in how to use them and provide accurate feedback to employees.[97]

Formal performance appraisals supply both managers and subordinates with valuable information; but subordinates often want more frequent feedback, and managers often want to motivate subordinates as the need arises. For these reasons many companies supplement formal performance appraisal with frequent **informal appraisals**, for which managers and their subordinates meet as the need arises to discuss ongoing progress and areas for improvement. Moreover, when job duties, assignments, or goals change, informal appraisals can give workers timely feedback concerning how they are handling their new responsibilities.

informal appraisal
An unscheduled appraisal of ongoing progress and areas for improvement.

Managers often dislike providing performance feedback, especially when the feedback is negative, but doing so is an important managerial activity.[98] Here are some guidelines for giving effective performance feedback that contributes to employee motivation and performance:

- *Be specific and focus on behaviors or outcomes that are correctable and within a worker's ability to improve.* Example: Telling a salesperson that he is too shy when interacting with customers is likely to lower his self-confidence and prompt him to become defensive. A more effective approach would be to give the salesperson feedback about specific behaviors to engage in—greeting customers as soon as they enter the department, asking customers whether they need help, and volunteering to help customers find items.

- *Approach performance appraisal as an exercise in problem solving and solution finding, not criticizing.* Example: Rather than criticizing a financial analyst for turning in reports late, the manager helps the analyst determine why the reports are late and identify ways to better manage her time.

- *Express confidence in a subordinate's ability to improve.* Example: Instead of being skeptical, a first-level manager tells a subordinate that he is confident that the subordinate can increase quality levels.

- *Provide performance feedback both formally and informally.* Example: The staff of a preschool receives feedback from formal performance appraisals twice a year. The school director also provides frequent informal feedback such as complimenting staff members on creative ideas for special projects, noticing when they do a particularly good job handling a difficult child, and pointing out when they provide inadequate supervision.

- *Praise instances of high performance and areas of a job in which a worker excels.* Example: Rather than focusing on just the negative, a manager discusses the areas her subordinate excels in as well as the areas in need of improvement.

- *Avoid personal criticisms and treat subordinates with respect.* Example: An engineering manager acknowledges her subordinates' expertise and treats them as professionals. Even when the manager points out performance problems to subordinates, she refrains from criticizing them personally.

- *Agree to a timetable for performance improvements.* Example: A first-level manager and his subordinate decide to meet again in one month to determine whether quality levels have improved.

LO 12-5 Explain the issues managers face in determining levels of pay and benefits.

In following these guidelines, managers need to remember *why* they are giving performance feedback: to encourage high levels of motivation and performance. Moreover, the information that managers gather through performance appraisal and feedback helps them determine how to distribute pay raises and bonuses.

Pay and Benefits

Pay includes employees' base salaries, pay raises, and bonuses and is determined by a number of factors such as characteristics of the organization and the job and levels of performance. Employee *benefits* are based on membership in an organization (not necessarily on the particular job held) and include sick days, vacation days, and medical and life insurance. In Chapter 9 we discuss how pay can motivate organizational members to perform at a high level, as well as the different kinds of pay plans managers can use to help an organization achieve its goals and gain a competitive advantage. As you will learn, it is important to link pay to behaviors or results that contribute to organizational effectiveness. Next we focus on establishing an organization's pay level and pay structure.

pay level The relative position of an organization's pay incentives in comparison with those of other organizations in the same industry employing similar kinds of workers.

Pay Level

Pay level is a broad comparative concept that refers to how an organization's pay incentives compare, in general, to those of other organizations in the same industry employing similar kinds of workers. Managers must decide if they want to offer relatively high wages, average wages, or relatively low wages. High wages help ensure that an organization is going to be able to recruit, select, and retain high performers, but high wages also raise costs. Low wages give an organization a cost advantage but may undermine the organization's ability to select and recruit high performers and to motivate current employees to perform at a high level. Either of these situations may lead to inferior quality or inadequate customer service.

In determining pay levels, managers should take into account their organization's strategy. A high pay level may prohibit managers from effectively pursuing a low-cost strategy. But a high pay level may be worth the added costs in an organization whose competitive advantage lies in superior quality and excellent customer service. As one might expect, hotel and motel chains with a low-cost strategy, such as Days Inn and Hampton Inns, have lower pay levels than chains striving to provide high-quality rooms and services, such as the Four Seasons profiled in "A Manager's Challenge."

Pay Structure

pay structure
The arrangement of jobs into categories reflecting their relative importance to the organization and its goals, levels of skill required, and other characteristics.

After deciding on a pay level, managers have to establish a pay structure for the different jobs in the organization. A **pay structure** clusters jobs into categories reflecting their relative importance to the organization and its goals, levels of skill required, and other characteristics managers consider important. Pay ranges are established for each job category. Individual jobholders' pay within job categories is then determined by factors such as performance, seniority, and skill levels.

There are some interesting global differences in pay structures. Large corporations based in the United States tend to pay their CEOs and top managers higher salaries than do their European or Japanese counterparts. Also, the pay differential between employees at the bottom of the corporate hierarchy and those higher up is much greater in U.S. companies than in European or Japanese companies.[99]

Concerns have been raised over whether it is equitable or fair for CEOs of large companies in the United States to be making millions of dollars in years when their companies are restructuring and laying off a large portion of their workforces.[100] Additionally, the average CEO in the United States typically earns over 360 times what the average hourly worker earns.[101] Is a pay structure with such a huge pay differential ethical? Shareholders and the public are increasingly asking this very question and asking large corporations to rethink their pay structures.[102] Also troubling are the millions of dollars in severance packages that some CEOs receive when they leave their organizations. When many workers are struggling to find and keep jobs and make ends meet, people are questioning whether it is ethical for some top managers to be making so much money.[103]

Benefits

Organizations are legally required to provide certain benefits to their employees, including workers' compensation, Social Security, and unemployment insurance. Workers' compensation helps employees financially if they become unable to work due to a work-related injury or illness. Social Security provides financial assistance to retirees and disabled former employees. Unemployment insurance provides financial assistance to workers who lose their jobs due to no fault of their own. The legal system in the United States views these three benefits as ethical requirements for organizations and thus mandates that they be provided.

Other benefits such as health insurance, dental insurance, vacation time, pension plans, life insurance, flexible working hours, company-provided day care, and employee assistance and wellness programs have traditionally been provided at the option of employers. The Health Care Reform Bill signed by President Barack Obama in March 2010 contains provisions whereby, starting in 2014, employers with 50 or more employees may face fines if they don't provide their employees with health insurance coverage.[104] Benefits enabling workers to balance the demands of their jobs and of their lives away from the office or factory are of growing importance for many workers who have competing demands on their scarce time and energy.

In some organizations, top managers determine which benefits might best suit the employees and organization and offer the same benefit package to all employees. Other organizations, realizing that employees' needs and desires might differ, offer **cafeteria-style benefit plans** that let employees choose the benefits they want. Cafeteria-style benefit plans sometimes help managers deal with employees who feel unfairly treated because they are unable to take advantage of certain benefits available to other employees who, for example, have children. Some organizations have success with cafeteria-style benefit plans; others find them difficult to manage.

As health care costs escalate and overstretched employees find it hard to take time to exercise and take care of their health, more companies are providing benefits and incentives to promote employee wellness. According to a survey conducted by Fidelity Investments and the National Business Group on Health, close to 90% of organizations provide some kind of incentive, prize, or reward to employees who take steps to improve their health.[105] For working parents, family-friendly benefits are especially attractive. For example, access to on-site child care, being able to telecommute and take time off to care for sick children, and provisions for emergency back-up child care can be valued benefits for working parents with young children.

Same-sex domestic partner benefits are also being used to attract and retain valued employees. Gay and lesbian workers are reluctant to work for companies that do not provide the same kinds of benefits for their partners as those provided for partners of the opposite sex.[106]

cafeteria-style benefit plan A plan from which employees can choose the benefits they want.

LO12-6 Understand the role that labor relations play in the effective management of human resources.

Labor Relations

Labor relations are the activities managers engage in to ensure that they have effective working relationships with the labor unions that represent their employees' interests. Although the U.S. government has responded to the potential for unethical and unfair treatment of workers by creating and enforcing laws regulating employment (including the EEO laws listed in Table 12.1), some workers believe a union will ensure that their interests are fairly represented in their organizations.

labor relations The activities managers engage in to ensure that they have effective working relationships with the labor unions that represent their employees' interests.

Before we describe unions in more detail, let's take a look at some examples of important employment legislation. In 1938 the government passed the Fair Labor Standards Act, which prohibited child labor and provided for minimum wages, overtime pay, and maximum working hours to protect workers' rights. In 1963 the Equal Pay Act mandated that men and women performing equal work (work requiring the same levels of skill, responsibility, and effort performed in the same kind of working conditions) receive equal pay (see Table 12.1). In 1970 the Occupational Safety and Health Act mandated procedures for managers to follow to ensure workplace safety. These are just a few of the U.S. government's efforts to protect workers' rights. State legislatures also have been active in promoting safe, ethical, and fair workplaces.

Unions

Unions exist to represent workers' interests in organizations. Given that managers have more power than rank-and-file workers and that organizations have multiple stakeholders, there is always the potential that managers might take steps that benefit one set of stakeholders such as shareholders while hurting another such as employees. For example, managers may decide to speed up a production line to lower costs and increase production in the hopes of increasing returns to shareholders. Speeding up the line, however, could hurt employees forced to work at a rapid pace and may increase the risk of injuries. Also, employees receive no additional pay for the extra work they are performing. Unions would represent workers' interests in a scenario such as this one.

Congress acknowledged the role that unions could play in ensuring safe and fair workplaces when it passed the National Labor Relations Act of 1935. This act made it legal for workers to organize into unions to protect their rights and interests and declared certain unfair or unethical organizational practices to be illegal. The act also established the National Labor Relations Board (NLRB) to oversee union activity. Currently the NLRB conducts certification elections, which are held among the employees of an organization to determine whether they want a union to represent their interests. The NLRB also makes judgments concerning unfair labor practices and specifies practices that managers must refrain from.

Employees might vote to have a union represent them for any number of reasons.[107] They may think their wages and working conditions need improvement. They may believe managers are not treating them with respect. They may think their working hours are unfair or they need more job security or a safer work environment. Or they may be dissatisfied with management and find it difficult to communicate their concerns to their bosses. Regardless of the specific reason, one overriding reason is power: A united group inevitably wields more power than an individual, and this type of power may be especially helpful to employees in some organizations.

Although these would seem to be potent forces for unionization, some workers are reluctant to join unions. Sometimes this reluctance is due to the perception that union leaders are corrupt. Some workers may simply believe that belonging to a union might not do them much good while costing them money in membership dues. Employees also might not want to be forced into doing something they do not want to, such as striking because the union thinks it is in their best interest. Moreover, although unions can be a positive force in organizations, sometimes they also can be a negative force, impairing organizational effectiveness. For example, when union leaders resist needed changes in an organization or are corrupt, organizational performance can suffer.

The percentage of U.S. workers represented by unions today is smaller than it was in the 1950s, an era when unions were especially strong.[108] In the 1950s, around 35% of U.S. workers were union members; in 2013, 11.3% of workers were members of unions.[109] The American Federation of Labor–Congress of Industrial Organizations (AFL-CIO) includes 56 voluntary member unions representing more than 12 million workers.[110] Overall, approximately 14.5 million workers in the United States belong to unions.[111] Union influence in manufacturing and heavy industries has been on the decline; more generally, approximately 6.7% of private sector workers are union members.[112] However, around 35.3% of government workers belong to unions.[113] Unions have made inroads in other segments of the workforce, particularly the low-wage end. Garbage collectors in New Jersey, poultry plant workers in North Carolina, and janitors in Baltimore are among the growing numbers of low-paid workers who are currently finding union membership attractive. North Carolina poultry workers voted in a union partly because they thought it was unfair that they had to buy their own gloves and hairnets used on the job and had to ask their supervisors' permission to go to the restroom.[114]

collective bargaining
Negotiations between labor unions and managers to resolve conflicts and disputes about issues such as working hours, wages, benefits, working conditions, and job security.

Collective Bargaining

Collective bargaining is negotiation between labor unions and managers to resolve conflicts and disputes about important issues such as working hours, wages, working conditions, and job security. Sometimes union members go on strike to drive home their concerns to managers. Once an agreement that union members support has been reached (sometimes with the help of a neutral third party called a *mediator*), union leaders and managers sign a contract spelling out the terms of the collective bargaining agreement.

Summary and Review

STRATEGIC HUMAN RESOURCE MANAGEMENT Human resource management (HRM) includes all the activities managers engage in to ensure that their organizations can attract, retain, and effectively use human resources. Strategic HRM is the process by which managers design the components of a human resource management system to be consistent with each other, with other elements of organizational architecture, and with the organization's strategies and goals. **LO 12-1**

RECRUITMENT AND SELECTION Before recruiting and selecting employees, managers must engage in human resource planning and job analysis. Human resource planning includes all the activities managers engage in to forecast their current and future needs for human resources. Job analysis is the process of identifying (1) the tasks, duties, and responsibilities that make up a job and (2) the knowledge, skills, and abilities needed to perform the job. Recruitment includes all the activities managers engage in to develop a pool of qualified applicants for open positions. Selection is the process by which managers determine the relative qualifications of job applicants and their potential for performing well in a particular job. **LO 12-2**

TRAINING AND DEVELOPMENT Training focuses on teaching organizational members how to perform effectively in their current jobs. Development focuses on broadening organizational members' knowledge and skills so they are prepared to take on new responsibilities and challenges. **LO 12-3**

PERFORMANCE APPRAISAL AND FEEDBACK Performance appraisal is the evaluation of employees' job performance and contributions to the organization. Performance feedback is the process through which managers share performance appraisal information with their subordinates, give them an opportunity to reflect on their own performance, and develop with them plans for the future. Performance appraisal gives managers useful information for decision making. Performance feedback can encourage high levels of motivation and performance. **LO 12-4**

PAY AND BENEFITS Pay level is the relative position of an organization's pay incentives in comparison with those of other organizations in the same industry employing similar workers. A pay structure clusters jobs into categories according to their relative importance to the organization and its goals, the levels of skill required, and other characteristics. Pay ranges are then established for each job category. Organizations are legally required to provide certain benefits to their employees; other benefits are provided at the discretion of employers. **LO 12-5**

LABOR RELATIONS Labor relations include all the activities managers engage in to ensure that they have effective working relationships with the labor unions that represent their employees' interests. The National Labor Relations Board oversees union activity. Collective bargaining is the process through which labor unions and managers resolve conflicts and disputes and negotiate agreements. **LO 12-6**

Management *in Action*

TOPICS FOR DISCUSSION AND ACTION

Discussion

1. Discuss why it is important for human resource management systems to be in sync with an organization's strategy and goals and with each other. [LO 12-1]

2. Discuss why training and development are ongoing activities for all organizations. [LO 12-3]

3. Describe the type of development activities you think middle managers are most in need of. [LO 12-3]

4. Evaluate the pros and cons of 360-degree performance appraisals and feedback. Would you like your performance to be appraised in this manner? Why or why not? [LO 12-4]

5. Discuss why two restaurants in the same community might have different pay levels. [LO 12-5]

Action

6. Interview a manager in a local organization to determine how that organization recruits and selects employees. [LO 12-2]

BUILDING MANAGEMENT SKILLS

Analyzing Human Resource Management Systems [LO 12-1, 12-2, 12-3, 12-4, 12-5]

Think about your current job or a job you have had in the past. If you have never had a job, interview a friend or family member who is currently working. Answer the following questions about the job you have chosen:

1. How are people recruited and selected for this job? Are the recruitment and selection procedures the organization uses effective or ineffective? Why?

2. What training and development do people who hold this job receive? Are the training and development appropriate? Why or why not?

3. How is performance of this job appraised? Does performance feedback contribute to motivation and high performance on this job?

4. What levels of pay and benefits are provided on this job? Are these levels appropriate? Why or why not?

MANAGING ETHICALLY [LO 12-4, 12-5]

Some managers do not want to become overly friendly with their subordinates because they are afraid that if they do so their objectivity when conducting performance appraisals and making decisions about pay raises and promotions will be impaired. Some subordinates resent it when they see one or more of their coworkers being very friendly with the boss; they are concerned about the potential for favoritism. Their reasoning runs something like this: If two subordinates are equally qualified for a promotion and one is a good friend of the boss and the other is a mere acquaintance, who is more likely to receive the promotion?

Questions

1. Either individually or in a group, think about the ethical implications of managers' becoming friendly with their subordinates.

2. Do you think managers should feel free to socialize and become good friends with their subordinates outside the workplace if they so desire? Why or why not?

SMALL GROUP BREAKOUT EXERCISE [LO 12-1, 12-2, 12-3, 12-4, 12-5]

Building a Human Resource Management System

Form groups of three or four people, and appoint one group member as the spokesperson who will communicate your findings to the class when called on by the instructor. Then discuss the following scenario:

You and your three partners are engineers who minored in business at college and have decided to start a consulting business. Your goal is to provide manufacturing process engineering and other engineering services to large and small organizations. You forecast that there will be an increased use of outsourcing for these activities. You discussed with managers in several large organizations the services you plan to offer, and they expressed considerable interest. You have secured funding to start your business and now are building the HRM system. Your human resource planning suggests that you need to hire between five and eight experienced engineers with good communication skills, two clerical/secretarial workers, and two MBAs who between them have financial, accounting, and human resource skills. You are striving to develop your human resources in a way that will enable your new business to prosper.

1. Describe the steps you will take to recruit and select (a) the engineers, (b) the clerical/secretarial workers, and (c) the MBAs.

2. Describe the training and development the engineers, the clerical/secretarial workers, and the MBAs will receive.

3. Describe how you will appraise the performance of each group of employees and how you will provide feedback.

4. Describe the pay level and pay structure of your consulting firm.

BE THE MANAGER [LO 12-4]

You are Walter Michaels and have just received some disturbing feedback. You are the director of human resources for Maxi Vision Inc., a medium-size window and glass door manufacturer. You recently initiated a 360-degree performance appraisal system for all middle and upper managers at Maxi Vision, including yourself, but excluding the most senior executives and the top management team. You were eagerly awaiting the feedback you would receive from the managers who report to you; you had recently implemented several important initiatives that affected them and their subordinates, including a complete overhaul of the organization's performance appraisal system. While the managers who report to you were evaluated based on 360-degree appraisals, their subordinates were evaluated using a 20-question BARS scale you recently created that focuses on behaviors. Conducted annually, appraisals are an important input into pay raise and bonus decisions.

You were so convinced that the new performance appraisal procedures were highly effective that you hoped your own subordinates would mention them in their feedback to you. And boy did they! You were amazed to learn that the managers *and* their subordinates thought the new BARS scales were unfair, inappropriate, and a waste of time. In fact, the managers' feedback to you was that their own performance was suffering, based on the 360-degree appraisals they received, because their subordinates hated the new appraisal system and partially blamed their bosses, who were part of management. Some managers even admitted giving all their subordinates approximately the same scores on the scales so their pay raises and bonuses would not be affected by their performance appraisals.

You couldn't believe your eyes when you read these comments. You spent so much time developing what you thought was the ideal rating scale for this group of employees. Evidently, for some unknown reason, they wouldn't give it a chance. Your own supervisor is aware of these complaints and said that it was a top priority for you to fix "this mess" (with the implication that you were responsible for creating it). What are you going to do?

THE WALL STREET JOURNAL CASE IN THE NEWS [LO12-4]

You're Awesome! Firms Scrap Negative Feedback

Managers Ease Up On Harsh Reviews; In Past, 'We'd Beat Them Down a Bit'

If you don't have anything nice to say, management has a tip: Try harder.

Fearing they'll crush, employees' confidence and erode performance, employers are asking managers to ease up on harsh feedback. "Accentuate the positive" has become a new mantra at workplaces like **VMware** Inc., **Wayfair** Inc., and the **Boston Consulting Group** Inc., where bosses now dole out frequent praise, urge employees to celebrate small victories and focus performance reviews around a particular worker's strengths—instead of dwelling on why he flubbed a client presentation.

The shift may annoy leaders who rose in a tough-love era in business, but executives say hard-edge tactics simply do more harm than good these days.

When employees' flaws are laid bare, "there's that mental 'ugh' and shrug of, 'This is who I am,' " says Michelle Russell, a partner at BCG.

Bit by bit, the consulting firm has changed the way managers evaluate employee performance. For years, those discussions focused largely on employee missteps and where they needed to improve.

"We would bring them in and beat them down a bit," says Ms. Russell. After the reviews, she observed some employees left the company as their confidence and performance slipped; others seemed rattled days or weeks later. Now, managers are expected to extol staffers' strengths during reviews and check-ins, explaining how the person can use his or her talents to tackle aspects of the job that come less naturally.

Firms Scrap Negative Reviews

Bosses are advised to mention no more than one or two areas that require development, Ms. Russell adds.

Some veteran managers dismissed the new approach as a feel-good initiative, she says. Others found they had to force consultants—so accustomed to homing in on their weaknesses—to listen to what they were doing well; says Ms. Russell.

Liz Gilliam, a project leader with the company, says she always zoned out during the positive parts of performance discussions with managers, but took notes whenever her bosses pointed out her flaws. Ms. Gilliam, 31 years old, found the negatives "disheartening" and "jarring," but admits she couldn't help obsessing, over them.

Managers now require her to pay attention to the positives—one forbade her to write down her weaknesses unless she jotted down the good things, too, and another made her transcribe her strengths on a white board. "It's a scary exercise," she says, but has given her new-found confidence.

Not that firms want to eliminate negative feedback entirely. Tough feedback sometimes motivates people better than praise does, management experts say. Jack Zenger and Joseph Folkman of leadership consultancy Zenger Folkman have found employees crave critiques more than gold stars.

Showing people how they stack up is the "emotionally loudest" type of feedback, according to Sheila Heen, a lecturer at Harvard Law School and co-author of "Thanks for the Feedback." Most employees feel unappreciated, Ms. Heen says, and criticism tends to overshadow appreciation or coaching, especially among young workers.

Still, companies that ramp up the positivity need to make sure they're not totally bypassing the evaluation of employees, she says.

Workers want to know where they stand, and they'll start listening for evaluation in all kinds of conversations if they're not getting it during a performance review, for example.

It can become an excuse for managers "to avoid the parts of the conversation they didn't want to have," Ms. Heen says. Problems can fester and employees will notice when their colleagues aren't pulling their weight. "That also is demoralizing," she says.

Maynard Webb, chairman of **Yahoo** Inc. and author of a 2013 book on work, recalls being yelled at by an executive at IBM in the early 1980s. With such feedback, "you just tried to make sure it didn't derail you," he says.

That same executive today would face disciplinary action, guesses Mr. Webb. "People expect to be treated differently," he says.

Lots of businesses remain devoted to toughness. At **Netflix** Inc., chief executive Reed Hastings's famed manifesto on the company culture likens the firm to a pro sports team, not a Little League squad, noting that "adequate performance gets a generous severance package."

VMware borrowed ideas from marriage counselors: boosting the ratio of positive-negative comments and having workers celebrate their wins.

The rising popularity of tools like Gallup's StrengthsFinder, which is designed to measure a person's talents in any of 34 areas, suggests how many more companies are taking a positive tack. About 600,000 people used the tool each year from 2001 through 2012, says Leticia McCadden, a spokeswoman for Gallup.

Since 2012, the number of users has jumped to 1.6 million a year. As of last year, Strengths Finder was used by 467 members of the Fortune 500.

Facebook, one of the best-known users of StrengthsFinder, has crafted a new management style attuned to the needs of 20-and 30-somethings that comprise most of its staff.

E-commerce company Wayfair teaches its managers how to make feedback "palatable," according to learning and development specialist Ashley Libitz, so that the company's hundreds of young workers, "not only understand they're doing a great job but exactly what it is they're doing great."

PricewaterhouseCoopers LLP, which hired nearly 9,000 employees and interns from universities last year, asks managers to hold "career outlook" discussions about employees' futures at the firm, rather than reviews centered on where they dropped the ball over the past year.

The firm also urges staff to send e-cards praising peers or subordinates, and allocates money for managers to dole out to further reward wins, according to Tim Ryan, a vice chairman at the company.

Caitlin Marcoux, a senior associate at the company, says she still gets told when she messed up. But she appreciates the extra dose of appreciation, which she says has helped to build her confidence. Without it, "I'll be a harsher critic on myself," she says.

Palo Alto, Calif., software company VMware Inc., is pushing managers to embrace Marshall Goldsmith's "feedforward" concept, which asks employees to suggest ideas for their own improvement in the future, rather than review past performance.

No judging, rating or critiquing is allowed, says Victoria Sevilla, who develops training for employees there.

"It doesn't depress [employees] into thinking, 'one more thing to develop, one more thing that's wrong,'" she says.

VMware has borrowed techniques from marriage counselors, such as increasing the ratio of positive to negative comments in the workplace and encouraging employees to celebrate their wins.

"You're really trying to get them in the moment where they're reliving the joy they felt," says Jessica Amortegui, a former VMware talent development executive.

Yahoo's Mr. Webb cautions that overly positive managers run the risk of ignoring problems festering in their workplace, making for a crisis down the line.

Overall, though, the evolution isn't a bad thing—people perform better when they're encouraged and inspired, he says. With softer tactics showing up everywhere from classrooms to football fields, it may be the direction things are headed anyway, he says.

"I don't think it's just management practices that are getting soft."

Questions

1. What are some of the potential advantages of providing employees with relatively positive performance appraisals and feedback?

2. What are some of the potential disadvantages of providing employees with positive performance appraisals and feedback?

3. What are some of potential advantages of providing employees with negative feedback?

4. What are some of the potential disadvantages of providing employees with negative feedback?

Source: Rachel Feintzeig, "You're Awesome! Firms Scrap Negative Feedback," The Wall Street Journal, February 11, 2015, B1, B5.

Endnotes

1. J.M. O'Brien, "100 Best Companies to Work For—A Perfect Season," Fortune, February 4, 2008, 64–66; "Four Seasons Employees Name Company to Fortune '100 Best Companies to Work For' List," www.fourseasons.com/about_us/press_release_280.html, February 22, 2008; "Four Seasons Hotels and Resort Named to Fortune List of the '100 Best Companies to Work For,'" http://press.fourseasons.com/news-releases/four-seasons-hotels-and-resorts-named-to-fortu . . ., February 24, 2010; "Four Seasons Hotels & Resorts—Best Companies to Work For 2012," Fortune, http://money.cnn.com/magazines/fortune/best-companies/2012/snapshots/85.html, April 23, 2012.; "Employer of Choice: Four Seasons Hotels and Resorts Named to FORTUNE List of the '100 Best Companies to Work For' for 17th Consecutive Year," employer-of-choice-four-seasons-hotels-and-resorts-named-to-fortune-list-of-the-100-best-companies-to-work-for-fo-17th-consecutive-year, April 23, 2014.; M. Moskowitz and R. Levering, "The 100 Best Companies to Work For," Fortune, February 3, 2014, 108–20; M. Moskowitz and R. Levering, "The 100 Best Companies to Work For," Fortune, March 5, 2015, pp. 140–54.

2. "Four Seasons Employees Name Company to Fortune '100 Best Companies to Work For' List"; "Employer of Choice: Four Seasons Hotels and Resorts Named to FORTUNE List of the '100 Best Companies to Work For' for 17th Consecutive Year."

3. O'Brien, "100 Best Companies to Work For—A Perfect Season"; "Four Seasons Hotels & Resorts—Best Companies to Work For 2012"; "Four Seasons Hotels—100 Best Companies to Work For 2014—Fortune, http://money.cnn.com/magazines/fortune/best-companies/2014/snapshots/91.html.

4. "Four Seasons Hotels and Resorts—About Us: Corporate Bios," www.fourseasons.com/about_us/corporate_bios/, February 24, 2010; "Four Seasons Hotels and Resorts Jobs / Hotel and Resort Career Search Site," http://jobs.fourseasons.com/Pages/Home.aspx, April 26, 2012.; "Four Seasons Holdings Inc.: Private Company Information," Businessweek, http://investing.businessweek.com/research/stocks/private/snapshot.asp?privcapId=357114, April 23, 2014.

5. O'Brien, "100 Best Companies to Work For—A Perfect Season."

6. Ibid.; "Creating the Four Seasons Difference," www.businessweek.com/print/innovate/content/jan2008/id20080122_671354.htm, February 22, 2008.

7. O'Brien, "100 Best Companies to Work For—A Perfect Season"; "Creating the Four Seasons Difference."

8. "Creating the Four Seasons Difference"; "Four Seasons Employees Name Company to Fortune '100 Best Companies to Work For' List."

9. M. Moskowitz, R. Levering, and C. Tkaczyk, "The List," Fortune, February 8, 2010, 75–88.

10. O'Brien, "100 Best Companies to Work For—A Perfect Season."

11. "Creating the Four Seasons Difference."

12. "Employer of Choice: Four Seasons Hotels and Resorts Named to FORTUNE List of the '100 Best Companies to Work For' for 17th Consecutive Year."

13. O'Brien, "100 Best Companies to Work For—A Perfect Season."

14. Ibid.

15. Ibid.

16. Ibid.

17. Ibid.

18. Ibid.; "Creating the Four Seasons Difference"; "Four Seasons Employees Name Company to Fortune '100 Best Companies to Work For' List"; "Employer of Choice: Four Seasons Hotels and Resorts Named to FORTUNE List of the '100 Best Companies to Work For' for 17th Consecutive Year."

19. J.E. Butler, G.R. Ferris, and N.K. Napier, Strategy and Human Resource Management (Cincinnati: Southwestern Publishing, 1991); P.M. Wright and G.C. McMahan, "Theoretical Perspectives for Strategic Human Resource Management," Journal of Management 18 (1992), 295–320.

20. AlixPartners Professionals, "Fitzpatrick, David A.," www.alixpartners.com/en/Professionals/tabid/670/EmployeeBio/FitzpatrickDavidA/Id/1709/Default.aspx, April 23, 2014.

21. L. Clifford, "Why You Can Safely Ignore Six Sigma," Fortune, January 22, 2001, 140.

22. J.B. Quinn, P. Anderson, and S. Finkelstein, "Managing Professional Intellect: Making the Most of the Best," *Harvard Business Review,* March–April 1996, 71–80.

23. Ibid.

24. "Looking for Ideas in Shared Workspaces. Established Companies Hope Interaction with Others Will Spark Collaboration," *The Wall Street Journal* (www.zappos.com/streetwear), March 20, 2012, http://about.zappos.com/press-center/media-coverage/looking-ideas-shared-workspaces-est. . ., April 23, 2012.

25. D. Garnick, "CEO Takes a Walk on the Whimsical Side," *Boston Herald,* Wednesday, May 20, 2009, http://about.zappos.com/press-center/media-coverage/ceo-takes-walk-whimsical-side, February 22, 2010; C. Palmeri, "Zappos Retails Its Culture," *BusinessWeek,* December 30, 2009, www.businessweek.com/print/magazine/content/10_02/b4162057120453.htm, February 22, 2010; "On a Scale of 1 to 10, How Weird Are You?" *The New York Times,* January 10, 2010, www.nytimes.com/2010/01/10/business/10corner.html?pagewanted=print, February 22, 2010; M. Chafkin, "Get Happy," *Inc.,* May 2009, 66–73; "Keeper of the Flame," *The Economist,* April 18, 2009, 75; M. Rich, "Why Is This Man Smiling," *The New York Times,* April 8, 2011.

26. 100 Best Companies to Work For 2010: Zappos.com—AMZN—from FORTUNE, "15. Zappos.com," http://money.cnn.com/magazines/fortune/bestcompanies/2010/snapshots/15.html, February 22, 2010; "Zappos, Best Companies to Work For 2012," *Fortune,* http://money.cnn.com/magazines/fortune/best-companies/2012/snapshots/11.html, April 23, 2012.; Moskowitz and Levering, "The 100 Best Companies to Work For." Fortune, February 3, 2014, pp. 108-120; Moskowitz and Levering, "The 100 Best Companies to Work For."

27. R. Wauters, "Amazon Closes Zappos Deal, Ends Up Paying $1.2 Billion," *TechCrunch,* November 2, 2009, http://techcrunch.com/2009/11/02/amazon-closes-zappos-deal-ends-up-paying-1-2-billion/, February 22, 2010.

28. J. McGregor, "Zappo's Secret: It's an Open Book," *BusinessWeek,* March 23 & 30, 2009, 62; "About.zappos.com," Tony Hsieh—CEO, http://about.zappos.com/meet-our-monkeys/tony-hsieh-ceo, February 22, 2010; Chafkin, "Get Happy."

29. Chafkin, "Get Happy"; "Keeper of the Flame."

30. "In The Beginning—Let There Be Shoes," about.zappos.com, http://about.zappos.com/zappos-story/in-the-beginning-let-there-be-shoes, February 22, 2010; Looking Ahead—Let There Be Anything and Everything," about.zappos.com, http://about.zappos.com/zappos-story/looking-ahead-let-there-be-anything-and-everything, February 22, 2010; J.B. Darin, "Curing Customer Service," *Fortune,* May 20, 2009, http://about.zappos.com/press-center/media-coverage/curing-customer-service, February 22, 2010.

31. Chafkin, "Get Happy"; "Keeper of the Flame."

32. "Zappos Core Values," about.zappos.com, http://about.zappos.com/our-unique-culture/zappos-core-values, February 22, 2010; "Zappos Family Core Values," about.zappos.com, http://about.zappos.com/our-unique-culture/zappos-core-values, April 23, 2012.

33. "From Upstart to $1 Billion Behemoth, Zappos Marks 10 Years," *Las Vegas Sun,* June 16, 2009, http://about.zappos.com/press-center/media-coverage/upstart-1-billion-behemoth-zappos- . . ., February 22, 2010; Chafkin, "Get Happy"; "Keeper of the Flame."

34. Chafkin, "'Get Happy"; "Keeper of the Flame."

35. Chafkin, "Get Happy."

36. C.D. Fisher, L.F. Schoenfeldt, and J.B. Shaw, *Human Resource Management* (Boston: Houghton Mifflin, 1990).

37. Wright and McMahan, "Theoretical Perspectives."

38. L. Baird and I. Meshoulam, "Managing Two Fits for Strategic Human Resource Management," *Academy of Management Review* 14, 116–28; J. Milliman, M. Von Glinow, and M. Nathan, "Organizational Life Cycles and Strategic International Human Resource Management in Multinational Companies: Implications for Congruence Theory," *Academy of Management Review* 16 (1991), 318–39; R.S. Schuler and S.E. Jackson, "Linking Competitive Strategies with Human Resource Management Practices," *Academy of Management Executive* 1 (1987), 207–19; P.M. Wright and S.A. Snell, "Toward an Integrative View of Strategic Human Resource Management," *Human Resource Management Review* 1 (1991), 203–225.

39. "Who's in Charge Here? No One," *The Observer,* April 27, 2003 (http://observer.guardian.co.uk/business/story/0,6903,944138,00.html); "Ricardo Semler, CEO, Semco SA," cnn.com, June 29, 2004 (http://cnn.worldnews.printthis.clickability.com/pt/cpt&title=cnn.com); D. Kirkpatrick, "The Future of Work: An 'Apprentice' Style Office?" *Fortune,* April 14, 2004 (www.fortune.com/fortune/subs/print/0,15935,611068,00.html); A. Strutt and R. Van Der Beek, "Report from HR2004," www.mce.be/hr2004/reportd2.htm, July 2, 2004; R. Semler, "Seven-Day Weekend Returns Power to Employees," workopolis.com, May 26, 2004 (http://globeandmail.workopolis.com/servlet/content/qprinter/20040526/cabooks26); "SEMCO," http://semco.locaweb.com.br/ingles, May 31, 2006; "Ricardo Semler, Semco SA: What Are You Reading?" cnn.com, May 31, 2006. (www.cnn.com/2004/BUSINESS/06/29/semler.profile/index.html); "About the Semco Group, *SEMCO,* www.semco.com.br/en/content.asp?content=1&contentID=610., April 24, 2012.

40. "Group Companies: Semco Capital Goods Division," *SEMCO,* www.semco.com.br/en/content.asp?content=7&contentID=611, April 24, 2012; "Group Companies: Pitney Bowes Semco," *SEMCO,* www.semco.com.br/en/content.asp?content=7&contentID=612, April 24, 2012.

41. R. Semler, *The Seven-Day Weekend: Changing the Way Work Works* (New York: Penguin, 2003); "SEMCO"; Semco Partners, http://semco.com.br/en/, April 23, 2014.

42. Semler, *The Seven-Day Weekend;* "SEMCO"; G. Hamel, *The Future of Management* (Cambridge, MA: Harvard Business Press, 2007).

43. A. Strutt, "Interview with Ricardo Semler," *Management Centre Europe*, April 2004 (www.mce.be/knowledge/392/35).

44. Semler, *The Seven-Day Weekend*.

45. Ibid.

46. R. Semler, "How We Went *Digital* without a *Strategy*," *Harvard Business Review* 78, no. 5 (September–October 2000), 51–56.

47. Semler, *The Seven-Day Weekend*.

48. Equal Employment Opportunity Commission, "Uniform Guidelines on Employee Selection Procedures," *Federal Register* 43 (1978), 38290–315.

49. R. Stogdill II, R. Mitchell, K. Thurston, and C. Del Valle, "Why AIDS Policy Must Be a Special Policy," *BusinessWeek*, February 1, 1993, 53–54.

50. J.M. George, "AIDS/AIDS-Related Complex," in L. Peters, B. Greer, and S. Youngblood, eds., *The Blackwell Encyclopedic Dictionary of Human Resource Management* (Oxford, England: Blackwell Publishers, 1997).

51. Ibid.

52. Ibid.; Stogdill et al., "Why AIDS Policy Must Be a Special Policy"; K. Holland, "Out of Retirement and into Uncertainty," *The New York Times*, May 27, 2007, BU17.

53. S.L. Rynes, "Recruitment, Job Choice, and Post-Hire Consequences: A Call for New Research Directions," in M.D. Dunnette and L.M. Hough, eds., *Handbook of Industrial and Organizational Psychology*, vol. 2 (Palo Alto, CA: Consulting Psychologists Press, 1991), 399–444.

54. "Kelly Services—Background," www.kellyservices.com/web/global/services/en/pages/background.html, April 24, 2012.

55. R.L. Sullivan, "Lawyers a la Carte," *Forbes*, September 11, 1995, 44.

56. E. Porter, "Send Jobs to India? U.S. Companies Say It's Not Always Best," *The New York Times*, April 28, 2004, A1, A7.

57. D. Wessel, "The Future of Jobs: New Ones Arise; Wage Gap Widens," *The Wall Street Journal*, April 2, 2004, A1, A5; "Relocating the Back Office," *The Economist*, December 13, 2003, 67–69.

58. The Conference Board, "Offshoring Evolving at a Rapid Pace, Report Duke University and The Conference Board," August 3, 2009, www.conference-board .org/utilities/pressPrinterFriendly .cfm?press_ID=3709, February 24, 2010; S. Minter, "Offshoring by U.S. Companies Doubles," *Industry Week*, August 19, 2009, www. industryweek.com/PrintArticle.asp x?ArticleID=19772&SectionID=3, February 24, 2010; AFP, "Offshoring by U.S. Companies Surges: Survey," August 3, 2009, www.google. com/hostednews/afp/article/ ALeqM5iDaq1D2KZU16YfbKrM PdborD7. . ., February 24, 2010; V. Wadhwa, "The Global Innovation Migration," *BusinessWeek*, November 9, 2009, www.businessweek.com/ print/technology/content/nov2009/ tc2009119_331698.htm, February 24, 2010; T. Heijmen, A.Y. Lewin, S. Manning, N. Perm-Ajchariyawong, and J.W. Russell, "Offshoring Research the C-Suite," 2007–2008 ORN Survey Report, *The Conference Board*, in collaboration with Duke University Offshoring Research Network.

59. The Conference Board, "Offshoring Evolving at a Rapid Pace"; Minter, "Offshoring by U.S. Companies Doubles"; AFP, "Offshoring by U.S. Companies Surges"; V. Wadhwa, "The Global Innovation Migration"; Heijmen et al., "Offshoring Research the C-Suite."

60. V. Wadhwa, "The Global Innovation Migration."

61. The Conference Board, "Offshoring Evolving at a Rapid Pace."

62. Ibid.; Minter, "Offshoring by U.S. Companies Doubles"; AFP, "Offshoring by U.S. Companies Surges"; Heijmen et al., "Offshoring Research the C-Suite."

63. R.J. Harvey, "Job Analysis," in Dunnette and Hough, *Handbook of Industrial and Organizational Psychology*, 71–163.

64. E.L. Levine, *Everything You Always Wanted to Know about Job Analysis: A Job Analysis Primer* (Tampa, FL: Mariner Publishing, 1983).

65. R.L. Mathis and J.H. Jackson, *Human Resource Management*, 7th ed. (Minneapolis: West, 1994).

66. Rynes, "Recruitment, Job Choice, and Post-Hire Consequences."

67. R. Sharpe, "The Life of the Party? Can Jeff Taylor Keep the Good Times Rolling at Monster. com?" *BusinessWeek*, June 4, 2001 (*BusinessWeek* Archives); D.H. Freedman, "The Monster Dilemma," *Inc.*, May 2007, 77–78; P. Korkki, "So Easy to Apply, So Hard to Be Noticed," *The New York Times*, July 1, 2007, BU16.

68. Jobline International, "Resume Vacancy Posting, Employment Resources, Job Searches," www. jobline.net, February 25, 2010.

69. www.jobline.org, Jobline press releases, May 8, 2001, accessed June 20, 2001.

70. R.M. Guion, "Personnel Assessment, Selection, and Placement," in Dunnette and Hough, *Handbook of Industrial and Organizational Psychology*, 327–97.

71. T. Joyner, "Job Background Checks Surge," *Houston Chronicle*, May 2, 2005, D6.

72. Ibid.; "ADP News Releases: Employer Services: ADP Hiring Index Reveals Background Checks Performed More Than Tripled since 1997," *Automatic Data Processing, Inc.*, June 3, 2006 (www. investquest.com/iq/a/aud/ne/ news/adp042505background.htm); "Employee Benefits Administration," *ADP*, www.adp.com/, April 25, 2012.

73. "Background Checks and Employment Screening from ADP," www.adp-es.co.uk/employment-screening/?printpreview51, April 25, 2012.

74. "ADP News Releases."

75. R.A. Noe, J.R. Hollenbeck, B. Gerhart, and P.M. Wright, *Human Resource Management: Gaining a Competitive Advantage* (Burr Ridge, IL: Irwin, 1994); J.A. Wheeler and J.A. Gier, "Reliability and Validity of the Situational Interview for a Sales Position," *Journal of Applied Psychology* 2 (1987), 484–87.

76. J. Flint, "Can You Tell Applesauce from Pickles?" *Forbes*, October 9, 1995, 106–8.

77. Ibid.

78. "Wanted: Middle Managers, Audition Required," *The Wall Street Journal*, December 28, 1995, A1.

79. I.L. Goldstein, "Training in Work Organizations," in Dunnette and Hough, *Handbook of Industrial and Organizational Psychology*, 507–619.

80. "Disney Workplaces: Training & Development," *The Walt*

Disney Company, 2010 Corporate Citizenship Report, http://corporate.disney.go.com/citizenship2010/disneyworkplaces/overview/trainingandde . . ., April 25, 2012.

81. N. Banerjee, "For Mary Kay Sales Reps in Russia, Hottest Shade Is the Color of Money," *The Wall Street Journal,* August 30, 1995, A8.

82. T.D. Allen, L.T. Eby, M.L. Poteet, E. Lentz, and L. Lima, "Career Benefits Associated with Mentoring for Protégés: A Meta-Analysis," *Journal of Applied Psychology* 89, no. 1 (2004), 127–36.

83. M. Khidekel, "The Misery of Mentoring Millennials," *Bloomberg Businessweek,* www.businessweek.com/printer/articles/102262-the-misery-of-mentoring-millennials, April 24, 2014.

84. P. Garfinkel, "Putting a Formal Stamp on Mentoring," *The New York Times,* January 18, 2004, BU10.

85. Ibid.

86. Allen et al., "Career Benefits Associated with Mentoring"; L. Levin, "Lesson Learned: Know Your Limits. Get Outside Help Sooner Rather Than Later," *BusinessWeek Online,* July 5, 2004 (www.businessweek.com); "Family, Inc.," *BusinessWeek Online,* November 10, 2003 (www.businessweek.com); J. Salamon, "A Year with a Mentor. Now Comes the Test," *The New York Times,* September 30, 2003, B1, B5; E. White, "Making Mentorships Work," *The Wall Street Journal,* October 23, 2007, B11.

87. Garfinkel, "Putting a Formal Stamp on Mentoring."

88. J.A. Byrne, "Virtual B-Schools," *BusinessWeek,* October 23, 1995, 64–68; "Michigan Executive Education Locations around the Globe," http://exceed.bus.umich.edu/InternationalFacilities/default.aspx, February 25, 2010.

89. "Top Distance Learning & Online MBA Programs," *Businessweek,* www.businessweek.com/bschools/rankings/distance_mba_profiles, April 24, 2014.

90. Fisher et al., *Human Resource Management.*

91. Fisher et al., *Human Resource Management;* G.P. Latham and K.N. Wexley, *Increasing Productivity through Performance Appraisal* (Reading, MA: Addison-Wesley, 1982).

92. J.S. Lublin, "It's Shape-Up Time for Performance Reviews," *The Wall Street Journal,* October 3, 1994, B1, B2.

93. J.S. Lublin, "Turning the Tables: Underlings Evaluate Bosses," *The Wall Street Journal,* October 4, 1994, B1, B14; S. Shellenbarger, "Reviews from Peers Instruct—and Sting," *The Wall Street Journal,* October 4, 1994, B1, B4.

94. C. Borman and D.W. Bracken, "360 Degree Appraisals," in C.L. Cooper and C. Argyris, eds., *The Concise Blackwell Encyclopedia of Management* (Oxford, England: Blackwell Publishers, 1998), 17; D.W. Bracken, "Straight Talk about Multi-Rater Feedback," *Training and Development* 48 (1994), 44–51; M.R. Edwards, W.C. Borman, and J.R. Sproul, "Solving the Double Bind in Performance Appraisal: A Saga of Solves, Sloths, and Eagles," *Business Horizons* 85 (1985), 59–68.

95. M.A. Peiperl, "Getting 360 Degree Feedback Right," *Harvard Business Review,* January 2001, 142–47.

96. A. Harrington, "Workers of the World, Rate Your Boss!" *Fortune,* September 18, 2000, 340, 342; www.ImproveNow.com, June 2001.

97. Lublin, "It's Shape-Up Time for Performance Reviews."

98. S.E. Moss and J.I. Sanchez, "Are Your Employees Avoiding You? Managerial Strategies for Closing the Feedback Gap," *Academy of Management Executive* 18, no. 1 (2004), 32–46.

99. J. Flynn and F. Nayeri, "Continental Divide over Executive Pay," *BusinessWeek,* July 3, 1995, 40–41.

100. J.A. Byrne, "How High Can CEO Pay Go?" *BusinessWeek,* April 22, 1996, 100–106.

101. A. Borrus, "A Battle Royal against Regal Paychecks," *BusinessWeek,* February 24, 2003, 127; "Too Many Turkeys," *The Economist,* November 26, 2005, 75–76; G. Morgenson, "How to Slow Runaway Executive Pay," *The New York Times,* October 23, 2005, 1, 4; S. Greenhouse, *The Big Squeeze: Tough Times for the American Worker* (New York: Alfred A. Knopf, 2008); "Trends in CEO Pay," *AFL-CIO,* www.aflcio.org/Corporate-Watch/CEO-Pay-and-the-99/Trends-in-CEO-Pay, April 26, 2012.

102. "Executive Pay," *BusinessWeek,* April 19, 2004, 106–110.

103. "Home Depot Chief's Pay in 2007 Could Reach $8.9m," *The New York Times,* Bloomberg News, January 25, 2007, C7; E. Carr, "The Stockpot," *The Economist, A Special Report on Executive Pay,* January 20, 2007, 6–10; E. Porter, "More Than Ever, It Pays to Be the Top Executive," *The New York Times,* May 25, 2007, A1, C7.

104. K. Garber, "What Is (and Isn't) in the Healthcare Bill," *U.S. News & World Report,* March 22, 2010, www.usnews.com/articles/news/politics/2010/02/22/what-is-and-isnt-in-the healthca . . ., March 29, 2010; S. Condon, "Health Care Bill Signed by Obama," Political Hotsheet CBS News, www.cbsnews.com/8301-503544_162-20000981-503544.html; T.S. Bernard, "For Consumers, Clarity on Health Care Changes," *The New York Times,* March 21, 2010, www.nytimes.com/2010/03/22/your-money/health-insurance/22consumer.html?sq=h . . .; CBSNews.com, "Health Care Reform Bill Summary: A Look At What's in the Bill," March 23, 2009, www.cbsnews.com/8301-503544_162-20000846-503544.html; Reuters, "Factbox: Details of final healthcare bill", March 21, 2010, www.reuters.com/article/idUSTRE62K11V20100321.

105. J. Wieczner, "Your Company Wants to Make You Healthy," "Pros and Cons of Company Wellness Program Incentives," WSJ.com, http://online.wsj.com/news/articles/SB1000142412788732339330457836025228415137 8, April 24, 2014.

106. S. Shellenbarger, "Amid Gay Marriage Debate, Companies Offer More Benefits to Same-Sex Couples," *The Wall Street Journal,* March 18, 2004, D1.

107. S. Premack and J.E. Hunter, "Individual Unionization Decisions," *Psychological Bulletin* 103 (1988), 223–34.

108. M.B. Regan, "Shattering the AFL-CIO's Glass Ceiling," *BusinessWeek,* November 13, 1995, 46; S. Greenhouse, "The Hard Work

of Reviving Labor," *The New York Times,* September 16, 2009, B1, B7.

109. S. Greenhouse, "Survey Finds Deep Shift in the Makeup of Unions," *The New York Times,* November 11, 2009, B5; "Union Members—2011," Union Members Summary, January 27, 2012, www.bls.gov/news.release/union2.nr0.htm; "Union Members Summary, Economic New Release," www.bls.gov/news.release/union2.nr0.htm.

110. www.aflcio.org, June 2001; "About Us," AFL-CIO, www.aflcio.org/aboutus; S. Greenhouse, "Most U.S. Union Members Are Working for the Government, New Data Shows," *The New York Times,* January 23, 2010, www.nytimes.com/2010/01/23/business/23labor.html?pagewanted=print; "About the AFL-CIO," www.aflcio.org/About; About the AFL-CIO, www.aflcio.org/About.

111. Greenhouse, "Most U.S. Union Members Are Working for the Government"; "Union Members—2011," Union Members Summary, January 27, 2012, www.bls.gov/news.release/union2.nr0.htm; Union Members Summary, Economic New Release, www.bls.gov/news.release/union2.nr0.htm.

112. Greenhouse, "Survey Finds Deep Shift in the Makeup of Unions"; "Union Members—2011," Union Members Summary, January 27, 2012, www.bls.gov/news.release/union2.nr0.htm; Union Members Summary, Economic New Release, www.bls.gov/news.release/union2.nr0.htm.

113. Greenhouse, "Most U.S. Union Members Are Working for the Government."

114. G.P. Zachary, "Some Unions Step Up Organizing Campaigns and Get New Members," *The Wall Street Journal,* September 1, 1995, A1, A2; "Union Members Summary, Economic New Release," www.bls.gov/news.release/union2.nr0.htm, April 24, 2014.

PART 6

13 Communication and Information Technology Management

Learning Objectives

After studying this chapter, you should be able to:

LO 13-1 Differentiate between data and information, list the attributes of useful information, and describe three reasons why managers must have access to information to perform their tasks and roles effectively.

LO 13-2 Explain why effective communication helps an organization gain a competitive advantage, and describe the communication process.

LO 13-3 Define information richness, and describe the information richness of communication media available to managers.

LO 13-4 Differentiate among six kinds of management information systems.

© Image Source/Getty Images RF

A smart wristband that has been synchronized with a smartphone. The wristband is a "wearable," a device that allows companies to keep track of workers and allows information to flow from one device to another.
© Haiyin Wang/Alamy RF

MANAGEMENT SNAPSHOT

Wearable Technology Tracks Employee Performance

How Can Managers Harness the Latest Technology to Improve Employee Efficiency and Effectiveness?

Imagine you are sitting at your desk writing a report on your computer. How will the boss know how productive you are? She could install a program that monitors the number of keystrokes you make on the computer or watch you from another cubicle. But there's a new way for the boss to know everything you do. Imagine that while you are working, you are wearing a sensor, just like your employee ID badge, on a lanyard around your neck.

The sensor picks up your body movements, voice inflections, and environmental factors like lighting and temperature. It records that you are sitting at your desk busily typing your report. After 30 minutes, you start to feel a bit fatigued. The badge notes that your pace has slowed. After an hour, you decide to take a short break before your upcoming meeting. The badge records your movements from your desk to the break room. In the break room, you run into a colleague who asks about your fantasy football team. You speak animatedly about how well it is doing. The device records to whom you are speaking (if the

other person is also wearing a sensor) and the level of enthusiasm in your voice. Then the badge tracks your movements from the break room to the conference room for your meeting. It then records who else is in the meeting. If you sit quietly at the meeting and do not contribute, the badge records that. If you nod your head or speak, the badge records that as well.

What is this sensor? It's called a "wearable." These devices allow companies to track where employees are, what they are doing, and how enthusiastically they are doing it. Wearables are somewhat like pedometers, but they do much more than measure steps. With wearables, companies can compare how animated a worker is around certain colleagues and how unanimated that worker is around others. It can tell in which meetings a worker participates and in which the worker prefers to keep quiet.

Wearables can come in the form of smart watches, eyeglasses, earpieces, badges, and other devices. For example, a small camera in a pair of "smart glasses" developed by Vuzix can be worn by distribution center workers to scan bar codes and provide information to the worker in a visual display. The glasses can warn workers if an item is fragile or needs to be picked up a certain way. The glasses also connect to software that can track the flow of workers throughout the distribution center. They can feed back information about which item the workers should pick up next and the fastest route to the item.[1]

Another organization that has used wearables is the Buffalo Bills' football team. The team has embedded a wearable called OptimEye from Catapult Sports in the players' shirts. The device measures speed, acceleration, and distance. The data provided by the OptimEye give the coaches a "Player-Load" statistic that allows them to consider whether a player is becoming fatigued. Fatigue is a common cause of injury. If the OptimEye shows that a player ran a lot in one practice, the coach might reduce the running requirement in the next practice to avoid injuring the player. Also, the data provided by the device allow different coaches on the team to see everything each player is doing. So if a player practices with the special teams coach and then with the defensive coach, both coaches will know how hard the player worked. In the long term, the team may be able to use all the data collected to gain new insights into overall player training.[2]

Wearables can provide valuable data that can be used to improve productivity. In fact, one study found the productivity of workers using wearables increased by 8.5% and their job satisfaction increased by 3.5%.[3] But there are problems as well.

Workers may feel that wearables impinge upon their privacy, that they are never alone at work, even in the bathroom. Also, workers may feel that the only purpose of the wearable is to improve outcomes in efficiency or productivity for the company.[4] Research indicates that when new technologies are touted as improving efficiency, workers tend to resent the meddling of management into their daily work lives.[5]

One organization that uses a wearable, Sociometric Solutions, suggests reassuring employees that their privacy is protected by letting them know what is being tracked, telling them that managers will see aggregate data, not each individual's data, and making participation voluntary. Companies also can present wearables as something that will help workers by making work safer or more interesting and autonomous. Ben Waber, the president and CEO of Sociometric Solutions, says, "What we're trying to do is really quantify what people have always felt to be unquantifiable. Things like, how are people interacting with each other? How do you talk to customers? How engaged are you in a conversation? And how is information flowing in an organization?"[6]

Overview

Even with all the advances in information technology, ineffective communication continues to take place in organizations. Ineffective communication is detrimental for managers, employees, and organizations and can lead to poor performance, strained interpersonal relations, poor service, and dissatisfied customers. For an organization to be effective and gain a competitive advantage, managers at all levels need to be good communicators—and the use of new IT is vital.

In this chapter we survey information systems and information technology in general, looking at the relationship between information and the manager's job. Then we describe the nature of communication and explain why it is so important for all managers and their subordinates to be effective communicators. We describe the communication media available to managers and the factors they need to consider when selecting a communication medium for each message they send. We consider the communication networks that organizational members rely on, and we explore how advances in information technology have expanded managers' communication options.

Finally, we discuss several types of information systems that managers can use to help themselves perform their jobs, and we examine the impact that rapidly evolving information systems and technologies may have on managers' jobs and on an organization's competitive advantage. By the end of this chapter, you will understand the profound ways in which new developments in information systems and technology continue to shape the way managers communicate and perform their functions and roles.

Information and the Manager's Job

LO 13-1 Differentiate between data and information, list the attributes of useful information, and describe three reasons why managers must have access to information to perform their tasks and roles effectively.

data Raw, unsummarized, and unanalyzed facts.

information Data that are organized in a meaningful fashion.

Managers cannot plan, organize, lead, and control effectively unless they have access to information. Information is the source of the knowledge and intelligence that they need to make the right decisions. Information, however, is not the same as data.[7] **Data** are raw, unsummarized, and unanalyzed facts such as volume of sales, level of costs, or number of customers. **Information** is data that are organized in a meaningful fashion, such as in a graph showing changes in sales volume or costs over time. Alone, data do not tell managers anything; information, in contrast, can communicate a great deal of useful knowledge to the person who receives it—such as a manager who sees sales falling or costs rising. The distinction between data and information is important because one of the uses of information technology is to help managers transform data into information in order to make better managerial decisions.

Consider the case of a manager in a supermarket who must decide how much shelf space to allocate to two breakfast cereal brands for children: Dentist's Delight and Sugar Supreme. Most supermarkets use checkout scanners to record individual sales and store the data on a computer. Accessing this computer, the manager might find that Dentist's Delight sells 50 boxes per day and Sugar Supreme sells 25 boxes per day. These raw data, however, are of little help in assisting the manager to decide how to allocate shelf space. The manager also needs to know how much shelf space each cereal currently occupies and how much profit each cereal generates for the supermarket.

Suppose the manager discovers that Dentist's Delight occupies 10 feet of shelf space and Sugar Supreme occupies 4 feet and that Dentist's Delight generates 20 cents of profit a box while Sugar Supreme generates 40 cents of profit a box. By putting these three bits of data together (number of boxes sold, amount of shelf space, and profit per box), the manager gets some useful information on which to base a decision: Dentist's Delight generates $1 of profit per foot of shelf space per day ([50 boxes @ $.20]/10 feet), and Sugar Supreme generates $2.50 of profit per foot of shelf space per day ([25 boxes @ $.40]/4 feet). Armed with this information, the manager might decide to allocate less shelf space to Dentist's Delight and more to Sugar Supreme.

Attributes of Useful Information

Four factors determine the usefulness of information to a manager: quality, timeliness, completeness, and relevance (see Figure 13.1).

QUALITY Accuracy and reliability determine the quality of information.[8] The greater its accuracy and reliability, the higher is the quality of information. Modern IT gives managers access to high-quality real-time information that they can use to improve long-term decision making and alter short-term operating decisions, such as how much of a particular product to make daily or monthly. Supermarket managers, for example, use handheld bar code readers linked to a server to monitor and record how demand for particular products such as milk, chicken, or bread changes daily so they know how to restock their shelves to ensure the products are always available.

TIMELINESS Information that is timely is available when it is required to allow managers to make the optimal decision—not after the decision has been made. In today's rapidly changing world, the need for timely information often means

Figure 13.1
Factors Affecting
the Usefulness of
Information

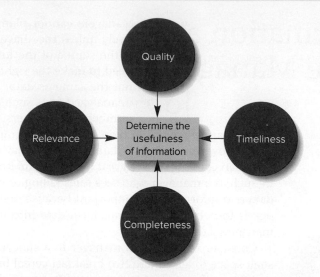

**real-time
information**
Frequently updated
information that reflects
current conditions.

information must be available on a real-time basis—hence the enormous growth in the demand for mobile computing devices such as smartphones.[9] **Real-time information** is information that reflects current changes in business conditions. In an industry that experiences rapid changes, real-time information may need to be updated frequently.

Airlines use real-time information about the number of flight bookings and competitors' prices to adjust their prices hourly to maximize their revenues. Thus, for example, the fare for flights from New York to Seattle might change from one hour to the next as fares are reduced to fill empty seats and raised when most seats have been sold. U.S. airlines make more than 100,000 fare changes each day. Obviously the managers who make such pricing decisions need real-time information about current market demand.

COMPLETENESS Information that is complete gives managers all the information they need to exercise control, achieve coordination, or make an effective decision. Recall from Chapter 5, however, that managers rarely have access to complete information. Instead, because of uncertainty, ambiguity, and bounded rationality, they have to make do with incomplete information.[10] One function of IT is to increase the completeness of managers' information.

RELEVANCE Information that is relevant is useful and suits a manager's particular needs and circumstances. Irrelevant information is useless and may actually hurt the performance of a busy manager who has to spend valuable time determining whether information is relevant. Given the massive amounts of information that managers are now exposed to and their limited information-processing capabilities, a company's information systems designers need to ensure that managers receive only relevant information.

**information
technology (IT)**
The set of methods or
techniques for acquiring,
organizing, storing,
manipulating, and
transmitting information.

What Is Information Technology?

Information technology (IT) is the set of methods or techniques for acquiring, organizing, storing, manipulating, and transmitting information.[11] A **management**

management information system (MIS) A specific form of IT that managers utilize to generate the specific, detailed information they need to perform their roles effectively.

information system (MIS) is a specific form of IT that managers select and use to generate the specific, detailed information they need to perform their roles effectively. Management information systems have existed for as long as there have been organizations, which is a long time indeed: Merchants in ancient Egypt used clay tablets to record their transactions. Before the computing age, most systems were paper-based: Clerks recorded important information on paper documents (often in duplicate or triplicate) in words and numbers; sent copies of the documents to superiors, customers, or suppliers; and stored other copies in filing cabinets for future reference.

Rapid advances in the power of IT—specifically the development of ever more powerful and sophisticated computer hardware and software—have had a fundamental impact on organizations and managers. Some recent IT developments, such as inventory management and customer relationship management (CRM) systems, contribute so much to performance that organizations that do *not* adopt them, or that implement them ineffectively, become uncompetitive compared with organizations that do adopt them.[12] In the 2010s much of the increasing productivity and efficiency of business in general has been attributed to the way organizations and their employees use advancing IT to improve their performance.

Managers need information for three reasons: to make effective decisions, to control the activities of the organization, and to coordinate the activities of the organization. Next we examine these uses of information in detail.

Information and Decisions

Much of management (planning, organizing, leading, and controlling) is about making decisions. For example, the marketing manager must decide what price to charge for a product, what distribution channels to use, and what promotional messages to emphasize to maximize sales. The manufacturing manager must decide how much of a product to make and how to make it. The purchasing manager must decide from whom to purchase inputs and what inventory of inputs to hold. The human relations manager must decide how much employees should be paid, how they should be trained, and what benefits they should be given. The engineering manager must make decisions about new product design. Top managers must decide how to allocate scarce financial resources among competing projects, how best to structure and control the organization, and what business-level strategy the organization should be pursuing. And regardless of their functional orientation, all managers have to make decisions about matters such as what performance evaluation to give to a subordinate.

To make effective decisions, managers need information both from inside the organization and from external stakeholders. When deciding how to price a product, for example, marketing managers need information about how consumers will react to different prices. They need information about unit costs because they do not want to set the price below the cost of production. And they need information about competitive strategy because pricing strategy should be consistent with an organization's competitive strategy. Some of this information will come from outside

Charts and graphs may be the clichéd centerpieces of managerial meetings, but the data they represent are key for making informed decisions.
© Jose Luis Pelaez Inc/Blend Images LLC RF

the organization (for example, from consumer surveys) and some from inside the organization (information about production costs comes from manufacturing). As this example suggests, managers' ability to make effective decisions rests on their ability to acquire and process information.

Information and Control

As discussed in Chapter 8, controlling is the process through which managers regulate how efficiently and effectively an organization and its members perform the activities necessary to achieve its stated goals.[13] Managers achieve control over organizational activities by taking four steps (see Figure 8.2): (1) They establish measurable standards of performance or goals; (2) they measure actual performance; (3) they compare actual performance against established goals; and (4) they evaluate the results and take corrective action if necessary.[14] The package delivery company UPS, for example, has a delivery goal: to deliver 95% of the overnight packages it picks up by noon the next day.[15] UPS has thousands of U.S. ground stations (branch offices that coordinate the pickup and delivery of packages in a particular area) that are responsible for the physical pickup and delivery of packages. UPS managers monitor the delivery performance of these stations regularly; if they find that the 95% goal is not being attained, they determine why and take corrective action if necessary.

To achieve control over any organizational activity, managers must have information. To control ground station activities, a UPS manager might need to know what percentage of packages each station delivers by noon. To obtain this information the manager uses UPS's own IT; UPS is also a leader in developing proprietary in-house IT. All packages to be shipped to the stations have been scanned with handheld scanners by the UPS drivers who pick them up; then all this information is sent wirelessly through UPS servers to its headquarters' mainframe computer. When the packages are scanned again at delivery, this information is also transmitted through its computer network. Managers can access this information to quickly discover what percentage of packages were delivered by noon of the day after they were picked up, and also how this information breaks down station by station so they can take corrective action if necessary.

Management information systems are used to control all divisional and functional operations. In accounting, for example, information systems are used to monitor expenditures and compare them against budgets.[16] To track expenditures against budgets, managers need information about current expenditures, broken down by relevant organizational units; accounting IT is designed to give managers this information. A twist on using technology to improve customer service is being used by Walt Disney World Resort. Instead of having employees use wearables (as described in the opening story), Disney is giving the wearables to the guests in the form of a wristband that works as a hotel room key, parking ticket, and charge card. The data collected will help Disney provide better customer service. For example, in the future, if a guest is wearing a wristband, a Disney employee can greet a visitor by name. The wristband collects a lot of important information about a guest.

From an employer's standpoint, there is a lot of information available on the Internet about employees and prospective employees. The accompanying "Management Insight" feature provides ideas on how that data can be used to make hiring and other workforce decisions.

MANAGEMENT INSIGHT

Big Data Helps Companies Find the Right Talent

How do you track the knowledge, skills, and abilities of every employee in an organization? This information was once stored in personnel files in the form of employee-written profiles and lists of knowledge, skills, and abilities created to match the organization needs. When a new project or a promotion came up requiring a new set of skills, the hiring manager would scan the current employees and check their profiles to see if the needed skills were available. If they were not in the organization's files, the organization might hire an outsider or bring in a contractor for the assignment.

Now there is software that can track the knowledge, skills, and abilities of employees without looking in the employee's file. This software looks at "big data" to find information about employees that is not formally listed in a file and may never have been mentioned to a manager. The software scans the Internet for information about each employee and compiles information from social media sites like Facebook and Twitter, blogs, comments on news stories, and other information posted on the Internet by the employee.

IBM's Smarter Workforce Institute offers products to help organizations locate the talent hidden within their own networks. Jonathan Ferrar, vice president of IBM's Smarter Workforce talent and workforce management division, called the products "a different way of finding people."[17] When using the system, a hiring manager can input the knowledge, skills, and abilities desired for a new position or project. The software searches current employees who fit the profile. The software also provides searches to help with recruitment and selection of quality candidates for jobs and provides help with the management of current employees, including on-boarding of new employees, compensation and rewards, training, performance appraisal, and employee engagement.[18]

Can a computer program do a better job of finding talent than a hiring manager with years of experience? Dr. Peter Cappelli, director of Wharton's Center for Human Resources, suggests that it can. A program can take different information into account than the average hiring manager can. "The industrial psychologists who've been working on this for a hundred years have their own sets of models. The great possibility of big data is in finding things that are outside these paradigms."[19]

Programs like those provided by the Smarter Workforce Institute help businesses to make sense of big data and leverage it for business success. Senior Vice President of the Information and Analytics Group at IBM Bob Picciano said, "Businesses and governments worldwide are being challenged to make sense of data and gather valuable insights from structured and unstructured data that are emerging from a variety of sources such as videos, blogs, and social networking sites. We are helping clients tackle these big data challenges in virtually every industry—from public safety to healthcare, retail, automotive, telecommunications, and everything in between."[20]

IBM's Smarter Workforce Institute offers products to help organizations locate the talent hidden within their own staff. Its software can track the knowledge, skills, and abilities of employees by scanning the Internet and compiling information about each employee from social media sites like Facebook and Twitter. © James Leynse/Corbis

LO 13-2 Explain why effective communication helps an organization gain a competitive advantage, and describe the communication process.

Information and Coordination

Coordinating department and divisional activities to achieve organizational goals is another basic task of management. As an example of the size of the coordination task that managers face, consider the coordination effort necessary to prepare between 500,000 and 1 million meals for the people who visit Disney parks and resorts every day. Combine that type of volume with Disney's efforts to get food locally, and logistics get complicated quickly. According to Executive Chef for Resorts Lenny DeGeorge, the supply chain for the restaurants at 18 Disney resorts in the United States and abroad depends on the location of the resort and what local growers and producers can provide. In Florida, for example, the company works with "Fresh from Florida" to find out what is in season and available. In Southern California, DeGeorge has some local growers providing organic produce. The longer growing season in Southern California also is a bonus for the restaurants around the Disneyland resort there.[21]

Starbucks has a program called "Origin Experience" that allows its employees to get involved in the logistics of the supply chain. This experience allows associates to travel overseas and meet Starbucks partners where the coffee beans are grown. The trips provide associates with a new perspective on the supply chain and the coffee that ends up in their stores.

The supply chain at Starbucks runs from the field where the coffee beans are grown to the cup of coffee poured by a friendly barista at a local shop. The supply chain spans 19 countries. From the field, the beans travel to one of six roasting centers, where they are prepared and then shipped to their final destination. The company makes more than 70,000 deliveries per day.[22]

In the Origin Experience, one store manager from Ohio flew to Costa Rica to see the process from "farm to cup." While there, the manager toured the fields where the coffee was grown and the mill where it was processed. She also sampled locally grown coffee and met local people. She traded email addresses with the farmer's children and they keep in touch to let her know how the growing season is going. In return, she tells them how sales are going in her store. Also as a result of the trip, she said she now thinks more like a farmer and works to make things sustainable in her store. Her new zeal for not wasting anything saves the store about 15 gallons of milk per week.[23]

Another associate traveled to Ecuador to visit a source of Starbucks coffee beans at a small farmer cooperative. The associate blogged about his impressions of the trip, including how one farmer used the training he received to develop an irrigation system. The associate also shared how thrilled the farmers were to taste the chocolate bars Starbucks sells that come from the cocoa pods they harvest.[24]

These visits help Starbucks employees learn about the supply chain and how to make it run more smoothly. The visits provide employees at the end of the supply chain with information about how things work at the beginning. Joseph Michelli, author of *Leading the Starbucks Way,* suggests that such trips can break down the silos in any organization and help employees understand their role in the supply chain.[25] Michelli suggests that such supply chain immersions and the subsequent stories told to customers strengthen the overall supply chain by improving the ties with vendors as well as making customers more comfortable with what the company is doing.

Communication, Information, and Management

communication The sharing of information between two or more individuals or groups to reach a common understanding.

Communication is the sharing of information between two or more people or groups to reach a common understanding.[26] First and foremost, communication, no matter how electronically based, is a human endeavor and involves individuals and groups sharing information and coordinating their actions. Second, communication does not take place unless a common understanding is reached. Thus, if you try to call a business to speak to a person in customer service or billing and you are bounced back and forth between endless automated messages and menu options and eventually hang up in frustration, communication has not taken place.

The Importance of Good Communication

In Chapter 1, we described how in order for an organization to gain a competitive advantage, managers must strive to increase efficiency, quality, responsiveness to customers, and innovation. Good communication is essential for attaining each of these four goals and thus is a necessity for gaining a competitive advantage.

Managers can *increase efficiency* by updating the production process to take advantage of new and more efficient technologies and by training workers to operate the new technologies and expand their skills. Good communication is necessary for managers to learn about new technologies, implement them in their organizations, and train workers in how to use them. Similarly, *improving quality* hinges on effective communication. Managers need to communicate to all members of an organization the meaning and importance of high quality and the routes to attaining it. Subordinates need to communicate quality problems and suggestions for increasing quality to their superiors, and members of self-managed work teams need to share their ideas for improving quality with each other.

Good communication can also help to increase *responsiveness to customers*. When the organizational members who are closest to customers, such as salespeople in department stores and tellers in banks, are empowered to communicate customers' needs and desires to managers, managers are better able to respond to these needs. Managers, in turn, must communicate with other organizational members to determine how best to respond to changing customer preferences.

Innovation, which often takes place in cross-functional teams, also requires effective communication. Members of a cross-functional team developing a new electronic game, for example, must effectively communicate with one another to develop a game that customers will want to play; that will be engaging, interesting, and fun; and that can potentially lead to sequels or derivative products. Members of the team also must communicate with managers to secure the resources they need for developing the game and to keep managers informed of progress on the project. Innovation in organizations is increasingly taking place on a global level, making effective communication all the more important, as illustrated in the accompanying "Managing Globally" feature.

MANAGING GLOBALLY

Global Communication Key to Success at GE Healthcare

GE Healthcare, which is headquartered in the United Kingdom, provides medical technology and services and makes medical imaging, diagnostic, and monitoring systems such as CT scanners. With more than 50,000 employees around the world, GE Healthcare has more than $18.3 billion in revenues.[27] To make the best scanners that meet the needs of health care professionals and patients around the world with next-generation technology, new product development and manufacture are truly global endeavors at GE Healthcare. Consider the development of the LightSpeed VCT scanner series (VCT stands for "volume controlled tomography"), which can perform a full-body scan in less than 10 seconds and yields a three-dimensional picture of patients' hearts within five heartbeats.[28]

The LightSpeed was developed through global collaboration. GE managers not only spoke with doctors (including cardiologists and radiologists) around the world to find out what their needs were and what kinds of tests they would perform with the LightSpeed but also gathered information about differences among patients in various countries. Engineers in Hino (Japan), Buc (France), and Waukesha, Wisconsin, developed the electronics for the LightSpeed. Other parts, such as the automated table that patients lie on, were made in Beijing (China) and Hino. Software for the LightSpeed was written in Haifa (Israel), Bangalore (India), Buc, and Waukesha.

As GE Healthcare learned, conference calls and emails are beneficial, but nothing replaces getting managers together for face-to-face discussions and problem solving.
© Doug Menuez/Getty Images RF

Effective global communication was a challenge and a necessity to successfully develop the LightSpeed series. As Brian Duchinsky, who was GE's general manager for global CT at the time, put it, "If we sat around in this cornfield west of Milwaukee, we wouldn't come up with the same breadth of good ideas. But yet, getting six countries on the phone to make a decision can be a pain."[29]

GE managers facilitated effective communication in a number of ways—participating in daily conference calls, making sure teams in different countries depended on one another, developing an internal website devoted to the LightSpeed, encouraging teams to ask one another for help, and holding face-to-face meetings in different locations. Although much communication took place electronically, such as through conference calls, face-to-face meetings were also important. As Bob Armstrong, who was GE's general manager for engineering at the time, indicated, "You need to get your people together in one place if you want them to really appreciate how good everyone is, and how good you are as a team."[30]

Effective communication is necessary for managers and all members of an organization to increase efficiency, quality, responsiveness to customers, and innovation and thus gain a competitive advantage for their organization. Managers therefore must have a good understanding of the communication process if they are to perform effectively.

Figure 13.2
The Communication Process

sender The person or group wishing to share information.

message The information that a sender wants to share.

encoding Translating a message into understandable symbols or language.

noise Anything that hampers any stage of the communication process.

receiver The person or group for which a message is intended.

medium The pathway through which an encoded message is transmitted to a receiver.

decoding Interpreting and trying to make sense of a message.

verbal communication The encoding of messages into words, either written or spoken.

nonverbal communication The encoding of messages by means of facial expressions, body language, and styles of dress.

The Communication Process

The communication process consists of two phases. In the *transmission phase,* information is shared between two or more individuals or groups. In the *feedback phase,* a common understanding is assured. In both phases, a number of distinct stages must occur for communication to take place (see Figure 13.2).[31]

Starting the transmission phase, the **sender,** the person or group wishing to share information with some other person or group, decides on the **message,** what information to communicate. Then the sender translates the message into symbols or language, a process called **encoding;** often messages are encoded into words. **Noise** is a general term that refers to anything that hampers any stage of the communication process.

Once encoded, a message is transmitted through a medium to the **receiver,** the person or group for which the message is intended. A **medium** is simply the pathway, such as a phone call, a letter, a memo, or face-to-face communication in a meeting, through which an encoded message is transmitted to a receiver. At the next stage, the receiver interprets and tries to make sense of the message, a process called **decoding.** This is a critical point in communication.

The feedback phase is initiated by the receiver (who becomes a sender). The receiver decides what message to send to the original sender (who becomes a receiver), encodes it, and transmits it through a chosen medium (see Figure 13.2). The message might contain a confirmation that the original message was received and understood or a restatement of the original message to make sure that it has been correctly interpreted; or it might include a request for more information. The original sender decodes the message and makes sure that a common understanding has been reached. If the original sender determines that a common understanding has not been reached, sender and receiver cycle through the whole process as many times as are needed to reach a common understanding.

The encoding of messages into words, written or spoken, is **verbal communication.** We also encode messages without using written or spoken language. **Nonverbal communication** shares information by means of facial expressions (smiling, raising an eyebrow, frowning, dropping one's jaw), body language (posture, gestures, nods, shrugs), and even style of dress (casual, formal, conservative, trendy). The trend toward increasing empowerment of the workforce has led some managers to dress informally to communicate that all employees of an organization are team members, working together to create value for customers.

Nonverbal communication can be used to back up or reinforce verbal communication. Just as a warm and genuine smile can back up words of appreciation for a job well done, a concerned facial expression can back up words of sympathy for a

Nonverbal cues, such as the intense look being exchanged by these people, can provide managers and employees with vital information that helps them make better decisions.
© Christopher Robbins/Digital Vision/Getty Images RF

personal problem. In such cases, the congruence between verbal and nonverbal communication helps to ensure that a common understanding is reached.

Sometimes when members of an organization decide not to express a message verbally, they inadvertently do so nonverbally. People tend to have less control over nonverbal communication, and often a verbal message that is withheld gets expressed through body language or facial expressions. A manager who agrees to a proposal that she or he actually is not in favor of may unintentionally communicate disfavor by grimacing.

Sometimes nonverbal communication is used to send messages that cannot be sent through verbal channels. Many lawyers are well aware of this communication tactic. Lawyers are often schooled in techniques of nonverbal communication such as choosing where to stand in the courtroom for maximum effect and using eye contact during different stages of a trial. Lawyers sometimes get into trouble for using inappropriate nonverbal communication in an attempt to influence juries.[32]

The Dangers of Ineffective Communication

Because managers must communicate with others to perform their various roles and tasks, managers spend most of their time communicating, whether in meetings, in telephone conversations, through email, or in face-to-face interactions. Indeed, some experts estimate that managers spend approximately 85% of their time engaged in some form of communication.[33] Effective communication is so important that managers cannot just be concerned that they themselves are effective communicators; they also have to help their subordinates be effective communicators. When all members of an organization are able to communicate effectively with each other and with people outside the organization, the organization is much more likely to perform highly and gain a competitive advantage.

When managers and other members of an organization are ineffective communicators, organizational performance suffers, and any competitive advantage the organization might have is likely to be lost. Moreover, poor communication sometimes can be downright dangerous and even lead to tragic and unnecessary loss of human life. For example, a recent study by Harvard University researchers found that changing how doctors communicate during shift changes reduced the risk of adverse events in patients by 30%. In addition, the researchers found that improving communications methods could also reduce the rate of medical errors by almost 25%.[34]

Information Richness and Communication Media

To be effective communicators, managers (and other members of an organization) need to select an appropriate communication medium for *each* message they send. Should a change in procedures be communicated to subordinates in a memo sent through email? Should a congratulatory message about a major accomplishment be communicated in a letter, in a phone call, or over lunch? Should a layoff announcement be made in a memo or at a plant meeting? Should the members of a purchasing team travel to Europe to cement a major agreement with a new supplier, or should they do so through conference calls and email messages? Managers deal with these questions day in and day out.

There is no one best communication medium for managers to rely on. In choosing a communication medium for any message, managers need to consider three factors. The first and most important is the level of information richness that is needed. **Information richness** is the amount of information a communication medium can carry and the extent to which the medium enables the sender and receiver to reach a common understanding.[35] The communication media that managers use vary in their information richness (see Figure 13.3).[36] Media high in information richness are able to carry an extensive amount of information and generally enable receivers and senders to come to a common understanding.

The second factor that managers need to take into account in selecting a communication medium is the *time* needed for communication, because managers' and other organizational members' time is valuable. Managers at AXA, a global financial services company, drastically reduced the amount of time they spent by using videoconferencing instead of face-to-face communication, which required managers to travel to locations around the world.[37]

The third factor that affects the choice of a communication medium is the *need for a paper or electronic trail* or some kind of written documentation that a message was sent and received. A manager may wish to document in writing, for example, that a subordinate was given a formal warning about excessive lateness.

In the remainder of this section we examine four types of communication media that vary along the three dimensions of information richness, time, and the availability of a paper or electronic trail.

Face-to-Face Communication

Face-to-face communication is the medium that is highest in information richness. When managers communicate face-to-face, they not only can take advantage of verbal communication but they also can interpret each other's nonverbal signals such as facial expressions and body language. A look of concern or puzzlement can sometimes tell more than a thousand words, and managers can respond to these nonverbal signals on the spot. Face-to-face communication also enables managers to

LO 13-3 Define information richness, and describe the information richness of communication media available to managers.

information richness The amount of information that a communication medium can carry and the extent to which the medium enables the sender and receiver to reach a common understanding.

Figure 13.3

The Information Richness of Communication Media

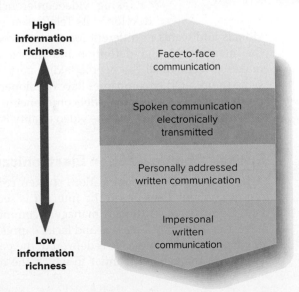

receive instant feedback. Points of confusion, ambiguity, or misunderstanding can be resolved, and managers can cycle through the communication process as many times as they need to, to reach a common understanding.

management by wandering around A face-to-face communication technique in which a manager walks around a work area and talks informally with employees about issues and concerns.

Management by wandering around is a face-to-face communication technique that is effective for many managers at all levels in an organization.[38] Rather than scheduling formal meetings with subordinates, managers walk around work areas and talk informally with employees about issues and concerns that both employees and managers may have. These informal conversations provide managers and subordinates with important information and at the same time foster the development of positive relationships. William Hewlett and David Packard, founders and former top managers of Hewlett-Packard, found management by wandering around a highly effective way to communicate with their employees.

Because face-to-face communication is highest in information richness, you might think that it should always be the medium of choice for managers. This is not the case, however, because of the amount of time it takes and the lack of a paper or electronic trail resulting from it. For messages that are important, personal, or likely to be misunderstood, it is often well worth managers' time to use face-to-face communication and, if need be, supplement it with some form of written communication documenting the message.

Advances in information technology are providing managers with new and close alternative communication media for face-to-face communication. Like AXA, other organizations use videoconferences to capture some of the advantages of face-to-face communication while saving time and money because managers in different locations do not have to travel to meet with one another.

In addition to saving travel costs, videoconferences sometimes have other advantages. Managers have found that decisions get made more quickly when videoconferences are used because more managers can be involved in the decision-making process and therefore fewer managers have to be consulted outside the meeting itself.

In spite of the popularity of electronic communication, face-to-face communication is still the medium that is highest in information richness. © Digital Vision/Getty Images RF

Taking videoconferencing a leap forward, Cisco Systems developed its TelePresence line of products, which enables individuals and teams in different locations to communicate live and in real time over the Internet with high-definition and life-size video and excellent-quality audio that makes it feel like all the people taking part, no matter where they are, are in the same room.[39] Other companies have developed similar products. What distinguishes these products from older videoconferencing systems is the fact that there are no delays in transmission and the video quality is sharp, clear, lifelike, and life-size.

Spoken Communication Electronically Transmitted

After face-to-face communication, spoken communication electronically transmitted over phone lines or via the Internet is second highest in information richness (see Figure 13.3). Although managers communicating over the telephone do not have access to body language and facial expressions, they do have access to the tone of voice in which a message is delivered, the parts of the message the sender emphasizes, and the general manner in which the message is spoken, in addition to the

Advancing the idea of videoconferencing, Cisco Systems developed its TelePresence product line, which enables individuals and teams in different locations to communicate live and in real time with high-definition video and excellent-quality audio. This technology makes it feel like all the people taking part, no matter where they are located, are in the same room. © Marketwire/AP Images

actual words themselves. Thus, telephone conversations have the capacity to convey extensive amounts of information. Managers also can ensure that mutual understanding is reached because they can get quick feedback over the phone and answer questions.

Voice mail systems also allow managers to send and receive verbal electronic messages over telephone lines. Voice mail systems are companywide systems that enable senders to record messages for members of an organization who are away from their desks and allow receivers to access their messages when away from the office. Video calling apps such as Skype and FaceTime enable people to communicate using voice and video over the Internet. They provide access to nonverbal forms of communication between sender and receiver, as well as enable individuals and businesses to conduct conference calls and interviews quickly and inexpensively. For example, some corporations may use Skype or FaceTime to interview potential candidates for job openings.[40]

Personally Addressed Written Communication

Lower than electronically transmitted verbal communication in information richness is personally addressed written communication (see Figure 13.3). One of the advantages of face-to-face communication and verbal communication electronically transmitted is that they both tend to demand attention, which helps ensure that receivers pay attention. Personally addressed written communications such as memos and letters also have this advantage. Because they are addressed to a particular person, the chances are good that the person will actually pay attention to (and read) them. Moreover, the sender can write the message in a way that the receiver is most likely to understand. Like voice mail, written communication does not enable a receiver to have his or her questions answered immediately, but when messages are clearly written and feedback is provided, common understandings can still be reached.

Even if managers use face-to-face communication, sending a follow-up in writing is often necessary for messages that are important or complicated and need to be referred to later. This is precisely what Karen Stracker, a hospital administrator, did when she needed to tell one of her subordinates about an important change in the way the hospital would be handling denials of insurance benefits. Stracker met with the subordinate and described the changes face-to-face. Once she was sure that the subordinate understood them, she handed her a sheet of instructions to follow, which essentially summarized the information they had discussed.

Email and text messages also fit into this category of communication media because senders and receivers are communicating through personally addressed written words. The words, however, appear on their computer screens, laptops, or mobile devices rather than on paper. Email use in business is so widespread that some managers find they have to deliberately take time out from managing their email to get other work done, including taking action on business strategies and coming up with new and innovative ideas. According to the Radicati Group, a marketing research firm, the average email account in corporations today receives about 18 megabytes of email and attachments every workday, and the volume is expected to increase over time.[41] To help employees effectively manage their email, many organizations provide in-house training programs or other guidelines to help employees learn how to use email more effectively as part of their daily workday.[42]

The growing popularity of email has also enabled many workers and managers to become telecommuters, people who are employed by organizations and work out of offices in their own homes. There are approximately 30 million telecommuters in the United States who work from home at least once a week.[43] Many telecommuters indicate that the flexibility of working at home enables them to be more productive while giving them a chance to be closer to their families and not waste time traveling to and from the office.

Unfortunately, the growing use of email has been accompanied by growing abuse of email. To avoid email abuse, managers need to develop a clear policy specifying what company email can and should be used for and what is out of bounds. Managers also should clearly communicate this policy to all members of an organization, as well as the procedures that will be used when email abuse is suspected and the consequences that will result when email abuse is confirmed. As described in the accompanying "Ethics in Action" feature, personal email and texting, along with Internet surfing at work, present managers with some challenging dilemmas.

ETHICS IN ACTION

Monitoring Employees' Email and Internet Use

A growing number of companies provide managers and organizations with tools to track the websites their employees visit and the email and social media messages they send. For example, network forensic software enables managers to record and replay everything that takes place on employees' computer monitors and can also track keystrokes. Currently, a majority of large corporations in the United States monitor their employees' email and Internet usage; the percentage is higher among organizations in certain industries.[44]

Monitoring employees raises concerns about privacy. Most employees would not like to have their bosses listening to their phone conversations; similarly, some believe that monitoring email and tracking Internet use are an invasion of privacy. Given the increasingly long working hours of many employees, should personal email and Internet use be closely scrutinized? Clearly, when illegal and unethical email use is suspected, such as sexually harassing coworkers or divulging confidential company information, monitoring may be called for. But should it be a normal part of organizational life, even when there are no indications of a real problem?

Essentially this dilemma involves issues of trust. And given that there is no federal legislation to protect employees from having their companies monitor

Intrusive monitoring policies by employers may have unintended negative consequences in organizations. © David Lee/Alamy

company-supplied machines such as computers, laptops, and cell phones, employees themselves can take steps to protect their own privacy.[45] Lewis Maltby, founder of the National Workrights Institute, which is devoted to safeguarding privacy at work, suggests that when sending sensitive or personal information, employees can use their own equipment (e.g., private cell phone or laptop) and an outside Wi-Fi provider so that their employing organization cannot access the information.[46] Employees also need to be careful about what email messages they send and avoid sending private and sensitive email on workplace systems. Once email messages are sent, they live on in the recipients' computers and systems and can potentially come back to haunt senders or be subpoenaed in a court of law.[47]

Impersonal Written Communication

Impersonal written communication is lowest in information richness and is well suited for messages that need to reach a large number of receivers. Because such messages are not addressed to particular receivers, feedback is unlikely, so managers must make sure that messages sent by this medium are written clearly in language that all receivers will understand.

Managers often find company newsletters useful vehicles for reaching large numbers of employees. Increasingly, companies are distributing their newsletters online and inviting employees to communicate through various channels with colleagues, customers, and others. For example, IBM's employee communications typically comes through the company's intranet, known internally as W3, and it has led a transformation from professional to user-generated content within the company.[48]

Managers can use impersonal written communication for various types of messages, including rules, regulations, policies, newsworthy information, and announcements of changes in procedures or the arrival of new organizational members. Impersonal written communication also can be used to communicate instructions about how to use machinery or how to process work orders or customer requests. For these kinds of messages, the paper or electronic trail left by this communication medium can be invaluable for employees.

Like personal written communication, impersonal written communication can be delivered and retrieved electronically, and this is increasingly being done in companies large and small. Unfortunately, the ease with which electronic messages can be spread has led to their proliferation. The electronic inboxes of many managers and workers are backlogged, and they rarely have time to read all the electronic work-related information available to them. The problem with such **information overload** is the potential for important information to be ignored or overlooked while tangential information receives attention. Moreover, information overload can result in thousands of hours and millions of dollars in lost productivity.

Some managers and organizations use blogs to communicate with employees, customers, investors, and the general public. A **blog** is a website on which an

information overload A superabundance of information that increases the likelihood that important information is ignored or overlooked and tangential information receives attention.

blog A website on which an individual, group, or organization posts information, commentary, and opinions and to which readers can often respond with their own commentary and opinions.

individual, group, or organization posts information, commentary, and opinions to which readers can often respond with their own commentary and opinions. Some top managers write their own blogs, and some companies, including Whole Foods and Oracle, have corporate blogs.[49]

social networking site A website that enables people to communicate with others with whom they have some common interest or connection.

A **social networking site**, such as Facebook, Twitter, or LinkedIn, enables people to communicate with others with whom they might have some common personal or professional interest or connection. Billions of people in the United States and around the world create custom profiles and communicate with networks of other participants via social networking sites. While communication through social networks can be work related, some managers are concerned that employees are wasting time at work communicating with their personal group of acquaintances through these sites.[50]

Advances in Information Technology

Advances in information technology have enabled managers to take gigantic leaps in the way they collect more timely, complete, relevant, and high-quality information and use it in more effective ways. To better understand the ongoing revolution in IT that has transformed companies and the way they do business, we need to examine several key factors of information technology.

The Effects of Advancing IT

The IT revolution began with the development of the first computers—the hardware of IT—in the 1950s. The language of computers is a digital language of zeros and ones. Words, numbers, images, and sound can all be expressed in zeros and ones. Each letter in the alphabet has its own unique code of zeros and ones, as does each number, each color, and each sound. For example, the digital code for the number 20 is 10100. In the language of computers it takes a lot of zeros and ones to express even a simple sentence, to say nothing of complex color graphics or moving video images. Nevertheless, modern computers can read, process, and store trillions of instructions per second (an *instruction* is a line of software code) and thus vast amounts of zeros and ones. This awesome number-crunching power forms the foundation of the ongoing IT revolution.

The products and services that result from advancing IT are all around us—ever more powerful microprocessors and PCs, high-bandwidth smartphones, sophisticated word-processing software, ever-expanding computer networks, inexpensive digital cameras and game consoles, and more and more useful online information and retailing services that did not exist a generation ago. These products are commonplace and are being continuously improved. Many managers and companies that helped develop the new IT have reaped enormous gains.

However, while many companies have benefited from advancing IT, others have been threatened. Traditional landline telephone companies such as AT&T, Verizon, and other long-distance companies the world over have seen their market dominance threatened by companies offering Internet, broadband, and wireless technology. They have been forced to respond by buying wireless cellphone companies, building their own high-powered broadband networks, and forming alliances with companies such as Apple and Samsung to make phones that will work on their networks. So advancing IT is both an opportunity and a threat, and managers have to move quickly to protect their companies and maintain their competitive advantage.

On one hand, IT helps create new product opportunities that managers and their organizations can take advantage of—such as online travel and vacation booking. On the other hand, IT creates new and improved products that reduce or destroy demand for older, established products—such as the services provided by bricks-and-mortar travel agents. Walmart, by developing its own sophisticated proprietary IT, has been able to reduce retailing costs so much that it has put hundreds of thousands of small and medium-size stores out of business. Similarly, thousands of small, specialized U.S. bookstores have closed in the past decade as a result of advances in IT that made online bookselling possible.

IT and the Product Life Cycle

product life cycle The way demand for a product changes in a predictable pattern over time.

When IT is advancing, organizational survival requires that managers quickly adopt and apply it. One reason for this is how IT affects the length of the **product life cycle**, which is the way demand for a product changes in a predictable pattern over time. In general, the product life cycle consists of four stages: the embryonic, growth, maturity, and decline stages (see Figure 13.4). In the *embryonic stage* a product has yet to gain widespread acceptance; customers are unsure what a product, such as a new smartphone, has to offer, and demand for it is minimal. As a product, like Apple's iPod, becomes accepted by customers (although many products are *not,* like BlackBerry's PlayBook tablet), demand takes off and the product enters its growth stage. In the *growth stage* many consumers are entering the market and buying the product for the first time, and demand increases rapidly. This is the stage iPhones and iPads passed through with great success. Of course these products' future success will depend on the value customers see in the collection of IT applications they offer—and how fast competitors such as Samsung and Google move to offer similar and less expensive tablet computers and smartphones.

Figure 13.4
A Product Life Cycle

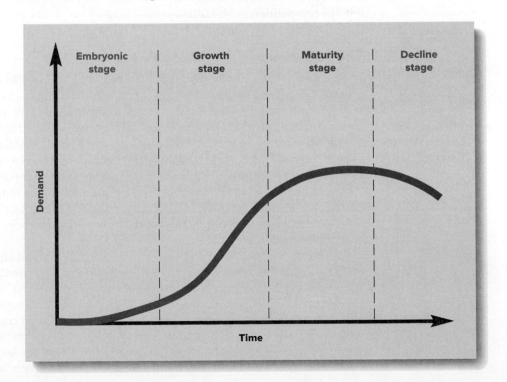

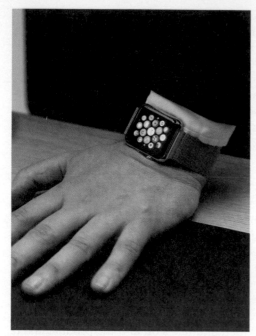

In the embryonic stage of its product life cycle, the Apple Watch is gaining widespread acceptance and is poised to enter the growth stage in the coming months. © Dave Stevenson/Alamy

The growth stage ends and the *maturity stage* begins when market demand peaks because most customers have already bought the product (there are relatively few first-time buyers left). At this stage, demand is typically replacement demand. The iPod transitioned to this stage after the launch of the iPod Touch. Its users had to decide whether to trade up to the more powerful version. In the iPod's maturing stage, the devices were still selling well. By the end of 2010, more than 275 million iPods were sold. In 2012, Apple made the last major upgrade to the iPod Touch.

Once a demand for a product starts to fall, the decline stage begins. This typically occurs when advancing technology leads to the development of a more advanced product, making the old one obsolete. In the case of the decline of the iPod, it was another Apple product that put the iPod into decline: the iPhone. When the iPhone launched in 2007, the late Apple cofounder Steve Jobs joked that it was "the best iPod we've ever made." The new Apple Watch was recently introduced by the company and has already entered its product life cycle with orders topping more than 1 million.[51]

In general, demand for every generation of a digital device such as a PC, smartphone, or tablet falls off when the current leaders' technology is superseded by new products that incorporate the most recent IT advances. One reason the IT revolution is so important for managers is that advances in technology are one of the most significant determinants of the length of a product's life cycle, as well as the level of competition in an industry.

The Network of Computing Power

The tumbling price of computing power and applications has allowed all kinds of organizations, large and small, to invest more into developing networks of computer services customized with the right mix of hardware and software to best meet their needs. The typical organizationwide computing **network** that has emerged over time is a four-tier network solution that consists of "external" mobile computing devices such as netbooks, smartphones, and tablet computers, connected to desktops and laptops, and then through "internal" rack servers to a company's mainframe (see Figure 13.5). Through wireless and wired communication an employee with the necessary permissions can hook into a company's IT system from any location—in the office, at home, on a boat, on the beach, in the air—anywhere a wireless or wired link can be established.

network Interlinked computers that exchange information.

The internal network is composed of "client" desktop and laptop PCs connected by Ethernet to the company's system of rack servers. The client computers that are linked directly to a server constitute a *local area network* (LAN), and most companies have many LANs—for example, one in every division and function. Large companies that need immense processing power have a mainframe computer at the center or hub of the network that can quickly process vast amounts of information, issue commands, and coordinate computing devices at the other levels. The mainframe can also handle electronic communications between servers and PCs situated in

Figure 13.5

A Four-Tier Information System with Cloud Computing

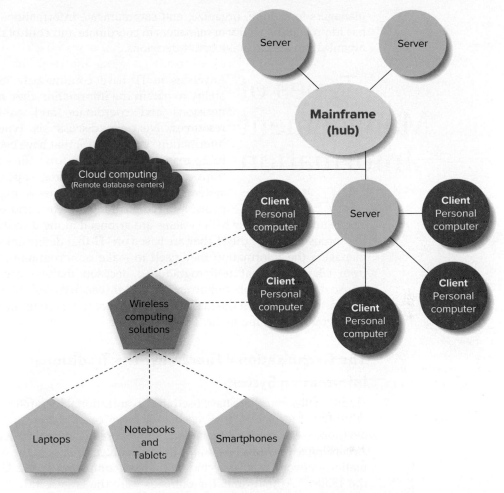

different LANs, and the mainframe can connect to the mainframes of other companies. The mainframe is the master computer that controls the operations of all the other types of computers and digital devices as needed and can link them into one integrated system. It also provides the connection to the *external* IT networks outside the organization; for example, it gives a user access to an organization's cloud computing services—but with high security and reliability and only from recognized and protected computing devices. For instance, a manager with a mobile device or PC hooked into a four-tier system can access data and software stored in the local server, in the mainframe, or through the Internet to a cloud-based computing solution hosted by an outsourcer whose database might be located anywhere in the world.

Just as computer hardware has been advancing rapidly, so has computer software. *Operating system software* tells the computer hardware how to run. *Applications software,* such as programs for word processing, spreadsheets, graphics, and database management, is developed for a specific task or use. The increase in the power of computer hardware has allowed software developers to write increasingly powerful programs that are also increasingly user-friendly. By harnessing the rapidly growing power of microprocessors, applications software has vastly increased the ability of managers to acquire, organize, and communicate information. In doing so, it also has improved the ability of managers to coordinate and control the activities of their organization and to make better decisions.

Types of Management Information Systems

LO 13-4
Differentiate among six kinds of computer-based management information systems.

Advances in IT have continuously increased managers' ability to obtain the information they need to make better decisions and coordinate and control organizational resources. Next we discuss six types of management information systems (MIS) that have been particularly helpful to managers as they perform their management tasks: transaction-processing systems, operations information systems, decision support systems, expert systems, enterprise resource planning systems, and e-commerce systems (see Figure 13.6). These MIS systems are arranged along a continuum according to the sophistication of the IT they are based on—IT that determines their ability to give managers the information they need to make nonprogrammed decisions. (Recall from Chapter 5 that nonprogrammed decision making occurs in response to unusual, unpredictable opportunities and threats.) We examine each of these systems after focusing on the management information system that preceded them all: the organizational hierarchy.

The Organizational Hierarchy: The Traditional Information System

Traditionally, managers have used the organizational hierarchy as a system for gathering the information they need to achieve coordination and control and make decisions (see Chapter 7 for a discussion of organizational structure and hierarchy). According to business historian Alfred Chandler, the use of the hierarchy as an information network was perfected by railroad companies in the United States during the 1850s.[52] At that time, the railroads were the largest industrial organizations in the United States. By virtue of their size and geographical spread, they faced unique problems of coordination and control. In the 1850s, they started to solve these problems by designing hierarchical management structures that provided senior managers with the information they needed to achieve coordination and control and to make decisions about running the railroads.

Daniel McCallum, superintendent of the Erie Railroad in the 1850s, realized that the lines of authority and responsibility defining the Erie's management hierarchy

Figure 13.6

Six Computer-Based Management Information Systems

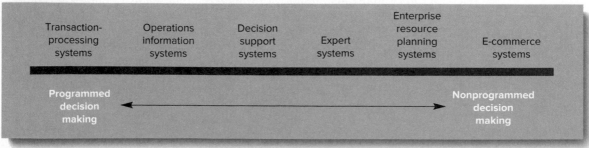

also represented channels of communication along which information traveled. McCallum established what was perhaps the first modern management information system. Regular daily and monthly reports were fed up the management chain so that top managers could make decisions about, for example, controlling costs and setting freight rates. Decisions were then relayed back down the hierarchy so they could be carried out. When performance gains from this system were publicized, many organizations imitated the railroads by using their hierarchies to collect, channel, and process information.

Although organizational hierarchy is a useful information system, it has several drawbacks. First, when too many layers of managers exist, it takes a long time for information and requests to travel up the hierarchy and for decisions and answers to travel back down. The slow communication can reduce the timeliness and usefulness of the information and prevent a quick response to changing market conditions.[53] Second, information can be distorted as it moves from one layer of management to another. **Information distortion**, changes in meaning that occur as information passes through a series of senders and receivers, reduces the quality of information.[54] Third, managers have only a limited span of control; so, as an organization grows larger and its hierarchy lengthens, more managers must be hired, and this makes the hierarchy an expensive (and sometimes ineffective) information system. The popular idea that companies with tall management hierarchies are bureaucratic and unresponsive to the needs of their customers arises from the inability of tall hierarchies to effectively process data and give managers timely, complete, relevant, and high-quality information. The management hierarchy is still the best information system available today—the one that results in the best decisions—*if* managers have access to the other kinds of management information systems discussed next.

Transaction-Processing Systems

A **transaction-processing system** is a system designed to handle large volumes of routine, recurring transactions. Transaction-processing systems began to appear in the early 1960s with the advent of commercially available mainframe computers. They were the first type of computer-based IT adopted by many organizations, and today they are commonplace. Bank managers use a transaction-processing system to record deposits into, and payments out of, bank accounts. Supermarket managers use a transaction-processing system to record the sale of items and to track inventory levels. More generally, most managers in large organizations use a transaction-processing system to handle tasks such as payroll preparation and payment, customer billing, and payment of suppliers.

Operations Information Systems

Many types of management information systems followed hard on the heels of transaction-processing systems in the 1960s. An **operations information system** is a system that gathers comprehensive data, organizes it, and summarizes it in a form that is of value to managers. Whereas a transaction-processing system processes routine transactions, an operations information system provides managers with information that they can use in their nonroutine coordinating, controlling, and decision-making tasks. Most operations information systems are coupled with a transaction-processing system. An operations information system typically accesses data gathered by a transaction-processing system, processes those data into useful

information distortion Changes in meaning that occur as information passes through a series of senders and receivers.

transaction-processing system A management information system designed to handle large volumes of routine, recurring transactions.

operations information system A management information system that gathers, organizes, and summarizes comprehensive data in a form that managers can use in their nonroutine coordinating, controlling, and decision-making tasks.

information, and organizes that information into a form accessible to managers. As described in the opening "Management Snapshot," the data collected by wearables could be part of an operations information system.

UPS uses an operations information system to track the performance of its thousands of ground stations. Each ground station is evaluated according to four criteria: delivery (the goal is to deliver 95% of all packages by noon the day after they were picked up), productivity (measured by the number of packages shipped per employee-hour), controllable cost, and station profitability. Each ground station also has specific delivery, efficiency, cost, and profitability targets that it must attain. Every month UPS's operations information system is used to gather information on these four criteria and summarize it for top managers, who are then able to compare the performance of each station against its previously established targets. The system quickly alerts senior managers to underperforming ground stations, so they can intervene selectively to help solve any problems that may have given rise to the poor performance.[55]

Decision Support Systems

decision support system An interactive computer-based management information system with model-building capability that managers can use when they must make nonroutine decisions.

A **decision support system** is an interactive computer-based system that provides models that help managers make better nonprogrammed decisions.[56] Recall from Chapter 5 that nonprogrammed decisions are decisions that are relatively unusual or novel, such as decisions to invest in new productive capacity, develop a new product, launch a new promotional campaign, enter a new market, or expand internationally. Although an operations information system organizes important information for managers, a decision support system gives managers a model-building capability and so provides them with the ability to manipulate information in a variety of ways. Managers might use a decision support system to help them decide whether to cut prices for a product. The decision support system might contain models of how customers and competitors would respond to a price cut. Managers could run these models and use the results as an *aid* to decision making.

The emphasis on the word *aid* is important, for in the final analysis a decision support system is not meant to make decisions for managers. Rather, its function is to provide valuable information that managers can use to improve the quality of their decision making.

Artificial Intelligence and Expert Systems

artificial intelligence Behavior performed by a machine that, if performed by a human being, would be called "intelligent."

Artificial intelligence has been defined as behavior by a machine that, if performed by a human being, would be called "intelligent." This behavior has already made it possible to write programs that can solve problems and perform simple tasks. For example, software programs variously known as *software agents, softbots,* or *knowbots* can be used to perform simple managerial tasks such as sorting through reams of data or incoming email messages to look for important ones. The interesting feature of these programs is that from "watching" a manager sort through such data, they can "learn" what the manager's preferences are when reviewing information. With this type of capability, these "smart" programs can take over some of the work for managers, freeing them up to work on other tasks. Many of these programs are still in the development stage but could be commonplace within the next several years.[57]

expert system A management information system that utilizes human knowledge embedded in computer software to solve problems that ordinarily require human expertise.

Expert systems, the most advanced management information systems available, incorporate artificial intelligence in their design. An **expert system** is a system that utilizes human knowledge embedded in computer software to solve problems that ordinarily require human expertise. Mimicking human expertise (and intelligence) requires technology that can, at a minimum, (1) recognize, formulate, and solve a problem; (2) explain the solution; and (3) learn from the experience.

Recent advances in artificial intelligence that go by names such as "fuzzy logic" or "neural networks" have resulted in computer programs that, in a simplistic way try to mimic human thought processes. Although artificial intelligence is still in the development stage, an increasing number of business applications are beginning to emerge in the form of expert systems.

Enterprise Resource Planning Systems

enterprise resource planning (ERP) systems Multimodule application software packages that coordinate the functional activities necessary to move products from the design stage to the final customer stage.

To achieve high performance, it is not sufficient just to develop a management information system within each of a company's functions or divisions to provide better information and knowledge. It is also vital that managers in the different functions and divisions have access to information about the activities of managers in other functions and divisions. The greater the flow of information and knowledge among functions and divisions, the more learning can take place, and this builds a company's stock of knowledge and expertise. This knowledge and expertise are the source of its competitive advantage and profitability.

Over the past 25 years, another revolution has taken place in IT as software companies have worked to develop enterprise resource planning systems, which essentially incorporate most MIS aspects just discussed, as well as much more. **Enterprise resource planning (ERP) systems** are multimodule application software packages that allow a company to link and coordinate the entire set of functional activities and operations necessary to move products from the initial design stage to the final customer stage. Some of the business applications in these software packages may include accounting, customer service management (CRM), human resources, manufacturing, and inventory and supply chain management.[58] Essentially ERP systems (1) help each individual function improve its functional-level skills and (2) improve integration among all functions so they work together to build a competitive advantage for the company. Today, choosing and designing an ERP system to improve how a company operates is the biggest challenge facing the IT function inside a company.

E-Commerce Systems

e-commerce Trade that takes place between companies, and between companies and individual customers, using technology and the Internet.

business-to-business (B2B) commerce Trade that takes place between companies using technology and the Internet to link and coordinate the value chains of different companies.

B2B marketplace An Internet-based trading platform set up to connect buyers and sellers in an industry.

business-to-customer (B2C) commerce Trade that takes place between a company and individual customers using technology and the Internet.

E-commerce is trade that takes place between companies and between companies and individual customers using technology and the Internet. **Business-to-business (B2B) commerce** is trade that takes place between companies using technology and the Internet to link and coordinate the value chains of different companies. The goal of B2B commerce is to increase the profitability of making and selling goods and services. Through the use of technology, B2B commerce increases profitability because it allows companies to reduce operating costs and may improve overall quality. A principal B2B software application is **B2B marketplaces**, which are Internet-based online trading platforms set up in many industries to connect buyers and sellers. To participate in a B2B marketplace, companies adopt a common software standard that allows them to search for and share information with each other. The companies can work together over time to reduce costs or improve quality.

Business-to-customer (B2C) commerce is trade that takes place between a company and individual customers using technology and the Internet. Using technology to connect directly to customers allows companies to avoid using intermediaries, such as wholesalers and retailers, who capture a significant part of the profit in the value chain. The use of websites and online stores also lets companies give their customers and other consumers much more information about the value of their products. This use of technology often allows companies to attract more customers and thus generate higher sales revenues.

In the 2010s, software companies such as Microsoft, Oracle, SAP, and IBM are using cloud computing to make their products work seamlessly while responding to global companies' growing demand for e-commerce software. Previously, their software was configured to work only on a particular company's internal website. Today, software must be able to network a company's IT systems to other companies, such as suppliers and distributors. The challenge facing managers now is to select e-commerce software that allows a seamless exchange of information between companies anywhere in the world. The stakes are high because global competitive advantage goes to the company that is first with a new major technological advance.

In summary, by using advanced types of MIS, managers have more control over a company's activities and operations and can work to improve its competitive advantage and profitability. The IT function has become increasingly important because IT managers decide which kind of hardware and software a company will use and then train other functional managers and employees how to use it effectively as part of daily business operations.

Limitations of Information Systems

Despite their usefulness, technology, in general, and management information systems, in particular, have some limitations. One potentially serious problem is that in all the enthusiasm for MIS, particularly in terms of efficiency, communications via computer networks decrease the vital element of human interaction. There is a strong argument that electronic communication should *support* face-to-face communication rather than replace it. For example, it would be wrong to make a judgment about an individual's performance merely by "reading the numbers" provided by a management information system. Instead, the numbers should be used to alert managers about individuals who may have a performance problem. The nature of this problem should then be explored in a face-to-face meeting, during which more detailed information can be gathered. One drawback of using technology such as email and teleconferencing is that employees spend too much time watching their computer screens and communicating electronically—and little time interacting with other employees. When this happens, important and relevant information may be missed due to the lack of human interaction, and the quality of decision making may deteriorate.

Summary and Review

INFORMATION AND THE MANAGER'S JOB Computer-based information systems are central to the operation of most organizations. By providing managers with high-quality, timely, relevant, and relatively complete information, properly implemented information systems can improve managers' ability to coordinate and control the operations of an organization and to make effective decisions. Moreover, information systems can help the organization attain a competitive advantage through their beneficial impact on productivity, quality, innovation, and responsiveness to customers. [LO 13-1]

COMMUNICATION AND MANAGEMENT Communication is the sharing of information between two or more individuals or groups to reach a common understanding. Good communication is necessary for an organization to gain a competitive advantage. Communication occurs in a cyclical process that entails two phases, transmission and feedback. [LO 13-2]

INFORMATION RICHNESS AND COMMUNICATION MEDIA Information richness is the amount of information a communication medium can carry and the extent to which the medium enables the sender and receiver to reach a common understanding. Four categories of communication media in descending order of information richness are face-to-face communication (includes videoconferences), electronically transmitted spoken communication (includes voice mail), personally addressed written communication (includes email), and impersonal written communication. [LO 13-3]

THE INFORMATION TECHNOLOGY REVOLUTION Over the past 30 years there have been rapid advances in the power, and rapid declines in the cost, of information technology. Falling prices, wireless communication, computer networks, and software developments have all radically improved the power and efficacy of computer-based information systems. [LO 13-4]

TYPES OF MANAGEMENT INFORMATION SYSTEMS Traditionally managers used the organizational hierarchy as the main system for gathering the information they needed to coordinate and control the organization and to make effective decisions. Today, managers use six main types of computer-based information systems. Listed in ascending order of sophistication, they are transaction-processing systems, operations information systems, decision support systems, expert systems, enterprise resource planning (ERP) systems, and e-commerce systems. [LO 13-4]

Management *in Action*

 ## TOPICS FOR DISCUSSION AND ACTION

Discussion

1. What is the relationship between information systems and competitive advantage? [LO 13-1]

2. Why is face-to-face communication between managers still important in an organization? [LO 13-2, 13-3]

3. Which medium (or media) do you think would be appropriate for each of the following kinds of messages that a subordinate could receive from a boss: (a) a raise, (b) not receiving a promotion, (c) an error in a report prepared by the subordinate, (d) additional job responsibilities, and (e) the schedule for company

holidays for the upcoming year? Explain your choices. [LO 13-3]

4. How can information technology help in the new product development process? [LO 13-3]

5. Many companies have reported that it is difficult to implement advanced management information such as ERP systems. Why do you think this is so? How might the roadblocks to implementation be removed? [LO 13-4]

Action

6. Ask a manager to describe the main kinds of information systems that he or she uses on a routine basis at work. [LO 13-1, 13-2]

BUILDING MANAGEMENT SKILLS

Diagnosing Ineffective Communication [LO 13-2, 13-3]

Think about the last time you experienced very ineffective communication with another person—someone you work with, a classmate, a friend, a member of your family. Describe the incident. Then answer the following questions:

1. Why was your communication ineffective in this incident?

2. What stages of the communication process were particularly problematic and why?

3. Describe any filtering or information distortion that occurred.

4. How could you have handled this situation differently so communication would have been effective?

MANAGING ETHICALLY [LO 13-2, 13-3]

In organizations today, employees often take advantage of their company's information systems. Email abuse is increasing, and so is the amount of time employees spend surfing the Internet on company time. Indeed, statistics suggest that approximately 70% of the total amount of time spent surfing the Internet is company time.

Questions

1. Either by yourself or in a group, explore the ethics of using IT for personal uses at work. Should employees have some rights to use these resources? When does their behavior become unethical?

2. Some companies keep track of the way their employees use IT and the Internet. Is it ethical for managers to read employees' private email or to record the sites that employees visit on the World Wide Web?

SMALL GROUP BREAKOUT EXERCISE [LO 13-2, 13-4]

Using New Information Systems

Form groups of three or four people, and appoint one member as the spokesperson who will communicate your findings to the whole class when called upon by the instructor. Then discuss the following scenario.

You are a team of managing partners of a large firm of accountants. You are responsible for auditing your firm's information systems to determine whether they are appropriate and up-to-date. To your surprise, you find that although your organization does have an email system in place and accountants are connected into a powerful local area network (LAN), most of the accountants (including partners) are not using this technology. You also find that the organizational hierarchy is still the preferred information system of the managing partners.

Given this situation, you are concerned that your organization is not exploiting the opportunities offered by new information systems to obtain a competitive advantage.

You have discussed this issue and are meeting to develop an action plan to get accountants to appreciate the need to learn, and to take advantage of, the potential of the new information technology.

1. What advantages can you tell accountants they will obtain when they use the new information technology?

2. What problems do you think you may encounter in convincing accountants to use the new information technology?

3. Discuss how you might make it easy for accountants to learn to use the new technology.

 BE THE MANAGER [LO 13-2, 13-3]

A Problem in Communication

Mark Chen supervises support staff for an Internet merchandising organization that sells furniture over the Internet. Chen has always thought that he should expand his staff. When he was about to approach his boss with such a request, the economy slowed, and other areas of the company experienced layoffs. Thus, Chen's plans for trying to add to his staff are on indefinite hold.

Chen has noticed a troubling pattern of communication with his staff. Ordinarily, when he wants one of his staff members to work on a task, he emails the pertinent information to that person. For the last few months, his email requests have gone unheeded, and his subordinates comply with his requests only after he visits with them in person and gives them a specific deadline. Each time, they apologize for the delay but say that they are so overloaded with requests that they sometimes stop answering their phones. Unless someone asks for something more than once, they feel a request is not particularly urgent and can be put on hold.

Chen thinks this situation is dysfunctional and could lead to serious problems in the near future. He realizes, however, that his subordinates have no way of prioritizing tasks and that is why some very important projects were put on hold until he inquired about them. Knowing that he cannot add to his staff in the short term, Chen has come to you for advice. He wants to develop a system whereby his staff will provide some kind of response to requests within 24 hours, will be able to prioritize tasks, identifying their relative importance, and will not feel so overloaded that they ignore their boss's requests and don't answer their phones.

Question

1. As an expert in communication, how would you advise Chen?

 FAST COMPANY CASE IN THE NEWS [LO 13-1, 13-2, 13-3]

How Google Humanizes Technology in the Workplace, and You Can, Too

Technology keeps us from interacting face-to-face more often, but Google is changing the way we adapt to this new era of communication.

The Internet turned 25-years-old a few weeks ago, a milepost that commemorates the day Tim Berners-Lee proposed the creation of a new kind of "information management system," and forever changed how we live and work.

That the Internet has enabled profound personal and organizational productivity gains since its launch is patently irrefutable. But at the same time, the Internet, along with its ever-growing progeny of applications, has an often unacknowledged dark side: Many of us have become overwhelmed by it.

Believing it's easier to communicate with people electronically, for example, we've stopped calling each other. According to MIT technology professor Sherry Turkle, we don't even e-mail people anymore—"our communication of choice is texting."

Perhaps because we're uncertain of the expectation of our bosses, or simply we are seduced by the prospect of what may be awaiting us every time we go on line, many of us now check our cell phones 150 times a day. Trends like these not only suggest that we're allowing technology to dehumanize us, our incessant connection distracts us from remaining present with other people, our work, and from sustaining any meaningful flow in our lives.

Using the occasion of the Internet's silver anniversary as an inflection point, I reached out to Google Human Resources Director, Dr. Todd Carlisle, to see if his firm has learned to more successfully utilize and integrate technology and even re-humanize it in their workplace. Here are five of his most useful insights:

1. Thoughtfully Mix It Up

According to Carlisle, the Google employees who rely on one kind of communication—for example, texting or e-mailing—for everything and never meet with people in person tend to receive low engagement scores from their direct reports. Consequently, his guidance to managers is that they should be very thoughtful in determining the best way to communicate in every situation.

Carlisle says he does a calculation every time he needs to speak with someone: If the conversation is going to be a two-minute back and forth, then he'll instant message them. If it's going to be longer than that, he'll instant message them to see if they have time to talk live. Then he must decide if it is better to speak on the phone or via a Google video-conferencing Hangout.

Carlisle insists that some messages are always best delivered in person, like sharing vision for the team, for example. Routinely being efficiency minded when

communicating will inevitably backfire, he says. "So I think what we're always talking about is, 'What are you trying to get across—and what's the best methodology?'"

One Google VP recently replaced his newsletter e-mail with a three-minute YouTube video. According to Carlisle, "after surveying people afterwards, we saw employees had better recollection of it, and overall more positive feelings toward the organization."

2. Let Technology Support Employees in Their Personal Lives

The day Carlisle and I met, he had an 8 p.m. meeting scheduled with a colleague in India; he told me directly that he had no intention of staying in the office until then. "I'll go home, put my kids to bed, and then take the Hangout from my living room. And the person in India will be getting ready to go to work (8:30 a.m.), so he's going to do the opposite. Before he takes his kids to school, he'll go to a quiet place, and we'll have our work meeting."

Much has been written about Google's penchant for workplace synchronicity—the notion that ideas get spread and enhanced via conversations employees have in the hallways and cafeterias. Nevertheless, the company makes no insistence that people are always in the office to take a meeting. "We care that people are happy and productive," says Carlisle, "and we're all trying to be flexible around the stuff that happens in life."

3. Leverage Technology to Give Employees Greater Voice

Traditionally in business, an organization's policies and procedures were crafted and communicated by people in a Human Resources

department, a process that excluded much, if any, involvement with line employees. According to Carlisle, Google sees its workers as the true subject matter experts, and purposely makes great use of its shared document technology to eliminate all "top-downness from decision making."

Recently, a group of individual contributors petitioned Carlisle to have their job titles revisited. Rather than take on the task himself, he challenged the team to brainstorm and produce the solution. Leveraging a suite of programs that enables people to collaboratively create documents and spreadsheets in real time, employees in Mountain View, India, and Dublin were able to post proposed titles, comment on what they liked and didn't like, and evolve the discussion until the task was completed.

"I'm certain the team will feel much more empowered [and engaged] by the outcome," says Carlisle, "because the new job titles weren't just handed down from the management team. They did it bottom up."

4. Go High-Tech and Low-Tech

Almost every meeting held today at Google makes use of the Hangout program to accommodate employees unable to attend, or who work in other locations. Wherever they are, meeting attendees are able to use the camera on their phone or computer and talk face-to-face with every person participating.

Despite having technology that so powerfully and conveniently unites people—and that their own company created—Google's founders and top executives have intentionally retained one old school element of leadership communication. Once a week, they make themselves available, live and in person, to Google headquarter employees (interactively beamed live to all other locations) in town hall meetings.

"This is not a high tech thing," says Carlisle. "This is a leader prioritizing transparency thing."

5. Encourage People to Disconnect

If you've ever checked e-mail after waking up at 3 a.m. to go to the bathroom, or felt compelled to respond to a boss's inquiry on a Saturday afternoon, it's consoling to know that, at least at Google, people are giving thought to whether "always being on" is good for us or our organizations.

According to new research on work-life balance, most of us now approach our jobs in one of two ways—we're either "Integrators" or "Segmentors." And, one of these methods, it seems, has the clear leg up on sustaining long-term productivity and overall human effectiveness.

Segmentors come to work, do their job, and go after a demanding day. At that point they are done. They turn their work-brain off and turn on their personal-brain. And the work-brain goes back on at 8:00 a.m. the next morning.

Integrators will come home at night, do some personal things, do a little work, check e-mail before going to bed, and then again first thing in the morning. Integrators have looser boundaries between work and life.

Internal research shows that some people say they prefer to segment and some say they prefer to integrate. But regardless of preference is on this, the data shows Google employees are happier with their overall well being when they segment.

One senior Google executive, someone who manages thousands of people in the organization, appears to be setting a more disciplined example. He's conveyed to his employees that he checks e-mail only three times a day (an hour in the morning, an hour after lunch, and an hour in the evening) making himself more available to be present in all of his human interactions.

Carlisle told me at the end of our conversation that Google is trying to "use technology in the most positive way." I believe him.

Questions

1. How does using the same form of communication with employees hinder a manager's ability to maintain a strong working relationship with direct reports?

2. What are some advantages and disadvantages of Google managers making themselves available live and in person to employees on a weekly basis?

3. Describe the characteristics of a Segmentor and an Integrator. Which type of employee are you?

Endnotes

1. H.J. Wilson, "The Hot New Thing in Business Attire Is Technology," *The Wall Street Journal,* accessed April 27, 2015, www.wsj.com; S. Leung, "How Wearable Technology Can (and Will) Change Your Business," *Salesforce Blog,* accessed April 27, 2015, https://www.salesforce.com.

2. Company website, "Buffalo Bills Case Study," www.catapultsports.com, accessed April 27, 2015.

3. C. Brauer, "Workplace Wearables: Your Boss Knows When You've Had a Good Night's Sleep?" *CNN,* accessed April 27, 2015, www.cnn.com.

4. B. Green, "How Your Boss Can Keep You on a Leash," *CNN,* accessed April 27, 2015, www.cnn.com.

5. Wilson, "The Hot New Thing in Business Attire Is Technology."

6. D. Gura, "If Your Company ID Badge Was a Tracking Device," *Marketplace Business,* accessed April 27, 2015, www.marketplace.org.

7. N. B. Macintosh, *The Social Software of Accounting Information Systems* (New York: Wiley, 1995).

8. C. A. O'Reilly, "Variations in Decision Makers' Use of Information: The Impact of Quality and Accessibility," *Academy of Management Journal* 25 (1982), 756–71.

9. G. Stalk and T. H. Hout, *Competing against Time* (New York: Free Press, 1990).

10. R. Cyert and J. March, *Behavioral Theory of the Firm* (Englewood Cliffs, NJ: Prentice-Hall, 1963).

11. E. Turban, *Decision Support and Expert Systems* (New York: Macmillan, 1988).

12. W. H. Davidson and M. S. Malone, *The Virtual Corporation* (New York: Harper Business, 1992); M. E. Porter, *Competitive Advantage* (New York: Free Press, 1984).

13. S. M. Dornbusch and W. R. Scott, *Evaluation and the Exercise of Authority* (San Francisco: Jossey-Bass, 1975).

14. J. Child, *Organization: A Guide to Problems and Practice* (London: Harper & Row, 1984).

15. Company website for UPS Supply Chain Solutions, "Contract Logistics—Retail," www.ups-scs.com, accessed April 27, 2015.

16. Macintosh, *The Social Software of Accounting Information Systems.*

17. T. Meek, "Big Data in HR: Finding In-House Talent in the Digital Age," *Forbes,* accessed April 27, 2015, www.forbes.com.

18. Company website, "Talent Management," www-03.ibm.com, accessed April 27, 2015.

19. E. Byrne, "Tomorrow's Recruitment: Big-Data Robots Bring Better Hires," *Forbes,* accessed April 27, 2015, www.forbes.com.

20. C. Versace, "Talking Big Data and Analytics with IBM," *Forbes,* accessed April 27, 2015, www.forbes.com.

21. J. Clampet, "Skift Q&A: The Man Who Feeds More Than 300,000 Disney Guests a Day," *Skift,* accessed April 27, 2015, http://skift.com.

22. K. Boyer, "Behind the Scenes at Starbucks Supply Chain Operations It's Plan, Source, Make & Deliver," *Supply Chain 24/7,* accessed April 27, 2015, www.supplychain247.com.

23. N. Cotiaux, "Starbucks Supply-Chain Program Holds Lessons for Small Businesses," *intuit.com,* accessed April 27, 2015, http://quickbooks.intuit.com.

24. Company website, "Cocoa Origin Trip Report—Ecuador," www.starbucks.com, January 10, 2011.

25. Cotiaux, "Starbucks Supply-Chain Program Holds Lessons for Small Businesses."

26. C. A. O'Reilly and L. R. Pondy, "Organizational Communication," in S. Kerr, ed., *Organizational Behavior* (Columbus, OH: Grid, 1979).

27. Company website, "GE Healthcare: Fast Facts," www.ge.com, accessed April 28, 2015.

28. Company website, "LightSpeed VCT Series," www.gehealthcare.com, accessed April 28, 2015; "New Scanner by GE Healthcare Advances Imaging Technology," *Wisconsin Technology Network,* June 21, 2004, www.wistechnology.com; S. Kirsner, "Time [Zone] Travelers," *Fast Company,* August 2004, 60–66.

29. Kirsner, "Time [Zone] Travelers."

30. Ibid.

31. E. M. Rogers and R. Agarwala-Rogers, *Communication in Organizations* (New York: Free Press, 1976).

32. J. Romig, "Listening to Nonverbal Cues," *Listen Like a Lawyer* (blog), accessed April 28, 2015, http://listenlikealawyer.com.

33. D. A. Adams, P. A. Todd, and R. R. Nelson, "A Comparative Evaluation of the Impact of Electronic and Voice Mail on Organizational Communication," *Information and Management* 24 (1993), 9–21.

34. S. Reinberg, "A Key Thing Doctors Can Do to Reduce Hospital Errors," *CBS News,* accessed April 28, 2015, www.cbsnews.com.

35. R. L. Daft, R. H. Lengel, and L. K. Trevino, "Message Equivocality, Media Selection, and Manager Performance: Implications for Information Systems," *MIS Quarterly* 11 (1987), 355–66; R. L. Daft and R. H. Lengel, "Information Richness: A New Approach to Managerial Behavior and Organization Design," in B. M. Staw and L. L. Cummings, eds., *Research in Organizational Behavior* (Greenwich, CT: JAI Press, 1984).

36. R. L. Daft, *Organization Theory and Design* (St. Paul, MN: West, 1992).

37. Company website, "Global Financial Services Firm Cuts Costs, Carbon Emissions," (case study), www.cisco.com, accessed April 28, 2015.

38. T. J. Peters and R. H. Waterman Jr., *In Search of Excellence* (New York: Harper and Row, 1982); T. Peters and N. Austin, *A Passion for Excellence: The Leadership Difference* (New York: Random House, 1985).

39. Company website, "Cisco TelePresence Overview," www.cisco.com, accessed April 28, 2015.

40. "Skype vs FaceTime: Looking for the Best Video Calling Experience on iOS," *Guiding Tech,* accessed April 28, 2015, www.guidingtech.com.

41. Company website, www.radicati.com, accessed April 29, 2015.

42. M. Johnson, "Business Email Etiquette: Proper from Subject to Closing," *udemy blog,* accessed April 29, 2015, https://blog.udemy.com.

43. K. Rapoza, "One in Five Americans Work from Home, Numbers Seen Rising over 60%," *Forbes,* accessed April 29, 2015, www.forbes.com.

44. "Is Your Employer Monitoring Your Internet Use?" *World Law Direct,* accessed April 29, 2015, www.worldlawdirect.

45. S.E. Ante and L. Weber, "Employers Have Latitude in Monitoring Workers," *The Wall Street Journal,* accessed April 29, 2015, www.wsj.com.

46. "Should Companies Monitor Their Employees' Social Media?" *The Wall Street Journal,* accessed April 29, 2015, www.wsj.com.

47. A. Tugend, "What to Think About before You Hit 'Send'," *The New York Times,* accessed April 29, 2015, www.nytimes.com.

48. S. Rosenbaum, "IBM: Communication and Curation Go Hand in Hand," *Forbes,* accessed April 30, 2015, www.forbes.com.

49. Nick Cicero, "The Top 10 Corporate Blogs of 2014," *Social Fresh,* accessed April 30, 2015, www.socialfresh.com.

50. Sharon Florentine, "6 Social Media Mistakes That Will Kill Your Career," *CIO.com,* accessed April 30, 2015, www.cio.com.

51. M. Swider, "Apple Watch Sold More in a Day Than Android Wear Did in 2014," *Tech Radar,* accessed April 30, 2014, www.techradar.com; D. Lee, "Apple's iPod: Is the End Nigh?" *BBC,* accessed April 30, 2105, www.bbc.com.

52. A. D. Chandler, *The Visible Hand* (Cambridge, MA: Harvard University Press, 1977).

53. C. W. L. Hill and J. F. Pickering, "Divisionalization, Decentralization, and Performance of Large United Kingdom Companies," *Journal of Management Studies* 23 (1986), 26–50.

54. O. E. Williamson, *Markets and Hierarchies: Analysis and Anti-Trust Implications* (New York: Free Press, 1975).

55. Company website, www.ups.com, accessed April 30, 2015.

56. Turban, *Decision Support and Expert Systems.*

57. B. Power, "Artificial Intelligence Is Almost Ready for Business," *Harvard Business Review,* accessed April 27, 2015, https://hbr.org.

58. F. Burnson, "Compare Enterprise Resource Planning (ERP) Software," *Software Advice,* accessed April 28, 2015, www.softwareadvice.com.

14

Operations Management: Managing Vital Operations and Processes

Learning Objectives

After studying this chapter, you should be able to:

LO 14-1 Explain the role of operations management in achieving superior quality, efficiency, and responsiveness to customers.

LO 14-2 Describe what customers want, and explain why it is so important for managers to be responsive to their needs.

LO 14-3 Explain why achieving superior quality is so important.

LO 14-4 Explain why achieving superior efficiency is so important.

© claudia veja/Moment/Getty Images RF

Airlines are always looking for ways to board passengers faster and more efficiently. What slows down boarding and departures? Passengers who jump the boarding line and those who pay for early boarding and clog the aisles while others try to board. © Image Source/Christopher Robbins RF

MANAGEMENT SNAPSHOT

Airlines Try Many Methods to Expedite Boarding Process

Why Is Efficiency Important?

Is it faster to board the back of the plane first? Or should airlines file in passengers with window seats first, followed by those with middle seats, followed by those with aisle seats? What about just assigning passengers to random groups and boarding that way? Or how about not assigning seats and just allowing passengers to sit wherever they want?

These were the questions some major airlines asked themselves recently in an effort to improve their on-time ratings. Late departures and arrivals cost airlines in more ways than reputation, so making sure boarding occurs in a timely manner is of great concern to the industry, as well as to passengers needing to make connecting flights.

Certainly the first two boarding options sound like they would be faster than the free-for-all of allowing random groups to board at the same time or allowing passengers to sit wherever they like. Surprisingly, two recent studies found that random boarding does work a little quicker than the other options, believe it or not.

One study was conducted by American Airlines, which spent two years studying ways to speed up the boarding process and landed on randomized group boarding for most passengers. The airline still gives families, military personnel, and travelers with elite status priority boarding. It also allows passengers the option of paying for early boarding if they choose.

Part of American's study had observers watch thousands of boarding processes to see where things bogged down. Carry-on bags were a big problem. Passengers were bringing large bags on board to avoid baggage fees. When the plane was boarded back to front, those waiting in the aisles to get to their seats would put their bags in overhead bins at the front of the plane, leaving no space for the bags of passengers who boarded later.

Using computer simulations, American not only found that the back-to-front boarding method was slower than the window-middle-aisle seat method, but it also discovered that putting passengers into random boarding groups allowed the plane to fill up faster. Using the random method, more passengers got to their seats at the same time than the two-at-a-time rate of the back-to-front method. Also, passengers were more likely to stow their bags in overhead bins closer to their seats than at the front of the plane. The new method even reduced the number of bags American checked at the gate by 20%.[1] More recently, American tweaked the system to add passengers without carry-ons to the list of priority boarders.[2]

Another study was done by MythBusters, the Discovery Channel television show that applies scientific methods to test various accepted ideas. In the episode on plane boarding, the MythBusters team sought to confirm the myth that "when boarding an airplane, boarding back-to-front is the slowest method."[3] On the program, the hosts built a plane replica, complete with seats and overhead bins. Volunteers tested the various boarding methods. To further simulate reality, 5% of the volunteers were told to disrupt boarding by such actions as sitting in the wrong seat or standing in the aisle for longer than needed. Professional flight attendants were hired to help with the process. The program measured two outcomes of each method tested: how long it took to board the plane and how satisfied the volunteer passengers were with each experience.

The method with the highest satisfaction rating was the "reverse pyramid," in which elite passengers boarded first followed by a complex set of zones that began with the rear window seats. That method allowed the plane to board in 15 minutes and 10 seconds. The method that allowed for fastest boarding was the one with no assigned seats. When used, the plane was boarded in 14 minutes and 7 seconds. Yet this method had the lowest satisfaction rating of all the methods attempted on the show.

The second-fastest method was boarding elite passengers first, followed by the window-middle-aisle seat method. This method received high marks for passenger satisfaction. This method is similar to one called the "Steffen Method," named for astrophysicist Jason Steffen who wrote a research paper with a mathematical approach to efficient boarding. In that method, passengers board in the window-middle-aisle seat method, but in assigned zones that keep them in different parts of the plane and allow simultaneous boarding.[4]

What slows down boarding? Many industry analysts and bloggers have listed the reasons. For one, many passengers board outside their "zone" or whatever method the airline is using, which makes the system less efficient. Some passengers may do this purposely and count on gate agents to look the other way. Second, other passengers pay for early boarding or are given early boarding as part of their frequent flier program, which has the same effect as those who jumped the line. Both the passengers who boarded with the wrong group on purpose and those who paid for the privilege may be in the aisle as others try to board or may be strapped into middle or aisle seats and will need to stand when the window seat passengers arrive. Third, sometimes after stowing a carry-on bag in the overhead bin, a passenger remembers something needed from the bag, stands up, and blocks the aisle while rummaging through the bag to find it.[5]

Probably the most cited culprit for slow boarding is baggage. Airlines started charging for checked luggage in 2008 when fuel prices went up. To avoid the fees, more passengers began using carry-on luggage. The extra luggage slows the boarding process by leaving passengers in the aisle longer. The extra luggage also frequently fills up the bins, requiring extra time and effort for airline personnel to gate-check the bags or take bags out of the cabin and place them with checked baggage in the cargo hold.

Why is the speed of boarding an airplane important? Airlines save $30 for every minute shaved off boarding times.[6] However, airlines appear to be making some of this money back in fees. U.S.-based airlines have increased their fees, despite making more than $3 billion from baggage fees in 2014. American Airlines, which collected more than $5 million in checked bags fees in 2014, increased its fee charged to passengers flying with more than two bags to $150 for the third bag and $200 per bag for additional bags.[7] Delta Airlines collected more than $1 billion in fees in 2013.[8]

Fees vary at different airlines, as do methods for boarding planes. Southwest Airlines continues to use the unassigned seat method of boarding. The airline assigns passengers to boarding groups and gives each passenger a boarding number within the group. Passengers line up in groups and in numerical order. Because seats are not assigned, each passenger selects a seat when on the plane.[9] Like American Airlines, most airlines use assigned seating and some type of boarding group system to put passengers on the planes—hoping for a speedy takeoff.

Overview As the "Management Snapshot" suggests, organizations don't always agree on the best way to conduct business. Companies in the same industry, such as the airline industry, can vary widely on their business practices. Some organizations may adopt the latest research and methods, while others use different strategies to try and stay competitive.

operations management
The management of any aspect of the production system that transforms inputs into finished goods and services.

In this chapter we focus on operations management techniques that managers can use to increase the quality of an organization's products, the efficiency of production, and the organization's responsiveness to customers. By the end of this chapter, you will understand the vital role operations management plays in building competitive advantage and creating a high-performing organization.

Operations Management and Competitive Advantage

Operations management is the management of any aspect of the production system that transforms inputs into finished goods and services. A **production system** is the system that an organization uses to acquire inputs, convert inputs into outputs, and dispose of the outputs (goods or services). **Operations managers** are managers who are responsible for managing an organization's production system. They do whatever it takes to transform inputs into outputs. Their job is to manage the three stages of production—acquisition of inputs, control of conversion processes, and disposal of goods and services—and to determine where operating improvements might be made in order to increase quality, efficiency, and responsiveness to customers and so give an organization a competitive advantage (see Figure 14.1).

Quality refers to goods and services that are reliable, dependable, or psychologically satisfying: They do the job they were designed for and do it well, or they possess some attribute that gives their users something they value.[10] *Efficiency* refers to the amount of inputs required to produce a given output. *Responsiveness to customers* refers to actions taken to meet the demands and needs of customers. Operations managers are responsible for ensuring that an organization has sufficient supplies of high-quality, low-cost inputs, and they are responsible for designing a production system that creates high-quality, low-cost products that customers are willing to buy.

Notice that achieving superior efficiency and quality is part of attaining superior responsiveness to customers. Customers want value for their money, and an organization whose efficient production system creates high-quality, low-cost products

LO 14-1 Explain the role of operations management in achieving superior quality, efficiency, and responsiveness to customers.

production system
The system that an organization uses to acquire inputs, convert the inputs into outputs, and dispose of the outputs.

Figure 14.1
The Purpose of Operations Management

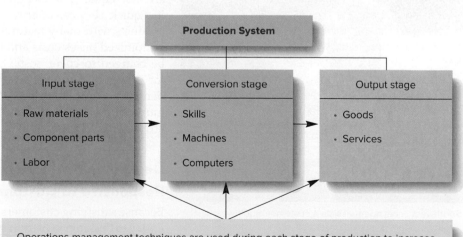

Operations management techniques are used during each stage of production to increase efficiency, quality, and responsiveness to customers in order to give the organization a competitive advantage.

is best able to deliver this value. For this reason, we begin by discussing how operations managers can design the production system to increase responsiveness to customers.

Improving Responsiveness to Customers

Organizations produce outputs—goods or services—that are consumed by customers. All organizations, profit seeking or not-for-profit, have customers. Without customers, most organizations would cease to exist. Because customers are vital to the survival of most organizations, managers must correctly identify customers and promote organizational strategies that respond to their needs. This is why management writers recommend that organizations define their business in terms of which customer *wants* or *needs* they are satisfying, not the type of products they are producing.[11]

operations manager A manager who is responsible for managing an organization's production system and for determining where operating improvements might be made.

LO 14-2 Describe what customers want, and explain why it is so important for managers to be responsive to their needs.

What Do Customers Want?

Given that satisfying customer demands is central to the survival of an organization, an important question is, What do customers want? To specify exactly what they want is not possible because their wants vary from industry to industry. However, it is possible to identify some universal product attributes that most customers in most industries want. Generally, other things being equal, most customers prefer

1. A lower price to a higher price.
2. High-quality products to low-quality products.
3. Quick service to slow service. (They will always prefer good after-sales service and support to poor after-sales support.)
4. Products with many useful features to products with few features.
5. Products that are, as far as possible, customized or tailored to their unique needs.

Of course, the problem is that other things are not equal. For example, providing high quality, quick service, after-sales service and support, products with many features, and products that are customized raises costs and thus the price that must be charged to cover costs. So customers' demands for these attributes typically conflict with their demands for low prices. Accordingly, customers must make a trade-off between price and preferred attributes, and so must managers.

A Southwest ticket agent assists a customer. Southwest's operating system is geared toward satisfying customer demands for low-priced, reliable, and convenient air travel, making it one of the most consistently successful airlines in recent years. To help keep flights on schedule, Southwest's workforce has been cross-trained to perform multiple tasks.
© Joseph Kaczmarek/AP Images

Designing Production Systems to Be Responsive to Customers

Because satisfying customers is so important, managers try to design production systems that can produce the outputs that have the attributes customers desire. The attributes of an organization's outputs—their quality, cost, and features—are determined by the organization's production system.[12] Since the ability of an organization to satisfy the demands of its customers derives from its production system, managers need to devote considerable attention to constantly improving production systems. Managers' desire to attract customers with improved products explains their adoption of many new operations management techniques in recent years. These include flexible manufacturing systems, just-in-time inventory, and, of course, the new information systems and technologies discussed in Chapter 13.

As an example of the link between responsiveness to customers and an organization's production system, consider how Southwest Airlines operates. One of the most consistently successful airlines in the United States, Southwest Airlines has been expanding rapidly. One reason for Southwest's success is that its managers created a production system uniquely tailored to satisfy the demands of its customers for low-priced, reliable (on-time), and convenient air travel. Southwest commands high customer loyalty precisely because its production system delivers products, such as flights from Houston to Dallas, that have all the desired attributes: reliability, convenience, and low price.

Southwest's low-cost production system focuses not only on improving the maintenance of aircraft but also on the company's ticket reservation system, route structure, flight frequency, baggage-handling system, and in-flight services. For example, Southwest offers a no-frills approach to in-flight customer service. No meals are served on board, and there are no first-class seats. Southwest does not subscribe to the big reservation computers used by travel agents because the booking fees are too costly. Also, the airline flies only one aircraft, the fuel-efficient Boeing 737, which keeps training and maintenance costs down. All this translates into low prices for customers. In addition, Southwest is one of the few airlines that does not charge baggage fees. Passengers can check two bags for free.[13]

Southwest's reliability derives from the fact that it has the quickest aircraft turnaround time in the industry. A Southwest ground crew needs only 15 minutes to turn around an incoming aircraft and prepare it for departure. This speedy operation helps to keep flights on time. Southwest has such quick turnaround because it has a flexible workforce that has been cross-trained to perform multiple tasks. Thus, the person who checks tickets might also help with baggage loading if time is short.

Southwest's convenience comes from its scheduling multiple flights every day between its popular locations and its use of airports that are close to downtown instead of more distant major airports.[14] Southwest's value chain management has given it a competitive advantage in the airline industry. Another company that has found a way to be responsive to customers by offering them faster service is Panera, which is profiled in the accompanying "Management Insight" feature.

MANAGEMENT INSIGHT

Technology Provides Faster Service for Customers at Panera

Panera is a bakery–café chain with more than 1,900 units located in both the United States and Canada. The chain is made up of three companies: Saint Louis Bread Co., Paradise Bakery & Café, and Panera Bread. Until recent years, the bakeries had been operating successfully with a traditional bakery–café model of offerings and service. That's until the company's CEO, Ron Shaich, had an epiphany. Always running late when driving his son to school in the mornings, Shaich would arrange for breakfast and lunch for his son by calling ahead to one of his stores and ordering. When he arrived at the store, his son would run in with his credit card, skip the line, and pick up the food. While the system worked for the Shaichs, it was not one that was available to everyone.

That's what gave Shaich the idea for Panera 2.0. Now customers can place orders via computer or mobile app. When the customer arrives at the restaurant, he or she can skip the line, pay for the ordered food, and either eat in or carry out. There also are touchscreen kiosks at the restaurants for customers who did not order ahead but who want to get through the line faster. And, of course, customers can still go to the register and place an order.[15]

One advantage of the new system is that it syncs with the MyPanera rewards program. The program remembers all orders that the customer places and currently has more than 19 million members. If a customer ordered a custom sandwich at one visit, the system remembers it and offers to place the same order at the next visit.

Panera began testing the system in 2011 and hopes to have it rolled out to all restaurants by 2016. And it has already seen users of Panera 2.0 and kiosk users increase the frequency of their visits. At one location, sales were up more than 50%.[16]

Until recently, Panera Bread had been operating its bakery–cafés in a traditional manner. Now, after CEO Ron Shaich got the idea for Panera 2.0, customers can place orders online, skip the store line, pay for the order, and eat in or carry out. The new system allows Panera to increase its efficiency and customer service satisfaction. © ZUMA Press, Inc/Alamy

The new system also has improved the order accuracy rates. The industry average is one in seven incorrectly fulfilled orders, many of the errors occurring during input at the register. "If we're in the to-go business, we have to be 100 percent accurate," Shaich says.[17] In addition to depending on the customer to enter the order correctly, employees double-check each order before it leaves the store.

Of course adding the system has meant changes for the employees at Panera. The information technology team has doubled. Operations have been affected as well. When customers place orders online or at a kiosk, it saves employees at the register from having to do so. Those employees can be redeployed to the kitchen to help keep up with the demand of incoming orders.

Once the system is in place at every Panera location, Shaich believes Panera will be one of the 10 largest e-commerce operators in the United States.

Customer Relationship Management

One operations strategy managers can use to get close to customers and understand their needs is **customer relationship management (CRM)**. CRM is a technique that uses IT to develop an ongoing relationship with customers to maximize the value an organization can deliver to them over time. By the 2000s most large companies had installed sophisticated CRM IT to track customers' changing demands for a company's products; this became a vital tool to maximize responsiveness to customers.

CRM IT monitors, controls, and links each of the functional activities involved in marketing, selling, and delivering products to customers, such as monitoring the delivery of products through the distribution channel, monitoring salespeople's selling activities, setting product pricing, and coordinating after-sales service. CRM systems have three interconnected components: sales and selling, after-sales service and support, and marketing.

Suppose a sales manager has access only to sales data that show the total sales revenue each salesperson generated in the past 30 days. This information does not break down how much revenue came from sales to existing customers versus sales to new customers. What important knowledge is being lost? First, if most revenues are earned from sales to existing customers, this suggests that the money being spent by a company to advertise and promote its products is not attracting new customers and so is being wasted. Second, important dimensions involved in sales are pricing, financing, and order processing. In many companies, to close a deal, a salesperson has to send the paperwork to a central sales office that handles matters such as approving the customer for special financing and determining specific shipping and delivery dates. In some companies, different departments handle these activities, and it can take a long time to get a response from them; this keeps customers waiting—something that often leads to lost sales. Until CRM systems were introduced, these kinds of problems were widespread and resulted in missed sales and higher operating costs. Today the sales and selling CRM software contains *best sales practices* that analyze this information and then recommend ways to improve how the sales process operates.

One company that has improved its sales and after-sales practices by implementing CRM is Empire HealthChoice Inc., the largest health insurance provider in New York, which sells its health care plans and products with more than 4,000 associates statewide. For years these agents were responsible for collecting all the customer-specific information needed to determine the price of each policy. Once they had collected the necessary information, the agents called Empire to get price quotes. After waiting days for these quotes, the agents relayed them back to customers, who often then modified their requests to reduce the cost of their policies. When this occurred, the agents had to telephone Empire again to get revised price quotes. Because this frequently happened several times with each transaction, it often took more than 20 days to close a sale and another 10 days for customers to get their insurance cards.

Recognizing that these delays were causing lost sales, Empire decided to examine how a CRM system could improve the sales process. Its managers chose a web-based system so agents themselves could calculate the insurance quotes online. Once an agent enters a customer's data, a quote is generated in just a few seconds. The agent can continually modify a policy while sitting face-to-face with the customer until the policy and price are agreed upon. As a result, the sales process can now be completed in a few hours.[18]

When a company implements after-sales service and support CRM software, salespeople are required to input detailed information about their follow-up visits to customers. Because the system tracks and documents every customer's case history, salespeople have instant access to a record of everything that occurred during previous phone calls or visits. They are in a much better position to respond to customers' needs and build customer loyalty, so a company's after-sales service improves. Cell phone companies like T-Mobile and Sprint, for example, require that telephone sales reps collect information about all customers' inquiries, complaints, and requests, and this is recorded electronically in customer logs. The CRM module can analyze the information in these logs to evaluate whether the customer service reps are meeting or exceeding the company's required service standards.

A CRM system can also identify the top 10 reasons for customer complaints. Sales managers can then work to eliminate the sources of these problems and improve after-sales support procedures. The CRM system also identifies the top 10 best service and support practices, which can then be taught to all sales reps.

Finally, as a CRM system processes information about changing customer needs, this improves marketing in many ways. Marketing managers, for example, have access to detailed customer profiles, including data about purchases and the reasons why individuals were or were not attracted to a company's products. Armed with this knowledge, marketing can better identify customers and the specific product attributes they desire. Traditional CRM systems were organized by having salespeople input customer information. Now social CRM systems can track customers on social media and put them on a company's radar. For example, if a Twitter user posts frequently about a topic relevant to the company or about the company's products, a CRM system can bring the user to the attention of the company as an important connection or a potential customer.[19] In sum, a CRM system is a comprehensive method of gathering crucial information about how customers respond to a company's products. It is a powerful functional strategy used to align a company's products with customer needs.

Improving Quality

As noted earlier, high-quality products possess attributes such as superior design, features, reliability, and after-sales support; these products are designed to better meet customer requirements.[20] Quality is a concept that can be applied to the products of both manufacturing and service organizations—goods such as a Toyota car or services such as Southwest Airlines flight service or customer service in a Wells Fargo branch. Why do managers seek to control and improve the quality of their organizations' products?[21] There are two reasons (see Figure 14.2).

LO 14-3 Explain why achieving superior quality is so important.

First, customers usually prefer a higher-quality product to a lower-quality product. So an organization able to provide, *for the same price,* a product of higher quality than a competitor's product is serving its customers better—it is being more responsive to its customers. Often, providing high-quality products creates a brand-name reputation for an organization's products. In turn, this enhanced reputation may allow the organization to charge more for its products than its competitors are able to charge, and thus it makes even greater profits. For example, in 2015 Lexus was ranked number one on the J.D. Power list of the 10 most reliable car brands for the fourth year in a row.[22] The high quality and dependability of Lexus vehicles enable the company to charge higher prices for its cars than the prices charged by rival auto makers.

Figure 14.2

The Impact of Increased Quality on Organizational Performance

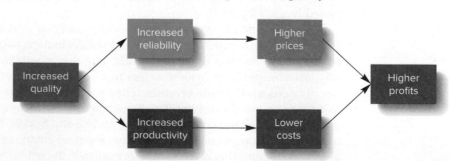

The second reason for trying to boost product quality is that higher product quality can increase efficiency and thereby lower operating costs and boost profits. Achieving high product quality lowers operating costs because of the effect of quality on employee productivity: Higher product quality means less employee time is wasted in making defective products that must be discarded or in providing substandard services, and thus less time has to be spent fixing mistakes. This translates into higher employee productivity, which means lower costs. The way management can have an impact on quality and cost is discussed in the accompanying "Management Insight" feature.

MANAGEMENT INSIGHT

Successful Discount Retailer Knows Customer Satisfaction Is Key

The TJX Companies Inc. sell clothes, shoes, handbags, and other fashions along with home decorating items at discounted prices. Its U.S. retail stores are T.J. Maxx, Marshalls, Sierra Trading Post, and HomeGoods. The company was founded in 1919 as the New England Trading Company and expanded into a chain of women's clothing stores. The sons of the founders built the Zayre department store in the 1950s; then came T.J. Maxx in 1976, which was created under the Zayre name. In a major restructuring in the late 1980s, the Zayre stores were sold and the company changed its name to TJX Companies. It later acquired Marshalls, HomeGoods, and Sierra Trading Post.

The company states its mission as delivering "a rapidly changing assortment of fashionable, quality, brand name and designer merchandise at prices generally 20 to 60 percent below department and specialty store regular prices, every day."[23] Aside from the savings, the main appeal of the stores is the "treasure-hunt shopping experience" in which the stores have different items and a different look—often a somewhat opposite experience to perusing the more static seasonal product lines found in traditional department stores. The company's business model allows it to perform well in almost any economic environment. TJX is able to sell high-quality name-brand merchandise at a discount by purchasing overstocks and canceled orders from other retailers. TJX buys up excess inventory at a steep discount, which it then passes on to the customer.[24]

TJX stores have no walls or physical dividers between departments. This allows the merchandise categories to expand or contract according to supply and demand. Inventory turns rapidly, which keeps stores fresh and allows the company to buy as it needs. "Our universe of over 16,000 vendors affords us tremendous flexibility, and we continue to strengthen our vendor relationships and build new ones to offer consumers even more exciting brands," said TJX CEO Carol Meyrowitz. "While we drive our top line, we expect to also drive our profitability through even better inventory management and a further improved supply chain."[25]

The supply chain is important to TJX's ability to deliver value and to properly stock each store. The retailer has more than 3,300 stores in six countries and plans to grow through new and remodeled stores, new distribution centers, and systems and supply chain improvements. Meyrowitz said the company will continue to invest in its supply chain over the next several years.[26]

Improving Efficiency

The third goal of operations management is to increase the efficiency of an organization's production system. The fewer the inputs required to produce a given output, the higher will be the efficiency of the production system. Managers can measure efficiency at the organization level in two ways. The measure, known as *total factor productivity,* looks at how well an organization utilizes all of its resources—such as labor, capital, materials, or energy—to produce its outputs. It is expressed in the following equation:

LO 14-4 Explain why achieving superior efficiency is so important.

$$\text{Total factor productivity} = \frac{\text{Outputs}}{\text{All inputs}}$$

The problem with total factor productivity is that each input is typically measured in different units: Labor's contribution to producing an output is measured by hours worked; the contribution of materials is measured by the amount consumed (for example, tons of iron ore required to make a ton of steel); the contribution of energy is measured by the units of energy consumed (for example, kilowatt-hours); and so on. To compute total factor productivity, managers must convert all the inputs to a common unit, such as dollars, before they can work the equation.

Though sometimes a useful measure of efficiency overall, total factor productivity obscures the exact contribution of an individual input—such as labor—to the production of a given output. Consequently, most organizations focus on specific measures of efficiency, known as *partial productivity,* that measure the efficiency of an individual unit. For example, the efficiency of labor inputs is expressed as

$$\text{Labor productivity} = \frac{\text{Outputs}}{\text{Direct labor}}$$

Labor productivity is most commonly used to draw efficiency comparisons between different organizations. For example, one study found that in 1994 it took the average Japanese automobile components supplier half as many labor-hours to produce a part, such as a car seat or exhaust system, as the average British company.[27] Thus, the study concluded, Japanese companies use labor more efficiently than British companies.

The management of efficiency is an extremely important issue in most organizations because increased efficiency lowers production costs, thereby allowing the organization to make a greater profit or to attract more customers by lowering its price. For example, in 1990 the price of the average personal computer sold in the United States was $3,000, by 1995 the price was around $1,800, and in 2015 it was around $379.[28] This decrease occurred despite the fact that the power and capabilities of the average personal computer increased dramatically during this time period (microprocessors became more powerful, memory increased, modems were built in, and multimedia capability was added).

Why was the decrease in price possible? Manufacturers of personal computers focused on quality and boosted their efficiency by improving the quality of their components and making PCs easier to assemble. This allowed them to lower their costs and prices yet still make a profit.

Facilities Layout, Flexible Manufacturing, and Efficiency

Another factor that influences efficiency is the way managers decide to lay out or design an organization's physical work facilities. This is important for two reasons. First, the way in which machines and workers are organized or grouped together

facilities layout
The operations management strategy whose goal is to design the machine–worker interface to increase production system efficiency.

flexible manufacturing
Operations management techniques that attempt to reduce the setup costs associated with a production system.

into workstations affects the efficiency of the production system. Second, a major determinant of efficiency is the cost associated with setting up the equipment needed to make a particular product. **Facilities layout** is the operations management strategy whose goal is to design the machine–worker interface to increase production system efficiency. **Flexible manufacturing** is the set of operations management techniques that attempt to reduce the setup costs associated with a production system.

FACILITIES LAYOUT The way in which machines, robots, and people are grouped together affects how productive they can be. Figure 14.3 shows three basic ways of arranging workstations: product layout, process layout, and fixed-position layout.

In a *product layout*, machines are organized so that each operation needed to manufacture a product is performed at workstations arranged in a fixed sequence. Typically, workers are stationary in this arrangement, and a moving conveyor belt takes the product being worked on to the next workstation so that it is progressively assembled. Mass production is the familiar name for this layout; car assembly lines are probably the best-known example. It used to be that product layout was efficient only when products were created in large quantities; however, the introduction of modular assembly lines controlled by computers makes it efficient to make products in small batches.

In a *process layout*, workstations are not organized in a fixed sequence. Rather, each workstation is relatively self-contained, and a product goes to whichever workstation is needed to perform the next operation to complete the product. Process layout is often suited to manufacturing settings that produce a variety of custom-made products, each tailored to the needs of a different kind of customer. For example, a custom furniture manufacturer might use a process layout so that different teams of workers can produce different styles of chairs or tables made from different kinds of woods and finishes. Such a layout also describes how a patient

Figure 14.3 **Three Facilities Layouts**

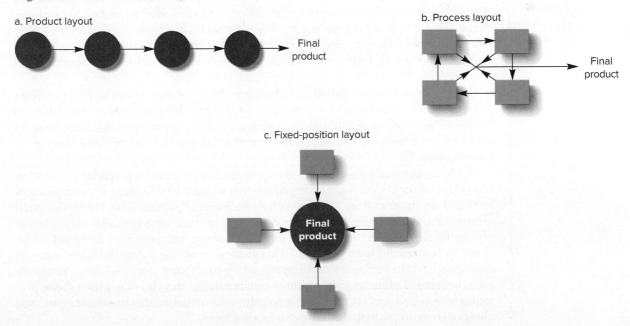

a. Product layout

Final product

b. Process layout

Final product

c. Fixed-position layout

Final product

might go through a hospital from emergency room to X-ray department, to operating room, to recovery, and so on. A process layout provides the flexibility needed to change a product, whether it is a PC or a patient's treatment. Such flexibility, however, often reduces efficiency because it is expensive.

In a *fixed-position layout,* the product stays in a fixed position. Its component parts are produced in remote workstations and brought to the production area for final assembly. Increasingly, self-managed teams are using fixed-position layouts. Different teams assemble each component part and then send these parts to the final assembly team, which makes the final product. A fixed-position layout is commonly used for products such as jet airlines, mainframe computers, and gas turbines—products that are complex and difficult to assemble or so large that moving them from one workstation to another would be difficult. Even companies that specialize in office design and layout have rethought their work spaces, as the accompanying "Management Insight" feature discusses.

MANAGEMENT INSIGHT

Steelcase Takes Its Own Advice When It Comes to Office Layout

Steelcase develops and manufactures office furniture, technology, and other office architecture. The Michigan-based company was founded in 1912 as the Metal Office Furniture Company. Its first patent was in 1914 on a metal wastebasket—an important item in an era when straw wastebaskets were fire hazards. The company went on to develop and sell many office products. In 1954, the company's name was changed to Steelcase.[29]

In the more than 100 years that the company has been around, workspace design has changed dramatically. Historically, workers used to jockey to be closer to the CEO's office. Like the organizational chart, the closer a person was to the CEO, the more power the person had. In today's business setting, however, information is power, and the design of the workspace should reflect and promote that sentiment.

In 2014, Steelcase published a study suggesting that the design of offices affects the emotional well-being of employees, which can have an impact on business results. The study suggested that workspaces can support positive emotions by encouraging a sense of belonging, helping workers see their worth, and promoting mindfulness.[30]

Steelcase does not just sell the products that make new workspaces possible—it has taken its own advice and changed its own workspaces to allow for communication and an open culture. All executive offices were moved onto floors designed around important issues facing the company. Instead of giving executives larger offices to signify their importance to the company, management assigned office space to "command-level projects." This change in office layout shifts the focus of meetings back to business and products and helps foster team building. The company believes that innovation requires collaboration, and the new office space promotes eye-to-eye contact, provides everyone with equal access to information, and allows people to participate and move around freely.[31]

FLEXIBLE MANUFACTURING In a manufacturing company, a major source of costs is the costs associated with setting up the equipment needed to make a particular product. One of these costs is the cost of production that is forgone because nothing is produced while the equipment is being set up. For example, components manufacturers often need as much as half a day to set up automated production equipment when switching from production of one component part (such as a washer ring for the steering column of a car) to another (such as a washer ring for the steering column of a truck). During this half-day, a manufacturing plant is not producing anything, but employees are paid for this "nonproductive" time.

It follows that if setup times for complex production equipment can be reduced, so can setup costs, and efficiency will rise. In other words, if setup times can be reduced, the time that plant and employees spend actually producing something will increase. This simple insight has been the driving force behind the development of flexible manufacturing techniques.

Flexible manufacturing aims to reduce the time required to set up production equipment.[32] Redesigning the manufacturing process so that production equipment geared for manufacturing one product can be quickly replaced with equipment geared to make another product can dramatically reduce setup times and costs. Another favorable outcome from flexible manufacturing is that a company is able to produce many more varieties of a product than before in the same amount of time. Thus, flexible manufacturing increases a company's ability to be responsive to its customers.

To realize the benefits of flexible manufacturing, General Motors built a plant in Lansing, Michigan, back in 2001 that can expand as the company sees fit. When it was first built, the company's Grand River Assembly plant was already more flexible than its other plants and was modeled after GM's innovative facilities overseas.[33] While some GM executives expressed concern that the site was too small to work well, the plant has received praise for its ability to manufacture a variety of car models as well as for its collaborative team management style and automation capabilities. In 2014, GM announced that a $174 million stamping facility would be added to the Grand River facility that would create or retain approximately 145 jobs.[34]

Just-in-Time Inventory and Efficiency

Inventory is the stock of raw materials, inputs, and component parts that an organization has on hand at a particular time. Just-in-time (JIT) inventory systems play a major role in the process of identifying and finding the source of defects in inputs. When an organization has a **just-in-time inventory system**, parts or supplies arrive at the organization when they are needed, not before. Under a JIT inventory system, defective parts enter an organization's production system immediately; they are not warehoused for months before use. This means that defective inputs can be quickly spotted. Managers can then trace a problem to the supply source and fix it before more defective parts are produced.

JIT systems, such as Toyota's *kanban* system, were originally developed as part of the effort to improve product quality; they have major implications for efficiency. Toyota's system is based on the delivery of components to the production line just as they are needed. This leads to major cost savings from increasing inventory turnover and reducing inventory holding costs, such as warehousing and storage costs and the cost of capital tied up in inventory.[35]

Although companies that manufacture and assemble products can obviously use JIT to great advantage, so can service organizations. Walmart, the biggest retailer in the United States, uses JIT systems to replenish the stock in its stores at least twice a week. Many Walmart stores receive daily deliveries. As soon as goods are purchased, new ones are ordered through Walmart's sophisticated supply chain. While the supply chain does a good job of getting goods to the stores, Walmart recently ran into some problems with stores that were so leanly staffed that there were not enough people to move goods from the storage area to store shelves. The company is working on implementing a new global replenishment system that should help improve inventory efficiencies.[36]

One drawback of JIT systems is that they leave an organization without a buffer stock of inventory.[37] Although buffer stocks of inventory can be expensive to store, they can help an organization when it is affected by shortages of inputs brought about by a disruption among suppliers (such as a labor dispute in a key supplier). Moreover, buffer stocks can help an organization respond quickly to increases in customer demand—that is, they can increase an organization's responsiveness to customers.

Even a small company can benefit from a kanban system, as the experience of United Electric Controls, headquartered in Watertown, Massachusetts, suggests. United Electric is the market leader in the manufacture of alarm and shutdown switches for industrial plant safety. At one time, the company simply stored all its inputs in a warehouse and dispensed them as needed. Then it decided to reduce costs by storing the inputs closer to their point of use in the production system. This led to inaccurate part counts and caused production stoppages due to a lack of inputs.

So managers decided to experiment with a supplier kanban system even though United Electric had fewer than 40 suppliers and they were up to date with its input requirements. Managers decided to store a three-week supply of parts in a central storeroom—a supply large enough to avoid unexpected shortages. They began by asking their casting supplier to deliver inputs in kanbans and bins. Once a week, this supplier checks the bins to determine how much stock needs to be delivered the following week. Other suppliers were then asked to participate in this system, and now more than 35 major suppliers operate some form of the kanban system.[38]

By all measures of performance, the kanban system has succeeded. Inventory holding costs have fallen sharply. Products are delivered to all customers on time. And new products' design-to-production cycles have dropped by 50% because suppliers are now involved much earlier in the design process so they can supply new inputs as needed.

Self-Managed Work Teams and Efficiency

Another efficiency-boosting technique is the use of self-managed work teams (see Chapter 11). The typical team consists of from 5 to 15 employees who produce an entire product instead of only parts of it. Team members learn all team tasks and move from job to job. The result is a flexible workforce because team members can fill in for absent coworkers. The members of each team also assume responsibility for work and vacation scheduling, ordering materials, and hiring new members—previously all responsibilities of first-line managers. Because people often respond well to being given greater autonomy and responsibility, the use of empowered self-managed teams can increase productivity and efficiency. Moreover, cost savings arise from eliminating supervisors and creating a flatter organizational hierarchy, which further increases efficiency.

The effect of introducing self-managed teams is often an increase in efficiency of 30% or more, sometimes much more. After the introduction of flexible manufacturing technology and self-managed teams, a GE plant in Salisbury, North Carolina, increased efficiency by 250% compared with other GE plants producing the same products.[39]

Process Reengineering and Efficiency

process reengineering

The fundamental rethinking and radical redesign of business processes to achieve dramatic improvements in critical measures of performance such as cost, quality, service, and speed.

Think of the major activities of businesses as processes that take one or more kinds of inputs and create an output that is of value to the customer. **Process reengineering** is the fundamental rethinking and radical redesign of business processes to achieve dramatic improvements in critical measures of performance such as cost, quality, service, and speed.[40] Customer relationship management can be thought of as a business process: Once a customer's order is received (the input), all the activities necessary to process the order are performed, and the ordered goods are delivered to the customer (the output). Process reengineering can boost efficiency because it eliminates the time devoted to activities that do not add value.

As an example of process reengineering in practice, consider how Ford Motor Company used it. One day a manager from Ford was working at its Japanese partner Mazda and discovered quite by accident that Mazda had only five people in its accounts payable department. The Ford manager was shocked, for Ford's U.S. operation had 500 employees in accounts payable. He reported his discovery to Ford's U.S. managers, who decided to form a task force to figure out why the difference existed.

Ford managers discovered that procurement began when the purchasing department sent a purchase order to a supplier and sent a copy of the purchase order to Ford's accounts payable department. When the supplier shipped the goods and they arrived at Ford, a clerk at the receiving dock completed a form describing the goods and sent the form to accounts payable. The supplier, meanwhile, sent accounts payable an invoice. Thus, accounts payable received three documents relating to these goods: a copy of the original purchase order, the receiving document, and the invoice. If the information in all three was in agreement (most of the time it was), a clerk in accounts payable issued payment. Occasionally, however, all three documents did not agree. Ford discovered that accounts payable clerks spent most of their time straightening out the 1% of instances in which the purchase order, receiving document, and invoice contained conflicting information.[41]

Ford managers decided to reengineer the procurement process to simplify it. Now when a buyer in the purchasing department issues a purchase order to a supplier, that buyer also enters the order into an online database. As before, suppliers send goods to the receiving dock. When the goods arrive, the clerk at the receiving dock checks a computer terminal to see whether the received shipment matches the description on the purchase order. If it does, the clerk accepts the goods and pushes a button on the terminal keyboard that tells the database the goods have arrived. Receipt of the goods is recorded in the database, and a computer automatically issues and sends a check to the supplier. If the goods do not correspond to the description on the purchase order in the database, the clerk at the dock refuses the shipment and sends it back to the supplier.

Payment authorization, which used to be performed by accounts payable, is now accomplished at the receiving dock. The new process has come close to eliminating the need for an accounts payable department. In some parts of Ford, the size of the accounts payable department has been cut by 95%. By reducing the head count in accounts payable, the reengineering effort reduced the amount of time wasted on unproductive activities, thereby increasing the efficiency of the total organization.

Managers at Ford Motor Company used process reengineering to improve the efficiency of their procurement process by simplifying it. Now, when one of Ford's dealers issues a purchase order to buy a collection of Ford vehicles for delivery to its lot, the dealer also enters the order into an online database. When the vehicles ordered arrive at the receiving dock for shipment by train, a clerk checks on a computer terminal to ensure that the specific shipment matches the purchase order and checks online with the dealer that the order is still correct. If it is, the vehicles are shipped. The use of process engineering has significantly cut down on the time accounts payable clerks spend to rectify complex vehicle orders that contain conflicting information. © Justin Sullivan/Getty Images News/Getty Images

In sum, managers at all levels have important roles to play in a company's effort to boost efficiency. Top management's role is to encourage efficiency improvements by, for example, emphasizing the need for continuous improvement or reengineering. Top management also must ensure that managers from different functional departments work together to find ways to increase efficiency. However, while top managers might recognize the need for such actions, functional-level managers are in the best position to identify opportunities for making efficiency-enhancing improvements to an organization's production systems. They are the managers who are involved in an organization's production system on a day-to-day basis. Improving efficiency, like quality, is an ongoing, never-ending process.

Operations Management: Some Remaining Issues

Achieving superior responsiveness to customers through quality and efficiency often requires a profound shift in management operations and in the culture of an organization. Many reports have appeared in the popular press about widespread disillusionment with JIT, flexible manufacturing, and reengineering. It is possible that many of the disillusioned organizations are those that failed to understand that implementing these systems requires a marked shift in organizational culture. None of these systems is a panacea that can be taken once, like a pill, to cure industrial ills. Making these techniques work within an organization can pose a significant challenge that calls for hard work and years of persistence by the sponsoring managers.

Managers also need to understand the ethical implications of the adoption of many of the production techniques discussed here. JIT, flexible manufacturing, and reengineering can all increase quality, efficiency, and responsiveness to customers, but they may do so at great cost to employees. Employees may see the demands of their job increase, or, worse, they may see themselves reengineered out of a job.

Is it ethical to continually increase the demands placed on employees, regardless of the human cost in terms of job stress? Obviously, the answer is no. Employee support is vital if an organization is to function effectively. What kinds of work pressures are legitimate, and what pressures are excessive? There is no clear answer to this question. Ultimately the issue comes down to the judgment of responsible managers seeking to act ethically.

Summary and Review

OPERATIONS MANAGEMENT AND COMPETITIVE ADVANTAGE To achieve high performance, managers try to improve their responsiveness to customers, the quality of their products, and the efficiency of their organization. To achieve these goals, managers can use a number of operations management techniques to improve the way an organization's production system operates. [LO 14-1]

IMPROVING RESPONSIVENESS TO CUSTOMERS To achieve high performance in a competitive environment, it is imperative that the production system of an organization responds to customer demands. Managers try to design production systems that produce outputs that have the attributes customers desire. One of the central tasks of operations management is to develop new and improved production systems that enhance the ability of the organization to deliver economically more of the product attributes that customers desire for the same price. Techniques such as JIT, flexible manufacturing, and process reengineering are popular because they promise to do this. Managers should analyze carefully the links between responsiveness to customers and the production system of an organization. The ability of an organization to satisfy the demands of its customers for lower prices, acceptable quality, better features, and so on depends critically on the nature of the organization's production system. As important as responsiveness to customers is, however, managers need to recognize that there are limits to how responsive an organization can be and still cover its costs. [LO 14-2]

IMPROVING QUALITY Managers seek to improve the quality of their organization's output because it enables them to better serve customers, to raise prices, and to lower production costs. The attempt to improve quality requires an organization-wide commitment; managers emphasize a strong customer focus, find ways to measure quality, set quality improvement goals, solicit input from employees about how to improve product quality, and design products for ease of manufacture. [LO 14-3]

IMPROVING EFFICIENCY Improving efficiency requires one or more of the following: improve quality, adopt flexible manufacturing technologies, introduce just-in-time inventory systems, establish self-managed work teams, and use process reengineering. Top management is responsible for setting the context within which efficiency improvements can take place by, for example, emphasizing the need for continuous improvement. Functional-level managers bear prime responsibility for identifying and implementing efficiency-enhancing improvements in production systems. [LO 14-4]

Management *in Action*

TOPICS FOR DISCUSSION AND ACTION

Discussion

1. Why is it important for managers to pay close attention to their organization's production system if they wish to be responsive to their customers? [LO 14-1]

2. "Total customer service is the goal toward which most organizations should strive." To what degree is this statement correct? [LO 14-2]

3. What is CRM, and how can it help improve responsiveness to customers? [LO 14-2]

4. What is efficiency, and what are some of the techniques that managers can use to increase it? [LO 14-4]

Action

5. Ask a manager how quality, efficiency, and responsiveness to customers are defined and measured in his or her organization. [LO 14-2, 14-3, 14-4]

6. Go into a local store, restaurant, or supermarket, and list the ways in which you think the organization is being responsive or unresponsive to the needs of its customers. How could this business's responsiveness to customers be improved? [LO 14-2]

BUILDING MANAGEMENT SKILLS
Managing a Production System [LO 14-1, 14-2]

Choose an organization with which you are familiar—one that you have worked in or patronized or one that has received extensive coverage in the popular press. The organization should be involved in only one industry or business. Answer these questions about the organization.

1. What is the output of the organization?

2. Describe the production system that the organization uses to produce this output.

3. What product attributes do customers of the organization desire?

4. Does its production system allow the organization to deliver the desired product attributes?

5. Try to identify improvements that might be made to the organization's production system to boost the organization's responsiveness to customers, quality, and efficiency.

MANAGING ETHICALLY [LO 14-1]

After implementing efficiency-improving techniques, many companies commonly lay off hundreds or thousands of employees whose services are no longer required. And frequently, the remaining employees must perform more tasks more quickly—a situation that can generate employee stress and other work-related problems.

In addition, these employees may experience "survivor's guilt" because they kept their jobs while many of their colleagues and friends were let go.

Questions

1. Either by yourself or in a group, discuss how to think through the ethical implications of using a new operations management technique to improve organizational performance.

2. What criteria would you use to decide what kind of technique is ethical to adopt and how far to push employees to raise the level of their performance?

3. How big a layoff, if any, would be acceptable? If layoffs are acceptable, what could be done to reduce their harm to employees?

SMALL GROUP BREAKOUT EXERCISE [LO 14-1, 14-2, 14-3, 14-4]
How to Compete in the Sandwich Business

Form groups of three or four people, and appoint one member as the spokesperson who will communicate your findings to the whole class when called on by the instructor. Then discuss the following scenario.

You and your partners are thinking about opening a new kind of sandwich shop that will compete head-to-head with Subway and ThunderCloud Subs. Because these chains have good brand-name recognition, it is vital that you find some source of competitive advantage for your new sandwich shop, and you are meeting to brainstorm ways of obtaining one.

1. Identify the product attributes that a typical sandwich shop customer wants the most.

2. In what ways do you think you will be able to improve on the operations and processes of existing sandwich shops and achieve a competitive advantage through better (a) product quality, (b) efficiency, or (c) responsiveness to customers?

BE THE MANAGER [LO 14-1, 14-3]

How to Build Flat-Screen Displays

You are an operations management consultant who has been called in by the management team of a start-up company that will produce flat-screen displays for PC makers like Apple and HP. The flat-screen display market is highly competitive, so there is considerable pressure to reduce costs. Also, PC makers are demanding ever-higher quality and better features to please customers. In addition, they demand that delivery of your product meet their production schedule needs. Management wants your advice on how best to meet these requirements. The company is in the process of recruiting new workers and building a production facility.

Questions

1. What kinds of techniques discussed in the chapter can help these managers to increase efficiency?

2. In what ways can these managers go about developing a program to increase quality?

3. What critical lessons can these managers learn from operations management?

THE WALL STREET JOURNAL CASE IN THE NEWS
[LO 14-1, 14-2, 14-3, 14-4]
Big Data Brings Relief to Allergy Medicine Supply Chains

A severe allergy season in parts of the country is pressing providers to get the right medicine to the right pharmacies at the right time.

Allergy sufferers in the U.S. have had a particularly rough time this spring, with April and May pollen levels in New York frequently surging 25% or more above the monthly average for the last three years, according to data from IMS Health Inc.

But unlike in 2010, when pharmacies around the northeastern U.S. sold out of allergy medications, advancing supply-chain technology has enabled pharmaceutical companies to keep their allergy-relief products in stock. Many vendors now are combining data from thousands of stores of different retailers and cross-referencing it with weather, pollen and other data to make sure they can meet consumer demand—and not miss out on potential sales.

"Traditionally about 6% to 10% of retail sales are lost because of out-of-stock problems," said Anuj Agrawal, vice president of product marketing at McLean, Va.–based Orchestro. The company has a team of scientists that help companies mine big data and better anticipate future demand. The company provides web-based software that allows clients to look at data reports, and to analyze and customize the data every day.

"It used to take [vendors] a week just to aggregate and organize the data before they could look at a report and figure out any insights," he said. "If it's taking you a week to organize the data and to see you have an out-of-stock somewhere, you're losing."

Bayer AG, maker of over-the-counter allergy medicine Claritin, said it has been using data to get ahead of seasonal trends. Mike DeBiasi, vice president of Bayer's U.S. allergy business, said his team started preparing the supply chain for spring six to nine months before the allergy season actually hit, using third-party software that looked at global warming information and modeled allergy and weather trends.

"There are much more advanced modeling tools that we use now . . . to project and predict weather trends and allergy suffering," said Mr. DeBiasi. He said allergy suffering has been particularly bad on the West Coast and in the Northeast this year because there has been relatively less rain, leaving more pollen particles in the air. "We had signs that were projecting heavier allergy suffering this year than we saw last year," Mr. DeBiasi said.

The allergy season typically starts in the south and moves north, the executive said. So as the season progressed in its usual pattern, Bayer closely monitored data coming in from retailers in the south to make sure the company was well stocked in regions to the north, to make sure inventory was plentiful going into the season, and winding down coming out.

The use of data in that way is critical to retailers as they try to operate lean supply chains and work with consumer goods that sell quickly.

Ash Patel, chief information officer at a Chicago-based data analytics firm Information Resources Inc., said his firm can use real-time data sources like Google Inc.'s flu index, temperature forecasts and even social media chatter to predict heightened demand for products like cough medicines Mucinex and Robitussin.

Still, the results aren't always simple. Mr. Patel said cold weather may drive up demand for cough medicine, but brutally cold weather drives sales down. "On the flip side, when the forecast is for 20 inches of snow, that drove stock-ups and people made extra trips to get everything they needed," he said.

"We never get it exactly perfect . . . it's more of an art than a science," said Mr. DeBiasi of Bayer. But "we're fully supplied in the U.S. marketplace for the most severe allergy season in recent history."

Questions

1. In what ways does Bayer's operations management system help improve the company's efficiency?

2. What are some of the advantages of using big data when it comes to increasing customer satisfaction? What are some disadvantages?

3. What strategies can companies employ to keep their supply chains lean while addressing the overall quality of their products?

Source: Loretta Chao, "Big Data Brings Relief to Allergy Medicine Supply Chains," *The Wall Street Journal*, May 26, 2015, www.wsj.com.

Endnotes

1. S. McCartney, "Airlines Go Back to Boarding School to Move Fliers onto Plane Faster," *The Wall Street Journal*, accessed May 7, 2015, www.wsj.com.

2. E. Chemi, "The Dumb Way We Board Airplanes Remains Impervious to Good Data," *Bloomberg Business*, accessed May 7, 2015, www.bloomberg.com.

3. C. Kitching, "We're Doing It All Wrong! The Fastest Way to Board a Passenger Plane Revealed," *Daily Mail*, accessed May 7, 2015, www.dailymail.co.uk.

4. N. Stockton, "There's a Better Way to Board an Airplane, But Airlines Aren't Using It," *Slate*, accessed May 7, 2015, www.slate.com.

5. C. Morran, "4 Things That Make Airline Boarding a Complete Mess," *Consumerist*, accessed May 7, 2015, http://consumerist.com.

6. D. Koenig, "The Airlines' Endless Quest for Better Boarding Procedures," *Huffington Post,* accessed May 7, 2015, www.huffingtonpost.com.

7. Company website, "Baggage," www.aa.com, accessed May 7, 2015.

8. P. Greenberg, "How Much Are Airlines Making from Ancillary Revenue?"*PeterGreenberg.com,* accessed May 7, 2015, http://petergreenberg.com.

9. Company website, "Boarding the Plane," https://www.southwest.com, accessed May 7, 2015.

10. The view of quality as including reliability goes back to the work of W. Edwards Deming and Joseph Juran. See A. Gabor, *The Man Who Discovered Quality* (New York: Times Books, 1990).

11. D. F. Abell, *Defining the Business: The Starting Point of Strategic Planning* (Englewood Cliffs, NJ: Prentice Hall, 1980).

12. M. E. Porter, *Competitive Advantage* (New York: Free Press, 1985).

13. Company website, www.southwest.com, accessed May 7, 2015.

14. J. Nicas, "As Southwest Goes Mainstream, Will Direct Flights Go Extinct?" *The Wall Street Journal,* accessed May 11, 2015, http://blogs.wsj.com.

15. L. Brown, "From iPad to Plate, Technology Speeding Up Food at Bread Co.," *St. Louis Post-Dispatch,* accessed May 11, 2015, www.stltoday.com.

16. B. Kowitt, "With Digital Ordering, Panera Makes a Big Bet on Tech," *Fortune,* accessed May 11, 2015, http://fortune.com.

17. Ibid.

18. Company website, "The Empire Difference," www.empireblue.com, accessed May 11, 2015; www.crm.com, 2012.

19. A. Nelson, "How Social Media and CRM Work Together Successfully," *Salesforce Marketing Cloud,* accessed May 11, 2015, www.exacttarget.com.

20. The view of quality as reliability goes back to the work of Deming and Juran; see Gabor, *The Man Who Discovered Quality.*

21. See also D. Garvin, "What Does Product Quality Really Mean?" *Sloan Management Review* 26 (Fall 1984), 25–44; P. B. Crosby, *Quality Is Free* (New York: Mentor Books, 1980); Gabor, *The Man Who Discovered Quality.*

22. Company website, "Vehicle Dependability Heavily Impacted by Owner Experiences with Technology," www.jdpower.com, accessed May 12, 2015.

23. Company website, "About Us," www.tjx.com, accessed May 12, 2015.

24. B. Kowitt, "Is T.J. Maxx the Best Retail Store in the Land?" *Fortune,* accessed May 12, 2015, http://fortune.com.

25. Company website, "Succeeding in All Types of Environments," www.tjx.com, accessed May 12, 2015.

26. Ibid.

27. J. Griffiths, "Europe's Manufacturing Quality and Productivity Still Lag Far behind Japan's," *Financial Times,* November 4, 1994, 11.

28. "Average Selling Price of Desktop PCs Worldwide from 2005 to 2015," *Statista,* accessed May 12, 2015, www.statista.com.

29. Company website, "About Steelcase," www.steelcase.com, accessed May 13, 2015.

30. B. Arantes, "How to Design Your Workspace to Encourage Positive Emotions at Work," *Fast Company,* accessed May 13, 2015, www.fastcompany.com.

31. G. Bradt, "Steelcase CEO on How Office Layout Impacts Corporate Culture," *Forbes,* accessed May 13, 2015, www.forbes.com.

32. P. Nemetz and L. Fry, "Flexible Manufacturing Organizations: Implications for Strategy Formulation," *Academy of Management Review* 13 (1988), 627–38; N. Greenwood, *Implementing Flexible Manufacturing Systems* (New York: Halstead Press, 1986).

33. L. VanHulle, "Lansing Grand River Plant's Milestone 'Means Confidence,'" *Lansing State Journal,* accessed May 13, 2015, http://archive.lansingstatejournal.com.

34. Company website, "GM Invests $63 Million in Lansing Delta Township Assembly Plant Expansion," https://media.gm.com, accessed May 13, 2015.

35. Company global website, "Just-in-Time: Philosophy of Complete Elimination of Waste," www.toyota-global.com, accessed May 13, 2015.

36. K. Souza, "Wal-Mart Slow to Roll Out New Replenishment System," The City Wire, accessed May 13, 2015, www.thecitywire.com; "Walmart's Inventory Struggles Offer Valuable Supply Chain Lesson," *Euro Supply Chain Jobs,* accessed May 13, 2015, https://www.eurosupplychainjobs.com; Paula Rosenblum, "How Walmart Could Solve Its Inventory Problem and Improve Earnings," *Forbes,* accessed May 13, 2015, www.forbes.com.

37. For an interesting discussion of some other drawbacks of JIT and other "Japanese" manufacturing techniques, see S. M. Young, "A Framework for Successful Adoption and Performance of Japanese Manufacturing Practices in the United States," *Academy of Management Review* 17 (1992), 677–701.

38. Company website, "Company Background," www.ueonline.com, accessed May 13, 2015; T. Stundza, "Massachusetts Switch Maker Switches to Kanban," *Purchasing,* November 16, 2000, 103.

39. J. Hoerr, "The Payoff from Teamwork," *BusinessWeek,* July 10, 1989, 56–62.

40. M. Hammer and J. Champy, *Reengineering the Corporation* (New York: Harper Business, 1993), 35.

41. Ibid.

Career Development

career The sum total of work-related experiences throughout a person's life.

Managers face several challenges both in the course of their own careers and in facilitating effective career management for their subordinates. A **career** is the sum total of work-related experiences throughout a person's life.[1] Careers encompass all of the different jobs people hold and the different organizations they work for. Careers are important to most people for at least two reasons. First, a career is a means to support oneself and one's loved ones, providing basic necessities and opportunities to pursue outside interests. Second, a career can be a source of personal fulfillment and meaning. Many managers find that making a difference in an organization and helping improve organizational efficiency and effectiveness are personally as well as financially rewarding.

Career development is a concern for managers both in terms of how their own careers unfold over time and how careers are managed in their organizations. In the development of their own careers, managers seek out challenging and interesting jobs that will develop their skills, lead to future opportunities, and allow them the opportunity to do the kind of work that will be personally meaningful. Similarly, in motivating and leading subordinates, managers need to be attuned to subordinates' career development. When careers (of both managers and rank-and-file employees) are effectively managed in an organization, the organization makes the best use of its human resources and employees tend to be motivated by, and satisfied with, their jobs.

Both employees and managers play an important role in effectively managing careers. For example, employees need to understand themselves, the kind of work they find motivating and fulfilling, and their own future aspirations for their careers. Employees then need to proactively seek the education, training, and kinds of work experiences that will help them to have the careers they want. Managers can motivate employees to make meaningful contributions to organizations by providing them with work assignments, experiences, training, and opportunities that contribute to employees' career development.[2]

Hewlett-Packard CEO (Meg) Whitman served in different posts for an array of companies, such as Stride Rite, FTD, Procter & Gamble, Disney, Hasbro, and eBay, before leading HP. © Gail Albert Halaban/Corbis/SABA

Types of Careers

While every person's career is unique, the different types of careers that people have fall into four general categories: steady-state careers, linear careers, spiral careers, and transitory careers.[3]

steady-state career A career consisting of the same kind of job during a large part of an individual's work life.

STEADY-STATE CAREERS A person with a steady-state career makes a one-time commitment to a certain kind of job that he or she maintains throughout his or her working life.[4] People with steady-state careers can become very skilled and expert at their work. A playwright who starts writing plays upon graduation from college and continues to write plays until retiring at age 70 has a steady-state career. So too does a dentist who maintains a steady dental practice upon graduation from dental school until retirement.

Some managers choose to have a steady-state career, holding the same kind of job during a large part of their work life, often becoming highly skilled and expert in what they do. A talented and creative graphic artist at a magazine publishing company, for example, may turn down promotions and other "opportunities" so that he can continue to work on designing attractive magazine spreads and covers, what he really likes to do. Similarly, some managers at Dillard's have steady-state careers as area sales managers because they enjoy the direct supervision of salespeople and the opportunity to "stay close to" customers.

linear career A career consisting of a sequence of jobs in which each new job entails additional responsibility, a greater impact on an organization, new skills, and upward movement in an organization's hierarchy.

LINEAR CAREERS A person who has a linear career moves through a sequence of jobs in which each new job entails additional responsibility, a greater impact on an organization, new skills, and upward movement in an organization's hierarchy.[5] The careers of many managers are linear, whether they stay with the same company or frequently switch organizations. A linear career traces a line of upward progress in the positions held.

Top managers in large corporations have moved through a series of lower-level positions in a variety of organizations before they became CEOs. Similarly, the assistant manager at the Red Lobster in College Station, Texas, started out in an entry-level position as a cashier. A linear career at Dillard's department stores may include the following sequencing of positions: executive trainee, area sales manager, assistant buyer, buyer, assistant store manager of merchandising, store manager, and divisional merchandise manager.[6] Managers' subordinates also may have linear careers, although some subordinates may have other types of careers.

spiral career A career consisting of a series of jobs that build on each other but tend to be fundamentally different.

SPIRAL CAREERS A person who has a spiral career tends to hold jobs that, while building off of each other, tend to be fundamentally different.[7] An associate professor of chemical engineering who leaves university teaching and research to head up the R&D department of a chemical company for 10 years and then leaves that position to found her own consulting firm has a spiral career. Similarly, a marketing manager in a large corporation who transfers to a job in public relations and then, after several years in that position, takes a job in an advertising firm has a spiral career. Those three jobs tend to be quite different from each other and do not necessarily entail increases in levels of responsibility.

transitory career A career in which a person changes jobs frequently and in which each job is different from the one that precedes it.

TRANSITORY CAREERS Some people change jobs frequently and each job is different from the one that precedes it; this kind of career is a transitory career.[8] A middle school teacher who leaves teaching after two years to work as an administrative assistant in a consumer products company for a year and then moves on to do carpentry work has a transitory career.

Career Stages

Every person's career is unique, but there are certain career stages that people generally appear to progress through. Even if a person does not progress through all the stages, typically some of the stages are experienced. Each stage is associated with certain kinds of activities, hurdles, and potential opportunities. Regardless of the extent to which a person experiences each stage, and regardless of the exact number of the stages, about which there is some disagreement among researchers, here we discuss five stages (see Exhibit A) that are useful to understand and manage careers.[9]

These career stages apply to managers and nonmanagers alike. Thus, understanding the stages is important for managers both in terms of their own career development and in terms of the career development of their subordinates. Importantly, and increasingly, these career stages are experienced by most people in a variety of organizations. That is, while in the past, at least some people might have spent most of their careers in a single organization (or in just a few organizations), this is becoming increasingly rare. Rapid changes in technology, increased global competition, environmental uncertainty, outsourcing, and the layoffs many organizations resort to at one point or another to reduce costs are just some of the factors responsible for people's careers unfolding in a series of positions in a number of different organizations. Thus, a boundaryless career, or a career that is not attached or bound to a single organization, is becoming increasingly common, and most people have a variety of work experiences in multiple organizations throughout their careers.[10]

boundaryless career A career that is not attached to or bound to a single organization and consists of a variety of work experiences in multiple organizations.

PREPARATION FOR WORK   During this stage, people decide what kind of career they desire and learn what qualifications and experiences they will need in order to pursue their chosen career.[11] Deciding on a career is no easy task and requires a certain degree of self-awareness and reflection. Sometimes people turn to professional career counselors to help them discover the kinds of careers in which they are most likely to be happy. A person's personality, values, attitudes, and moods impact the initial choice of a career.[12]

After choosing a career area, a person must gain the knowledge, skills, and education necessary to get a good starting position. A person may need an undergraduate or graduate degree or may be able to acquire on-the-job training through an apprenticeship program (common in Germany and some other countries).

ORGANIZATIONAL ENTRY   At this stage, people are trying to find a good first job. The search entails identifying potential opportunities in a variety of ways (such as reading advertisements, attending career/job fairs, and mining personal contacts), finding out as much as possible about alternative positions, and making oneself an attractive candidate for prospective employers. Organizational entry is a more challenging stage for some kinds of careers than for others. An accounting major who knows she wants to work for an accounting firm already has a good idea of her opportunities and of how to make herself attractive to such firms. An English major who wants a career as an editor for a book publisher may find entry-level positions that seem a "good" start to such a career few and far between and may decide her best bet is to take a position as a sales representative for a well-respected publisher. More often than not, managers

Exhibit A Career Stages

do not start out in management positions but rather begin their careers in an entry-level position in a department such as finance, marketing, or engineering.

EARLY CAREER   The early-career stage begins after a person obtains a first job in his or her chosen career. At this stage there are two important steps: establishment and achievement. *Establishment* means learning the ropes of one's new job and organization—learning, for example, specific job responsibilities and duties, expected and desired behaviors, and important values of other organizational members such as the boss.[13] A person who has acquired the basic know-how to perform a job and function in the wider organization is ready to take the second step. *Achievement* means making one's mark, accomplishing something noteworthy, or making an important contribution to the job or organization.[14]

The achievement step can be crucial for future career progression. It is a means of demonstrating one's potential and standing out from others who are aspiring to become managers and are competing for desired positions. Downsizing and restructuring have reduced the number of management positions at many large companies, making it very important for individuals to manage the early-career stage effectively and thus increase their chances of advancement. By identifying where and how you can make a truly significant contribution to an organization, you can enhance your career prospects both inside and outside the organization.

Some people find that seeking out and gaining the assistance of a mentor can be a valuable asset for the early-career and subsequent stages. A **mentor** is an experienced member of an organization who provides advice and guidance to a less experienced worker (the protégé, or mentee). The help that a mentor provides can range from advice about handling a tricky job assignment, dealing with a disagreement with a supervisor, and what kind of subsequent positions to strive for, to information about appropriate behavior and what to wear in various situations. Mentors often seek out protégés, but individuals also can be proactive and try to enlist the help of a potential mentor. Generally, especially good potential mentors are successful managers who have had a variety of experiences, genuinely desire to help junior colleagues, and are interpersonally compatible with the would-be protégé. Research has found that receiving help from a mentor is associated with an increase in pay, pay satisfaction, promotion, and feeling good about one's accomplishments.[15]

MIDCAREER   The midcareer stage generally occurs when people have been in the workforce between 20 and 35 years. Different managers experience this stage in quite different ways. For some managers, the midcareer stage is a high point—a time of major accomplishment and success. For other managers, the midcareer stage is a letdown because their careers plateau.

Managers reach a **career plateau** when their chances of being promoted into a higher position in their current organizations or of obtaining a more responsible position in another organization dwindle.[16] Some managers inevitably will experience a career plateau because fewer and fewer managerial positions are available as one moves up an organization's hierarchy. In some organizations upper-level positions are especially scarce because of downsizing and restructuring.

Plateaued managers who are able to come to terms with their situation can continue to enjoy their work and make important contributions to their organization. Some plateaued managers, for example, welcome lateral moves, which give them the chance to learn new things and contribute in different ways to the organization.

mentor An experienced member of an organization who provides advice and guidance to a less experienced worker.

career plateau A position from which the chances of being promoted or obtaining a more responsible job are slight.

Some find being a mentor especially appealing and a chance to share their wisdom and make a difference for someone starting out in their field.

LATE CAREER   This stage lasts as long as a person continues to work and has an active career. Many managers remain productive at this stage and show no signs of slowing down.

Effective Career Management

effective career management
Ensuring that at all levels in the organization there are well-qualified workers who can assume more responsible positions as needed.

Managers face the challenge of ensuring not only that they have the kind of career they personally desire but also that effective career management exists for all employees in their organization. Effective career management means that at all levels in the organization there are well-qualified workers who can assume more responsible positions as needed and that as many members of the organization as possible are highly motivated and satisfied with their jobs and careers. As you might imagine, effectively managing careers in a whole organization is no easy task. At this point, however, it is useful to discuss two important foundations of effective career management in any organization: a commitment to ethical career practices and accommodations for workers' multidimensional lives.

COMMITMENT TO ETHICAL CAREER PRACTICES   Ethical career practices are among the most important ingredients in effective career management and, at a basic level, rest on honesty, trust, and open communication among organizational members. Ethical career practices include basing promotions on performance, not on irrelevant considerations such as personal friendships and ties, and ensuring that diverse members of an organization receive the career opportunities they deserve. Supervisors must never abuse their power to make career decisions affecting others and must never behave unethically to advance their own careers. Managers at all levels must abide by and be committed to ethical career practices and actively demonstrate this commitment; they must communicate that violation of these practices will not be tolerated; and they must make sure that organizational members who feel that they were not ethically treated can communicate their concerns without fear of retaliation.

ACCOMMODATIONS FOR WORKERS' MULTIDIMENSIONAL LIVES   Effectively managing careers also means being sensitive to and providing accommodations for the multiple demands that many organizational members face in their lives. The dual-career couple is now the norm rather than the exception, the number of single parents is at an all-time high, and more and more midcareer workers need to care for their elderly and infirm parents. By limiting unnecessary moves and travel, adopting flexible work arrangements and schedules, providing on-site day care, and allowing workers to take time off to care for children or elderly parents, managers make it possible for workers to have satisfying and productive careers while fulfilling their other commitments.

Careers are as important for managers' subordinates as they are for managers themselves. Understanding the many issues involved in effectively managing careers helps ensure that both managers and their subordinates will have the kinds of careers they want while helping an organization achieve its goals.

Endnotes

1. J. H. Greenhaus, *Career Management,* (New York: Dryden Press, 1987).

2. L. Lovelle, "A Payday for Performance" *Business Week,* April 18, 2005, pp. 78–80.

3. M. J. Driver, "Careers: A Review of Personal and Organizational Research," in C. L. Cooper and I. Robertson (eds.), *International Review of Industrial and Organizational Psychology,* (New York: Wiley, 1988).

4. Ibid.

5. M. J. Driver, "Careers: A Review of Personnel and Organizational Research," in C. L. Cooper and I. Robertson, eds., *International Review of Industrial and Organizational Psychology,* (New York: Wile y, 1988).

6. *Career Path* (recruitment material provided by Dillard's, Inc., 1994).

7. J. H. Greenhaus, *Career Management,* (New York: Dryden Press, 1987).

8. M. B. Arthur, "The Boundaryless Career: A New Perspective for Organizational Inquiry," *Journal of Organizational Behavior* 15 (1994), 295–306; M. B. Arthur and D. M. Rousseau, *The Boundaryless Career: A New Employment Principle for a New Organizational Era* (New York: Oxford University Press, 1996), 237–55; "Introduction: The Boundaryless Career as a New Employment Principle," in M. B. Arthur and D. M. Rousseau (eds.) *The Boundaryless Career: A New Employment Principle for a New Organizational Era* (New York: Oxford University Press, 1996), 3–20; L. T. Eby et al., "Predictors of Success in the Era of the Boundaryless Career," *Journal of Organizational Behavior* 24 (2003), 689–708; S. C. deJanasz, S. E. Sullivan and V. Whiting, "Mentor Networks and Career Success: Lessons for Turbulent Times," *Academy of Management Executive* 17, no. 4 (2003), 78–91.

9. N. Griffin, "Personalize Your Management Development," *Harvard Business Review,* March 2003, 113–19.

10. Driver, "Careers: A Review of Personal and Organizational Research."

11. Greenhaus, *Career Management.*

12. J. L. Holland, *Making Vocational Choices: A Theory of Careers* (Englewood Cliffs, NJ: Prentice Hall, 1973).

13. Greenhaus, *Career Management.*

14. Ibid.

15. G. Dreher and R. Ash, "A Comparative Study of Mentoring Among Men and Women in Managerial, Professional, and Technical Positions," *Journal of Applied Psychology* 75 (1990), 525–35; T. A. Scandura, "Mentorship and Career Mobility: An Empirical Investigation," *Journal of Organizational Behavior* 13 (1992), 169–74; D. B. Turban and T. W. Dougherty, "The Role of Protégé Personality in Receipt of Mentoring and Career Success," *Academy of Management Journal* 37 (1994), 688–702; W. Whitely, T. W. Dougherty, and G. F. Dreher, "Relationship of Career Mentoring and Socioeconomic Origin to Managers' and Professionals' Early Career Success," *Academy of Management Journal* 34 (1991), 331–51.

16. T. P. Ference, J. A. F. Stoner, and E. K. Warren, "Managing the Career Plateau," *Academy of Management Review* 2 (1977), 602–12.

Glossary/Subject Index

A

Ability tests, 414

Accuracy, 196, 441

ACHIEVEMENT ORIENTATION A worldview that values assertiveness, performance, success, and competition, 149

Achievement-oriented behaviors, 350

Acquired immune deficiency syndrome (AIDS), 102–103, 409

Activity ratios, 273, 274

Ad hoc committees, 253, 375

ADA (Americans with Disabilities Act), 99, 408

Adaptive cultures, 284–285

Adjourning, 381

ADMINISTRATIVE MANAGEMENT The study of how to create an organizational structure and control system that leads to high efficiency and effectiveness.

Administrative model, 166–169

ADMINISTRATIVE MODEL An approach to decision making that explains why decision making is inherently uncertain and risky and why managers usually make satisfactory rather than optimum decisions, 166

Age, 98–99

Age Discrimination in Employment Act, 98, 99, 408

Agile companies, 22

Aging of population, 98, 138

AGREEABLENESS The tendency to get along well with other people, 47

AIDS (acquired immune deficiency syndrome), 409

AIDS awareness training, 103

Allocating authority, 248–251

Alternative courses of action, 91, 171, 172, 177

Alternatives

    assessing, 171–173

    choosing among, 173

    generating, 171

    implementing, 173

    learning from feedback, 174–175

Ambiguous information, 169

AMBIGUOUS INFORMATION Information that can be interpreted in multiple and often conflicting ways, 168

Americans with Disabilities Act (ADA), 99, 408

Annual meeting, 64

Annual planning cycle, 200

Apple Watch, 58

APPLICATIONS SOFTWARE Software designed for a specific task or use, 459

ARBITRATOR A third-party negotiator who can impose what he or she thinks is a fair solution to a conflict that both parties are obligated to abide by.

Artificial intelligence, 462–463

ARTIFICIAL INTELLIGENCE Behavior performed by a machine that, if performed by a human being, would be called "intelligent," 462

ASA (attraction-selection-attrition) framework, 59

Assessment center, 414

Asynchronous technologies, 377

Attitude, 51, 53–56

ATTITUDE A collection of feelings and beliefs, 53

ATTRACTION-SELECTION-ATTRITION (ASA) FRAMEWORK A model that explains how personality may influence organizational culture, 59

Authority, 36, 248–251

AUTHORITY The power to hold people accountable for their actions and to make decisions concerning the use of organizational resources, 36

Autonomy, 237

B

Background checks, 413

Background information, 412–413

Backward vertical integration, 211

Barriers

    distance and culture, 144–145

    trade and investment, 143–144

Barriers to entry, 133–134

BARRIERS TO ENTRY Factors that make it difficult and costly for an organization to enter a particular task environment or industry, 133

Bay of Pigs invasion, 176

B2B MARKETPLACE An Internet-based trading platform set up to connect buyers and sellers in an industry, 463

B2B NETWORK STRUCTURE A series of global strategic alliances that an organization creates with suppliers, manufacturers, and distributors to produce and market a product, 254

Behavior appraisal, 419–420

Behavior control, 277

    bureaucratic control, 280–282

    direct supervision, 278

    management by objectives, 278–280

Behavior model of leadership, 345–347

    consideration, 345

    initiating structure, 346–347

BEHAVIORAL MANAGEMENT The study of how managers should behave to motivate employees and encourage them to perform at high levels and be committed to the achievement of organizational goals.

Belongingness needs, 312

BENCHMARKING The process of comparing one company's performance on specific dimensions with the performance of other high-performing organizations, 289

Benefits, 424–425

Big five personality traits, 45–47, 49

    agreeableness, 47

    conscientiousness, 47

    extraversion, 45–46

    negative affectivity, 47

    openness to experience, 47, 49

Big, hairy, audacious goals (BHAGs), 201

BLOG A website on which an individual, group, or organization posts information, commentary, and opinions and to which readers can often respond with their own commentary and opinion, 455-456

Body weight, 105

Bonus, 324–325

BOTTOM-UP CHANGE A gradual or evolutionary approach to change in which managers at all levels work together to develop a detailed plan for change, 289

BOUNDARY SPANNING Interacting with individuals and groups outside the organization to obtain valuable information from the environment.

BOUNDARYLESS CAREER A career that is not attached to or bound to a single organization and consists of a variety of work experiences in multiple organizations, 496

BOUNDARYLESS ORGANIZATION An organization whose members are linked by computers, email, computer-aided design systems, video teleconferencing, and cloud-based software, and who rarely, if ever, see one another face-to-face, 255

BOUNDED RATIONALITY Cognitive limitations that constrain one's ability to interpret, process, and act on information, 167

Brainstorming, 179–180

Brand loyalty, 134–135

BRAND LOYALTY Customers' preference for the products of organizations currently existing in the task environment, 134

Buffer stocks of inventory, 486

BUREAUCRACY A formal system of organization and administration designed to ensure efficiency and effectiveness, 36

Bureaucratic control, 280–283

    problems with, 281–282

BUREAUCRATIC CONTROL Control of behavior by means of a comprehensive system of rules and standard operating procedures, 280

Concentration on a single industry, 210–211
CONCENTRATION ON A SINGLE INDUSTRY
Reinvesting a company's profits to strengthen its competitive position in its current industry, 210

Conceptual skills, 13
CONCEPTUAL SKILLS The ability to analyze and diagnose a situation and to distinguish between cause and effect, 13

CONCURRENT CONTROL Control that gives managers immediate feedback on how efficiently inputs are being transformed into outputs so that managers can correct problems as they arise, 267

Confidence, 57–58, 93
CONSCIENTIOUSNESS The tendency to be careful, scrupulous, and persevering, 47

CONSIDERATION Behavior indicating that a manager trusts, respects, and cares about subordinates, 345

Contingency models of leadership, 347–352
    Fiedler's contingency model, 347–349
    House's path–goal theory, 349–350
    leader substitutes model, 350–351
CONTINGENCY THEORY The idea that the organizational structures and control systems managers choose depend on—are contingent on—characteristics of the external environment in which the organization operates, 230

Continuity, 196
Control process, 268–270
Control systems, 265, 266–268
CONTROL SYSTEMS Formal target-setting, monitoring, evaluation, and feedback systems that provide managers with information about how well the organization's strategy and structure are working, 266

Controlling, 10–11, 66–67, 265, 266. *See also* Organizational control
CONTROLLING Evaluating how well an organization is achieving its goals and taking action to maintain or improve performance; one of the four principal tasks of management, 10

COO (chief operating officer), 13
Coordinating functions and division, 247–253
CORE COMPETENCY The specific set of departmental skills, knowledge, and experience that allows one organization to outperform another, 15

CORE MEMBERS The members of a team who bear primary responsibility for the success of a project and who stay with a project from inception to completion,
252

Corporate scandals, 66, 83
CORPORATE-LEVEL PLAN Top management's decisions pertaining to the organization's mission, overall strategy, and structure, 198

Corporate-level strategy, 198
    concentration on a single industry, 210–211
    diversification, 213–216
    international expansion, 216–220
    vertical integration, 211–213
CORPORATE-LEVEL STRATEGY A plan that indicates in which industries and national markets an organization intends to compete, 209

Creativity
    emotion-laden process, 357
    entrepreneurship and, 180–183
    group, 179–180
    individual, 178–179
CREATIVITY A decision maker's ability to discover original and novel ideas that lead to feasible alternative courses of action, 177

CRM (customer relationship management), 478–480
Cross-cultural team, 374
Cross-departmental responsibility, 12
Cross-functional teams, 104, 253, 374
CROSS-FUNCTIONAL TEAM A group of managers brought together from different departments to perform organizational tasks, 247

Cross-functioning, 38
Cross-training, 21
Culturally diverse management team, 150
Culture
    adaptive, 284–285
    declining barriers, 144–145
    national. *See* National culture
    organizational. *See* Organizational cultures
Current ratio, 273, 274
Customer relationship management (CRM), 478–480
CUSTOMER RELATIONSHIP MANAGEMENT (CRM) A technique that uses IT to develop an ongoing relationship with customers to maximize the value an organization can deliver to them over time, 478

Customer service, 23
Customers, 475
    ethics, 89
    performance appraisals by, 421
    responsiveness to, 372, 476–480
CUSTOMERS Individuals and groups that buy the goods and services that an organization produces, 132

D

DATA Raw, unsummarized, and unanalyzed facts, 441

Day-care facilities, 104
Days sales outstanding, 273, 274
Death penalty, 83
Debt-to-assets ratio, 273, 274

DECENTRALIZING AUTHORITY Giving lower-level managers and nonmanagerial employees the right to make important decisions about how to use organizational resources, 251

Decision making
    administrative model, 166–169
    assess alternatives, 171–173
    choose among alternatives, 173
    classical model, 166, 167
    for entrepreneurs and managers, 161–162
    entrepreneurship and creativity, 180–183
    generate alternatives, 171
    group, 175–176
    implementing chosen alternative, 173
    information and decisions, 443–444
    learning from feedback, 174–175
    managerial, 162–169
    need for, 170–171
    nonprogrammed, 165–166
    organizational learning and creativity, 176–180
    programmed, 163–165
    in response to opportunities, 163
    in response to threats, 163
    steps in process, 169–175
DECISION MAKING The process by which managers respond to opportunities and threats by analyzing options and making determinations about specific organizational goals and courses of action, 163

DECISION SUPPORT SYSTEM An interactive computer-based management information system that managers can use to make nonroutine decisions, 462

Decisional role and diversity, 106
Decline stage, 458
DECODING Interpreting and trying to make sense of a message, 449

DEFENSIVE APPROACH Companies and their managers behave ethically to the degree that they stay within the law and abide strictly with legal requirements.

DELPHI TECHNIQUE A decision-making technique in which group members do not meet face-to-face but respond in writing to questions posed by the group leader, 180

Demand forecast, 409
DEMOGRAPHIC FORCES Outcomes of changes in, or changing attitudes toward, the characteristics of a population, such as age, gender, ethnic origin, race, sexual orientation, and social class, 138

DEPARTMENT A group of people who work together and possess similar skills or use the same knowledge, tools, or techniques to perform their jobs, 11

Deregulation, 139
Development, 404, 415–418

Intelligent, 462

INTEREST GROUP An informal group composed of employees seeking to achieve a common goal related to their membership in an organization, 378

Intermediate-term plans, 199

INTERNAL LOCUS OF CONTROL The tendency to locate responsibility for one's fate within oneself, 49

Internal recruiting, 412
International expansion, 216–220
Internet, 27, 125–126, 145, 219, 220, 288, 411, 454–455

INTERNET A global system of computer networks.

INTERPERSONAL JUSTICE A person's perception of the fairness of the interpersonal treatment he or she receives from whomever distributes outcomes to him or her, 316

Interpersonal role and diversity, 106
Interview, 413–414
Intranet, 174, 254, 381, 455

INTRANET A companywide system of computer networks.

Intrapreneur, 290

INTRAPRENEUR A manager, scientist, or researcher who works inside an organization and notices opportunities to develop new or improved products and better ways to make them, 53

Intrapreneurship, 182–183

INTRINSICALLY MOTIVATED BEHAVIOR Behavior that is performed for its own sake, 303

Introverts, 45

INTUITION Feelings, beliefs, and hunches that come readily to mind, require little effort and information gathering, and result in on-the-spot decisions, 165

Inventory, 485–486

INVENTORY The stock of raw materials, inputs, and component parts that an organization has on hand at a particular time, 85

Inventory turnover, 273, 274
Investment, 143–144
iPod, 457–458
Irrelevant information, 442
Islamic Sabbath, 150
IT revolution, 456

J

Japan
  merit pay plan, 325
  operating budgets/challenging goals, 277
  safety needs, 312

JARGON Specialized language that members of an occupation, group, or organization develop to facilitate communication among themselves, 64

JIT (just-in-time) inventory system, 485–486
Job analysis, 38, 409

JOB ANALYSIS Identifying the tasks, duties, and responsibilities that make up a job and the knowledge, skills, and abilities needed to perform the job, 411

Job characteristics model, 236–237
Job description, 411

JOB DESIGN The process by which managers decide how to divide tasks into specific jobs, 233

Job enlargement, 234–236

JOB ENLARGEMENT Increasing the number of different tasks in a given job by changing the division of labor, 235

Job enrichment, 234–236

JOB ENRICHMENT Increasing the degree of responsibility a worker has over his or her job, 235

Job interview, 413–414
Job satisfaction, 53–56

JOB SATISFACTION The collection of feelings and beliefs that managers have about their current jobs, 53

JOB SIMPLIFICATION The process of reducing the number of tasks that each worker performs, 234

JOB SPECIALIZATION The process by which a division of labor occurs as different workers specialize in different tasks over time, 38

Job specification, 411
Job-specific skills, 15

JOINT VENTURE A strategic alliance among two or more companies that agree to jointly establish and share the ownership of a new business, 220

Judgment, 165
Justice rule, 91–92

JUSTICE RULE An ethical decision is a decision that distributes benefits and harms among people and groups in a fair, equitable, or impartial way, 91

Just-in-time (JIT) inventory system, 485–486

JUST-IN-TIME (JIT) INVENTORY SYSTEM A system in which parts or supplies arrive at an organization when they are needed, not before, 485

K

Kanban, 485–486

KNOWLEDGE MANAGEMENT SYSTEM A company-specific virtual information system that systematizes the knowledge of its employees and facilitates the sharing and integration of their expertise, 255

L

Labor productivity, 482
Labor relations, 406, 425–427

LABOR RELATIONS The activities that managers engage in to ensure that they have effective working relationships with the labor unions that represent their employees' interests, 425

LAN (local area network), 458
Landline telephone companies, 456
Language, 64–65
Laptop, 458
Large customers, 206
Large suppliers, 206
Late career, 498

LATERAL MOVE A job change that entails no major changes in responsibility or authority levels, 412

Layoff decisions, 85
Layoffs, 55

LEADER An individual who is able to exert influence over other people to help achieve group or organizational goals, 106

LEADER–MEMBER RELATIONS The extent to which followers like, trust, and are loyal to their leader; a determinant of how favorable a situation is for leading, 348

Leader substitutes model, 350–351
Leaders and leadership, 10, 337
  behavior model, 345–347
  charismatic leader, 353–354
  contingency models, 347–352
  cross-cultural differences, 340
  emotional intelligence, 356–357
  empowerment, 343
  Fiedler's contingency model, 347–349, 351
  gender, 355–356
  groups and teams, 379
  House's path–goal theory, 349–351
  leader substitutes model, 350–351
  managerial tasks, 339–340
  personal leadership style, 339–340
  power, 340–343
  stages of group development, 381
  trait model, 344
  transformational leadership, 352–355

LEADERSHIP The process by which an individual exerts influence over other people and inspires, motivates, and directs their activities to help achieve group or organizational goals, 339

LEADERSHIP SUBSTITUTE A characteristic of a subordinate or of a situation or context that acts in place of the influence of a leader and makes leadership unnecessary, 350

Name Index

Company Index